The World's Search for Sustainable Development

Addressing a forty year period, when science legitimized policy debates around natural resource use for urbanization and when international cooperation evolved from concerns on environmental risk posed by discrete issues to universal goals of human wellbeing within ecological limits, this book presents a practitioner's analysis on the implications of urbanization as the global mega-trend:

- The urban middle class, expected to triple by 2050, is the driver shaping societal functions – housing, mobility and food; key production systems, such as energy, that steer these arrangements; and dominant institutions, policies, technologies and thinking that sustain them.
- Consumption (the substance of societal well-being) and production (transformation of natural resources), both, impact planetary limits in different but significant ways.
- Disproportionate burdens on the global ecosystem require policy focus not only on globalised material flows and related scarcity but also on the patterns of global use and distribution of natural resources.
- The transformation will require going beyond shorter-term economic efficiency and optimization strategies as it is a social process rather than a physical problem.

Rather than focus on institutions, the book explores drivers, trends and patterns of natural resource usage. It inquires, why interdependence has not been matched by knowledge and policy frameworks; why effective global governance mechanisms should not be now framed around the rural-urban divide rather than between countries; how re-emerging countries, China and India, are harnessing new ideas for post-industrial services and knowledge economy that are not based on increasing use of energy, giving hope that global natural systems will continue to maintain their resilience as the basis for a good life for all.

Mukul Sanwal obtained a Master's degree in Public Administration from Harvard University. He joined the Indian Administrative Service in 1971. He represented India at the Rio Conference in 1992 as a lead negotiator for the Climate Change Treaty. He joined the UN in 1993 as policy adviser to the Executive Director of United Nations Environment Programme and later to the Executive Secretary of the United Nations Framework Convention on Climate Change till 2007. He was part of the group of scientists that contributed to the award of the Nobel Peace Prize for 2007 to the Intergovernmental Panel on Climate Change. He has contributed significantly to national/international journals and think tanks in the areas of sustainable development, climate policy, governance and global strategic affairs.

"…. This book presents an authentic and sophisticated voice of the developing world on a theme of global significance. Given the fact that the fate of efforts to address the challenge of sustainable development will lie in the actions of countries like China, India and Indonesia, coming to terms with this call for reframing and will be a necessary condition for success in addressing the challenge of sustainable development going forward."

— **Oran R. Young**, Professor Emeritus
Institutional and International Governance, Environmental Institutions, Bren School of Environmental Science and Management, University of California (Santa Barbara)

"…. The book explores sustainable development from the perspective of developing countries, with both practical and forward-looking indications. This book has provided in-depth and comprehensive discussion on the necessity, barriers and challenges faced by developing countries in pursuing sustainable development, including analysis of the significance, effects and problems of existing international cooperation mechanisms. The author has also proposed innovative thoughts and solutions for international cooperation that will be of great significance for global environment security and resource conservation."

— **Jiahua Pan**, Director-General
Institute for Urban & Environmental Studies
Chinese Academy of Social Sciences, Beijing

"…. combines a broad historical background with innovative insights that add value to the existing literature on sustainable development and climate change, notably in going beyond familiar political, economic and technological parameters to consider the social dimensions, and it stands out in conveying the perspective of the emerging economies of the South while drawing on his personal hands-on experience of international negotiations."

— **Michael Zammit Cutajar**, Executive Secretary
United Nations Climate Change secretariat (1991–2002)

The World's Search for Sustainable Development

A Perspective from the Global South

Mukul Sanwal

CAMBRIDGE
UNIVERSITY PRESS

4381/4 Ansari Road, Daryaganj, Delhi 110002, India

Cambridge University Press is part of the University of Cambridge.

It furthers the University's mission by disseminating knowledge in the pursuit of education, learning and research at the highest international levels of excellence.

www.cambridge.org
Information on this title: www.cambridge.org/9781107122666

© Mukul Sanwal 2015

This publication is in copyright. Subject to statutory exception and to the provisions of relevant collective licensing agreements, no reproduction of any part may take place without the written permission of Cambridge University Press.

First published 2015

A catalogue record for this publication is available from the British Library

Library of Congress Cataloguing in Publication data
Sanwal, Mukul, 1949-
The world's search for sustainable development : a perspective from the global south/ Mukul Sanwal.
    p. cm.
Includes bibliographical references and index.
Summary: "Traces the evolution of sustainable development and climate change from the time it emerged in international consultations and agreements"– Provided by publisher.
ISBN 978-1-107-12266-6 Hardback
1. Sustainable development – International cooperation.   2. Sustainable development – Government policy – Developing countries.   I. Title.
HC79.E5S26625 2015
338.9'27–dc23 2015011576

ISBN 978-1-107-12266-6 Hardback

Cambridge University Press has no responsibility for the persistence or accuracy of URLs for external or third-party internet websites referred to in this publication, and does not guarantee that any content on such websites is, or will remain, accurate or appropriate.

Dedicated to my parents, whose dreams inspired me to adopt a lifelong concern for the rural poor, an understanding of the dimensions of poverty and the perseverance to support their moving into the urban middle class.

Contents

Preface	*xi*
Acknowledgments	*xv*
Abbreviations	*xvii*

INTRODUCTION   **1**

1. Social Dimension of Sustainability   3
   - 1.1   The importance of a developing country perspective   4
   - 1.2   How is this different to the current approach   6
   - 1.3   Dimensions of the 'common concern' on environment and human well-being   7

CONSUMPTION IN AN UNEQUAL WORLD: FRAMING INTERNATIONAL
COOPERATION   **11**

2. Geopolitics of the Global Environment   13
   - 2.1   Politics around modifying consumption   14
   - 2.2   Limitations of natural sciences and risk-based regulatory approaches   18
   - 2.3   Potential of social sciences for growth within ecological limits   24
   - 2.4   Urbanization and interlinked natural and social systems   26
   - 2.5   Global limits   31
3. Natural Science – Policy – Institutions Interface   34
   - 3.1   Politics of the interaction between scientists and policymakers   36
   - 3.2   Political basis of the role and design of expert organizations   38
   - 3.3   Case studies: framing key global concerns: 1972–2012   41
   - 3.4   Grand scientific challenges of the twenty-first century   63
4. Focus on Developing Countries   72
   - 4.1   Bridging the divide   73

viii | Contents

4.2	Global politics and national means of implementation	74
4.3	The negotiation process	77
4.4	Different world views of re-emerging and industrialized economies	82
4.5	Strategic role of the United States – documents	84

5. Limitations of Multilateral Environmental Agreements 94

5.1	Distinction between global and local concerns	94
5.2	Sharing responsibility but not prosperity	97
5.3	Reframing the global environmental concern	100
5.4	New forms of international cooperation	103

CLIMATE POLICY: GLOBAL TO NATIONAL 111

6. Political Origins of Climate Policy 113

6.1	Understanding global carbon management	115
6.2	Flawed stress on projections of production patterns	118
6.3	Middle-class consumption as the problem and the solution	121

7. Questions on the Framework 124

7.1	Market-based approaches are not leading to a technological transformation	124
7.2	Transparency in national reporting	126
7.3	Differentiation between countries	127

8. Burden Shifting Rather than Burden Sharing 131

8.1	Changing scope of the negotiations	131
8.2	Copenhagen and the changing balance of power	133
8.3	Reframing the equity principles	135

9. Development of a Shared Vision 140

9.1	New policy approaches for the stalemated process	140
9.2	Longer term cooperation to support change	142
9.3	Importance of national actions	143

10. The Middle Class and Global Ecological Limits 147

10.1	Carbon budget, societal transformation and urbanization	147
10.2	Multilateral negotiations in a multipolar world	148
10.3	Centrality of human well-being	150

11. The New Climate Regime 154

11.1	Re-emergence of China and India	154
11.2	Emerging climate regime	155
11.3	Moving away from current and per capita emissions	157
11.4	Limitations of international environmental law	158
11.5	Leadership by China and India	160

SUSTAINABLE DEVELOPMENT: NATIONAL TO GLOBAL   **167**

12.   Conceptual and Institutional Foundation   169

     12.1   Dimensions of universalism   169

     12.2   Importance of diversity   173

     12.3   Understanding human well-being   175

     12.4   Implications for the multilateral system   177

13.   Politics within the United Nations   179

     13.1   Setting the agenda   179

     13.2   Evolution of the issues   181

     13.3   Multilateral negotiations   184

     13.4   Governance arrangements   186

     13.5   Evolving institutional arrangements   190

14.   Limitations of the Building Blocks of Sustainability   194

     14.1   Economic sustainability: modifying natural resource use   194

     14.2   Environmental sustainability: enhancing ecosystem services   195

     14.3   Social sustainability: local development and conservation   197

15.   Use of Natural Resources   200

     15.1   Urbanization   200

     15.2   Transport   203

     15.3   Electricity   206

     15.4   Energy transformation   207

16.   Distribution of Natural Resources   211

     16.1   Mega-trends and the decreasing stock of natural resources   211

     16.2   Myth of the environmental impact of the rural population   212

     16.3   Land-use change and statistics   213

     16.4   Globalization and sustainable natural resource management   214

CONSUMPTION IN A MORE EQUAL WORLD: SHAPING
SOCIETAL FUNCTIONS   **217**

17.   Geoeconomics of Human Well-being   219

     17.1   Urban Design   219

     17.2   Diet   220

     17.3   Behaviour   221

18.   Social Science – Policy – Society Interface   223

     18.1   Interrelated systems and the environmental perspective   223

     18.2   Policy implications of current patterns of natural resource use   225

     18.3   Longer term trends in natural resource use   226

x | Contents

19.	Reframing the 'Common Concern' From a Physical to a Social Problem	229
	19.1 Measuring sustainability and human well-being	229
	19.2 Re-defining ecological limits and global interdependence	231
	19.3 Redistribution in the use of natural resources	232
20.	Developing a Shared Global Vision	235
	20.1 New role of the social sciences	235
	20.2 New policy framework	237
	20.3 New understanding of global interdependence	238
	20.4 New forms for sharing technology	241
	20.5 New global rules	243

**GEOPOLITICS TO GEOECONOMICS: RURAL–URBAN DIVIDE, RATHER THAN
BETWEEN COUNTRIES** **247**

21.	Urban Areas: Sustainable Development and Human Well-being	249
	21.1 Consumption more important than production	249
	21.2 Shaping the transformation	251
	21.3 Middle class as the driver of global change	256
22.	Rural Areas: Climate Change, Fragile States and Human Security	262
	22.1 Political dimension	264
	22.2 Scientific dimension	266
	22.3 Legal dimension	268
	22.4 Policy dimension	270
	22.5 Development dimension	270
23.	Global Sustainable Development Goals	274
	23.1 Societal well-being in the twenty-first century	274
	23.2 Integrated global agenda	277
	23.3 Redefining national security	279
	23.4 Reviewing governance reform	280
24.	Transformative Impact of the Re-Emergence of China	285
	24.1 Urbanization as the global mega trend	287
	24.2 Stress on modifying consumption patterns: case studies	291
	24.3 Weakening natural science framework	298
	24.4 Emerging social science framework	300
	24.5 Governance focus on use and distribution, not scarcity, of natural resources	300

THE ASIAN CENTURY **303**

25.	Moving from Ideas to Reality will Depend on How Asia Structures its Urban Future	305

Index *313*

Preface

'Earth provides enough to satisfy every man's needs, but not every man's greed'.
Mohandas Karamchand Gandhi

Urbanization – as a social process, physical transformation of natural resources and creator of wealth – is one of the most powerful, irreversible and visible anthropogenic forces on Earth. More than half of the world's population already lives in urban areas and by 2050 three-fourth of the population is likely to be concentrated in cities; nearly half of global GDP growth between 2010 and 2025 will come from 440 cities, most of them in Asia, which will have two-third of the world's GDP in 2050.

With urbanization, and its intensive natural resource use, emissions of carbon dioxide increased three times between 1950 and 1970 and doubled between 1972 and 2012 and they will more than double between 2012 and 2035. The industrialized countries[1] share has come down from two-third to two-fifth, and in 2035, it is anticipated that with one-sixth of the global population their share will remain at 30 per cent. The share of Asia, with half the world population, will rise to only 40 per cent because energy consumption per capita will remain less than half that of the industrialized countries as the re-emergence of China demonstrates. Asia will move to a services and knowledge-based economy, and unlike the earlier Industrial Revolution, the Information Technology Revolution spearheaded by India, is not based on increasing use of energy. China's median age will be 47 by 2030, compared to 40 in the United States and 32 in India and the working age population (between 15 and 64) in China will shrink by 11 per cent between 2014 and 2030, that is over 107 million fewer people; this trend will reduce future demand. Global overconsumption will also be reduced with the demographic transition in industrialized countries as one-fifth of their population is expected to be 65 or older by 2035. The Asian century will happen largely outside the North–South framework and will in-turn reshape the geopolitics and geoeconomics of global governance and natural resource use around the rural–urban divide rather than between countries.

Scientific expert opinion has been used to describe the patterns, trends and drivers of natural resource use in terms of global environmental change. In 2000, one-seventh of the human population

---

[1] The terms industrialized countries and emerging countries refers to developed and developing countries. Re-emerging countries are the ancient civilizations of China and India.

in industrialized countries in cities accounted for half of global energy use and this pattern of energy use came about because, for example, in the United States, cheap energy, low cost capital and real prices for non-petroleum imports fell by more than a third as infrastructure was being developed between 1950 and 1970 and again between 1970 and 1990 when the urban transformation was taking place, allowing consumers to continue enjoying *de facto* gains in living standards[2].

As a result global governance structures and rules are characterized by asymmetries in terms of access, scope and outcomes. While developing countries must abide by and/or shoulder the effects of global governance rules and regulations, they have had limited influence in shaping them; important areas of interest to them are currently not covered, or sparsely covered, while other areas are overregulated with divergent rules and provisions leading to a shrinking of policy space for developing countries[3]. This book provides the intellectual background of how this arrangement came about with respect to one of the most important global concerns by tracing the evolution of global environmental concerns, in 1972, sustainable development, in 1987, and climate change, in 1992, as distinct from economic development up until their again coming together in a new integrated framework with a common set of global goals, in 2012, in a multipolar world.

The discussion and analysis is based on my decade and a half experience within the United Nations, which has shaped my understanding of the framework that was established, as well as its limitations and potential. It includes the politics of framing issues, agenda setting, multilateral processes and outcomes of global conferences. In addition, five forms of material — papers of the United States State Department, United Nations Archives, United Nations publications, Reports of the Secretary-General of the United Nations to support multilateral processes and studies of management consulting firms analysing global trends – that reflect the thinking within governments, international institutions and global research not directly supported by any government, are quoted extensively and can serve as data for further research by others. Moving away from the dominant environmental and economic academic theoretical constructs, which continues to be dominated by researchers in industrialized countries, helps to understand the origins and continuation of an institution-focussed framework that has lasted for over 40 years. Consequently, the way the argument has been developed in this book different dimensions of the issues have been discussed, even at the risk of some repetition. This book presents the perspective of re-emerging and developing countries to better understand global trends, future of international cooperation and governance for achieving sustainable development.

The book assesses past and present natural resource use to analyse global change as well as effective and socially desired ways of dealing with the impacts on the planet, recognizing that the impacts of production and consumption have different characteristics. Besides the introductory chapter/section it has five sections: the first two consider global environmental change and climate change, and the later sections analyse the evolution of sustainable development and global well-being. The transformative geo-economic shift to Asia is already reframing global politics and the China–United States Climate Agreement of November 2014, outside the United Nations framework, and the Asian Infrastructure Investment Bank established by China in

---

[2] Richard Dobbs, Sree Ramaswamy, Elizabeth Stephenson, and S. Patrick Viguerie. 2014. Management intuition for the next 50 years, McKinsey Quarterly September 2014, McKinsey and Company.
[3] Committee for Development Policy, Policy Note: Global governance and global rules for development in the post-2015 era. United Nations, June 2014. The Committee is an expert body of the United Nations Economic and Social Council composed of 24 members serving in their personal capacity.

October 2014, outside the Bretton Woods framework, are examples. Future natural resource use will largely be within a cooperative framework between re-emerging and developing countries, instead of the post-colonial North–South divide.

The first section explains global environmental change, climate change and sustainable development in an unequal world, and emphasizes that management of natural resources, including trade, is at the heart of this global concern. Politics, rather than science, shaped the way the issue was framed in technical terms as global risk around symptoms rather than the national causes of the problems, thereby requiring global collective action and limiting national policy space in developing countries. How this mode of governance was defined, established and legitimized in a globalizing world is necessary to understand what can be done to modify global governance for sustainable development, in an even more interdependent world. The analysis is illustrated with extensive use of archival material and United Nations reports of the first global conference in 1972 as well as case studies of subsequent major environmental concerns. The details will be of interest primarily to researchers as current assessments, including the reports of the Intergovernmental Panel on Climate Change, rely exclusively on scientific and academic research published in peer-reviewed journals, whose authors are based almost exclusively in industrialized countries.

The second and third sections have a more in-depth treatment of different dimensions of the evolution of climate change from a global to a national concern and the evolution of sustainable development from a national to a global concern. The institutional arrangements reflected, rather than shaped, patterns, trends and drivers of natural resource use. Achieving sustainable development and addressing climate change are closely related concerns and involve trade-offs and synergies between multiple objectives, attention to interactions between different types of policies, and the need for transformational change in systems[4]. This modification of the institution-focussed conceptual framework is a result of the principle of 'common but differentiated responsibilities', which was the last principle to be negotiated in the Rio Declaration in 1992, and it led to the interplay between universality and diversity providing policy space to developing countries till the emergence of the new world order.

The fourth section considers the interlinked concerns of global environmental change, climate change and sustainable development in a more equal world. A broader group of stakeholders, including social scientists are developing a different conceptual framework, that is not based on multilateral treaties or the market, and is based on patterns, trends and drivers of natural resource use, shaped by the transformative impact of the re-emergence of China and India.

The fifth section reinforces the importance of framing and considers the emergence of a global rural–urban divide in international relations, as urbanization, economic growth, trade and geopolitics shifts to developing countries in Asia. The politics is no longer around the framings based on the natural sciences and differentiated rights and obligations in multilateral environmental agreements but around the social sciences, societal functions and global goals. For example, climate-resilient pathways are enabled by urban transformations that facilitate both adaptation and mitigation rather than treat them as separate policy areas. Increasing interdependence of cities on flows of goods and services is a megatrend in the transformation from poverty to middle-class levels of well-being involving three times the population that shifted to cities prior to 1970 when the current governance architecture was instituted to support particular patterns of natural resource use. The leadership of the re-emerging countries and the nature of these shifts give more hope for sustainability than at any time in the past as global goals are now shaped by a service and knowledge-based, not industrial, economy; the quest for markets for services rather than natural resources as the basis of well-being will lead to greater equity and coherence in the global agenda.

---

[4] IPCC Fifth Assessment Synthesis Report, 2014.

The objective of the book is to rethink the conceptual basis of conventional approaches to studying global change from the perspective of developing countries. I explore the possibilities for turning into reality the vision of shared prosperity for the 9 billion people that will soon inhabit this planet. Internationally traded goods and services already constitute 60 per cent of world production, indicating the very high level of interconnectedness between national economies and the role of trade in balancing locations of urban demand with sources of rural supply. With market forces stretching into most parts of the world, conferring global market values on land, water, energy, forests and minerals, the analytical focus is shifting even more sharply from scarcity of natural resources to their distribution and use or consumption in cities. Global policy is moving away from its narrow focus on governance 'of' sustainable development to the broader concern with governance 'for' sustainable development.

For example, the focus of multilateral cooperation around climate governance has become a part of the political, economic and security debate because of the perceived competition for scarce resources. Why has the issue been framed in terms of dealing with the scarcity of natural resources, the symptoms, rather than the causes of the problem, the use of energy, and the result of an inexorable trend in human civilization – urbanization – enabled by a globalizing economy and supported by multilateral rules? Are the political causes related to collective action problems of states shifting pollution across national boundaries or are they motivated by control over ecosystem services outside national borders and natural resource use beyond planetary limits, both linked to a market economy? Why have consumption patterns in cities not been the focus of inquiry and why megatrends are only now being researched with the re-emergence of China and India? Social scientists are now arguing that environmental issues should no longer be considered in physical terms but rather as social problems concerning people, symptoms of a dysfunctional society and matters of governance and fairness[5]. This reframing will support new forms of international cooperation that are not framed by international experts supporting national agendas but rely on exchanging experiences, developing knowledge networks and sharing human well-being and prosperity.

This book explores the role of ideas, and not just power and influence, to explain the way in which natural resource use, global governance and globalization evolved with urbanization reaching saturation levels in industrialized countries, with three-quarters of the population having shifted to urban areas by the 1970s. The social dimension is becoming relevant as China, with seven times that population, nears the completion of its urbanization around 2030 and 1 billion Indians are expected to reach urban middle-class levels of well-being by 2050 as Asia accounts for two-thirds of global GDP. An understanding of the dynamics of this transformation offers insights into the three dominant interacting processes of global interdependence, governance and human well-being. Sustainability is about the use and distribution, and not the scarcity, of natural resources.

References

National Intelligence Council, Global Trends 2030: Alternative Worlds. 2012, United States of America. See also, Key World Energy Statistics 2013, International Energy Agency, Paris, 2014.

---

[5] ISSC/UNESCO. 2013. *World Social Science Report 2013: Changing Global Environments*. Paris: OECD Publishing and UNESCO Publishing.

Acknowledgments

The book draws heavily on documents of the United States Department of State, including declassified diplomatic correspondence, as well as on reports of the United Nations and its Specialized Agencies, studies of Management Consultancies and Think-tanks. This material provides a perspective different from the mainstream literature, and a related objective is to make this material readily accessible for further work in better understanding a complex challenge.

This book also builds on the following articles:

The China–US Climate Agreement – A Victory for the Planet, and for Developing Countries, Vol. 2 No. 2, *Chinese Journal of Urban and Environmental Studies*, (2014), 2014.

Global Sustainable Development Goals are about the Use and Distribution, not Scarcity of Natural Resources: Will the Middle Class in the USA, China and India Save the Climate as Its Incomes Grow. *Climate and Development*, 4 (4), 2014.

Post-2015 Global Agenda: Are the Political Decisions on Climate Change Shifting to a New Forum in the United Nations as It Comes Together with Sustainable Development and Security? *Climate and Development* 6 (2), 2014.

Fresh thinking needed on sustainable development, *Economic and Political Weekly*, Vol. XLIX No. 31, 02 August 2014.

The Rise and Fall of Global Climate Policy: Stockholm to Rio 1992, to Rio + 20 and Beyond. *Chinese Journal of Environmental and Urban Studies* 1 (1), 2013.

Why is the UN Security Council Discussing Climate Change? *Strategic Analysis* 37 (6), 2013.

Rio +20, Climate Change and Development: The Evolution of Sustainable Development (1972–2012). *Climate and Development* 4 (2): 157–166, 2012.

Climate Change and the Rio + 20 Summit: A developing Country Perspective. *Climate and Development,* 3 (2011) 1–5.

Global Governance: International Cooperation to Achieve Sustainable Development: Modifying Longer Term Trends. Paper presented at the 2nd UNITAR–YALE Conference on Environmental Governance and Democracy: *Strengthening Institutions to Address Climate Change and Advance a Green Economy,* Yale University, September 2010.

Leadership in the Climate Negotiations, *Economic and Political Weekly*, Vol. XLV No. 33, 14 August 2010.

Climate Change and Global Sustainability: Need for a New Paradigm for International Cooperation. *Climate and Development* 2 (2010), 2010.

Reflection on the Climate Negotiations: A Southern Perspective. *Climate Policy* 9 (2009), 2009.

G8 and India on Climate Change, *Economic and Political Weekly*, Vol. XLIII No 29, 19–25 July 2008.

Sustainable Development and Climate Change, *Economic and Political Weekly*, Vol. XLIII No 15, 12–18 April 2008, India.

Evolution of Global Environmental Governance and the United Nations, *Global Environmental Politics*, Vol. 7, No. 3, August 2007, USA.

What Drives Environmental Policy? *Environment Policy and Law*, Vol. 36, No. 3–4, July 2006, Germany.

Trends in Global Environmental Governance: The Emergence of a Mutual Supportiveness Approach to Achieve Sustainable Development. *Global Environmental Politics*, 4: 4, November 2004, USA.

Sustainable Development, the Rio Convention and Multilateral Cooperation. *Colorado Journal of International Environmental Law and Policy* Vol. 4, No. 1, Special Number on the United Nations Conference on Environment and Development (UNCED), 1993, USA.

The Sustainable Development of all Forests, *Review of European Community & International Environmental Law*, Special Number on the UN Conference on Environment and Development, Vol. 1, Issue 3, 1992, UK.

I express my gratitude to those colleagues and friends in the Government of India and the United Nations who shared their insights, to all those who facilitated my interaction with students in China and in the United States and to the time and effort others have put into improving the work.

I also express my special gratitude to my wife who had the patience to bear with me as I worked on this book and to my two sons who encouraged me at all times.

Abbreviations

ADB	Asian Development Bank
AIIB	Asian Infrastructure Development Bank
BRICS	Brazil, Russia, India, China and South Africa group
EC	European Commission
EU	European Union
FAO	Food and Agriculture Organization of the United Nations
GHG	Greenhouse gases
ECOSOC	Economic and Social Council of the United Nations General Assembly
ICSU	International Council for Science
ISSC	International Social Science Council
IEA	International Energy Agency
IPBES	International Platform on Biodiversity and Ecosystem Services
IPCC	Intergovernmental Panel on Climate Change
OECD	Organization for Economic Cooperation and Development
UN	United Nations
UNCED	United Nations Conference on Environment and Development
UNCTAD	United Nations Conference on Trade and Development
UNFCCC	United Nations Framework Convention on Climate Change
UNEP	United Nations Environmental Programme
UNESCO	United Nations Educational, Scientific and Cultural Organization
UNHABITAT	United Nations Human Settlements Programme
UNIDO	United Nations Industrial Development Organization

INTRODUCTION

'"Only one Earth" marked a watershed in the evolution of humanities relationship with the earth and global concern about the environment'

United Nations Conference on the Human Environment, 1972

'Sustainable development is development that meets the needs of the present without compromising the ability of future generations to meet their own needs'

Our Common Future: World Commission on Sustaianble Development, United Nations, 1987

'... Protecting and managing the natural resource base for economic and social development'.

'The Future We Want', Outcome document of the 2012 United Nations Conference on Environment and Development, United Nations.

'Sustainable development calls for robust economic development and a long term convergence in living standards between rich and poor countries in ways that are socially equitable and respect planetary boundaries'

Sustainable Development Network, United Nations, at the launch of 'The World in 2050: Pathways towards a sustainable future', March 2015.

'... we have a hard time grasping what it means to live within planetary limits ... transforming key systems such as transport, energy, housing and food systems lies at the heart of long-term remedies ... as well as redesign of systems that have steered these provisioning systems and have created unsustainable lock-ins: finance, fiscal, health, legal and education'

The European Environment - state and outlook 2015: synthesis report, European Environment Agency, 2015

'... China wants to write the rules for the worlds's fastest growing region ... why would we let that happen? We should write those rules'

President State of the Union Address January 15, 2015.

'... To build a community of common destiny ... The interests of others must be accommodated while pursuing one's own interests, and common development must be promoted while seeking one's own development ... security should be given equal emphasis as development, and sustainable development surely provides a way to sustainable security'.

Keynote Speech by H.E. Xi Jinping, President of the People's Republic of China, at the Boao Forum for Asia Annual Conference 2015, 28 March 2015

Social Dimension of Sustainability

In a unipolar, and post-colonial world, assured access to low-cost natural resources shaped economic growth pathways: industrialization, urbanization and lifestyles. A multipolar world is not able to keep commodity prices low modifying longer term trends shaping economic growth: urban design, community attitudes and individual decisions affecting natural resource use consumption patterns are taking place in an increasingly services oriented and knowledge-based economy, giving hope for finally moving sustainability from ideas to reality. In the twenty-first century, with unprecedented interdependence, wealth and inequality, sustainability is about the use and distribution, not scarcity, of natural resources – the neglected social dimension of sustainable development.

The impact of human activity on the global environment increased dramatically after 1950; by 1970, three-fourths of the population of industrialized countries had moved to cities, and the 'American way of life' soon became the 'Western way of life' as Europe rebuilt its cities, but at half the level of natural resource use in the United States. What is considered economic development is really based on use of natural resources for infrastructure and energy, electricity for lighting, heating, cooling and mechanical power, and oil powered cars, trucks and aircraft for transportation of people and industrial food production. High energy consumption affected every aspect of daily life with the promise of large houses in the suburbs, low price fuel, fast travel and foreign holidays, dining out, weekly shopping and new fabrics. Infrastructure–production and lifestyle–consumption systems reflected technological advances as well as social values and worldviews, which combined with low commodity prices, have led to path dependency of a high natural resource use and high carbon system. The citizens of these countries, until recently, were not even aware that two-third of the total national emissions of carbon dioxide emissions come from the residential, commercial and transport sectors which together constitute urban economic activity. Such was the power of ideas, institutions and rules that the imbalance being created in the planet was first described as global environmental change and later, to accommodate developing countries concerns, as sustainable development, without requiring any action at the personal level in the industrialized countries.

Re-emerging China and India, with three times the population of the industrialized countries[1], are adopting an 'Asian way of life' that is less energy intensive and wasteful, not so much focused on accumulation of material goods and with values and behaviour shaped by very different ancient civilizations. Half of China is already living in cities with denser urban design and smaller homes,

---

[1] The difference rises to 15 times in comparing the population that shifted to urban areas in the mid 20th century with the urbanization taking place in the 21st century.

greater reliance on public rail transport, more internal than foreign travel for recreation and greater preference for local food with much less waste. In this transformation, the largest mitigation and adaptation opportunities are going to be in rapidly urbanizing areas where urban form and infrastructure are not yet locked-in [IPCC, 2014].

This book analyses the challenges of global interdependence; the value judgments in the science–policy interface of how sustainable development has been framed in an unequal world in terms of human impacts of a growing population on nature rather than the nature of the activities and consumption patterns as rural agrarian populations shifted to cities. An institutional focus was adopted – interplay of agency, architecture, accountability and legitimacy, to which equitable allocation of resources and adaptiveness of governance systems was later added (Bierman, 2014) – instead of analysing patterns, trends and drivers of natural resource use. Europe's consumption footprint is double that of its own biological productive capacity, and hence human well-being depends on ecological capacity from elsewhere [WWF, 2013]. The United States ecological footprint is even greater. These patterns of natural resource use were shaped by the trend, in real terms, of oil and gas, metal and food prices remaining flat or falling throughout the twentieth century and they have increased by an average of 260, 176 and 120 per cent, respectively, since 2000 as a result of a combination of strong demand, notably from China and rising supply costs, shaping very different consumption patterns in the twenty-first century [McKinsey and Co, 2013]. Despite this increase, in 2010, emerging economies made up 40 per cent of the world's GDP and by 2025 this number is predicted to be over 70 per cent, largely in Asia. This trend is going to continue as the global economy doubles by 2030 and doubles again by 2050 driven by the re-emerging economies with very different norms, consumption patterns and practices.

Very different societal values are leading to different trends of natural resource use in the re-emerging countries, which will in turn shape institutions for a new world order that will dilute the North–South divide between countries for an urban–rural divide, as most of these flows will take place between developing countries requiring new forms of international cooperation. The book draws more on practice and policymaking rather than international relations theory, or approaches based on economics and political science, which are analytically rigorous but do not describe reality accurately.

1.1 The importance of a developing country perspective

Sustainable development, the way it was framed, was a deliberate construct to bridge the growing divide around natural resource management between industrialized countries that had become urban by the 1970s, and the much larger population in countries which had earlier emerged from colonialism after the 1950s, from where natural resources were sourced and were expected to urbanize in the coming years. The intellectual conceptualization of sustainable development had three elements: it encompassed a common concern for the global environment while supporting economic growth in different degrees in all countries; international cooperation was to be achieved through expert groups, treaties and institutional bargaining among autonomous actors with different perceptions of problems and interests; and the agenda was identified by and the outcomes were shaped by the industrialized countries, and reflected their priorities. Since the United Nations did not, and does not even now, play a role in economic policies, the way the issues were defined in physical terms, as 'scarcity', and in technical terms, as chemical agents, focussed attention on the symptoms and linked them to development as an additional cost. This paradigm reflected the capacity for strategic thinking built up in the United States to deal with the Cold War, which could easily be applied to other issues in order to secure their national interest.

At the international level, the management of finite natural resources raised two issues: sharing global common resources and collectively managing transnational problems. International environment law, formulated through a political process, shaped policy less in dealing with environmental damage and more in industrialized countries securing rights over natural resources outside national boundaries: the oceans, biological diversity and the atmosphere. The way the issues were framed around these related but distinct concerns served the interests of industrialized countries with maximum benefits and minimum obligations for them. For example, gaining access to biological diversity to support the next wave of growth through the biotechnology industry was a key policy objective of the Rio Conference in 1992, leading to products eventually, covering healthcare, energy and industrial and agriculture sectors. The market capitalization of these companies in the United States, Europe, Canada and Australia increased from $4 billion in 1994 to $400 billion in 2006 and rose to $792 in 2013 with revenues of $92 billion and the global biotechnology industry is expected to exceed $320 billion in 2015, only now with China and India playing an increasing role in development of bio-drugs [Ernst and Young, 2014].

The process of international norm creation for the global commons began in 1972, in Stockholm. International cooperation, shaped by global treaties in 1992, in Rio, evolved into concepts of public–private partnership in 2002, in Johannesburg, and, into global goals in 2012, again in Rio. In this 40-year span, countries moved from being connected, to becoming interconnected and now interdependent on each other. This evolution reflects globalization: the global spreading of industrialization to old colonies and beginning of the shift of their rural populations to urban areas and into the middle class as consumers driving economic growth, and natural resource use. With understanding of the interdependence of environmental challenges and social and economic systems, the focus of inquiry and policy is now shifting to modification of longer term trends in urban consumption patterns, or 'lifestyles' of the rich worldwide, with an emerging rural–urban rather than the historical North–South divide.

Since sustainable development was projected as a technical subject describing scarcity in particular sectors rather than analyzing the causes, it was not designed to solve the problem. The objective was to divert attention from activities in industrialized countries to what was happening in developing countries. The refusal of developing countries to agree to a partitioning of the atmosphere at Copenhagen, in 2008, was the turning point and reflected their growing power to be able to reject formulations presented by industrialized countries and the gradually lessening leverage exercised by multilateral financial institutions that were established outside the United Nations. The subsequent China–United States climate deal, November 2014, recognizes human well-being within ecological limits and does not adopt a purely risk management perspective.

Within the United Nations, the evolution of sustainable development reflects three related but distinct discourses. First, the tension between the traditional focus of the organization on sectors, or the specialized agencies, and the growing need to consider distribution as environmental considerations are raised in broader cross-cutting areas. The post-Rio 2012 global goals are now leading to an enhanced role for the Economic and Social Council as the World Trade Organization and World Bank lose their relevance in the opening of markets and means of implementation. Second, just as the 2002 World Summit on Sustainable Development was a dialogue among major stakeholders from government, civil society and the private sector on new partnerships, signalling an end to the gap between the public and private sectors in international cooperation, in the future many sustainable development concerns will be treated outside the framework of the United Nations, for example, by cities, suggesting the need for new formulations and institutions, such as the Compact of Mayors launched at the 2014 United Nations Climate Summit. Third, the geopolitical shifts have also had an impact on international civil servants and the leadership of the specialized agencies is now considering distribution issues, broadening the science linkage. The conditions are ripe for a new framework, or paradigm, for the related global concerns of management of natural resources and human well-being.

1.2 How is this different to the current approach

Urbanization led to growth slowing in the industrialized countries in the 1970s, and one outcome was to establish global institutions and rules to seek natural resources in the global commons. In addition, natural resources like forests and biological diversity were sought to be characterized as global environmental goods. International environmental law was conceptually an extension of the rules that had led to the flow of commodities for their industrialization and infrastructure at low costs, did little to reduce global environmental damage and increased wealth and income gaps between and within countries. The harmonization of the free-market system has a natural tendency towards increasing the concentration of wealth and policy proposals assume this growing concentration of wealth is not only inevitable, but the thing that matters most [Piketty, 2014]. Increase in wealth in turn led to increase in natural resource use, in urban and not in rural areas, as well as inequality, and 'sharing of the pie' with the bottom 40 per cent of people is only now gaining traction even with the International Monetary Fund; for example, the United States economy's per capita gross domestic product has grown by more than $6,000 since 1999 but the median income has declined by more than $4,000. Consequently, changing the way we think about society, and a focus on distribution, supports the adoption of low-carbon models different from the current high-carbon socio-technical systems; growing inequality is now raising important questions of global social justice and human rights, for example, as the poorest billion are responsible for less than 5 per cent of global emissions and need carbon space for their economic growth. This acknowledgement has come about with geopolitical shifts, underlining the importance of the way the issues are framed. For the first time, the Intergovernmental Panel on Climate Change in its fifth assessment report, in 2014, has identified ethics and justice along with economic analysis as guidance for policymakers [IPCC, 2014]. In this view, the exercise of individual choices or lifestyles may need to become more austere, if everyone has to get equal access to energy, for example, instead of treating the integrity of ecosystems as more important by those who already have access to energy.

The scientific effort to understand global change has been, and to an extent continues to be, framed by the natural sciences that investigate, monitor and document environmental damage. The planetary boundaries that are set involve judgments about what constitutes an acceptable risk. Consequently, the policy framework is such that the assessment of what is and what is not relevant has also been determined by the natural sciences. The responses have, therefore, been issue based, addressed in a piecemeal manner focused on sectors and countries rather than trends and goals at the global level; the outcome is incremental with partial solutions, while also limiting which analyses are deemed possible and relevant. For example, it is only now that the Intergovernmental Panel on Climate Change is considering '"key factors", it is still not considering "drivers", and identifies them as: 'population size, economic activity, energy use, land use patterns, technology change and climate policy' in the Synthesis Report. The Report still does not distinguish between the excessive resource use by some while others' increase in natural resource use is questioned because of planetary limits. It is only now beginning to be recognized that social science, along with the natural sciences, enables us to better imagine the future we want.

Sustainability is a political challenge, as choices have to be made about human well-being within ecological limits and how countries understand themselves and the world their citizens wish to live in. While there are no alternatives to physical infrastructure, alternative growth models and urban design can have a transformative impact with a greater potential than that of new technologies, by modifying consumption patterns as the urban middle class increases three times by 2050; energy efficiency is now recognized as a fuel by the Intergovernmental Panel on Climate Change, the International Energy Agency and McKinsey and Company. Natural resource use in cities, energy use, transport, food and water consumption are social processes where environmental impacts are linked with the economies which collectively shape us just as society shapes the natural environment;

they are not independent silos, as we have been considering since the Report of the Brundtland Commission in 1987. Achieving global well-being within planetary limits, as the essential challenge of sustainable development, questions the consumption patterns that define prosperity in terms of material resources for a greater focus on the qualitative aspects of well-being.

In the new paradigm, industrial pollution, scarcity of natural resources, degradation of ecosystems and planetary limits are seen as symptoms of the way consumption and production have been organized as human populations shifted from their century's long dependence on their local environment as agricultural producers to becoming urban consumers depending on global trade in natural resources for the goods and services required to maintain their well-being and lifestyles. Even adaptation to the adverse effects of climate change has so far been researched in terms resilience of ecological systems and is only now being seen in terms of social systems, considering adaptive livelihood systems in the context of wider transformational changes.

1.3 Dimensions of the 'common concern' on environment and human well-being

The architecture and contours of international cooperation around the environment were shaped by the United States, as the major user of natural resources and the most powerful state. The United States set the global agenda in a manner that characterized the global environment as a 'common concern', with a set of agreed rules for its management. The increasing scarcity and interdependence was not reflected in sharing natural resources. Using the leverage of cheap loans from multilateral financial institutions to debt laden countries enabled multinational corporations to enter, extract and keep commodity prices low and was an incentive for international cooperation in three areas: a key role for scientists, and later non-governmental organizations, in shaping ideas and the agenda; countries working together to share gains, again defined by the scientists; and, with institutions increasing transparency, preventing cheating and monitoring compliance of elements also identified by scientists. The continuing problem with these processes is the absence of a common understanding on how broader social change and human well-being will take place.

Both the establishment and the evolution of the treaty-based regimes were shaped by ideas developed by groups of scientists and scholars in industrialized countries, with the agenda and new global rules projected to represent impartial expertise rather than politics. The conceptions of appropriate behaviour were expected to change the way states looked at costs and benefits as well as perceptions of their interests and roles in the multilateral system. Developing countries remain reluctant partners in this arrangement, as they gradually became aware, with the implementation of multilateral environmental agreements, that their policy space had been restricted while industrialized countries had gained access to key natural resources within their borders; for example, access to biological diversity without sharing the benefits of biotechnology.

In other ways as well, the institutional approach did not deliver the global benefits it was designed to secure. For example, in 1992, technology was considered as the key to solving the world's problems, but the intellectual property right regime of 1995 worked against its transfer. In 2002, it was realized that there would be no lasting change without modifying knowledge systems and lifestyles to develop qualitatively different growth pathways. However, the 10-year 'framework of programs on sustainable consumption and production' of the United Nations remains voluntary. In 2012, new 'green growth' was also considered largely in terms of efficiency of production patterns, without addressing the underlying drivers of related urban middle class consumption.

The way global sustainable development policymaking is evolving poses three challenges. These concerns are reviewing the approaches for understanding and assessing the change that has taken place; identifying those trends that need to be modified rather than adopt a broad focus on production and consumption; and ensure a long-term perspective in policymaking that incorporates global links allied to social rather than regulatory transformations. A more holistic approach to environmental problems focuses on 'restraint', in particular uncontrolled consumerism, and requires altering behaviour instead of the sole focus on new markets for reshaping production patterns, as social considerations are weighed alongside environmental and economic ones. This transformation will be difficult, for example, designing cities around reducing the need to travel, and the determining factor will be societal change. The United Nations continues to be best place to generate strategic knowledge leading to deepening coherence of the global agenda in order to support a common understanding on patterns of resource use that are in principle common for all.

The way the problem is now being framed also challenges the 'universalism' that has dominated the global agenda for a stronger recognition of 'diversity' as a part of the architecture, because there will be different sets of solutions for countries at different levels of industrialization and urbanization, or different levels of development. The shift from a focus on the symptoms to the causes of the problem focuses on urban consumers as the drivers of change in all countries. Norway, in April 2015, followed in the footsteps of a host of other countries, including the UK, Ireland, Finland and Denmark to put in place legislation adopting a carbon budget as the best way to slash emissions and increase the role of renewable energy in the energy mix, without relying on a global treaty or markets; as the Prime Minister pointed out, "there is a need to transform Norwegian society". The United Kingdom adopted a Carbon Budget system in 2008 as the best way to make the transition (UK, 2014). The emerging framework is still not stressing equitable sharing of the global commons, or natural resources, to meet the scale of the demand. It will need a new type of international cooperation as re-emerging countries shape their urban future establishing linkages with other developing countries.

There is also a contradiction between ecological, economic and technological interdependence and the political fragmentation within the United Nations, which continues to see global issues, for example, sustainable development, trade, technology and finance, as separate issues because they have been treated as technical concerns. For example, asymmetries in power and capacities are reflected in the use of the dispute settlement mechanism of the World Trade Organization in terms of access and retaliatory measures; so far 40 per cent of cases have been between developed countries while another 22.2 per cent of cases involved developed countries requesting the investigation of middle-income countries that are industrializing [Lee et al., 2014]. Increasing globalization raises the question of global governance with norms that consider the various human activities as parts of a single system to share both responsibility towards the environment and prosperity of all human beings. With geopolitical shifts the old frameworks are being challenged with China establishing new financial institutions in Asia, where three-fourth of future growth is going to take place.

Since 1972 some 500 million Chinese, which is more than the urban population of the United States and Europe in 1972, have moved to cities and an equal number is expected to shift by 2030. This is now a part of the global mega-trend driving natural resource use, and 750 million Indians are also expected to be living in cities in 2030. Therefore, the issue that must now be debated is how to manage the Asian century, or transformation, and the rural–urban complementary flows that will shape politics within and between nations in the interim period. One difference with the previous wave of urbanization is that it was driven by access to and use of low-cost commodities and industrial production, the Asian Century will be shaped in a greater degree by the global services and knowledge economy, for example, renewable energy, biotechnology, nanotechnology and information technology, enabling a different growth model, urban design, consumption patterns and social concerns; as well as shaping a different type of international cooperation that is not based on the North–South divide.

For example, in 2012, flows of goods, services and finance reached $26 trillion, with knowledge-intensive flows nearly half of total flows, or 36 per cent of global GDP, 1.5 times the level in 1990, and expected to triple by 2025 [MGI, 2014]. In 2013, labour mobility covered 232 million persons, largely from Asia, and is a factor in reducing wage differences between countries; India obtained $70 billion by way of remittances in 2014. Information and Computer Technology has a unique footprint in Asia: export revenues in 2011 accounted for nearly a quarter of exports, twice the global average; cloud computing is expected to generate 10 million jobs and will transform traditional business models and productivity; more than half of the global growth in frontier technologies, such as photovoltaics and semiconductors, is in Asia, and India had a 40 per cent share of global revenues of knowledge and legal process outsourcing. India is a hub for manufacture of generic biotechnology-based pharmaceuticals. These trends challenge the linear path of progress and will enable Asia to jump technology cycles [ADB, 2013] as well as earlier patterns, trends and drivers of natural resource use.

This is the context in which the book analyses the evolution of sustainability within the United Nations. The developments reflect the power of ideas, persuasion and pressure. The objectives and processes were shaped by international civil servants, natural and social scientists and think-tanks, mainly in industrialized countries. The way the issues have been framed explains why the outcomes did not lead to the professed results, as they served national interests of industrialized countries. The book also explores new social science inputs, forms of international cooperation in a multipolar world and the best ways societies can modify consumption and production patterns to pursue sustainable development paths for well-being of their citizens while reducing the causes of risk to the planet. People are now at the centre of sustainable development, the challenges call for a transformation of social systems and new ideas are now coming from re-emerging countries. They are focusing on how to facilitate a broadly acceptable societal change, which will be supported rather than driven by technology. While much can be learned from the experience of the industrialized countries, much more will need to be learned from the initiatives in China, India and other developing countries that are now rapidly urbanizing, and managing the rural–urban divide until their population moves into the middle class, with new global governance arrangements, processes and rules 'to build a community of common destiny'.

References

ADB. 2013. 'Innovative Asia: Advancing the Knowledge-Based Economy: The Next Policy Agenda'. Philippines: Asian Development Bank, Manila.

Biermann, 2014, *Earth System Governance World Politics in the Anthropocene*, Frank Bierman, The MIT Press, October 2014.

Ernst and Young. 2014 *Beyond Borders: Unlocking Value*. Global Biotechnology Report 2014.

IPCC. 2014. Working Group III, 'Mitigation of Climate Change'. 'Chapter 12: Human Settlements, Infrastructure and Spatial Planning'. 5th Assessment Report. Intergovernmental Panel on Climate Change.

Lee, Keun, Wonkyu Shin, and Hochul Shin. 2014. 'How large or small is the policy space?' WTO Regime and Industrial Policy, Background Paper for the Sixteenth Session of the United Nations Committee for Development Policy.

McKinsey and Co, Resource Revolution: Tracking global Commodity Markets – Trends Survey 2013.

MGI. 2014. '*Global Flows in a Digital Age: How Trade, Finance, People, and Data Connect the World Economy* McKinsey Global Institute, 2014'.

NIC. 2008. Global Trends 2025: A Transformed World, November 2008, National Intelligence Council 2008-003.

Piketty, Thomas. 2014. *Capital in the Twenty-First Century*. Trans Arthur Goldhammer. Belknap Press/Harvard University Press.

UK, 2014, Meeting Carbon Budgets – 2014 progress report to Parliament, Government response to the sixth annual progress report of the Committee on Climate Change. URN 14D/364. Crown Copyright 2014.

WWF, 2005. *The Ecological Footprint 3*, World Wildlife Fund 2005.

CONSUMPTION IN AN UNEQUAL WORLD: FRAMING INTERNATIONAL COOPERATION

'...Long-range policy planning to cope with global environmental problems must take account of the total ecological burden. This burden tends to increase with population, growth and with the level of economic activity, whereas the capacity of the environment to provide essential inputs to production and to absorb unwanted outputs from consumption is fundamentally limited. The problem of managing total ecological burden will remain even after world population is stabilized. Controlling that burden by systematic reduction in per capita production of goods and services would be politically unacceptable. A concerted effort is needed to orient technology toward making human demands upon the environment less severe'.

'US Priority Interests in the Environmental Activities of International Organizations', prepared by the Committee on International Environmental Affairs of the State Department, Report by Task Force III of the Committee on International Environmental Affairs, Washington, December 1970. Foreign Relations of the United States, Foreign Relations 1969–1976, Documents on Global Issues 1969–1972, Vol. E-1, Chapter V, International Environment Policy, Edited by Susan K. Holly and William B. McAllister, Office of the Historian, Bureau of Public Affairs, US Department of State, 2005.

'...Urbanization is the product of a major long term, worldwide, socio-economic process– centuries old evolution in man's way of life from the rural agricultural life pattern to the urban-industrial way of life ... urbanization has changed the nation with seventy five percent of its people living in urban areas...

We must see ourselves not only as victims of environmental degradation but as environmental aggressors and change our patterns of consumption and production accordingly ... different patterns of growth from ours may improve the quality of life without environmental degradation'.

Stockholm and Beyond: Report of the Secretary of State's Advisory Committee on the 1972 United Nations Conference on the Human Environment, May 1972, Department of State Publication 8657, International Organization and Conference Series 101, Washington DC

'Will the growing awareness of the concepts of "one earth" and "one environment" in fact lead–as it should–to the nobler concept of "one humanity", and to a more equitable sharing of environmental costs and a greater international interest in, and responsibility for, the accelerated development of the less industrialized world? Or will it become a narrow concern of the industrialized world, leading to many awkward confrontations with the developing countries rather than to a new era of international cooperation?'

Report on Development and Environment by Secretary-General for UN Conference on the Human Environment to the General Assembly, Maurice Strong, UN General Assembly Document A/CONF.48/10, 22 December 1971.

Geopolitics of the Global Environment

2

The global environmental concern has been shaped by an interrelated conceptual and normative framework. A two-track approach of mainstream sciences formed an extensive literature, which was provided to the public in a simplified form by the experts and to the science–policy interface informing multilateral treaties to establish processes of research, dialogue, negotiation and conflict resolution. Both streams have been entirely funded by the industrialized countries. The scientific research reflected their interests in shifting the focus away from the global impact of material requirements of infrastructure and the consumption of three-quarters of their own population which had moved to cities by the 1970s on to the larger agricultural, poor and growing population in developing countries arising from colonialism. With one-third of the global population, industrialized countries were already consuming three-quarters of the global natural resource, facilitated by an international system where the real price of these resources declined by a third between 1950 and 1970, and non-petroleum commodity prices again declined by a similar extent between 1990 and 2012. Fearing a similar trend of natural resource use in developing countries will raise prices and seeking to secure rights to natural resources outside national boundaries for continuing rapid growth, as their growth rates faltered from 1970 with urbanization, industrialized countries shaped the intellectual framework, agenda and rules on global environmental change, climate change and sustainable development within the United Nations.

Since the 1970s, the mainstream scientific understanding of the global environment and sustainable development has gone through three phases. The initial research focused on describing, measuring and monitoring what is happening to nature by collecting evidence of the adverse impacts of human activity, which at that time was evident in the developing countries, supplying commodities to the developed countries. This was followed with predictions of what could happen, as it was assumed that developing countries would follow the growth models of industrialized countries. Since the focus remained on the future and the newly industrializing countries, the explanation as to why these activities were leading to environmental degradation, particularly the expansion of agriculture into forest areas, was largely seen in terms of descriptions of the 'tragedy of the commons' and sociological theories, ignoring an earlier trend when the industrialized countries were at similar stages of development. We now know that the assertion that international regulation is needed to check 'free riders' was not evidence based. Recent research documents that there is little evidence that environmental regulation impacts international competitiveness; the effect of current environmental regulations on where trade and investment take place is negligible compared to other factors such as market conditions and the quality of the local workforce, and there is ample evidence that environmental regulations encourage businesses to undertake innovation in clean technologies and discourage research and development in conventional polluting technologies [Grantham Research Institute, 2014].

The intensive global research, data and concern on finding solutions to climate change, a commons problem, pointed to activities in both the industrialized and developing countries. As developing countries began conducting their own research, including on the increasing consumption in their countries, the limitations of earlier prescriptions based on sectoral environmental problems and reliance only on pricing and technology for solutions were exposed, leading to considering the interconnectedness of the social and natural system as a single agenda. An analysis of patterns, trends and drivers of natural resource use in a globalized world reveals consumption patterns of the growing urban middle class rather than poverty-ridden rural population growth driving global environmental degradation, with modification of longer term trends as the solution.

How this transformation is to be achieved was also first raised in the 1970s. A political decision was taken by the United States, as the super power at that time, to develop mechanisms to involve the developing countries and focus deliberations in the United Nations first on technical issues and later on efficiency improvements rather than on the more politically sensitive consumption patterns. We now know that this framework successfully postponed the needed systemic societal changes, and with the global middle class set to triple by 2050, the burden has shifted to developing countries in the form of global goals, with sustainable consumption for the first time becoming a part of the global agenda, in the post-2015, sustainable development agenda. In the period 1990–2012, total aggregate emissions of the United States have increased [UNFCCC, 2014]. United States President, Barack Obama, described China's commitment on peaking of its carbon dioxide emissions by 2030, as 'important because if China, as it develops, adopts the same per capita carbon emissions as advanced economies like the United States or Australia, this planet doesn't stand a chance, because they've got a lot more people' [China Daily, 2014]. Clearly, China, India and other developing countries do not aspire to consumption patterns in the United States transforming sustainable development from ideas to reality.

2.1 Politics around modifying consumption

The real global challenge is the nature of the increasing urban consumer demand. The increased affluence of the urban middle-income population, or middle class, with higher average incomes than in rural areas leads to lifestyles reflecting energy and natural resource-intensive consumption patterns that are produced by energy-intensive industries, and during their lifecycle lead to growing amounts of waste, both solid waste and carbon dioxide. Poor urban public transport planning despite growing demand for transportation encourages car ownership. The urban diet is largely processed food and meat with high levels of energy use as well as waste. Globally, urban households are much more energy intensive than rural populations, even as family size is becoming smaller, with a converging standard of living worldwide.

Global concerns like environmental change, climate change and sustainable development are not about how poor countries and their growing rural populations can best manage conservation of local natural resources and develop with the assistance of industrialized countries but rather about evolving a global consensus on a model, or framework, for moving poor rural populations into the urban middle class within global ecological limits, with a focus on modifying consumption patterns. A number of international conferences on Global Sustainable Consumption Governance in the period between 1972 and 2012, especially after 1992, produced reports where fundamental issues were discussed and insights developed on conceptual frameworks and indicators, while the most crucial questions relating to drivers, trends and patterns of natural resource use have been excluded in the outcomes because of the way the issues were framed, as there has been no political agreement on the actions required to be taken in industrialized countries.

The current framing was supported by a research agenda and intellectual framework that shaped the deliberations within the United Nations. In 1947, Harry Truman, President of the United States, said 'our foreign relations, political and economic, are indivisible and bound up completely with a third objective: re-establishment of world trade', and natural resources formed the bulk of that trade. In the period 1950–1970, United States emissions of carbon dioxide from fossil fuel use increased 3 per cent annually, with a corresponding increase in natural resource use, as it completed its urbanization[1]. The International Monetary Fund, World Bank and General Agreement on Trade and Tariffs supported low commodity prices through worsening terms of trade, debt and structural adjustment loans. In 1971, the United States moved away from the gold standard leading to the collapse of the Bretton Woods System of fixed exchange rates. In 1972, a new legal framework was established in the United Nations with the twin objectives of maintaining patterns of natural resource use, on which the prosperity of their citizens now depended, and securing rights to natural resources outside national boundaries, defined in terms of the global commons, diluting national sovereignty of developing countries as these resources were located in those countries or to which they had a claim.

The United States, as the super power and the leading economy, successfully framed global concerns around three objectives. Firstly, keeping the focus away from the causes of the global environmental problem which had been identified by the 1970s as sustainable consumption and production and securing access to identified natural resources with a future economic potential , for example, the oceans and sea-bed. This was successfully achieved by initially shifting the search for solutions to technological change, with innovation and diffusion of environmentally more benign technology considered to have a growing need [Jesse Ausubel et al., 1995]. This approach changed with assertiveness of the developing countries since 2000 following the acceptance of the principle of 'common but differentiated responsibilities' in the Rio Declaration in 1992, reluctantly by the industrialized countries, and the acceptance of intellectual property rights in the World Trade Organization in 1995, reluctantly by the developing countries. Secondly, global treaties also began to establish commitments with respect to natural resource management along with obligations affecting their distribution as well as rights to natural resources outside national boundaries, for example, designating biological diversity as a global resource to spur advances and profits in biotechnology. Thirdly, on-going negotiations became a part of the framework in which a resolution occurred only when developing countries agreed to compromise their gains in an earlier negotiation. For example, though Agenda 21 in 1992 included a reference to transfer of technology on 'favourable' terms to developing countries in the negotiated outcome of the High Level Policy Forum of the United Nations in 2014 the agreement has been diluted to 'mutually agreed' terms.

While the United States is no longer in a position to set a universal agenda, it retains the intellectual capacity and influence to modify efforts to establish a new agenda that stresses diversity in the obligations based on levels of development. For example, the High-Level Segment of the first session of the UN Environment Assembly adopted a Ministerial Outcome Document, in June 2014, pledging the promotion of sustainable consumption and production patterns which was, however, defined as sustainable lifestyles and resource efficiency and without a specific focus

---

[1] China's emissions in the period 2001–2008 increased 10 per cent annually.

on modifying individual consumption patterns. In the debate leading up to adoption of this document Ministers discussed whether or not to include mention of the principle of common but differentiated responsibility in the Document. For the first time, since 1992, this principle is not specifically mentioned in a negotiated text, and the final Document merely reaffirms commitment to the full implementation of the Rio+20 outcome document and 'all the principles' of the 1992 Rio Declaration on Environment and Development. Similarly, the text of the Sustainable Development Goals incorporates this principle only in the preamble. These developments are signalling the emergence of a new framework on global environmental governance that would not rely on laws but on common environment and development goals, or sustainable development goals, which includes modifying consumption and production patterns in specific sectors without focusing solely on actions to be taken by countries or individuals.

The global research agenda was also entirely funded by the industrialized countries and evolved to respond to their changing requirements, political and economic. The initial analysis of global patterns of natural resource use was later discarded as it implied a comparison between countries and considered the distribution of natural resources. Instead the focus shifted to particular sectors, like energy, food and water, with a stress on local factors of production without considering their global distribution and consumption. For example, it was acknowledged that wealthy nations had more than a century to address the environmental issues of industrialization and urbanization and, even after the global concern was recognized, have not been able to modify longer term trends in natural resource use and that newly developing countries are now required to take measures in an accelerated time frame that will affect their industrialization and urbanization [Weizsacker, 1998]. However, policy emphasis remains on the impact on planetary limits of population increasing from 3.7 billion in 1970 to 7 billion in 2012, ignoring the fact that, for example, 15 per cent of the population in industrialized countries consumed half of global energy in 1992, automobiles in the United States doubled between 1970 and 1990 with the number in developing countries remaining around 10 per cent of this level of car ownership, and per capita incomes in the industrialized countries increased at twice the rate in the developing countries because of urbanization, manufacturing and trade.

The causes and consequences of declining trends in prices of natural resources in the twentieth century have also been ignored because of the implications for wasteful 'lifestyles' in industrialized countries. Economic growth in the industrialized countries was enabled by overall declining global market prices for most natural resources including fuel, metals, and food. Natural resources (energy and materials) in many industries amounted to as little as 5 per cent of total cost; the focus was on labour productivity while productivity in manufacture and use was ignored leading to increase in waste, including carbon dioxide emissions. The enormous growth in economic activity and consumption in China, India and other emerging economies has now led to average prices of primary materials becoming four times higher than long-term price levels of the last two decades of the twentieth century.[2] The re-emerging countries are now focusing on improvements in resource efficiency in the material-intensive sectors of the economy such as the iron and steel and cement industries, in housing and transport as well as in the food provision sector, and more efficient use of energy and water. However, further modification of longer term trends in consumption patterns will be required to house, clothe, feed and transport 9.6 billion people by the middle of this century under the ongoing 'second wave of urbanization', as the global urban population is projected to reach 5 billion in 2030 and 6.25 billion in 2050.

---

[2] In 2014, commodity prices declined 14 per cent from their 10-year average with the Chinese economy shifting from infrastructure to consumption led 7 per cent growth rates

Increasing levels of natural resource use, scarcity of ecosystem services and planetary limits have led to the idea of sustainability evolving through four overlapping phases over the past 40 years. Three phases were driven by the interests of industrialized countries with a focus on issues and sectors and the recent more holistic one reflects geopolitical shifts influenced by the emerging countries shaping comprehensive responses to the threats. The first two phases were based on the natural sciences and essentially described the impacts for policymakers and public opinion and were followed by the social sciences searching for solutions with a focus on production and later consumption patterns. The fourth phase is still emerging; for example, according to the *The Future We Want*, the outcome document of the United Nations Conference on Sustainable Development (Rio+20) in 2012, 'fundamental changes in the way societies consume and produce are indispensable for achieving global sustainable development'.

Each of these four phases has evolved approximately over durations of 5–10 years and have considered, respectively, the magnitude of the human impact on physical limits in nature and description of the changes taking place in ecosystems over time (the symptoms); examination of the scope of the economic, social and institutional dimensions of the impacts (assessment and valuation of the changes); modifying production patterns through new technology and developing market-based frameworks to deal with scarcity (increasing efficiency) and considering both environmental and social risks as interlinked by looking at the patterns, trends and drivers of natural resource use and how to meet the needs of 9 billion people within global ecological limits (modifying identified longer term consumption patterns).

The conceptual framework has emphasized fairness, or equity, while the research focus, largely financed by industrialized countries and the agenda of the multilateral negotiation framework has been on future environmental damage and economic analysis to develop new markets and reduce costs in industrialized countries. This has two related but distinct dimensions with respect to international cooperation. First, the focus is on the future use of natural resources that will take place in developing countries as they industrialize and urbanize rather than historical patterns of resource use to understand longer term trends. Second, discussions around the means of implementation focus on support to developing countries in capacity building, which is expected to lead to equity. As the focus has been on solving a political problem of securing a global consensus through ambiguous language in the agreements rather than solving the problem itself, contrasting perspectives continue on the relationship between environmental, economic, social, technological and institutional change. Equity for developing countries, political feasibility of solutions in industrialized countries and broader considerations of least cost effectiveness that has been pushed as the dominant framework conflict with one another leading to an uneasy compromise.

For example, population growth is considered as the driver of environmental degradation, but in the advance of civilization, population growth has not been a driver for the rise, for example, in energy demand. In developing countries, rapid growth in population after 1950 did not lead to a corresponding rise in energy use. In industrialized countries, a gradual increase in population led to a rapid increase in energy use with urbanization. It was only when developing countries began to industrialize and urbanize that their total demand for energy increased around 2000. The explanation for the environmental crisis lies in the nature of industrialized societies, technological change was the enabler rather than driver, that led to the establishment of infrastructure, shift of rural population to urban areas and widespread growth in incomes leading to high levels of natural resource use, particularly energy, consumption-based lifestyles and high levels of waste, like emissions of carbon dioxide.

Modifying consumption patterns is now on the global agenda because of the re-emergence of China and India reflected in urbanization and growth of their middle class, related geopolitical shifts and growing influence of developing countries. Even at the World Summit on Sustainable

Development (WSSD), in 2002, the sustainable consumption Plan of Implementation was formulated in the weakest possible language, with a call for governments to '*encourage* and *promote* the development of a 10-year framework of programmes' in support of regional and national, not global, initiatives. This was also the last item to be agreed at the conference. Sustainable consumption continues to be framed in terms of improvement in efficiency, and the only advance has been that life cycle analysis was included in an agreed United Nations document for the first time.

Recognition of the increasing role of the private sector introduced new ideas. The International Chamber of Commerce and the World Business Council for Sustainable Development's Report on sustainable consumption for the WSSD also for the first time looked at the demand rather than on the supply side and considered the key role of consumers in shaping markets. It, however, identified increasing eco-efficiency as the contribution of industry to sustainable consumption and did not discuss any role for business in driving and reducing overconsumption. It limited behavioural change to providing information to consumers about the social and environmental effects of their choices, and lifestyles. The report of the High Level Panel on the Post-2015 Development Agenda considers sustainable consumption and production as a cross-cutting issue and does not suggest it as a stand-alone goal. Sustainable consumption and production is included in the future Sustainable Development Goals as a stand-alone goal, rather than as a cross-cutting issue represented in targets across a number of goals in the post-2015 development agenda, in a diluted form without any reference to actions by individual citizens or consumers.

A 10-year research programme, Future Earth, with three themes – Dynamic Planet, Global Sustainable Development and Transformations towards Sustainability – is now reframing sustainable development science from the perspective of the Earth system and how humans interact with it to understanding the longer term trends that need to be modified for meeting the needs of 9 billion people, as the Earth's life-support system is going to be further transformed with the re-emergence of China and India and economic growth in other developing countries. While technological change continues to be considered as a major enabler of long-run economic growth, it is now recognized in this reframing that there are complex interdependencies where technologies and their institutional and social settings evolve together in the process of urbanization leading to a situation where the shift is not only about reforming the science by including the social sciences but also complete reframing in the way sustainable development is defined.

2.2 Limitations of natural sciences and risk-based regulatory approaches

Natural scientists brought the issue of environmental damage to global attention but did not analyse the activities in the twentieth century that caused the problem, as the global economy grew 14-fold and global energy consumption increased sixfold in the 20th century. The extent of these environmental changes caused by human beings is considered to have become a driving force, even though they are symptoms and not the drivers of the changes.

The impact of increasing natural resource use is reflected in deforestation, biodiversity loss, collapse of fish stock, water scarcity and the pollution of soil and water supplies, and these changes were highlighted. For example, an estimated two-thirds of the world's ecosystem services have been degraded or over-used since the mid-twentieth century as the global economy has grown more than five times. However, the impacts continued to be described in terms of production, that is, increased deforestation, land use change, use of biomass and water resources, and reduction in biodiversity rather than in terms of consumption, that is, the use of minerals for infrastructure and demand for food in cities because the stress is on the status of ecosystems and not on the activities that generate the range of impacts. Similarly, the symptoms, or changes to the biochemical flow patterns, for example, the carbon and nitrogen cycles, have been described by the Millennium Ecosystem Assessment, in 2005, without analysing the causes. As the framework did not link environmental degradation to the patterns, trends and drivers of natural resource use, it drew attention only to scarcity, stressing that continuing growth of the global economy leads to concerns that natural resources will not be available to meet the needs of an estimated 9 billion people that are expected to achieve the level of well-being enjoyed in the industrialized countries.

Environmental change was initially used interchangeably with sustainable development and defined as a global concern in very broad terms. Two parallel tracks emerged, shaped by legislation and by economists.

A beginning was made with considering natural resource use through a compartmentalized approach that separated parts of the consumption and production cycles. In the late 1960s and early 1970s, some of the first environmental legislation was enacted globally. These initiatives were based around single-issues, reactive, site-specific and suggested 'end-of-pipe' measures. These addressed either 'sustainable consumption' or 'cleaner production' and ignored the linkages. In the 1980s, a systems perspective began to be adopted, with an increasing focus on 'cleaner production' in environmental policymaking, considering the technology of the production process and not just treatment of the waste after it was produced. In the 1990s, cleaner production was seen as a way of increasing eco-efficiency, including waste minimization, and as a means of integrating in production the precautionary principle that was set out in the 1992 Rio Declaration on Environment and Development. Reduction in environmental damage, it was felt, would occur through cleaner production at the 'point of generation' rather than at the 'end-of-pipe' stage, during and not at the end of the production process. The next step was a shift to considering the consumption of the products by advocating life cycle solutions, partnerships and voluntary initiatives, working in tandem with the private sector and other stakeholders. At the same time, there was a shift in focus from targeting single companies, adversarial stances and regulation, to consumer and civil society empowerment and systemic solutions in terms of the life cycle of the product.

The concept of resource efficiency looks at the relationship between economic activity and resource use and measures resource use by unit of economic activity. Resource efficiency can be expressed as resource productivity (economic output per unit of resource use) or resource intensity (resource use per unit of economic output). Productivity and intensity are inverse measures. Measuring resource productivity allows for comparison of trends with other factor productivities, whereas intensity focuses more on the environmental and resource use aspects of economic activities. This framework did not consider consumption patterns, and there are few examples of successful consumption policies anywhere in the world.

Material efficiency at the country-level improved throughout the entire second half of the twentieth century with technological advances. The global trend in improving manufacturing efficiency as economies matured reversed at the beginning of the twenty-first century, driven by a large shift of economic activity from material-efficient economies such as Europe and Japan to much less resource-efficient economies such as China and India, as they largely outsourced their material-intensive production to developing countries. However, there is no improvement in absolute material use once global resource extraction is attributed to final consumption in these countries. Recent research shows that the use of non-domestic resources is, on average, about threefold larger than the physical quantity of traded goods, emphasizing the need for consumption-based accounting of natural resource use [Wiedmann et al., 2013].

The continuing and sharp increase in natural resource use in the re-emerging countries after 2000 has led to the emergence of more holistic approaches. The notion of 'planetary boundaries' moved beyond the earlier focus on individual sub-systems of processes considered in isolation to considering the Earth System as an integrated complex system with an identifiable safe operating space for development and evolution, with increasing focus on carbon dioxide emissions and planetary limits to absorb the waste [Rockstrom et al., 2009]. Still no attempt was made by mainstream science to relate these concerns to the patterns, trends and drivers of natural resource use in order to find solutions. This analysis was left to non-governmental policy analysts seeking to understand the causes and solutions in order to support private sector investment rather than aid flows. A report by McKinsey Global Institute, in 2011, identified that three-quarters of resource efficiency improvements would come from a small number of activities including improving the energy efficiency of buildings, promoting a modal split in transport favouring public transport, renewable energy, and greater eco-efficiency of heavy industries specially iron and steel and cement. Delivering the required improvements in resource productivity, it was argued, will be a large and complex public policy agenda. It will require an improved knowledge base, enhanced capacity of government agencies to identify policy tools, implementation pathways and monitoring strategies, as well as a very large initiative around training and retraining workers especially in the material- energy- and waste-intensive sectors of the economy. Even in this report, consumption patterns and 'lifestyles' were not questioned because local rather than global ecological limits were being considered.

In the second track, economists took the lead in interpreting environmental change and sustainability in the 1960s and 1970s, with valuation of environmental assets and the costs and benefits of various regulatory and policy initiatives. A number of formulations translated these elements into economic analysis. For example, that future generations should be able to enjoy the same freedoms, economic opportunities and level of economic welfare available to the present generation. The elements of what constitutes such welfare, however, were not defined.

Economists then turned their attention, in the 1980s and 1990s, to the role played by natural capital in economic development, refining techniques for measuring the value of environmental damage, the cost savings that could be gained by market-based solutions, and specified the institutional conditions required for implementation of the different policy initiatives. The focus on the well-being of future generations meant there was no need for regulatory command-and-control approaches or to analyse the patterns of urbanization followed in industrialized countries because the stress was on future scarcity rather than current use and distribution of natural resources. When it became apparent that natural resources are essential for human welfare, the view emerged that ecosystem services are at risk and the many goods and services they provide are the most undervalued elements of natural capital because they are not traded.

The continuing acceleration of growth of the world economy, now driven by urbanization in China, raised the question that the human footprint may soon exceed the Earth's carrying capacity. The current pattern of economic development, it was argued, continues on an unsustainable path because the true costs to society of the consumption of natural resources are not allocated, and 'getting the prices right' was considered an important policy measure to create the necessary incentives making them transparent to consumers, so that prices reflect the full costs of resource use to society. This explains the thrust for a global carbon price to reduce energy use in re-emerging countries and market-based frameworks to share marginal costs of measures taken by industrialized countries. No attempt has been made at the international level to measure the increasing costs of ecological scarcity globally or how best the poor in developing countries can move into the middle class to eradicate poverty. Such analysis would have also brought out the importance of making a distinction between the measures that need to be taken in countries with different levels of consumption, challenging the universalism that environmental treaties established.

Analytical results to identify the best possible policy outcome based on techniques like cost-benefit analysis have also given way to more process oriented open dialogue with policymakers. The Millennium Ecosystem Assessment (2005) used the concept of payments for environmental services to assess the value people attach to ecosystems, in order to develop price signals which will, in the long term, give incentives for sustainable development, even though this is not the market value of the resource. However, these ideas have not been mainstreamed in the economic system to a degree that they start modifying trends in the desired direction. It is now being argued that in addition to 'getting the prices right', there is a need to go beyond economic valuation to recognize the role of policy in controlling excessive environmental degradation, and implementation requires effective and appropriate information, incentives, institutions, investments and infrastructure [TEEB, 2010]. The focus, however, has remained on developing countries, and their economic growth path was expected to rebuild natural and social capital as economic assets and as sources of global and national benefits, because it continues to be assumed that the rural poor, who directly depend on nature, will remain rural and dependent on agriculture.

At the same time, for economies in industrialized countries, the emphasis has been on the efficiency with which labour, capital and resources, inputs to production, are utilized. The stress is on technological innovation so that more output can be produced for any given input. Efficiency forms the basis of the concept of 'decoupling', where production processes, goods and services are redesigned to use less material or natural resources. The question whether the global economy can continue to grow without breaching planetary limits is ignored. In this framing, the focus has been on relative decoupling, to reduce the material intensity per unit of output, where resource use and its impact declines only relative to GDP, but not in absolute terms.

The numerous publications from bodies of the United Nations on 'low-carbon transformation' or the 'green economy' prepared for the Rio+20 Conference in 2012 put stress on combined benefits of interactions between the economy and the environment in terms of economic efficiency. The focus continued to be on determining an appropriate monetary value to natural capital to provide incentives to reduce its exploitation and degradation. This framework was presented as applicable to both industrialized and developing countries, through the use of pricing instruments like carbon taxes, tradable carbon permits, and the removal of fossil fuel subsidies. The expectation was that increased prices of energy will lead to enhanced productivity through better designs and new operating systems and keep emissions of the waste carbon within planetary limits. Natural ecosystems would benefit from new systems of planning and management that value the services they offer, such as clean water and fresh air, providing local benefits. In addition, greening the construction sector, waste recycling, and low-tech renewable energy generation could all generate substantial numbers of jobs because they are labour-intensive.

The focus, however, remains only on specific elements, for example, technological, financial or governance aspects, which are discussed largely from a national rather than from a global perspective. Moreover, apart from the use of fossil fuels in energy systems, other longer term trends, such as urbanization, ecosystem services at the global level and the rise of the global middle class are not investigated in detail, including the possibility that the remaining global carbon budget will soon be exhausted. It is not only that nearly 2 billion people continue to be poor but also the overwhelming majority of the global population is still excluded from the well-being enjoyed by a few, which requires society to undergo a fundamental transformation to ensure future prospects of all within planetary limits. For example, while steps have been taken towards energy system de-carbonization, the greater potential of emissions reduction from the use of environmentally friendly public transport for commuting is not examined.

The close interconnectedness between global environmental, economic and social trends is now beginning to be recognized. The important role of new technologies providing wider economic and social benefits as well as protecting the environment has been acknowledged, but downplayed in the conclusions or actions, because of the international dimensions related to transfer of technology. For example, calls for a large reduction in the use of materials in the economy, by at least a factor of four, did not examine the global implications of the terms on which innovative technology would be available [Weizsacker, 1998]. The Organization for Economic Co-operation and Development (OECD) has adopted the concept of resource decoupling, defined as breaking the link between 'environmental bads' and 'economic goods', in their policy paper 'Environmental Strategy for the First Decade of the 21st Century' (adopted by OECD Environment Ministers in 2001), with emphasis on the life cycle approach. For the European Union, however, it also meant using less material, energy, and water and land resources for the same economic output while not leading to global reductions in natural resource use. Decoupling should really consider both the amount of resource use linked with economic activity and the environmental impacts associated with this resource use at all stages of the life cycle, as these impacts are different and lead to a disruption of the national and global ecosystem services that are essential to human well-being, as in the case of carbon dioxide.

Perspectives also vary in defining the idea of restraint – the focus has not been on the rich who have to make 'lifestyle changes' to consume fewer natural resources, but rather on the poor adopting 'appropriate technologies' that will improve well-being marginally with fewer demands on natural resources. The potential for a substantial increase in energy efficiency was raised quite early with the increase in consumption patterns in industrialized countries. It was argued that these changes will offer market opportunities for businesses and they should grasp the changes, both for the environment and profits, and business took this up and analysed the potential profits in detail [McKinsey & Co, 2010]. However, it was only in 2013 that the International Energy Agency (IEA) recognized that half of the reductions in energy use could come from efficiency improvement, making it essentially a fuel [IEA , 2013]; yet the *New Climate Economy Report: Better Growth, Better Climate*, produced by the Global Commission on the Economy and Climate in September 2014, while recognizing urbanization as a major driver for the future transformation does not include energy efficiency in the suggested policy measures[3], because actions would need to be taken primarily in industrialized countries.

The fundamental questions remain unanswered – whether greening the economy, through prices and technology – will modify longer term trends enough to shift the current unsustainable path of the global economy and its neglect of the social dimension, which has been considered in terms of relief from poverty and not moving rural populations into the urban middle class. With geopolitical shifts, scientific findings pointing towards increasing levels of environmental damage are leading to a more holistic view, with two opposing priorities.

First, Earth System Governance is being stressed with a focus on the co-evolution of human and natural systems in a way that secures the sustainable development of human society, but without suggesting a new framework for sharing global prosperity within planetary limits. These shifts reflect new scientific evidence that both production and consumption patterns are affecting the resilience of ecosystems to provide services for human well-being, and because of the global

---

[3] The Commission has operated as an independent body, supported by seven governments and its programme of work has been conducted by research institutions led by the World Resources Institute, USA.

nature of the problem and the urban transition necessary for the shift of the rural poor into the middle class, the response requires more than local conservation and enhancing resource efficiency as an important response option. Economists have yet to be able to answer the question how a continually growing economic system can fit within a finite ecological system. The only response to this challenge is to suggest – as some economists do – that growth in dollars is 'decoupled' from growth in physical throughputs and environmental impacts, but how that can be done has not been explored. Germany's push for electricity supply in 2050 coming from renewable energy sources is an important initiative because it assumes a high degree of energy efficiency and focuses on changes within the country and not in developing countries, and China capping carbon dioxide emissions when its urbanization is completed in 2030 reflects confidence that its urban middle class will not adopt the 'American way of life'.

Second, developing country researchers have continued to give importance to the needs of the rural poor raising distributional questions of control and sharing of any profits arising from their use, but at the local level. While they have supported grassroots struggles, they have not analysed patterns of natural resource use at the global level. The struggle of the Brazilian rubber tappers, led by Chico Mendes, started on trade union rights. The campaign of the Ogoni people of Nigeria, led by Ken Saro-Wiwa, began on social justice. The Chipko movement in India, mainly of women, began by protecting trees. The worldwide growth of the anti-globalization and anti-capitalism protests that have taken place during meetings of the world's politicians and businesses leaders linked these struggles across the world, but were soon neutralized, and industrialized country funding on social science research focused on 'development as freedom'. This social resistance has been described by some as a political struggle as well as 'social capital' by others, giving it a cultural, rather than an economic, dimension with a national focus while avoiding any questioning of the global asymmetries in the use of natural resources and governance institutions.

There is now an emerging consensus that governments are expected to play a key role in nudging business, changing taxes and subsidies, supporting targeted research and dissemination of information for social and political action that involves weaker sections of society – indigenous groups, the poor and women and the defence of common property resources usually owned by forest dwellers. Even here, environmental protection has been given greater importance, with the argument that the values that 'existing cultures' placed in their environments need to be formally expressed in terms of markets and prices. Markets, however, stress the benefits of ecosystem services for businesses, and providing incentives for investing in natural capital for the green economy, unrelated to conservation of natural resources and local social benefits. In the interest of conservation, the tropical forest, for example, becomes, literally, a global resource; before the benefits of bio-diversity can be commoditized and traded, they must first be privatized, and their ownership clarified for the genetic material to be patented without requiring any sharing the benefits with the host population and country. The optimal policy to deal with a global environmental problem recommended by economic theory requires a globally uniform price equal to the marginal damage caused by the pollution, without considering the social dimension.

The way the issue has been framed puts stress on giving the stock of natural resources, or 'critical natural capital', priority over the flows of income that depends upon it. Enhancement of ecosystem services is also considered at the national level, as a policy failure of developing countries, rather than consider distribution at the global level, for example, the global carbon budget which is a commons sink, and unrestricted use is a failure of global governance. It was only in 2013 that the Intergovernmental Panel on Climate Change recognized ethics and justice as policy issues and that emission reductions should be measured in terms of the carbon budget, modifying the Kyoto framework of the peaking of emissions and steady periodic reductions in emissions in all countries. In the future climate framework differentiation will be between countries based on levels of development, or urbanization, and not just incomes.

2.3 Potential of social sciences for growth within ecological limits

We are at a transition where the thrust of the argument is shifting from patterns of natural resource use in rural areas, with examples of how access to sustainably managed natural resources at the local level can draw people out of poverty, to considering urban consumption as having a much more significant impact on natural resource use, but the conclusions are still not targeting individual consumption patterns.

Access to energy services, which is linked with global ecological limits, developing renewable energy and measures to enhance energy efficiency to reduce the dependency on fossil fuels are being analysed, but without comparing per capita use of energy. The sustainable management of water is considered more important than energy in the efforts to eliminate poverty, since poor people's lives are closely linked to access to water for agriculture, and its multiple uses and functions, even though cities depend even more on water supplies and a much higher consumption per capita. Marine resources as a source of food and employment shape the livelihoods more in developed countries than in developing countries, but the scarcity in the oceans, a global commons like the atmosphere, is not emphasized when environmental crises are considered and there is no global treaty for this common environmental resource. The capacity of agriculture to be able to feed 9 billion people by 2050 without further degrading and polluting land is considered in terms of supply – current farming practices representing over 70 per cent of the world's freshwater resources and contributing to over 13 per cent of greenhouse gas (GHG) emissions – ignoring demand patterns as half of these emissions arise in processing and transport. The rate of forest deforestation is described but its reasons are seldom analysed; in Brazil, two-third of such land is used for livestock and one-third for soybean cultivation, mostly for export. Even forest conservation and sustainable management is now increasingly seen in terms of the green economy; as sources of new materials such as bio-based plastics, bio-fuels and in renewable energy strategies.

So far the current framework has supported increase in economic activity as natural resources and ecosystem services continue to be available, and planetary limits have not been reached. The sink constraints of the atmosphere and the limited capacity to absorb waste carbon dioxide present a new situation. Despite global primary energy efficiency increases and the carbon intensity per unit of output decreasing by about a third, absolute reductions in emissions have not been possible. Concern has, therefore, been raised about the use of energy and the system it creates of technologies, policies and institutions and increasing demand driven by middle class lifestyles unrelated to the impact on others. The speed and scale of the urban transformation requires not only correcting current failures and incentives but also establishing new structures so that some people do not have to be deprived of material benefits, like access to electricity, and have to give up key freedoms. Increased investment in public goods and social infrastructure, like public transport, is expected to support this societal shift from private interests to the public good and shared prosperity.

With geopolitical shifts supporting new research in the re-emerging countries, recognition of the importance of the social dimension of sustainable development has led to a better understanding of the different pathways that will be required in industrialized and developing countries. For example, historically the emphasis on energy-related development began by focusing on energy poverty, followed by building up infrastructure as part of industrialization, then on widening access and finally on tackling the environmental externalities associated with growth in energy use and urban consumption. The overriding question for developing countries is how to move away from this historical pattern to an integrated, concurrent approach shaped by the sheer magnitude of numbers and inequality as well as energy access and climate stabilization objectives [Grubler, 2004]. There are significant benefits from a global perspective on a sustainable energy transition, despite difficulties in developing an integrated national approach because of capital constraints, costly technology and lack of a successful model.

With the increasing number of scientists in developing countries researching multilateral concerns, science is increasingly becoming global and new questions are being asked by social scientists and old assumptions are being questioned. Human activity continues to generate change in industrialized countries and the rates will accelerate because of the larger population in developing countries. The majority now resides in cities relying on extensive supply chains and trade in natural resources; a development that also distinguishes their impact on ecosystem services from the impact of local, rural and poor populations. It is now being realized that the institutions, organizations and mechanisms for global governance of the human relationship with the natural environment, in particular the global biochemical cycles because of planetary limits, were not designed to deal with the problems as we now understand them. We now know that

- Undesirable environmental impacts on ecosystem services arise in the phases of extraction, production/manufacture as well as consumption/use with demand driving supply.
- These impacts are caused by changes made to natural systems such as land cover change and resource extraction, and by economic activities causing carbon dioxide emissions as a waste, and the two are interrelated, but with different characteristics.
- The degree to which resource use causes adverse impacts depends not only on the amount of resources used, but also on the types of resources used and on the ways in which they are used.

These shifts are leading to a rethinking of the science–policy–society nexus for understanding societal functions and the context in which the activities impacting on the environment take place. Risk-based regulatory approaches are not able to deal with aspects of sustainability because it is cross-cutting in nature, involves a high degree of uncertainty and requires data that is just not available. Risk assessment works best for chemical and physical agents that have already been emitted, partly because the nature and degree of impact is better understood and can be monitored. Instead of asking the question 'what action can be taken given the risk', the emerging approach is to 'maximize social and economic and environmental benefits with as little harm as possible'. That is, shifting the focus from environmental damage to augmenting ecosystem services and sustainable consumption, and in this re-framing three related but distinct elements are emerging.

First, identification of trends in natural resource use has relied on risk analysis and quantitative forecasting even though the systems addressed and their linkages are not fully understood, assumptions are not clearly stated and a lot of the empirical data is not available. What is needed is an approach based on historical patterns of natural resource use to identify the longer term trends that need to be modified. Consequently, attention is shifting to global drivers such as urbanization, technologies, trade patterns and consumption along with demographics of ageing. Many of these changes are interdependent and their full impact will emerge over decades and we do not understand them fully.

Second, the transformation of energy systems, which will be the key element of the transition to sustainability, has taken centuries for full coverage and, even more important, the drivers of previous energy transitions have been the development of end products or services that were made possible by innovative and new forms of energy but not by the existing and old ones. So far end-use services and technologies, the most promising emission reduction option, have not been adequately considered in the analysis of sustainable development, climate and scenarios as well as in public investments in research and development.

Third, there is no consensus on whether and how the way the institutions of the global economy operate can be modified to deliver a societal and economic transformation that will be needed before new global rules can be established. Absolute decoupling in resource use and production patterns will require significant changes in government policies, corporate behaviour, and consumption patterns by citizens of all countries. The doubling of per capita material use due to the provision of infrastructure for urbanization is a necessary part of the process of economic development as there are no substitutes, and modifications in longer term trends in subsequent consumption patterns are most effective when urbanization is complete and depend on urban design, and subsequent individual actions [WBGU, 2014]. In the next 20 years, $100 trillion dollars will be invested in infrastructure, providing the opportunity to make the energy, urban and consumption transformation.

A new branch of economics is focusing on human well-being, understanding and assessing people's happiness. According to the Easterlin paradox beyond a certain point in improvement of their material circumstances, countries do not get happier and content as they get richer and living standards improve [Easterlin, 2003]. For example, the U.S. economy has tripled since 1960 but its citizens are not necessarily three times happier. While basic living standards are essential for happiness, after the baseline has been met happiness varies more with quality of human relationships than income. For governments, policy goals other than increasing GDP, could include high employment and high-quality work; a strong community with high levels of trust and respect, which government can influence through inclusive participatory policies; improved physical and mental health; support of family life and a decent education for all. The environmental debate could be importantly recast by changing the fundamental objectives from economic growth to building and sustaining the quality of lives in cities, and building a wider sense of common identity among all peoples with each other as the only possible way forward for human thriving [World Happiness Report, 2013].

2.4 Urbanization and interlinked natural and social systems

Urbanization shapes increasing levels of natural resource use by humans who have entered into the middle class; rural populations everywhere are poor and also live in balance with nature. Buildings consume one-third of global energy and produce one-fifth of the carbon dioxide emissions. Urban design and related 'lifestyles' shape three areas which account for nearly three-quarters of carbon dioxide emissions, and natural resource use, currently with high levels of wastage and potential for reductions without affecting middle-class lifestyles. These areas are electricity use in buildings, personal transport and diet. Instead of framing the sustainable development question as one of scarcity of natural resources, the key global policy issue is reducing waste and modifying consumption patterns to ensure equitable access to energy, transport and food for the emerging urban middle class [OECD, 2014].

2.4.1 Urban design

Urban areas are engines of economic activity and growth. Urbanization is the driver for the increased demand for materials and energy, as it alone enables well-being of all people and their ability to enjoy a lifestyle equivalent to that in industrialized countries, where three-quarter of the population had moved to urban areas by 1970. Around half of the global population now lives in cities. By 2050, about 75 per cent of the population are likely to be city dwellers, nearly 7 billion people, out of a total global population of 9 billion, compared with less than 30 per cent in 1950, when the total population was 2.5 billion. By 2050 more than half of the world's GDP is likely to be earned in developing countries, against a third in 2010. Urban expansion creates infrastructures that have a long lifespan and will impact immediately on material and in the longer term on energy and other natural resources demand, and later consumption patterns impacting on ecosystem services and finally planetary limits. This makes it necessary to avoid investments that lock society into existing knowledge, policy frameworks and technologies limiting innovation options.

Urban societies existed in China, India and the Middle East thousands of years ago, but only a very small proportion, less than 5 per cent, of the total population lived in cities. In 1750, the largest cities were Beijing, the capital of China, and Fatehpur Sikri, near Agra, at that time the capital of Mughal India. Even today the majority of the global urban population lives in Asia and is expected to double in the next two decades because of the rate of economic development. Africa is the least urbanized continent because of the different colonial past and continuance of its economic structures focusing on mineral extraction and its export. The highest relevant urban growth rates are in African countries due to the comparatively low initial base. While urban growth is likely to take the form of mega cities in Asia, settlements with less than 500,000 inhabitants are likely to predominate in Africa. Currently, also, more than half of the urban population does not live in mega cities but in smaller settlements. Latin America's middle class has grown 60.3 per cent since 2003, according to the Inter-American Development Bank. During that period, the population living in poverty declined by 34 per cent. Altogether, the World Bank puts the middle class at about 30 per cent of Latin America's population, and this number has remained stable. At the global level, it is expected that population growth will stagnate in rural areas around 2020, largely because of migration, and future growth in population and wealth will mainly take place in cities worldwide. Since the early twentieth century, the global urban population has grown from around 165 million people, or around 10–15 per cent of the total population, to around 3.5 billion at present, and continues to grow rapidly.

Globally, the urban building sector accounts for half of electricity use, less than two-third of the rural population has access to electricity, and about two-fifth of humanity, or 2.7 billion people, continues to rely on traditional biomass, such as wood, dung and charcoal. The poorest three-quarters in rural areas use only about 10 per cent of global energy, and urban areas already use around three-quarters of global final energy, because of manufacturing, commercial production, services and demands of human well-being and an equivalent share of natural resource use [GEA, 2012]. The scale of the urban transition in the industrialized countries accounts for the increasing emissions of GHGs beyond the capacity of the planet to absorb the waste. By 1950, industrialized countries had reached full access to electricity, and carbon dioxide emissions doubled in the period 1950–1970 because of urbanization and again doubled in the period 1970–2000 because of the consumption patterns of the population that moved into the urban middle class. In 2005, emissions peaked in the United States and earlier in the European Union, assisted by outsourcing of production to developing countries and energy efficiency responding to rising energy prices, while urban transport emissions continue to rise.

Cities support rapid economic growth because of the concentration and integration of investment and employment opportunities that enable increasing levels of productivity. The service sector provides higher-income jobs than manufacturing, as well as greater availability and access to goods, services and public facilities, enabling improved education, health and quality of life. These conditions encourage migration from rural areas for a better life, higher income and natural resource use in urban areas. The use of natural resources in the urbanization process is largely determined initially by the density of the urban structures and subsequently on a continuing and in some cases increasing basis by the level and lifestyle of human well-being, or income, and for the industrialized countries, each of these factors, looked upon independently, was responsible for roughly a doubling of the rate at which natural resources are used [Krausmann et al., 2008].

Urban design and related consumption patterns also explain the different levels of natural resource use even for countries at similar levels of well-being. For example, Japan and many European countries use half the natural resources, about 13 tons/capita, as compared with the United States, Australia and Finland, even though levels of income and well-being are not very different. Trends in developing countries are similar, with countries such as China and India using resources at the rate of about 5 tons/capita in the year 2000, compared to Brazil and South Africa, where the resource use is almost two times that level. Densely populated areas need less construction material, use public infrastructure more frequently and thus more efficiently and have less need for transport fuels, save space and provide more efficient supply of energy for heating or cooling of buildings. More dense forms of living enable for lower consumption of many natural resources at the same levels of material comfort. For example, the emissions in New York City are one-third of the average for the United States.

In the absence of a global consensus on conservation of natural resources, the trend in current lifestyles reflects societal patterns of consumption unrelated to need. In Japan, residential and commercial sectors directly and indirectly accounted for 35 per cent of total GHG emissions in 2012, these have increased by nearly 60 per cent since 1990 and half of Japanese emissions come from the residential, commercial and transport sectors which together represent urban economic activities [Kuramochi, 2014]. In the United States, GHG emissions in 2012 have increased 8 per cent since 1990, buildings consume 39 per cent of all energy use, 74 per cent of electricity, and are responsible for 38 per cent of carbon emissions, the transportation sector in the United States accounts for approximately 27 per cent of total GHG emissions, making it the second-largest emissions source (behind electricity generation), with approximately eight vehicles in the United States for every 10 people [Damassa et al., 2012]. The differences between industrialized countries are as significant as with developing countries.

As the bulk of future global urban growth is expected to take place in Asia, China and India are likely to become the most important world consumer market in the future. China is likely to overtake the United States by 2025 to become the world's biggest consumer market, with India as the third largest. These markets will define their own lifestyles and spending patterns and will shape global market development and trends. Future global sustainability will depend first on urban design and later on consumption patterns in China and India, both of which are continental size economies. Policy changes currently being adopted in China suggest that, for example, motorized personal vehicle ownership rates are not expected to increase significantly, and cities have begun to impose limits on new vehicle registration. The concentrated structure and efficiencies of scale in cities in these countries offer major opportunities to reduce energy demand and minimize pressures on natural resources, and surrounding lands, even though we do not have one single, functioning, low-carbon model city.

How urban areas are designed, built and organized will have a strong impact on natural resource use and emissions of GHGs. Once built, it is difficult to modify cities and the individual behaviour adapted to the systems, locking in energy- and resource-intensive lifestyles. Planners in developing countries face multiple environmental, social and economic problems at lower income levels, or earlier in the process of economic development, than was the case in countries that are now industrialized. They are already changing the way in which urban dwellers live, work and interact, modifying the structures, technologies and practices of industrialized countries in designing their urbanization transition.

2.4.2 Energy

Since nearly half of humanity living in developing countries is still deprived of the benefits of industrialization and urbanization, these countries will account for around three-fourth of the increase in global economic output and nearly 90 per cent of the increase in demand for electricity till 2035. Even though China because of its large population will become the largest energy consumer, using nearly three-fourth more energy than the United States, the second-largest consumer, the per-capita energy consumption in 2050 in China is likely to be less than half the level in the United States and in India even less than half of the levels in China. This dynamics can only be understood in terms of patterns, trends and drivers of energy use.

Renewable energy, in the form of firewood for cooking, heating and lighting, solar energy for heating and drying, hydro-energy or wind power for pumping or irrigation, was the only source of energy until the industrial revolution and remains the primary energy source for a great number of rural people in many developing countries, forming as much as half of humanity. Modern renewable energies today deliver less than one-fifth of the global electricity supply, and meet one-tenth of the heating needs of industry and buildings. Nuclear energy started to make major contributions to the electricity supply in the 1970s, and most of the current nuclear power plants were built between 1970 and 1990, and at that time they contributed one-fifth to global electricity generation, and currently there are more than 400 operational nuclear reactors worldwide. Barriers to an increasing use of nuclear energy include concerns about safety in operations, concerns about disposal of waste, and high costs. Fossil fuels, particularly coal, enabled industrialization and their use grew till the 1970s when a saturation level in infrastructure development was reached in industrialized countries. The share of fossil fuels in global energy supply has been steadily coming down with the 1970s as an important turning point, though they continue to have the major share. The share of fossil fuels in global energy supply seems to have peaked with the growing shift to a services economy.

Future trends in energy use with respect to carbon dioxide emissions remain uncertain. Four-fifths of the total energy-related carbon dioxide emissions that should be emitted for remaining within the global carbon budget are already 'locked-in' by the existing power plants, buildings, factories and transportation networks. Replacing coal fired with highly efficient natural gas combined cycle plants can bring down emissions by half. There is a limited potential for substitution of oil as the fuel for transportation, making demand for oil less responsive to changes in the oil price. According to the IEA, even though the subsidy cost per unit of output is expected to decline, most renewable-energy sources will need continued support in order to compete in electricity markets. Nuclear energy could rise by more than 70 per cent over the period to 2035, without this it would be difficult for developing countries to meet the growing demand for electricity. How these developments interact will depend on national policies and circumstances rather than globally agreed arrangements to reduce growth in emissions of carbon dioxide.

While reliance continues to be on new technologies to address problems of global environmental change, there is increasing evidence that 'technological fixes' simply shift the source of the problem and create new problems, for example, electric cars need to be charged. Despite the potential of reducing wasteful use of energy, the focus remains on relative 'decoupling' in three areas, to transition to a circular economy and reducing natural resource use per unit of output, but not yet on conserving resources.

First, recycling systems as part of extended manufacturer and consumer responsibility are gaining significance worldwide; for example, China has legislation for creating a circular economy, the 'Circular Economy Law of the People's Republic of China. These remain policy-based initiatives rather than new business models with incentives for manufacturers to design recycling-friendly products. Manufacturing aluminium from recycled material, for example, requires only 5 per cent of the energy needed for producing the same amount of raw aluminium from bauxite, and this also applies to a number of metals. Recycling systems, however, require transport and enhanced energy consumption limiting their adoption largely to urban areas, which are both production and consumption sites. Second, efforts are being made to organize production processes such that secondary products and waste heat from one process, along with used products, can form the basis for further production processes. This creates a material flow cycle so that both the introduction of new raw materials and the disposal of non-usable residue can be reduced to a minimum. Third, the actual use of long life consumer products like household appliances, electronics, networked products or vehicles not only involves use of considerably less energy in production but also reduces the problem of disposal of the product. Designs in developing countries that make repairs possible, extending the lifespan of the product, need to be adopted more widely [WBGU, 2011].

The dominant trend from historical energy technology transitions – steam power relying on coal and its displacement by electricity and petroleum-based technologies – is that supply-side transformations are driven by end-use applications that deliver a new, improved or different energy service. The two major energy technology transitions since the Industrial Revolution were not driven by resource scarcity or by direct economic signals such as prices; oil has always been more expensive than coal. The diffusion of steam and gasoline engines, as well as electric motors and appliances, was the driver for innovation and structural changes in the energy supply. This trend highlights the critical importance of end-use technologies, consumers, and the demand for energy services such as heating, lighting, mobility and power in technological change of the energy system.

In this transition, initially cost has not been as important as performance. The thermal conversion efficiency of the first atmospheric steam engines was around 1 per cent only, and it took a century to improve this to around 20 per cent, and another century to attain current efficiency of steam turbines of 40 per cent. The modest performance benefits of steam engines was sufficient to substitute for horse power, and costs started coming down some 100 years later, which then led to widespread use. In the case of electricity, the first innovation was the incandescent light bulb, and the new demand led to changes in generation and distribution on the supply side. Electricity significantly altered production patterns where steam engines were centrally driving belts to a number of machines. Electric lighting was much easier to use than gas for lighting. Railways and cars provided faster service and more flexible and private form of transport, respectively. The trend in private mobility illustrates a general characteristic of energy transitions where efficiency gains are overtaken by increase in demand for the service leading to widespread expansion.

Major energy transitions are associated with step-changes in both the quantity and the quality of energy services provided through end-use technologies. It took steam power in the UK close to 100 years (to the 1860s) to gain a 50 per cent market share in total installed horsepower, gradually displacing wind and waterpower. It took some 40 years (to the 1920s) for electric drives to account for 50 per cent of all prime movers in the United States industry leading to a dramatic increase in the quantity of the service demanded. Currently, car and truck engines comprise nearly three-quarters of all energy conversion capacity in the United States, exceeding the thermal capacity of electric power plants by a factor of about 10. China's aim of securing 20 per cent of its electricity generation in 2030 through renewable energy, equal to the current generation from coal and 70 per cent of its total capacity, will require a transformation of the transmission grid. Though transitions may be catalysed by innovations that create new, better or qualitatively different energy services, these transitions are subsequently driven and sustained by dramatic falls in the effective cost of providing energy services.

End-use efficiency, on the other hand, requires modifying consumption patterns in buildings, domestic appliances, industry and transport. These areas involve many actors, institutions, technologies, norms and behaviour patterns, while the supply side of electric power generation is based on units, making technical changes easier to implement. It is now recognized that end-use efficiency is the most important factor in the continuing decrease of the energy intensity of economic output and consumption in buildings. This has historically, since the beginning of the industrial revolution, been more important than changes in economic structure, shifts to the tertiary sector and technical improvements. Every unit of power that is saved has a multiplier effect as it replaces three units of primary energy and their emissions if the energy is generated using fossil fuel [IIASA, 2011]. Both renewable energy and energy efficiency are necessary for the energy transformation to sustainable development as the world transitions to the knowledge economy, whose defining feature is not increased use of energy.

2.5 Global limits

Human well-being depends on the consumption of goods and services, their production depends on the transformation of natural resources and both impact on the global environment in different ways. In the context of urbanization, middle class levels of human well-being and increased demand for energy, the argument that there are limits to growth is not a new one.

In the 1970s, studies commissioned by the Club of Rome had drawn attention to the limits of resource availability. The need to consider placing certain limits on total world production and consumption was also recognized by the Brundtland Commission in its report, in 1987, which noted that the concept of sustainable development did imply limits, although they might need to be imposed gradually. The report recommended that 'those who are more affluent adopt lifestyles within the planet's ecological means and the Chairman's Foreword took note of the fact that many of the development paths of the industrialized nations are clearly unsustainable. Arguments for limits have since then gained urgency because of the sink constraints of the planet to absorb the waste carbon dioxide of human activity, in particular from the use of energy.

The arguments around limits, and scarcity, are now being reframed in terms of the use and distribution of natural resources. Cross-country data show that the quality of life does not improve much beyond a certain level of per capita income of about $10,000, and there are no significant additional gains in human development (as measured by the human development index) beyond the energy-use level of about 110 gigajoules (GJ), or 2 tons of oil equivalent (toe) per capita. It has been computed that the Human Development Index (HDI) increases hugely from 0.2 to 0.75 as per capita electricity consumption increases from 0 to 1,000 units per year. However, increase of electricity consumption from 1,000 to 9,000 units per capita leads to a small increase in HDI. While capping the use of energy from fossil fuel is being considered by China, there is as yet no model for 'prosperity without growth'. In fact, on the basis of consumption patterns in industrialized countries, it has been argued that there is a 'dilemma of growth' – while the current pattern of growth is unsustainable[4], the current structure of the economy and of society is such that an economy without growth is unstable, and sustainability will require major structural transformations of economies and societies [Jackson, 2009].

Societal change will have to be the driver for the transformation. The speed and scale of the technological transformation will require government support for its design and implementation, which will in turn be possible to the extent required, only if there is a societal consensus. Moreover, reliance cannot be placed on yet to be developed technologies, and the changes in production patterns, including generation of electricity, are not likely to be sufficient. With nearly three-fourth of the human population shifting from rural to urban areas as part of the process of economic development, global patterns of natural resource use will be in, and determined by, cities. As incomes rise, consumption patterns shift to spending on housing and household goods and services,

---

[4] Personal consumption constitutes 70 percent of the GDP of the United States.

for example, small appliances. The settlement pattern and size of the house, in turn, determines these spending patterns. While the percentage of the income spent on food declines, consumption patterns shift to protein-rich food leading to pressure on land for livestock production and for feed. The production of waste also increases in cities along with the increase in resource use. These trends suggest that polices for modifying consumption patterns, through societal and individual behaviour changes, will be critical in enabling the change in growth pathways for the transformation to sustainable development within global ecological limits. Changes in consumption patterns affect end-use demand and lifestyles as well as drive production patterns and technologies.

The social value system will have to change from a focus on reducing damage to nature and considering the importance ecosystem services provide to support life to considering ecological limits with the global commons as a resource to be shared with all humankind. It is only then that economic well-being of all, or emergence of a global middle class, can be ensured within the planetary limits. This change in values will need to inform a new conceptual framework for understanding the drivers of natural resource use and shaping of public opinion for actions at the individual level. They will also need to be reflected in the way we measure progress; not just in terms of economic activity but also in terms of trends in resource use, to provide feedback and assess the level of changes being made. These shifts will be part of the societal transformation that will be needed to enable changes in consumption patterns, and will be much more difficult that the technological transformation in production patterns.

The nature–social science–technology–policy interface will need new institutions, as hubs for knowledge brokerage which could serve to identify relevant studies from trusted sources, assess the quality of scientific information and communicate up-to-date knowledge to national governments. Another option is for a kind of 'consensus panel' among global researchers for synthesizing and presenting the main findings. The message from governments should be that sustainability is a fundamental necessity and not a choice requiring changes in thinking, practices, policies and lifestyles.

International cooperation will be an important driver for the transformation to sustainable development because trends and impacts are increasingly globalized and governance arrangements inadequate to deal with them. Since the 'sink' constraints of the planet are considered as a 'global good', a transformation to safeguard ecosystem services is possible only through the efforts of all countries. In particular, cooperation will be needed for the development and deployment of new technologies and exchange of experiences in affecting societal change. The development pathways of countries like China and India, while providing infrastructure, are also reviewing the urbanization model adopted by industrialized countries to be less energy and resource-intensive in a services driven and knowledge-based economy. Shifting to new urban design and lifestyles is also easier for them as they are still building their infrastructure. Industrialized countries, on the other hand, have to modify existing patterns of resource use in their factories and cities, as well as consumption patterns of their citizens. Exchange of experiences will benefit both.

References

Ausubel, Jesse, Iddo Wernick, and David Victor. 1995. 'The Environment Since 1970'. *US Global Change Research*, Vol. 1, no. 3.

China Daily. 2014. 'Obama Hails Climate Deal'. *China Daily*, November 18.

Damassa, Thomas, Nicholas Bianco, Taryn Fransen and Jennifer Hatch. 2012. *GHG Mitigation in the United States: An Overview of the Current Policy Landscape*. Working Paper. World Resources Institute, Washington, DC.

Easterlin, Richard A. 2003. 'Explaining Happiness'. *Proceedings of the National Academy of Sciences* 100 (19): 11176–83.

GEA: 2012. 2012: *Global Energy Assessment – Toward a Sustainable Future*. Global Energy Assessment Cambridge University Press, Cambridge and New York and the International Institute for Applied Systems Analysis, Laxenburg, Austria.

Grantham Research Institute. 2014. 'The Impacts of Environmental Regulations on Competitiveness'. Policy Brief November 2014. Programme on 'Growth and the economy', sponsored by the Global Green Growth Institute, London School of Economics and Political Science, London.

Grubler, Arnuf. 2004. *Technology and Global Change*. Cambridge University Press, Cambridge.

IIASA. 2011. Lessons from the History of Technology and Global Change for the Emerging Clean Technology Cluster. Interim Report IR-11-001, prepared for the UN World Economic and Social Survey 2011 by the International Institute for Applied Systems Analysis, Austria.

IEA. 2013. *Redrawing the Energy-Climate Map: World Energy Outlook Special Report*, International Energy Agency, Paris.

Jackson, Tim. 2009. *Prosperity Without Growth–Economics for a Finite Planet*. Earthscan, UK.

Krausmann F., Fischer-Kowalski M., Schandl H., and Eisenmenger N. 2008. 'The Global Sociometabolic Transition'. *Journal of Industrial Ecology*. 12: 637–56.

Kuramochi, Takeshi. 2014. *GHG Mitigation in Japan: An Overview of the Current Policy Landscape*. Working Paper. World Resources Institute, Washington, DC.

McKinsey & Co. 2010. *Energy Efficiency: A Compelling Global Resource, McKinsey Sustainability and Resource Productivity*, McKinsey and Company.

MEA. 2005, Millennium Ecosystem Assessment, Island Press. Island Press, Washington DC.

OECD. 2014. '*Cities and Climate Change: Policy Perspectives – National Governments Enabling Local Action*', September 2014, Paris.

Rockstrom Johan, Will Steffen, Kevin Noone, Åsa Persson, F. Stuart Chapin, III, Eric F. Lambin, Timothy M. Lenton, Marten Scheffer, Carl Folke, Hans Joachim Schellnhuber, Björn Nykvist, Cynthia A. de Wit, Terry Hughes, Sander van der Leeuw, Henning Rodhe, Sverker Sörlin, Peter K. Snyder, Robert Costanza, Uno Svedin, Malin Falkenmark, Louise Karlberg, Robert W. Corell, Victoria J. Fabry, James Hansen, Brian Walker, Diana Liverman, Katherine Richardson, Paul Crutzen & Jonathan A. Foley. 2009. 'A Safe Operating Space for Humanity'. *Nature*. 461: 472–75

TEEB. 2010. *The Economics of Ecosystems and Biodiversity*. Progress Press, Malta.

UNFCCC. 2014. National greenhouse gas inventory data for the period 1990–2012, 17 November 2014, FCC/SBI/2014/20, United Nations.

WBGU. 2011. *World in Transition: A Social Contract for Sustainability*. German Advisory Council on Global Change, Berlin.

WBGU. 2014. *Special Report – Climate Protection as a World Citizen Movement*. German Advisory Council on Global Change, Berlin.

Weizsacker, Ernst U. von. 1998. *Factor Four: Doubling Wealth and Halving Resource Use – A Report to the Club of Rome*. Earthscan, London.

Wiedmann, Thomas O., Heinz Schandl, Manfred Lenzen, Daniel Moran, Sangwon Suh, James West, and Keiichiro Kanemoto. 2013. 'The Material Footprint of Nations'. *Proceedings of National Academy of Sciences USA*. 1220362110v1-201220362

World happiness Report. 2013. *The Earth Institute*. Columbia University, New York.

Natural Science – Policy – Institutions Interface

3

The way global expert organizations frame environmental issues determines what exactly the 'problem' is that needs to be assessed, shapes the discourse on how it should be 'resolved' and has framed the nature, scope and agenda of international environmental treaties[1].

The development of our understanding of the different dimensions of global environmental change, climate change and sustainable development requires a significant involvement of scientific expertise in policy formulation and implementation. While the international political process is open in procedural terms, it has been informed by consensual natural science to persuade officials to adopt certain policies in a manner that the debate, discussion and compromise reflects expert 'consensus' on the nature of the global environment and the ecosystem services it provides; the symptoms rather than the human activities that have caused the problem. The framing of natural resource use as environmental changes, which were in turn framed as global universal risks that demand collective action, is itself questionable because significant decisions can be taken at the national level. For example, if climate change risks were framed differently in terms of energy use rather than increase in global temperature then different forms of political action would have opened up, as is happening now with the China–United States deal on climate change, in November 2014, and the de-coupling of global emissions of carbon dioxide from economic growth, also in 2014, outside the multilateral climate treaty and markets.

The current framework delivered results in identifying global concerns till political decision making shifted to national policy implementation, which was very different from setting the agenda by identifying the extent of environmental damage and its impact on the economy and society to support universal solutions. Global environmental change, climate change and sustainable development stand out as areas where the industrialized countries successfully shifted attention from their consumption and production patterns of natural resource use by shaping the way the issues were defined in terms of global goods. They developed the global agenda in 1972 with the help of the scientific community and secured agreement of reluctant partners in developing countries. This framework has continued to shape international cooperation for 40 years and, with the re-emergence of China and India, is only now being challenged. As industrialized countries are seeking to shift the focus to national actions, but within a universal regime while developing countries are insisting on recognition of diversity

---

[1] This chapter has extensive quotes from published material without editing or changes as 'case studies', with the objective of drawing attention of researchers to this material.

in the architecture of the regimes to ensure fairness for countries at different levels of development. The most tangible outcome has been to provide industrialized countries rights to natural resources outside national boundaries, which they needed to sustain economic growth, as by the 1970s three-quarters of their population had moved to cities and economic growth had begun to slow.

Prior to 1992, developing countries were largely unconcerned about the substantive issues related to global environmental discussions, based on their view that the deliberations had little relevance for them. As the social sciences gradually became more important in understanding the problems of natural resource use and seeking solutions, which involved finance and linkages with other negotiations, foreign ministries began seeking a controlling role from meteorologists, biologists and economists. The debates were no longer about scientific enquiry on the assessments of physical aspects of nature but about the principles governing natural resource use and allocations between countries involving distribution, and positions hardened as the policy space started to get restricted.

Academic research priorities, however, continue to be largely shaped and financed by governments in industrialized countries, with issues periodically identified to reflect their shifting priorities; for example, the emergence and decline of global emissions trading and the role of markets. These efforts have included having a say in identification of researchers and continuing funding that served to build a community of experts who had worked together on these issues to develop reports within the multilateral system, as a form of 'soft power'. The situation began to change with the extensive capacity building and national reporting under the Climate Change Convention, because it built a wider community of experts with fewer restrictions on the agenda as well as developing a statistical base for analysis by an even wider group in developing countries.

With the increasing globalization and the re-emergence of China and India, global trends began to be produced by consultants working for business groups, occasionally supported by governments and business associations in developing countries. These analyses reflected the need for a more varied and diffuse agenda for countries at different levels of development and did not project a single perspective, making a consensus on management of the environment more contentious, but without suggesting a new framework for the global natural resource management and sharing of the resources. These reports have largely been written from the perspective of new markets and have supported the shift to looking at consumption rather than production patterns; one outcome has been to shift the focus of carbon dioxide emissions from production to consumption patterns with the finding that end use should be the policy concern as it covers nearly three-quarters of global emissions and natural resource use.

More recently, the appointment of developing country officials in high positions within the United Nations has modified the responses of these bodies to analyzing sustainability in the reports produced for the Rio+20 Conference by focusing on consumption patterns – UN Energy focusing on adequate access led by UNIDO, impact of food waste and livestock on natural resource use and emissions of greenhouse gases analysed by the FAO, recognition that urbanization is shaped by public transport stressed by UN HABITAT, global environmental concerns as social rather than physical problems highlighted by UNESCO, and recognition for the first time of Ethics and Justice in the reports of the IPCC – with a number of these analytical studies being published in 2013.

An immediate impact has been on the think-tanks of the G7 industrialized countries, with the International Energy Agency recognizing for the first time energy efficiency essentially as a conventional fuel, also in 2013, and requiring action in industrialized countries, 5 years after independent policy analysts, like McKinsey and Company not connected with governments, identified that end-use technologies and services are the single most important long-term emissions reduction option, in line with historical patterns, that can reduce half of the cumulative emissions over the twenty-first century. The European Commission also now acknowledges on its website that sustainable development will not be brought about by policies only: it must be taken up by the society at large as a principle guiding the many choices each citizen makes every day, along with the big political and economic decisions that have to be made. This transformation requires profound changes in thinking, in economic and social structures and in consumption and production patterns.

After 40 years, it is now becoming clear that in the relationships between countries and with the world economy and society, it is not the tipping points in nature that alone should be considered but also the social tipping points; that is, measures that can tip production and consumption patterns, or economic structures and societal systems, into sustainable development. This is really a reiteration, as consumption and production factors had been identified as early as the 1970s as the primary cause of global environmental change.

3.1 Politics of the interaction between scientists and policymakers

The role of the science–policy interface has been to provide authoritative justification for identifying the environmental issue by the adoption of a particular framework, approach or course of action, with diplomats shaping the further development of the issue-based regime, with continued assistance by the scientists. This group of experts, largely known to each other, usually working with each other on joint projects, and developed consensual opinion that was adopted to influence agenda-setting in the intergovernmental negotiations [Hass et al., 1993]. The interaction between scientists, academics and policymakers can be characterized as more political than scientific and varied depending on the economic importance of the issue area and the choice of scientists. For example, most of the funding was for complex systems such as climate change and biological diversity, which are non-linear by nature – there are uncertainties about chain reactions through the system which are not directly proportional to the size of the triggers. The way the issues have been defined based on the natural sciences, future climate and biodiversity risks are not based on data that can be directly observed, require scientific and policy judgments as the full scientific data are not available at the time decisions have to be made, further reinforcing the importance of the way the issue is framed.

In this arrangement, two trends of the process have generated debate. First, the continuing dominance of natural scientists, even in the analysis and policy development of the causes and consequences of global environmental degradation, has kept the focus on describing the symptoms rather than analysing the longer term trends and drivers causing the problem; for example, atmospheric scientists in the climate regime and conservation biologists in the biodiversity regime. Second, the chairs and the members of the scientific panels and advisory groups advising intergovernmental negotiating processes, even those selected by United Nations bodies like the Intergovernmental Panel on Climate Change, which lists the experts who wrote each of its chapters, have been dominated by scientists trained and largely working in the industrialized countries, or those who had migrated there. With geopolitical shifts, the result has been that the concept of 'expert' has increasingly become contested as they provide inputs into the policy process, and concerns related to public trust and credibility are now questioning the defining role that national influence and economic interests play in scientists framing policy debates in particular ways within the United Nations.

The intellectual power of the framing has been such that the role of these bodies has been to influence the public debate in particular ways, rather than be incorporated directly in policy shifts which require economic changes. This has meant that issues are characterized as technical and scientific, even though they reflect national interests and have to be debated by diplomats in political terms. The lack of success in dealing with global environmental degradation can be explained by the way the issues have been framed ignoring difficulties inherent in taking hard decisions that are needed, and which have been postponed or ignored. The reality is that the underlying causes of the global environmental problems have been successfully avoided by industrialized countries, and a crisis situation has emerged because the trends can no longer be ignored with the re-emergence of China and India requiring them to take national actions – a major political achievement of the industrialized countries.

The way the issue has been framed has also determined the research questions and the scientific and academic literature that has emerged from within donor agencies, international agencies largely funded by them, research activities entirely funded by them or from individuals and groups seeking to respond to donor thinking in this regard. Similarly, most of the current attempts seeking to develop environmental capacity in developing countries have been funded by donor agencies. Both the coordinated research in industrialized countries and the related capacity building in developing countries have led to the establishment, and reinforcement, of a global epistemic community. The wide range of sponsored educational and capacity building programs have also co-opted a generation of developing country environmental scientists and policy analysts to an industrialized country view that international cooperation focused largely on actions in developing countries is necessary to meet the challenge of global environmental change, defined in terms of safeguarding ecosystem services and planetary limits.

The concern comes up most often as a criticism about the lack of implementation, particularly about the promises that are now a part of every environmental treaty and institution. The result is that when the dominant scholarship on global environmental governance, located in the industrialized countries, discusses the issue of effectiveness they have focused on the ecological aspects of effectiveness; for example, which ecological issues have been tackled, how and how well [Victor et al., 1998; Young and Oran, 1999; Miles et al., 2002; Haas et al., 2003; Mitchell et al., 2006].

The developing country concerns are about the means of implementation for effectiveness that stresses diversity, or levels of development, and is significantly different to and at odds with a universal approach largely relying on markets. Their focus has been on the developmental aspects of global environmental governance, or what they consider as global sustainable development governance and the well-being of their population, now seeking middle-class status within ecological limits [Agarwal and Narain, 1992; see also, Sanwal, 2004]. However, the way the issue of natural resource use and the global environment has been framed has not been seriously questioned.

This is largely because modelling ignored social science research on distribution-related concerns, just as sustainable development has been framed in term of silos: environmental, economic and social. The different perspectives have now only begun to be integrated in a multidisciplinary approach by the research and academic communities in industrialized and developing countries, as well as by international institutions. For the first time, the report of the Intergovernmental Panel on Climate Change released in 2014 has a chapter on 'Social, Economic and Ethical Concepts'. However, the analyses of equity perspectives remain limited in number, scope and impact in reframing the global concerns. In the climate negotiations for a new regime, a strong political position has been taken by the developing countries to give equal importance to mitigation and adaptation and vulnerability only in 2014. The re-emergence of China has raised issues that are important for the rural poor moving into the middle class and are also now being researched by management consultancies analysing emerging markets. Research on the role of lifestyles in determining consumption patterns in the industrialized countries is of even more recent origin, though the implications for global environmental change are still not considered central enough to reframe the global concern.

From the time the global environment concern was framed, in 1992, with a common understanding on the agenda and during the climate negotiations, developing countries have stressed the importance of equity and justice. They were successful only in incorporating these considerations in the Rio Declaration, in 1992. Such was the power of the way the issue was framed, and consensual

38 | The World's Search for Sustainable Development

science that had been developed, that since then these governments have not been able to develop an alternative framework. Consequently, the divide between the positions of industrialized countries and developing countries has also not yet been bridged. The Brazilian proposal on determining historical responsibility at Kyoto, in 1997, was modified by the United States, and was agreed as the Clean Development Mechanism with a focus on private sector finance. This effort reflected both the intellectual capacity in the United States to reshape distributional concepts in terms of the possibility of new finance as well as being the isolated scientific alternative framework incorporating sustainable development principles in the Climate Change Convention.

Equity is raised by the developing countries in every meeting with no substantial outcome, leading to the criticism that it is really an excuse for not taking on commitments. The policy of the developing countries towards the global concerns has been of denial; that developed countries have to take the lead while they do not have to take any measures. Consequently, their research focus has continued over the past 40 years to be on trade and macroeconomic issues, as the most visible aspect of global change. The China–United States climate deal of November 2014, outside the multi-lateral process, stands out because China was able to secure a bilateral agreement linking its peaking of carbon dioxide emissions to the completion of its urbanization rather than solely to environmental considerations.

The development and implementation of the major international research programs (i.e. the International Geosphere-Biosphere Program, the World Climate Research Program, International Human Dimensions Program and Future Earth), while progressively taking into account concerns of developing countries, has not supported research capacity building in developing countries, and these global initiatives remain dominated by scientists from industrialized countries, constituting up to four-fifth of the participants involved. This has helped to shape the global agenda but has had limited effectiveness at the national level. The global research agenda does not include the priorities of developing countries, it provides a template for the kinds of research to be performed that does not cover the issues of relevance to them and does not provide incentives for their researchers to contribute to questioning the international efforts, further reinforcing the original framing [Sagar, 2000].

A related result has been that policy development and public opinion in developing countries continues to be shaped by the scientific and academic work being done in industrialized countries, despite apprehensions that it does not reflect the diversity of their national circumstances and does not integrate equity into the universal framework, which is at best tweaked for specific negotiations. This gap was recognized quite early, leading to the START initiative–Global Change System for Analysis, Research and Training, in 1992. It was established to develop a system of regional networks of collaborating scientists and institutions, conduct research on regional aspects of global change, assess the impacts of regional findings, and provide regionally important integrated and evaluated information to policymakers. However, only 2 of the 9 members of the first START Scientific Steering Committee were from developing countries and the initiative had some political impact on the UNCED, but very little impact on capacity building in developing countries. It was only in 2013 that the Chinese Academy of Social Sciences began publishing a peer reviewed publication–the 'Chinese Journal of Urban and Environmental Studies', with World Scientific publishing.

3.2 Political basis of the role and design of expert organizations

Expert organizations are now providing expert knowledge, rather than expert science, to the major intergovernmental bodies and the industrialized countries continue to shape their priorities and ways of working, though with a lesser impact on the political process than earlier. The model of the IPCC has been extended to the Intergovernmental Platform on Biodiversity and Ecosystem Services (IPBES).

A new global body for expert knowledge is being formed to serve the United Nations Convention on Combating Drought and Desertification as well as an international science advisory mechanism for disaster risk reductions. Most recently, the UN Secretary-General Ban Ki-moon in January 2014 established a Scientific Advisory Board (SAB) on sustainable development. The central function of the Scientific Advisory Board is to provide advice on science, technology and innovation (STI) for sustainable development to the UN Secretary-General and to Executive Heads of UN organizations. Among its many functions, the Board will contribute to strengthening the linkage between science and policy and ensuring that up-to-date and rigorous science is appropriately reflected in high-level policy discussions within the UN system. Its role remains uncertain as the International Social Science Council (ISSC) has independently reviewed the negotiations on the sustainable development goals and directly submitted its recommendations to the political process [ISSC, 2015]. Expert bodies in the Multilateral Environmental Treaties are established under the Conference of the Parties and are part of the institutional structure and composed of government representatives, unlike expert organizations like the Scientific Advisory Board which are set up outside the intergovernmental bodies to whom they provide the expert knowledge.

The IPCC was established to serve a political purpose. In 1988, the Toronto Conference, convened by non-state actors, called for a 20 per cent reduction in emissions of greenhouse gases by 2005. This development worried the United States as it would involve policy actions to be taken by it and other industrialized countries in which developing countries were not included to share the burden[2]. The United States successfully diverted global attention onto atmospheric research away from the causes of the problem based on production and consumption patterns of energy use. The new body was designed, at a time when there were few developing country scientists engaged in global environmental concerns, to maintain political control through the selection and type of autonomy given to scientists engaged in the assessment process, and this helped to shape the agenda of the subsequent climate negotiations.

The IPCC framed climate change around global average temperature as the pre-eminent indicator of risk, which continues to be the reference point around which both scientific knowledge has been assessed and different policy options evaluated. In 1990, the IPCC compared two climate models and in 2014 it compared 40 models running at higher spatial resolution and focused on more complex components of the Earth system, yet these improvements have not reduced the spread of uncertainty in the model projections, and their role in policy formulation is now being questioned [Ryan et al., 2014]. Despite this analytical rigour, because of the approach adopted, the range of policy choices that are compatible with the current scientific findings is limited to improving climate predictions and suggesting new economic policy instruments, neglecting a large number of policy alternatives including adaptation, consumption and equity which are raised in the political debate and in the negotiations. The thrust now is on a carbon budget placing climate change impacts in relation to other drivers/pressures, indicating the importance of economic and environmental co-benefits, and while the question of 'ethics' has been raised social concerns have not modified the framework. As a result, the political discussions about climate change, and the popular perceptions of 'global warming' continue to be selective and restrictive.

The IPCCs chosen style of risk assessment and communication has also led to a unitary approach to represent scientific consensus as a single voice, while not acknowledging or inviting diverse voices or perspectives. Focusing on consensus, the IPCC has not found it difficult to continue with the earlier framing by excluding issues where no consensus exists (e.g., the global energy balance, geological data). As an example of 'group think', Richard Tol, convening lead author of one of the chapters of the IPCC report on Adaptation, Working Group II, dissociated himself from the Summary for Policy Makers

---

[2] NASA climate expert, James Hansen, also asserted before a Senate panel that statistics showed "the greenhouse effect has been detected and is changing our climate now."

(SPM) in 2014, objecting to the deletion of an important policy statement in the earlier drafts that "many of the more worrying impacts of climate change really are symptoms of mismanagement and underdevelopment … with later drafts putting more and more emphasis on the reasons for concern about climate change". He also observed that "the SPM omits that better cultivars and improved irrigation increase crop yields. It shows the impact of sea level rise on the most vulnerable country, but does not mention the average. It emphasizes the impacts of increased heat stress downplays reduced cold stress. It warns about poverty traps, violent conflict and mass migration without much support in the literature".

The IPCCs emphasis on peer-reviewed research to underpin its consensus-based statements also excludes alternative forms of expertise – such as reports of management consultancies and the United Nations bodies, which, as a rule, are rarely published in these forums, and also ignores more localized and informal forms of knowledge. As a response to these shortcomings, the IPCC has introduced new guidelines for the integration of 'grey literature'. Starting out with relatively few formalized rules in 1988, the IPCC has gone through three major revisions, in 1993, 1999, and 2010. However, the reform is limited to procedures and management structures to improve the transparency of its processes, rather than the content of the science and knowledge.

Since the early 1990s, the level of participation of developing countries in the IPCC assessment process has been a concern, because it is the authoritative body to provide a state-of-the-art global assessment of the scientific literature on the issues in the global climate debate. There has been only limited change, even though developing country participation has been on the agenda of almost every IPCC Bureau meeting. Industrialized country experts continue to be in leadership roles, shaping agendas. There are no agreed criteria for selection of participants, who are invited on the basis of their work in joint research projects and peer-reviewed articles in journals that are present only in industrialized countries, reinforcing personal connections and donor-driven academic networks that subscribe to the agreed framework. As developing countries are increasingly conducting their own research, these studies will contribute to the credibility, legitimacy and policy relevance of future reports of the IPCC.

The limited number of 'experts' in developing countries researching the topics that fall within the scope of way the climate issue has been framed led to the role of these governments being limited to procedures and management structures to improve the transparency of the processes. The focus has been with criteria for evaluating scientific evidence, setting standards for knowledge validity, selecting experts, organizing review procedures, and demarcating mandates between scientific and political institutions – without going into the research questions that these bodies should answer. These bodies assess the most recent scientific research produced worldwide relevant to an understanding of global environmental change in relation to a particular policy-relevant problem, even though there is no consensus on the problem itself. The result is that their output, referred to as an authoritative assessment of relevant scientific research and peer-reviewed publications, can be highly disaggregated and not readily accessible to policymakers requiring a summary, which also provides the opportunity to those who have framed the issue to highlight certain approaches and exclude others.

Unlike in the case of the IPCC, the negotiation process to overcome disconnect between science and policy needs for the conservation of biological diversity has been relatively transparent and open, has included a thorough gap analysis of information needs and the explicit involvement of developing country experts. This was possible because the politically controversial area of access to genetic resources and related biotechnology was excluded. Governments agreed to establish a permanent, globally orchestrated organization on the lines of the IPCC, but with important modifications. After 7 years of intense negotiations, the Intergovernmental Science-Policy Platform on Biodiversity and Ecosystem Services (IPBES) was formally established in 2012 under the auspices of UNEP. Different options concerning the governance structure of the platform were explored, instead of simply implementing the IPCC design, involving a broad range of stakeholders and a multidisciplinary expert approach from the beginning.

The conceptual framework of the IPBES recognizes the multiplicity of knowledge systems and does not institute a global but multi-scale assessment and complements this process by setting up three additional working areas, namely knowledge generation, capacity building, and policy support. Instead of taking scientific, peer-reviewed knowledge as the gold standard, the IPBES plenary considered the relevance and credibility of different forms and sources of knowledge and experience in relation to serving the broad range of tasks the IPBES decided to tackle. As a result, the IPBES agreed on establishing a task force for strengthening the quality of indigenous peoples' participation in the platform's deliverables. It has also recognized that an exclusive focus on universal economic valuation is not an adequate response to the complexity of biodiversity loss and has taken on board a differentiated conceptualization of the values of biodiversity and of its benefits for human well-being, recognizing uncertainties, divergent world views, and relevant local and indigenous knowledge to produce a diverse range of possible interventions, policy options and scientific validity [Beck, Silke et al., 2014].

The experience with the IPCC and similar bodies that set the agenda for multilateral negotiations are an essential part of the framework where industrialized countries are willing to delegate only limited authority to global expert organizations. They continue to safeguard their national interests by controlling key processes such as the nomination of experts or the drafting of summaries for policymakers. Consensus-based procedures do not also allow for divergent opinion to be recognized by restricting policy options to the earlier framings. The result is that the advice is not neutral. The underlying rationale of global expert organizations is to serve a political purpose; this is changing, but in a limited way.

3.3 Case studies: framing key global concerns: 1972–2012

Politics has been the defining factor in how every major issue on the global environment, climate change and sustainable development is understood, as attention was diverted away from natural resource use, or consumption and production patterns, to the symptoms, or impacts on nature, characterized first as global environmental change and climate change and later as sustainable development. This framing, based on international environmental law and 'common concern', was shaped as much by strategic thinking and intellectual capacity as by influence and power of the industrialized countries, and in turn shaped agendas, concerns and solutions in universal terms ignoring diversity and levels of development. The result has been restrictions on the policy space in developing countries with minimal impacts on industrialized countries and limited success in dealing with the problem[3].

3.3.1 The 'Grand Bargain': International environmental law

Stockholm conference on the Human environment, 1972

The approach adopted, of defining the problem of global environmental change as a technical and sectoral issue of pollution control rather than modifying consumption and production patterns because of their combined impact on ecological limits, has shaped the definition and objective of global environmental change, climate change and sustainable development since the Stockholm Conference on the Human Environment, in 1972. The deliberations within the United States show that while the importance of dealing with the causes rather than the symptoms of the problem were recognized, because of political considerations the concerns were framed as a technical issue.

---

[3] This section is based on extensive quotes from documents, statements and reviews

42 | The World's Search for Sustainable Development

The report prepared in the run-up to the first United Nations Conference on the Human Environment in 1970, noted that

> 'Long range policy planning to cope with global environmental problems must take account of the total ecological burden. This burden tends to increase with population growth and with the level of economic activity, whereas the capacity of the environment to provide essential inputs to production and to absorb unwanted outputs from consumption is fundamentally limited. The problem with managing total ecological burden will remain even after world population is stabilized. Controlling that burden by systematic reduction in per capita production of goods and services would be politically unacceptable. A concerted effort is needed to orient technology towards making human demands upon the environment less severe' [US, 1970].

Kurt Waldheim, the Secretary-General of the United Nations at the time of the Stockholm Conference, also recognized that the causes of the problem lay in resource use in industrialized countries but laid it out before the intergovernmental process with a focus on the future actions in developing countries signalling the further politicization of the issue–'the South is also beginning to realize that the North which consumes two-thirds of the world's resources might damage irremediably the oceans, earth and atmosphere which are the sources of life for all. The North is worried by the great number of people in the South, who continue to increase. These large numbers if multiplied by increased consumption and industrialization will be a main factor in tomorrow's world environment'.

Stockholm also marks the beginning of the global concern around climate change at the political level. The Conference discussed a scientific report sponsored by the Massachusetts Institute of Technology, USA, on 'Inadvertent Climate Modification', characterized it in terms of climate variability rather than climate change, and it remains a more accurate characterization than global warming.

At Stockholm, at the request of China, a special working group reviewed the text of the draft declaration signalling its strategic interventions in these conferences, reflecting its status, not as a member of the Group of 77, but as an associate member retaining the flexibility of acting independently[4].

Sustainable development

The conclusions of the Brundtland Report, 1987, the origin of the term sustainable development in a political text within the United Nations, were also adapted to serve the national interests of industrialized countries.

Jim MacNeill, the Secretary-General of the Commission, points out:

> 'Just 10 years after Stockholm, the UN reported that global environmental trends were getting worse. There were many reasons for this, but one stands out above all others and it applies as much today as it did then. We discussed it at some length in "Our Common Future". Briefly, we found that the environmental-protection agenda that nations' adopted before and after Stockholm tackled only the "symptoms" of environmental degradation; it completely ignored the "sources". The sources were to be found not in our air, soil, and waters, which were the focus of the environmental-protection agenda, but in a whole range of perverse public policies, especially our dominant fiscal and tax policies, our energy policies, and our trade, industry, agriculture, and other policies'.

He goes on to stress that sustainable development 'raises profound questions about our values, and about our relationship with nature, on whose integrity and stability all life depends. ... We

---

[4] Originally published in Sanwal (2011).

had defined sustainable development in several ways: ethical, social, and ecological. They were all interrelated, but there were two that I thought were quite basic. The first referred to the need to live within nature's limits. Development was sustainable, we said, if, at a minimum, it did not endanger the natural systems that support life on earth – the atmosphere, the waters, the soils, and the living beings. Later we pointed out that current forms of development drew too heavily on already overdrawn accounts of ecological capital and that they could not be extended into the future without bankrupting those accounts. We further said that, while we may show profits on the balance sheets of our generation … our children will inherit the losses'.…

'The second element referred to consumption levels. Development was sustainable, we said, if it was "based on consumption standards that are within the bounds of the ecologically possible and to which all can reasonably aspire. … Today, of course, nobody remembers those definitions. In 1987, only one definition grabbed the headlines, and it stuck. It is the one that features the need for intergenerational equity, framed as, 'development which meets the needs and aspirations of the present generation without compromising the ability of future generations to meet their own needs". I have always regretted that turn of events. Intergenerational equity is obviously an important feature of any viable definition of sustainability, but standing alone to the exclusion of others, it does not make sense'.

He also points out that 'Rio was a political success. It produced several major agreements … nowhere in those agreements will you find a single word in which the assembled governments committed themselves to actually do something … The journey to a more sustainable world is barely underway, even though we have made a significant amount of progress'

He concludes by saying that 'the Brundtland Commission report paid particular attention to the interrelationships among the three goals of environmental, economic and social development, noting two-way connections between any given pair. In particular, noting that social development was necessary for sustaining both economic development and environmental protection, the Commission observed that a world in which poverty is endemic will always be prone to ecological and other catastrophes' and that the distribution of power and influence within society lies at the heart of most environment and development challenges. It emphasized that sustainable development is not a goal applicable only to developing countries but must be a goal of developed countries as well. However, the commonly accepted definition of sustainability takes as its starting point only one element, portrayed as the consensus, within the World Commission on Environment and Development' [MacNeill, 2013].

Climate change

In the 1970s, within the United States, the scientists were not certain as to the causes of the climate problem and considered anthropogenic causes the least significant.

'Climatologists are studying various factors that possibly influence climate. Among them are solar activity, changes in the earth's orbit and rotation, volcanic activity, and the impact of mankind. Orbital changes and solar activity affect the heat energy available to the climate system. Carbon dioxide, dust and other atmospheric substances added to the atmosphere by man and volcanoes affect the distribution of heat within the system and the flow of heat in and out of the system. Heat produced by man's activities may also contribute directly to climatic changes' [CIA, 1978].

At this time, UNESCO's Man and Biosphere Program (1971–1984) involved members of the natural science community to study the collective impact of human activity on the global environment as a system or set of closely interlocking systems. The new international collaborative research programme did not reflect this range of possible causes of the problem. It was led by researchers in the atmospheric sciences, and it brought together other scientists of this discipline across national borders and across different disciplines. Other disciplines, as well as the social sciences, were kept out even though the experts were examining both the causes and impacts of global environmental change. Climate change was defined in terms of increase in global temperature or global warming.

Climate policy was defined in 1988 in the United Nations resolution 43/53 in terms of environmental damage; 'climate change as a common concern of human kind', with a focus on emissions of carbon dioxide–the symptom and not the cause of the problem. It was a short step to the current emphasis in agendas for intergovernmental cooperation and frameworks suggesting universal solutions with the objective of de-carbonization of energy supply, by substituting one technology by another. This ignores the potential for recognizing diversity, for example, in energy efficiency, which we now know would have a deeper impact; de-carbonization will be a co-benefit and not the driver for modifying energy systems because climate policy is very different to energy policy.

A focus on human well-being suggests an energy policy providing reliable, adequate and least cost energy services to half of humanity who are at present deprived of the benefits of industrialization, urbanization and increased incomes. Providing this energy will require diversification of supply and that will include de-carbonization. The difference is that the emphasis would then be on renewable energy technologies rather than the still to be commercialized and more controversial carbon capture and storage (CCS) technology. It would still take into account the requirement of climate policy to increase the supply of energy in a manner that is within ecological limits, but the emphasis would be with respect to the areas, geographies and technologies needing change with attendant political implications. Both policies will ultimately be driven by societal change.

Based on the experience with other pollutants, like sulphur dioxide and ozone, it was argued that scientists – epistemic communities – could provide a diagnosis of 'the problem' to policymakers, with solutions also driven by science. The assumption within policymakers that a shared understanding of the problem would facilitate a solution is correct, except that there was no real agreement on the nature of the problem – is it an environmental problem where the burden of controlling the damage should be shared or a resource to be equitably shared. Even as these perspectives are subject of debate, based largely on research in developing countries, it is increasingly becoming clear that climate change is more than just an environmental problem because it is integral to the process of economic development, infrastructure, urbanization and middle class lifestyles, not just modern energy with emissions as a by-product [Girod et al., 2009].

Biological diversity

Biodiversity and related biotechnology are issues where industrialized countries were able to use the decentralized structure of the United Nations, as developing countries were largely represented in the United Nations Environment Programme at the technical level, to develop a framework in terms of environmental commitments while ensuring the development of their economic interests. The Convention on Biological Diversity was the central focus of the industrialized countries at the Rio Conference in 1992.

Biodiversity became a global issue from the mid-1980s, when the first environmental release of a genetically modified organism took place. This technological development influenced changes in the theory and practice of nature conservation concerning the increase in species extinction, safety considerations and the expansion of genetic engineering with the entry of industrial interests into areas from which they had so far been excluded. The Convention on Biological Diversity is based on the concept of 'common concern of mankind' for sustainable use of biological resources, but through the development of the market. It established a commercial framework with provisions relating to international cooperation. It also established a hierarchy of norms with the obligation, as members of the WTO, to adopt intellectual property rights and a market framework, constraining national action in developing countries. This arrangement established a system of biodiversity ownership consisting of three mutually reinforcing components – molecular biology, IPRs and international treaties, negating the emphasis on compensatory payments for access to biological resources.

The commoditization of biological resources was presented not only as an incentive to biodiversity conservation but also as a lever for the recognition of the rights of rural communities, which was being pushed by NGOs. However, community rights, recognized by the Convention, do not enjoy recognition and protection comparable with that of intellectual property rights; unlike the rights protected by the rules of the WTO, their violation does not entail retaliation by governments. Even the possibility of getting compensation requires recognition of the intellectual property rights of the industries. The choice of a property rule was not required by the nature of biological diversity, and it served to confirm a *de facto* situation, that is, turning the privileges of the transnational firms that were already exploiting genetic resources into legal rights, which could be patented.

The legal regime applied to genetic resources prior to the negotiation of the new convention had taken into account the notion of common heritage of humankind to plant genetic resources for food and agriculture, promoted by the Food and Agriculture Organization (FAO) in its International Undertaking on Plant Genetic Resources in 1983 and established their universal availability. It envisaged a multilateral fund to which contributions would be made by industrialized countries to pay ex-post compensation to the farmers as an acknowledgment of the past contribution of their resources and related knowledge to the development of agriculture. This arrangement was not extended to biological diversity. The attempt to ensure the goals of efficiency and equity through a common framework subjected the achievement of the latter to the pursuit of the former. The text of the Convention only seems to establish the claims for national sovereignty over natural resources.

The compromise in the Convention on Biological Diversity led to the definition of biological diversity as a 'common concern of mankind' and not just a national resource or property. The recognition of national sovereignty within this framework gave developing countries where these resources are situated some leverage in maintaining control over and the right to benefit from use of their genetic resources in biotechnology. While developing countries were able to negotiate a reframing from an environmental to a sustainable development Convention, the sharing of benefits with those who had conserved the genetic resources was nullified by the 'interpretative statement' recorded to the treaty by the European Union and by the United States in Agenda 21 pushed by their seed, pharmaceutical and chemical industry. The European Union refused to share the technology and profits from the resulting biotechnology and the United States refused to ratify the treaty. In 1992 their $8 billion biotechnology industry was the most dominant in the world, and they did not want to dilute the later TRIPS Agreement of 1995 on intellectual property rights in the World Trade Organization, and open the door to compulsory licensing arrangements imposed by developing countries. Both statements convert sustainable use under the conservation treaty into a trade convention.

European Community

Declaration:

Within their respective competence, the European Community and its Member States wish to reaffirm the importance they attach to transfers of technology and to biotechnology in order to ensure the conservation and sustainable use of biological diversity. The compliance with intellectual property rights constitutes an essential element for the implementation of policies for technology transfer and co-investment.

For the European Community and its member States, transfers of technology and access to biotechnology, as defined in the text of the Convention on Biological Diversity, will be carried out in accordance with article 16 of the said Convention and in compliance with the principles and rules of protection of intellectual property, in particular multilateral and bilateral agreements signed or negotiated by the Contracting Parties to this Convention.

The European Community and its Member States will encourage the use of the financial mechanism established by the Convention to promote the voluntary transfer of intellectual property rights held by European operators, in particular as regards the granting of licences, through normal commercial mechanisms and decisions, while ensuring adequate and effective protection of property rights.

United States of America

Declaration: (Upon adoption)

1. In signing the Final Act, the United States recognizes that this negotiation has drawn to a close.

2. The United States strongly supports the conservation of biodiversity and, as is known, was an original proponent of a convention on this important subject. We continue to view international cooperation in this area as extremely desirable.

3. It is deeply regrettable to us that—whether because of the haste with which we have completed our work or the result of substantive disagreement—a number of issues of serious concern in the United States have not been adequately addressed in the course of this negotiation. As a result, in our view, the text is seriously flawed — in a number of important respects.

4. As a matter of substance, we find particularly unsatisfactory the text's treatment of intellectual property rights; finances, including, importantly, the role of the Global Environment Facility (GEF); technology transfer and biotechnology.

5. In addition, we are disappointed with the development of issues related to environmental impact assessments, the legal relationship between this Convention and other international agreements, and the scope of obligations with respect to the marine environment.

6. Procedurally, we believe that the hasty and disjointed approach to the preparation of this Convention has deprived delegations of the ability to consider the text as a whole before adoption. Further, it has not resulted in a text that reflects well on the international treaty-making process in the environmental field.

Source: Handbook of the Convention on Biological Diversity.

The initial drafts of the Convention prepared by the UNEP secretariat had reflected the views of industrialized countries seeking to define biodiversity located within national borders as a 'global commons'. This was opposed by developing countries as they would have had to give others a right of access to their genetic resources. The way biodiversity is considered at the international level has since changed linking it even more closely to global markets. In 1992, the concern was with biodiversity as a natural resource and the economic aspects were distinct. The 2010 Nagoya Protocol explicitly recognizes 'the interdependence of all countries with regard to genetic resources for food and agriculture', emphasising the economic importance of biodiversity for human well-being, without moving forward on sharing the resulting biotechnology and making any reference to pharmaceuticals, where the real profits lie [Boisvert et al., 2002].

Basel convention

The Basel Convention was negotiated in 1989 following international outrage due to illegal transnational shipping of hazardous waste. Trade in hazardous wastes and 'radioactive waste' had become a big business in the late 1970s. This trade continued to increase as industrialized countries faced increasingly stringent environmental regulations and as they continued to generate increasing quantities of hazardous waste. Industries in the United States alone exported over 160,000 tons of hazardous waste each year, which was nearly 95 per cent of all hazardous waste.

Industrialized countries placed the issue on the global agenda and the UNEP Governing Council in 1982 mandated a group of experts to evolve guidelines and principles on environmentally sound management and transportation of hazardous wastes to legalize the trade, rather than an outright ban on exports of hazardous material. As the public outcry against the illicit dumping of hazardous wastes increased, several technical working groups continued to meet on the need to come up with a comprehensive global convention on the control of trans-boundary movement of hazardous wastes, guidelines were approved by the UNEP Governing Council in 1987, and after negotiations lasting 2 years the Global Convention on the Control of Trans-boundary Movements of Hazardous Wastes was enacted in Basel, Switzerland, in March 1989, as the Basel Convention. At the Conference, Africa advocated a complete ban on trans-boundary movement of hazardous wastes rather than mere regulation or control based on consent.

The Basel Convention had two overall purposes: to encourage the environmentally sound management of hazardous wastes and to protect developing countries from receiving hazardous wastes without prior consent. It did not make the trade illegal. The Convention was also not about modifying production patterns to reduce the generation of wastes but was carefully crafted to maintain flexibility for trans-boundary movement, or trade, of wastes. The provision for the protection of the sovereign right of every state to ban the import of hazardous wastes for transit or disposal was incorporated in the preamble, without any legal force. However, one of the initial, unexpected, consequences was the subsequent negotiation of separate regional agreements banning all imports of hazardous wastes to developing nations in specific regions.

African leaders believed that Basel's regulatory regime would merely legitimize a practice they found unacceptable and declared the hazardous waste trade 'a crime against Africa and the African people'. They feared that poor states, needing cash for development, could be given incentives to ignore the disastrous consequences of the hazardous waste trade. African leaders were concerned that Africa would become a dumping ground for hazardous waste from industrialized countries.

The United States strongly opposed an outright ban on trans-boundary shipments of hazardous waste characterizing it as a free trade issue. The argument was that prohibition was against individual liberty and would conflict with freedom of contract and free trade. There were other countries that did not favour an outright ban, also for economic reasons. For example, in the Netherlands, domestic environmental conditions and regulations made safe disposal of waste costly and they exported most of domestic production of hazardous waste. Some developing countries, such as the Philippines and India, relied on processing imported lead-acid batteries as a source for lead.

In the face of this opposition during the negotiations, the Organization of African Unity Council of Ministers passed a resolution (the Cairo Guidelines) in 1988 stating that the import of hazardous waste into Africa was a crime against Africa and its people and that states should introduce import bans and adhere to the provisions of the Cairo Guidelines. The Resolution also requested African countries to reach a consensus on a common African position to deal with the inadequacies of the draft Convention and to ensure that their unity was not disrupted until the draft Convention was adopted. The OAU member states refused to sign the Basel Convention during 1989 and 1990. In July 1989, they passed a resolution with a mandate to draft a reciprocal commitment of African states among themselves, aimed at the implementation and effective prohibition of the import of hazardous wastes into Africa. Thereafter, a working group was set up to draft a Convention to provide for and effectively ban the import of hazardous waste into Africa and to manage hazardous waste generated within Africa. On 30th January, 1991, the Bamako Convention was adopted at the Pan-African Conference on Environment and Sustainable Development in Africa. It imposed strict and unlimited criminal liability on importers of hazardous wastes into Africa and was a response to the shortcomings of the Basel Convention.

The Bamako Convention led to the amendment of the Basel Convention, in 1995, in which signatory parties agreed to an immediate ban on the export of hazardous wastes intended for final disposal from OECD to non-OECD countries. They also agreed to ban, by 31 December 1997, the export of wastes intended for recovery and recycling. Since 1995, the Basel Ban has been the dominant goal and activity of the Basel Convention. [Ogunlade, 2010]

Montreal protocol

The United States and the then 12-nation European Community (EC) dominated the market for CFCs together accounting for more than 80 per cent of the world's output in 1974, with half the global output in the United States. Despite shared political, economic and environmental values, they had markedly different views on the potential threat to the ozone layer, based on the commercial interests of their chemical industry.

The ozone depletion theory seemed to capture the imagination of the American public because of the United States space program, who were more sensitized than Europeans to events in the stratosphere. Congress, media, and environmental and scientific organizations in the United States were quick to voice concern. In contrast, for many years, there was no countervailing voice in Europe to the powerful chemical industry. The otherwise environmentally conscious European public accorded higher priority to such closer-to-home problems as acid rain and oil spills.

On both sides of the Atlantic, the chemical, automobile and other related industries adamantly denied any linkage between growing CFC use and the long-term stability of the stratospheric ozone layer. Industrialists mobilized research and public relations efforts to highlight the scientific uncertainties, the necessity of CFCs for modern lifestyles, the infeasibility of substitutes and the presumed high costs and economic dislocations associated with controls on these chemicals.

The United States banned CFCs as propellants for non-essential aerosol sprays in early 1978, affecting nearly $3 billion worth of sales in a wide range of products. Similar action was taken by Canada, a relatively small producer, and by Sweden, Norway, Denmark, and Finland, all importing countries and located in the polar latitudes where the danger of cancer from the 'hole' in the Ozone layer is more acute. In contrast, under heavy pressure from such companies as Britain's Imperial Chemical Industries, France's Atochem, and Germany's Hoechst, the European Community waited until 1980 before enacting painless measures, fully supported by industry, which gave an appearance of control while permitting unhampered CFC expansion for two more decades. After its aerosol ban, the United States lost its market pre-eminence. EC exports rose by 43 per cent from 1976 to 1985 and averaged almost one-third of its production. In contrast, the United States now consumed virtually all it produced.

The European Commission based its ozone position largely on the 'self-serving data and contentions of a few big companies. European industry's primary objective was to preserve market dominance and to avoid the costs of switching to alternative products for as long as possible'. Both industry and government officials felt that panic had driven Americans into the 1978 aerosol ban and that the United States had only itself to blame for any market losses. Reflecting the close EC industry–government linkages, company executives often served on official delegations to the negotiations.

Natural Science – Policy – Institutions Interface | **49**

According to Benedick, 'during the Montreal Protocol negotiations in 1987 we actually came across an official EC instruction drafted on an Atochem corporate letterhead'.

In 1983, the United States, along with others in the Toronto Group, proposed a provision to eliminate CFCs in non-essential aerosols, mirroring the actions taken several years earlier by them. They argued that a worldwide aerosol ban was clearly feasible, as substitutes were now available. The European Community rejected this idea and countered with a proposal to cap new production capacity. Correctly, European Community representatives pointed out that growing non-aerosol uses could eventually cancel out aerosol reductions. The Toronto Group responded that while the European Community proposal was theoretically elegant, it was practically ineffectual: under the European Community cap, currently underutilized European capacity would permit millions of additional tons of CFCs to be released over the next 20 years. Moreover, such a cap would lock in existing market shares and was therefore biased against countries with little or no surplus capacity, such as the United States.

As Benedick points out, 'whatever the intrinsic merits of the respective proposals each of the two contending blocs favoured an agreement that would require no new controls for itself and considerable adjustment for the other group of countries. Faced with this stalemate over regulatory strategies, the negotiators decided to return to the original idea of a research convention, which would at least provide a framework for any future agreement to control ozone-depleting substances'.

Over initial European objections, the Toronto Group pushed through a last-minute resolution in the Vienna Convention on Protection of the Ozone Layer, 1985, directing UNEP to reopen diplomatic negotiations with a 1987 target date for agreement on a binding CFC control protocol. This resolution simultaneously promoted an innovative scientific fact-gathering and consensus-building process, in the form of informal workshops under UNEP sponsorship, which proved critical to the future formal negotiations.

American companies had long resented the competitive advantage that their European rivals had achieved by escaping regulation in the late 1970s. Not surprisingly, American industry did not want any further U.S. regulatory action that was not also binding on the other major producer countries. Hence, in September 1986, the Alliance for Responsible CFC Policy, a coalition of about 500 producer and user companies, announced its support for international controls on CFCs.

This unexpected development broke industry's united front practically on the eve of the protocol negotiations and caused concern in Europe. Some European industrialists had suspected all along that the United States was using the ozone scare to cloak commercial motivations. They now claimed that American companies had endorsed CFC controls in order to enter the profitable European export markets with substitute products that had been secretly developed.

Significantly, DuPont also announced in 1986 that it could develop substitutes within about 5 years, but that 'neither the marketplace nor regulatory policy ... has provided the needed incentives' to justify the required investments. Now the incentives were there, and DuPont–the world's largest producer of CFCs–committed itself, even before any national government did, to cease the production of all CFCs and halons by the end of the century.

In an effort to counteract the influence of Imperial Chemical Industries on the U.K. position, some U.S. environmental organizations visited their British counterparts, who had not hitherto been active on this issue, in order to brief them on the significance of ozone layer depletion. Their efforts met with success, and British activists soon caused pointed questions to be raised in Parliament about the government's position. This even resulted in an official protest from Her Majesty's Government.

Final success on the control schedules at Montreal is attributable to a combination of factors. According to Benedick these included 'the American diplomatic and information campaign, which prompted Japan and the Soviet Union, among others, to agree on the need for stronger controls; the vigorous efforts of such delegations as Canada, Austria, Denmark, Egypt, Finland, New Zealand, Norway and others; the growing influence of the Federal Republic of Germany within EC councils; and the personal interventions by UNEP's Executive Director Tolba at the negotiating table and behind the scenes with key developing country governments'.

Under the Montreal Protocol, developing countries agreed to phase out their use of ozone-depleting substances, with a deadline for phasing out the production of CFCs, and were able to obtain a multilateral fund providing grants to enable adoption of less harmful substitutes, funded by contributions from developed countries. The United States agreed to this as without precedent and subsequent funds like the Global Environment Facility have limited their role to supporting capacity building and not industrial transformation.

According to Benedick, the agreed charter for the ozone fund was an exceptional innovation in multilateral cooperation. Procedures and terms of reference had been devised incorporating delicate checks and balances among donors and recipients. The Parties to the Protocol exercised the ultimate authority over the new financial mechanism. The 14-member Executive Committee represented the Parties in overall supervision and administration of the fund, which would have only a small central secretariat. The three principal collaborating multilateral institutions were assigned specific responsibilities under interagency agreements with the Executive Committee. Regular consultations among the cooperating agencies were planned, and the heads of the organizations invited to meet at least annually with the Executive Committee. The arrangement had important implications for future approaches to global problems requiring North–South cooperation, where policy changes and governance were linked to financing with the Bretton Woods Institutions who approached environmental problems through markets [Benedick, 2004].

The Montreal Protocol introduced hydroflourocarbon (HFC) to phase out hydrochlorofluoro-carbon (HCFC), an interim substitute for chlorofluorocarbon (CFC). Both HCFC and CFC damage the stratospheric ozone layer that blocks harmful ultraviolet rays. HFCs are greenhouse gases, which are over 2,000 times more potent than carbon dioxide, and this was known when it was adopted. In the past decade, the use of HFC has grown by 8–10 per cent annually, mostly in the United States, Europe, Japan and Australia, and mostly for use in their air-conditioning and refrigerator sector. The United States is now pushing developing countries where demand is going to rise steeply for a phase out HCFC, raising the question should they first phase into HFC and then phase out of it because it is bad for climate change? Or should they leapfrog to new substances, good for both ozone and climate? The same companies that first invented CFC and then profited from its phase-out are now ready with another alternative. United States companies such as DuPont and Honeywell are promoting hydrofluoroolefins (HFOs) for air-conditioning and HFC-1234yf for car air-conditioning. But these new generation chemicals are good for ozone, have less global-warming potential, but are still not good for climate because they are energy-inefficient. These indirect emissions (due to energy use) from appliances will add to climate change.

Alternative technologies, rated on the basis of their lifecycle energy emissions, are also available. For instance, some companies are moving to hydrocarbons, such as propane and butane, for refrigeration and air-conditioning. The United States still does not approve this shift, arguing flammability problems associated with these off-patented technologies. Politics rather than science remains the determining factor.

Common but differentiated responsibilities

At the Rio Conference on Environment and Development, in 1992, the 'grand bargain' was based around international environmental law as the framework for global environmental governance in order to reconcile the differing and competing concerns of developed and developing countries. The framework was conceptualized in terms of mutual rights and obligations of polluting and victim states. It was argued that interdependence in terms of contributions and solutions required cooperation, but there was no common understanding on the form of international cooperation.

During the negotiations on the Rio Declaration, the conference secretariat led by Maurice Strong, had prepared a draft of the 'Earth Charter', which they were not able to circulate because the G77 and China came out with their own draft. This draft, unlike the usual draft decisions, incorporated the major points of the industrialized countries making it difficult for them to reject it outright as a basis for negotiations.

The principle of 'common but differentiated responsibilities (CBDR)' was incorporated in the Rio Declaration despite the opposition of all the industrialized countries. This was the last clause to be agreed and was pushed by the Chairman, Tommy Koh, as it was a part of the communiqué of Ministers of Environment of the industrialized countries issued in the run up to Rio. You can oppose it when the Declaration is put up for adoption, Tommy Koh told the negotiators, and I will then ask you whether you are prepared to go on record against your own Ministers.

The notion of CBDR is based on the application of equity in general international law, as one means to formally integrate environment development at the international level and as a way to make one country's commitments more 'just' relative to the commitments of other countries, or more proportional by modifying application of universal agreements. CBDR only evolved as an international principle in the climate and biodiversity treaties in the 1992 United Nations Conference on Environment and Development (UNCED). It was originally spelt out in Principle 7 of the Rio Declaration as 'soft law'. The principle gained particular prominence in the context of negotiations on international climate policy, but is also relevant for other negotiations; for example, global sustainable development goals.

Earlier, international environmental law had been guided by principles based on sovereign equality and reciprocity between states, around the 1972 Stockholm Declaration Principle 21–'states sovereign right to exploit their own resources pursuant to their own environmental policies' with the caveat … 'to ensure that activities within their jurisdiction or control do not cause damage to the environment of other States or of areas beyond the limits of national jurisdiction'.

The Vienna Convention for the Protection of the Ozone Layer, 1987 Montreal Protocol differentiates responsibilities according to capabilities by highlighting 'the circumstances and particular requirements of developing countries' in its preamble and by relating Parties' 'general obligations' to 'the means at their disposal and their capabilities', such as delayed compliance for developing countries and a special fund to facilitate implementation in the form of special treatment.

CBDR comprises two core conceptual elements. The first element concerns states' common responsibility for environmental protection at the national, regional and global levels. The second element concerns the need to take into account differing national circumstances in relation to each state's contribution to the particular environmental problem and its capacity to reduce the threat of it. Therefore, the architecture itself provides for diversity rather than universality, with special treatment based on levels of development.

Politically, the climate convention has also been shaped by two distinct framings – climate change was framed as an environmental issue, to which pollution control is the answer, and second, climate change was linked to the sustainable development framework highlighting intra- and intergenerational equity and emphasizing the minor contribution of developing countries to current global environmental problems, their limited capacities to deal with them and poverty reduction as their overriding political priority. The elusive balance between these opposing perspectives reflects the lack of agreement on CBDR, and is a source of continuing tension.

The use of law to produce global collective benefits was itself a political decision to secure rights to natural resources outside national boundaries, and industrialized countries did not anticipate the incorporation of the CBDR in a negotiated text, as it raised the important question of burden sharing. When the Rio Declaration was adopted at Rio, the United States recorded a reservation and has repeated this reservation whenever this provision is introduced by developing countries in any negotiated text. Because of this interpretative statement, or non-acceptance by the United States, an amended principle has been adopted in the climate and biodiversity treaties. This compromise, or accommodation, changes its nature, scope and thrust–'common but differentiated responsibilities and respective capabilities', by balancing the impact of earlier economic growth with that of future economic growth. However, the central feature remains unaffected where the architecture is not based on universalism but includes diversity, and it shaped negotiations over a 20-year period. Whether or not to consider this principle as outdated is the key issue in the negotiations on a new climate regime and global sustainable development goals to be agreed in 2015.

Statement of the United States

Principle 7 of the Rio Declaration on Environment and Development

As the United States of America stated for the record at the 1992 United Nations Conference on Environment and Development, the United States understands and accepts that principle 7 of the Rio Declaration on Environment and Development highlights the special leadership role of developed countries, based on their industrial development, experience with environmental protection policies and actions, and wealth, technical expertise and capabilities. The United States does not accept any interpretation of principle 7 that would imply a recognition or acceptance by the United States of any international obligations or liabilities, or any diminution of the responsibilities of developing countries under international law.

The phrase 'common but differentiated responsibilities' is contained in the second sentence of Rio principle 7, which provides that 'in view of the different contributions to global environmental degradation, States have common but differentiated responsibilities'. The United States interprets references to common but differentiated responsibilities in the Plan of Implementation in this manner.

US Department of State, Diplomacy in Action, 51. U.S. interpretive statement on World Summit on Sustainable Development declaration

------

The principle of common but differentiated responsibilities that emerged at the Rio Conference, in 1992, did not specify what is to be done and paid for and by whom and for what purpose. The Oxford Handbook of International Environmental Law subsequently raised the important issue of legitimacy that 'international environmental law continues to struggle with the complaint that it reflects the concerns of developed countries more than those of developing countries … in the ongoing debates over whether developing countries, for example, should preserve biological resources of global concern or should reduce their greenhouse gas emissions and, if so, how much financial support developed countries should provide for such efforts' [Bodansky, 2007].

Personal knowledge as Co-Chair of the negotiations on the Rio Declaration. Some portions originally published in Sanwal (2011).

Forests

The United States proposed a global forest convention in 1990 and continued to take the lead in the negotiations. The United States as well as international organizations like the Food and

Agriculture Organization, emphasized the tropical forests' global values, such as their role as carbon sinks and their biodiversity as the 'common heritage of mankind'. This framing would amount to acknowledging the value placed on forests by people outside forest areas who receive no other direct benefit from the forests. This conceptual framework implied that citizens in industrialized countries were entitled to some of the benefits inherent in forests in the developing countries and thus should have a say in their use. Negotiations for a global forest convention began in the United Nations as a part of the preparations for the 1992 UN Conference on Environment and Development (UNCED), but soon stalled because of North–South politics.

In 1990, the European Union and the G-77 were discussing a deal on two protocols within the climate change regime, which was being negotiated at that time. The European Union was proposing a forest protocol to the proposed Framework Convention on Climate Change treating forests as carbon dioxide sinks, while the G-77 was proposing an energy protocol in order to shift attention away from the developing countries as the source of carbon emissions. The United States opposed any framework to regulate energy use as that would replace the current framework of limiting increase in global temperature. To pre-empt a deal, the United States suggested negotiation of a new forest convention to the European Union. The developing countries argument was that forests are local natural resources, and their global aspects were addressed in the biodiversity convention, carbon sequestration was addressed in the climate convention and trade was addressed within the WTO.

The developing countries, however, remained ambivalent because of the pressure on them. Their opposition was led by Malaysia, at that time the world's largest producer of tropical timber, asserting that the 'message that developing countries did not know how to manage their forest resources and therefore they would have to take the lead … impeded the full utilization of our resources and putting them at the disposition of the transnationals'. Malaysia also referred to 'compensation for opportunity cost foregone'. Arguing that, 'we wish to underline the supremacy of our sovereignty over our forests. We are certainly not holding them in custody for those who have destroyed their own forests, and now try to claim ours as part of the heritage of mankind . . . Our message is clear; we are prepared to play our part in the great environmental effort. We are prepared to sustainably use our sovereign forest resources. However, we require financial resources and technology to carry out our environmental obligations'.

India alone continued with its opposition to a forest convention till the end. At the final negotiations, only India opposed any reference to even treating forests as a 'common concern of mankind', as all the other developing countries, including Malaysia, had instructions at that stage not to oppose a convention. At Rio India's Minister, Kamal Nath, did not relent; Emil Salim, The Minister of Forests of Indonesia, sitting next to him candidly stated that he supported that stand but had instructions not to speak, and Malaysia was in a similar position. The stalemate between Minister Nath and William Reilly, Administrator of the United States Environment Protection Agency and leading their delegation, continued for over 2 hours with all other countries maintaining a studious silence. Ambassador Akao of Japan then intervened to say that in view of the opposition of India, there was no point in continuing with the negotiations, and the United States reluctantly agreed. India was opposed to a forest convention because its forests were not wildernesses areas, but 10 per cent of the total population lived in and were dependent on those resources.

With economic growth emissions from deforestation or conversion of forest land for agriculture and cities has now come down from 25 to 15 per cent of global emissions without a treaty or the market. The global role of tropical forests is now considered in Reducing Emissions from Deforestation and forest Degradation while promoting conservation, sustainable management of forests and enhancing forest carbon stocks (REDD+), to provide carbon offsets, and is part of the international framework

54 | The World's Search for Sustainable Development

for action being considered in the Climate Convention. Economic benefits for industrialized countries remain the primary consideration for multilateral action [Davenport, 2005].

Personal knowledge, represented India in the negotiations at UNCED.

Modifying consumption patterns

Despite continuing recognition of the need to modify consumption patterns, and references in major conferences since 1992, no actions have been proposed at the international level in the negotiated outcomes. Recognizing the political sensitivity of the issue, the United Nations has restricted it focus to resource efficiency and the dominance of economic reasoning ignoring the social aspects; even though it acknowledged the importance of all the three dimensions of sustainable development.

At the United Nations Conference on Environment and Development, held in Rio in 1992, it was recognized in the text that 'the major causes of the continued deterioration of the global environment are the unsustainable patterns of consumption and production, particularly in industrialized countries, which is a matter of grave concern, aggravating poverty and imbalances', but there was no separate programme of action to support modification of these trends. Ten years later, the World Summit on Sustainable Development, in 2002, reiterated that 'fundamental changes in the way societies produce and consume are indispensable for achieving global sustainable development', but was only able to agree to a weak 'framework of programmes' at the regional and national, rather than at the global, level; and, as the last item to be agreed.

With increasing scientific evidence of continuing deterioration of the global commons the United Nations, in a perceptively titled report, 'Human Development Report, 2007/8, Fighting Climate Change: Human Solidarity in a Divided World', focused on global change, and stated that the 'fundamental challenge is the way we think about progress. ... carbon intensive economic growth is symptomatic of a deeper problem ... that the economic model which drives growth, and the profligate consumption in rich countries that goes with it, is unsustainable'. Such a perspective suggests a much deeper cut in resource use patterns in industrialized countries than in developing countries, including the fast developing ones, and was not followed up.

The annual publication of The World Watch Institute also observed in 2010 that changing lifestyles will be necessary, 'as the world's climate cannot be saved by technology alone. The way we live will have to change as well ... the things we may need to learn to live without–oversized cars and houses, status based consumption, easy and cheap world travel, meat with every meal, disposable everything–are not necessities or in most cases what makes people happy'.

Within the European Commission, the recognition that continuing current patterns of resource use is not an option emerged on the policy agenda in 2011, reversing a four-decade-old framework on single solutions around the environment ignoring such impacts. According to the European Commission, profound changes would be needed in thinking, in economic and social structures and in consumption and production patterns.

The recent report of the Secretary-General of the United Nations to the Preparatory Committee for the Rio+20 Summit in 2012 also pointed out that 'the main challenge facing humanity now is to sustain the process of poverty eradication and development while shifting gears. Developed countries must shrink environmental footprints as fast and as far as possible while sustaining human development achievements. Developing countries must continue to raise their people's living standards while containing increases in their footprints, recognizing that poverty eradication remains a priority. This is a shared challenge with a goal of shared prosperity'. For implementing this vision, the report stresses that public policy for a green economy must extend well beyond the current reliance on 'getting prices right' to fundamentally shift consumption and production patterns onto a more sustainable path. This perspective was not reflected in the negotiated outcome document, but sustainable consumption was finally considered as a key element in the transition to sustainable development.

Expert bodies then began to dilute the requirement of modifying consumption patterns. The UN Secretary-General's High-Level Panel on Global Sustainability laid out its vision for the kind of world we want in 2050, in the following terms: 'To eradicate poverty and reduce inequality, make growth inclusive, and production and consumption more sustainable, while combating climate change and respecting the range of other planetary boundaries'. This definition blurs the distinction between poverty, climate change and sustainable development that emerged in 1992 while saying nothing about the trade-offs involved or laying out an overarching goal.

In the negotiations of the Sustainable Development Goals (SDGs), the Co-chair's Zero-draft (June 2014): Introduction and Proposed Goals and Targets on Sustainable Development for the Post-2015 Development Agenda, Goal 12–Promote sustainable consumption and production patterns stresses production patterns–chemical, hazardous, food and other waste; business practices and public procurement; dissemination of environmentally sound technologies and capacity building; sustainable tourism–which is really old wine in new bottles. The key issue of modifying consumption patterns is limited to providing information to 'ensure that people everywhere have information and understanding needed to live sustainable lifestyles', and as such may not even be included in the monitoring arrangements.

The Ministerial Declaration of the 2014 high-level segment of the Economic and Social Council and the high-level political forum also refers to 'changing unsustainable and promoting sustainable patterns of consumption and production', diluting its original thrust. The focus has been on institutional arrangements–establishment of a Trust Fund, Board and Secretariat, National Focal Points, regional meetings, programs, inter-agency coordination with the United Nations, and the Global Sustainable Development Report drawing attention to trends, issues, policy approaches and long-term implications of today's actions. The outcome of international cooperation should really be broad consensus on societal transformation leading to directional shifts in global economic growth pathways, rather than fine tuning the architecture of global environmental governance and the science–policy interface.

An effective approach should reach beyond consumption as an economic activity taking place in markets based on monetary values and stress non-material contributions to a 'good life'. It must also consider people not only in terms of their function as consumers, but as citizens, considering the quality of services linked to resource management. The current approach also ignores the distinction between production and consumption, or business and households (*Lorek and Fuchs (2011), EC (2011).*

Part originally published in Sanwal (2011).

Energy

Energy use is divided into three types–travel energy (gasoline, jet fuel, etc.), household energy (electricity, gas, coal, etc.), and finally 'embedded energy', which refers to the amount of energy required to make a particular object, for example, food.

We now know that two-thirds of the global environmental damage has been caused by carbon dioxide emissions as a result of current patterns of resource use, primarily energy. As it has significant implications for the question of climate change, energy was not included in the Millennium Development Goals despite being an essential element of economic growth. The United Nations has now stressed 'Sustainable Energy for All', ignoring the trade-offs to be made at the global level by stressing

56 | The World's Search for Sustainable Development

national decision-making and the goal of universal energy access a 'first among equals' of the three sustainable energy goals, with the other two goals relating to renewable energy and energy efficiency.

Energy access for developing countries has also been defined very differently to the way the concept is understood in Europe and North America, as new energy connections and related consumption in developing countries is expected to increase by a very small amount, consequently emissions also increase minimally. The International Energy Agency, in its World Energy Outlook, 2013, defines 'initial threshold' for energy access to be 250 kWh for rural households and 500 kWh for urban households, assuming five persons per household. This is 50–100 kWh per person per year, and the IEA assumes an increase in demand to 750 kWh/year by 2030, compared with the global average of 3,000 kwh in 2010–the average for the United States is 13,400 kWh, Germany 7,200 kWh and Greece 5,200 kWh, in 2010. The World Bank includes use of appliances but sees the consumption rising to only 420 kWh per capita per year. The IEA also considers that the opportunity costs of the meagre amount of electricity around $700 billion till 2030 will be 'unacceptable' to developing country governments; stressing the need to move away from grid-based energy to decentralized renewable energy systems, which would cost only 10 per cent of that amount, or $70 billion, as they would not be connected to the electricity grid.

It is not appropriate to frame the global concern of access to energy only in terms of minimal household energy use, because the course of development followed by all industrialized nations shows that energy has links to all sectors of the economy, and is necessary to sustain continued economic growth. Recognition of the scale of the challenge will make assured and affordable electricity part of the national agenda and impact not only on the global carbon budget but also on the transformational change needed in policies, institutions and investment, and move away from trade-offs to seeing opportunities through fostering innovation.

The many complex global scenarios that elaborate longer term trends in future energy systems, and by implication the related greenhouse gas emissions have also not included a societal transformation and instead have focused on the objective of avoiding a global rise in mean temperature of more than 2°C. Most models assume that the energy system, because of path-dependency or inertia, will see a gradual and limited change from a projected business-as-usual path. There is only now recognition of the role of energy efficiency in reducing emissions of carbon dioxide but lack of data prevents incorporation of this trend in models shifting the focus of changes to the supply side, and generation technologies, instead of changes in consumption patterns largely in industrialized countries [United Nations, 2013; The Future We Want, 2013; The Energy Access Imperative, 2014].

Finance

Finance was reluctantly included in the framework agreed in 1972 and it continues to dominate the negotiations, with the outcomes dealing with current political problems rather than the problem itself.

'The rich countries made many promises to help poor countries to achieve the MDGs in 2000 starting with the "partnership goal". Those promises were also solemnly made at the Conference on Financing for Development at Monterrey, Mexico (March 2002); the G8 Gleneagles Summit (June 2005) and at subsequent Summits. But they are not fulfilled. And there is no practical recourse to enforce the fulfillment of these commitments, other than the relatively weak level of public opinion' [Sachs, 2013].

In the 2009 Copenhagen Accord of the United Nations Framework Convention on Climate Change (UNFCCC), developed countries agreed to the joint mobilization of $100 billion annually by 2020 to address the needs of developing countries. As an initial step, they also committed to provide $30 billion in new and additional finance – so-called fast-start finance – between 2010 and

2012. A preliminary assessment of fast-start finance finds that commitments were exceeded, and $35 billion were mobilized between 2010 and 2012. However, this has mostly not been additional to traditional ODA – 80 per cent of these flows were also counted as ODA, and were paid out with similar modalities, largely through bilateral channels. Fast-start finance has benefitted middle-income countries disproportionally, often focused on leveraging private financing flows – less than half of it was delivered as grants. Climate financing more broadly remains focused on mitigation, while financing for adaption – critical for the most vulnerable countries – is lacking [United Nations, 2014].

In the negotiations leading to the third Financing for Development conference, to be held in Addis Ababa, Ethiopia, from 13 to 16 July 2015, developed countries are stressing the role of domestic resource mobilization, multi-stakeholder partnerships and private finance and blended finance in development financing rather than grants or loans on concessional terms.

3.3.2 Intergovernmental panel on climate change

The First World Climate Conference, held in 1979, did not make any calls for policy action and only initiated a series of workshops. The International Conference on the Assessment of the Role of Carbon Dioxide and other Greenhouse Gases in Climate Variations and Impacts at Villach, in 1985, first recommended exploration of 'alternative polices and adjustments' as future global energy demand would determine concentration increases and suggested that targets and timetables were the way forward. The participants recommended a strategy that relied on technical- and science-based research to establish target emission or concentration limits to regulate the rate of change of global mean temperature within specific parameters. The Executive Director of UNEP subsequently called for a climate convention. In order to avoid an international framework based on policies and measures, the United States initiated the process of setting up the Intergovernmental Panel on Climate Change (IPCC), in November 1988, with 'official experts' as the politically favoured means of climate change assessment, addition of other greenhouse gases to the computation of climate change and with the express purpose of engaging developing countries. The hasty conversion of the outcome into an intergovernmental mechanism with experts from the atmospheric sciences internationalized the issue and focused on the symptoms rather than the causes of the problem. The initiative was motivated by the desire of the United States to buy time and delay a potentially costly political response based on energy use, in addition to involving developing countries, as they were absent in the earlier deliberations. Two months after the IPCC was established, in January 1989, the UN General Assembly adopted a resolution proposed by Malta on 'Protection of Global Climate for present and future generations of mankind'. Thus, the IPCC started off with both assessing knowledge to advise policy and directly help shape policy itself [Agarwal, 1998].

Despite its political origins, the IPCC attracted a large number of scientists because they were all part of an 'epistemic community'. It also adopted the criteria of increase in global temperature as the 'definition' of climate change, since that time popularly considered as global warming, rather than study climate variability and adopt a carbon budget or sustainable development perspective, which was being pushed by developing countries, with Brazil in the forefront.

Within the 'scientific' framework, IPCC authors are instructed to be policy-relevant, without being policy-prescriptive, and the Summary for Policy Makers (SPM) is designed to provide an agreed output based on an assessment of the recent science acceptable to all governments. With developing countries questioning the policy relevance of some statements in the summary with implications for the on-going negotiations, the broader question of how best to assess complex multidisciplinary

58 | The World's Search for Sustainable Development

science is now being raised. Their policy relevance remains controversial because problems have emerged in each of the reports, as they are issued before major rounds of climate negotiations.

Methane controversy prior to the negotiation of the climate treaty
In 1991, the World Resources Institute, a United States think tank, listed country emissions of greenhouse gases in the form of a scientific index based on the global warming potential of greenhouse gases, ignoring their lifetime in the atmosphere, which is more than 100 years for carbon dioxide and only 15 years for methane but 56 times higher global warming potential. It also included CFCs even though their destructive impact on the ozone layers has a negative impact on global warming. In addition, carbon dioxide emissions from deforestation were included. This framework put Brazil, China and India third, fourth and fifth, respectively, in the list of the biggest polluters of the atmosphere.

Following on the framework focusing on increase in temperature to define climate change, the IPCC also adopted this calculation and the industrialized countries began to use it in their reports and publications, to add to their scientific value in the on-going negotiations on the climate treaty.

The index's figures and assumptions were challenged immediately, and characterized as 'environmental colonialism', and soon lost their relevance in the negotiations [WRI, 1991, Agarwal and Narain, 1991].

Focus on receding glaciers in the Himalayas prior to the Copenhagen conference
The Himalayas have the third largest ice mass on the planet, after the Arctic/Greenland and Antarctic regions.

The IPCC Fourth Assessment Report (2007) argued that 'Glaciers in the Himalaya are receding faster than in any other part of the world and, if the present rate continues, the likelihood of them disappearing by the year 2035 and perhaps sooner is very high if the Earth keeps warming at the current rate. Its total area will likely shrink from the present 500,000 to 100,000 km² by the year 2035'.

The Government of India, in their review comment, had pointed out that 'this is a very drastic conclusion. Should have a supporting reference otherwise should be deleted'. The scientific evidence actually showed that glaciers in the Western Himalayas were expanding because of increased precipitation and the pace of change in glaciers in the Himalayas is similar to that of other glaciers in the world.

On being challenged, the IPCC said the paragraph 'refers to poorly substantiated estimates of rate of recession and date for the disappearance of Himalayan glaciers. In drafting the paragraph in question, the clear and well-established standards of evidence, required by the IPCC procedures, were not applied properly'. Reliance had been placed on a single 3-year study, funded by Sweden, which found that of 10 glaciers measured in the region all are shrinking, with a marked acceleration in loss of ice between 2002 and 2005; these did not include the major glaciers feeding the main rivers.

Impacts not based on the time period under consideration
A review by the Netherlands Environmental Assessment Agency observed that the Working Group II Summary for Policy Makers in the fourth assessment is more focused on the negative impacts of climate change than the underlying report, an approach agreed to by participating governments [PBL, 2010].

An official evaluation of the IPCC also found that many of the conclusions in the 'Current Knowledge about Future Impacts' section of the Working Group II Summary for Policy Makers were based on unpublished or non-peer-reviewed literature, and imprecise statements have been made without reference to the time period under consideration or to a climate scenario under which the conclusions would be true. It observed that all of the factors that affect carbon dioxide emissions and mitigation costs in top-down models are uncertain, and uncertainty about them increases with the length of the projection. In the long run, costs of substitution depend on advances in technology, which are highly uncertain and may themselves depend on assumptions about policies. It noted that the authors reported high confidence in statements for which there is little evidence, such as the widely quoted statement that agricultural yields in Africa might decline by up to 50 per cent by 2020. The evaluation stressed that the IPCC should make the process and criteria for selecting participants for scoping meetings more transparent.

The beginning of change within the IPCC

As the 'IPCC has come under heightened scrutiny about its impartiality with respect to climate policy and about the accuracy and balance of its reports', in March 2010, the UN and the IPCC jointly commissioned the alliance of national scientific academies–the Inter Academy Council (IAC)–to conduct an independent evaluation of the procedures and processes of the IPCC. The staff for the review came from the United States and United Kingdom with no one from developing countries.

Despite acknowledging 'continuing credibility of the IPCC assessments themselves' and 'controversies over the value and importance of particular classes of evidence', the IAC focused only on processes of assessment and quality assurance rather than on the content of IPCC reports. The evaluation noted that the IPCC assessment process is complicated by several challenges that have arisen or become more acute in recent years, and 'the growing influence of developing nations has changed the geopolitical context for making decisions on climate change'. It also noted that as the potential influence of IPCC assessments on governmental decisions that would affect the energy sector becomes increasingly clear, the IPCC finds itself in the heart of a political debate with serious economic consequences.

The Committee found that with major advances in climate science, heated controversy on some climate-related issues, and an increased focus of governments on the impacts and potential responses to changing climate, a wide variety of interests have entered the climate discussion, leading to greater overall scrutiny and demands from stakeholders. It observed that the Working Group II Summary for Policy Makers contains many statements that are not supported sufficiently in the literature, not put into perspective, or not expressed clearly. The Committee also recommended that Lead Authors document that they have considered the full range of thoughtful views, even if these views do not appear in the assessment report. It noted that consensus-based decision-making procedures have led to negotiations and a minimum outcome accepted by all parties at that time.

The Council also stressed that the IPCC establish criteria for selecting participants for the scoping meeting, where preliminary decisions about the scope and outline of the assessment reports are made; for selecting the IPCC Chair, the Working Group co-chairs, and other members of the Bureau; and for selecting the authors of the assessment reports. It also noted that the requirement of unanimity also leads to the fact that scientific findings and views deviating from the mainstream are systematically ignored or excluded, and most of the experts continue to come from the developed countries. The IPCC reforms addressed not so much the causes (such as the perceived lack of public accountability of the content) as merely the symptoms (e.g., the lack of transparency of existing procedures) of the problem [Inter Academy Council, 2010].

The Fifth Assessment Report, 2014, is more sober in its conclusions. For example, it acknowledges that 'current data sets indicate no significant observed trends in global tropical cyclone frequency over the past century'. It also points out that 'current alarmist predictions of massive flows of so-called "environmental refugees" or "environmental migrants" are not supported by past experiences of responses to droughts and extreme weather events and predictions for future migration flows are tentative at best'. It acknowledges that the rate of warming between 1998 and 2012 'is smaller than the rate calculated since 1951', and it predicts modest temperature increases through 2035 of between 1°C and 1.5°C , because 'the innate behaviour of the climate system imposes limits on the ability to predict its evolution'.

60 | The World's Search for Sustainable Development

3.3.3 Emergence of a social science perspective

IPCC Fifth Assessment Report: 2014: Main Points and Analysis

Prior to the approval by governments of the Intergovernmental Panel on Climate Change (IPCC)'s 'Summary for Policymakers' of Working Group I on the 'Physical Science Basis', intense debates took place on several key issues. For the first time, major concerns raised by developing country governments were referred to contact groups or informal consultations for resolution. This reflected the increased understanding of the issues and the increased power of China and these countries in being able to secure their interests. However, the interventions were reactive, designed to correct the text on points of detail, rather than develop an entirely new framework based on equity considerations[5].

Attempts to introduce a new income-based criteria in the negotiations
Working Group II of the IPCC focuses on how to mitigate the emissions that cause global warming. The 'Summary for Policymakers' (SPM) has elements analysing historic emissions trends by country income groups, which were considered drivers of emissions, based on a World Bank framework used by its experts in analysing economic growth. Patterns, trends and drivers of emissions show an equally strong correlation with urbanization and lifestyles. Income criteria would shift the commitments being negotiated in the new climate regime towards the re-emerging countries and was successfully deleted by developing countries [Wible, 2014].

Evaluation of climate models: climate change or climate variability?
In the section on 'evaluation of climate models' in the June version of the draft prepared by the IPCC, there was a statement that 'there is very high confidence that models reproduce the more rapid warming in the second half of the 20th century and cooling immediately following large volcanic eruptions. Models do not generally reproduce the observed reduction in surface warming trend over the last 10–15 years. There is medium confidence that this difference between models and observations is to a substantial degree caused by unpredictable climate variability, with possible contributions from inadequacies in the solar, volcanic, and aerosol forcings used by the models and, in some models, from too strong a response to increasing green-house gas forcing'.

Following comments by various governments prior to the meeting in Stockholm, the authors amended the above paragraph to read as follows: 'The long-term climate model simulations show a trend in global-mean surface temperature from 1951-2012 that agrees with the observed trend, despite differences between simulated and observed trends over the past 10-15 years (very high confidence)'.

'The observed reduction in surface warming trend over the period 1998-2012 as compared to the period 1951-2012, is due in roughly equal measure to a reduced trend in radiative forcing and a cooling contribution from internal variability, which includes a possible redistribution of heat within the ocean (medium confidence). The reduced trend in radiative forcing is primarily due to volcanic eruptions and the timing of the downward phase of the 11-year solar cycle. However, there is low confidence in quantifying the role of changes in radiative forcing in causing the reduced warming trend. There is medium confidence that internal decadal variability causes to a substantial degree the difference between observations and the simulations; the latter are not expected to reproduce the timing of internal variability'.

Venezuela sought clarification over the 'very high confidence' judgement by the authors while China said that the paragraphs above were new and amount to an evaluation of the climate models.

---

[5] Reporting by the South Centre in the South Bulletin.

Natural Science – Policy – Institutions Interface | **61**

It wanted to know the advantages and disadvantages of the models and said the June version of the SPM draft had this. Similar sentiments were expressed by Saudi Arabia.

The United States said the paragraphs did relate to the evaluation of the models and it is about observations in a broader context and not just 10–15 years. Switzerland said that one could not test models in 15 years.

Following consultations with the authors, the following compromise was reached at around 2 am: 'The long-term climate model simulations show a trend in global-mean surface temperature from 1951–2012 that agrees with the observed trend (very high confidence). There are, however, differences between simulated and observed trends over periods as short as 10–15 years (e.g., 1998–2012)'.

'The observed reduction in surface warming trend over the period 1998-2012 as compared to the period 1951-2012, is due in roughly equal measure to a reduced trend in radiative forcing and a cooling contribution from internal variability, which includes a possible redistribution of heat within the ocean (medium confidence). The reduced trend in radiative forcing is primarily due to volcanic eruptions and the timing of the downward phase of the 11-year solar cycle. However, there is low confidence in quantifying the role of changes in radiative forcing in causing the reduced warming trend. There is medium confidence that internal decadal variability causes to a substantial degree the difference between observations and the simulations; the latter are not expected to reproduce the timing of internal variability. There may also be a contribution from forcing inadequacies and, in some models, an overestimate of the response to increasing greenhouse gas and other anthropogenic forcing (dominated by the effects of aerosols)'.

Emission reductions required by 2050: accounting for uncertainty

Under the discussion on 'Future global and regional climate change', the draft prepared by the IPCC stated that: 'Projections of changes in the climate system are made using a hierarchy of climate models … These models simulate changes based on a set of scenarios of anthropogenic forcing's. A new set of scenarios, the Representative Concentration Pathways (RCPs), was used for the new climate model simulations … In all RCPs, atmospheric CO_2 concentrations are higher in 2100 relative to present day as a result of a further increase of cumulative emissions of CO_2 to the atmosphere during the 21st century'.

One aspect that was discussed in this regard related to 'carbon and other biogeochemical cycles'. Member States were asked to consider the following statement: 'Based on Earth System Models, following RCP2.6 requires by 2050 an average emission reduction of 50% (range 14% to 96%) relative to 1990 emissions, and requires, about as likely as not, sustained net removal of CO_2 from the atmosphere by the end of the 21st century'.

China expressed concerns as to how one single figure is obtained and asked how the 50 per cent figure was obtained when this is not what the ranges indicate. It also said that no information has been provided from other scenarios and that only one scenario is considered. Saudi Arabia said that members are talking about projections that would resonate with policymakers. It can be misleading to talk about a range from 14 to 96 per cent. It wanted the entire paragraph deleted. Russia also had similar concerns.

A contact group was formed to address this issue. Following the discussions, the following paragraph was agreed to: 'By 2050, annual CO_2 emissions derived from Earth System Models following RCP2.6 are smaller than 1990 emissions (by 14% to 96%) … By the end of the 21st century, about half of the models infer emissions slightly above zero, while the other half infers a net removal of CO_2 from the atmosphere'.

Carbon budget: a range rather than an absolute amount

In the discussion on 'climate stabilization', Member States were asked to consider the following paragraph: 'Limiting the warming caused by anthropogenic CO_2 emissions alone to likely less than 2 degrees C relative to pre-industrial, will require cumulative CO_2 emissions from all anthropogenic sources to stay below about 1000 GtC since the beginning of the industrial era. This amount is reduced to about 800 GtC when accounting for non-CO_2 forcings as in RCP2.6. An amount of 545 [460 to 630] GtC, was already emitted by 2011'.

China raised concerns that the cumulative reductions required to stay below 2°C are not consistent with the figures in the underlying assessment report of WG1 which reflect that emission reductions should be in the range of 800–2500 GtC between 1750 and 2100. The United States said that the IPCC is supposed to be policy neutral and the information needs to be presented in a neutral way.

Informal consultations were held in this regard and the text which was agreed is as follows: 'Limiting the warming caused by anthropogenic CO_2 emissions alone with a probability of >33%, >50%, and >66% to less than 2 degrees C since the period 1861-1880, will require cumulative CO_2 emissions from all anthropogenic sources to stay between 0 and about 1560 GtC, 0 and about 1210 GtC, and 0 and about 1000 GtC since that period respectively. These upper amounts are reduced to about 880 GtC, 840 GtC, and 800 GtC, respectively, when accounting for non-CO_2 forcings as in RCP2.6. An amount of 531 [446 to 616] GtC, was already emitted by 2011'.

South Bulletin Feb 4, 2014, published by South Centre.

Ethics and justice

While recognizing the role of economics in climate policy choices, the IPCC Fifth Assessment Report for the first time stresses the limits of economics in addressing some ethical values and considerations of justice that cannot be easily monetized. The report also emphasizes how economic methods – even when monetizing is possible – implicitly involve significant ethical assumptions. In its first four assessments in 1990, 1995, 2001, and 2007, IPCC relied almost exclusively on economic analysis of policy alternatives, rather than ethics and justice in its guidance to policymakers on how to develop climate law and policy[6].

In a new chapter on the Social, Economic, and Ethical Concepts, the IPCC now admits expressly that in prior IPCC Reports 'ethics has received less attention than economics', and raises some new issues, even though the report continues to be focused on maximizing efficiency. The new issues include:

How should the burden of mitigating climate change be divided among countries? It raises difficult questions of fairness, and rights, all of which are in the sphere of ethics (IPCC, 2014. WG III, Ch. 3, p. 11); and

The methods of economics are limited in what they can do. ... They are suited to measuring and aggregating the well-being of humans, but not in taking account of justice and rights (IPCC, 2014, AR5, WG III, Ch. 3, p. 24).

In addition, the Working Group III AR5 report also has a new chapter on Sustainable Development and Equity which contains a number of conclusions that have important ethical and justice implications. They include:

Given the disparities evident in consumption patterns, the distributional implications of climate response strategies are critically important (IPCC, 2014, AR5, WG III, Ch. 4, p. 9);

[T]he eventual effectiveness of a collective action regime may hinge on equitable burden sharing, the absence of actors who are powerful enough to coercively impose their preferred burden sharing arrangements, the inapplicability of standard utilitarian methods of calculating costs and benefits, and the fact that regime effectiveness depends on long-term commitments of members to implement its terms (IPCC, 2014, AR5, WG III, Ch. 4, p. 17);

---

[6] Adapted from the blog of Donald Brown–Ethics and Climate.

There is a basic set of shared ethical principles and precedents that apply to the climate problem… [and] such principles… can put bounds on the plausible interpretation of equity in the burden sharing context…[and] are important in establishing what may be reasonably required of different actors. (IPCC, 2014, AR5, WG III, Ch. 4, p. 48); and

[T]here is now a consensus that methods of cost-benefit analysis that simply add up monetary-equivalent gains and issues are consistent and applicable only under very specific assumptions … which are empirically dubious and ethically controversial. (IPCC, 2014, AR5, WG III, Ch. 4, p. 54)

One common problem with IPCC's treatment of the ethical dimensions of climate change policymaking is that the text often leaves the impression that while policymakers should consider ethical questions in developing climate change policies they are free to ignore what ethics requires of nations. The organizational structure of the working groups tends to inherently divide natural and human systems, and the disciplinary bias is apparent in the selection of coordinating lead authors, who are predominantly natural scientists and economists. Since authorship is by invitation, this anomaly will not change with a transformation of the leadership and structure [Carey, 2014].

The geopolitical changes of the twenty-first century have led to changes in the assessments of the IPCC and an increasing role of the social sciences in responding to global challenges, but the dominant approach remains based on the natural sciences because developing countries scientists have yet to make the shift at the national level to adopt these changes. Also, as the IPCC acknowledges in its report to the fortieth session, held in October 2014, 'for a range of reasons there is relatively less input (including involvement of scientists and the use of non-English language literature) from developing countries into the IPCC process'. Only China has given importance to sustainable development research in the Chinese Academy of Sciences. The Fifth Assessment Report marks a significant change where debates have moved from arguments over scientific merits to a political discussion on how to respond to scientific findings [IPCC, 2014a, 2014b, 2014c].

3.4 Grand scientific challenges of the twenty-first century

Reframing global environmental change from a physical to a social concern

It is the first time that a UN Secretary-General has set up a Scientific Advisory Board on Science and Technology, in September 2013, to bring together leading scientists in an effort to influence and shape negotiations in the United Nations to advance sustainable development. The High-Level Political Forum on Sustainable Development has a strengthened interface between science and policy, so that the latest scientific findings are reflected in the high-level policy discussions. The Global Sustainable Development Report will build on existing assessments and provide an evidence-based instrument to support policymakers. The advisory body has been established in UNESCO, but it reflects the challenges as seen by the donors and not by the scientific community.

The functions of the Board reflect in general the broad objective identified by scientists in the International Council for Science (ICSU), based on the social sciences – it will bring together in a coherent manner the collective capacity of all relevant scientific fields, with due regard to social and ethical dimensions of sustainable development. The fields will span a broad spectrum, from the basic sciences, through engineering and technology, social sciences and humanities, ethics, health, economic, behavioural, and agricultural sciences, in addition to the environmental sciences, which are more commonly associated with sustainability.

The type of recommendations that would be made and the advice to the UN Secretary-General is, however, based on the Belmont Challenge led by donor agencies, and continues to focus on the natural sciences–up-to-date scientific issues relevant to sustainable development, including advice on "'assessments and digests" around concepts as "planetary boundaries", "tipping points" and "environmental thresholds"…'. This implies that the Secretary-General will articulate scientific issues which have attracted widespread attention in contemporary affairs reflecting the perspectives of the natural sciences and broad concerns of the donors rather than the social science community. This has led to a situation where the International Council of Science has independently stressed that the main problem with the process for global Sustainable Development Goals is the absence of a common understanding on how broader social change will take place, it is important to agree on what the world would look like once all the goals are fully achieved, and they suggest that this meta-goal should be 'a prosperous, high quality of life that is equitably shared and sustainable' [ICSU, ISSC, 2015].

Thirty years after the first global environmental research programme established by the natural science community, the social science community began an effort to re-frame the issues in the science–policy linkage for global change. This was a response to the changing global context and the failure of past efforts at understanding the transformation to sustainable development. In February 2009, ICSU started a consultative Visioning Process, in cooperation with the International Social Science Council (ISSC), for integrated, policy relevant Earth System research, to consider global sustainability in the context of global environmental change and not just environmental damage.

In June 2009, the world's main funders of environmental change research–United States and the United Kingdom – established a new, high-level body called the Belmont Forum. The objective was to align international resources for the delivery of the science-derived knowledge and capabilities that society needs to address environmental change. ICSU and ISSC both joined the Forum's membership. In October 2010, the funders from the Belmont Forum, ICSU and ISSC met to discuss the visions and implementation options that emerged from both the Belmont and Visioning processes. It was agreed that there are significant opportunities for convergence between these two processes: both in terms of substantive priorities and in the next steps towards their implementation. It was also recognized that there was a need to engage representatives of operational service organizations (e.g. WMO) – who are crucial in the delivery of services on the basis of new scientific knowledge. However, differences in the approaches adopted remained, as the social scientists focused on longer term trends, social change and human well-being within planetary limits while the donors focus remains on short-term technical arrangements and markets to reduce risk and enhance ecosystem services.

ICSU–2009

ICSU's Earth System Science for Global Sustainability: The Grand Challenges, finalized in 2010, acknowledges that our existing knowledge falls well short of what can be considered integrated solutions. It called for exploring social transformations in the world that can overcome barriers to sustainability, and consider the full social–environmental global system rather than independent components of that system recognizing that none of the challenges can be fully addressed without progress in addressing the other challenges.

The research challenge has been identified as determining the institutional, economic and behavioural changes that can enable effective steps toward global sustainability:

1. What institutions and organizational structures are effective in balancing the trade-offs inherent in social–environmental systems at and across local, regional and global scales and how can they be achieved?

2. What changes in economic systems would contribute most to improving global sustainability, in the context of global environmental change, and how could they be achieved?
3. What changes in behaviour or lifestyle, if adopted by multiple societies, would contribute most to improving global sustainability, in the context of global environmental change, and how could they be achieved?
4. How can institutional arrangements prioritize and mobilize resources to alleviate poverty, address social injustice and meet development needs under rapidly changing and diverse local environmental conditions and growing pressures on the global environment?
5. How can the need to curb global environmental change be integrated with the demands of other interconnected global policy challenges, particularly those related to poverty, conflict, justice and human security?
6. How can effective, legitimate, accountable and just, collective environmental solutions be mobilized at multiple scales? What is needed to catalyse the adoption of appropriate institutional, economic or behavioural changes?

ICSU recognized that global change exposes gaps in social institutions, including governance and economic systems for managing emerging global (and local) problems. The time and spatial scales of global change differ fundamentally from the types of problems that humanity has addressed in the past. Currently, decision-makers have incentives that favour short-term and private benefits, rather than long-term and collective benefits. It recognized that addressing the problems of global change, including unsustainable resource use, pollution of the global commons, growing resource demand resulting from growing per capita consumption will require addressing fundamental questions of governance, economic systems and behaviour.

Belmont challenge–2010

The Science agendas are to a considerable extent shaped by funding agencies (SAB, 2014). The Belmont Challenge, initiated by United States and the United Kingdom funding agencies shifted the priority research challenges to those that deliver welfare and economic benefits to society, which were expressed in terms of solutions for adaptation and mitigation, and very different to the transformation ICSU had sought. The stress was on innovative technical solutions to environmental change which will drive opportunities for markets and equitable economic and social development, rather than a focus on sustainability. This research agenda focuses on

1. Identification of strategies needed to reduce vulnerability to change (mitigation or adaptation),
2. Comparative analyses (costs and benefits) of different mitigation and adaptation strategies, based on whole-system, whole-lifecycle impacts, vulnerability and risks. Include assessments of the trade-offs,
3. Strategies to manage the trade-offs, and
4. Comparative analysis of different approaches towards risk reduction requiring development of risk models, and multidisciplinary quantitative analysis of their outputs. Identifying any potential unintended consequences of changes with the risk models able to integrate quantitative and qualitative information.

It sought knowledge of 'tipping points' (critical thresholds at which rapid, non-linear environmental change will occur that will disrupt well-being of society) and strategies for avoiding, adapting and enhancing resilience to them, requiring integration of 'impact' and 'response' research. It stressed knowledge of technical and socio-economic innovations that can overcome barriers to sustainability and likely options for international trade in managing the Earth System. The concern is with sectors and not populations.

The research challenge was identified as:

1. Enabling effective transitions to low-carbon, resource-efficient economies, through assessing whole-system impacts and trade-offs for innovation options in sectors such as energy, agriculture, water and waste,
2. Providing an evidence base for development, auditing and regulation of new markets for trading ecosystem services, such as carbon sequestration, nitrogen fixation, water purification, etc.,
3. Monitoring and forecasting to protect property and infrastructure, reducing economic losses from damage and degradation and providing confidence for investment,
4. Improving health and well-being through reduced vulnerability to natural hazards and pollution, and
5. Lifting people out of poverty through supporting innovative unsustainable development pathways towards Millennium Development Goals.

The Belmont Challenge document also acknowledged that ICSU has identified some priority needs for information on strategies and trade-offs including and reproduced them without linking them to the outputs: How can global energy security be provided entirely by sources that are renewable and have neutral impacts on other aspects of global sustainability; How can competing demands for scarce land and water be met over the next half-century – while dramatically reducing land use greenhouse gas emissions, protecting biodiversity and maintaining or enhancing other ecosystem services; How can ecosystem services meet the needs for improving the lives of the world's poorest peoples and those of developing regions (such as safe drinking water and waste disposal, food security, and increased energy use) within a framework of global sustainability? While a reference was made to these concerns, they are not reflected in the conclusions.

The focus remained on comparative analysis of different approaches towards risk reduction, development of risk models, and multidisciplinary quantitative analysis of their outputs. The priorities were also identified as technical issues:

- Assessments of risks, impacts and vulnerabilities, through regional and decadal-scale analysis and prediction,
- Information on the state of the environment, through advanced observing systems,
- Enhanced environmental information service provision to users.

This was stated to be inter- and trans-disciplinary research which would take account of coupled natural, social and economic systems with effective integration and coordination mechanisms to address interdependencies and marshal global resources. The priority foci, however, remains limited to sectoral concerns – Coastal Vulnerability, Freshwater Security, Ecosystem Services, Carbon Budgets and most vulnerable societies. This formulation ignores social science research that an effective response to global change will also require much greater understanding of the interrelations between global environmental change, global poverty and development needs, and global justice and security.

ISSC: Transformations to Sustainability–2013

The International Social Science Council has subsequently focused on identifying the longer term social transformations associated with pathways to sustainability, influenced both by the Belmont Challenge and the earlier Grand Challenges. 'Transformations to Sustainability' is a new Sida-supported programme that will fund and promote research on innovative processes of social transformation to secure equitable and durable solutions to some of the urgent global problems such as climate change, biodiversity loss, food security, poverty and inequality–with social considerations as one of the main elements.

The focus shifted from the economic, social and institutional systems in place to policies related to political, economic and cultural values, changes in institutional structures and individual behaviours, large-scale systems changes and technological innovations that reduce the rate, scale and magnitude of global environmental change and its consequences. The research challenge is identified as determining what can be done to transform economic systems, measures, goals and development policies for global sustainability.

The following questions have been identified in an attempt to bring together the earlier identification of the 'Grand Challenges' and the 'Belmont Challenge', as well as bringing together the natural and social sciences:

- How can freshwater, clean air and food be sustainably secured for the world population today and in the future?
- How can governance be adapted to promote global sustainability?
- What risks is humanity now facing as global growth and development place unprecedented pressures on ecosystems? What are the risks of crossing tipping points with serious implications for human societies, and the functioning of the Earth system, and the diversity of life on earth?
- How can the world economy and industries be transformed to stimulate innovation processes that foster global sustainability?
- In a rapidly urbanizing world, how can cities be designed to sustain a high quality of life for more people and have a sustainable global footprint that considers the human and natural resources they draw on?
- How can humanity succeed in a rapid global transition to a low-carbon economy that secures energy access for all?
- How can societies adapt to the social and ecological consequences of a warming world, and what are the barriers, limits and opportunities to adaptation?
- How can the integrity, diversity and functioning of ecological and evolutionary systems be sustained so as to sustain life on earth and ecosystem services, and to equitably enhance human health and well-being?
- What lifestyles, ethics and values are conducive to environmental stewardship and human welfare and how might these contribute to support a positive transition to global sustainability?
- How does global environmental change affect poverty and development, and how can the world alleviate poverty and create rewarding livelihoods which help achieve global sustainability?

An effective response to global change requires much greater understanding of the interrelations between global environmental change, global poverty and development needs and global justice and security. For example, how will global environmental change influence progress toward the goals of preventing and eradicating poverty and hunger and improving human health? Determining how to achieve changes in social organizations, institutional arrangements and human behaviour is just as important as establishing what changes are desirable. How does global environmental change shift the agenda for sustainable development in the world?

This framing recognizes individuals, not just policymakers, as a fundamental unit. It forces attention to a new level of detail on how information about the environment and feedback on thresholds being reached and breached can impact social changes and actions. How can timely actions be undertaken at multiple geographical and geopolitical scales, where the nature and scale of the issues involved means that the actors have widely differing – and disconnected – values, interests and power? How can we better understand the role of individual decisions within diverse settings as the building block of societal decisions? How can we better understand the factors shaping individual behaviour, values and perceptions of threats and risks and how those values and perceptions influence both individual action in relation to global change and the potential for collective action? The research outcomes are expected to influence individuals, who will then incorporate this information along with other factors such as institutions or policies, to make decisions that then aggregate to impact society and the environment.

Future earth 2025 vision

The science community is now focusing on societal challenges and a new type of science to contribute to a sustainable and equitable world in which people can thrive. Future Earth will inspire and create ground-breaking interdisciplinary science to address eight focal challenges that research needs to address in order to achieve a sustainable and equitable world.

These are to

1. *Deliver water, energy, and food for all, and manage the synergies and trade-offs among them,* by understanding how these interactions are shaped by environmental, economic, social and political changes.
2. *Decarbonise socio-economic systems to stabilize the climate* by promoting the technological, economic, social, political and behavioural changes enabling transformations, while building knowledge about the impacts of climate change and adaptation responses for people and ecosystems.
3. *Safeguard the terrestrial, freshwater and marine natural assets underpinning human well-being* by understanding relationships between biodiversity, ecosystem functioning and services, and developing effective valuation and governance approaches.
4. *Build healthy, resilient and productive cities* by identifying and shaping innovations that combine better urban environments and lives with declining resource footprints, and provide efficient services and infrastructures that are robust to disasters.
5. *Promote sustainable rural futures to feed rising and more affluent populations* amidst changes in biodiversity, resources and climate by analysing alternative land uses, food systems and ecosystem options, and identifying institutional and governance needs.
6. *Improve human health* by elucidating, and finding responses to, the complex interactions among environmental change, pollution, pathogens, disease vectors, ecosystem services, and people's livelihoods, nutrition and well-being.
7. *Encourage sustainable consumption and production patterns that are equitable* by understanding the social and environmental impacts of consumption of all resources, opportunities for decoupling resource use from growth in well-being, and options for sustainable development pathways and related changes in human behaviour.
8. *Increase social resilience to future threats* by building adaptive governance systems, developing early warning of global and connected thresholds and risks, and testing effective, accountable and transparent institutions that promote transformations to sustainability.

Future Earth, sponsored by the Science and Technology Alliance for Global Sustainability, is an informal partnership and the International Social Science Council (ISSC) and the United Nations

Educational, Scientific and Cultural Organization (UNESCO) currently co-chair the Alliance. Future Earth aims to provide knowledge and support to accelerate transformations to a sustainable world and brings together the other initiatives.

The World Social Science Report

The World Social Science Report 2013, prepared by the International Social Science Council and co-published with UNESCO and the OECD, concludes that social science needs to be at the heart of understanding and responding to global challenges such as climate change, pollution, resource limits and planetary boundaries to economic growth, and asserts that global environmental change, including climate change, is a social and not a physical problem. This report is perhaps the only United Nations publication that could not initially be downloaded online and was initially distributed by the OECD on payment–again, reflecting the politics around the issue.

A scientific review of the global sustainable development goals says that the Sustainable Development Goals (SDGs) offer a "major improvement" over their predecessors, the Millennium Development Goals (MDGs), with a greater understanding of the interplay between social, economic and environmental dimensions. However, the "ultimate end" of the sustainable development goals in combination is not clear. It, therefore, strongly calls for defining and drawing up a Meta-Sustainable Development Goal – a prosperous, high quality of life that is equitably shared and sustained. The recomendation is that the overarching goal should also be reflected in the new metrics for measuring progress towards it, as this could stimulate progress towards moving beyond using GDP (Gross Domestic Product) as a proxy for the overarching goal (ICSU, ICSSC, 2015).

The transformation of the intellectual and conceptual framework defining global concerns will really depend on the extent to which China, India and other emerging countries support new academic and policy research to contribute to and further develop the understanding of global change.

References

Agarwal, A. and S. Narain. 1991. Global Warming in an Unequal World: A Case of Eco-colonialism. Center for Science and Environment, New Delhi.

Agarwal, A. and S. Narain, 1992. Towards a Green World: Should Environmental Management be Built on Legal Conventions or Human Rights? Centre for Science and Environment, New Delhi.

Beck, Silke. Maud Borie, Jason Chilvers, Alejandro Esguerra, Katja Heubach, Mike Hulme, Rolf Lidskog, Eva Lövbrand, Elisabeth Marquard, Clark Miller, Tahani Nadim, Carsten Neßhöver, Josef Settele, Esther Turnhout, Eleftheria Vasileiadou, Christoph Görg. 2014. Towards a Reflexive Turn in the Governance of Global Environmental Expertise. The Cases of the IPCC and the IPBES. *GAIA–Ecological Perspectives for Science and Society*. 23(2): 80–87.

Belmont Forum. 2010. The Belmont Challenge: A Global, Environmental Research Mission for Sustainability.

Benedick, Elliot. The Improbable Montreal Protocol: Science, Diplomacy, and Defending the Ozone Layer. Case Study prepared for the 2004 Policy Colloquium of the American Meteorological Society, USA.

Bodansky, Dan, Jutta Brunee, Ellen Hay. 2007. *Oxford Handbook of International Environmental Law*. New York: Oxford University Press.

Boisvert, Valerie, and Armelle Caron. 2002. 'The Convention on Biological Diversity: An Institutionalist Perspective of the Debates'. *Journal of Economic Issues*. XXXVI(1): 150–66.

Carey, Mark, Lincoln C. James and Hannah A. Fuller, 2014, 'A new social contract for the IPCC'. *Nature Climate Change*, 4 December 2014.

Central Intelligence Agency, National Foreign Assessment Center, Relating Climate Change to its Effects: A Research Paper, GC 78-10154, August 1978.

Davenport, Deborah S. 2005. 'An Alternative Explanation for the Failure of the UNCED Forest Negotiations'. *Global Environmental Politics* 5:1, February 2005.

Dubash, Navroz K., Marc Fleurbaey, and Sivan Kartha. 2014. 'Political Implications of Data Presentation'. *Science* 4: 36–7.

EC. 2011. Communication from the Commission to the European Parliament, The Council, The European Economic and Social Committee and the Committee of the Regions: A Resource-Efficient Europe–Flagship initiative under the Europe 2020 Strategy, Brussels, 26.1.2011, COM(2011) 21 final.

Edenhofer, Ottmar, and Jan Minx. 2014. 'Mapmakers and Navigators, Facts and Values'. *Science* 4: 37–8.

Future Earth 2025 Vision. 2014. Future Earth- Research for Global Sustainability, November 2014. International Council for Science, Paris.

Girod B., A. Wiek, H. Mieg, and M. Hulme. 2009. 'The Evolution of the IPCC's Emissions Scenarios'. *Environmental Science and Policy*. 12(2): 103–118. doi: 10.1016/j.envsci.2008.12.006.

Hass, Peter M., Robert O. Keohane, and Marc Levy, ed. 1993. *Institutions for the Earth: Sources of Effective Environmental Protection*. MIT Press: Cambridge.

Haas, Peter M., Robert O. Keohane, and Marc A. Levy, eds. 2003. *Institutions for the Earth: Sources of Effective International Environmental Protection*. MIT Press, Cambridge

ICSU. 2010. Earth System Science for Global Sustainability: The Grand Challenges. International Council for Science, Paris.

ICSU, ISSC. 2015. Review of the Sustainable Development Goals: The Science Perspective. International Council for Science, Paris.

InterAcademy Council, Climate Change Assessments: Review of the Process and Procedures of the IPCC, Committee to review the Intergovernmental Panel on Climate Change, October 2010.

Intergovernmental Panel on Climate Change (IPCC). 2014a. *Working Group I, Physical Science Basis*. New York: Cambridge University Press.

Intergovernmental Panel on Climate Change (IPCC). 2014b. *Working Group II, Impacts, Adaptation and Vulnerability*. New York: Cambridge University Press.

Intergovernmental Panel on Climate Change (IPCC). 2014c. *Working Group III, Mitigation of Climate Change*. New York: Cambridge University Press

International Social Science Council. 2012. Transformative Cornerstones of Social Science Research for Global Change, ISSC, May 2012.

ISSC/UNESCO. 2013. World Social Science Report 2013: Changing Global Environments. Paris: OECD Publishing and UNESCO Publishing, Paris.

Lorek, S. and Fuchs, D. 2011. 'Strong Sustainable Consumption Governance–Precondition for a Degrowth Path? *Journal of Cleaner Production*

MacNeill, Jim. 2013. 'Brundtland Revisited', Canada International Council, February 4, 2013.

Miles, E. L., A. Underdal, et al. 2002. *Environmental Regime Effectiveness: Confronting Theory with Evidence*. Cambridge, MA: MIT Press.

Mitchell, Ronald B., William C. Clark, David W. Cash, and Nancy M. Dickson (ed). *Global Environmental Assessments–Information and Influence*. Cambridge: MIT Press.

Ogunlade, Adebola. 2010. Can the Bamako Convention adequately safeguard Africa's environment in the context of trans-boundary movement of hazardous wastes? University of Dundee.

PBL. 2010. Assessing an IPCC assessment. An analysis of statements on projected regional impacts in the 2007 report. Report|05-07-2010, PBL Netherlands Environmental Assessment Agency.

Ryan Sarah, E. Cris Hebdon and Joanna Dafoe 2014. 'Energy Research and the Contributions of the Social Sciences: A Contemporary Examination'. *Energy Research and Social Science*. 3(2014): 186–97.

SAB. 2014. UN System Priorities related to science for sustainable development: Background paper on items 4 and 5 of the SAB terms of reference, January 2014, Scientific Advisory Board of the Secretary General of the United Nations, hosted by UNESCO.

Sachs, J. 2013. The Challenge of Sustainable Development and the Social Sciences. World Social Science Report: 2013. Changing Global Environments. ISSC/UNESCO, 2013.

Sagar, Ambuj. 2000. 'Capacity Development for the Environment: A View for the South, A View for the North'. *Annual Review of Energy and Environment* 25: 377–439.

Sanwal, Mukul. 2004. 'Trends in Global Environmental Governance: The Emergence of a Mutual Supportiveness Approach to Achieve Sustainable Development'. *Global Environmental Politics*. 4(4): 16–22.

Sanwal, Mukul. 2011a. Global Vision for Rio + 20 and Beyond: Patterns, Trends and Drivers in the Evolution of Sustainable Development (1972–2012), Economic and Political Weekly.

Sanwal, Mukul. 2011b. Vision for Rio + 20: Transition to a low carbon economy and society-climate change, eradication of poverty and Sustainable Development.

The Energy Access Imperative: Power for All. June 2014, SE4ALL Initiative. United Nations.

The Future We Want. Background Paper for Global Energy Consultation, United Nations, 2013. The consultation was co-led by UN-Energy and the UN Secretary-General's Sustainable Energy for All (SE4ALL) Initiative.

United Nations, 2014. Report of the Secretary-General, International financial system and development, A/69/50 dated 25 July 2014, United Nations, New York.

US, 1970. 'US Priority Interests in the Environmental Activities of International Organizations', prepared by the Committee on International Environmental Affairs of the State Department, Report by Task Force III of the Committee on International Environmental Affairs, Washington, December 1970. Foreign Relations of the United States, Foreign Relations 1969–1976, Documents on Global Issues 1969–1972, Volume E-1, Chapter V, International Environment Policy, edited by Susan K. Holly and William B. McAllister, Office of the Historian, Bureau of Public Affairs, US Department of State, 2005.

Victor, David G, Kal Raustiala and Eugine B. Skolnikoff. 1998. *The Implementation and Effectiveness of International Environmental Agreements: Theory and Practice*. Cambridge, MA: MIT Press, Cambridge.

Victor, David G. Reyer Gerlagh, Giovanni Baiocchi. 2014. 'Getting Serious about Categorizing Countries. *Science* 4: 34–6.

Wible, Brad. 2014. 'IPCC Lessons from Berlin: Did the "Summary for Policymakers" become a Summary by Policy-makers?' *Science* 345 (6192): 34–7.

WRI. 1991. *World Resources 1990–91*. World Resources Institute. Oxford University Press, New York.

Young, Oran R, ed. 1999. *The Effectiveness of International Environmental Regimes: Causal Connections and Behavioral Mechanisms*. Cambridge: MIT Press

Focus on Developing Countries 4

The institutional framework and the rules under which global environmental change, climate change and sustainable development policy evolved have failed to give legitimacy to the shape of the response. This has led to continuing differences on the nature and scope of international cooperation between countries at different levels of development[1].

The way the issue was framed reflected the interests and concerns of the United States, and other industrialized countries, as the developing countries focused primarily on the means of implementation. The United Nations facilitated a consensus by developing a common understanding around the science as it was developed in industrialized countries and supported the positions they were taking. The divide was bridged with the argument that long-term development was necessary to combat the poverty that contributed to pollution and that such growth also depended on dealing with short-term environmental problems. Increased resources to apply to a global problem, characterized as 'additionality', helped overcome concerns related to global economic inequities.

The common understanding of global environmental change was shaped by deliberations within the United Nations reflecting its planetary dimensions, multilateral character and relation to national policy. From the beginning, there has been a tension in combining growing concerns on a range of global environmental issues with equally severe existing national socio-economic issues, and this dichotomy continues till today. A political perspective was adopted in 1972 to shift attention from the consequences of the industrial revolution and the movement of three-fourth of the population from rural to urban areas in industrialized countries, which had led to certain consumption patterns with a significant global impact. The issue was defined as a scientific and technical concern rather than dealing with the activities that led to the problems, that is, unsustainable consumption and production patterns.

The objective of first World Conference on the Human Environment, in 1972, was to take political decisions for international cooperation in the context of the use of natural resources with an environmental impact beyond the limits of national jurisdiction. As the United Nations observed, the delicately balanced life support systems were already overtaxed [United Nations Press Note, 1972].

---

[1] This chapter quotes from declassified confidential documents of the United States Department, the United Nations and international organizations with the objective of providing material for further research as these have not so far been used in the analyses by academics and others.

While there was no common understanding on how this problem concerned all nations, participation of developing countries implied their acceptance of interdependence in patterns of natural resource use.

The new interrelationship between environment and development was recognized as a controversial issue, and developing countries, represented in the consultations largely at the expert level by economists, perceived international cooperation in terms of additional costs as well as potential trade restrictions, to which the industrialized countries, keen to ensure their participation, agreed reluctantly and only partially. Maurice Strong, the Secretary General of the Stockholm Conference, in his address to the Conference highlighted the 'total deterioration of our common environment', which at that time was solely caused by the industrialized countries. Though the issue of imbalance in global patterns of resource use was raised, it was not made an integral part of the framework for international cooperation which concerned rights to natural resources outside national boundaries for industrialized countries and the means of implementation at the national level for developing countries.

4.1 Bridging the divide

Developing countries came to Stockholm quite reluctantly. They questioned the need for such a conference and viewed it as a threat to their interests. Some developing countries viewed the Conference as an attempt to 'ratify and even enhance existing unequal economic relations and miring them in poverty forever'. Other developing countries pointed out that industrialized countries wanted to 'slow planetary industrialization in order to replenish the spoiled ecosphere', after they had used cheap natural resources for their industrialization, urbanization and removal of poverty. Reflecting this perspective was the statement from Ivory Coast at the Stockholm Conference that it would prefer more pollution problems 'in so far as they are evidence of industrialization'. Developing countries were contesting both the need for the Conference and the agenda, that is, why the United Nations should consider global environmental issues as a priority.

From the very beginning, developing countries had a mixed reaction to the environment issue. Most treated concern for the environment as a luxury which only the rich nations could afford, while others viewed it as central to the development process itself. To obtain the participation of developing countries for the Stockholm Conference, the United Nations took steps to relate the environmental issue to their existing domestic priorities. To achieve this aim, the environmental problem was defined very broadly, in terms of the human environment, to include not only industrial pollution but also soil erosion and depletion, inadequate sewage facilities and health centres, shortages of water supplies and housing, and malnutrition and water-borne diseases, so that it would be of direct relevance to the principal economic and social priorities of developing countries.

The United Nations sought to bridge the political gap with the help of development economists. Key experts in the United Nations and its reports shaped official debates and multilateral decisions on sustainable development. They developed the formulation of basic human needs as the overriding objective, which environmental sustainability also had to meet by broadening its scope to include, for example, health and water, in addition to industrial pollution. An 'epistemic' community of experts became the means of shaping the multilateral framework of discrete treaties. This group remains dominated by experts from industrialized countries and its role in shaping political concerns became limited only when experts from developing countries began to question the assumptions, methods and frameworks that were adopted.

Instead of considering the world's physical interdependence, the focus was shifted to additional funding to the developing countries, already struggling to meet the expectations that independence aroused. As well as an instrument of humanitarianism or foreign policy, international assistance now served to maintain the stability of the global environment and of those who depend on it and share it. Such assistance was initially characterized as an obligation of the developed to the developing countries, as their high levels of economic welfare were achieved at the expense of the global environment. Developing countries, as they were at that time agricultural economies and societies, did not see the global environment as a resource to be shared. Their focus remained on local national resources and argued that if they were to be deprived of the rights to unbridled resource exploitation, the availability of low-cost environmentally disruptive industrial processes and the use of the commons to assimilate waste – in that order of importance, as elements by which development of the industrialized world was advanced – then additional funds equivalent to these benefits foregone should be forthcoming; the unresolved issue was, and remains, under what circumstances?

This perspective was not readily accepted by industrialized countries. The principle 'polluter must pay' (where all costs, long-term as well as short-term, indirect as well as direct, social as well as economic, are to be met by those responsible for such costs), and the principle of 'optimum natural resource management' (where environmental control measures will result in the best use of a country's resources over time) taken together led the interests of development and environment being met, in the long term if not the short term, and it was difficult to argue the principle of 'additionality'. The one clear instance in which additional funds could be provided by the international community, the industrialized countries felt, would occur when a developing country acted specifically to safeguard the environmental quality of an international common property resource, which at that time were the oceans and atmosphere.

The conflicting interpretations on the increased flow of financial resources have continued to exist, reducing its operational significance as a source of funds distinct from development assistance, even as developing countries agreed to treat natural resources, including national ones like biological diversity, and their use by other countries as a 'common concern of mankind'. The way the issue was framed, additional finance was limited in scope and served to solve political problems raised in individual negotiations rather than the underlying problem itself.

4.2 Global politics and national means of implementation

The scientists in the United States had correctly diagnosed the global environmental problem and its societal roots, but its National Report to the Stockholm Conference framed the issue in terms of the symptoms and not the causes of the problem, because that served domestic and global interests of a country using half the world's resources.

> The Government's Advisory Committee adopted a scientific approach and stated the problem quite clearly in terms of the urban way of life. 'In a larger sense, 20th century man has come to the realization that the dimensions of the human environment include not only all ecological systems, whether natural or manmade, but also a multitude of social and cultural values – all of which react and interact between and among one another. … Moreover, man's exploitation of his environment has brought a degree of affluence that has drawn dangerously near to embracing a philosophy of the invincible sovereignty of man without regard for the inevitable reactions that govern all other life systems … not force us to abandon growth but to redirect it … This goal will not be easy to achieve because it implies a balancing of individual freedom with responsibility to others. To attain this balance difficult value decisions must be made … The task mankind faces will demand the wholehearted cooperation of both motivated citizens and motivated governments.

If the world intends to capture the full potential of goal-directed scientific and technological change, then it seems imperative that social changes must keep pace. Only in this way can the quality of human environment be maintained at a level that will allow generations yet unborn to share the resources which they rightly deserve.

Urbanization is the product of a major long term, worldwide, socio-economic process – centuries old evolution in man's way of life from the rural agricultural life pattern to the urban-industrial way of life ... urbanization has changed the nation with seventy five per cent of its people living in urban areas.

'We must see ourselves not only as victims of environmental degradation but as environmental aggressors and change our patterns of consumption and production accordingly ... different patterns of growth from ours may improve the quality of life without environmental degradation' [Stockholm and Beyond, 1972]'.

The National Report of the United States to the Conference, however, adopted a more political approach and framed the issue in terms of international cooperation and shifted the focus onto developing countries. It stated that 'The Stockholm Conference is intended to be a worldwide convocation to stimulate action on environmental problems which affect the interests of all nations. It will provide both a challenge and an opportunity to come to grips with the issues posed by the potentially adverse impact on the environment that might result from rapid economic development in the LDCs'.

For the developing countries, multilateral deliberations on the global environmental concerns were influenced by the parallel deliberations on a New Economic Order. They were concerned over detrimental economic and social trends and a growing disparity between per capita incomes. Lacking scientific capacity to understand global trends, they came together to develop institutional arrangements to better understand the effects of trade from the increasing demand for commodities, which was to them the most visible sign of the industrialization and urbanization taking place in industrialized countries. As a result of their efforts, the Economic and Social Council Resolution 1785 (XVII) of 8 December 1962 mandated the convening of the first UN Conference on Trade and Development (UNCTAD), and later, on the basis of United Nations General Assembly Resolution 1995 (XIX) of 30 December 1964, the Conference acquired an institutional character of its own as an organ of the General Assembly. The primary purpose of the Conferences of UNCTAD was 'to serve as an agent of accelerated development for all countries by means of formulating and carrying into effect new development-oriented trade policies through the combined efforts of the entire international community ... That would be equitable and advantageous to all countries' (Report of UNCTAD II, ch. IV, para. 40).

At the conclusion of UNCTAD I, in 1964, a Joint Declaration presented by 77 Developing Countries was adopted, which stated that 'this unity has sprung out of the fact that facing the basic problems of development they have a common interest in a new policy for international trade and development ... The developing countries have a strong conviction that there is a vital need to maintain, and further strengthen, this unity in the years ahead. It is an indispensable instrument for securing the adoption of new attitudes and approaches in the international economic field'. These developments informed the stand the developing countries, as the G77, were to take in the preparations for the Stockholm Conference on the Human Environment.

In this context, three factors shaped international negotiations on the global environment; in 1967 Sweden had proposed a global conference to the United Nations General Assembly to "facilitate co-ordination and to focus the interest of member countries on the extremely complex problems related to the human environment."

First, the developing countries played little part in developing the substantive agenda as their focus was on the means of implementation, in particular additional finance. However, the agreed target of 1 per cent of national income of financial resources to be provided to developing countries included reservations by the donors which were recorded and actual disbursements soon stabilized in absolute terms and declined as a proportion of the steadily increasing gross national product of developed countries. While in 1961, the flow of development financing to developing countries amounted to 0.87 per cent of gross national product of developed countries, it came down to 0.62 per cent in 1966.

The G77 as a negotiating block, at the third conference of the NAM in Lusaka in 1970, set out their goals of international cooperation in terms of three policies focused on additional resources to attain equitable development. First, alleviate the problem of debt by increasing the net flow of financial transfers from developed to developing countries, distinguishing between investment for development and investment for commerce. Second, transfer of technology to developing countries to expand research opportunities and to improve educational systems. Third, protecting the prices of raw materials by creating systems to process raw materials and attain the advantages of value-added sales, and preference for products from developing countries to diversify their economies.

Their declaration stated that 'traditional approaches, isolated measures and limited concessions are not enough. The gravity of the problem calls for the urgent adoption of a global strategy for development requiring convergent measures on the part of both developed and developing countries … Special measures in the field of finance, technical assistance and marketing, including financing of research, abolition of subsidies and granting of preferences should be taken to improve the competitive position of natural products of developing countries that are affected by the competition of synthetics and substitutes originating from developed countries … Each developed country should comply with the target of a minimum 1 per cent of its gross national product for net financial flows, in terms of actual disbursements, by the end of the Development Decade'.

The Swedish observation on 'Financial Resources for Development: Total Inflow of Public and Private Resources' (Resolution 61) which also set targets is illustrative of the view of the donors. It stated that, 'Sweden voted in favor of this resolution as a whole in recognition of the vital importance of an increased net transfer of real resources to the developing countries. Sweden would, however, have preferred a text which emphasized the primary role of official development assistance in these transfers. The Swedish Government maintains serious reservations about the definition of the traditional one per cent target. This target does not reflect the true net transfer of resources, as reverse flows of investment income and interest payments are not deducted. The phrase 'minimum net amount' in the resolution is therefore misleading. Furthermore the traditional target includes transactions which are not subject to government control and no government can consequently make firm commitments with regard to these transactions. However, on the assumption that private flows will not decrease sharply, Sweden should reach the 1 per cent target before the middle of the decade'. On this same resolution, the delegation for the United Kingdom of Great Britain and Northern Ireland observed very succinctly: 'The delegation abstained on this resolution because they were unable to subscribe to the target for official development assistance.'

These divergent views on international cooperation were incorporated into various United Nations forums, including the Founex meeting of developing country economists to prepare for the Stockholm Conference, as 'additionality' of financial resources, and this approach to seek funds continues in each negotiation on the global environment. The question of debt and later intellectual property rights remains unresolved for good reason because growth in industrialized countries has been and continues to be built upon the control of intellectual property and financial globalization.

The second factor shaping negotiations was that the developing countries were, and still are, divided on a basic disagreement on the outcome of international negotiations, in part shaped by their levels of debt, industrialization and urbanization, leading many to make requests for accommodation in the existing arrangement rather than re-shaping the agenda. In 1974, the NAM submitted a draft Declaration on the Establishment of a New International Economic Order, and it was passed by the General Assembly without dissent, even the United States, still smarting under the economic shock of the unity of the developing countries under OPEC in increasing oil prices, while opposed to it in principle saw it as 'a significant political development'.

The industrialized countries then invoked a policy of 'divide and rule' with success. At the G7 meeting in 1975, Kissinger stated the United States view: 'With cooperation we can separate the moderates from the radicals with OPEC, the LDCs from the OPEC countries, and prevent a lot of other PECs' [Henry Kissinger, 1999]. As a consequence of this strategy, in 1976, the United States was able to reject calls for the establishment of the 'New International Economic Order' and the key issue became the common resolve of the G7 to keep the IMF and the World Bank out of control of the United Nations, while they supported limited financial assistance to deal with the political problems within the United Nations.

In the meeting of UNCTAD, in 1976, Kissinger, Secretary of State of the United States, proposed the creation of a modest International Resources Bank to create a bond market as advances and insurance for commodity sales, and avoided the political questions of power in economic relations. Of the special action program of 'urgent' $1 billion, only one-fifth was disbursed and the $6 billion commodities fund only secured $470 million. It was a step in breaking the unity of the NAM/G77 on a new economic order. Later when the Charter of Economic Rights and Duties of States was taken up, six countries voted against it (Belgium, Denmark, Luxembourg, United Kingdom, United States and West Germany, and there were 10 abstentions), signalling the beginning of the opposition to the initiatives of developing countries.

The third factor in the negotiations was that only China drew the right lessons from the rapid global growth after World War II and recognized the importance of industrialization rather than continuing reliance on agriculture, rural development and aid; one indicator of the seriousness of the exercise was the remarkable increase in the number of its scientists – from 500 in 1949 to 30,000 in 1988.

4.3 The negotiation process

The progress of the negotiations at Stockholm, and later in all environmental negotiations, is an illustration of, what has been described with only some justification as the 'geometry of imperialism', because the way the issues were framed and the agenda was set was really the success and failure of strategic thinking. The developing countries 'petitioned' the global bodies while the industrialized countries 'acted', and in each successive round of negotiations, the unity of the developing countries around their original position weakened in favour of the formulations presented by the industrialized countries and by the United Nations officials. This process enabled industrialized countries to achieve their policy objectives of securing what they defined as rights to global commons, while developing countries focused on the immediate means of implementation, or additional but limited finance.

This was the backdrop of the UN General Assembly Resolution 2398 (XXIII) on Problems of the Human Environment (3 December 1968), as one of the main problems facing developed and developing countries, and it included a reference to 'the possibilities for increased international cooperation, especially as they relate to economic and social development, in particular of the developing countries'. UN General Assembly Resolution 2657 (XXV) on the UN Conference on the Human Environment (7 December 1970) recommended the inclusion in the agenda for the second and third sessions of the Preparatory Committee of one or more specific items relating to economic and social aspects in order to safeguard and promote the interests of developing countries. This was an attempt at reconciling the global and national environmental policies with the national development plans and priorities of developing countries. It also recommended that the Preparatory Committee for the United Nations Conference on the Human Environment in 1972, consider the financing of possible action in this field to ensure that additional resources are provided to developing countries in the context of the protection of the environment.

The UN General Assembly Document A/CONF.48/PC/9 (26 February 1971) proposed that Development and Environment should be one of the six main subjects of the Conference Agenda and indicated that the following elements should be considered:

(a) Environmental policies as a component of comprehensive development planning, taking specially into account the particular problems, interests, needs and priorities of developing countries; link and relationship to strategy for the Second Development Decade.

(b) Environmental problems, priorities, perspectives and actions concerning developing countries.

(c) Impact of national and international environmental action on economic growth; impact of economic growth on the human environment.

(d) Means of calculating costs of environmental factors in economic transactions and of providing for allocation of such costs; development of criteria and techniques for evaluation and presentation of social factors in cost-benefit analysis of alternative policies and actions; means and criteria for relating economic growth indicators to quality of life factors.

(e) Fiscal implications of planning, conserving and developing natural resources and of environmental programmes for decontamination of air, treatment of water and elimination of industrial wastes.

(f) Environmental consideration in the choice of location of new industries on national and international level with particular reference to new industries in areas of lower industrial concentration, for example, developing countries.

(g) Resources required for meeting needs for environmental quality at different stages of economic development; implications for alternative use of resources and resource flows; financing of international programmes of environmental action, technical cooperation and assistance – all with particular reference to developing countries.

(h) Implications of environmental issues for international trade, technical and development assistance, including technology transfer, its required cost and financing.'

In February 1971, the Second Session of the Preparatory Committee for the UN Conference on the Human Environment, held at Geneva, had a separate agenda item on 'additionality'. The principle itself was first introduced and discussed at a meeting of experts convened at Founex, Switzerland, from 4–12 June 1971. The meeting was called by the Secretary General of the UNCHE to examine the relevance of environmental issues to the developing countries. The Founex Panel, as it became known, was composed of 27 eminent economists, sociologists, and environmentalists, with Mahbub-ul-haq taking the lead role in preparing the text. The panel undertook to assess the implications of the new environmental concern for the traditional development priorities of the developing countries in contrast to the earlier technocratic approach [Tolba, 1998]. The report also described as environmental a wide range of problems falling within the traditional concerns of the developing countries – from water supply to soil conservation, from sewage control to deforestation. These broader aspects of the environment gained such impetus that they dominated the Conference agenda and Action Plan, and the list of priorities emerging from the First Session of the UNEP Governing Council.

The results of the deliberations of these experts came to be known as the 'Founex Report: Panel of Experts on Development and Environment, Final Report of Meeting Additional Financing for the Developing Countries for Environmental Progress'. The panel was tasked with answering questions being posed by developing countries, such as:

How would actions taken by the more industrialized nations affect them?

What was likely to be the availability of technical assistance?

What would happen to the markets they required for their own development?

What attention was likely to be given to the kind of environmental problems which directly affected them?

In its final report the panel pointed out that,

'additional aid funds will be required to subsidize research on environmental problems for the developing countries, to compensate for major dislocations in the exports of the developing countries, to cover major increases in the cost of development projects owing to higher environmental standards, and to finance restructuring of investment, production or export patterns necessitated by the environmental concern of the developed countries. A suitable mechanism for the channelling of these funds should be devised.

We have also discussed the question of who pays for the higher costs arising out of the environmental concern and how the burden is to be shared between the developed and the developing world. Looking at the problem strictly from the point of view of the developing countries, it is quite clear that additional funds will be required to subsidize research for environmental problems for the developing countries, to compensate for major dislocations in the exports of the developing countries, to cover major increases in the cost of development projects owing to higher environmental standards and finance restructuring of investment, production or export patterns necessitated by the environmental concern of the developed countries. There was some discussion on how these additional funds should be provided. A proposal was made that a Special Fund should be set up specifically for this purpose. It was, however, felt that the consideration of a Special Fund was premature at this stage and the additional funds could as well be channelled through the existing international machinery so long as they could be clearly earmarked for the above-stated objectives, and clearly recognized as being additional. While the precise mechanism for the channelling of additional funds could not be discussed by us in any comprehensive manner, it was generally agreed that additional resource flows in one form or another will be needed ... The developed countries should ensure that their growing environmental concern will not hurt the continued development of the developing countries'.

The specific areas eligible for additional funding – environmental research, incremental costs of development projects attributed to environmental measures and disruption of developing country exports due to decreased demand or new requirements arising from environmental concern in the industrialized countries – were cited more explicitly at the Founex meeting than at any subsequent forum. It is interesting to note that the last item relates to the disruption of international trade resulting from environmental measures, which later emerged as the principle of compensation.

The report also considered the systemic issues with respect to trade but did not pursue them further at the conference, and merely asked for more research and specific studies:

'4.4 there is a fear that the insistence of the developed countries on rigorous environmental standards of products exchanged in international trade may well give rise to a "neo-protectionism". Many of the developed countries will be loath to see their production and employment suffer if their export prices rise as environmental standards is enforced; they may try to argue that imports from the developing countries based on less rigorous environmental standards should either be taxed or banned. The import-competing sectors and organized lobbies are likely to join in this outcry. Agricultural products may be the first to suffer. Some industrial products, notably chemicals, may fare no better. And from specifics, the argument can quickly go on to a general level. Why be liberal in admitting the products of the developing countries if they are the outgrowth of a "sweated environment"? The humanitarian concern for environment can far too easily become a selfish argument for greater protectionism. The developing countries still confront the argument of "sweated labour"; the argument of "sweated environment" will be equally fallacious but even harder to beat.

4.5 … In certain cases, the possibility of channelling additional aid toward adapting export industries in developing countries to the new requirements in developed countries or towards a diversification of their exports should also be studied. …

4.6 As a first step, it appears necessary to draw advance attention to the implications of environmental concerns for the continued growth of international trade. Appropriate procedures for prior notification, consultation and co-ordination will be needed to avoid adverse effects for world trade arising from national measures designed to promote pollution control. Conflicts of trade interests arising in this area should be resolved through existing and evolving arrangements and procedures. In this connection, the existing GATT framework – under which most of the industrialized countries have assumed specific rights and obligations – should be further used to mitigate such problems so as to reduce the fears of developing countries that a desire for a better environment may lead to an increase in protectionism.

4.7 It is important that the dimensions of this problem should be carefully defined and more concrete information accumulated so as to serve as the basis of international action. We therefore recommend that a number of specific studies be undertaken to analyse the implications of the current environmental concern for trade disruption. First, a comprehensive study should be made, possibly by UNCTAD, of the major threats that may arise to the exports of the developing countries, the character and severity of such threats, and the corrective action that may be possible. Second, the FAO should continue its present useful work on food standards considerations, including contamination, and seek to establish agreed environmental standards and guidelines for the export of foodstuffs. Third, the GATT should undertake to monitor the rise of non-tariff barriers on grounds of environmental concern and bring out pointedly any such trends in its Annual Reports.

4.9 Aid priorities and project appraisal may also, it is feared, be distorted by an excessive tendency by the developed countries to apply their own environmental standards unthinkingly to the developing countries. To the extent that aid priorities are influenced by, and are an extension of, the current concerns in the developed countries, it is inevitable that they will respond to the growing environmental concern. Aid donors may well believe that projects meant for environmental improvement should claim a fairly high priority in the developing countries while the latter may give these projects a lower priority in the context of their own competing needs'.

The Secretary General of the Conference in his report to the Third Session of the Preparatory Committee for the UN Conference on the Human Environment held at New York in September 1971. UN General Assembly Document A/CONF.48/PC.11 (30 July 1971), acknowledged that in the discussions at the Third Session of the UNCHE Preparatory Committee most developing countries expressed their reluctance to act without 'additionality':

'In view of the limited resources at their disposal and in view of the goals for development set by the International Development Strategy for the Second United Nations Development Decade, developing countries were reluctant to divert their goals and resources to an area of lesser priority for them … The need was emphasized for augmenting the resources available to developing countries by extending technical cooperation and financial assistance for the purpose of coping with their environmental problems. Such assistance could also help in maintaining the order of priorities in their national development plans'.

He also sounded a note of caution on the scope of 'additionality':

'Series of "Action Proposals": Development planning

The governments of the developing countries should consider taking the necessary action to allow for environmental factors within the framework of their own development strategies. This may involve redefining development policies and adjusting planning techniques. There may need to be a general broadening of development plans to allow for a redefinition of priorities and dimensions in the light of each country's cultural and social values and stage of economic development'.

Later in his Report to the General Assembly on Development and Environment, the Secretary General for the UN Conference on the Human Environment, Maurice strong pointed out that UN General Assembly Document A/CONF.48/10 (22 December 1971), 'One of the principal questions that arises from the increased concern with the human environment is what the cost to achieve various higher levels of environmental quality will be – since our knowledge of the magnitude of those costs is still limited at present – and how the costs should be distributed among the nations of the world. Developing countries are understandably concerned that because of their inherently weak position in international trade and control of technology, they may be forced to bear an unfairly heavy share of these costs. Will the growing awareness of the concepts of "one earth" and "one environment" in fact lead – as it should – to the nobler concept of "one humanity", and to a more equitable sharing of environmental costs and a greater international interest in, and responsibility for, the accelerated development of the less industrialized world? Or will it become a narrow concern of the industrialized world, leading to many awkward confrontations with the developing countries rather than to a new era of international cooperation?'

In December 1971, during its 26 Session, the UN General Assembly adopted Resolution 2849 (XXVI) on development and environment which, for the first time, gave official recognition to the principle of additionality. The perspective of the developing countries has been best articulated in UN General Assembly Resolution 2849 (XXVI): 'Pollution of world-wide impact is being caused primarily by some highly developed countries as a consequence of their own high level of improperly planned and inadequately coordinated industrial activities, and that, therefore, the main responsibility for the financing of corrective measures falls upon those countries to provide additional technical assistance and financing, beyond the targets indicated in the International Development Strategy for the Second United Nations Development Decade and without affecting spheres, to enable developing countries to enforce those new and additional measures that might be envisaged as a means of protecting and enhancing the environment'. The Resolution strongly argued for an acceleration of the flow of resources to the developing countries. It was carried with 85 votes in favour, 34 abstentions, with the United States and the United Kingdom voting against it.

Later, in his Progress Report to the next session of the Conference, UNCHE Document A/CONF.48/CRP.1 (31 May 1972), the Secretary General of the Conference again sought to bridge the divide: "additionality" is not merely designed to satisfy the environmental aspects of development, but makes a case for increasing the resources devoted to environment and development cannot be easily separated and distinguished. Thus what is involved in "additionality" in the broadest sense of that word is not merely an added dimension to development projects but the provision of greater resources for such basic needs as water, sewage, etc. which are required to provide a decent environment for human life in the developing countries ... "additionality" in its narrower sense covers the additional financing required for measures taken specifically or primarily in order to protect or enhance the human environment. ... The initial reaction of some of the governments of the industrialized countries with which the Secretary General of the Conference has consulted pursuant to operative paragraph 9 of General Assembly resolution 2849 (XXVI) has been to tend to consider expenditures needed to cover additional costs of projects flowing from environmental considerations as integral parts of sound development programmes and, as such, not distinguishable from other aspects of such programmes. In the view of some of these countries, such expenditures may not justify special appropriations or special financial handling ... the new perceptions of the basic interdependence of the more industrialized countries with the developing world which the environment issue points up makes an added case for a reconsideration by the industrialized countries of their development policies, aid flows and development assistance performance, as a basis for the new dimensions of international co-operation required to preserve and enhance our planetary environment for all mankind'.

The UN General Assembly passed Resolution 3002 (XXVII), 15 December 1972, which recommended in operative paragraph No. 4, 'respect for the principle that resources for environmental programmes, both within and outside the United Nations system, be additional to the present level and projected growth of resources contemplated in the International Development Strategy, to be made available for the programmes directly related to development assistance'. The Resolution also refers to the fact that funds available for the environment "will tend to be scarce in relation to the needs", but nevertheless supports the priorities of the developing countries for additional funding. The Resolution was carried with 74 in favour, 26 abstentions, and 3 against. A few donor countries (e.g. Australia and United States) claimed that efforts to implement the principle of additionality were already in progress.

The Report of the United Nations Conference on the Human Environment held at Stockholm on 5–16 June 1972. UN General Assembly Document A/CONF.48/14 (3 July 1972), also included a reference that '... for the developing countries most of the environmental problems are caused by under-development ... In the industrialized countries environmental problems are generally related to industrialization and technological development', but this statement did not determine the framework that was established.

4.4 Different world views of re-emerging and industrialized economies

The developing country world view, even in 1990, did not see the environmental problem arising out of urbanization and industrialization, as the United states had correctly analysed as far back as 1972 when its own urbanization had led to a shift of three-fourth of the population out of agriculture. On the contrary, developing countries stressed that it was important to '... ward off excessive migration to urban areas'. Consequently, the developing countries (except China) continued to see the population remaining in rural areas, with the need for financial resources for the welfare of the rural poor. For them, the environmental negotiations were a part of the fight to create space for political sovereignty, economic development, and social justice, and, unlike the industrialized countries in 1970 they were still not considering patterns of natural resource use for urbanization and industrialization and the resulting ecosystem scarcity and planetary limits.

The South Commission, in 1990, laid out their position in some detail, with a continuing lack of understanding of global patterns and trends of natural resource use, as well as reliance on the multilateral system for additional finance and without focusing on including in the agendas actions to be taken by developed countries. 'The damage to the environment is increasingly viewed with concern by decision-makers and public opinion. This concern could be a powerful motive for harnessing the collective energies of the international community for the removal of poverty and underdevelopment, which are the principal causes of environmental stress in the South ... The North is responsible for the bulk of the damage to the environment because of its wasteful lifestyle. However, poverty is also a great degrader of the environment, and an effective strategy for the removal of poverty is, in the final analysis, a strategy for protecting the environment ... The South's development strategies must take explicit account of the finite character of the world's natural capital ... The South should not shirk its responsibilities towards future generations ... should the North be prepared to finance a substantial part of the cost of switching to environment-sensitive patterns of growth and consumption in the south, a negotiated agreement could provide for reciprocal obligations on the part of the governments of the South'.

'It is only through reform of the international system governing flows of trade, capital and technology that the global environment for development can be improved. It is precisely this reform that is the object of the South's demand for a comprehensive dialogue with the North. And it should be the South's position in the various North-South discussions that which are now under way'.

'With different national priorities, individual countries are often unable to withstand the pressures selectively exerted upon them by the North. Furthermore, inadequate appreciation of the long-term implications of matters under negotiation leads some of them to break ranks with other countries of the South without realizing that this would harm the broader interests of all – including their own ... The ability of governments to control events within national borders is drastically constrained by the external environment ... In view of their weaknesses and vulnerabilities, it is therefore of critical importance for all developing countries to try to secure an adequate degree of institutionalized protection of their independence and freedom of action through a multilateral regime, backed up by a strengthened United Nations' [The South Commission, 1990].

The perspective of the South Commission is indicative of the lack of capacity within developing countries to do their own research and define a clear strategy. Consequently, their preferences and goals were not able to impact on international agenda setting, relegating the developing countries to a mostly defensive position. By the 1990s, their focus had also shifted to South–South cooperation and the role of locomotives of the South, rather than shaping the multilateral agenda, where resource flows continued to become detrimental to their growth. For example, in 1981, the net flow of capital to the developing countries was $35.2 billion. In 1987, $30.7 billion left the developing countries for Western banks.

The geopolitical situation began to change around 2000 with the commodity boom driven by China's industrialization and urbanization and, with rising commodity profits improving Latin American finances, more foreign direct investment becoming available and the developing countries began trading more among themselves. In June 2003, at the margins of the Group of Eight gathering in Evian, France, IBSA (the India-Brazil-South Africa Dialogue) emerged keen to 'maximize the benefits of globalization' and promote sustained economic growth. Brazilian Foreign Minister Celso Amorim defined it at the time as 'an ideology in the best sense of the word – an ideology of democracy, diversity, tolerance, a search for cooperation'. The BRICS was created as a group in

2009 out of the BRIC-IBSA union with the addition of China and Russia. Discussions on a new development bank, a BRICS Bank began in 2009 and the New Development Bank was founded in 2014. China and Brazil have also set up a $30 billion currency swap deal to pay for trade instead of using the United States dollar. However, no new global framework has been suggested by them.

The focus on ideas and scientific analysis remained important in international cooperation. Except for China, none of the other developing countries analysed historical trends in the civilizational shifts from rural agricultural poverty to urban industrial middle class status for their citizens as well as the relation of global natural resource use to national environmental change and continued to see these changes in terms of poverty and aid for the rural poor. This perspective enabled the industrialized countries to shape the discourse around consensual, or harmonized, natural science and legal rights to resources outside national boundaries and with multilateral institutions monitoring arrangements, opening markets and resolving disagreements and disputes, while keeping multilaterally agreed national actions out of the agenda as that would bring in issues related to re-distribution – these continue to be outside the agenda of the United Nations.

Prashad points out in *The Darker Nations*, in 2007, that the Third World was a project, not a place, and in *The Poorer Nations*, in 2012, he sees the Third World, or Global South, as a term that properly refers not to geographical space, but to a series of protests against neo liberalism [Prashad, 2007, 2012]. While this situation is changing with the BRICS, there is as yet no new vision for global sustainable development. The 38th Annual Meeting of Ministers of the G77 and China on 26 September 2014, reaffirmed the strategic objective for the post-2015 agenda of the United Nations on the lines of the statements made by the G77 and China at its inception in 1964: 'developing an international enabling environment for sustainable development, by addressing the questions of trade, reform of the international financial system, global economic governance, debt, repatriation of illicit funds, cooperation in the fields of finance and technology, in order to support the efforts of developing countries to achieve sustainable development'. Cleary, this worldview has been, and remains, the only substantive concern that unites the current number of 175 countries of the G77 and China on global governance. It remains to be seen whether they will now focus on a 'means-ends continuum' on how the change they seek will actually take place, and adopt a new meta-goal for global governance – 'a prosperous, high quality of life that is equitably shared and sustainable' – on the lines of the advice from the International Social Science Council [ICSU, ISSC, 2015]. Only in 2015, speaking at the Boao Forum on 28 March 2015, (the forum is conceived as the Asian version of the World Economic Forum, at Davos, and its theme this year is "Asia's New Future: Toward a Community of Common Destiny") China's President Xi Jinping sketched out a vision for a new Asian order, and presented China as a partner willing to "jointly build a regional order that is more favourable to Asia and to the world". China has established a new bank to fund in infrastructure in Asia and released an action plan for "one belt, one road" which will include roads, rail, ports, oil and gas pipelines, fibre optic networks as well as funding for information technology, biotechnology and new energy. Customs and other regulations that might impede trade and investment are also to be smoothed out. The alternate to United States dominated sources of credit led Lawrence Summers, former United States Treasury Secretary to note that the United States had "lost its role as the underwriter of the global economic system.

4.5 Strategic role of the United States – documents

The United States had established strong institutional capacities to develop global strategies for the long term as a way of maintaining its status as the only superpower. Originally set up in the Cold War era, this capacity continued to work on natural resources, environmental concerns, climate change and sustainable development. The strategy of maintaining intellectual superiority contributed to the ability to influence much larger number of countries and set the global development agenda in the United Nations. For example, the G7, formed in 1974, was essentially an anti-developing country not an anti-Soviet Union mechanism.

The United States national report on the human environment prepared for the United Nations Conference on Human Environment, June 1972, Stockholm, Sweden, diagnosed the problem of global environmental change with a clarity that the rest of the world is only now achieving. In large measure because of the way the issue was framed in physical terms and not as a social problem, the United States has been able to continue to shape the global agenda over a 40-year period.

[1] U.S. PRIORITY INTERESTS IN THE ENVIRONMENTAL ACTIVITIES OF INTERNATIONAL ORGANIZATIONS

Salient Features of Man-Made Environmental Problems

(a) The defining characteristic of an environmental problem is the current or prospective existence of some condition, trend, or deficiency in the environment which adversely affects human welfare. Man-made environmental problems arise because of the side effects of normal socio-economic activity in contrast to such natural phenomena such as earthquakes and typhoons. In this respect, environmental pollution is an unintended consequence of the modern way of life.

(b) Broadly speaking, the extent of pollution in any country or throughout the world is determined by (1) population size, growth, and distribution (especially trends in urbanization); (2) industrialization and the modernization of agriculture, along with concomitant increases in consumption; and (3) the technology on which contemporary society are based. None of these factors is the sole cause and, in any particular country or during any period of time, one may be a more important contributor to environmental deterioration than the others. For the world as a whole, these three basic variables determine the nature and magnitude of the total ecological burden (i.e. the totality of all demands which human activity puts upon the environment). The management of this burden will require a high degree of international cooperation in the years ahead.

Environmental Affairs in the International Arena

(c) The basic objective of international cooperation on environmental problems is threefold (1) to prevent further deterioration of the environment, (2) to reduce, and if possible to eliminate, the pollution that already exists, and (3) to improve the quality of life for both present and future generations. Competing and conflicting national interests on environmental issues can create or exacerbate international tension. In political terms, the underlying purpose of cooperative efforts to resolve these issues is to reduce or forestall this tension; but international cooperation might also have more specific aims such as strengthening an intergovernmental organization that serves U.S. interests, securing mutual advantages in international trade, or improving the U.S. image abroad.

(d) Remedial and preventive action on environmental problems can often be undertaken at the local, subnational, or national level. However, effective control of environmental deterioration sometimes requires the cooperation of several, most, or all countries. International co-operation is frequently desirable even though it may not be necessary. At the very least, nations can profit by sharing their experience with domestic pollution problems and by exchanging information on factors affecting the quality of man's environment.

(e) There is a compelling need for international cooperation in preventing and correcting pollution in any part of the natural environment which is shared by several countries and which therefore functions as a commons. This applies particularly to the atmosphere and the oceans, but also applies to rivers and lakes on international boundaries. The rationale for cooperation on such matters as land use, conservation, and development of inland water resources is critically affected by the sovereign rights of national powers. Apart from territoriality, the basic factor affecting the need for international cooperation in these cases is the economic interdependence of nations.

(f) Long-range policy planning to cope with global environmental problems must take account of the total ecological burden. This burden tends to increase with population, growth and with the level of economic activity, whereas the capacity of the environment to provide essential inputs to production and to absorb unwanted outputs from consumption is fundamentally limited. The problem of managing total ecological burden will remain even after world population is stabilized. Controlling that burden by systematic reduction in per capita production of goods and services would be politically unacceptable. A concerted effort is needed to orient technology toward making human demands upon the environment less severe.

(g) The issues posed by the continual growth of world-wide demands upon the environment are primarily important for long-range planning, but they also require long lead times for resolution. Cooperative efforts to devise and implement technical solutions to global environmental problems may need to be supplemented by two admittedly difficult measures. One is to move toward zero population growth more rapidly; the other is to re-orient human values, especially in regard to national self-interest versus the interests of all mankind [Stockholm and Beyond, 1972].

------

[2] US NATIONAL REPORT

Effective action on many global environmental problems, including the management of total ecological demand, requires not only international cooperation but also long-range planning. New questions about means and ends will undoubtedly emerge in the course of planning for the satisfaction of future needs and wants within the constraints imposed by a finite environment and the uncertainties inherent in the development of new technologies. It may be necessary to devise new forms of multinational decision-making in order to resolve environmental issues affecting the interests of all mankind.

(z) For the nations of the world, the most difficult political issue posed by future environmental problems is likely to be the need for genuine commitment to goals that transcend national interests. Another crucial problem is the need for increasing the power of intergovernmental organizations to act. Improvements in existing mechanisms for international cooperation may be insufficient unless they enable multinational organizations to execute programs which nations do not or cannot carry out alone and to enforce decisions which subordinate sovereign rights to human rights. Perhaps this ultimate goal will be regarded as attainable when nations become accustomed to thinking of the environment as a heritage that can be used more rationally and improved for the welfare of future generation' [US National Report, 1972]

------

[3] US OBJECTIVES

The United States, alone among all the countries participating, had very clear priorities for the Stockholm Conference – 'The overall U.S. objective for the Conference is to raise the level of national and international awareness and understanding of environmental problems and to increase national, regional and global capabilities to recognize and solve those problems which have a serious adverse impact on the human environment. By doing so, we will maintain and improve our overall international economic, competitive position as other countries adopt control measures comparable to our domestic programs'.

> 323. *Memorandum from the President's Assistant for National Security Affairs (Kissinger) to President Nixon, Washington, June 8, 1972*
>
> Washington, June 8, 1972.

------

[4] US DIPLOMATIC EFFORTS

The United States, more than other industrialized countries, invested a lot of political capital in the preparations for the Stockholm Conference.

> 306. *Letter From the Scientific Attache (Hudson) at the Embassy in Brazil to the Director of the Office of Environmental Affairs (Herter), February 12, 1971*
>
> Washington, October 8, 1970.
>
> Embassy of the United States of America
>
> Rio de Janeiro
>
> February 12, 1971
>
> Christian A. Herter, Esquire Office of Environmental Affairs Bureau of International Scientific and Technological Affairs
>
> Department of State
>
> Washington, 20520
>
> Dear Chris:
>
> As I have regained a more current assessment of the situation here in Brazil, vis-a-vis environmental matters, following my leave, a thought has occurred to me which I would like to pass along to you. As you know, one of the standard Department procedures, especially where international organizations or activities such as the upcoming Stockholm Conference are concerned, when they run into trouble, is to attempt to mount a demarche by all of the "friendlies" on the poor little fellow who happens to be too "unenlightened" to appreciate fully the merits of our position. Having participated in more of these than I would like to remember, I have invariably been impressed by their ineffectiveness and sometimes even outright counter productivity.
>
> Since the environment is an important subject to the present administration and to mankind as a whole, I would like to suggest an alternative to last-minute concerted approaches. I think we can anticipate without much difficulty that there is going to be a continuation of the feeling among many of the underdeveloped countries that being concerned about the environment is, in the final analysis, a rich man's game. This feeling may well, in fact, be present at a low level even with countries which

88 | The World's Search for Sustainable Development

may be pragmatically willing to go along for "what's in it for them". While we know this is not just a rich man's game, we also know that it is sometimes very difficult to persuade otherwise someone whose major goal must be development.

Accordingly, my suggestion would be that you give consideration now to identifying those countries where we are likely to have the most opposition and associate them with ourselves or specific "friendlies" of like mind and set into motion now, while we still have time, a well thought-out program of gradually informing and hopefully converting the key policy makers wherever that seems necessary. Certainly, our Canadian colleagues would be willing to join in such an operation and I think many of our other friends who share our concern in the environment would prefer to establish long term persuasive relationships with the policy makers of specific underdeveloped countries where they may have influence by virtue of past association or a special relationship rather than face the last minute crash approach.

[5] US CONCERNS IN SEEKING INTERNATIONAL COOPERATION

The United States was concerned about the position Africa was taking.

> 322. *Intelligence Note REC 11 Prepared by the Bureau of Intelligence and Research, Washington, May 31, 1972*
>
> Washington, May 31, 1972.
>
> Intelligence Note
>
> Bureau of Intelligence and Research
>
> May 31, 1972
>
> Stockholm Environment Conference: African Position
>
> Within the past few months there have been indications that some African representatives may strongly challenge developed countries' "doctrine" on environmental matters at the upcoming Stockholm Conference—perhaps as strongly as Brazil has done on previous occasions. While they may be overridden by more moderate view of other African representatives, their views linking environment and development will be with us in the years to come.

"give far more weight to the preoccupations of the industrialized countries than to the more serious ones of the developing countries." The group also states that the problems to be discussed at Stockholm are of a political nature and urges representation there by African cabinet ministers backed by experts. The group recommends that "all African countries should demand a reappraisal of all the regulations, methods and models, imposed from abroad which have so far governed the economic decision of some African countries and which have led to a ruinous exploitation and waste of their natural resources."

Dakar Group Proposes Reparations. The group contends that African nations have a "right to reparation by countries which have partially based (and continue to base) their growth on this exploitation." The talk of reparations does not appear to mean actual reparations, but rather compensation in the form of increased foreign aid. The "polluters-must-pay" principle for ongoing activities is endorsed. The proposed strategy is to attempt to split the Americans from the Europeans at the Stockholm Conference by saddling the Europeans with the onus of colonial exploitation in Africa through talk of reparations.

A Self-Centered Development Model? The Dakar group does not see any conflict between development and environment, provided development is "within the framework of a model specifically designed to serve the interests of Africa's population." Although the model is not spelled out, there is a hint of it in the group's call for an examination of all mining and power projects "in the perspective of long-term self-centered development." The group also calls for regional cooperation, particularly with regard to river basins and coastal areas.

On population growth and labor the group proposes stating that:

> They reject the argument according to which a halt to population growth, advocated in certain quarters as a way of halting the advance of the "colored peril", is one of the preconditions for development and for safeguarding the human environment in Africa.

> They reject the idea of African people being simply considered as a factor of production, as cheap labour, which only worsens inequalities in the international division of labour or the use of Africans to feed the growth of the advanced industrialised countries.

> The Ideas Will Linger After the Rhetoric Dies. It is doubtful that such polemic language will end up in the proposed "joint African stand," if one is adopted, but this direction of thinking may well surface.

The Dakar group's proposals reflect not only an increasing African militancy on development matters, but an attempt to link a series of development-related issues. Thus, the Stockholm Conference on the Human Environment is seen as a forum for going beyond purely environmental matters into political, social, trade, and economic questions. The basic position worked out in Dakar in April 1972 likely will reappear in some form at the UN Conferences on the Law of the Sea in 1973 and on World Population in 1974 as well as in other forums.

------

[6] US EVALUATION OF THE STOCKHOLM CONFERENCE

From the perspective of the United States, the Stockholm Conference was a success.

> 324. *Memorandum from the Chairman of the Council on Environmental Quality (Train) to President Nixon, Washington, June 19, 1972*

> Washington, June 19, 1972

> Memorandum

> For the President

> Subject:

> UN Conference on the Human Environment

> From:

> Russell E. Train

> Executive Office of the President Council on Environmental Quality

> 722 Jackson Place, N. W.

> Washington, June 19, 1972

> The UN Conference on the Human Environment

> It is my personal assessment that the Conference was a success. The United States played a strong role and gained practically all of its objectives.

> The United States proposal for a $100 million Environmental Fund (your personal initiative in your February 1972 Environmental Message) provided the single concrete proposal which helped

pull the entire action program together. Our commitment of $40 million toward the Fund was matched by about $25 million in specific pledges by other governments. A number of other expressions of general support were given.

------

[7] US RESPONSE TO THE G77

The increasing unity of the G77 in the United Nations was a serious cause of concern for the United States.

42. *Briefing Memorandum from the Assistant Secretary of State for International Organization Affairs (Lewis) to Secretary of State Kissinger, Washington, March 3, 1976*

Department of State Briefing Memorandum

March 3, 1976

To: The Secretary

Through: P - Mr. Sisco

E - Mr. Robinson

From: IO - Samuel W. Lewis [SWL initialed]

Strategy for Multilateral Diplomacy in 1976

The Role of the United Nation

Widening fissures have been opening in the solidarity of nonaligned coalitions. Although majorities existed at the last UNGA for some highly objectionable resolutions, it is probably of more long-range significance that radical leaders found it increasingly difficult to produce overwhelming majorities for extreme resolutions. (A more detailed analysis of the "breaking up of the blocs" is attached).

But despite these generally favorable elements, the fundamental features of the problem remain. We are dealing in the UN framework with countries deeply dissatisfied with the cards they were dealt when they became nations. Their impatience to narrow gulfs of inequality, to remove quickly what they regard as fundamental injustices, will ensure that it remains a formidable task to muster support for what may actually be feasible, gradual, partial, practical measures.

Build up our new operational capacity to relate multilateral and bilateral diplomacy, so that we create more incentives and deterrents to promote more responsible behavior in international organizations, less gratuitous hostility, greater readiness to deal with issues on their individual merits, continued erosion of bloc voting, and overall, more support for U.S. positions on critical issues.

We should do everything in our power to avoid conflict with the LDCs over legalistic formulas, as opposed to concentrating on the merits of concrete substantive proposals. ... political goals of redistributing representation and power ... Radicals among the poor insist that what they want is a larger share of the world product. Others among the poor agree with the rich, for the most part, that sustained growth is the best guarantee the poor have of developing their economies [*Global International Relations, 1969–1976*].

------

[8] US INTELLIGENCE COMMUNITY

The intelligence community of the United States also took an early interest in international conferences, indicating the importance attached to the outcomes in terms of national security and the opportunity to formulate adequate response strategies to achieve those outcomes:

"The Stockholm Conference is intended to be a worldwide convocation to stimulate action on environmental problems which affect the interests of all nations. It will provide both a challenge and an opportunity to come to grips with the issues posed by the potentially adverse impact on the environment that might result from rapid economic development in the LDCs.

Recommendations for action by national governments and by international bodies will be considered at the Conference. Emphasis will be given to (1) programs designed to help developing countries minimize or forestall the adverse effects on the environment that result from rapid industrialization and unplanned urbanization, and (2) problems that are difficult or impossible to solve by one country alone or whose solution would be greatly facilitated by multilateral agreements, including cooperative arrangements within the UN framework.

A draft Declaration on the Human Environment will be submitted for debate. It will probably be a statement of general principles about the rights and obligations, of men, nations, and international organizations in regard to the environment. Differences in attitudes toward environmental pollution on the part of the developing countries and the industrialized states will be difficult to reconcile. There is a good chance that the substance of any declaration accepted by a majority of the participants will be fairly ambiguous in order to allow for different interpretations consistent with diverse national interests [*Bureau of Intelligence and Research, 1970*].

[9] CONTINUING ASYMMETRY OF POWER

The asymmetry of power has continued to impact on global environmental negotiations underlining the political, rather than scientific, basis of the outcomes.

> A leaked document from the British Government Communications Headquarters (GCHQ) describes the agency's role to uncover negotiation positions by other countries.
>
> The document has been exposed by the Danish broadsheet *Dagbladet Information* that obtained it from Edward Snowden. The GCHQ appears to have intercepted online communication and accessing delegate email accounts, according to other documents seen by *Dagbladet Information*. The GCHQ appears to have spied on the UN climate summits between COP13 in 2007 and COP16 in 2010, according to the leaked document dated from February 2011.
>
> According to an NSA document leaked by Mr. Snowden, the agency spied on key countries at the summit. The NSA document stated that: "Leaders and negotiating teams from around the world will undoubtedly be engaging in intense last-minute policy formulating; at the same time, they will be holding sidebar discussions with their counterparts, details of which are of great interest to our policymakers ... Signals intelligence will undoubtedly play a significant role in keeping our negotiators as well informed as possible throughout the negotiations."
>
> [Kasper Jon Larsen, 2014]

------

[10] POLITICS AROUND THE COPENHAGEN ACCORD

> Embassy dispatches show America used spying, threats and promises of aid to get support for Copenhagen accord Seeking negotiating chips, the US state department sent a secret cable on

31 July 2009 seeking human intelligence from UN diplomats across a range of issues, including climate change. The request originated with the CIA. As well as countries' negotiating positions for Copenhagen, diplomats were asked to provide evidence of UN environmental "treaty circumvention" and deals between nations.

Getting as many countries as possible to associate themselves with the accord strongly served US interests, by boosting the likelihood it would be officially adopted. A diplomatic offensive was launched. Diplomatic cables flew thick and fast between the end of Copenhagen in December 2009 and late February 2010, when the leaked cables end.

The accord promised $30bn (£19bn) in aid for the poorest nations hit by global warming they had not caused. Within two weeks of Copenhagen, the Maldives foreign minister, Ahmed Shaheed, wrote to the US secretary of state, Hillary Clinton, expressing eagerness to back it.

By 23 February 2010, the Maldives' ambassador-designate to the US, Abdul Ghafoor Mohamed, told the US deputy climate change envoy, Jonathan Pershing, his country wanted "tangible assistance", saying other nations would then realise "the advantages to be gained by compliance" with the accord. "Ghafoor referred to several projects costing approximately $50m (£30m). Pershing encouraged him to provide concrete examples and costs in order to increase the likelihood of bilateral assistance." The Maldives were unusual among developing countries in embracing the accord so wholeheartedly, but other small island nations were secretly seen as vulnerable to financial pressure. The confidential cable records a blunt US threat to Zenawi, Prime Minister of Ethiopia: sign the accord or discussion ends now. Zenawi responded that Ethiopia will support the accord, but has a concern of his own: that a personal assurance from Barack Obama on delivering the promised aid finance is not being honoured.

Any linking of the billions of dollars of aid to political support is extremely controversial – nations most threatened by climate change see the aid as a right, not a reward, and such a link as heretical. But on 11 February, Pershing met the EU climate action commissioner, Connie Hedegaard, in Brussels, where she told him, according to a cable, "the Aosis [Alliance of Small Island States] countries 'could be our best allies' given their need for financing".

The pair were concerned at how the $30bn was to be raised and Hedegaard raised another toxic subject – whether the US aid would be all cash. She asked if the US would need to do any "creative accounting", noting some countries such as Japan and the UK wanted loan guarantees, not grants alone, included, a tactic she opposed. Pershing said "donors have to balance the political need to provide real financing with the practical constraints of tight budgets", reported the cable.

Along with finance, another issue in the global climate negotiations, currently continuing in Cancún, Mexico, is trust that countries will keep their word. Hedegaard asks why the US did not agree with China and India on what she saw as acceptable measures to police future emissions cuts. "The question is whether they will honour that language," the cable quotes Pershing as saying.

US determination to seek allies against its most powerful adversaries – the rising economic giants of Brazil, South Africa, India, China (Basic) – is set out in another cable from Brussels on 17 February reporting a meeting between the deputy national security adviser, Michael Froman, Hedegaard and other EU officials. Froman said the EU needed to learn from Basic's skill at impeding US and EU initiatives and playing them off against each in order "to better handle third country obstructionism and avoid future train wrecks on climate".

Hedegaard is keen to reassure Froman of EU support, revealing a difference between public and private statements. "She hoped the US noted the EU was muting its criticism of the US, to be constructive," the cable said. Hedegaard and Froman discuss the need to "neutralise, co-opt or marginalise unhelpful countries including Venezuela and Bolivia", before Hedegaard again links financial aid to support for the accord, noting "the irony that the EU is a big donor to these countries". Later, in April, the US cut aid to Bolivia and Ecuador, citing opposition to the accord.

Any irony is clearly lost on the Bolivian president, Evo Morales, according to a 9 February cable from La Paz. The Danish ambassador to Bolivia, Morten Elkjaer, tells a US diplomat that, at the Copenhagen summit, "Danish prime minister Rasmussen spent an unpleasant 30 minutes with Morales, during which Morales thanked him for [\$30m a year in] bilateral aid, but refused to engage on climate change issues."

After the Copenhagen summit, further linking of finance and aid with political support appears. Dutch officials, initially rejecting US overtures to back the accord, make a startling statement on 25 January. According to a cable, the Dutch climate negotiator Sanne Kaasjager "has drafted messages for embassies in capitals receiving Dutch development assistance to solicit support [for the accord]. This is an unprecedented move for the Dutch government, which traditionally recoils at any suggestion to use aid money as political leverage. "Later, however, Kaasjager rows back a little, saying: "The Netherlands would find it difficult to make association with the accord a condition to receive climate financing."

Perhaps the most audacious appeal for funds revealed in the cables is from Saudi Arabia, the world's second biggest oil producer and one of the 25 richest countries in the world. A secret cable sent on 12 February records a meeting between US embassy officials and lead climate change negotiator Mohammad al-Sabban. "The kingdom will need time to diversify its economy away from petroleum, [Sabban] said, noting a US commitment to help Saudi Arabia with its economic diversification efforts would 'take the pressure off climate change negotiations.'"

The Saudis did not like the accord, but were worried they had missed a trick. The assistant petroleum minister Prince Abdulaziz bin Salman told US officials that he had told his minister Ali al-Naimi that Saudi Arabia had "missed a real opportunity to submit 'something clever', like India or China, that was not legally binding but indicated some goodwill towards the process without compromising key economic interests".

WikiLeaks cables reveal how US manipulated climate accord

Guardian 3 Dec 2010.

References

Bureau of Intelligence and Research. 1970. Major International Conferences on the Environment: 1971–1972. ITE Foreign Relations of the United States, 1969–1976, Volume E–1, Documents on Global Issues, 1969–1972, Document 300D, October 8.

Global International Relations of the United States. 1969–1976. Ve–1, Documents on Global International Relations, 1969–1972.

ICSU, ISSC. 2015. Review of the Sustainable Development Goals: The Science Perspective. Paris: International Council for Science (ICSU).

Kasper Jon Larsen. 2014. UK intelligence allegedly spied on UN climate talks. Climate-dev November 1, 2014.

Kissinger, Henry. 1999. *Years of Renewal*. New York: Simon and Schuster. p. 677.

Prashad, V. 2007. *The Darker Nations: A Biography of the Short-Lived Third World*. New Delhi: Leftword Books.

Prashad, V. 2012. *The Poorer Nations: A Possible History of the Global South*. London: Verso.

Stockholm and Beyond. 1972. Report of the Secretary of State's Advisory Committee on the 1972 United Nations Conference on the Human Environment, May 1972, Department of State publication 8657, International Organization and Conference Series 101, Washington, DC.

The South Commission. 1990. *The Challenge to the South: Report of the South Commission*. Oxford University Press, New York.

Tolba, Mostapha K. 1998. *Global Environmental Diplomacy: Negotiating Environmental Agreements for the World 1973–1992*. MIT Press.

United Nations Press Note. 1972. P.R. HE 121, 24 May 1972.

U.S. National Report on the Human Environment, Prepared for: United Nations Conference on Human Environment, June 1972, Stockholm, Sweden.

Limitations of Multilateral Environmental Agreements

5

The most successful environmental agreement, the Montreal Protocol, focused on modifying production and consumption patterns but the subsequent agreements, whether issue-based, sectoral or economy-wide, focused on symptoms and not the causes of the environmental problem and have, therefore, had limited success. An independent review by the United Nations has also concluded that 'the current framework of international environmental governance is weakened by institutional fragmentation and specialization and lack of a holistic approach to environmental issues and sustainable development' [UN JIU, 2008][1].

A legal framework was important for industrialized countries for three reasons. First, it created rights and obligations with respect to the global environment which was defined to include natural resources outside national boundaries – biodiversity, carbon budget and forests. Second, it facilitated trade – hazardous substances, biotechnology and new markets. Third, the way the issues were framed around future natural resource use meant weak commitments for them and there were provisions for reservations and interpretative statements – used, for example, for common but differentiated responsibilities, biotechnology. The developing countries, having recently emerged from colonialism, focused on two related but distinct issues; sovereignty over natural resources within territorial boundaries and on the means of implementation for global environmental concerns. They perceived these elements as enabling them to supplement their development efforts, particularly finance and capacity building. In all these agreements, economic interests predominated, with the industrialized countries shaping the agenda around the intellectual, but not scientific, 'common concern' for the global environment framed in a manner that looked only at the impact of human activity on natural resources rather than their use for human well-being.

5.1 Distinction between global and local concerns

The Stockholm Conference on the Human Environment, in 1972, for the first time made a distinction between global and local environmental problems and recognized the social factors behind many global problems. However, both industrialized and developing countries were uneasy with the resulting compromise because it implied a trade-off between environment and development. The Rio Conference on Environment and Development, in 1992, continued to treat environment as a

---

[1] Parts of this chapter were first published in Sanwal (2004, 2007).

separate policy issue and focused on the promotion of multilateral environmental agreements as the way to make environment and development compatible. The Rio Conference, in 2012, focused on global goals ending this dichotomy, as well as the differentiation between developed and developing countries, with urbanization becoming a mega-trend.

International law was adopted as the framework for global environmental governance in order to reconcile the competing priorities and concerns of industrialized and developing countries. The legal framework was based on the argument that interdependence of responsibilities and solutions required cooperation. The use of law to produce global collective benefits raised the important question of burden-sharing between countries at different levels of economic development. However, the principle of common but differentiated responsibilities that emerged at the Rio Conference, in 1992[2], did not specify what is to be done and paid for by whom and how much, and developing country concerns were shifted to the Preamble of treaties rather than to substantive sections; the differentiation, however, made the treaties politically acceptable to developing countries.

The result has been an uneasy, and ineffective, compromise. The Oxford Handbook of International Environmental Law notes that '... international environmental law continues to struggle with the complaint that it reflects the concerns of developed countries more than those of developing countries ... in the on-going debates over whether developing countries, for example, should preserve biological resources of global concern or should reduce their greenhouse gas emissions and, if so, how much financial support developed countries should provide for such efforts' [Bodansky et al., 2007].

While considerable progress has been made in identifying environmental issues of common concern, even after 40 years of discussion, considerably less progress has been made in developing a shared conceptualization of international cooperation in the North-South context of burden sharing and the means of implementation. This topic arises in every serious discussion in the context of implementing multilateral environmental agreements and is a source of considerable tension, preventing the development of a common understanding of sustainable development.

Finance has really served to deal with political problems rather than the problem itself. For example, a study of international support for adaptation to climate change concluded that the various funds are not technically adequate for responding to developing countries' needs, both because of the complex design of the funds and the poor implementation of the guidance provided by the Conference of the Parties[Mohner et al., 2007]. The European Policy Institute assessing the extent to which the EU has lived up to existing financial commitments made for supporting implementation of the Kyoto Protocol concluded that there is lack of clarity in defining what is new and additional, the information communicated to the UNFCCC is unreliable or not provided, and the annual amount provided to multilateral funds 'falls well short' of the commitment [Pallermaerts et al., 2009].

The situation with respect to technology transfer has been no different. Chapter 34 of Agenda 21, titled 'Transfer of Environmentally Sound Technology, Cooperation and Capacity-Building', contains the earliest reference to the issue, and sets out the key parameters involved. It identifies the need for 'favorable' access to and transfer of environmentally sound technologies to developing countries, as well as building up of endogenous economic, technical and managerial capabilities for the efficient use and further development of transferred technology; and calls on Governments, the private sector and research institutes to play their role in technology transfer (paragraph 34.4). In his closing statement, Maurice Strong, the Secretary-General of the Conference, observed 'on

---

[2] This was the last principle to be agreed, very reluctantly by developed countries, in the Rio Declaration, to which the United States recorded a reservation, and was included in the Climate Convention with a reference to 'respective capabilities' to accommodate that reservation.

technology transfer, we have agreement. But the degree of full commitment to the basic principles of that agreement is still evolving and we cannot yet measure how deep that commitment is' [United Nations, 1992]. Subsequent negotiations have only diluted these provisions and the Sustainable Development Goals, negotiated in August 2014, provided for technology transfer on 'mutually agreed' terms.

Recent work by the United Nations stresses that the key question for the transition to sustainability is to enable developing countries, especially the low-income countries that also have low rates of electricity usage and availability of food, to access, utilize and afford renewable energy and agriculture technologies. The options and challenges associated with the fundamental technological transformation to more efficient and renewable energy technologies and with transforming agricultural technologies to guarantee food security, without further degrading land and water resources, have been analysed. The conclusion is that this technological revolution is different to the earlier ones because of the speed and scale of change needed, governments rather than markets will have to take a leading role. It will require implementation of investment and incentive schemes designed to accelerate green technological innovation, structural change directed towards sustainable production and consumption. Strengthened international cooperation will also be needed if developing countries are to effect the necessary technological transformation without compromising their aspirations regarding growth and poverty reduction [United Nations, 2011]. As against these assertions, a publication co-authored by the OECD concluded that 'there is no visible effect of the Kyoto Protocol on technology transfer' [Dechezlepretre et al., 2008], even though public sector for R&D on renewable energy at \$21 billion in 2010 is much more than \$14 billion expenditure spent by the private sector [Amin, 2011]. There is no agreement in the various multilateral forum – World Trade Organization, World Intellectual Property Organization, and the United Nations Convention on Climate Change – on developing global rules for a new role for governments in enabling the sharing of innovative technologies.

An independent evaluation of aid effectiveness concluded that implementation continues to be looked upon as a technical and bureaucratic process rather than a wider societal engagement to bring about change [Wood et al., 2011]. Overall, the evaluation finds that country ownership has advanced farthest, with alignment and harmonization progressing more unevenly, and managing for development results and mutual accountability advancing least. Lack of transparency emerged as a critical concern. For example, moving from responsibilities to capabilities, it is evident that developing countries are not able to afford the same level of subsidy support for renewable energy technologies as Europe and North America, as they respond to the pressing need for electricity.

Discussions within the World Bank on sustainability illustrate the problems with approaches that had their origin in Agenda 21, the set of programmes agreed at the Rio Conference in 1992. An independent evaluation of the World Bank's support for environmental sustainability after 15 years considered the extent of integration of environmental concerns in economic policies and concluded that the project approach pays insufficient attention to longer term sustainable development and affecting larger forces. The Advisory Panel reviewing the evaluation went beyond a sector-based approach and flagged four areas of strategic importance for promoting sustainable development – transitioning towards a low carbon economy coupled with expanding clean and affordable energy access to the poor; preserving biodiversity while improving rural livelihoods; improving resource productivity; and, protecting water resources, coupled with expanding access to water and sanitation. It also recommended collaboration among a large number of development partners [World Bank, 2008]. This reorientation, to stress the social dimension, reflects both the lack of success with the current approach and an important shift from considering on-going activities to modification of longer term trends to support human well-being.

Moreover, even after 20 years, industrialized countries have not been able to modify longer term trends, as they had agreed to do under Article 4.2(a) of the Climate Convention. In the period 1990–2005, industrialized countries emissions rose by 1.35 Gt, and overall emissions remained limited only because of the reductions of 1.76 Gt in the Economies in Transition following the economic collapse of the Soviet Union [Levin and Bradley, 2010]. According to UN data for the European Commission, emissions from the energy sector, accounting for 80 per cent of total GHG emissions, increased by 2.2 per cent in the period 1990 and 2006 and emissions from energy industries increased by 3.7 per cent – while transportation emissions increased 25.8 per cent [UNFCCC, 2009]. Emissions in Japan and the United States have increased in double digits till 2005. Technological innovations have often led to greater resource consumption.

5.2 Sharing responsibility but not prosperity

The conceptual framework of the United Nations Conference on Environment and Development was based on two interlinked premises. The first was the distinction between global and local environmental problems, as a means of getting countries to help solve problems they did not cause. It continued with the earlier recognition that developing countries, and now also economies in transition, should be supported with financial resources for taking measures leading to global benefits. The second premise was the focus on regulation, and the assumption that global concerns require multilateral treaties for burden sharing as the basis for international cooperation. The framing of environmental issues based on these premises created a dichotomy between international cooperation and national action because it failed to recognize the local causes of global problems and the local impacts of proposed global-level solutions. For example, the 'Hague Report' summarizing the main conclusions of the Hague Symposium, held on 25–27 November 1991, and attended by about 40 leading thinkers from all over the world, identified six basic policy messages, one of which was that 'sustainable development models must avoid the false distinction between national and global environmental problems' [Pronk and Mahbubul Haq, 1992]. This global–local dichotomy has made on-going negotiations on the design and implementation of sustainable development into a diplomatic exercise, in which the single most important issue affecting negotiations has been continuing disagreements first on the subject of financing and later burden sharing.

The framework established the separation of the technological and social processes in international cooperation. Mostafa Tolba, the only developing country head of the United Nations Environment Program since it was established in 1972, perceptively noted that in the early 1970s developing countries were suspicious of considering the global environment as a public issue, in large part because it was at that time defined primarily as a technical problem of pollution abatement [Tolba, 1998]. The Stockholm Conference on the Human Environment, in 1972, attempted to break the impasse by recognizing the socio-economic factors behind many environmental problems, but in terms of special treatment of developing countries, while still dealing with the symptoms rather than the causes of the problem. The Brundtland Commission's coining a new term and the definition of sustainable development in 1987 was an attempt to bridge that political gap, but still within the dominant intellectual and conceptual framework.

The Rio Conference on Environment and Development in 1992, took a different approach towards international cooperation, by focusing on the promotion of multilateral environmental agreements as a way to make environment and development compatible. The large number of interpretative statements from industrialized countries on substantive issues of concern to developing countries clearly indicates that there was at best a fragile consensus, achieved with the use of ambiguous text papering over differences on important issues outside this framework. For example, the principle of common but differentiated responsibilities, considered a key element of international environmental law, has never been accepted by the United States, and it recorded a reservation [United Nations, 1992].

Based on these assumptions, the institutional response that emerged from Rio has also proved inadequate to the task. Rather than discussing how national responses to global concerns will be shaped and integrated, it was based on bargaining over mutual restraints at the international level with periodic review of national communications. The institutional response also focused on pursuing collaboration at the project level, through the Global Environment Facility, on the pattern of development aid projects, largely for capacity building, or, more recently, the Clean Development Mechanism, which is also project based. While this approach avoids conflicts and difficult decisions and is easier to formulate, it does not generate the necessary national political will to address problems that need to be solved in the broader institutional sphere.

The institutional responses further tended to consider the environment as a distinct and separate policy issue, rather than looking at economic activity or social patterns that led to the environmental problem in the first place. This has made the mainstreaming of national environmental policy making difficult, especially as environmental considerations continue to be regarded as potential barriers to economic growth.

Agenda 21, the Programme of Action agreed at Rio, sought to replace the notion of a trade-off between environment and development with national programs listing win-win options. The policy problem was seen largely as one of improving technology in order to reap both economic and environmental benefits. This led to a broad consensus that market-based instruments provide the most efficient means of inducing technical change. But this approach ignored the fact that local problems can attain global dimensions, requiring more strategic and sectoral, rather than just unit or project level, technological change.

With respect to the technology question, since Rio in 1992, the discussion at the scientific and technical level has largely remained limited to calls for more multidisciplinary scientific research, development of indicators and clearing houses, adapting economic instruments, technical fixes, or greater participation of non-state actors to meet the challenges. These are important measures and lead to better understanding of the complex issues. But their treatment has been 'additive' rather than 'integrative' in nature and has been insufficient for the modification of longer-term trends that requires reassessment of underlying social, economic, ecological and governance paradigms. The focus on technological regulation alone also reflects an inadequacy in the policy dialogue in understanding the requirements for mutually supportive transformations. More must be done to bring technology developments more fully into the institutional response to global environmental problems, and on a broader scale.

As a result of collaborative long-term international research efforts, far-reaching technological breakthroughs that can be seen as public goods, like the green revolution in agriculture, can be achieved. Taking a more integrative approach to technology will ensure that further technological developments of this kind occur. Diffusion of these technologies for efficiency, productivity and reduced environmental impacts, particularly in technology-dependent domains like agriculture and energy, would be facilitated by economic growth in developing countries. In this approach, for example, while economic growth may provide a boost to such developments, future energy systems with low carbon dioxide emissions need not be associated with costs higher than those of systems with high emissions [Grubler et al., 2002].

However, since Rio much of the scholarship on international environmental cooperation has been primarily concerned with the formation of regimes and their implementation [Nazli Choucri, 1995; Miles et al., 2002]. Generally adopting a state-centric approach, the focus has been on various aspects of effectiveness, including the strategic use of incentives [Barrett, 2003]. A common conclusion is that the United Nations has a limited capacity to solve problems involving the relationship between environment and development [Young, 1997]. More recently, the concerns have been expressed in terms of the dimensions of effective governance: agency, architecture, accountability and legitimacy; equitable allocation of resources; and adaptiveness of governance systems [Bierman, 2014]. Even after more than 40 years of such deliberations, states are still discussing the global environmental agenda, the effectiveness of institutions and establishing expert groups on scientific and methodological questions to further implementation of multilateral environmental agreements.

The 2002 World Summit on Sustainable Development (WSSD) framed the issue of international cooperation somewhat differently from the Rio Conference in 1992, which adopted an institution-focused approach. It focused much more on the underlying activities that cause environmental degradation, and specifically narrowed in on three areas – the eradication of poverty, modification of consumption and production patterns and the protection of the national resource base for economic growth. The consideration of consumption and production patterns was seen as an essential element of the 'sustainability transition' [Kates et al., 2003]. This approach was based less on the principle of 'common but differentiated responsibilities' and more on the principle of 'shared responsibility and prosperity' to determine 'what should be done' rather than 'who should do what.' The new framework moves beyond Agenda 21 in seeking to resolve the global dimensions of common concerns and to understand how the problems can be solved locally.

Globalization, through the expansion of global trade and investment, also led to a large degree of overlap between so-called global environmental concerns and national sustainable development objectives. Because of this integration, it is now increasingly acknowledged that global-level environmental problems do not necessarily imply that the appropriate governance institutions would be international or intergovernmental. Indeed, the current era of globalization has seen a shift in power from the national level to the global and local levels, for example, cities, and at all levels from the public to the private sector. As human activities that impact the global environment take place in cities and through activities of the citizens and the private sector, there has been a growing recognition that it is important to look beyond states and to identify ways to harness the practical knowledge of business and local communities to alter trends that lead to global scale environmental problems [ILO, 2004].

The experience of the last 40 years of global environmental negotiations suggests that a new and different approach to international cooperation is required to move beyond the current impasse and operationalize sustainable development. This new approach should highlight the dangers of the local–global dichotomy, encourage the development and use of innovative technology as part of a broader formulation of policy, and see globalization as a potentially positive force for the shift of rural populations into urban areas. Cutting across each of these areas, the approach needs to look beyond the state to other stakeholders as contributors to the dialogue on sustainable development that does not rely solely on issue-based networks or state-centred conference diplomacy.

The way the global concern has been framed, and the agenda developed to link environment and development while only considering environment as a global concern has led to the current impasse on the steps to be taken to keep global growth within planetary limits. In the initial deliberations, scientists took the lead, adopted an issue-based approach, and social and economic dimensions were treated as ancillary to the environmental problem. This led to parallel governance processes separating science and policy, with the former focusing on setting the agenda and the latter focusing on bringing together diverging views of industrialized and developing countries on sharing the burden for global environmental protection through multilateral environmental agreements. Problems that have since appeared with the implementation of these agreements are leading to recognition that the social and economic dimensions are as relevant as the environmental aspects, and measures for environmental protection are part of a larger societal response to global change.

A new approach towards international cooperation is emerging that combines the knowledge of practitioners with an emphasis on innovation and exchange of experiences, to take advantage of the opportunities provided by increasing flows of trade, investment and technologies to promote the transition to sustainable development. The recognition at the WSSD and at Rio+20 that these are essential means of implementing sustainable development responds to the concerns of a much larger section of the world population than the earlier approach of imposing restrictions based on multilateral environment agreements on the use of natural resources for safeguarding the interests of future generations. The nature of the shifts experienced over the past decade requires wholly new perspectives for international cooperation that are not based on institutional hierarchies but rather on decentralized networks of multiple actors. Sustainable development is no longer the exclusive concern of governments. It requires an integration of scientific and technological advice with the fragmented knowledge of the various sectors and levels at which policy, technology and behavioural shifts are needed.

The principle of 'shared responsibility and prosperity' recognizes not only the relationships between states but also the relationship between cities, international regimes and non-state actors. It suggests modalities of cooperation between international regimes, including the relationship between trade, environment and development, to be based on forms of cooperation other than legal arrangements, because it assumes synergies rather than conflict [Logomasini, 2006]. It recognizes the potential of the regional level in developing harmonized approaches and sharing experiences for solutions to common problems. It requires institutions oriented towards the broader development and application of new technologies that have characteristics of a public good, involving international partnerships between the public and private sectors.

The common understanding of sustainable development has now changed to focus on urbanization as new insights modify, or even redefine, the multilateral consensus. Therefore, it is appropriate to focus on collaborative strategic approaches to global environmental governance that will unite the diverse constituencies through institutional innovation.

5.3 Reframing the global environmental concern

The defining feature of global environmental governance has been the development of multilateral environmental agreements catalysed by the United Nations. Research attention has consequently focused on institutional design of environmental regimes, ignoring the causes of the problem, which were not covered in these arrangements because the treaties deal with the symptoms of the problem. The research studies have also ignored new policy approaches that are emerging at the national level from the experience with these multilateral environmental agreements, for example, modifying consumption patterns, technology policies and urban design. As the focus has been on 'burden sharing' and related 'economic efficiency' at the global level, limited attention has been paid to actions at the national level that would decouple environmental degradation from economic growth by modifying consumption patterns.

The long impasse over how to achieve sustainable development is largely the product of the way the agenda has been framed in global efforts to link environment and development. The adoption of an issue-based approach, with social and economic dimensions treated as ancillary to the environmental problem, led to reliance on international law to promote international cooperation [Sanwal, 2004]. As environmental degradation has continued unabated, endless international negotiations and treaties have only created the illusion of progress on global environmental threats and the current approach to dealing with global environmental problems is clearly inadequate [Speth, 2004].

Multilateral environmental agreements, by providing forums for regular dialogue, have achieved results in problem solving only in terms of refining and deepening understanding of the problems. This learning has questioned not only the way the issues have been framed but also how the problem-solving strategies are defined and how the results are evaluated. The resulting policy shifts now focus on areas that are very different from the way the agenda has been framed in the past – which focused on responsibilities, rights and obligations of states, and the tensions inherent in burden and benefit sharing. This strategic shift has been evident since 2002, following the World Summit on Sustainable Development, in at least six policy areas.

1. *Arrangements that consider the environment as a distinct and separate policy issue are not suitable means to deal with longer-term transitions that require mainstreaming into national economic development strategies and private sector investment decisions.*

There are numerous early examples where the importance of economic development has been recognized as integral to addressing environmental problems. The Delhi Ministerial Declaration on Climate Change and Sustainable Development, adopted at the eighth session of the Conference of the Parties to the Convention on Climate Change in 2002, linked climate with energy and sustainable development, saw climate change as largely an economic challenge, and recognized the development priority of access to energy services. It also stressed international cooperation for the development of new technologies, through private sector involvement, investments and supportive public policies [FCCC, 2003].

A review of its first 10 years conducted by the sixth session of the Conference of the Parties to the Convention on Biological Diversity in 2002 found that the nature and scope of the measures for implementation require making complex and integrated policy choices that call for coordination and strong political will at the national level. It also found that the Convention will succeed in ensuring sustainable use and level of conservation that benefits everyone only if its importance is recognized in the wider context of economic development and global change, and those mechanisms for engaging the private sector in implementation need to be identified [UNEP/CBD, 2002; UNEP, 2002b]. A further example is the Convention to Combat Desertification, which has been characterized as a multilateral instrument for development cooperation [Kjellen, 2003].

2. *New approaches to global environmental governance incorporate strategic planning, outline future goals, rather than merely describing what could happen within a decade.*

Strategic planning has been adopted in a variety of forums, from governments, to regional bodies, to international treaties and other international mechanisms. The United Kingdom, for example, has announced that it will be integrating reduction of emissions of greenhouse gases as a key element of energy policies [United Kingdom, 2003]. The European Commission has been researching strategic linkages between climate change, technology and energy polices [European Commission, 2003].

Strategic planning has also taken place under international environmental treaty frameworks, such as the Convention on Biological Diversity [UNEP/CBD 2002; UNEP 2002b] and the Multilateral Fund for the Implementation of the Montreal Protocol [UNEP/Ozl 2002; UNEP 2002a]. The Convention on International Trade in Endangered Species of Wild Fauna and Flora (CITES) adopted a strategic plan in 2000 for international trade in wild fauna and flora to be conducted in a sustainable manner, through deeper understanding of the economic issues and involvement of civil society [CITES, 2000]. A re-examination of global biodiversity and forest conservation conventions and mechanisms has been considered to ensure that these foster and support community conservation, through new institutional models [Molnar, 2004]. The non-legally binding Strategic Approach to

International Chemicals Management (SAICAM), adopted in 2006, has a strong cross-sectoral dimension, including involvement of nongovernmental actors and impact on regional processes [Logomasini, 2006].

3. *Role of new considerations, such as markets and external forces, has taken on key importance as the focus shifts from identifying the scale of the damage to implementation of measures to mitigate that damage.*

The Millennium Ecosystem Assessment, published in 2005, confirms the importance of ecosystem services and markets. It argues that 'most resource management decisions are most strongly influenced by ecosystem services entering markets ... the most important public policy decisions affecting ecosystems are often made by agencies and policy arenas other than those charged with protecting ecosystems'. It notes, for example, that 'forest management is influenced more strongly by actions outside the forest sector, such as trade policies and institutions, macroeconomic policies, and policies in other sectors such as agriculture, infrastructure, energy, and mining, than those within it' [MEA, 2005]. Since current arrangements adopt a sectoral approach, it is not surprising that a survey of initial impacts of the Assessment, 1 year after the release of the technical reports, found a mixed policy impact [Reid, 2006].

4. *Globalization and the recognition that investment, technology and trade are essential means of implementation have changed the context within which future actions to protect the environment will be undertaken.*

The Environmental Performance Index, developed to assess effectiveness of polices [Esty, 2006], identifies two main drivers of environmental performance. First, policy choices affect performance, because at every level of development some countries achieve environmental results that far exceed their peers. Second, governance structures are vital to support pollution control and natural resource management. In addition, because of globalization, industrialization and urbanization issues are being redefined in socio-economic terms for example, it is now recognized that addressing biodiversity requires changes in the way resources are used and benefits distributed that goes beyond conservation [Le Prestre 2002; UNEP 2006b]. Increasing global investment flows provide opportunities for the integration of environmental concerns in the broader sustainable development agenda. It is also widely recognized that protecting and managing the natural resource base of economic and social development depends on changing consumption and production patterns and is essential for the eradication of poverty [UN, 2002].

5. *Technology is expected to be a key driver for change, linking knowledge with action.*

Since local environmental problems attain global dimensions when they are caused by human impact whose scale is deep and scope wide, they require technical change at the strategic level, rather than at the unit, or project level. Recent calls for environmental governance reform reflect a realization that, given the scale of global environmental problems, there are limits to what can be achieved through action at the sector level alone. New technologies are also necessary. For example, the goal of the International Partnership for the Hydrogen Economy was to organize, evaluate and coordinate multinational research, development and deployment programs that advance the transition to a global hydrogen economy.

Even a price on carbon dioxide emissions, on its own, will not be enough to deal with global warming [Socolow, 2006]. A paper prepared by the OECD argued that despite efforts spanning 15 years countries have found it extremely difficult to construct a regime that will limit emissions of greenhouse gases, and while these efforts will continue, and 'governments are relying on technology to provide solutions, not treaties' [OECD, 2006].

6. *Entirely new policy instruments oriented towards partnerships between public and private sectors are increasingly important.*

The new information to support environmental policy-making will come from science as well as from practitioners, in particular, the technologies and forms of organization adopted by governments, private sector and civil society. For example, market creation and sharing of benefits is considered the most direct approach to solving the problem of biodiversity decline, by making biodiversity-related policy more compatible with economic development [OECD, 2004]. In this arrangement, there is no need to worry about compliance, as there will only be coordination problems in contrast to cooperation problems. Building an economy that will sustain economic progress requires worldwide effort between governments, private sector and local communities, particularly cities.

5.4 New forms of international cooperation

The scale of current global change, with the re-emergence of China and India, underlines the need for new thinking on global environmental policy. At the United Nations Conference on the Human Environment, held in Stockholm in 1972, it was argued that '... the major environmental problems of the developing countries are essentially of a different kind. They are predominantly problems that reflect the poverty and very lack of development of their societies ... these are problems no less than those of industrial pollution' [Founex, 1971]. These concerns shaped the conceptual framework of global environment governance in the last century – treating the environment as a separate policy issue and creating a distinction between global and local environmental problems. This paradigm is losing its relevance because of changes in the global political economy, with the spread of urbanization.

Sustainable development gained prominence in the international lexicon in 1987, in the Report of the World Commission on Environment and Development, *Our Common Future* [World Commission on Environment and Development, 1987]. As the Secretary-General of the World Commission, Jim MacNeill, has recently pointed out that Report defined sustainable development in several ways – ethical, social and ecological. But only one definition, the one focused on intergenerational equity, grabbed the headlines. The Report also put forward a number of broad directions that development must take if it is to be sustainable. The failure thus far to merge environment with economics in the process of decision-making has been characterized by MacNeill as the 'forgotten imperative of sustainable development' because consumption and production factors were not considered the central element [MacNeill, 2006].

As a society goes through the processes of urbanization, industrialization and services economy, public concern, rules, rights and willingness to pay shift in favour of environmental protection, which is seen in terms of natural resource use [Cole, 2005]. In 2005, the combined output of China, India and other developing countries accounted for more than half of world GDP, with countries other than China and India together making up three-quarters of the total increase in developing countries GDP [The Economist, 2006]. It has been forecast that Brazil, China, India and Russia would be the worlds' six largest economies by the middle of this century [Wilson 2005]. These countries are set to give the world economy its biggest boost in history, because it is markedly different from the industrial revolution which involved only one-third of the world's population. The total number of cars in China and India combined could rise from around 30 million today to 750 million by 2040—more than all the cars on the world's roads today. The price of oil has doubled in the last 3 years, and buses and light rail have seen a sharp growth while sales of SUVs have declined sharply in America, forcing changes in lifestyles in ways that reduces the environmental damage. As incomes rise in developing countries with urbanization, city dwellers worry more about pollution and natural resource use – this is now happening in China. China and India are preparing national programs to mitigate and adapt to climate change and are willing to discuss these concerns at the global level. At the same time, they are also looking at new forms of urban design as their rural population shifts to the urban middle class.

The emerging global consensus around a new paradigm has three implications for the relevance of, and interactions between, international organizations, governments and non-state actors. First, the focus on results marks a shift from the earlier emphasis on establishing global norms to actions that are demand-driven and country-based, and do not require multilateral agreement. Second, the recognition of the key role of capital markets and innovation in economic growth shifts the focus from government or multilateral aid to investment as the driver of international cooperation and the spread of new technologies. This is significant, as the single most important factor affecting international cooperation has been continuing disagreement on the nature and amount of financial assistance. Third, implementation requires going beyond traditional forms of cooperation between nation-states to global networks of state and non-state actors, particularly the private sector and cities sharing innovative technologies and urban design experiences. For example, tools such as life cycle analysis have not been found to be useful and have not even been mentioned in the guidelines of the Global Reporting Initiative 2006 [UNEP, 2006a].

At the same time, the world community expects the United Nations to continue to provide intellectual leadership by developing a new conceptual approach relating to goals, strategies and institutions for a global sustainable development policy for the current century, just as it did four decades ago to meet the environmental challenges of the twentieth century [Berg, 2006]. The strategic framework for managing global environmental change should really incorporate new tools and instruments, including knowledge management, involvement of the private sector, regional and city-based thematic partnerships and cooperation amongst developing countries. It should also incorporate an operational focus for an approach that provides a differentiated response to different categories of countries based on levels of development. The challenge in supporting countries in formulating a long-term vision for environmentally sustainable and equitable global growth is to strengthen national institutions with new knowledge, as the basis for dealing with drivers and trends leading to global environmental problems.

The focus of the strategic framework for the global environment needs to shift in the direction of developing a common understanding of welfare gains from ecosystem services. Such a shift will support integration of environmental issues in economic and social policies and will help to address selected environmental challenges. Framing issues around global and national ecosystem services will determine strategic goals, impact on other policy arenas and alter policy objectives. For example, ecosystem services can be reflected through recognition of their limited capacity to absorb waste (carbon dioxide, chemicals), as an integral part of the incomes of the poor (forests), as the economic and social gains from new products (biodiversity), and augmentation of water supply and agricultural productivity (watershed management). The global environmental-sustainable development strategy will then focus on influencing the drivers of economic growth, that is, urbanization, capital markets and institutional innovation.

Ecosystem services are the most direct way that nature affects the population shift and transition from rural to urban areas, but many ecosystem services do not flow directly through markets or lack a market price that reflects their full economic value. For example, at the local level, the livelihoods of the rural poor, natural resource needs of the urban middle class and the conservation and sustainable use of natural resources are so intimately intertwined that they are best addressed through an integrated approach, irrespective of whether the primary motivation is development or environmental conservation. It is estimated that environmental wealth accounts for 26 per cent of the total wealth of low-income countries, versus 13 per cent of wealth in middle-income countries and only 2 per cent of wealth in developed countries [Hamilton, 2005]. Even though environmental sustainability has been one of the Millennium Development Goals, a focus on environmental sustainability is lacking in most poverty reduction strategy papers, and only the Least Developed Countries seem to be really concerned about natural resources [Bojo, 2003]. It is the local NGOs in developing countries, as well as researchers, have highlighted the gap between global policy-making institutions and local resource-users [Adger, 2001]. Garnering the political will to halt ecosystem degradation caused by increasing demand from city dwellers will depend on demonstrating to policy-makers and society at large the full contribution made by ecosystems to the shift out of poverty and into the middle class as well as to national economic growth and urban lifestyles.

The lead is now being taken by a very different set of non-state actors. For example, Goldman Sachs, a global investment bank, adopted a comprehensive environmental policy that acknowledges the value of ecosystem services and is funding a new Centre for Environmental Markets for broadening the application of social and environmental factors into loaning and investment activities [Piasecki, 2006]. JPMorgan has brought out a corporate bond index designed to reduce exposure to issuers' financial risks arising from climate change [JPMorgan, 2007]. As part of the buyout deal of a Texas power utility, the private equity groups have agreed not to build eight coal burning power plants, invest $400 million in helping consumers to use energy more efficiently, build a pilot 'clean coal' plant and invest more in alternate energy. The NGO Environmental Defense greeted the new strategy as a 'watershed moment in America's fight against global warming'[The Economist, 2007]. Companies are seeking competitive advantage in a carbon constrained future, even though governments are offering little guidance on how policies might change [Lash, 2007].

Environmental action is important for the private sector as the transition to sustainable development will both alter existing markets and create new ones. The call for regulation to address the impacts of climate change is now coming from management consultancies, investment banks and reinsurance companies, as the viability of the global economy depends on government intervention to promote the necessary changes in the world's urban, transport and energy infrastructure [Hoffman, 2006]. The focus of analytical work is shifting from population/scarcity issues and ecosystem management to use in cities and distribution of natural resources along with harnessing the power of entrepreneurs. For example, there are case studies combining private investment with sustainable use of natural resources in a way that produces a satisfactory return on the capital invested [Price Waterhouse Coopers, 2007].

In the future partnerships between governments, scientists, private sector and nongovernmental organizations will develop commercial solutions for environmental problems. New multilateral institutions will gain authority as nodes of networks dealing with specific technological and institutional issues, rather than issues related to the scarcity of natural resources. Analysis of good practices will help to define how and under what circumstances the public and private sectors can work more closely together, to gain a better understanding of what works and for consideration of initiatives to support government action.

It is also important to link local viability, distinctive perspectives and global benefits. If a problem has been identified at the global level, it does not mean that solutions can only be found at that level. The potential of the regional, and sub-regional or city level, for sharing lessons learned on solutions to common problems is to be encouraged. A promising approach is through committees of experts on the OECD model, for example, facilitating implementation of clusters of Multilateral Environmental Agreements. South–South cooperation around science and technology on issues such as technology transfer, which have traditionally divided countries, will not only serve to bridge the political divide between developed and developing countries that presently characterizes the multilateral system, but also provide elements for sharing prosperity.

The United Nations will, therefore, need to play a catalytic role at three levels. First, it should undertake analytical work to inform the policy dialogue especially with regard to the economic impact of global ecosystem services on human well-being in the shift of rural populations to urban areas. Second, it should promote dissemination of good practices to support implementation, such as institutional strategies for improved consumption patterns, new markets and practices and information on technologies for environment-related infrastructure. Third, it should promote new programs at the regional and global levels in partnership with the private sector, civil society and cities. An example is the Expert Group on Climate Change and Sustainable Development, catalysed by the United Nations to recommend innovative approaches for mitigation and adaptation to climate change for consideration by the United Nations Commission on Sustainable Development [SEG, 2007]. Another example is the identification of urbanization for discussion in the first meeting of the High-Level Policy Forum established at Rio+20, in 2012, to replace the Commission on Sustainable Development, which was held in July 2014.

The United Nations is at a crossroads as it seeks to identify the particular contribution it can make in supporting international cooperation for environmentally sustainable global growth or sustainable development. A new conceptual framework provides opportunities for the multilateral system to act as a knowledge broker and nurture concepts that are not based on the traditional divides but on mutual supportiveness; develop new problem-solving strategies that can have an influence on other policy arenas; work with a range of actors; devolve governance to the regional level and deliver a differentiated response to countries at varying levels of development. The defining feature of global environmental governance and sustainable development in this century will not be multilateral environmental agreements but interactive clusters of institutions and processes galvanizing capital markets, enabling sharing of new technologies and supporting societal action in cities.

The notion of a 'common concern' around the global environment will need to be replaced with a clear means-ends continuum or 'theory of change' underpinning the new framework around global goals. The ultimate end of the Sustainable Development Goals in combination and how the goals would contribute to achieving that ultimate end, would require a common understanding of what world would look like once all the goals are fully achieved. Policy makers, therefore, need to agree on an overarching global goal as a meta-goal – "a prosperous, high quality of life that is equitably shared and sustainable" [ICSU, ISSC, 2015].

References

Adger, W. Neil, Tor A. Benjaminsen, Katrin Brown, and Hanne Sverstad. 2001. 'Advancing a Political Ecology of Global Environmental Discourses'. *Development and Change* 32 (4): 681–715.

Amin, Adnan. 2011. Harnessing the Potential of Renewable Energy, article in Climate Change Policy and Practice, IISD, July 22 2011.

Barrett, S. 2003. *Environment and Statecraft: The Strategy of Environment Treaty-Making*. Oxford University Press, New York.

Berg, Robert J. 2006. 'The UN Intellectual History Project: Review of a Literature'. *Global Governance* 12: 325–41.

Biermann, Frank. 2014. *Earth System Governance: World Politics in the Anthropocene*. MIT Press.

Bodansky, Daniel, Jutta Brunne, and Ellen Hay. 2007. *The Oxford Handbook of International Environmental Law.* Oxford University Press.

Bojo J. and R. C. Reddy. 2003. 'Poverty Reduction Strategies and the Millennium Development Goal on Environmental Sustainability: Opportunities for Alignment'. *Environmental Economic Series*. Paper no 92. Environment Department Papers. Washington, DC: World Bank.

CITES. 2000. Decision 11.1, Strategic Plan for the Convention, Decisions of the Conference of the Parties to CITES.

Cole, Mathew A., and Eric Neumayer. 2005. Environment Policy and Environmental Kuznets Curve: Can Developing Countries escape the Detrimental Consequences of Economic Growth? In *Handbook of Global Environmental Politics,* edited by Peter Dauvergne. Cheltenham, UK: Edward Elgar.

Dechezlepretre, Antonie, Matthieu Glachant, and Yann Maniere (of CERNA) and Ivan Hascic, Nick Johnstone (OECD). 2008. Invention and Transfer of Climate Change Mitigation Technologies on a Global Scale: A study Drawing on Patent Data, December 2008.

Depledge, Joanna. 2006. 'The Opposite of Learning: Ossification in the Climate Change Regime'. *Global Environmental Politics* 6 (1): 1–22.

Esty, Daniel, Marc A. Levy, Tanja Srebotnjak, Alexander de Sherbin, Christine H. Kim, and Bridget Anderson. 2006. *Pilot 2006 Environmental Performance Index.* New Haven, CT: Yale Centre for Environmental Law and Policy.

European Commission. 2003. *World Energy, Technology and Climate Policy Outlook—2030.* Directorate General for Research—Energy, European Commission.

FAO. 2007. *State of the World's Forests.* Rome: Food and Agriculture Organization of the United Nations.

FCCC. 2003. Delhi Ministerial Declaration on Climate Change and Sustainable Development, Report of the Conference of the Parties on its Eighth Session, held at New Delhi, Decision 1/CP.8, FCCC/CP/2002/7/Add.1, 2003.

Founex. 1971. Development and Environment: Report and Working Papers of Experts Convened by the Secretary General of the United Nations Conference on the Human Environment, June 4–12, 1971, Founex, Switzerland.

Grubler, Arnuf, Nebojsa Nakicenovic, and William D. Nordhaus. 2002. *Technological Change and the Environment.* Washington, DC: Resources for the Future.

Hamilton, K., G. Ruta, A. Markandaya, S. Pedroso, P. Silva, M. Ordoubadi, G-M Lange, L. Tajibaeva, L. Gronnevet, and M. Dyoulgerov. 2005. *Where is the Wealth of Nations? Measuring Capital for the 21st Century.* Washington, DC: World Bank.

Hoffman, Andrew J. 2006. Getting Ahead of the Curve: Corporate Strategies that Address Climate Change. Report prepared for Pew Centre on Global Climate Change. Arlington, VA, October.

ICSU, ISSC (2015): Review of the Sustainable Development Goals: The Science Perspective. Paris: International Council for Science (ICSU).

ILO. 2004. *A Fair Globalization: Creating Opportunities for All.* International Labour Organisation Geneva: ILO Publications.

JPMorgan. 2007. 'JENI-Carbon Beta'. North American Corporate Research, 27 February.

Kates, Robert W., and Thomas M. Parris. 2003. Characterizing a Sustainability Transition: Goals, Targets, Trends, and Driving Forces. *Proceedings of the National Academy of Sciences* 100 (14).

Kjellen, Bo. 2003. The Saga of the Convention to Combat Desertification: The Rio/Johannesburg Process and the Global Responsibility for the Dryland's. *RECIEL* 12 (2): 127–132.

Lash, Jonathan, and Fred Wellington. 2007. 'Competitive Advantage on a Warming Planet'. *Harvard Business Review*, March.

Le Prestre, Philippe. 2002. 'The Convention of Biological Diversity: Negotiating the Turn to Effective Implementation'. *ISUMA: Canadian Journal of Policy Research* Fall: 92–98.

Levin, Kelly and Bradley, Rob. 2010. Comparability of Annex I Emission Reduction Pledges, Working Paper. World Resources Institute, February 2010.

Logomasini, Angela. 2006. The UN's Strategic Approach to Chemicals Management. Paper No. 104. Washington, DC: Competitive Enterprise Institute, March.

MacNeill, Jim. 2006. The Forgotten Imperative of Sustainable Development. *Environmental Policy and Law* 36(3–4): 167–170.

Mee, Laurence D. 2005. The Role of UNEP and UNDP in Multilateral Environmental Agreements. *International Environmental Agreements* 5: 227–263.

Miles, Edward, Arild Underdal, Steinar Andresen, Jorgen Wettestad, Jon Birger Skjaerseth, and Elaine M. Carlin. 2002. *Environmental Regime Effectiveness: Confronting Theory with Evidence*. Cambridge, MA: The MIT Press.

MEA. 2005. *Ecosystems and Human Well-being: Synthesis*. Millennium Ecosystem Assessment Washington, DC: Island Press.

Mohner, A and R.J.T. Klein. 2007. *The Global Environment Facility: Funding for Adaptation or Adapting to Funds?* Stockholm Environment Institute.

Molnar, Augusta, Sara J. Scherr, and Arvind Khare. 2004. *Who Conserves the World's Forests? Community Driven Strategies to Protect Forests and Respect Rights*. Washington, DC: Forest Trends.

Nazli Choucri, Nazli. ed. 1995 *Global Accord: Strategies for Sustainability and Institutional Innovation*. Cambridge, MA: The MIT Press.

_____. 2006. Do we have the Right R&D Priorities and Programmes to Support the Energy Technologies of the Future? Report prepared by Richard Doornbosch and Rt. Hon. Simon Upton. SG/SD/RT(2006)1. Paris: OECD.

OECD. 2004. *Handbook of Market Creation for Biodiversity: Issues in Implementation*. Paris: OECD.

Pallermaerts, Mark, and Jonathan Armstrong. 2009. Financial Support to Developing Countries for Climate Change Mitigation and Adaptation: Is the EU Meeting its Commitments? Institute for European Environmental Policy, Brussels, January 2009.

Piasecki, Bruce, and Peter Erasmus. 2007. 'A Better Shade of Green for Wall Street'. *Wall Street Journal*, April 3.

Price Waterhouse Coopers. 2007. Sustainable Investments for Conservation: The Business Case for Biodiversity. Price Waterhouse Coopers.

Pronk, Jan, and Mahbubul Haq. 1992. *The Hague Report: Sustainable Development From Concept to Action*. The Hague, The Netherlands: Ministry of Development Cooperation, United Nations Development Programme, and the United Nations Conference on Environment and Development.

Reid, Walter. 2006. *Millennium Ecosystem Assessment: Survey of Impacts*. Stanford, CA: Stanford Institute for the Environment.

Sanwal Mukul. 2004. 'Trends in Global Environmental Governance: The Emergence of a Mutual Supportiveness Approach to Achieve Sustainable Development'. *Global Environmental Politics* 4:4.

Sanwal Mukul. 2007. 'Evolution of Global Environmental Governance and the United Nations' *Global Environmental Politics* 7(3).

SEG. 2007. Confronting Climate Change: Avoiding the Unmanageable and Managing the Unavoidable. Scientific Expert Group on Climate Change. Report prepared for the 15th session of the United Nations Commission on Sustainable Development, Sigma Xi, Research Triangle Park, NC, and the United Nations Foundation, Washington, DC, February.

Socolow, Robert H., and Stephen W. Pacala. 2006. A Plan to Keep Carbon in Check. *Scientific American* 295(3): 50–57.

Speth, James Gustav. 2004. *Red Sky at Morning: America and the Crisis of the Global Environment—A Citizen's Agenda for Action*. New Haven, CT: Yale University Press.

The Economist. 2006. 'The New Titans: A survey of the world economy,' September 16.

_____. 2007. 'Eco-warriors at the gate,' March 3.

Tolba, Mostafa K. 1998. *Global Environmental Diplomacy: Negotiating Environmental Agreements for the World, 1973–1992*. Cambridge, MA: MIT Press.

UN JIU. 2008. Management Review of Environmental Governance within the United Nations System, JIU/REP/2008/3. Joint Inspection Unit, United Nations, Geneva.

UNEP. 2002a. Report of the Fourteenth Meeting of the Parties to the Montreal Protocol on Substances that Deplete the Ozone Layer, 2002. UNEP/Ozl/Pro/14/9.

_____. 2002b. Report of the Open-ended Intersessional Meeting on the Strategic Plan, National Reports and Implementation of the Convention on Biological Diversity, 2002. UNEP/CBD/COP/6/5.

_____. 2006a. Industry as a Partner for Sustainable Development. UNEP, October.

_____. 2006b. Report of the Conference of the Parties of the Convention on Biodiversity, 2006.

_____. 2006c. Summary of the Second Biodiversity Outlook, 2006. UNEP/CBD/COP/8/12.

UNEP. 2011. Global Trends in Renewable Energy Investment 2011: Analysis of trends and Issues in the Financing of Renewable Energy, United Nations Environment Programme and Bloomberg Finance, 2011. UNEP/CBD/COP/6/26.

UNFCCC. 2009. Report of the Individual Review of Greenhouse Gas Inventories of the European Community submitted in 2007 and 2008, FCCC/ARR/2008/EC dated 29 April 2009.

United Kingdom Government. 2003. *Energy White Paper 2003.*

United Nations, 1992. Report of the UN Conference on Environment and Development, Rio de Janeiro, 3–14 June 1992. United Nations Publication, Sales No. E.93.I.8 and corrigenda.

United Nations. 1972. Report of the UN Conference on the Human Environment, Stockholm, 5–16 June 1972. United Nations Publication, Sales No. E.73.II.A.14 and corrigenda.

United Nations. 2002. Report of the World Summit on Sustainable Development, Johannesburg, South Africa, 26 August–4 September 2002. UN/A/CONF.199/20.

United Nations. 2011. *World Economic and Social Survey: The Great Green Technological Transformation.* Department of Economic and Social Affairs, United Nations, New York 2011.

Wilson, Dominic, and Roopa Purushotham. 2005. *Dreaming with BRICS.* Goldman Sachs.

Wood, B; Betts, J; Etta, F; Gayfer, J; Kabell, D; Ngwira, N; Sagasti, F; Samaranayake, M. *The Evaluation of the Paris Declaration, Final Report*, Copenhagen, May 2011.

World Bank. 2008. Environmental Sustainability: An evaluation of World Bank Group Support. The Independent Evaluation Group, The World Bank, 2008.

World Commission on Environment and Development. 1987. *Our Common Future.* Oxford, UK: Oxford University Press.

Young, Oran R., ed. 1997. *Global Governance: Drawing Insights from Environmental Experience.* Cambridge, MA: The MIT Press.

CLIMATE POLICY: GLOBAL TO NATIONAL

'Change in the Earth's climate and its adverse effects are a common concern of humankind'

United Nations Framework Convention on Climate Change, 1992.

'The social sciences must help to fundamentally reframe climate and global environmental change from a physical into a social problem'.

ISSC/UNESCO, 2013, World Social Science Report 2013: Changing Global Environments. OECD Publishing and UNESCO Publishing, Paris.

'Behavior, lifestyle and culture have a considerable influence on energy use and associated emissions … in particular when complementing technological and structural change. Emissions can be substantially lowered through changes in consumption patterns, adoption of energy savings measures, dietary change and reduction in food wastes. … outcomes seen as equitable can lead to more effective cooperation.'

IPCC, Fifth Assessment Synthesis Report, 2014.

'Choices made in cities today about long lived urban infrastructure will determine the extent and impact of climate change, our ability to achieve emission reductions and our capacity to adapt to changing circumstances'.

International Energy Agency, 'Cities and Climate Change: Policy Perspectives – National governments enabling local action', September 2014

"… the Presidents of China and the United States announced their respective post-2020 actions on climate change, recognizing that these actions are part of the longer range effort to transition to low-carbon economies, mindful of the global temperature goal of 2°C. The United States intends to achieve an economy-wide target of reducing its emissions by 26%–28% below its 2005 level in 2025 and to make best efforts to reduce its emissions by 28%. China intends to achieve the peaking of CO_2 emissions around 2030 and to make best efforts to peak early and intends to increase the share of non-fossil fuels in primary energy consumption to around 20% by 2030. Both sides intend to continue to work to increase ambition over time …: In response to growing urbanization and increasingly significant greenhouse gas emissions from cities and recognizing the potential for local leaders to undertake significant climate action, China and the United States will establish a new initiative on Climate-Smart/Low-Carbon Cities…"

China-US Joint Announcement on Climate Change Beijing, China, 12 November 2014

Political Origins of Climate Policy

6

Climate change is being reframed as the scientific understanding shifts its focus from carbon dioxide emissions since 1850 to the growth of emissions till 2050, because policy decisions taken now will shape the future trajectory, till stabilization of concentration levels takes place with developing countries aging as fast as industrialized countries are now aging. As climate policy moves from the global to the national level the understanding of the issue, the way longer term perspectives are integrated in urbanization and the parameters of international cooperation are being redefined to focus on national actions. The prospects for success are greatest if China, India and United States pull together to forge a new vision for sustainable economic development in the twenty-first century [WWI, 2013][1].

The shift is taking place in five areas – a concern with climate variability, rather than change, for the period up to 2050 when three-quarter of the world population would be living in cities; framework based on cumulative emissions of the past and the future, rather than a focus on current emissions, and how they could change over time as part of the carbon budget, which will be a range rather than a number; moving away from considering short-term policies and measures to long-term drivers for natural resource use, focusing on transformations; rejecting multilaterally determined national emissions reduction obligations, reflecting the symptoms, to nationally determined actions for dealing with the causes, while also shifting from risk management to global goals; modifying climate policy to understand the carbon budget as a monitoring, rather than allocation, tool as countries accord primacy to meeting the energy needs of the urban middle class in determining the scale and scope of the measures to be taken.

The reframing reflects social science research on global megatrends shaping the structure of society. The limitations of quantitative risk analysis, forecasting and the inter-linkages are becoming apparent because increasingly sophisticated computer models depend on data that is not available and assumptions require value judgments to be made. Current approaches to risk analysis and quantitative forecasting are problematic since the systems addressed and their dynamics are not well understood, assumptions are often non-transparent, and necessary data are not always available [EEA, 2011]. It is not just the uncertainty and complexity but also the recognition of diversity that is driving the shift away from universality, and reliance on markets, to longer term transformations at the national level and behavioural change. Recent research establishes that growth and climate

---

[1] Parts of this section was first published in Sanwal (2009, 2010).

protection are rival objectives only in high-income countries, which are called upon to modify their overuse of natural resources to enable a global sustainability transition. The political difficulties of this reality are obvious, and the crucial question for multilateral cooperation in climate policy is how far from the global welfare and climate optimum is it necessary to deviate in order to win acceptance in industrialized countries of global sustainable development.

There has been no globally determined action on climate change over a period of more than 20 years because ethics and fairness requires significant action by industrialized countries to decarbonize to a far greater degree than other nations. Whether responsibility for climate change should be determined by a country's full emissions or just some of them, and whether it is a resource-sharing problem of a common resource distributing national entitlements or a burden-sharing exercise assigning national emissions targets implies the application of justice principles to one or the other, determines how to measure climate change and helps identify potential solutions. Equity could refer to per capita national emissions entitlements, the sharing of decarbonization burdens, in terms of mitigation costs or percentage reductions in relation to a baseline. The Kyoto Protocol is a modified version of this burden-sharing approach, with national emissions caps assigned an average reduction of 5 per cent from 1990 baselines. This version does nothing to change the highly inequitable resource sharing between industrialized and developing countries, and the question remains how much a country's past emissions record and future emissions should be taken into account in determining the adequacy of national actions [ISSC and UNESCO, 2013]. The political problem with determining an allocation criteria has led to a re-framing: '... The solution to climate change is energy policy. If we make the right choices about how we build buildings, how we transport people, what we do with respect to providing electricity and power to our countries, this problem gets solved' [Kerry, 2014].

The conceptual framework has evolved slowly, but steadily. Climate change first came onto the global agenda in the Stockholm Programme of Action in 1972. With limited progress under the Climate Convention (1992), Kyoto Protocol (1997) and Copenhagen Accord (2009), the theme of the Rio+20 World Summit (2012) was the transition to a low-carbon economy in the context of eradication of poverty and sustainable development. The Sustainable Development Goals, negotiated in August 2014, include a goal to 'take urgent action to combat climate change and its impacts ... and ... integrate climate change measures into national policies, strategies, and planning', signifying a shift away from legally binding commitments to global goals as the basis for international cooperation to meet the challenge. The new climate treaty will no longer be the fulcrum for climate policy, as its relevance shifts to becoming the central forum for monitoring the status of emissions of greenhouse gases (GHGs), with States beginning to take autonomous action.

After a 20-year period of continuing negotiations, since 1992, with prospects for legally binding commitments fading, the global concern around climate change is now being re-framed in terms of modifying longer term trends in consumption and production patterns. This shift may succeed in securing international cooperation in a manner that the focus on percentage reductions in GHGs, which considered symptoms rather than the causes of climate change, was not able to achieve. Reconciling competing resource needs with respect to maintaining lifestyles of a small part of the global middle class and requirements of the rest of the middle class as they emerge out of poverty is at the core of the climate negotiations, and the global biophysical limits to growth should mean lifestyle changes not depriving the poor. New rules to establish national carbon budgets as a monitoring tool, shifting the focus from flows to stocks of carbon in the atmosphere now suggested by the Intergovernmental Panel on Climate Change (IPCC), will be more scientific, lead to sustainability of global well-being and blur the North–South divide.

The climate negotiations at Copenhagen, in 2008, were a turning point because China took the initiative to express views different to those expressed by industrialized countries and questioned the framework to partition the atmosphere that was being suggested. It also brought out that the outcomes of multilateral diplomacy through conferences could no longer be determined by a small group of countries in the G7. Redistribution has so far been kept out of the agenda of the United Nations, and new global goals and rules to share both responsibility and prosperity can lead to a new world order that will also be more equitable. The unresolved issue is whether in writing their urban future China and India will shape an alternative global vision adopting a sustainable development perspective.

China's emissions are now higher than the emissions of the United States. The two largest emitters, responsible for over one-third of global emissions, arrived at a climate deal, in November 2014, breaking the deadlock on what developing countries should do. The deal re-frames the issue away from a single peaking year to where a country's past and future emissions record is taken into account in determining the adequacy of national actions. The United States has agreed to cut net GHG emissions by 12–14 per cent of 1990 levels and China could increase its emissions by around 30 per cent till 2030, by then China will complete its urbanization and it will have a GDP per capita of $20,000 [CITI Bank, 2014]; differentiated levels of economic growth and demographic change should result in both countries achieving equal levels of well-being by 2050, differently defined by each country for itself.

China will increase the non-fossil fuel share of all energy to around 20 per cent by 2030, putting up additional 800–1,000 GW of nuclear, wind, solar and other zero emission generation capacity – more than all the coal-fired power plants that exist in China today and close to total current electricity generation capacity in the United States; in 2014, in China renewable energy investments exceeded $83 billion, followed by the United States at $38 billion. Shifting the criteria for review of actions taken by developing countries from emissions reduction to longer term transformations, in an increasingly interdependent world, is more important for the social and economic development of growing economies than for the mature economies of industrialized countries. It also reframes the earlier sole emphasis on environmental risk, or increases in average global temperature, with the requirement of human well-being within planetary limits, at comparable levels of development for all countries.

6.1 Understanding global carbon management

Natural and human factors drive climate change by altering the Earth's energy budget. Emissions represent what goes into the atmosphere, as about a quarter of the total emissions are taken up by the oceans and another quarter by the biosphere, in this way reducing the amount of carbon dioxide in the atmosphere. Concentrations represent what remains in the atmosphere after the complex system of interactions between the atmosphere, biosphere and the oceans and determine the increase in global temperature.

At present there is a net uptake of the Sun's energy by the Earth system; that is, more energy is entering the Earth system than is being lost back to space. Along with the waste carbon dioxide from human energy use, the outcome is an increase in heat energy stored by the Earth. This imbalance is driving the rise in global temperature, and the most recent report of the Intergovernment Panel on Climate Change [IPCC, AR5], notes that over 90 per cent of the energy accumulated between 1971 and 2010, that is, excess heat, are stored in the ocean which has also absorbed 30 per cent of the carbon dioxide emissions; only 1 per cent of the increase in energy is stored in the atmosphere. That report concluded that the total cumulative carbon dioxide emissions since the start of the industrial era would need to be limited to about 1,000 Gt of carbon for emissions from human activities to result in a maximum warming of less than 2°C relative to pre-industrial levels. About half of this amount had already been emitted by 2011, and a significant proportion of climate change is probably irreversible on a human timescale. Depending on the size of emission cuts, the rise in global mean surface temperature in the atmosphere at land and ocean surfaces by the end of the twenty-first century is more than two-thirds certain to be between the ranges 2.6–4.8°C and 0.3–1.7°C. By 2050, as by then three-quarter of the global population will be in cities, urban design and related consumption patterns will be the key global concern [IPCC, 2014].

According to the Fifth Assessment Report of the IPCC average global temperatures rose by 0.85°C in 1880–2012; sea levels rose by 3.2 mm a year in 1993–2010, twice as fast as in 1901–2010; the acidity of the ocean's surface has risen by 26 per cent since 1800. Natural systems have been impacted; Arctic sea ice is shrinking by around 4 per cent a decade, the Greenland and Antarctic ice sheets are losing mass and marine species are shifting to find cooler waters in the Poles. There is no evidence of impacts on human welfare; 'low confidence' that the frequency and extent of floods have been affected by climate change, and while heat and drought may have reduced yields of maize and wheat, there has been little effect on rice and soya beans. Most importantly, the climate has exceptionally long response times and the concentration of carbon dioxide in the atmosphere means that the expected rise in surface temperatures till 2050 will not be disruptive.

Whether and when the current climate variability will turn into significant climate change remains uncertain. Geological and historical records show that there have been climate shifts in the past independent of human activity. Observations of the oceans, which absorb most of the heat from increased temperatures, are not available for a long enough period to understand changes in the oceans and effect on climate. Details of processes such as evaporation and the flow of radiation through clouds are uncertain and can enhance or reduce the climate impact. Understanding these uncertainties is important for policy, because human additions to carbon dioxide in the atmosphere by the middle of the twenty-first century are expected to directly shift the atmosphere's natural greenhouse effect by only 1–2 per cent. There are also computational challenges in describing the dynamics and interactions of the various components of the Earth system – the atmosphere, the oceans, the land, the ice and the biosphere of living things – some parts of the models rely on known physical laws while other parts involve technically informed estimation, with marked differences in their details, projections and the energy balance [IPCC, 2013].

For example, even though the human influence on climate was much smaller in the past, the models do not account for the fact that the rate of global sea-level rise 70 years ago was as large as what we observe today – about one foot per century. There is also a lot we do not know; Arctic warming is occurring twice as fast as the global average, while in the Antarctic sea, ice has expanded over 20 million km^2 for the first time in the past 35 years, and the World Meteorological Organization notes it is too soon to say whether the annual maximum has been reached. There are scientific uncertainties as well as data uncertainties in projecting the future.

Climate change influences the Earth's surface temperature, the sea level as well as the amount, timing and intensity of precipitation. On land, these changes affect freshwater availability and quality, surface-water run-off and groundwater recharge, and the spread of water-borne disease vectors. Many coastal zones, mountains and areas prone to river floods are particularly vulnerable, as are urban areas where most of the population will be living by mid-century. New opportunities may also arise in some sectors and temperate regions. The major impacts of climate change will only become visible several decades from now, and public opinion and policy responses are both made difficult as there is also no scientific agreement on how much warming would result from increased concentrations of greenhouse gases in the atmosphere by 2050. Climate change over the next few decades is largely governed by levels of greenhouse gases already in the atmosphere and the amount of mitigation action assumed in scenarios has little impact in the near-term, as around 2050 all countries should be urbanized and with middle class populations living in a built environment whose design will shape both mitigation and adaptation.

As the Intergovernmental Panel on Climate Change points out, 'anthropogenic greenhouse gas emissions are mainly driven by population size, economic activity, lifestyle, energy use, land-use patterns, and technology and climate policy', and cumulative emissions of carbon dioxide will largely determine global mean surface warming only by the late twenty-first century and beyond. Carbon dioxide emissions have tripled between 1970 and 2010, constituting three-fourth of the increase in total greenhouse gases, and half the increase in cumulative concentration of carbon dioxide in the atmosphere has occurred in the last 40 years. Buildings use the most energy and account for one-third of emissions, while transport and industry each account for a little more than one-quarter of final energy use and emissions. In 1850, in a rural agricultural economy and society, carbon dioxide emissions were still around 2 Gt per year, of which emissions from land-use changes were responsible for around 10 times the amount of emissions from the use of fossil fuels. With urbanization and industrialization, cumulative carbon dioxide emissions have tripled from 420 Gt in 1970 to 1,330 Gt of carbon dioxide in 2010; per capita emissions in industrialized countries are more than two times higher than in developing countries, and between 1990 and 2010 consumption-based emissions increased by 5 per cent in industrialized countries along with increases in GDP. On average, per capita energy use in developing countries in Asia is one-third that of developed countries, but consumption-related emissions differ by a factor of five, because of embedded carbon in traded goods.

By 1950, annual emissions of carbon dioxide amounted to 5 Gt carbon, rising in 1970 to 27 Gt of carbon, around three-quarters of which were attributable to fossil sources from infrastructure development and urbanization in industrialized countries, as developing countries were still rural and poor. Around 1980, emissions exceeded the capacity of the planet to absorb the waste carbon dioxide, before China began to industrialize. In 1990, emissions had increased to around 32 Gt of carbon, four-fifth from industrialized countries, one-quarter of which was from the United States, and around one-tenth from China. In 2010, emissions had risen to 49 Gt of carbon, with China (having four times the population) emitting one-quarter and the United States slightly more than one-eighth of global emissions. Accounting for emissions based on where a product is consumed rather than where it is manufactured still puts China at the top, but with a narrower gap to the United States, and China now accounts for 22 per cent of global consumption emissions while the United States accounts for 18 per cent of global emissions.

In terms of carbon dioxide emissions since the Industrial Revolution started in the eighteenth century, the United States accounts for nearly 28 per cent of the world's cumulative emissions from energy and industry and China's share is less than 10 per cent. Currently, global emissions are around 50 Gt of carbon and are estimated to rise to 60 Gt of carbon in 2020. Industrialized countries have yet to effectively cap their carbon dioxide emissions; United States carbon dioxide emissions in 2012 exceeded those in 1992. Since major growth in emissions is expected to occur in developing countries, as their rural population moves to cities into the middle class and try to catch up economically with the industrialized world, the future of global sustainability will be decided in Asia, in particular China and India, as two-third of global GDP is expected to come from there in 2050.

China's per capita emissions have reached levels in the European Union; levels in the United States are more than two times higher and those in India are still one-quarter those of China – and sectoral shares are also quite different for the industrialized and emerging countries. Increases in the volume of consumption have offset emissions reduction caused by structural change and efficiency improvements. Climate change will bring new challenges to States ability to share scarce natural resources.

The basic assumptions of global environmental sustainability that were laid out 40 years ago no longer hold. This common understanding was based on the historical responsibility of industrialized countries for causing the pollution – they would do whatever has to be done and support developing countries through provision of financial resources and technology. The modest scale of pledges at Copenhagen, accounting loopholes in the Kyoto Protocol and lack of political support for modification of longer term trends – 'the American way of life is not up for negotiation' – has been a cause of concern at the climate negotiations. In the period 1990–2005, industrialized countries emissions rose by 1.35 Gt of carbon, and their overall emissions remained limited only because of the reductions of 1.76 Gt of carbon in the Economies in Transition following the economic collapse of the Soviet Union. While global emissions remained constant in 2009, for the first time since 1992 because of the drop in economic activity, they again increased as industrialized countries grow out of recession. Recent analysis also establishes that market mechanisms will not lead to the required technological transformation for a sustainability transition [Committee on Climate Change, 2009; IEA, 2010]. The industrialized countries have not modified longer term trends, as they had agreed to do under Article 4.2.a. of the Climate Convention.

There are limits to the total ecological burden the planet can sustain. Without industrialized countries sharply reducing their resource use and emissions of carbon dioxide immediately other countries cannot get their fair share of the global commons, or global carbon budget for eradication of poverty. As the Nobel Prize winner Joseph Stiglitz pointed out in his address to the International Economics Association, held in Istanbul in June 2008, the transition to a low-carbon economy will require a new economic model – changed patterns of consumption and innovation, as 'only through changes in patterns of demand will adverse effects of climate change on developing countries be mitigated'. Stiglitz also stressed that in the case of global carbon management, the key problem is how to allocate emission rights, currently valued at about $2 trillion annually, that is 5 per cent of global GDP, and the 'only serious defensible principle is equal emission rights per capita, adjusted for past emissions … as a process of slowly easing in emission rights would increase inequities associated with past emissions'. Even if this entails large redistribution, it is not clear why this should be treated differently than other property rights, except in terms of geopolitics.

National carbon budgets are emerging in the reports of the Intergovernmental Panel on Climate Change as the most appropriate indicator for remaining within agreed limits in increase of global temperature. The carbon budget is also an appropriate indicator for measuring sustainability – sustainable use of atmospheric and terrestrial natural resources, and for assessing national strategies. The United Kingdom already has legislation establishing a national carbon budget. A report of the National Academy of Sciences of the United States on limiting the magnitude of future climate change, published in May 2010, also concluded that the 'policy goal must be stated as a quantitative limit on domestic GHG emissions over a specified time period – in other words a GHG emissions budget … national shares of global emissions need to be agreed at the multilateral level as the basis for developing and assessing domestic strategies' [NAS, 2010].

The re-framing is leading to results. According to the International Energy Agency special report on energy and climate that will be released on 15 June 2015, worldwide emissions of carbon dioxide in 2014 were the same as in 2013, without either a climate-change treaty or a global carbon price. In the European Union, GDP went up by 1.4 per cent in 2013 but carbon dioxide emissions from energy use fell by 6 per cent driven by energy efficiency measures in buildings and vehicles, while in the United States there was a marginal increase. In China, as manufacturing and heavy industry decline as a share of GDP (and services increase) demand for coal is dwindling. According to China's national bureau of statistics, coal consumption fell by almost 3 per cent in 2014 – pushing carbon dioxide emissions down slightly.

6.2 Flawed stress on projections of production patterns

According to the recent scientific consensus arising from an international consultative process, the social and biophysical sub-systems are intertwined such that the system's conditions and responses to external forcing are based on the synergy of the two sub-systems. Environmental problems should not be defined as discrete problems and are increasingly being understood as symptoms of a particular economic growth path. Consequently, the full global system has to be studied rather than its independent components, as none of the challenges can be fully addressed without addressing the other challenges. The key scientific insight is that in actions for achieving global sustainability, environmental change and social transformations are tightly intertwined. Current research trends on how to meet global challenges focus on societal dynamics as both the root of environmental problems and the potential solution to them [ICSU, 2010; WBGU, 2011].

The policy problem is that climate change has been framed in physical terms of temperature increase or global warming. One objective was to require coordinated global reductions, and the attendant emissions targets and timetables pit old against new emitters. The related objective was a framework of international cooperation focused on the environmental impact of future growth that will take place largely in developing countries while ignoring consumption patterns in industrialized countries that led to the global crisis in the first place, and which will need to change. The shared vision of the Cancun Agreements, 2010, was a compromise recognizing the substantial opportunities from a paradigm shift towards building a low-carbon society. Giving centrality to human well-being, which serves to clarify our understanding of a very complex issue, has yet to be accepted as the basis for the future climate regime.

A more holistic view, however, has led to the recognition that hypothetical global scenarios on which international cooperation is based bear no relationship to trends in resource use and the real options confronting policy makers. For example, different energy economies and greenhouse gas emission profiles lead to different economic and environmental impacts for countries in pursuing a harmonized policy approach. Existing models focus on specific policy areas and sectors such as energy and transport, and they cannot capture fully the impact of resource use on ecosystems, enterprises, the economy and society as a whole, or the interdependence of policy measures and longer term trends [Frank Ackerman et al., 2011]. Depending on the type of natural resource use, between 24 and 56 per cent of the associated total footprint of Europe occurs outside. For example, the share of urban land in Belgium is almost twice as high as in the Netherlands, despite a population density that is one third lower because of more planning restrictions, more compact urban settlements, and a lower share of detached detached houses (EEA, 2014).

Scenarios are also not able to capture the 'decoupling' taking place in developing countries driven by social rather than environmental considerations with respect to urbanization. In China, India, and in other developing countries, societal notions of well-being and consumption patterns are reflected in sectoral shares very different to those in industrialized countries. These shifts as a part of urbanization will lead to per capita energy use remaining below most other countries with similar GDP levels. In the re-emerging countries, per capita carbon dioxide levels are not likely to increase significantly despite rising per capita GDP, partly because their urbanization responds not just to an industrial but also a services and knowledge-based economy. Developing countries are likely to settle into the status of countries like Germany, rather than the United States, in terms of resource use, and this could well be the global norm in terms of 'happiness' in 2050. Recent reviews of China's actions to reduce energy and carbon intensity challenge the many analyses projecting continued exponential growth for China. Energy demand is likely to plateau around 2030 because of the saturation effects (appliances, residential and commercial floor area, roadways, railways, fertilizer use, etc.), deceleration of urbanization, energy efficiency, low population growth, change in exports mix to high value-added products and shift to consumption, with carbon dioxide emissions expected to stabilize around 2030 owing to continuous energy efficiency improvements as well as spread of renewable energy in the power sector [Zhou et al., 2011].

Scenarios are also not able to model the evolution of a large number of disparate energy end-use applications using consistent assumptions covering a range of sectors from transport to manufacturing and home appliances. Modellers usually respond to the problem of insufficient behavioural data by omitting behavioural considerations entirely while nevertheless incorporating overly optimistic estimates of future technological innovation. In such cases, the output of the models will likely overweight the potential of unproven technologies such as carbon capture and storage of hydrogen fuel cells while underweighting the potential of energy efficiency technologies such as controls for building lighting with the use of LED bulbs [AAAS, 2011]. The Intergovernmental Panel on Climate Change has also acknowledged that its emissions reduction scenarios do not take into account lifestyle changes [IPCC, 2007].

Another reason for the focus on energy supply rather than on end-use technological change is the way energy statistics are maintained. Currently, they cover economic activities and sectors as part of the energy system and end-use data are covered under industrial and consumer goods markets. Consequently, consumption data are generally not available as their primary purpose is to provide a service in the form of mobility, lighting and heating. It is, therefore, challenging to derive plausible and consistent scenario assumptions on energy efficiency. As model structure influences model outcomes, the implication is that the scenarios are based on trends and consequently stress production and generation of electricity rather than consumption patterns and the role of end-use services and transportation in driving technological change. Analysis of patterns, trends and divers of resource use confirms that energy efficiency and end-use technologies through rapid penetration by 2050 of energy efficiency, including low energy buildings constitute first rank options to cope with severe climate constraints. An inter-model comparison of stringent climate stabilization targets concluded that all models pay considerably less attention to end-use energy efficiency technologies than to supply-side technologies, which could create a bias towards favouring carbon intensity improvement and changing the fuel mix [Edenhofer et al., 2010].

Trends in industrialized countries highlight the limitations of only considering production patterns, for example, the carbon dioxide emissions from the fuel mix of electricity generation. The paradox is that while global energy intensity – final energy use per unit of GDP, largely driven by technology – fell by 26 per cent in the period 1990–2005, energy use per capita – largely driven by increase in wealth – increased more than 6 per cent in industrialized countries and less than 1 per cent in developing countries. Consequently, even though carbon dioxide emissions from manufacturing have not increased, overall emissions increased 15 per cent in industrialized countries, in this period; over two-thirds of the electricity generated is used in buildings, and more than half of the carbon dioxide emissions are now coming from the services, households and travel sectors, they account for more than half the increase in global emissions since 2005, and it is expected that emissions from transportation (largely for leisure) will exceed half of global emissions in 2050 [IEA, 2010].

It has now become clear that international cooperation based on multilateral agreements around long-term issues, like climate change, has to focus on alternative patterns and processes in the human use of nature in industrialized and developing countries which result in trade-offs for socio-economic systems. These are very different to focusing only on global environmental systems; the successful Montreal Protocol also focused on consumption and production patterns. Market mechanisms have not led to the required technological transformation for a sustainability transition, because they have focused only on the production sector, and when policies focused on economic growth have confronted policies focused on emission reduction, it is economic growth that wins out every time. International cooperation on economy-wide issues, unlike discrete issues and sectors, is also difficult because while globalization increases the rewards in coordinating policies, the interests of the citizens in major economies need to converge and domestic costs should not be high for the implementation of a multilateral agreement. That is why the climate regime established by industrialized countries, led by the United States, continues to address only their interests of securing their lifestyles – their emissions from manufacturing are steady since 1990 because manufacturing has moved overseas while consumption emissions of their urban middle class continues to rise – while ignoring the long-term transformations around global well-being and rise of the urban middle class, shifting from rural poverty, in developing countries. Clearly, the challenge of climate change will need a new regime where the future will be very different from the past and recognition of the interests of developing countries will be a part of the architecture.

6.3 Middle-class consumption as the problem and the solution

Over two-thirds of global emissions of carbon dioxide till 2000 occurred in the industrialized countries in the period after 1970, caused by the demands of urban lifestyles, rather than from industrialization as infrastructure had reached saturation levels and manufacturing moved overseas; half of all cumulative emissions are also from the industrialized countries. Greenhouse gas emissions are driven ultimately by consumption of the urban middle class. By 1970, three-quarter of the population of the United States and Europe has moved to cities, and total emissions in terms of carbon dioxide increased by 8 Gt of carbon in the 1970s, 6 Gt in the 1980s and 2 Gt in the 1990s levelling of reflecting the urban consumption in industrialized countries, and 10 Gt in the 2000s, reflecting the re-emergence of China and India – in the last 40 years per capita emissions more than doubled in Asia while remaining stable in other developing countries. As there are limits to the total ecological burden the planet can sustain, the global policy issue is what form international cooperation should take for supporting urbanization in developing countries in the context of the slow pace of modification of lifestyles and some adverse longer term trends in industrialized countries.

Industrialized countries are seeking to maintain their energy use per capita, as they do not want to modify their lifestyles by increasing the cost of energy or through regulation. Instead there are calls for a carbon price applied across all countries; including market-based cooperative frameworks, for sharing marginal costs of measures, as they define them, with developing countries. Their analysts, therefore, consider the economic potential of countries and adjustments only in developing countries, ignoring the required changes needed in the industrialized country economy and society. For example, these studies suggest that avoiding emissions from tropical deforestation can be done at relatively low cost, reducing carbon prices for measures taken in industrialized countries by up to 40 per cent in 2020 [OECD, 2009], rather than ranking measures across all countries. Consequently, in the world energy related carbon dioxide abatement scenario up to 2050, prepared by the International Energy Agency, most of the reductions come from developing countries – China 27 per cent, India 12 per cent, United States 11 per cent, industrialized Oraganization for Economic Co-operation and Development (OECD) other than Europe 10 per cent and OECD Europe 7 per cent [IEA, 2010]. Not surprisingly, all policy scenarios for proposed emissions reductions show relatively larger reduction in GDP growth for developing countries than for developed countries (Joachim Schleich et al., 2010). This approach based on economic efficiency, temperature limits and a global price for carbon focuses on environmental impacts of future growth of developing countries, rather than on industrialized country patterns of natural resource use and is the cause of the impasse in the negotiations on how best to deal with the challenge of climate change.

The way science has been used in current scenarios of the future, up to 2050, the focus is on 'flows' of greenhouse gases, whereas climate change is caused by their 'stock', or, concentration in the atmosphere. For bending the curve from a reference line to an acceptable global emissions pathway international cooperation, defined by industrialized countries in terms of sharing the costs, requires a peaking year. However, determining the reference line and the assumptions about national and global economies remains controversial, and even the Intergovernmental Panel on Climate Change is moving towards considering a global carbon budget, which is a physical quantity, easily determined and more transparent. Moving from prices to quantities and the economics of human development as the basis for international cooperation will require agreement on quantitative limits for sharing the remaining global carbon budget. Even though cumulative per capita emissions are correlated to cumulative per capita GDP, developing countries will have to make do with the budget currently available to a developed country, like Germany, and also move away from debates around historical responsibility to considering the global carbon budget for the period 1970–2050, when the issue first came onto the global agenda. The principle of common but differentiated responsibilities and respective capabilities will then be interpreted in terms of 'taking responsibility corresponding to the development level' of the country [Jiang, 2010], and should have wider acceptability and legitimacy.

Developing countries recognize that the context in which sustainability is being discussed at the multilateral level has changed since the Climate Convention was negotiated in 1992. In 2005, for the first time, since colonialism and the dawning of the industrial age, developing countries accounted for more than half of global GDP at purchasing–power–parity (PPP). Their growth prospects suggest that the challenge lies in devising national strategies, as rural populations shift to urban areas, for development of infrastructure and urban design that will also move to a low-carbon economy and society. However, at current levels of technology, developing countries will have to follow many trends followed by industrialized countries. Therefore, key issues for deliberation in the climate negotiations, and in the sustainability discussions, are agreement on criteria to enable behavioural change and sharing of technological innovation for renewable energy, urbanization and transportation as the drivers for making the transition to sustainable development.

The deliberations, rather than seeking to maintain lifestyles, should really be seen as an opportunity to discuss options for making the societal transformation to achieve sustainable development. The global community would then ask a very different set of questions, instead of the current narrow focus on mitigation, adaptation and burden sharing, and frame the issue differently in terms of sustainable development. They would, for example, need to identify which longer term trends in resource use should be modified, and the best way of doing so at the national level. At the international level, they would need to lay out a timetable for joint research and development of new technologies, as well as mechanisms for their transfer, to meet the scale and speed of the response. In each of these areas, developing countries would need to take actions to shape urbanization, and equity would then be redefined as patterns of resource use that can in principle be adopted by all countries.

The analytical and policy focus needs to shift from economic sectors to urban areas. As the Intergovernmental Panel on Climate Change points out, 'urban areas account for more than half of global primary energy use and energy related CO_2 emissions, and contain a high proportion of the population and economic activities at risk from climate change. In rapidly growing and urbanizing regions, mitigation strategies based on spatial planning and efficient infrastructure supply can avoid lock-in of high emission patterns. Mixed use zoning, transport oriented development, increasing density, and co-locating jobs and homes can reduce direct and indirect energy use across sectors. Compact and in-fill development of urban spaces and intelligent densification can save land for agriculture and bioenergy and preserve land carbon stocks. Urban adaptation provides opportunities for incremental and transformational adjustments towards resilience and sustainable development. Reduced energy and water consumption in urban areas through greening cities and recycling water are examples of mitigation action with adaptation benefits. Building resilient infrastructure systems can reduce vulnerability of urban settlements and cities from coastal flooding, sea level rise and other climate induced stresses' [IPCC, 2014].

Developing countries as they urbanize, with ten times the population than the earlier phase of urbanization, are now responsible for half of the growth in emissions since 1950, but the increase in carbon dioxide emissions from energy use at 3 per cent per annum in the 2000s is only twice that between 1980 and 2000. This will change as their focus shifts from considering eradication of poverty, or extreme poverty at the national level, to developing models and frameworks to enable the population shift to cities and into the middle class. Sharing innovative energy technology can keep this growth within planetary limits; for example, 38 per cent of the cumulative emission reductions required by 2050 could come from increased energy efficiency [IEA, 2014].

References

AAAS. 2011. 'Beyond Technology: Strengthening Energy Policy through Social Science'. A Report of the American Academy of Arts and Sciences, Cambridge, MA.

Ackerman, Frank, Ramón Bueno, Sivan Kartha, and Eric Kemp-Benedict. 2011. Comparing Climate Strategies: Economic Optimization versus Equitable Burden-Sharing. Stockholm Environment Institute, Working Paper US-1104.

CITI Bank. 2014. These 6 Huge Trends Are Completely Reshaping the World Economy. 2014.

Committee on Climate Change. 2009. Meeting Carbon Budgets – The Need for a Step Change. Progress Report to Parliament, Committee on Climate Change, UK, October 2009.

EEA. 2011. *The European Environment – State and Outlook 2010: Assessment of Global Megatrends*, European Environment Agency, Copenhagen.

EEA, 2014, *Environmental indicator report 2014: Environmental impacts of production-consumption systems in Europe*, European Environment Agency, Copenhagen, Denmark.

Edenhofer, O B. Knopf, T. Barker, L. Baumstark, E. Bellevrat, B. Chateau, P. Criqui, M. Isaac, A. Kitous, S. Kypreos, M. Leimbach, K. Lessmann, B. Magne, S. Scrieciu, H. Turton, Vuuren, D. van. 2010. 'The Economics of Low Stabilization: Model Comparison of Mitigation Strategies and Costs'. *The Energy Journal* 31: 11–48.

ICSU. 2010. Earth System Science for Global Sustainability: The Grand Challenges, International Social Sciences Council, Paris, Oct 2010.

IEA. 2009. *Worldwide Trends in Energy Use and Efficiency: Key Insights from IEA Indicator Analysis*. International Energy Agency, Paris.

IEA. 2010. *Energy Technology Perspectives 2010: Scenarios and Perspectives till 2050*. International Energy Agency, Paris.

IEA. 2014. *Energy Technology Perspectives*, International Energy Agency, Paris.

IPCC. 2013. *Climate Change, 2013: The Physical Science Basis*. Fifth Assessment Report – AR5, Intergovernmental Panel on Climate Change, Geneva.

IPCC. 2014. *Fifth Assessment Synthesis Report*, Intergovernmental Panel on Climate Change, Geneva.

ISSC and UNESCO. 2013. *Changing Global Environments*. World Social Science Report 2013. Paris: OECD Publishing and UNESCO Publishing, Paris.

Jiang, Chen. 2010. China and the UN – A long standing partnership, *Beijing Review*, Vol. 53 No. 39, September 30, 2010.

Kerry, John. 2014. Secretary of State of the United States, Ministerial Meeting of the Major Economies Forum on Energy and Climate Change, held on 21 September 2014. Press release, US Department of State, Washington

NAS. 2010. *Limiting the Magnitude of Future Climate Change*. Washington: National Academies Press.

OECD. 2009. *The Economics of Climate Change* Mitigation. OECD, Paris.

Schleich, Joachim, Vicki Duscha, and Everett B. Peterson. 2010. Environmental and economic effects of the Copenhagen pledges and more ambitious emissions reduction targets. German Federal Environment Agency.

UK CCC. 2009. Meeting Carbon Budgets – The need for a step change, Progress report to Parliament Committee on Climate Change, October 2009.

WBGU. 2011. *The World in Transition: A Social Contract for Sustainability – Summary for Policymakers*, German Advisory Council on Global Change, Berlin.

WWI. 2013. *Vital Signs*. Chapter 1: China, India, and the New World Order, World Watch Institute, Washington, DC.

Zhou Nan, David Fridley, Michael McNeil, Nina Zheng, Jing Ke, and Mark Levine. 2011. China's Energy and Carbon Emissions Outlook to 2050, LBNL-4472E, China Energy Group, Lawrence Berkeley National Laboratory.

Questions on the Framework

7.1 Market-based approaches are not leading to a technological transformation

It is now being recognized that the global rules – institutional architecture, system of global agreements, organizations and policy approaches – we have in place have not proved effective in making the transition to a low-carbon economy, and the United Nations has pointed out, in a recent report to the Economic and Social Council, that sustainable development is unattainable within the existing international frameworks [United Nations, 2011][1].

Under the current framework for international cooperation around burden sharing, the corollary of financial transfers to developing countries is putting a price on greenhouse gas emissions for sharing marginal costs of measures for meeting multilaterally agreed emission reduction targets in developed countries. Environment policies in industrialized countries have been directed at specific impacts, imposing additional costs, and have met with variable success because, for example, mitigation actions may reduce emissions but do not necessarily stimulate a transformation of industrial policy. Setting the price signal and emissions cap at the right level has proven politically difficult, and the effectiveness of the European Trading Scheme in promoting low-emissions investment is being questioned. Japan has concluded that an emissions trading scheme will hamper investments in key industries and that forcing companies to accept allocated emission caps, as in Europe because of its special circumstances of countries at different levels, would not work in Japan. The United States has also deferred a discussion on a 'cap and trade' system, as well as economy-wide emissions reduction commitments.

Modifying longer term trends in consumer behaviour by setting a price on carbon has not been successful anywhere. Energy demand is quite inelastic, and balancing between the levels of the price, incentive for innovation and acceptance by the public has not been easy. Economic theory suggests that the marginal cost of emissions should be equal to the marginal cost of the environmental damage, and these estimates range from $15/ton to $300/ton of carbon, while the average historical price of carbon credits is less than $6, and declined to less than $5 in 2013. The uncertainty, extent and timing of damage lead to subjective pricing where public goods are concerned. Even with a global carbon

---

[1] This chapter draws on material first published in (Sanwal, 2012, 2013).

price industry would find it more efficient to shift manufacture, as has happened for economic reasons even from the United States with no carbon price, or seek higher allocations to make windfall profits by raising prices for consumers, as has happened in Europe. The experience of the European Union, at the forefront of global efforts to deal with climate change through 'third-party' emissions reductions, also shows that the primary policy objective remains economic growth and well-being, and reliance continues on low-cost 'offsets' from developing countries and economies-in-transition to meet targets. Most important of all, alternative technology is not yet available in a form that it can be adopted by companies without further support from governments, as in the case of renewable energy technologies.

Putting a price on carbon does not also support investment in research, because unlike pharmaceuticals, engineering goods cannot be easily patented, and public funding on a long-term basis will be necessary. According to World Bank estimates, the second phase of the carbon trading scheme of the European Union could end with an overall surplus of 970 $MtCO_2e$, which could be carried over ('banked') for use from 2013 onwards, accounting for almost 40 per cent of the 'reduction' target that the EU claims will be required of power companies and industries allowing the scheme to continue without any domestic emissions reductions until at least 2017 [World Bank, 2010]. The experience with 20 years of efforts largely in the European Union to reduce emissions directly by creation of a market for carbon has not reduced emissions, as it has been focused on renewable energy and forests, neither has it supported a technological shift for decarbonization of energy supply because the price of carbon credits remains low. Offsets are not a part of company strategies in the United States to reduce emissions. The one clear result has been large and rising increases in costs of electricity to consumers (as much as two-fifth increase in the United Kingdom), along with the important market role played by government through regulation and purchases of credits from abroad.

Recent research also shows that legislation, regulation and consumer demand have failed to influence corporate behaviour, which continues to focus on traditional business objectives, paying little more than lip service to environmental objectives. Legislation and regulations have been laxly formulated and consumers influenced, if at all, by media reports. Sustainability has not as yet become a part of business strategy. For example, the UK Carbon Trust points out that despite the UK adopting ambitious new carbon targets, only 59 per cent of FTSE 100 companies have clear, robust targets to cut emissions. Carbon markets are in the middle of a fundamental crisis and must be understood in relation to the politics involved in their development, maintenance and operation [Stephen et al., 2014].

There is now an emerging consensus that no single policy instrument will be sufficient to tackle the wide range of sources and sectors emitting GHGs. Energy efficiency is expected to provide most of the reductions of carbon dioxide over the next two decades, with the International Energy Agency now considering it as essentially a 'fuel.' Even where carbon dioxide emissions are duly priced, specific incentives are needed for supporting the early deployment of renewable energy technologies by reducing their costs, and wealth transfers from consumers to utilities under emissions trading is being subject to further scrutiny. The UK Low Carbon Transition Plan, while recognizing the role of technology, criticizes the fact that the entire reduction in emissions of carbon dioxide from the energy sector – which is the largest source of emissions – is expected to come from carbon credits and there would be no technological transformation. Recent policy experience establishes that market mechanisms, such as emissions trading that target only the production sectors, themselves will not lead to the required technological transformation for a sustainability transition. A combination of technology development, market mechanisms and government policies will be needed to influence the actions of millions of energy consumers, from large factories to individual households. Governments are now promoting strategies to encourage more environmentally sustainable household consumption patterns and behaviour, including the phasing out of CFL light bulbs for LED bulbs, the introduction of energy performance labels for homes, and the provision of tax incentives to purchase alternative-fuelled vehicles [OECD, 2011].

7.2 Transparency in national reporting

There are three problems with the way emissions reduction are accounted under the current framework. First, recognition of the use of offsets in meeting national targets has led to a situation where the total amount of surplus emissions credits is large enough to allow many of these countries to follow a business-as-usual pathway until after 2020, while still complying with the currently announced emission reduction targets. Over reliance on offsets also allows industrialized countries to keep on polluting, and 'additionality' of the credits is difficult to assess. The majority of industrialized countries have also announced, rather than legislated, their emission reduction pledge, and until mechanisms are adopted to carry out these emission reductions, there is a chance that even these low pledges will not be met, as in the second commitment period of the Kyoto Protocol. Recent estimates show that these loopholes would allow industrialized countries to increase actual domestic greenhouse gas emissions by 7–10 per cent, that is, 2–3 Gt, and overall reductions in emissions of industrialized countries would be only around 3 per cent below 1990 levels in 2020, when the new regime is to be established.

Second, the rules, guidelines and methodologies for determining, reporting and reviewing reductions in emissions have loopholes. Generous emission targets under the Kyoto Protocol, in the form of surplus allowed allowances, have added as much as 1.4 Gt of 'hot air' per year that can be sold even though they do not represent any real reductions in emissions. Emissions from the land-use sector can vary significantly from year to year and the choice of including them, as well as the choice of a base year, can make a significant difference in defining the stringency of a given country' target by shifting the baseline. As domestic legislation in some countries accounts for emissions from agriculture, comparability and assessment exercises have been difficult and contentious, and these could amount to as much as 1 Gt for the industrialized countries and the proposals under discussion can further weaken the rules.

For example, the choice of a base year can have significant implications on the magnitude of the emission reduction pledge for any given country, and many countries, including the United States, are now choosing 2005 instead of 1990 as the base year. Canada's recent pledge of a target of 17 per cent reduction from the 2005 level will amount to 3 per cent above the 1990 level excluding emissions from the land-use and forest sector. Moreover, the 2.1 Gt of abatement committed by industrialized countries till 2020 includes 1.5 Gt that has already been captured by the impact of the economic downturn on lowering the business as usual emissions. Absolute emission reduction is the only measurement relevant to the goal of stabilizing the global climate [Bradley et al. 2010].

Third, the context in which emissions reductions takes place has been ignored in the current approach. Industrialized countries have exported their 'dirty' industry to developing countries where emissions have risen partly as a result of this shift. Economic researchers at Carnegie Mellon University in Pennsylvania have come up with a fully quantified measure of China's export-related emissions using standard money flow models and official China emissions data. The team, led by Christopher Weber, found that in 2005, China emitted 1.7 billion tons of greenhouse gases from its export-related sectors, 33 per cent of the national total, up from an estimated 12 per cent of total emissions in 1987 [Peters et al., 2011]. Britain's apparently creditable performance is less the result of a well-designed policy than the 'dash for gas' in the 1980s, spurred by the hostility to the coal industry of its then prime minister, Margaret Thatcher, and attempts to get a renewable energy industry going have not succeeded. It has been observed that policies that are effective, efficient and politically palatable have proved elusive everywhere. For example, in power generation, the current combination of markets and market instruments (the electricity markets and the EU ETS) are now considered to be poorly designed to deliver required long-term decarbonization [Committee on Climate Change, 2009].

The way the Kyoto Protocol has been negotiated, Annex I countries would be in compliance even as their emissions increased. The emerging market mechanisms provide allocation of emissions allowances for industrialized countries to themselves. They also earn emissions credits from emissions reductions of developing countries, moving towards a commoditization of carbon, based on an inequitable occupation of atmospheric space and allocation based on annual flows, thereby disregarding the stock of historical emissions. This approach is now being questioned even by its proponents [Prins et al., 2010].

The UN Secretary-General set up a Panel on sustainability in 2010 charged with recommending how a 50 per cent reduction in global emissions can be brought about by 2050; a target first proposed by the G7. While such Panels, as a part of the United Nations framework, have more legitimacy than other groupings, like the G20 and the Major Economies Forum, the deliberations continue to be driven by developed countries seeking to legitimize their over occupation of carbon space, but have yet to be accepted by developing countries as the forum for negotiations. Another Panel on Climate Finance also set up by the Secretary-General of the United Nations was not able to come with an agreed approach to transaction-based sources of international finance in order to provide the $100 billion promised at Copenhagen, largely because developing countries have opposed the composite measures under consideration, as they will have a greater incidence on developing countries than on industrialized countries. One reason for this impasse is that industrialized countries began to argue that the challenge of climate change is too complex for the 'cumbersome' current institutions to deal with, and informal institutions outside the Climate Convention decision making structure have been advocated [Keohane et al., 2011; Bodansky, 2011].

Outcomes under the climate regime will now be driven by choices made by developing countries on the evolution of climate governance, as they will have a say in the structures that will shape the way they will report their national actions and open them for review. The policy issue before developing countries is how best to navigate the different processes while simultaneously shaping the agenda in the multilateral negotiations to retain the priority of enabling the shift of their rural and poor populations to urban areas and middle-class levels of resource use and well-being. As developing countries are taking the leadership in emissions reduction, climate change is now synonymous with sustainable development, considering both environmental damage and social transformations in order to secure human well-being. Equity is, therefore, being redefined in terms of access to electricity, infrastructure and innovative technology, or patterns of resource use that are in principle common for all [IPCC, 2007].

7.3 Differentiation between countries

The gap between the stated concern for the environment and the nature and scope of the design and implementation of the actions – the way the problem has been defined and monitored, implementation sought through the market and cooperative action designed around workshops to discuss implementation issues – has led to a situation where evolution of the climate regime has focused on institutional arrangements that shift the deliberations on international cooperation away from the commitments of industrialized countries, through three distinct but related tracks.

The lengthy negotiations on the Kyoto Protocol and its rules (1994–2001) were dominated by largely successful efforts of developed countries to shift the focus to flows rather than stocks of carbon, reduce the scope and costs of measures they would be taking through offsets, like the Clean Development Mechanism (CDM) projects and now tropical forest sinks (REDD), securing accounting loopholes (in the way emission limits were assigned and in the definition of terrestrial sinks) and a weak compliance system (where any shortfall would be met in the next commitment period). Consequently, there is no real obligation to cap emissions of carbon dioxide.

The second track has been to keep developing countries engaged in capacity building projects (Global Environment Facility), expert groups (technology transfer) and programmes of action (adaptation). The only tangible result has been to increase awareness, and adoption of new energy or agriculture technology has not been enabled by meeting incremental costs promised in the Convention, despite countries submitting projects and lists of technologies they need. The various funds are not technically adequate for responding to developing countries' needs for adaptation, both because of the complex design of the funds and the poor implementation of the guidance provided by the Conference of the Parties [Mohner and Klien, 2007], and there is no visible effect of the Kyoto Protocol on technology transfer [Dechezlepretre, 2008]. The European Policy Institute assessing the extent to which the European Union has lived up to existing financial commitments made for supporting implementation of the Kyoto Protocol has concluded that there is a lack of clarity in defining what is new and additional, the information communicated to the United Nations is unreliable or not provided, and the amount provided to multilateral funds (about $4 billion in grant funds) falls well short of the commitment [Pallermaerts, 2009]. This inaction must be seen in the context of the recognition that consideration of development can no longer be left to other forums and institutions but must be addressed in an integrated manner through measures to deal with climate change [WESS, 2009].

The third track, since the ratification of the Kyoto Protocol, has focused on an agenda that would blur the differentiation between developed and developing countries with respect to emissions reduction commitments. In the annual meetings of the Conference of the Parties, the negotiations for the second commitment period of the Kyoto Protocol have come to an impasse, despite a specific commitment in Article 3.9 of the Protocol to that effect. The Parties to the Protocol argue that they will take commitments only if the United States does so, and the latter will take commitments only if China, now the largest emitter, takes on legally binding commitments. Hilary Clinton, Secretary of State of the United States, is reported to have told the European Union as early as 2001 that 'Kyoto is dead'.

Outside the multilateral framework, with the re-entry of the United States in the negotiations, the G8 Summit at Heiligendamm, in 2007 (relying on, as we now know, a biased report of the Intergovernmental Panel on Climate Change (IPCC)) called for a new framework and global goal for emissions to be halved by 2050, with further action to be based on the principle of common but differentiated responsibilities and capabilities. It set up a dialogue process (2007–2009) to build trust with, and recognize the role of, the major emerging economies (Brazil, China, India, Mexico and South Africa) for developing a common understanding on climate change, and initiated analytical work on technology cooperation and energy efficiency through the OECD and the IEA. At the G8 Summit in L'Aquila, in 2009, leaders of the major developing countries were invited, and all major emitting countries reiterated the importance of keeping the increase in average global temperature below 2°C. This set the stage for intense political pressure at Copenhagen, later in 2009, for internationalization of mitigation action. The subsequent stress on international consultation and analysis of national actions in developing countries had the objective of negating the current agreement that poverty eradication is the overriding priority of developing countries. With environmental effectiveness based on future emissions as the benchmark for review of national policies and strategies, as in the case of the industrialized countries, differentiation based on historical responsibility was effectively diluted.

Environmental considerations were not served because temperature increase is caused by the concentration of carbon dioxide in the atmosphere, and not just by current emissions. Under the bottom-up approach that emerged at Copenhagen, current pledges are estimated to be around 11–19 per cent below 1990 levels, and fall far short of the range of emission reductions (25–40 per cent) that the IPCC notes would be necessary for stabilizing concentrations of carbon dioxide at 450 ppm. The pledges of industrialized countries also amount to only about 2–2.5 Gt as they want to maintain their energy use per capita. The climate conundrum is that China's planned domestic action of 20 per cent reduction in energy intensity of GDP by the end of 2010 over 1990 levels as a part of its current national plan will reduce 1.5 billion tons per year, which is more than the 4 per cent reduction planned in the United States till 2020, and China is on course to meet this target. The cumulative emissions of the United States are more than three times those of China, yet it has pledged to reduce half of what China has pledged to reduce by 2020. Announcements by developing countries to change the trajectory of their growth amount to 5 Gt that is more than the 4 Gt reduction commitments of the developed countries [Ecofys, 2009].

The United States climate envoy Todd Stern, having shifted the discussion from responsibility to capability, said in a speech in October 2010 that a 'new paradigm' was needed since industrialized nations now account for just 45 per cent of world emissions, a share that is set to fall to 35 per cent by 2030. The Cancun Agreements, in December 2010, instead of the multilaterally agreed emissions reduction targets of the Kyoto Protocol, secured agreement on a shared target for all countries where deep cuts in greenhouse gases are required according to science, and previously agreed temperature goal. Differentiation would then be on the modalities of action and measurement; industrialized countries taking the lead in cutting greenhouse gases with low carbon strategies and guidelines to assess domestic action in developing countries.

As future increase in emissions would be in developing countries, because of their urbanization, they would need to do more than their fair share. The sequencing of the negotiations, using recent science in the IPCC AR4 in 2007 on severity of impacts to get agreement on temperature increase before new science in the IPCC AR5 in 2014 stressed the carbon budget, ignored the natural resource needs for human well-being and was able to focus on emission reduction as the criteria taking and assessing national action, with developing countries fighting to retain the principle of common but differentiated responsibilities once they realized the implication of what they had agreed earlier.

References

Bodansky, Daniel. 2011. A Tale of Two Architectures: The Once and Future Climate Change Regime. Working Paper Series. March 2011. http://ssrn.com/abstract=1773865.

Bradley, Rob and Kelly Levin. 2010. Comparability of Annex I Emission Reduction Pledges. Working Paper. World Resources Institute. February 2010.

Committee on Climate Change. 2009. Meeting Carbon Budgets – The Need for a Step Change. Progress Report to Parliament. Committee on Climate Change, October.

Dechezlepretre, Antonie, Matthieu Glachant, and Yann Maniere (of CERNA) and Ivan Hascic, Nick Johnstone (OECD), Invention and Transfer of Climate Change Mitigation Technologies on a Global Scale: A Study Drawing on Patent Data, December 2008.

Höhne, Niklas, Michiel Schaeffer, Claudine Chen, Bill Hare, Katja Eisbrenner, Markus Hagemann, Christian Ellermann, Ecofys, Climate Analytics and the Potsdam Institute for Climate Impact Research. 2009. Copenhagen climate deal – how to close the gap?

IPCC. 2007. *Climate Change 2007: Synthesis Report. Summary for Policymakers*, Intergovernmental Panel on Climate Change, Geneva.

Keohane, Robert, and David G. Victor. 2011. 'The Regime Complex for Climate Change'. *Perspectives on Politics* 9 (1): 7–23.

McKinsey Global GHG Abatement Cost Curve, version 2, and Project Catalyst. 2009. Towards a Global Climate Agreement, Climate Works Foundation and European Climate Foundation, 2009, and Project Catalyst, Scaling up Climate finance, Sept 2009 for a discussion on providing resources to developing countries to make the required reductions.

Mohner, A and R.J.T. Klein. 2007. *The Global Environment Facility: Funding for Adaptation or Adapting to Funds?* Stockholm Environment Institute.

OECD. 2011. *Greening Household Behavior: The Role of Public Policy*. OECD, Paris.

Pallermaerts, Mark, and Jonathan Armstrong, Financial Support to Developing Countries for Climate Change Mitigation and Adaptation: Is the EU Meeting its Commitments? Institute for European Environmental Policy, Brussels, January 2009.

Peters, Glen P., Jan C. Minx, Christopher L. Weber, and Ottmar Edenhofer. 2011. 'Growth in Emission Transfers via International Trade from 1990 to 2008. *Proceedings of National Academy of Sciences* 108 (21): 8903–08.

Prins, Gwyn, Isabel Galiana, Christopher Green, Reiner Grundmann, Atte Korhola, Frank Laird, Ted Nordhaus, Roger Pielke Jnr, Steve Rayner, Daniel Sarewitz, Michael Shellenberger, Nico Stehr and Hiroyuki Tezuko. 2010. *The Hartwell Papers: A New Direction for Climate policy after the Crash of 2009*, Institute for Science Innovation and Society, University of Oxford and McKinder Programme for the study of Long Wave events, London School of Economics, UK, May, 2010.

Project Catalyst. 2009. Taking Stock – the Emission Levels Implied by the Current Proposals for Copenhagen, Climate Works Foundation and European Climate Foundation, December 9 2009.

Sanwal, Mukul. 2012. 'Rio +20, Climate Change and Development: The Evolution of Sustainable Development (1972–2012)'. *Climate and Development* 4 (2) 157–166.

Sanwal, Mukul. 2013. 'The Rise and Fall of Global Climate Policy: Stockholm to Rio 1992, to Rio + 20 and Beyond'. *Chinese Journal of Environmental and Urban Studies* 1 (1).

Stephen, Benjamin, and Richard Lane. 2014. *The Politics of Carbon Markets*. UK: Routledge.

United Nations. 2009. *World Economic and Social Survey 2009*, United Nations.

United Nations. 2011. *World Economic and Social Survey*: The Great Green Technological Transformation, Department of Economic and Social Affairs, United Nations, New York 2011. p. 167.

World Bank. 2010. *State and Trends of the Carbon Market 2010*. World Bank, Washington.

Burden Shifting Rather than Burden Sharing

8.1 Changing scope of the negotiations

Actions in developing countries, rather than emissions reductions limited to industrialized countries, soon became the central issue in the climate negotiations. Having secured a broad agreement on limiting increase in global temperature to 2°C, industrialized countries began insisting on a global goal of halving emission levels by 2050, which continues to focus on future flows rather than historical stocks of carbon, even though science dictates that concentration and not emissions of greenhouse gases (GHGs) causes increase in global temperature and that, too, over a long period of time. A doubling of the atmospheric concentration of carbon dioxide corresponds to global warming of 2.3–4.5°C within the 68 per cent confidence interval, but only by 2150. The causes of the melting of the Greenland Ice Shield as well as West Antarctic Ice Shield, each containing enough ice to raise the global sea-level by around 5 m, are also not clear as sea levels have risen some 7 m in pre-historic times from the sun's energy because of the orbital oscillations of the earth. As industrialized countries continue to set the agenda, these scientific findings and uncertainties have been disregarded in the negotiations; they would allow an over-shooting of emissions in developing countries, to allow for the rural poor to move into the urban middle class, before declining assisted by aging populations[1].

The Convention requires as an 'aim' that industrialized country emissions should have peaked at 1990 levels by the year 2000 – modified longer term trends. As industrialized country emissions have continued to grow, developing countries see the global goal, with its implications for a peaking year, as a threat to their future economic growth and an effort to alter the agreed balance of rights and obligations in the climate treaty.

This approach, even if controversial principles and provisions of the Convention related to equity are not taken into account, will shift the burden to developing countries. First, it is argued that since emissions from developing countries will account for half of the global emissions by 2050, they must take on emission reduction commitments now. Global attention is sought to be focused on the increasing emissions from China and India, even though three-quarters of the electricity generated goes for industrial production and any reduction in emissions will have a direct impact on economic growth and eradication of poverty, unlike in industrialized countries where consumption by households' accounts for two-thirds of the electricity generated, and reductions will impact only on (wasteful) lifestyles. Moreover, while the major share of emissions in developing countries is

---

[1] This chapter draws on material first published in Sanwal (2012, 2013).

from food production, mobility (for leisure) has the largest share in emissions of industrialized countries. As developing countries still have to build their infrastructure, urbanize and shift poor rural populations to cities with opportunities for employment and well-being, the global leaders should really discuss how their economic growth can take place in an environmentally sustainable manner.

Second, the global concern should be about the use and distribution of natural resources, and not just scarcity. Despite the stress on 'prices', ecosystem services delivered outside national boundaries – by the atmospheric and terrestrial natural resource – have been ignored, effectively setting their value to zero in decision making. The current framework ignores the fact that energy and ecological services are directly related to human well-being. Development of infrastructure, urbanization, manufacturing and food production all need carbon space, and are essential for economic growth. For example, the per capita generation of electricity in India is one-fifteenth that of the United States. Estimates suggest that currently, worldwide 1.6 billion people lack access to electricity. The key global climate policy issue is that without industrialized countries sharply reducing their emissions immediately other countries cannot get their fair share of the carbon budget for eradication of poverty and for the shift of their population to middle-class levels of living.

A third shortcoming is the current international approach of setting emissions targets at the point of production rather than consumption, amidst increasing globalization of the world economy. For example, it is estimated that China's export-related emissions account for one-third of its emissions [Jiahua et al., 2008]. It has, thus, become easier for industrialized countries to slow the growth in their emissions and meet their targets at the expense of developing countries – in effect, exporting their emissions.

At the same time, all scientific assessments conclude that developing countries, rather than industrialized countries, will bear the adverse impacts of climate change with huge economic costs. According to recent research, agricultural output in developing countries is expected to decline by 10–20 per cent by 2080 affecting their food security. Agricultural growth has also been found to be four times more effective in reducing poverty than growth in other sectors. As the main determinant of a countries' adaptive capacity is economic wealth, such unprecedented adverse impacts of climate change will severely constrain development and lock the rural poor in long-term poverty traps. Meeting this challenge will require major new investments, for example, in agricultural research to develop new drought-resistant crop varieties and insurance schemes. UNDP has estimated the annual costs of adapting to climate change to be $86 billion in 2015, while the amount pledged, not committed, to date for adaptation (cumulatively, not per year) is $300 million.

Although adaptation is often a response to specific climate risks at a given time and in a given context, a recent preliminary analysis by the United Nations Environment Programme highlights that adaptation challenges also require global action. The assessment focuses on gaps in developing countries in three important areas: finance, technology and knowledge and argues that the cost of adapting to climate change in developing countries is likely to reach two to three times the previous estimates of $70–100 billion per year by 2050 of the Intergovernmental Panel on Climate Change's Fifth Assessment Report, which were based largely on World Bank figures from 2010. The report highlights that there is a need to accelerate the propagation and international transfer of technologies for adaptation, many of which already exist. As an example of successful technologies, the report looks at scientifically developed seeds, which can be used to sustain agriculture within the context of a changing climate [UNEP, 2014].

However, the Third United Nations Conference on Disaster Relief, held at Sendai in March 2015, The Sendai Framework for Disaster Risk Reduction 2015–30, is weak on international cooperation as industrialized countries agreed to provide "adequate and sustainable support" to the developing countries – a lesser commitment than the "additional and predictable" phrasing of earlier drafts. Developing countries had agreed to give up their demand for "additional and predictable" finance, in exchange for clearer commitment to technology support, but the United States objected, wanting to keep in the qualifier "as mutually agreed" in respect to technology transfer.

A large share of the burden of adaptation will inevitably fall on national budgets of developing countries, and they have to accept this responsibility. For example, India already spends about 3 per cent of its GDP on adaptation. However, such an international understanding should be contingent on the industrialized countries providing funding for natural disaster insurance, a provision that exists in the Climate Convention, as well as joint research for the development of drought-resistant seeds, etc. on the lines of the green revolution. This framework would allow countries to move onto a new era of global cooperation on a common concern, rather than remain bogged down in details of how much of the increasing severity of current drought, floods and cyclones are caused by climate change, as well as the share of mitigation that developing countries should bear.

In this context, the approach adopted by China and India for sustainable development has taken the first steps for an alternate policy framework, instead of a narrow focus on mitigation action more suited for industrialized countries. Their focus on activities that generate global change, placing resource conservation, environmental protection and economic development on equal footing, is showing good progress. The 11th Five year Plan of China (2006–2010) had set a target to reduce energy use per unit of GDP by 20 per cent by 2010 compared to 2005, which is going to be achieved. China has more efficient coal-fired plants than the United States and is becoming the major world market for such plants, as well as for renewable energy [IEA, 2009]. In 2009, it approved a national target for increasing the use of renewable sources to 15 per cent of energy use and committed to lowering carbon dioxide emissions by 40–45 per cent of 2005 levels by 2020. On World Environment Day, June 2009, China issued a nationwide call for a 'low carbon lifestyle'. The National Action Plan on Climate Change developed by India, in 2008, also seeks shifts in development growth pathways to achieve sustainable development through demand-side management, renewable energy, and conservation of forests and water resources. India plans to cut carbon intensity by 20–25 per cent below 2005 levels by 2020. Announcements by developing countries at Copenhagen to change the trajectory of their growth amount to more than the mitigation commitments of the industrialized countries.

8.2 Copenhagen and the changing balance of power

It was widely reported that at Copenhagen in 2009 China rejected unilateral cuts in greenhouse gas emissions by industrialized countries. A UK Minister wrote in the Guardian that 'we did not get an agreement on 50 per cent reductions in global emissions by 2050 or on 80 per cent reductions by developed countries. Both were vetoed by China, despite the support of a coalition of developed and the vast majority of developing countries' [Miliband, 2009]. A furious Angela Merkel, German Chancellor, is reported to have demanded 'why can't we even mention our own targets?' [Lynas, 2009]. A commentator from China explains the Chinese position in terms of safeguarding equity, pointing out that, cuts of both global greenhouse gas emissions by 50 per cent and that of industrialized countries by 80 per cent by 2050, would amount to a partitioning of the atmospheric resource and would mean that emissions in developing countries are only allowed to increase by 15 per cent by 2050 relative to their 1990 levels [Zhang, 2010]. Developing countries now have the power to resist imposition of rules that are detrimental to their interests.

The failure of Copenhagen also showed that the top-down approach will not lead to a global emissions target, or allocation criteria for sharing the carbon budget, and events after Cancun in 2010 suggest that a bottom-up process of country pledges is not a viable option either, as the pledges are not part of an agreed framework and conditional. Not surprisingly, with the refusal of a number of Parties to agree to a second commitment period of the Kyoto Protocol, climate talks remained stalled over disagreements on the future agenda. The shared vision of the Cancun Agreements also recognizes the substantial opportunities from a paradigm shift towards building a low carbon society and equitable access to sustainable development. The strategic issue here is whether the negotiations should consider a new strategy to tweak the climate regime or a new paradigm focused on human well-being will be necessary to ensure global sustainability.

As we now have to deal with resource scarcity in terms of 'sinks' – the capacity of the planet to absorb waste carbon dioxide generated by human activity – there is a global consensus on the biophysical limits to growth. According to recent analyses, in this context, what really matters is the total greenhouse gas budget we allow ourselves, because of the scientific uncertainty associated with the relation between temperature increase, emission rates and concentration targets, which cannot be accurately inferred from quantities we can observe. However, there is as yet no consensus whether political decisions on equitably sharing the global commons (the new paradigm) are a precondition for agreement on a global rule-based system or incremental steps to develop a rule-based system on the basis of the Cancun Agreements (the old paradigm) will lead to equitable outcomes.

The Copenhagen Accord, by shifting the focus on 'what' has to be done, from 'how' it should be done, has redefined the principle of common but differentiated responsibilities and respective capabilities in terms of levels of development as the basis of burden sharing. The internationalization of mitigation action requires benchmarks against which national actions will be legislated and assessed. Moving the multilateral discourse on climate change away from percentage reductions in emissions, equitable access to atmospheric space or nationally determined actions has the potential to transcend the binary division of the world into two groups, Annex I and non-Annex I, and shape the transformation of the world economy and human activity.

Climate policy is at a crossroads. The Copenhagen Accord has transformed the global climate discourse, fostered new groupings of countries and created a policy vacuum at the global level. As future increases in global emissions of carbon dioxide are going to come from developing countries, they have to be innovative in modifying growth pathways in order to achieve sustainable development. They have so far resisted taking far reaching policy measures because of the fear that it would lead to shifting the burden of dealing with climate change and its adverse effects onto them. They are now developing their vision of a climate constrained future, to impact on global trends, in terms of climate justice, transparency and a societal response to natural resource use and distribution.

A new global climate policy framework is emerging because the multilateral process is in danger of losing its legitimacy as industrialized countries have been steadily increasing their emissions since 1990. The key issue of modifying longer term trends, requiring around 14 Gt of emissions abatement by 2020, will have a greater impact on the policy space for future economic growth than the concurrent negotiations on world trade. The global discourse must, therefore, revolve around a new approach where the carbon budget of cumulative emissions will be used for reviewing nation actions, and not as the basis for national actions. The political problem of burden sharing cannot be solved through technocratic solutions.

This perspective challenges recent analysis describing Copenhagen as 'something of a failure', suggesting that 'policymakers must give up on a binding deal and begin to look outside the UN process'. The key issue of the negotiations at Copenhagen, as the United States and the European Union reminded the delegates at the opening session, was not the amount of reduction in emissions but when national emissions will peak, that is, the sharing of the carbon budget or environmental space. Speaking to the press at Copenhagen, China's Minister for Science and Technology also acknowledged that their emissions would peak in the period 2030–2040. He identified improved energy efficiency of power plants, buildings and transport and changed consumer behaviour as well as nuclear energy and other forms of renewable energy as the areas where future energy savings would come from. China is prepared to take on its fair share of the burden of meeting the challenge of climate change and subsequent negotiations will revolve around defining what is fair, or just, in terms of levels of development.

Though industrialized countries can no longer avoid capping their emissions, they do retain the power for making the required reductions based on an equitable distribution, as defined by them; as yet their 'way of life is not up for negotiation'. Initial steps have, however, begun to be taken by them to modify consumption patterns outside the negotiation framework. For example, in Japan, the Low-Carbon City Promotion Act, 2012, aims to promote cross-sectoral emissions reductions through the development of compact cities to achieve both low-carbon urban development and more efficient city administration. The Act provides tax breaks for certified energy efficient buildings that reduce primary energy consumption by more than 10 per cent compared to the reference level. It also provides incentives for low-carbon measures such as home energy management systems, water saving measures, the use of timber as building materials and 'heat-island' prevention measures. In addition, it requires that municipalities formulate Low-Carbon City Development Plans. Since such initiatives have yet to gain political acceptance in the United States and European Union, the changing power balance continues to pit old against new emitters as well as the less industrialized countries against the fast developing countries, and the resulting fragmentation and conflict has become more pronounced.

While China, and also India, now have the influence to refuse unacceptable deals, they face the dilemma that they must also be responsive to the concerns of other developing countries. In the current situation where their rapid economic growth is perceived by the least developed countries to be at variance with their concerns for adaptation to the adverse effects of climate change. They must, therefore, project a credible vision with a larger purpose than national self-interest to re-establish solidarity amongst developing countries.

Developing countries are now formulating their vision of a climate-constrained future in terms of a strategic framework to impact on modifying longer term trends, and India provides an interesting case study. For 8 years after the Rio Conference, in 1992, national policymakers were in a state of denial. When the annual climate conference was held in Delhi, in 2002, India stated what it would not do – per capita emissions will never exceed the developed country average. While the National Action Plan on Climate Change announced in 2008 focuses on energy efficiency and demand side management, at Copenhagen India announced targets for reducing carbon intensity of GDP. However, India, China and other developing countries have yet to develop a vision of the transformation of the global economy and human activity to secure the well-being of all citizens. India's Prime Minister Narendra Modi, speaking at UNESCO in April 2015, used a United Nations forum to begin a dialogue focusing on consumption patterns – "a change in lifestyle, because the emission reduction that we seek will be the natural outcome of how we live".

It is now being recognized that energy and ecological services in cities, just like capital and technology, are directly related to human well-being, as they enable the development of infrastructure, urban services, manufacturing and food production. Equity has also been redefined by the Cancun Agreements in terms of access to sustainable development. Therefore, the climate negotiations are beginning to recognize that both global temperature and greenhouse gas concentration limits are needed as the basis for long-term co-operation to meet the climate challenge. These findings suggest that new criteria centred on sustainable development, or different peaking years, are now on the research and the policy agenda.

8.3 Reframing the equity principles

At Copenhagen, according to the Centre for European Policy Studies, the industrialized countries were seeking a multilateral agreement on 50 per cent reduction in global emissions by 2050, peaking of developing country emissions around 2020–2030 and offering to reduce 80 per cent of their own emissions by 2050. A single number serves as a powerful communication tool, but like the economic indices, the underlying data and assumptions are important but seem an unnecessary distraction to most persons other than to professionals in this field. The 80 per cent cut collectively in developed country emissions by 2050 would have fixed their share of the atmospheric space at 2 t of carbon dioxide equivalent per capita per year, leaving developing countries to fight amongst themselves for less than half of that amount over the coming decades.

Recent analysis shows that industrialized countries accounting for 20 per cent of the world's population in 2005 have already contributed around 75 per cent of the cumulative carbon dioxide emissions (from energy) until 2000, and above 50 per cent of the cumulative emissions since then. Given the range of pledges listed at Copenhagen, these countries will have used up about 25–30 per cent of the total remaining greenhouse gas budget stock by 2050. And, meanwhile, some of the emerging economies such as China, India, Brazil, Mexico, Korea and South Africa are about to consume the remaining part, potentially curbing the economic growth ambitions of the least-developed and other countries whose per capita emissions are below the global average and have been growing more slowly [WRI, 2010].

The countries with low per capita emissions collectively might need as much carbon budget as the developed countries are about to take up from now until 2050, if they were to merely reach per capita greenhouse gas emissions of 4 t carbon dioxide equivalent by 2030 and maintain that level until 2050. Many would expect such per capita emissions as reasonable in order to make possible the approximately 8 per cent annual economic growths needed to lift people out of poverty and into the middle class. In all likelihood, currently existing and affordable technologies will not enable this kind of economic growth without a significant per capita carbon emissions increase. During the review of the Copenhagen Accord starting in 2016, the target might be strengthened, as the Accord suggests, leaving an open question on how this might actually happen.

An approach based on carbon justice, or equity, would reserve a part of the remaining carbon budget of cumulative emissions for the countries with per capita greenhouse gas emissions below the global average in 2005, which combined account for a population of roughly 3 billion. Taking their combined total GHG emissions in 2005 as a starting point (corresponding to almost 2 tons per capita, excluding land use and forestry emissions), assuming a linear increase to 4 t per capita in 2030 that remains constant until 2050 while keeping for the sake of simplicity the 3 billion population fixed over the whole 2005–50 period, results in a cumulative 4.25 Gt, that is, one-third of the remaining carbon budget [CEPS, 2009].

As Nicholas Stern has pointed out 'if the allocation of rights to emit in any given year took greater account both of history and of equity in stocks rather than flows, then rich countries would have rights to emit which were lower than 2 tons per capita (probably even negative). The negotiations of such rights involve substantial financial allocations: at $40 per ton of carbon dioxide equivalent a total world allocation of rights of, say, 30 Gt (roughly the required flows in 2030) would be worth $1.2 trillion per annum' [Stern, 2009]. Clearly, industrialized countries will strongly oppose bearing this burden arguing that when they were urbanizing between 1950 and 1990 carbon was not a global concern. They will need to consider bearing the burden of securing atmospheric space for the countries with low per capita emissions to enable them to grow up to the global average; even this would require them to take steps which would not find popular acceptance.

Clearly, national emissions reduction schemes based on the 'targets and timetables' approach are inadequate, and despite making reference to being guided by 'science' the Copenhagen Accord makes no mention of cumulative emissions, because in the scientifically credible framing of mitigation it is cumulative emissions that matter [Kevin Anderson and Alice Bows, 2011]. Even though cumulative per capita emissions are correlated to cumulative per capita GDP, and the cumulative emissions of an average Chinese in the period 1850–2005 are less than one-tenth, and now half of those of an average American, developing countries will have to make do with the carbon budget that is available to Germany, for example. They will need to move away from debates around historical responsibility to focus on drivers and trends, like urbanization. The interpretation of the principle of common but differentiated responsibilities and respective capabilities will then also recognize levels of development and should have global acceptability and legitimacy.

The Millennium Development Goals agreed in 2000 did not include energy, and as part of the re-appraisal of current approaches, a new poverty index recently developed by the United Nations stresses lack of services such as electricity as a key factor in determining poverty [UNDP, 2010]. While it is agreed that individuals' access to electricity should be seen in incremental levels of basic human needs, productive uses and modern society needs, 'basic human needs' is the level that is commonly used for forecasts related to growth in developing countries emissions from universal energy access. Consequently, the International Energy Agency assumes that 1.4 billion rural poor without access to electricity (the United Nations Development Programme computes much a larger number) will each need only 100 kwh annually – a floor fan, two compact fluorescent bulbs and a radio – for about 5 hours each day, which would, therefore, increase developing country emissions by a negligible 3 per cent till 2050. Others argue that this figure is too low, and the aim should be to achieve a higher per capita electricity use (the developed country average is 1,000 kwh) for the 4–5 billion rural poor that will move to urban areas along with development of industry and infrastructure needed for the eradication of poverty and urbanization [AGECC, 2010]. The World Economic and Social Survey, 2011, points out that eradication of poverty will require an almost 10 times increase in availability of modern energy sources by those now counted as poor [UN, 2011].

The United Nations has called for a commitment to three complementary goals by 2030, of ensuring universal access to modern energy services that are affordable and combine basic needs and productive uses to 2–3 billion people as well as reducing global energy intensity by 40 per cent and increasing the share of renewable energy to 30 per cent. While there is no common understanding, even within international organizations, of how the resulting increased emissions from developing countries will be accommodated in the transition to sustainable development, it is clear that peaking of carbon dioxide emissions will depend on shifts in patterns of resource use in industrialized countries and on the availability of innovative energy technologies in developing countries as part of their urbanization and industrialization. Placing adequate and affordable energy access as a central element in the framework of sustainable development/low-carbon green economy requires political decisions for reconciling competing resource needs with respect to maintaining lifestyles and growth of the global middle class. This issue is now at the centre of the deliberations on modification of longer term trends in patterns of resource use and remains extremely contentious.

There is also still no agreement among countries on the public policies needed to establish a global technology sharing regime to accelerate emission reductions that is going to be as important as behavioural changes in countries staying within their share of the global carbon budget. Since the 1990s, following the Uruguay Round of the World Trade Organization, protecting private intellectual property rights by enforcing exclusive use and deployment by its owner is the dominant global approach. Internationally, spurring green technological development will require a wider mix of public sector strategies, which guarantee a commercial incentive substantial enough to enable private parties through the use of subsidies and public purchases of technology at reasonable cost in their research undertakings, while constraining monopolistic practices which restrict diffusion and further development. Public policy tools could include global funding for research, to be placed in the public domain for widespread dissemination under the same modality utilized in the green revolution in new seeds and food agriculture in the 1960s and 1970s. Where exclusive private-sector rights of use to vital technology are a hindrance to the development of other needed technology or to widespread use, the technology regime must have a mechanism (such as exists in certain areas of public health) for granting a 'compulsory license' that places such technology in the public domain. International public technology policymaking can provide an integrating theme to promote greater coherence between the disparate entities of the multilateral system, environment and trade, whose common objective is to support the transition to global sustainable development.

The relationship with the global trading regime remains an unresolved issue. The role of market mechanisms and offsets, as well as the possibility of providing any legality to border tax adjustments action under the WTO, is questionable. Here too, as long as a country is within its fair share of the carbon budget of cumulative emissions, there would be no unfair competitive advantage. The best way forward is to monitor national action in terms of equitable shares the carbon budget of cumulative greenhouse gases, while reserving a portion for the growth of developing countries whose per capita emissions are currently below the global average, so that patterns of resource use are common for all citizens.

The principle of common but differentiated responsibilities and respective capabilities is being re-defined and a cooperative framework is emerging. The focus has so far been on 'responsibility' in terms transfer of financial resources, which has been provided as development assistance rather than as an entitlement. The amount of less than $4 billion that has been made available to the financial mechanism of the Convention (the Global Environment Facility) is insignificant. A High Level panel will now study potential sources of revenue to provide $100 billion a year by 2020. For the first time, transfers of financial resources are being considered subject to verification. The majority of new funding will go for adaptation in the least developed countries and will be provided over the long term. A new fund has been established under the Convention as well as a new mechanism for technology transfer, but their substantive impact remains uncertain.

The deliberations at the multilateral level should really be seen as an opportunity to discuss options for making the societal transformation to modify production and consumption patterns as part of a long-term macrostructural transformation to achieve urbanization and sustainable development. They would, for example, need to identify which longer term trends in patterns of resource use should be modified, and the best way of doing so at the national level. At the international level, they would need to agree on criteria to treat the global carbon budget as a monitoring, rather than allocation, tool and lay out a timetable for joint research and development of new technologies, as well as mechanisms for their transfer, to meet the scale and speed of the response. Only the least developed countries will continue to need financial support for sustainable economic growth, rather than just for measures to reduce pollution, blurring the distinction between environment and development that emerged at Rio in 1992 as well blurring the 40-year-old North–South divide around the global environment.

The political divide in the climate negotiations continues to adopt an institutional perspective and focuses on whether it is time to end the differentiation between developed and developing countries. The existing division of countries in the Convention follows the United Nations classification, largely based on per capita incomes, and a change must be considered in the United Nations because of the impact on other areas, including the trade regime. The implication is that modification of longer term trends at the national level will be enabled, rather than directed, by new global rules that provide policy coherence in a multipolar world to support the transformation in natural resource use for human well-being, re-shaping international relations. The universalism that was imposed with international environment law as the organizing principle is now giving way to a recognition of diversity recognizing urbanization as a mega-trend and global sustainable development goals as the organizing principle. Therefore, in the transition, it is necessary to incorporate both perspectives in the information, national actions, assessment and agenda in the new climate regime and its future evolution. This arrangement alone will support the needed transformation, pave the way for global goals that balance fairness and adequacy and move away from the current 'institutional' approach to the global, and national, challenge.

References

AGECC. 2010. Energy for a Sustainable Future, The Secretary-General's Advisory Group on Energy and Climate Change, April 2010.

Anderson, Kevin and Alice Bows. 2011. 'Beyond 'Dangerous' Climate Change: Emissions Scenarios for a New World'. *Philosophical Transactions of the Royal Society A* 369 (1934): 20–44.

CEPS. 2009. The Copenhagen Accord: A first stab at deciphering the implications for the EU, comment by Christian Egenhofer and Anton Georgiev, Centre for European Policy Studies, 25 December 2009.

Lynas, M. 2009. How Do I know China Wrecked the Copenhagen Deal? I Was in the Room, *The Guardian,* 23 December, 2009.

Miliband, E. 2009. The Road from Copenhagen. *The Guardian,* 20 December, 2009.

Pan, Jiahua, Ying Chen, Wengiin Wang, and Chenxi Li. 2008. Carbon Budget Proposal: Global Emissions Under Carbon Budget Constraint in an Individual Basis for an Equitable and Sustainable Post-2012 International Climate Regime. Research Centre for Sustainable Development, Chinese Academy of Sciences, Beijing, December 2008.

Sanwal, Mukul. 2012. 'Rio +20, Climate Change and Development: The Evolution of Sustainable Development (1972–2012)'. *Climate and Development* 4 (2) 157–166.

Sanwal, Mukul. 2013. 'The Rise and Fall of Global Climate Policy: Stockholm to Rio 1992, to Rio + 20 and Beyond'. *Chinese Journal of Environmental and Urban Studies* 1 (1).

Stern. 2009. Action and Ambition for a Global Deal at Copenhagen, UNEP, 2009.

UNEP. 2014. *The Adaptation Gap Report – A Preliminary Assessment Report.* United Nations Environment Programme November 2014.

UN. 2011. World Economic and Social Survey: The great green technological transformation, Department of Economic and Social Affairs, United Nations, New York.

UNDP. 2010. *Human Development Report: The Real Wealth of Nations – Pathways to Human Development,* United Nations Development Programme, November 2010.

WRI. 2010. *Climate Analysis Indicators and Tools.* World Resources Institute, Washington, DC.

Zhang, Zhong Xiang. 2010. Copenhagen and Beyond: Reflections on China's Stance and Responses. In *Climate Change Policies: Global Challenges and Future Prospects*, edited by Emilio Cerdá and Xavier Labandeira (Editors). Edward Elgar.

Development of a Shared Vision

9

9.1 New policy approaches for the stalemated process

The Intergovernmental Panel on Climate Change has now acknowledged that how the burden of mitigating climate change should be divided among countries raises difficult questions of fairness, and rights, all of which are in the sphere of ethics [IPCC, 2014a]. How this fits into the four distinct policy measures for emission reductions – the Kaya identity – remains an unresolved issue. These elements are wealth, population, energy intensity (units of energy per unit of GDP) and carbon intensity (carbon produced per unit of energy). These levers involve population shifts from rural poverty to urban middle-class levels of well-being, consumption patterns, energy efficiency and modifying the fuel mix and how they interact with one another. The outcome is not dependent on a multilateral treaty or market, but on the substance of societal well-being.

The Intergovernmental Panel on Climate Change has now also observed that the methods of economics are concerned with value as well as measuring and aggregating the well-being of humans but not in taking account of justice and rights [IPCC, 2014b]. For example, there could be an overlap between the financial instruments with carbon pricing, because both policies address the same market failure and the high initial cost of the technology, but high prices have little impact on the practices that reflect societal change. Similarly, for the generation sector, energy efficiency standards have been found to be as effective as prices in reducing emissions. There is evidence of a stark trade-off between distributional impacts and policy efficiency depending on how the revenue is distributed. Carbon prices are also not applicable to long-lived assets, like building and transport infrastructure, where life cycle assessment of costs is involved.

According to projections of the International Energy Agency, global energy supply is estimated to increase three times by 2050, without including the requirements of access to energy by the poor. In contrast, during the past 100 years, energy use largely in industrialized countries increased 16 times. If a distinction is made between electricity demand and transportation, a very different picture emerges, as transportation emissions are projected to be half of the global emissions of carbon dioxide in 2050. This leads to two approaches for 50 per cent reduction in carbon dioxide emissions: first, focus on consumption patterns, end-use efficiency and transportation, or, second, focus on the production side and decarbonization of the fuel mix for generation of electricity. The scope and scale of the transformation needed is such that we need a social as well as a technological transformation.

Achieving cost and performance improvements in supporting technological change have in the past depended on governments. First, currently very little is invested in research by the energy sector, because energy is cheap, and the supply from one source is no different to that from another source. At the same time, in the United States, public sector investment in health is around $30 billion and the private sector spends twice as much. Second, the new energy technologies have high capital costs with low running costs but also a low profit stream without a clear market niche. Nuclear energy was widely adopted because of government, rather than market, support. Third, Europe's Emissions Trading Scheme, despite putting a price on carbon has not led to a technological shift, in part because of the volatility of the carbon price, which remains dependent on political factors.

The International Energy Agency is now recognizing that establishing least cost policies for decarbonization will not rely solely on putting a price on carbon, or on the market, and will also need energy efficiency policies and public support for research and development, otherwise the price would be too high to gain public acceptance. The mix of these policies will also differ according to national circumstances as the cost advantages are clearer at the demand rather than the supply side. For example, energy efficiency in buildings and in electric vehicles will require new financing mechanisms. On the other hand, price increases in electricity and transport can have significant wider costs to the economy as a whole affecting economic output, employment and welfare. The International Energy Agency is also acknowledging the limitations of models, as they are not able to include market barriers and the assumptions made, for example, on trade balances, have a high level of subjectivity. The conclusion is that fairness for developing countries and political feasibility in industrialized countries conflicts with least cost effectiveness.

The International Energy Agency is now putting energy efficiency at the core of the policy response to reducing end-user demand, which also leads it to be considered essentially as a fuel. However, despite being cost-effective, these technologies and practices have not been extensively adopted because the barriers to the delivery of energy efficiency cannot be addressed by carbon price at any level. Full information on the energy performance of different technologies and the costs and benefits of energy-efficiency measures is usually not available. For example, the energy efficiency of appliances is usually not known to consumers, so that they are unable to see the impact of increase in energy prices on individual appliances. Similarly, monthly electricity bills say little about the use of individual appliances. Split incentives occur where, for example, the landlord put the heating equipment but the tenant pays the bill. Load planning has to be done to integrate intermittent renewable energy technologies into the electricity grid. The policy measures for these market failures are regulations, such as minimum energy performance standards, energy performance labelling and consumer feedback tools such as smart meters, as well as financial instruments such as grants, subsidies and financing public–private partnerships [IEA, 2011]. The halt in emissions growth in 2014 has been attributed to changing patterns of energy consumption in China and OECD countries. In China, 2014 saw greater generation of electricity from renewable sources, such as hydropower, solar and wind, and less burning of coal. In OECD economies, recent efforts to promote more sustainable growth – including greater energy efficiency and more renewable energy – are producing the desired effect of decoupling economic growth from greenhouse gas emissions [IEA, 2015].

At the international level, there are important precedents on institutional responses on how best to support and manage innovation with respect to access to new technologies. The Global Fund to Fight AIDS, Malaria and TB in seeking significant and undefined innovations choose not to identify and specify the nature of the research or pick 'winners'. Instead it invited applications for new ideas in treatment and for new drugs, subjected them to a rigorous review process, and worked with applicants, including funding them through grants in successive cycles, while discontinuing support for the

142 | The World's Search for Sustainable Development

failures. The Global Alliance for Vaccines and Immunization (GAVI) has made market commitments to the pharmaceutical industry to develop vaccines for developing countries on the lines of the success, in the 1970s, of the Consultative Group on International Agricultural Research (CGIAR) providing new seeds and practices which led to the Green Revolution in wheat and rice. These successes are important precedents for similar international cooperation in sharing innovative renewable energy technologies.

The Report of the Secretary-General of the United Nations to the Preparatory Committee for the Rio+20 Summit in 2012 also observed that 'the main challenge facing humanity now is to sustain the process of poverty eradication and development while shifting gears. Developed countries must shrink environmental footprints as fast and as far as possible while sustaining human development achievements. Developing countries must continue to raise their people's living standards while containing increases in their footprints, recognizing that poverty eradication remains a priority'. For implementing this vision, the Report stressed that public policy for a green economy must extend well beyond the current reliance on 'getting prices right' to fundamentally shift consumption and production patterns onto a more sustainable path.

9.2 Longer term cooperation to support change

States have to go beyond the current approach to carbon policy based on assessing and managing risks posed by pollutants. An analysis of the diplomatic interaction since 1992 shows that the annual meetings of the 'United Nations Framework Convention on Climate Change' (UNFCCC) have not discussed how countries will modify longer term trends, as they had all agreed to do in the Climate Convention; industrialized countries specifically under its Article 4.2(a). The evolution of the climate regime has only led to new institutional arrangements, expert groups and workshops serving to solve political problems rather than the problem to be solved.

The two decades 'diplomatic game', including the decisions on 'new and additional financial resources, transfer of technology and capacity building' and establishing a new trust fund, continues in a form that implementation has not increased the level of political commitment. The Green Fund is expected to channel $100 billion a year to poor nations by 2020, but this enhanced amount remains an intention, there is no commitment, and it is not clear how much will be provided on a grant or concessional basis. A new technology mechanism will shift international cooperation beyond the current focus on capacity building and needs assessment to public–private partnerships, but the stress remains on information sharing, and it is silent on intellectual property rights. In return, industrialized countries secured agreement on guidelines for international measuring, reporting and verification of nationally appropriate mitigation action in developing countries, without defining what these are. These steps were widely seen as saving the United Nations climate process from collapse, even though they did not address the core ethics issue of determining 'who has to do what and by when'.

Recent research has also questioned the foundation of the Climate Treaty, the rigorously reviewed national emissions inventories, arguing that these statistics do not depict a true state of affairs. They ignore the fact that most industrialized countries have increased their consumption-based emissions faster than their territorial emissions. Net carbon dioxide emissions transfers via international trade from developing to developed countries increased from 0.4 Gt in 1990 to 1.6 Gt in 2008 – more than the Kyoto Protocol emissions reductions [Peters et al., 2011]. While production-based emissions are needed for global climate models, policy responses for stabilization of greenhouse gases require consumption-based data, because human activity in urban areas is the key driver for global change.

There is no agreed approach to deal with the challenge of climate change and its adverse effects, because of the different perspectives of industrialized and developing countries. Many see climate change in terms of environmental damage, and the most popular image is of polar bears floating on ice floes. Hence, any agreement, despite the consensus that world temperatures must not rise above 2°, that does not focus on global emissions reductions is considered flawed. For others, the human impacts are more important, whether it is recurrent drought in Darfur or one billion rural poor lacking assured access to modern energy and three-quarter of the global population living in cities by 2050 with actions to be taken in the context of enabling those countries sustainable development within planetary limits.

Industrialized countries, most notably the European Union, have argued that it would be very costly to make the structural changes necessary to achieve even the meagre targets they are proposing for themselves, and find it necessary to meet their targets in developing countries, where they say the measures are cheaper to achieve, through the carbon market, and this is one definition of fairness. For them long-term cooperation is about reducing costs for them and is now being defined in terms of the relationship to the technical and economic potential of countries.

Developing countries need to develop an alternate approach to shape the shared vision, rather than just focus on the architecture of the new arrangement. For example, the way legally binding commitments under the Kyoto Protocol are being ignored highlights the limitations of international environmental law, and new approaches for long-term cooperation must be explored. Similarly, traditional concerns of safeguarding sovereignty need to be revisited while dealing with global concerns, and any review of national actions will not be intrusive if it is fair. That means reporting is restricted to data elements and benchmarks agreed to assess performance as the gap between the tons of carbon reduced/avoided and the fair share of the carbon budget for that country. The question that should be asked, and the annual climate conferences have not asked, is how to make the transformation to sustainable development happen. How can our complex social and economic systems interact with a complex planetary system undergoing rapid change to create a future we all want? With per capita emissions varying by more a factor of 10, a truly shared vision must ensure the right to sustainable development for all.

In October 2008, as part of an initiative by the International Geosphere-Biosphere Programme, a group of economists, sociologists, historians, ecologists, climatologists, oceanographers, biogeochemists, biologists, chemists and others met in Lund, in Sweden to draw up a vision for the planet in 2050. They identified the global goal as improvement in human well-being in line with sustainable development, with a new model of growth where by consumers considered their needs rather than their wants, so controlling material consumption. The trade-offs in the kinds of deep structural change that will be necessary are very different to a focus only on national emissions of carbon dioxide. This is because the world will replace and add massive amounts of new capital stock during the next decade, and 'catching up' on emissions reduction post-2020 is not a viable option.

9.3 Importance of national actions

In developing countries, the domestic response to climate change is being shaped by a strategic perspective of the future and not just by the focus (of the Copenhagen Accord) on global temperature limits. Pathways to a low-carbon economy are identifying and considering options and giving a predominant role to the private sector. This shift is breaking the traditional bureaucratic mould for policymaking of putting new wine in old bottles by adopting inappropriate developed country models or emission reduction targets that do not take into account levels of development. International cooperation is also not being seen as a precondition for these measures, because in a growing economy, with new technology there is no need to shift the burden onto others.

High emissions/GDP in industrialized countries is a symptom of energy consumption growing rapidly in the transport, household and service sectors, driven by rising passenger travel and freight transport, appliance energy use by households and a rapid expansion in the urban service economy. Two-thirds of end-use energy will soon be in these sectors. For example, India with 10 per cent of emissions from the transport and residential sectors, energy-use per capita one-fifth of industrialized country levels and 300 million people waiting to move into towns, the problem must be framed in terms of urban design, transportation options and lifestyles.

The strategic policy issue for decoupling energy use from economic growth will not just be developing energy efficiency standards and de-carbonizing energy – as developed countries are doing – but rather a modal shift in transport patterns to railways and modifying the nature of the urbanization process itself, in particular new land-use patterns that minimize need for personal transportation and maximize natural resource use. Moving beyond energy efficiency to conservation of energy is a necessity, because actions taken now as new cities are established will largely determine trends for many decades to come. The societal response to resource use, distribution and scarcity is very different in developing countries compared with the industrialized countries, as innovation here is driven by need and not by greed. The interaction between poverty, societal forces and technology has already led to new products and services. The private sector has to be further challenged to make major emitters, like China and India, global leaders in innovation for sustainable development.

Policy frameworks tailored to social value creation need to be developed through public–private–people partnerships (PPP) to chart new pathways in transportation and urbanization; new instruments to impact on modifying consumption patterns and innovative policies for augmenting services provided by critical natural resources – energy, water, forests. The required shifts will come from infrastructure decisions, new institutions, changing values, norms and behaviour and innovative technology. For example, Indian firms have established themselves as cutting-edge innovators targeting the poor – some 500 million consumers. That trend surfaced with the Nano, the small car costing $2,000 produced by Tata Motors and has resulted in a number of products for people with little money who aspire for a better life. The products are not just cheaper versions of well-established models available in developed countries, but have taken design and manufacturing to a whole new level in the way they use resources.

A level playing field, or equity, requires that the multilateral process, as a matter of priority, determine fair criteria for burden sharing to provide the benchmark against which national actions will be assessed. Under this framework, all countries would then take long-term measures, including cooperative action, to keep within their carbon budget, and be subject to international monitoring to ensure transformational change. Patterns of resource use must be common for all countries. The Intergovernmental Panel on Climate Change has now unequivocally stated that 'the evidence suggests that outcomes seen as equitable can lead to more effective [international] cooperation', putting the onus on countries like India and China to suggest a new climate policy framework to give life to the languishing climate negotiations.

In its recent Synthesis Report, the Intergovernmental Panel on Climate Change has concluded that there will be 'severe, widespread, and irreversible impacts' on people and the natural world, to which developing countries will have to adapt; it has recommended 'phasing out fossil fuels by the end of the century', which primarily concerns industrialized countries whose industrialization, urbanization and lifestyles have been largely responsible for most of the emissions permissible if dangerous climate change is to be avoided; it has suggested that 'global emissions need to fall by 40–70 per cent by 2050 with multiple pathways to achieve this objective'; and, also for the first time, it has given prominence to 'ethics and justice' in how countries can cut emissions.

The policy relevance of the scientific advice that there is now a '95 per cent' certainty on the anthropogenic causes of climate change, 'cumulative emissions of CO_2 largely determine global mean surface warming by the late 21st century and beyond', requiring 'substantial and sustained reductions' in emissions of greenhouse gases is primarily for the public and policymakers in industrialized countries. This is because they have so far not accepted the need to modify longer term trends in the use of energy and shifts in energy systems, have questioned their historical responsibility in causing the problem and are not even discussing economy-wide measures in their national legislatures. For developing countries what is new is that they have to take meaningful action for both reducing the growth of emissions and adapting to the adverse impacts, largely from their own resources. There is also a new chapter in the Report of the IPCC on 'Social, Economic and Ethical Concepts', modifying the earlier reliance exclusively on economic analysis of policy alternatives in the guidance to policymakers.

For all countries, the Report points to the needed transformation. It stresses the importance of 'a wide range of analytical approaches for evaluating expected risks and benefits, recognizing the importance of governance, ethical dimensions, equity, value judgments, economic assessments and diverse perceptions and responses to risk and uncertainty ... Behavior, lifestyle and culture have a considerable influence on energy use and associated emissions ... in particular when complementing technological and structural change. Emissions can be substantially lowered through changes in consumption patterns, adoption of energy savings measures, dietary change and reduction in food wastes'. Clearly, there will be many pathways and time frames for the transformation.

The main Reports of the IPCC provide the evidence. Half of the cumulative emissions of carbon dioxide from human activity in the period 1750–2010 have occurred in the period after 1970; urban areas are responsible for three-quarter of these emissions and energy use. In an interdependent world, urban dietary patterns have changed with meat production, accounting for a quarter of world's greenhouse gas emissions, and one-third of world food production is wasted. The value of world trade in natural resources is a quarter of world merchandise trade and world transport energy use doubled in the last 40 years and is expected to double again by 2050. Buildings and the transport sector are each responsible for about one-third of final energy consumption. In a more equal world, the shift from a focus on the symptoms to the causes of the problem also focuses on urban consumers as the drivers of change in all countries.

The way the problem is now being framed challenges the 'universalism' that has dominated the global agenda for a stronger recognition of diversity as a part of the architecture, because there will be different sets of solutions for countries at different levels of industrialization and urbanization or different levels of economic and social development. There are calls for developing countries to take the lead for the review of national actions in terms of modification of longer term trends, with a mix of trends in per capita cumulative emissions and per capita GDP since 1950 for assessing the measures being taken. This will ensure the interplay of environmental and sustainable development considerations that the Intergovernmental Panel on Climate Change has now stressed.

A comparative characterization of GHG emissions illustrates why a separate framework to review national actions of developing countries is needed. In 2012, out of a total global emissions of 32.7 trillion metric tons,[1] China's share was 8.55, or 26.1 per cent; the United States, 5.27, or 16.1 per cent; Europe, 4.26 of GHG, or 13.0 per cent; and India's share, with a population comparable to China's and four times that of the United States, was 1.83 or 5.6 per cent; this is only 40 per cent of the United States', and 21 per cent of China's share. Comparing emissions per capita per year of the large countries has the United States at 14.1 metric tons per capita; Japan at 9.42; Europe at 7.12, about half of the figure for the United States; China at 6.05; and India at 1.47, comparable with Africa at 1.11. The per capita GHG for India is only a third or 32 per cent of the world average. This diversity is only now being recognized in the climate negotiations.

---

[1] US Energy Information Administration data.

Developing countries will now consider the framework for reviewing their national actions, and it is likely to be based on the scientific consensus in the Fifth Assessment Report of the IPCC—'the evidence suggests that outcomes seen as equitable can lead to more effective [international] cooperation', therefore, the stress on the use and distribution, not just scarcity, of natural resources. The universalism being pushed by the industrialized countries will have to recognize diversity as part of the architecture, and this could well be a peaking year of 2050 for India and the other developing countries.

Global emissions will have peaked by 2050 because, despite the growth of emissions in some developing countries, China, whose emissions will have peaked by 2030, will be ageing as fast as industrialized countries are now ageing. As climate policy transitions away from annual emission reductions towards integrating longer-term transformations in national policy, the parameters of international cooperation are also being redefined with the North–South divide becoming blurred around a rural–urban divide, as most of the future emissions are going to take place in cities in Asia. As two-thirds of future global growth is going to take place in Asia, the Asian giants should now take the lead in the sustainability transformation as part of their economic growth, for sharing responsibility and prosperity.

In 1988, natural science was used to focus on increase in global temperature and emissions of carbon dioxide, the term 'global warming' was coined to define a global concern and a scientific body, the Intergovernmental Panel on Climate Change, was established by the United States. In 2014, following the release of the Fifth Assessment Report of the Panel, which for first time included social science inputs, China was able to re-frame the issue in terms of longer term energy transformations. The focus has shifted from the global symptoms to the national causes of the problem of natural resource use, ecosystem services and planetary limits, outside the framework of international environmental law and as part of global sustainable development goals.

Countries have begun to consider climate change as a social and energy rather than a physical and environmental problem, because longer term transformations rather than shorter term emission reductions matter; sustainability is about the use and distribution, not scarcity, of natural resources. As two-thirds of future global growth, urbanization and increase in emissions of carbon dioxide is going to take place in Asia, the Asian giants are now taking the lead in sharing responsibility and prosperity for the global transformation to sustainable development. Global climate policy will no longer be debated around the North–South divide, 'burden sharing' or the 'means of implementation' but in terms of supporting transformations, sharing policy experiences, establishing knowledge networks and technology transfer in a South–South context. With China taking the lead in accepting responsibility for global concerns and in developing renewable energy technologies, future international cooperation will depend on its willingness to transfer these technologies to other developing countries on concessional terms.

References

China Daily. 2014. 'Obama Hails Climate Deal'. *China Daily*, November 18.

Climate Action Tracker, China and the US: How does their climate action compare? Policy Brief, 21 October 2014.

IEA. 2011. Summing up the Parts: Combining Policy Instruments for Least Cost Climate Mitigation Strategies. International Energy Agency, September 2011, Paris.

IEA, 2015. *Special Report on Energy and Climate*, International Energy Agency, June 2015, Paris.

IPCC. 2014a. *Working Group III, Mitigation of Climate Change*. Intergovernmental Panel on Climate Change Cambridge University Press, New York.

_____. 2014b. *Working Group III*, Chapter 3, Intergovernmental Panel on Climate Change, pp. 24–25.

Peters, Glen P., Jan C. Minx, Christopher L. Weber, and Ottmar Edenhofer. 2011. 'Growth in Emission Transfers via International Trade from 1990 to 2008'. *Proceedings of National Academy of Sciences of the United States of America* 108(21): 8903–08.

The Middle Class and Global Ecological Limits

10

10.1 Carbon budget, societal transformation and urbanization

New data, based on national communications, released by the United Nations shows that emissions from the United States increased over 15 per cent in the period 1990–2008 and will increase another 7 per cent by 2020 [UNFCCC, 2011]. Recent research in the United States assumes that 200 Gt of carbon dioxide equivalent will be available in the period 2012–2050; while for 2008, annual emissions from the United States were 7 Gt. The scientific analysis is unambiguous, and notes that this budget is 'based on "global least cost" economic efficiency criteria for allocating global emissions among countries, and using other criteria, different budget numbers could be suggested, for instance, some argue that based on global "fairness" concerns, a more aggressive U.S. emission reduction effort is warranted' [NAS, 2010]. A climate budget framework provides a sound basis for global and domestic policy.

After Copenhagen, with agreed limits on increase in global temperature, global policy requires early agreement at the multilateral level on quantitative limits on emissions and allocation criteria for the scarce atmospheric resource. The IPCC has also shifted its emphasis to the remaining global carbon budget, because scientifically for an agreed temperature limit, the carbon budget is a more appropriate framework. However, the industrialized countries, having failed at Copenhagen to secure a partitioning of the atmosphere are now against a legally binding regime that would impose restrictions on them, signifying an end to the global climate policy enunciated in 1992.

Developing countries recognize that the context in which sustainability is being discussed at the multilateral level has changed since the Rio Conference and negotiation of the Climate Convention, in 1992. In 2005, developing countries accounted for more than half of global GDP at purchasing–power–parity (PPP), their prospects for economic growth enables them to devise national strategies for development of infrastructure necessary for eradication of poverty that will also move to a low-carbon middle-class economy and society, blurring the way emissions are characterized as 'industrial' emissions with a focus on production factors, while ignoring urban consumption.

Consumption, and not only production, is now being seen as a determinant of sustainable development. Governments report data on direct emissions of the various sectors to the United Nations on a regular basis, but there is no agreed methodology and reporting of the attribution of environmental impact, such as, consumption on the basis of process chains and lifecycle analyses.

An analysis of the greenhouse gas footprint, that is, direct and indirect emissions (excluding land-use change) for eight consumption categories and 87 countries or regions for the year 2001 allocated production-related emissions on a pro-rata basis to the components of macroeconomic demand (household consumption, government consumption, investments, net trade) in order to include spatial shifts of environmental pressure caused by trade. The analysis shows that processes causing greenhouse gas (GHG) emissions benefit humans by providing consumer goods and services. It showed that 72 per cent of overall emissions were related to household consumption, 10 per cent could be allocated to government consumption, and 18 per cent were connected to investments. The analysis also shows that this benefit, and hence the responsibility for emissions, varies by purpose or consumption category and is unevenly distributed across and within countries, for example, food and services are more important in developing countries, while mobility and manufactured goods rise fast with income and dominate in rich countries and; food is the consumption field which has the most impact on overall emissions, followed by operation and maintenance of shelter and mobility. If only carbon dioxide emissions are considered, on the other hand, food has much less influence, with shelter and mobility dominating. The importance of public services and manufactured goods has not yet been sufficiently appreciated in climate policy, and national policy priorities will depend on development status and country-level characteristics [Hertwich and Peters, 2009].

A consumption-based analysis of the emissions also shows that the impact which consumers have on climate change mitigation is not limited to their own country; in 2004, 23 per cent of global carbon dioxide emissions from fossil energy carriers (6.2 Gt carbon dioxide) and were related to internationally traded goods. The majority were exports to industrialized nations from China and other newly industrializing countries. For example, the net emissions 'imported' by Germany in this way amounted to 2.8 t carbon dioxide per capita, and including these its emissions per capita increase from 10.7 t carbon dioxide to 13.5 t carbon dioxide for 2004; the carbon intensity of economic activity in developing countries now lagging behind that in developed countries by less than half a decade [Stephens et al., 2010].

The development and implementation of the new climate regime should take into account the new science. The mandate now is to ensure 'the highest possible mitigation efforts by all Parties' for 'aggregate emission pathways consistent with having a likely chance of holding the increase in global average temperature below 2 °C or 1.5 °C above pre-industrial levels'. Under the present emissions pathway 6 °C is more likely by the end of the century, as all countries want others to bear the burden, and it has been difficult to arrive at a consensus on the principles for the new regime, leading to a questioning whether a multilateral legal framework of rights and obligations is the appropriate one.

10.2 Multilateral negotiations in a multipolar world

The defining feature of the United Nations Framework Convention on Climate Change (UNFCCC) was the allocation of effort to combat climate change largely on the basis of per capita income, and countries considered to be developed were listed in an annex to the Convention. The central feature of the climate negotiations in the first 20 years of the climate regime has been the efforts of developed, or industrialized, countries to end this differentiation. During this period, the developing countries' primary stress was on the principle of 'common but differentiated responsibilities and respective capabilities' focused on short-term needs of 'means of implementation', like finance, technology and market mechanisms, rather than allocation of effort between the designated groups of countries. For example, even at Durban, in 2011, in the context of maintaining the distinction, the developing countries pushed for extension of the Kyoto Protocol without identifying emissions targets required by science for industrialized countries, because of a lack of agreement amongst them on the reduction required. Consequently, there is still no common understanding of an 'equitable' approach to climate policy, as different countries emphasize 'differentiated responsibilities', 'common responsibilities' and 'respective capabilities', leading to continuing North–South tension.

Climate policy inside the UNFCCC, as well as outside it, has been driven by the United States and, after ending 'differentiation' based on international environmental law, it established the new framework around global goals, through a well-thought-out strategic set of steps.

The United States viewed the Kyoto Protocol, 1997, with its emission reduction commitments only for industrialized countries, as a 'dichotomous' distinction as incomes and emissions continued to rise in many countries considered to be 'developing' countries, reflecting the general pace of global economic growth. The United States re-engaged in the climate negotiations by convening the Major Economies Forum, and in July 2009 leaders of 17 industrialized and developing countries agreed that 'peaking of global emissions should take place as soon as possible', with large developing countries recognizing the need to reduce their greenhouse gas emissions, over a longer time span than the others. This was formalized in the Copenhagen Accord of December 2009 and Cancun Agreements of November 2010 blurring the distinction between countries established on the basis of per capita incomes. Some distinction remained in the nature of the measures or actions, with developed countries alone required to make economy-wide reductions, and this was also diluted at Durban, in 2011.

The eighteenth round of climate meetings, in December 2012, ended with agreement of all countries taking on commitments of a similar legal nature, limited emission reductions by the industrialized countries and few resources for the developing countries. Though this has been the case over the years, the difference this time was that adaptation, or 'loss and damage', has now been accepted to be as important as mitigation in dealing with climate change and its adverse effects; this was later diluted in Warsaw, in November 2013, as no new mechanism was created and 'loss and damage' was included in the arrangements for adaptation.

As the scientific assessment by the Intergovernmental Panel on Climate Change (IPCC) has now made clear, efforts to combat global climate change and the pursuit of sustainable development are two sides of the same coin, but this understanding has yet to be integrated into the climate change debate and the climate negotiations. As global emissions now have to remain within an agreed limit, reductions have very different implications for economies where growth has stabilized and for those that will continue to grow. To ensure equity of outcomes, the new regime has to allow for convergence of global living standards within global ecological limits for it to have any legitimacy in developing countries, because emissions, standards of living and global ecological limits are inter-linked, and cannot be considered in isolation.

All the analyses suggest that the most rapid growth of the middle class will occur in Asia, with India somewhat ahead of China over the long term. Their chances of becoming richer will be substantially greater in cities, and the volume of urban construction for housing, office space, and transport services over the next 40 years could roughly equal the entire volume of such construction to date in world history. Up to now less than one billion people have accounted for three-quarters of global consumption; during the next two decades, new and expanded middle classes in the developing world could create as many as two billion additional consumers. Urban centres are engines of productivity, generating roughly 80 per cent of economic growth, giving a boost to long-term competitiveness and social and political stability, and the health of the global economy will be increasingly linked to how well countries earlier considered developing do – more so than the traditional West. As these countries enjoy a rapid increase in their power, they will need to think about their future in new ways.

A multipolar world is now marked by wide differences regarding how to manage the international system of natural resource management. The developing countries have been calling for a more

150 | The World's Search for Sustainable Development

democratic process for international relations instead of established powers setting the agenda and the rules, disputing perceptions of an open, liberal order which has allowed emerging powers to prosper and rise. As the recent authoritative analysis by the National Intelligence Council of the United States notes equality, openness and fairness are not just values to be applied to domestic setups, but also pertain to the broader international order (NIC, 2008). With the dilution of the legal basis for differentiation and the related shift towards national action, a convergence is emerging around a new agenda that acknowledges the role of energy in human well-being.

10.3 Centrality of human well-being

Discordant values among the key players and lingering suspicions mean that technology, markets and societal change are likely to have a more important impact in reducing carbon emissions than globally agreed emission reduction commitments. The expanded exploitation and use of cheaper and cleaner natural gas could overtake coal, resulting in significant emission reductions for the United States and other big emitters such as China and India. Other technological advances in renewable technologies would also shift the debate on climate change by making mitigation efforts less burdensome on productivity. The fact that no single nation or bloc of countries will have the political or economic leverage to drive collective action means that continued multilateral advances will be difficult to forge, raising the question whether a treaty requiring agreed emission reduction is a precondition for sustainability, or the focus should shift to modification of longer term trends at the national level as that puts human well-being at the centre.

The IPCC has now given a good basis for both international and national action. The 'carbon budget' was the last part of the Policymakers Summary to be decided, and the subject of hours of heated discussions. Industrialized countries were rightly concerned that the on-going climate negotiations would now focus on how to allocate the remaining 'carbon budget' fairly among countries. The political implication is clear. Annual emission targets, expressed in terms of annual or per capita emissions, pit old against new emitters and point the finger at economic growth in developing countries, ignoring the historical emissions of the industrialized countries. The problem is that these annual targets also deal with the symptoms and ignore the causes of these emissions. The focus has so far been on short-term measures like energy efficiency in industry and gases other than carbon dioxide that will postpone measures to deal with the central issue of energy and carbon dioxide emissions; the carbon budget will focus policy on the drivers of urbanization and long-term sustainable development goals.

A carbon budget will consider the activities that generate these emissions in the course of economic development and urbanization, leading to very different conclusions than those taken in 1988, when the IPCC was established. A carbon budget recognizes that the bio-physical and social systems are intertwined such that the system's conditions and responses to external forcing, like increases in carbon dioxide in the atmosphere, are based on the synergy between the two sub-systems. Consequently, the full global system will be studied rather than its individual components, as none of the challenges can be fully studied without addressing the other challenges. So far the projections about the future have focused on environmental damage rather than patterns, trends and drivers of natural resource use, and the International Energy Agency suggests that global emissions should peak by 2017 to avoid 'infrastructure lock-in' ignoring the growth aspirations of developing countries rural poor, as well as its own research, supporting recent research by McKinsey, that the greatest emission reduction potential is in demand-side management in developed countries, with 30 per cent reductions at no additional cost.

While all countries have adopted a cautious approach in the negotiations at the domestic level they have begun to take steps to modify longer term trends with energy efficiency and benefits extend beyond improvements in competitiveness which has been the traditional concern. Europe and Japan have taken steps for efficiency improvements in buildings, North America in motor vehicles, parts of the Middle East in air conditioners, and China and India have taken steps for energy pricing reforms. The overall result has been to bring down costs for industry, reduce energy prices on household budgets (the share of energy in household spending has reached very high levels in the European Union) and on import bills (the share of energy imports in Japan's GDP has risen sharply). Looking at trends till 2035, the International Energy Agency concludes that the potential for energy efficiency is still far from exhausted, as two-thirds of the economic potential of energy efficiency remains to be tapped; barriers include subsidies which continue to be important in the energy sector and fossil-fuel subsidies were estimated to be $544 billion in 2012 [IEA, 2013].

The energy sector is being transformed without needing a multilateral agreement. Unconventional oil and gas and renewable energy are modifying the distribution of the world's energy resource, making importers like the United States into exporters and able to get their power producers using coal to cut emissions; China also has vast new gas reserves and is going to cap emissions by 2030. Urban design, policies and technologies show that patterns of resource use which shaped the links between economic growth, energy demand and energy-related carbon dioxide emissions in industrialized countries are being weakened.

Global climate policy is being reframed, moving away from an exclusive focus on emissions, the symptoms, to the causes of the problem, use of energy, and new sustainable development architecture. At the Ministerial Meeting of the Major Economies Forum on Energy and Climate Change, held on 21 September 2014, John Kerry, Secretary of State of the United States, stressed out that 'the solution to climate change is energy policy. If we make the right choices about how we build buildings, how we transport people, what we do with respect to providing electricity and power to our countries, this problem gets solved'. India pointed out that its energy needs would grow at least four times, and reiterated its rejection of a universal approach as it needed more time for emission reduction. Speaking at the UN Climate Summit, on 23 September, Vice-Premier Zhang Gaoli said China is willing to 'take on international responsibilities that are commensurate with our national conditions and actual capabilities', and laid stress on expanding renewable energy and lowering emissions intensity. At the United Nations General Assembly (UNGA) in 2014 India's Prime Minister reiterated that the principle of a 'balance of collective action' must continue to shape the architecture of the new climate regime.

The most recent science on climate change supports a shift to a sustainable development perspective. The Fifth Assessment Report of the Intergovernmental Panel on Climate Change released in 2013–2014, for the first time

- concludes that cumulative emissions of carbon dioxide are the dominant factor determining the global mean surface warming, that is, the use of energy, and it now nudges international cooperation around the global climate budget;
- includes a chapter on 'Ethics and Justice' and its importance in dealing with the problem and strengthening international cooperation;
- emphasizes that sustainable development and equity provide a basis for assessing climate policies; and
- stresses that climate resilient pathways are sustainable development trajectories that combine adaptation and mitigation to reduce climate change and its impacts.

An alternative sustainable development framework is emerging, as there is no agreement on how to include 'fairness' into the Kyoto framework of focusing on current emissions of Parties that are at different levels of development. This framework could have four elements. First, reporting on energy use and peaking, or the global carbon budget as that alone directly relates to global temperature increase. Second, establish new rules for sharing renewable energy and agriculture technologies and financial resources to enable all countries to modify their growth pathways. Third, recognize levels of development in the national actions of all countries so that they contribute their fair share to the global effort in accordance with global trends in use of energy. Fourth, the annual meetings of the Climate Convention should discuss how best to modify longer term trends in energy use, provide access to adequate and affordable energy to all keeping related emissions of carbon dioxide within planetary limits, exchange experiences on adaptation to support climate resilient growth pathways and assess the aggregated effects of the steps taken by the Parties. This framework will be fully in accordance with the Objective of the Climate Convention and replace the Kyoto framework which has not found universal acceptance. The experience of the successful Montreal Protocol is that the focus must be on modifying consumption, measures that are practical, have clarity and enhance international cooperation.

According to the Preamble of the Climate Convention 'change in the climate and its adverse effects is a common concern of mankind' and developing countries are now insisting that the new regime be re-framed to recognize that actions to respond to climate variability are as important as carbon management. In parallel with these negotiations, international bodies outside the treaty framework which are not bound by the existing legal framework of burden sharing are furthering international cooperation in areas that continue to be debated within the former and responding to the concern of the developing countries for a global focus on sustainable development. For example, the Fourth High-Level Round Table of the International Treaty, Food Crops and Food Security in a Changing Climate, catalyzed by the Food and Agriculture Organization (FAO), recognizes the interconnectedness between climate change, agricultural productivity, food security and biodiversity in a new forum of global governance based on 'shared dependence of all nations' on natural resources, in this case genetic diversity. The New York Communiqué, October 2014, stresses that climate change presents unprecedented challenges for global food production. Rising temperatures, water scarcity and increased occurrence of droughts and floods are likely to precipitate further problems such as rising soil salinity and the emergence of new crop pests and diseases. It recognizes that unless we are able to develop climate-resistant food crops, we risk the breakdown of global food systems and the very serious consequences that this will have for agricultural productivity and food security, particularly for the poorer sections of society. It proposes relying on plant genetic diversity, and this treaty agrees to equitably share the benefits through an 'open platform to support technology co-development and transfer' with a 'benefit sharing fund'.

The way forward is to recognize the value of both 'pledges' from all countries and establishing multilaterally determined indicators for the assessment of nationally determined actions; a hybrid climate agreement is emerging based on a core of national action with elements to ensure adequacy of these actions that cover both mitigation and adaptation in a sustainable development framework. This needs agreed criteria based on the evolution over time of per capita emissions, per capita GDP and energy intensity. 'The OECD Development Co-operation Report 2014: Mobilizing Resources for Sustainable Development' makes recommendations on how to mobilize further resources, as for example, through smart use of ODA to leverage additional resources and mitigate risks; policy reform to improve the environment for investment in developing countries to mobilize domestic resources and to combat illicit flows; and innovative mechanisms such as a levy on airline tickets or a financial transaction tax. It also considers combatting climate change, promoting peace and security, and creating a fair and equal trading system as global public goods; integrating and widening the current scope of global public goods.

To respond to this shift in global governance, and international cooperation, developing countries must now set the sustainable development agenda, because in the coming years, they will be making increasing demands on ecological resources, as they consume vast quantities of natural resources for infrastructure, urbanization and food security, as well reaching planetary limits. The annual meetings of the Conference of Parties (COP) would then no longer focus on 'conference diplomacy' and review the level of annual emission reductions. The governments would establish informal 'networks for innovation' and address modification of consumption and production patterns, as well as food security, to understand how best to make the transition to global sustainability while ensuring human well-being.

References

Davis and Ken Caldeira. 2010. 'Consumption Based Accounting of CO_2 Emissions'. *Proceedings of National Academy of Sciences of the United States.* 107(12): 5687–92.

Hertwich, Edgar G. and Glen P. Peters. 2009. Carbon Footprint of Nations: A Global, Trade-Linked Analysis. *Environmental Science and Technology.* 43(16): 6414–6420.

IEA. 2013. *World Energy Outlook.* International Energy Agency, Paris.

Ken Caldera and Stephen J. Davis. 2011. 'Accounting for Carbon Dioxide Emissions: A Matter of Time'. *Proceedings of National Academy of Sciences of the United States.* 108(21): 8533–34.

NAS. 2010. *Limiting the Magnitude of Future Climate Change.* National Academy of Sciences. National Academies Press, Washington.

NIC. 2008. *Global Trends 2015: A Transformed World,* National Intelligence Council, NIC 003-2008, Washington DC, USA.

UNFCCC. 2011. Compilation and Synthesis of Fifth National Communications-Policies, Measures and Past and Projected Future Greenhouse Gas Emission Trends of parties included in Annex I to the Convention, FCCC/SBI/2011/inf. 1/Add. 23 May 2011.

The New Climate Regime

11.1   Re-emergence of China and India

According to an analysis of economic trends by the Organization for Economic Co-operation and Development (OECD), the think-tank of the developed countries, around 2030 Asia will be the world's powerhouse just as it was prior to 1800. This suggests that these countries will define standards of living, natural resource use, global values and international cooperation [OECD, 2012;][1].

First, though it is now universally acknowledged that countries gain in influence more because of the size of the economy than the strength of their military, the global implications of the rising economic power of Asia have yet to be grasped. Currently, the OECD has two-third of global output compared to one-fourth in China and India, and by 2060, these two countries will have a little less than half of world GDP with OECDs share shrinking to one-quarter. The new giants are expected to establish new institutions and shape new global rules rather than challenge the international system which led to their rise.

Second, in addition to changes between States there will be changes in country shares of global GDP, largely driven by ageing populations. China is expected to surpass the United States around 2020 to become the largest economy in the world. India's GDP will equal that of the Euro area in 2030 and in 2060 it will exceed that of the United States, increasing from 11 to 18 per cent as a share of global GDP while China's share will remain at 28 per cent during this period, as its dependency ratio will quadruple, and the relative share of both the United States and the Euro area will decline. The working age population of China has peaked, while India has half its population – 650 million people who are less than 25, out of which 400 million are less than 15 years old, presenting a very different set of challenges compared to the other powers.

Third, living standards will rise but differences will persist. Both China and India will experience more than sevenfold increase in income per capita by 2060, but China could equal and India is expected to be little more than half of current U.S. levels – with a significant impact on patterns of natural resource use and emissions of carbon dioxide. While education, skills and productivity can enhance standards of living, by 2030 demand for food and energy is expected to rise 50 per cent and water stress has the potential of interstate conflict. Clearly, drivers, trends and patterns of natural resource use are more important for the re-emerging countries to meet rising aspirations of the middle class than for other countries having to reduce their emissions of greenhouse gases.

---

[1] This chapter draws on material first published in Sanwal (2012, 2013, 2014)

Fourth, there is as yet no common understanding on what the world will look like once all the global sustainable development goals are fully achieved. The emerging scientific consensus is that the meta-goal should be 'a prosperous, high quality of life that is equitably shared and sustainable' [ICSU, ISSC, 2015]. In the absence of a global consensus, global convergence of levels of well-being while keeping middle-class aspirations within global ecological limits will remain the most important national policy issue for both China and India. Therefore, new values based on the principle of shared responsibility and prosperity will have to be the basis for international cooperation; redistribution has so far been kept outside the United Nations system. All developing countries cannot and will not aspire to achieve the 'American way of life', and the United Nations has begun work on replacing per-capita income with another indicator of 'happiness'. New global rules for the use and distribution of natural resources to raise standards of living for all will be vital for continued global growth, and for global peace and prosperity.

China and India will have to reconstruct international relations theory, as the focus of both realists and idealists is on material force and material benefit, whereas we now need a global vision of equitable distribution and sharing of natural resources and technology. This will support a new model of sustained growth different to the finance led United States consumption and Chinese production-based models. A shared vision of prosperity for four billion people who have yet to benefit from globalization and join the middle class, based on finance, and China has reserves of $4 trillion, and innovation jointly developed between China and other countries, will provide the legitimacy to reshape the future global order to overcome global ecological limits, and avoid conflict.

There is limited appreciation of the way multilateral rule-making is being redefined. The lack of reference to the principle of common but different responsibilities in its original form in the emerging framework is a sign of geopolitical change, as well as the changing nature of the aspirations of the G77 from eradication of poverty to sustainable development. Loans from the World Bank are losing their earlier power of leverage (China's soft loans to Africa already exceed those provided by the World Bank) and a robust Dispute Settlement Mechanism in the World Trade Organization is now increasingly used by the developing countries without fear of undue retaliation. In the absence of negotiated solutions, the WTO is becoming a forum to channel complaints on market access arising from balancing national climate-related energy policies and international trade – China entering the global renewable energy market and Japan at the forefront of energy efficiency goods – and where large numbers of consumers are involved the decisions can have a significant environmental impact [Silva-Send, 2013]. Differentiation is gradually being diluted in political, economic and social terms in both the climate regime and the global sustainable development goals, which now include climate change. Sustainability is now being discussed in the United Nations Economic and Social Council, and not in parallel frameworks focusing on issues and sectors. Multi-lateral arrangements are in a state of flux.

11.2 Emerging climate regime

The world is at a defining moment, much like at the end of World War II when the United States established the multilateral system, putting economic concerns under the Bretton Woods Institutions with 'one dollar one vote' and keeping political concerns in the Security Council where the victors had a veto, while humanitarian and environmental concerns went to the United Nations with its 'one country one vote'. It has become clear that in a multipolar world, the new global challenges can no longer be dealt with in a fragmented system.

The climate treaty, negotiated in Rio in 1992, was an experiment in bringing together environment and development to reconcile a continually growing global economy within a finite global ecosystem. However, international environmental law has not been able to resolve how to accommodate the rising living standards of all those who have so far been excluded from the benefits of globalization through burden sharing. Post-Rio 2012, development and environment are coming together around global sustainable development goals to shape patterns, trends and drivers of global change. The new rules to be developed for the post-2020 climate regime are considering aggregate emissions pathways rather than just percentage reductions in emissions of greenhouse gases. The distinction between climate change, development and sustainable development is blurring because of the recognition that natural resource use is shaped by the consumption patterns of the urban middle class.

The political problem is that the billion richest accounts for over 70 per cent of world consumption with the poorest billion accounting for only 1 per cent of natural resource use, and how the ecological limits are approached depends on lifestyles and associated consumption. These in turn depend on what is used, and how and what is regarded as essential for human well-being. The industrialized countries, are reluctant to even put the longer-term trends of natural resource use on the global agenda. They continue to see the collective response in terms of new rules for intervention to meet environmental risks in countries, primarily the least developed countries, that are not urbanizing rather than for societal and technological transformations. A redefinition of national security is being pushed by them raising the question whether traditional roles of national states and international agreements will prove adequate for dealing with the adverse effects of climate change as a 'threat multiplier'. The deliberations in the Security Council on this issue mirror those in the climate forum and have ignored the complex interactions between human activities, ecological limits and international cooperation. Addressing fragility is now being suggested as critical to address poverty in all countries, and not only the conflict-ridden, with a stress on inclusive institutions and norms and targets for monitoring aid spending on global peace, security and conflict resolution [OECD, 2015].

The policy issue for China and India is whether to continue with the comfortable but fraying principle of environmental law, 'common but differentiated responsibilities and respective capabilities' agreed in 1992, even as the context in which that was framed has changed. This is because deliberation has shifted to other forums, and there is the need to acknowledge the significance of the different concerns coming together around human well-being and take a more forward looking approach of the interplay between universality and diversity. For example, new researches like the World Economic Forum's 'Global Risk Report, 2013', state that severe income disparity is a greater disruptive risk by likelihood and impact than climate change. By shifting the global agenda from environmental risk as the overriding concern to seeking human well-being within ecological limits, these countries are shaping the new global goals to focus on the gaps in the Millennium Development Goals (MDG), because eradicating poverty has been central to the agenda of the United Nations since it was established in 1948 with limited success.

This new global vision will have five key elements.

First, the reduction in poverty in recent decades has been overwhelmingly dependent on the rapid growth in China, which alone accounts for three-fourths of the global reduction and did not adopt an MDG-focused policy. A review of past trends suggests that two-thirds of poverty reduction depends on growth and one-third on equality; poverty will be eradicated only when all have assured access to affordable services, like energy, food, housing, transport, education, health and employment that urban areas provide. A consensus is needed to define global goals around middle-class standards of living that ensure both exercise of universal rights and provide economic opportunities.

Second, the key global concern should be modifying longer term trends in consumption and production patterns to determine how standards of living can be raised within ecological limits. Developing countries will shift to urbanization and manufacturing to provide employment and services. This transformation will need to limit the use of natural resources while still achieving high standards of living, and will require a review of existing global rules (e.g. intellectual property rights) and new rules (e.g. energy efficiency and joint research on sharing agriculture biotechnology).

Third, the guiding principle for the new partnership should be a functional view of the principle of common but differentiated responsibilities and respective capabilities for acknowledging diversity; and 'sharing responsibility for the Planet and prosperity of the People'. The MDGs, for example, did not include adequate and affordable energy, which is essential for growth, because it has a global environmental impact and was controversial. They also framed development cooperation narrowly as essentially an aid-driven relationship and ignored other policy instruments like trade, investment and technology transfer. New goals will need new rules and a new partnership, or 'global deal'.

Fourth, all the analyses suggest that the most rapid growth of the middle class will occur in Asia. China and India are still building their infrastructure, and according to BPs forecasts in its 'Energy Outlook 2030', energy-use per capita is predicted to increase at a similar rate to that in industrialized countries in the period 1970–2011, and despite energy intensity of GDP in 2030 being less than half of the level in 1970, incomes and population are expected to drive a 40 per cent increase in global primary energy use. Currently, per capita generation of electricity in India is one-fifteenth and in China one-fifth that of the United States and the use of cheap and widely available coal will continue because of the imperatives of growth, which also provides opportunities for reshaping the pattern of demand or lifestyles.

Fifth, in the face of continuing reluctance of the industrialized countries to modify longer term trends in consumption and production patterns, which they had committed to under the Convention, and geopolitical shifts in the power of developing countries, a rigid environmental perspective giving sole consideration to risk management is giving place to a more flexible sustainable development perspective of economic growth within ecological limits. Temporarily overshooting of the global temperature limits using carbon budget or paths over time rather than an end-point is gaining prominence amongst scientists and is likely to be reflected in any new agreement. International cooperation will then be seen in terms of sharing technological development and exchanging experiences on societal transformations that will lead to emissions reduction, and not the other way round.

11.3   Moving away from current and per capita emissions

The Prime Ministers of India and China stayed away from the UN Climate Summit, held on 23 September 2014 in New York, convened by the United States Secretary-General, signalling a lack of confidence that such meetings outside of the formal United Nations negotiations are going to produce an outcome that will be fair to them. They are now crafting a response that secures middle-class well-being of their populations, protects the global climate and has the support of the majority of countries.

The most recent science on climate change supports a shift to a sustainable development perspective. The 'World Social Science Report, 2013', produced by the United Nations (UNESCO), concludes that we must 'reframe climate and global environmental change from a physical into a social problem'. New rules for sharing technology will make the pie bigger while placing restrictions on emissions of carbon dioxide from the use of energy will allow some to take a larger slice.

The United States and the European Union are pushing for a political agreement that will 'update' the Climate Treaty, of 1992, with voluntary pledges to enact laws to cut emissions of carbon dioxide, while continuing to use the provisions for reporting, review and assessment of national action. Countries would be legally required to enact domestic climate change policies but would voluntarily pledge to specific levels of emissions cuts and to channel money to poor countries to help them adapt to climate change. Countries might then be legally obligated to report their progress toward meeting those pledges at meetings held to identify nations that did not meet their cuts.

Industrialized countries are reluctant to discuss the implications of elements of the new climate agreement in the climate negotiations, because what is being suggested is not 'updating' the Climate treaty but amending its defining feature – the principle of common but differentiated responsibilities – not through a legal amendment but by a political agreement of specifying emission reduction. Industrialized countries are already obligated to reduce emissions and it would be replaced with voluntary pledge while requiring developing countries to agree to a similar arrangement, whereas the treaty recognizes the low per capita emissions of developing countries and that their emissions will grow to enable eradication of poverty. The result will be as the 'OECD Environmental Outlook to 2050' points out that its member countries will contribute over 20 per cent to the increase in global emissions till 2050, when their per capita emissions will be nearly two times that of the others.

Second, according to the *Report of the Secretary-General, International Financial System and Development*, released in 25 July 2014, in the 2009 Copenhagen Accord of the United Nations Framework Convention on Climate Change, developed countries agreed to the joint mobilization of $100 billion annually by 2020 to address the needs of developing countries. A preliminary assessment of fast-start finance finds that 80 per cent of these flows were also counted as ODA and were paid out with similar modalities, largely through bilateral channels. Less than half of it was delivered as grants. Most of the $200 now pledged in the New York Summit will come from institutional investors, commercial banks and insurance companies. Climate financing more broadly remains focused on mitigation, while financing for adaption – critical for the most vulnerable countries – is lacking.

Third, economic concerns continue to dominate national policy making in industrialized countries. For all the concern about the global environment, currently, in the European Union, coal-fired electricity generation capacity has been ramped up, and carbon emissions have been on the rise, fuelled by imports of cheap United States coal. Developing countries, learning from the developed countries, must be cautious in international negotiations while being aggressive at home.

The United States, as the largest emitter, ensured it had no measurable commitments in the Climate Treaty in 1992, did not ratify the Kyoto Protocol in 1997, the European Union reneged on its commitment in the Kyoto Protocol for a second commitment period and since the Copenhagen Conference, in 2009, these countries have insisted that developing countries, irrespective of their level of development, also take on similar commitments. Developing countries, led by India and China, have begun to consider at the national level an alternative vision.

11.4   Limitations of international environmental law

A key question now being asked is whether the principles and instruments of international environmental law are the best way of framing global climate change and developing international cooperation for its solutions? The new High Level Political Forum (HLPF) on Sustainable Development recently established in the United Nations (A/67/L.72 dated 27 June 2013) to replace the Commission on Sustainable Development will review progress of all major conferences and result in a 'negotiated ministerial declaration', blurring the distinction with arrangements like the climate treaty. Recent science argues for goals that consider both people and planet [Nature, 2013]. The sustainable development goals, now being negotiated for the post-2015 global agenda will define sustainable development including climate change, as well as international cooperation at least for the next 30 years, and will be more transformative than the previous period.

In an interdependent world, the patterns, trends and drivers of global change are at the heart of the climate negotiations. The central issue of global environmentalism is a set of interlinked concerns – how much more growth can the planet survive? How can poorer nations raise their living standards to parity with the 'developed' world? And within both rich and poor countries, how can a fairer distribution of the benefits of growth be realised? The key problem of our time is the possibility of pursuing three goals simultaneously: ecological sustainability, economic development and a more equitable distribution of wealth within and among nations and will now need to be resolved by developing countries, because that is where growth is taking place.

The central feature of climate change is aggregate emission pathways and related national measures, and they reflect changing patterns of energy use and evolve with economic development. In the industrial stages of development, an economy largely consumes energy to produce goods. In the more mature stages of development, as incomes grow, energy use becomes more important in supporting urban living, transport and diet based on 'lifestyles', not needs. The overriding global goal of human well-being follows from new information on the science, analysis of trends, drivers for change and forms of international cooperation, and climate policy is really about middle-class standards of living and central to the domestic agenda of all countries.

Instead of the narrow focus on mitigation, adaptation and burden sharing as add-ons to be implemented through international environmental law and global markets, the building blocks of global sustainability are now moving towards a transformation in the way all countries use natural resources. For example, the Academies of Sciences of the United States and China have recently intensified their cooperation in renewable energy technology development, cost reduction or deployment outside the climate treaty [NAS, 2010].

The IPCC Fifth Assessment Reports (AR5) conclude that the cumulative emissions of CO_2 are the dominant factor determining the global mean surface warming [IPCC, 2013]. The IPCC has also concluded that global CO_2 emissions from fossil fuel combustion are within 8 per cent uncertainty (i.e. in 90 per cent confidence interval), while uncertainties for CO_2 emissions from other sources have an order of ±50 per cent, uncertainty for global emissions of CH_4, N_2O and the F-gases are about 20, 60 and 20 per cent, respectively. Therefore, national carbon budgets, within a given range rather than an absolute number, can safeguard the ecological health of the planet, ensure policy space for developing countries to eradicate poverty and focus on the transformation of the world economy and human activity, leading to patterns of resource use that are common for all countries. Climate governance has to be conceptualized in terms of strategies that will modify patterns of resource use rather than in terms of multilateral environmental agreements that will determine a balance of rights and obligations.

The scope, structure, design and implementation of a fair future agreement, to balance the interests of the major economies, should be focused on monitoring national actions rather than determining these actions, and be based on three elements.

First, as global emissions now have to remain within an agreed limit range, reductions have very different implications for economies that will continue to grow and where growth has stabilized. As emissions, standards of living and global ecological limits are interlinked, and cannot be considered in isolation, the new regime has to allow for convergence of global living standards within global ecological limits for it to have any legitimacy in developing countries.

Second, an understanding, rather than agreed global criterion, for sharing the carbon budget is a precondition for national actions to be endorsed and reviewed in terms of fairness, otherwise developed countries lack of ambition will get international approval to the detriment of the others as energy use reaches the planet's ecological limits before comparable levels in standards of living are achieved. Therefore, what is 'fair' must focus on natural resource use, different peaking dates or concentration of carbon dioxide in the atmosphere should shape the multilateral reporting and assessment of national actions in terms of effects on emissions pathways over the long term, as global growth will continue till at least 2060.

Third, the international review of national actions should, therefore, consider national circumstances, or levels of development, as well as related international cooperation on sharing technological development and exchanging experiences on societal transformations – the modification of longer term trends in consumption and production patterns that generate carbon dioxide – rather than consider only the effects of those activities expressed in terms of emissions reductions.

Review of nationally determined actions should include qualitative measures and quantitative aims. A transformation, rather than incremental change, alone will modify the increase in global temperature. In the new regime, national action and global rules should consider societal and technological transformations, moving away from requiring equitable access to the atmospheric resource along with a focus on environmental risks, while still seeking fairness. In the Lima Call for Climate Action 'fairness' is referred to in terms of national circumstances rather than historical responsibility, reflecting the earlier China–United Announcement. By recognizing that China's emissions of carbon dioxide will continue to grow till 2030, the United States adopted a sustainable development perspective, subordinating to it the earlier approach of sole focus on emissions reduction and limiting increases in global temperature. The shift responds to the global policy dilemma of balancing human well-being, energy use and related reductions in concentrations of carbon dioxide in the atmosphere.

The two largest emitters, responsible for over one-third of global emissions, unexpectedly announced their respective post-2020 actions on climate change, 'recognizing that these actions are part of the longer range effort to transition to low-carbon economies, mindful of the global temperature goal of 2°C.' They addressed the knotty problem raised by the global agreement in 2010 on keeping increases in global temperature below 2 degrees centigrade, which placed the issue of planetary limits at the centre of climate change negotiations, with a focus on peaking years; a peaking year shifts the focus to sharing the global carbon budget. The deal reframes historical responsibility by moving away from a single peaking year and links emissions reductions to transformation of the energy system.

Concretely, the United States is expected to cut net greenhouse gas emissions by 12–14 per cent of 1990 levels by 2025. China is expected to increase its emissions by around 30 per cent and 20 per cent of its energy will come from renewables in 2030. By this time it will have completed its infrastructure development and urbanization process, and will have a GDP per capita of $21,000 – a level half that of Germany, which most developing countries aspire to instead of the consumerism in American urban regions. Even more important, the gap between per capita energy use and emissions in China and the United States will converge to around 10–12 tonnes per capita by 2030; China's population is also expected to start decreasing from this year onward [MIT-Tsinghua, 2014].

11.5 Leadership by China and India

The policy implication of the 'China-US Joint Announcement on Climate Change' in November 2014, accounting for over one-third of global greenhouse gas emissions, has been to break the deadlock on what developing countries should do by re-framing the issue.

China will increase the non-fossil fuel share of all energy to around 20 per cent by 2030, putting up additional 800–1,000 GW of nuclear, wind, solar and other zero emission generation capacity by 2030 – more than all the coal-fired power plants that exist in China today and close to total current electricity generation capacity in the United States. Shifting the criteria for review of actions taken by developing countries from emissions reduction to longer term transformations, in an increasingly interdependent world, is more important for the social and economic development of growing economies than for the mature economies of industrialized countries. In updating the 20-year-old

Climate Convention, the Announcement makes equity a part of the architecture and responds to the finding by the Intergovernmental Panel on Climate Change that 'the evidence suggests that outcomes seen as equitable can lead to more effective international cooperation'. It has four implications for the global climate policy.

First, it re-frames the political divide on whether it is time to end the differentiation between industrialized and developing countries. The existing division of countries in the Convention follows the United Nations classification, largely based on per capita incomes. In the Announcement, the focus has now shifted from who has to do what, or burden sharing under international environmental law, to what has to be done and how, as part of global sustainable development goals.

Second, by recognizing that China's emissions of carbon dioxide will continue to grow till 2030, the Announcement adopts a sustainable development perspective as against the current approach of focusing on increases in global temperature, which is really the symptom and not the cause of the problem. This shift responds to the policy problem that there is no agreed pathway to balance human well-being, energy use and related reductions in emissions of carbon dioxide, and how this shift will best come about has now been has made the focus of the deliberations in the annual meetings on climate change. For example, it tacitly recognizes the complex reality that a focus on total emissions ignores human well-being, and the Announcement recognizes different time frames for peaking of emissions of carbon dioxide; peaking is really about sharing the global carbon budget.

Third, it recognizes the evolution in our understanding of the problem, as modification of longer term trends at the national level will be enabled, rather than directed, by new global rules that provide policy coherence in a multipolar world to support the transformation in natural resource use. The Announcement states that urbanization is a major trend in the twenty-first century, and cities worldwide account for a significant per cent of global greenhouse gas emissions. The United States and China will share city-level experiences with planning, policies, and use of technologies for sustainable, resilient, low-carbon growth, smart infrastructure for urbanization and set new city-level goals. This responds to the causes of the growth of emissions of carbon dioxide in the civilizational trend – shift of rural populations to cities and middle-class levels of well-being. This process had been completed in the industrialized countries by the 1970s and three-quarters of the population of China will move into cities by 2030 and provides the context for the causes and solutions to the climate problem.

Four, the unresolved issue is whether the Announcement will save the Planet. The Intergovernmental Panel has suggested that 'global emissions need to fall by 40–70 per cent by 2050 with multiple pathways to achieve this objective', and it will be debated whether the Agreement supports the required reduction in emissions. The European Union has already taken steps in this direction and the pressure now builds up on Australia, Canada and Japan. India is also taken a decision to expand its solar energy programme to 15,000 MW over the next 5 years and deforestation rates have come down from their peak in Brazil. The focus now shifts to a global sustainable development goal for all countries to generate 20 per cent of their electricity requirement from renewable sources, and how best to achieve it.

United States President Barack Obama described China's commitment of peaking its carbon dioxide emissions by 2030 as 'important because if China, as it develops, adopts the same per capita carbon emissions as advanced economies like the United States or Australia, this planet doesn't stand a chance, because they've got a lot more people' [China Daily, 2014]. Clearly, this was an important incentive for the United States, and the statement suggests that it will be on such parameters that the agreement will be sold to the United States Senate and to other industrialized countries – peaking safeguards the environment and is a practical solution to a very complex problem of international cooperation.

China is confident that as it reaches saturation levels of infrastructure development by the 2030s, its subsequent 'lifestyle'-related emissions will not increase to the same level as happened in the United States because its activity levels are very different. For example, the average U.S. citizen consumes more than four times the electricity of the average Chinese; in the United States floor space per inhabitant is roughly twice and energy use per square metre of floor area in the residential sector is three times that in China. Car ownership is 10 times higher in the United States than in China, though the difference is declining China has still lower emissions per car and stronger vehicle emission standards [Climate Action Tracker, 2014].

At the climate conference at Lima, in December 2014, doing away with the legal differentiation between countries at different levels of development has brought centre-stage the political problem of balance between contributions of countries that are required to cap their emissions (industrialized countries) and countries that will do so later (developing countries), in a manner that will ensure that the late developers can continue to use energy for infrastructure, urbanization and moving their rural poor into the urban middle class. The China-United States Climate Announcement and the subsequent Lima Call for Climate Action, which reflects that understanding, makes mitigation and adaptation an integral part of the urban transformation taking place in China, and in India. This paradigm shift is based on the use and distribution, not scarcity, of natural resources and re-frames the nature and scope of national actions creating new nodes for international cooperation. An understanding of its dimensions is important in analysing the factors shaping the architecture and evolution of the new climate regime as the global climate, sustainable development and geopolitical agendas come together. No country has substantially reduced poverty without urbanization and greatly increasing the use of energy; most economic activity would be impossible without energy. An analysis of the patterns of natural resource use shows that while renewable energy is a substitute for coal in the generation of electricity, there is no practical substitute for cement and steel required for infrastructure development; global construction accounts for half of natural resource use. The climate paradox is that emissions will have to rise before they can come down.

Critically, the Announcement also recognized the evolution in our understanding of the climate problem with urbanization as a mega-trend and driving force. No country has developed without the shift of population from agriculture and cities are centres of innovation and growth. Urbanization – as a social phenomenon, physical transformation of natural resources and generator of wealth – is one of the most powerful, irreversible and visible anthropogenic forces on Earth. These are social processes where environmental impacts are linked with the economies which collectively shape us just as society shapes the natural environment; they are not independent silos, as we have been considering since the Report of the Brundtland Commission in 1987. It is very possible that defining peaking points until the process of urbanization is completed in India and other late developing nations – effectively replicating the China–United States deal forms a part of the new global consensus and eventual global treaty.

Two-third of future global growth is going to take place in Asia and the issue at the heart of the climate negotiations is really how to support the Asian giants in managing this transformation. The issue is no longer whether and to what extent China and India will modify their growth pathways to reduce carbon dioxide emissions because of the national policies of these countries and the emerging evidence that they are de-coupling economic growth from carbon dioxide emissions; they are no longer relying on their low historical emissions as reasons for not taking national actions.

These approaches are supported by national policy actions, which are more significant than in industrialized countries because of differences in levels of development. China installed more renewable energy capacity in 2013 and in 2014 than Europe and the remaining Asia Pacific region combined and accounts for two-thirds of global solar panel production, 90 per cent of installed biogas systems and 40 per cent of newly installed wind capacity in 2013 [IRENA, 2014]. India is seeking investments of US $100 billion over 7 years to boost the domestic solar energy capacity by 33 times to 100,000 megawatts by 2022. They are both aiming for renewables contributing around 20 per cent to total electricity generation by 2030; whereas in 2040, in the United States, the share of renewables is likely to be around 16 per cent [EIA, 2014]. As the United Nations points out the global challenge is to develop a broad consensus on what kind of urbanization will nurture sustainable growth [Clos, 2015]. It has been estimated that fast-urbanizing cities in Asia could potentially reduce total global energy use in cities by more than 25 per cent from business as usual [Creutzig, Felix, 2015].

The transformation in the use of energy has strong public support in these countries. Air pollution has become a persistent problem for most Chinese major cities. Even more important, China sees economic opportunity in upgrading its industry and developing new growth poles for its economic development and now identifies its core interest in climate change negotiations as a free and fair trade of environmental goods and international cooperation in renewable and clean energy technology research development [Zhou Ji, 2014]. The Chinese lead negotiator in climate change, the deputy director of NDRC, Mr Xie Zhenhua told the media after the China–United States Announcement that the international agreement will be an external pressure which in turn forces China to change the conventional way of development to a cleaner and more energy efficient way that will also improve the environment [Xinhua News, 2014].

India's Prime Minister Narendra Modi has also called for a paradigm shift in attitudes towards climate change. At the meeting of the National Council on Climate Change, in January 2015, he stressed that, instead of focusing on emissions and cuts alone, he wants the focus to shift to reviewing what the country has done for clean energy generation, energy conservation and energy efficiency, 'and what more can be done in these areas'. He has also called for a consortium of all nations who have the greatest solar energy potential and world leaders to join hands for innovation and cutting-edge research that would reduce the cost of solar energy, making it more accessible to people [PMO, 2015]. India's middle class is likely to follow the patterns of natural resource use of China [Indo-German Expert Group, 2015].

New approaches are coming from re-emerging countries in Asia as they are now the drivers of global growth, their transformative change is modifying longer term trends and their evolving national interests are impacting on the negotiation process. The understandings between the United States, China and India show that the three countries, at very different levels of development, are willing to collaborate on global multilateral governance. The United States now recognizes that efforts to address climate change will only be sustainable if they also serve a larger purpose of fostering prosperity and well-being for citizens around the globe [US Department of State, 2015] and considers climate change a top strategic rather than just an environmental risk [National Security Strategy, 2015].

A universal climate regime will need to reflect the concerns of countries which are late developers and where energy demand, and carbon dioxide emissions, will continue to increase till their rural populations move to cities and into the middle class, around 2050. The new framework will have to provide a technical definition for the principle of 'common but differentiated responsibilities' that reflects the needs of the services and knowledge economy that is not dependent on increasing use of energy, focusing on international cooperation goals rather than burden sharing obligations. For example, a global 'aim' for a 20 per cent share of renewable energy in electricity generation, energy efficiency improvement of 20 per cent and reduction of demand for personal urban transportation of 20 per cent of 2010 levels by 2030 is feasible, and in line with goal 7 of the Global Sustainable Development Goals.

The G20 has already agreed on 'Principles on Energy Collaboration' and a 'Action Plan on Voluntary Cooperation on Energy Efficiency' identifying increased collaboration on energy as a priority and targeting energy efficiency improvements as a means of addressing the rising demands of sustainable growth and development. India's Prime Minister Narendra Modi had made a proposal at the G20 meeting, in Brisbane in November 2014, to set up a global virtual centre for clean energy research and development, with adequate public funding, which will fund collaborative projects in diverse sources of clean energy, smart grids, energy efficiency, stressing the need to make renewable, especially solar energy competitive with conventional energy.

Global well-being is expected to converge around 2050 and carbon dioxide emissions will also have peaked by then because despite the growth of emissions in developing countries, China, having capped its emissions in 2030, will be ageing as fast as industrialized nations are now ageing, and industrialized countries will have reduced their emissions by 80 per cent according to their current trajectories and statements.

By 2060, Germany's population will shrink by one-fifth, one-third of Japan will be over 65 years old, as will China with 450 million elderly, and by 2050 the United States and European Union will be using 25% less energy per capita than today (McKinsey global Institute, 2015). As climate policy transitions towards integrating longer-term transformations in national policy, the parameters of international cooperation are also being redefined.

' The demographic deficit is now spreading to China as the human population is getting older, with implications for emissions. In 1990 only a small share of the global population lived in the few countries with fertility rates substantially below those needed to replace each generation—2.1 children per woman, and now about 60 percent of the world's population lives in countries with fertility rates below the replacement rate. The European Commission expects that by 2060, Germany's population will shrink by one-fifth, and the number of people of working age will fall from 54 million in 2010 to 36 million in 2060, a level that is forecast to be less than France's. In 2014, the share of China's population older than 60 reached roughly 15 percent; demographers predict that figure will double by 2050, reaching the equivalent of nearly 450 million people, or about one-quarter of the world's elderly, China's median age will skyrocket, from roughly 35 to 46. China is projected to add only 25 million by 2050, compared with 80 million in the United States (McKinsey Global Institute, 2015). These trends support China's aim to cap emissions of carbon dioxide in 2030 and by 2050 the United States and European Union will be using 25% less energy per capita than today.

Individual interest of countries drives the success of collective action. For meeting the global challenge of climate change, China, India and the United States are now seeing the climate treaty as an opportunity to respond to global trends to transform their energy use rather than seeking a balance of rights and obligations to insulate themselves from any obligations under that treaty. The principle of 'common but differentiated responsibilities', pushed by developing countries in 1992, responded to their national priority of poverty alleviation. The shift of agricultural populations into the urban middle class is now the defining feature of the transformation underway in China and India, and is reframing 'fairness' in terms of the needs of the 21st century, ending over 20 years of acrimonious debate on differentiation between those who have to take the lead and those who have to do less, and the Climate Convention is no longer the forum driving international cooperation and national action on climate change and its adverse effects. With China's growth rate declining to 7 percent, from the earlier 10 percent, and the impact of renewable energy and efficiency measures in China, European Union and United States, emissions of carbon dioxide from the energy sector plateaued in 2014, for the first time in 40 years without an economic crisis, multilateral treaty or market mechanisms and with the global economy expanding by 3 percent (IEA, 2015).

References

ADB. 2013. Asian Development Bank, *Innovative Asia: Advancing the Knowledge-Based Economy: The Next Policy Agenda*, Asian Development Bank, Philippines.

Clos, Joan. 2015. *Building Better Cities,* Joan Clos, Executive Director, United Nations Human Settlements Programme, McKinsey Global Institute, January 2015.

Creutzig Felix, Baiocchi Giovanni, Bierkandt Robert, Pichler Peter-Paul, Seto, Karen. 2015. 'A Global Typology of Urban Energy Use and Potentials for an Urbanization Mitigation Wedge'. *Proceedings of the National Academy of Sciences.* doi: 10.1073/pnas.13155451.

Damassa, Thomas, Nicholas Bianco, and Taryn Fransen with Jennifer Hatch. 2012. 'GHG Mitigation in the United States: An Overview of the Current Policy Landscape.' Working Paper, World Resources Institute, Washington, DC.

Ecofys. 2014. China and the U.S: How does their climate action compare? Climate Action Tracker, Policy Brief, 21 October 2014.

EIA. 2014. *Annual Energy Outlook 2014, Report Number: DOE/EIA-0383(2014).* U.S. Energy Information Administration, Washington, USA.

ICSU, ISSC (2015): Review of the Sustainable Development Goals: The Science Perspective. Paris: International Council for Science (ICSU).

IEA. 2014. *World Energy Outlook – 2014.* International Energy Agency, Paris.

IEA, 2015, *Global Energy Related Emissions of Carbon Dioxide Stalled in 2014,* Press release March 13, International Energy Agency, Paris.

IRENA. 2014. *RE Roadmap 2030: A Renewable Energy Road Map.* International Renewable Energy Agency, June 2014, Abu Dhabi.

Indo-German Expert Group. 2015. *Sustainable Lifestyles: Pathways and Choices for India and Germany* – Policy paper, Indo-German Expert Group on Green and Inclusive Economy, Jan 2015, GIZ, Berlin.

MIT-Tsinghua. 2014. *An Energy Outlook for China*, MIT-Tsinghua China Energy and Climate Program, Beijing.

McKinsey Global Institute. 2015. 'The four global forces breaking all trends', *McKinsey Insights and Publications,* April 2015.

NAS. 2010. The Power of Renewables: Opportunities and Challenges for China and the United States, Committee on U.S.-China Cooperation on Electricity from Renewable Resources; National Research Council; Chinese Academy of Sciences; Chinese Academy of Engineering, National Academy of Sciences, USA, November 2010.

National Security Strategy. 2015. The White House, February 2015, Washington, DC.

OECD. 2012. Looking to 2036: Long Term Global Growth Prospects – A going for growth Report, OECD Economic Policy papers 03, OECD, Paris.

_____. 2015. States of Fragility 2015: Meeting Post-2015 Ambitions. *OECD,* 2015, Paris.

PMO. 2015. Website, Prime Minister's Office, India.

Sanwal, Mukul. 2012. 'Rio +20, Climate Change and Development: The Evolution of Sustainable Development (1972–2012)'. *Climate and Development* 4 (2): 157–166.

Sanwal, Mukul. 2013. 'The Rise and Fall of Global Climate Policy: Stockholm to Rio 1992, to Rio + 20 and Beyond'. *Chinese Journal of Environmental and Urban Studies.* 1 (1).

Sanwal, Mukul. 2014. 'Post-2015 Global Agenda: Are the Political Decisions on Climate Change Shifting to a New Forum in the United Nations as It Comes Together with Sustainable Development and Security?' *Climate and Development* 6 (2): 93–95.

Silva-Send, 2013, Climate Change Disputes and the World Trade Organization:National energy policies and International Trade Liability, Nilmini Silva-Send, *San Diego Journal of Energy & Climate Law*, Vol 4, 195, 2012-13.

Xinhua News. 2014. '*Xie Zhenhua: The China–US Joint Announcement on Climate Change is a New Shining Point in Sino-US Relations*', Sun Bo: Xinhua News, 25 November, 2014.

Zou Ji. 2014. '*The Four Impacts of the China-US Joint Announcement on Climate Change*', China Dialogue, 11 December, 2014.

SUSTAINABLE DEVELOPMENT: NATIONAL TO GLOBAL

'Sustainable Development is development that meets the needs of the present without compromising the ability of future generations to meet their own needs'

Our Common Future, Report of the World Commission on Environment and Development 1987, United Nations.

'The Rio Conference or Earth Summit, was a major success in raising public awareness on the need to integrate environment and development

The Rio Declaration, in Principle 7, stated that 'States shall cooperate in a spirit of global partnership to conserve, protect and restore the health and integrity of the Earth's ecosystem. In view of the different contributions to global environmental degradation, States have common but differentiated responsibilities. The developed countries acknowledge the responsibility that they bear in the international pursuit to sustainable development in view of the pressures their societies place on the global environment and of the technologies and financial resources they command'

United Nations Conference on Environment and Development, 1992.

'Poverty eradication, changing consumption and production patterns, and protecting and managing the natural resource base for economic and social development are over arching objectives of, and essential requirements for sustainable development'

The Johannesburg Declaration on Sustainable Development – Political Declaration, World Summit for Sustainable Development, 2002

'The conceptual framework ... emphasises the challenge of understanding and exploring avenues for human development within Earth system boundaries. This fundamental, holistic, understanding is the basis for developing transformative pathways and solutions for global sustainability'.

Future Earth (2013) Future Earth Initial Design: Report of the Transition Team. Paris: International Council for Science (ICSU).

'A new global social contract, political will and mutual trust will be needed to achieve the shared vision of a sustainable future.'

Report of the Secretary General to the General Assembly, 69th session, Implementation of Agenda 21, the Programme for the Further Implementation of Agenda 21 and the outcome of the World Summit on Sustainable Development and of the United Nations Conference on Sustainable Development, A/6/ August, 2014.

'Sustainable development calls for robust economic development and a long term convergence in living standards between rich and poor countries in ways that are socially equitable and respect planetary boundaries'

Sustainable Development Network, United Nations, at the launch of 'The World in 2050: Pathways towards a sustainable future', March 2015.

Conceptual and Institutional Foundation

12

The evolution of sustainable development over a 40-year period is characterized by periodic development of new intellectual frameworks, institutions and rules around prioritizing issues related to demand for natural resources, ecosystem services, energy use within planetary limits and urbanization. There is now a new dimension to the global concern, which was first defined in terms of giving priority to global environmental change, then as climate change and later as sustainable development. Increasing consumer demand from the shift of rural populations to cities led by the re-emergence of China and India is now shifting economic growth, geopolitics and science from considering scarcity to considering the use and distribution of natural resources in cities. This transformation is not based on negotiated outcomes at the multilateral level, but rather seeks to modify patterns, trends and drivers of natural resource use[1].

The need for international cooperation to respond to the global environmental consequences of natural resource use, or rights to global commons, was first recognised in 1972, evolved in terms of enhancing services provided by the ecosystem, or biodiversity and related biotechnology, in 1992, and the 'sink' constraints of the planet have now taken natural resource scarcity to a new dimension, for keeping within the carbon budget. These shifts highlight the interdependencies of a globalized society in using natural resources for providing development opportunities for all people and their shift to cities. The various mechanisms evolved through global negotiations to deal with natural resources fall short because they are not located within a larger debate on dealing with human well-being and instead focus only on limiting damage, and ignore distribution in the context of scarcity. Globalization makes clear that the United Nations is best placed to support a common understanding on patterns of resource use that are in principle common for all by generating strategic knowledge, and will lead to deepening coherence of the future global agenda.

12.1 Dimensions of universalism

The Charter, of the United Nations, agreed in 1945, assigns governments a responsibility to work for peace, freedom, human rights and social and economic progress for all people, but is silent on the role of environmental issues in achieving these goals. Within the United Nations the issue of management of the global environment was framed at the conceptual and institutional levels to set

---

[1] This part draws on Levin et al. (2010); Sanwal (2012)

a new agenda for securing rights over natural resources outside territorial boundaries. In order to frame the issues in global terms to secure acceptance and international cooperation, this framework defined 'common concerns' as well as national rights and obligations, with measures to be taken in terms of the inter linkages between natural resource use, ecosystem services and planetary limits. The scientific and academic papers supporting this framework focused on universality to support new markets through new technical means for harmonization of actions, ignoring demands of developing countries for recognition of diversity to enable their social and economic development. The balance between universality and diversity has characterized academic research and multilateral negotiations; continuing tension is inherent in the way the issue was framed.

Initially, the United Nations held major population conferences in Rome in 1954 and in 1964, discussing connections between natural resources, population growth and development, as well as how these issues should be addressed by the international community. Presenting such arguments, *Paul Ehrlich's The Population Bomb (1968)*, which examined risks associated with a quickly accelerating population, gained widespread public and political attention; even though it did not distinguish between growth in numbers of the poor in developing countries and population shift of three-quarter of the population of developed countries to the urban middle class and their accelerating consumption. In September 1968, the Intergovernmental Conference of Experts on a Scientific Basis for a Rational Use and Conservation of the Resources of the Biosphere (the so-called Biosphere conference) was held under the auspices of United Nations Educational, Scientific and Cultural Organization (UNESCO). It called for comprehensive international and domestic environmental management and stressed that environmental issues were closely connected to societal issues, reflecting the intensive use of natural resources for infrastructure development in North America and Europe, after 1950, because of urbanization. An increase in transnational transportation and flows of capital, resources, materials, substances, communication infrastructure and concepts of globalization reinforced the interdependence between countries and people based on patterns and trends of natural resource use. At the same time, during the period from 1955 to 1971 United Nations' membership grew rapidly, as former colonies became independent nations, and by 1972, there were 132 members of the United Nations. At the political level, beginning at the Bandung conference in Java in 1955, many developing countries took on a more independent role in international politics, proclaiming themselves to be a third force, beside the Eastern and Western blocs.

This was the context of the 'explanatory memorandum' from Sweden to U Thant, Secretary-General of the United Nations in May 1968, outlining why the United Nations should organize a global conference on the problems of the human environment. The memorandum stated that 'problems of human environment should be understood both as human influence on the natural environment (e.g. creation of air and water pollution, wastes and soil erosion) and the influence of natural surroundings on human health and living conditions (e.g. expansion of shantytowns, urbanization and rising crime levels)'. The relationship between human societies and the environment was defined in terms of symptoms and in physical terms and there was no mention of resource management or of the societal issues identified by the scientists.

The focus was not on implementation, but on the architecture of rights over natural resources outside national boundaries through the development of international environmental law and related principles, agreements, organizations and programs, as well harmonizing national action. The Stockholm Conference was organized around the theme of *Only One Earth* and the Stockholm Declaration called for *a common outlook* and laid down *common principles* for policy action, as specified in, for example, the Stockholm Action Plan. Once this universalism was established, the idea of giving up sovereignty through the creation of a powerful United Nations Environment Organization was resisted by the industrialized countries, and they did not accept anything beyond a coordinating mechanism.

The Stockholm Conference on the Human Environment held in 1972 laid out a weak institution, as the Brussels Group – including Belgium, France, Germany, the United Kingdom, and United States – worked on the margins to undermine the new United Nations Environment Programme (UNEP) even as it was being established, reflecting the politics around the way the issues of the global environment were framed [Gill et al., 2002; Linner et al., 2003]. As a result, the Stockholm Conference decided to recommend that the United Nations General Assembly set up a program to act as coordinator and catalyst of multilateral cooperation on the environment, rather than as an international regulatory organization, with specific issues prioritized for global action; the decision was adopted with 93 states in favour, 30 abstentions (most industrialized countries), with one country opposed to the establishment of even a weakened UNEP (United States).

At Stockholm, industrialized countries focused on global rules, rather than institutions, and stressed that all countries and people are bound together by common fundamental interests and goals on environment and development (United Nations Conference on the Human Environment (UNCHE) Country Reports). It was recognized that the industrialized countries could not resolve global problems without active cooperation by the developing countries. Many politicians and experts from developing countries acknowledged the increasing global interdependence, but questioned central conceptual aspects of this process calling for the creation of a new legal framework, institutions and practices that did not reflect differences in situations and interests between industrialized and developing countries. Their argument was that most pollution was caused by industrialized countries and consequently they alone had responsibility for finding solutions; developing countries argued that most of their environmental problems were related to local development issues such as limited access to clean drinking water, land and soil erosion and inadequate housing standards (Country Reports to UNCHE). As such, they called for more human and financial aid from industrialized countries to address these issues, which, it was argued, would improve the ability for more effective environmental management and was connected to calls for a new international economic order that would be more geared towards the conditions and interests of developing countries. The outcome was minor changes in the international economic system, and industrialized countries succeeded in securing rights to natural resources outside national boundaries and agreement on the need for concerted action on international environmental issues, as defined by them and without specifying the measures to be taken.

Out of the 132 UN member states, 113 attended the Stockholm Conference (the Eastern Bloc boycotted the Conference), and only a few raised the issue of a need for assessing the long-term viability of current levels of production and consumption. Mr L. Sico Mansholt, President of the European Economic Commission, declared in a speech to the plenary, that 'the organs of the U.N. are going to specify exactly what standard of living this percent of the world population (who are living on lower economic standards than people in the industrialized countries) can actually reach, taking into account the limits of resources and energy and the equilibrium of the ecosphere. And if we are to be sincere in our promise to close the gap between the rich and poor nations we must be ready to accept the consequences for our own rate of growth and its direction. Thus it is time to ask: Are our present social structures and production methods defensible?' The outcome of the conference, however, focused on technical issues.

The first major international attempt to revisit conceptual issues relating to environment and development post-1972 was the symposium on Patterns of Resource Use, Environment and Development Strategies that was held in Cocoyoc, Mexico, October 8–12, 1974. The symposium was organized jointly by UNEP and the United Nations Commission on Trade and Development (UNCTAD), as a multilateral meeting to examine connections between environmental protection issues and issues relating to global redistribution of economic and social resources. This agenda reflected a return to the organizing of

172 | The World's Search for Sustainable Development

expert meetings rather than political meetings, but this time initiated by a body of the United Nations led by Mostafa Tolba from Egypt, who directed UNEP from 1975 till 1992 and since then no one from a developing country has been appointed as Executive Director of UNEP.

The Declaration noted that 'the evils which flow from excessive reliance on the market system' had led to a failure to fulfil the development goals of the UN Charter for most of the world's population. Such a failure was not believed to be caused by a lack of physical resources, but by misuse as well as economic and social misdistribution within and across countries. Participants at the symposium argued that any solution to these problems could not be found in a continued reliance on free market mechanisms. It was believed that the notion of an automatic 'trickling down' of wealth from rich countries to poor countries had been disproved, similar to several of the statements that were made at the Stockholm Conference. Instead, it was argued, a new international economic system had to be created that specifically took into account the dire situation of developing countries brought about by the enforced low prices of raw materials from developing countries which had contributed to pollution and waste generation in industrialized countries. In its stand on international economic and trade issues, the Cocoyoc Declaration was linked to calls by intellectuals and representatives of many developing countries for a revision of the international economic and trade system, which they believed favoured the interests of industrialized countries over the economic and social needs of developing countries. These efforts contributed to the UN Declaration and Programme of Action on the Establishment of a New International Economic Order, which was proclaimed by the UN General Assembly in May 1974. The United States responded by withdrawing financial contributions to UNEP[2].

This was the background for the setting up of the Independent Commission on International Development Issues chaired by Willy Brandt in 1977. Seeking a common ground between North and South, its two reports stressed the existence of mutual dependence: industrialized countries needed developing countries for their wealth of natural resources and markets, and developing countries needed industrialized countries for their development. The Reports pointed out that the 'strain on the global environment derives mainly from the growth of the industrial economies, but also from that of world population. It threatens the survival and development opportunities of future generations. All nations have to cooperate more urgently in international management of the atmosphere and other global commons, and in the prevention of irreversible ecological damage' [Brandt Commission, 1980, 1983]. As in the case of the World Conservation Strategy, 1981, and the World Charter of Nature, 1983, prepared by the International Union for the Conservation of nature (IUCN) in parallel with the social science oriented Brandt Commission, the focus of the Brandt Commission was on formulating common interests, goals and responsibilities. There was no review why despite the fact that governments had made strong political commitments 'based on respect for the individual and the common good' and several policy responses had been formulated, most negative environmental trends had not been reversed and many development-related concerns of the world's poorest had not been addressed. The reports are a comprehensive solutions-oriented analysis of critical global economic issues, but they had no practical impact on policy, as the conclusions were not supported by the United States.

The broadening of the agenda from the environment to sustainable development has been a complex process. The purpose of the Brundtland Commission, 1987,[3] was to formulate another agenda that would gain the support of both developed and developing countries. Under the slogan

---

[2] However, an informal understanding continued for two decades–that the Deputy Executive Director, Secretary of the Governing Council and Chief of Personnel would be from the USA.

[3] The Commission was established by the United Nations in 1983 to reflect about ways to save the human environment and natural resources and prevent deterioration of economic and social development.

of 'a common future' – similar to the idea of 'only one earth' that was promoted at the Stockholm Conference – the Brundtland Commission argued that different conditions and needs in the North and the South resulted in different responsibilities for taking action towards a more sustainable future. The Commission also considered 'development' issues, now defined in terms of population, food security, species and ecosystems, energy, industry and human settlements.

Sustainable development was intended by its proponents to even more clearly link developing countries into the framework designed by industrialized countries. The Commission identified three factors that caused the growing equity gap between and within countries: an increase in population, the current structure of international economic relations and the increase in per capita consumption by parts of the world population (WCED, 1987). The Commission provided eight principles to guide domestic action: Review Growth, Change in the Quality of Growth, Conserve and Enhance the Resource Base, Ensure a Sustainable Level of Population, Re-orient Technology and Manage Risks, Integrate Environmental and Economics in Decision-Making, Reform International Economic Relations and Strengthen International Cooperation. The emphasis was shifted to resource use and distribution at the national level. In the 'Tokyo Declaration', which was issued at its final meeting, the Commission called upon all countries to integrate sustainable development into their domestic policymaking and policy goals.

The Stockholm Conference had revealed significant disagreements among countries regarding the issues which should be prioritized and countries' economic and political responsibilities. The decade after the Stockholm Conference further polarized the North–South relationship over environment and development and related prioritizing of issues, the handling of issues, and financial and political responsibilities, which the Brundtland Commissions papered over. The subsequent major political events, efforts and policy developments served to build a new generation of multilateral rules and institutions for according rights to natural resources outside national boundaries, opening trade opportunities and harmonizing national actions irrespective of levels of development, which benefitted industrialized countries resource needs and markets but did little to deal with the global environmental problem resulting from urbanization, manufacturing and consumption patterns of middle-class 'lifestyles'.

12.2 Importance of diversity

The world order shaped by the United States after the Second World War was based on international law to regulate relations between states. The natural resources of the global commons were sought to be managed through the new field of international environmental law. The network of rules and institutions supported global trade rules that facilitated flow of natural resources and commodities to the industrialized countries and the sale of manufactured goods in return, leading to unprecedented prosperity for less than a quarter of the global population. Globalization linked the global community but did not lead to stability, security and fairness to prepare for the global middle class tripling in size by 2050. Planetary limits require equally unprecedented levels of global cooperation with respect to the use and distribution of natural resources. The problem here is that new approaches and rules will have to be devised, in which the central feature is the recognition of diversity and fairness, for the concept of a 'global citizen' to emerge. Social science research is already suggesting how human societies can organize the use and distribution of limited natural resources while modifying certain patterns and trends of resource use, rather than middle class standards of living; these conclusions have to be converted into a political consensus.

The grand bargain integrating environment and development agreed at Rio, in 1992, secured a balance of rights and obligations for burden sharing between countries at different levels of development by incorporating the principle of common but differentiated responsibilities. It remains an uneasy compromise, as the industrialized countries did not accept responsibility for their past actions and developing countries focused on financial resources. The result has also not been able to effectively deal with unintended consequences of natural resource use, ecosystem services and planetary limits.

Reviewing developments since 1972, the conclusions of a diplomat are that the basic flaw was in agenda setting, as "insufficient attention has been paid to national policies of industrialized countries. Since Stockholm, the substantive focus has been on developing countries. Yet, a change to more sustainable production and consumption patterns must be driven by the richer countries who use a disproportionate part of the world´s resources and who still continue to be global role models. This is in line with the principle of common but differentiated responsibility agreed in Rio and remains valid even with the later rise of several emerging economies. The reasons that such a major flaw in agenda setting developed can be partly ascribed to political design of some leading industrialized countries such as the activities of the secret Brussels group in the early, crucial, agenda setting stage before the Stockholm Conference. Later, the South´s dependence on financial assistance from the North has also been a major factor". (Lars-Göran Engfeldt, 2009).

Consequently, Sustainable Development is at a cross-road, as we move towards analysing why current arrangements which focus on management of the global environment are dysfunctional, and what might be done about it. A better understanding has emerged of how to make the transition to sustainability, driven largely by the intensive academic research, data, and business concern and policy experience around climate change. The reappraisal of the current system of international cooperation is an acknowledgement that the global policy response requires a strategic shift from merely considering environmental damage and resource productivity, or the symptoms, to enhancing and equitably sharing ecosystem services and treating the global commons as an economic resource. While each country has its own vision of well-being and fairness in defining the criteria for sharing the global commons, an analysis of patterns, trends and drivers of national resource use since 1972 suggests that transforming societies towards living in balance with the natural environment will be necessary as the global middle class triples in size, and will also lead to more equity and coherence of the global agenda.

The issue remains inherently political. The choice is for either affluence with persistent disparity and tension or moderation with prospects for equity and coherence. If there is to be some kind of prosperity for all world citizens, the Western model needs to be superseded, making room for ways of living, producing, and consuming that leave only a light footprint on the earth [Sachs, 2010]. While the average Southeast Asian used 3.3 tons of materials in 2008, the average North American used 27.5 tons – eight times as much. People are consuming so much as it stems from decades of engineering of a set of cultural norms, values, traditions, symbols, and stories that make it feel natural to consume ever larger amounts – of food, energy and material. Policymakers changed laws, marketers and the media cultivated desire, businesses created and aggressively pushed new products, and over time 'consumers' deeply internalized this new way of living. These and countless other lifestyle choices are in the aggregate undermining the well-being of countless humans, today and for centuries into the future [Assadourian, 2010; Costanza et al., 2012].

New thinking has been enabled and supported by the shift in global power as regional power blocs become increasingly important in multilateral negotiations. The key factors enabling the global shift of economic power from the industrialized economies to the emerging economies are the higher rates of productivity and income growth in these economies, which are outpacing those in industrialized economies. Other important drivers are similar to those underlying continued economic growth: population shifts from rural to urban areas, continuing technological innovation and diffusion of technologies, favourable economic policies and integration at regional and global level [Maddison, 2001]. Fast-growing countries may even gain more in economic influence than their growth rates suggest when their middle-class consumers grow in numbers and start to spend discretionary income on modern, short-cycle consumer goods, becoming attractive export markets for industrialized countries. For example, the BRIC countries are already able to exercise power at international negotiations on economic matters (such as trade barriers and product standards) as well as in climate change, and other environmental and sustainable development negotiations.

Global sustainable development should be about big thinking beyond just green growth, develop new levels of international cooperation and take political decisions to change the relationship between human activities and nature for a sustainable planet. Global goals provide the opportunity to answer the question how a continually growing economic system can fit within a finite ecological system. Natural resources underpin the functioning of the global economy and the quality of life of all citizens, and the concern over limits is not new. What is new is the scientific evidence that the planet will soon not be able to absorb the waste carbon dioxide of infrastructure development, industrial activity, urbanization and excessive consumption. The policy response has to be a new form of international cooperation to equitably share the carbon space in the global commons[4], because of the impacts on other drivers of human well-being. A low carbon green economy is now considered synonymous with sustainable development and has been defined as one that results in improved human well-being and social equity, while significantly reducing environmental risks and ecological scarcities, requiring a significant paradigm shift across entire societies [Jackson, 2009; UNEP, 2011; WBGU, 2011]. The outcome should, therefore, focus on the social rather than the environmental dimension of sustainable development, and lay the ground for supporting a qualitatively different economic model.

12.3 Understanding human well-being

The distinguishing feature of economic development is the population shift from rural to urban areas, and rising levels of GDP per capita correspond to levels of urbanization. Rising levels of income lead to rising levels of resource use. Currently, over half the human population lives in cities, consuming three-quarters of all natural resources and responsible for over three-quarters of the world's energy-related carbon dioxide, with transport, industry and building sectors being the largest contributors; this level will rise as urbanization continues in developing countries. Spatial organization, density and lifestyle choices determine trends in natural resource use. With all economies being increasingly driven by the urban services sector, and not just by industrialization, global environmental change is being driven by the lifestyles of the middle class worldwide.

The limits to growth concerns not just ecosystem scarcity but also the impact on individual welfare, through reduced options of future generations. The use of energy and technology has led to economic growth and the shift out of agriculture to urban areas has contributed to the increase in consumption of natural resources, defining current levels of human well-being. This has clearly occurred along an unsustainable pathway. According to the report of the *UK Sustainable Development Commission – Prosperity without Growth: the Transition to a Sustainable Economy* [Jackson, 2009], once prosperity ceases to mean increasing consumption of material goods, then the focus shifts towards the capabilities that citizens will need to 'participate meaningfully and creatively in the life of society … Humans can still flourish and yet reduce their material impact on the environment'. However, increased efficiency of production, or relative decoupling, in most cases has led to decreased

---

[4] The atmosphere and the oceans serve as global commons for the waste carbon dioxide of human activity, and 'sinks' include national forests.

consumption; absolute decoupling, or conservation of resources to keep within ecological limits, will not happen without societal change. Designing strategies for a decoupling of economic activity from undesirable environmental impacts requires an improved understanding of trends and their drivers. While adopting a global perspective in outlining the magnitude of the challenge, it is important to assess actual past trends rather than project resource consumption into the future.

Growth pathways for countries follow three somewhat consecutive phases of development of electricity coverage, infrastructure for industrialization and urbanization, which in turn leads to higher levels of income and well-being reflected in population shifting from rural to urban areas and later rising wealth and consumption patterns in cities. References made to 'leapfrogging' by developing countries with introduction of new technology to modify production patterns ignore the infrastructure needs which depend on energy and natural resources. Skipping a 'dirty' stage of development considers only environmental degradation arising out of certain technologies for industrialization, ignoring the subsequent impact on ecosystem services, largely through use of energy – electricity and transport – and diet of the urban population in cities. At the same time, developing countries enjoy an advantage as they are still establishing their physical and technological infrastructures, but the notion of staying within ecosystem thresholds presupposes societal change to shift to a new growth pathway – public transport instead of personal mobility that is not even considered for industrialized countries. Innovation now needs to be focused on patterns of resource use that are common for all.

For example, the emerging scientific consensus challenges current perspectives on the rise in global temperatures as a result of future emissions as well as the nature of international cooperation required to deal with the consequences. According to an international consultative process conducted by the International Council for Science and the International Social Science Council, the social and biophysical sub-systems are intertwined such that the system's conditions and responses to external forcing are based on the synergy of the two sub-systems. Consequently, the full global system has to be studied rather than its independent components, as none of the challenges can be fully addressed without addressing the other challenges. For example, we know that half the global carbon budget has already been exhausted, but there is no consensus on the patterns, trends and drivers that led to this situation (ICSU, 2010). For developing countries, the critical sustainable development issue is policy space for urban design, building urban infrastructure in a way that will modify longer term trends in consumption patterns while ensuring basic services, employment and well-being, or equitable access to sustainable development.

It has also now become clear that international cooperation based on multilateral agreements around long-term economy-wide issues, like climate change, is different to sectoral issues like the ozone problem, as alternative patterns and processes in the human use of nature in developed and developing countries result in trade-offs for socio-economic systems that are very different to those focusing only on environmental systems. Recent research establishes that growth and climate protection are rival objectives only in high-income countries, consequently when policies focused on economic growth have confronted policies focused on emission reduction it is economic growth that wins out every time. At the global level, this has led to downplaying the fact that the largest emission reduction potential consistent with human well-being worldwide is on the consumption side, in the building and transportation sectors and diet. The issue has so far been framed to focus on production patterns to avoid industrialized countries needing to modify certain consumption patterns, even though developing countries need to take immediate steps to modify their urbanization pathways as they will shape future consumption patterns. One reason is that it suggests a new framework, as demand-side management also does not need global market mechanisms to offset mitigation amounts and costs. It only needs new forms of international cooperation to develop a global vision of well-being, as is evident from the transformative impact of the rise of China.

Moving away from earlier notions of equity around the divisive historical responsibility principle, global public policy has begun to focus on enhancing ecosystem services though fundamental shifts in consumption and production patterns onto a more sustainable path based on per capita resource use. The new paradigm by making social development goals – human well-being supported by sustainable energy and ecosystem services – as the central objective rejects the way the issue has been framed around environmental damage, as well as targets and timetables, that have shaped the definition and objectives of sustainable development since the Stockholm Conference on the Human Environment, held in 1972.

In this paradigm, the choice is not between preservation and exploitation of nature, rather the stress is on conservation through modifying patterns of natural resource use. There is the recognition that market-based mechanisms will not lead to a technological transformation, and new technologies also require a societal transformation. The new vision of sustainable development stresses adoption of patterns of resource use that are in principle common for all countries. A common understanding is needed of resultant shifts in global growth pathways that are not just based on negotiated commitments at the multilateral level to regulate on-going activities. The focus should be on working with a range of actors at different levels to generate strategic knowledge and exchange experiences for understanding and modifying longer term trends in patterns of resource use. The objective should be to increase resource conservation and productivity in the new cities, and decouple economic growth there from resource use and its environmental impact; which will be facilitated by the corresponding shift from an industrial to a services and knowledge economy.

12.4 Implications for the multilateral system

The implication for the global rule based system is that the policy focus has to be on urban design and behavioural change to reduce natural resource use by modifying demand, reducing consumption of energy, water from buildings, eliminating food wastage and modal shifts in transport. The key global challenge to support industrialization and urbanization is making energy available to those who do have it at present, and aspire to middle class well-being, in an environmentally sustainable manner. In this framework, international cooperation would review progress in three areas – monitoring deviations from multilaterally agreed national carbon budgets or peaking years, development and sharing of innovative renewable energy and agricultural biotechnologies, and developing new concepts of well-being suited to a service and knowledge-based economy.

Energy remains the unresolved political issue related to international cooperation around the equitable sharing of the global commons, and the transition to sustainability, as the poorer three-quarters of the world's population currently use only 10 per cent of the world's energy. Development of infrastructure, urbanization, manufacturing and food production are essential for economic growth and needs natural resources, including energy and related carbon space. Driven by equity concerns raised in the climate negotiations, the global community has begun to ask a very different set of questions instead of the current narrow focus on mitigation, adaptation and burden sharing. For example, the need to ensure access to and availability of affordable and adequate modern energy for the rising middle class as the key element of sustainable development is now recognized. However, there is no common understanding, even within international organizations, of how the resulting increased emissions from developing countries will be accommodated in the transition to sustainable development.

Global carbon management provides an integrating theme bringing together all natural resources – energy, biodiversity, water and food – as well as the global policy agenda around access to resources and development of markets. An equitable allocation of the global commons into national carbon budgets will link climate change (patterns of resource use), biological diversity (ecosystem services) and the national sustainable development goals (middle class well-being within ecological limits). National carbon budgets are also the most appropriate currently available indicator for measuring the sustainable management of natural resources, the sustainable use of atmospheric, ocean and terrestrial natural resources, as well as assessing national strategies for making the transition to sustainability. Global goals agreed at the multilateral level provide development opportunities for all people within the boundaries of the natural environment and they will require very different relations between the State, markets and citizens than under the current framework for international cooperation focused on the physical environment.

The global goal of ensuring human well-being requires a new perspective to the international debate as the United Nations struggles to find a consensus and suggests a broader focus centred on patterns of resource use that can in principle be adopted by all countries. The key scientific insight is that in actions for achieving global sustainability environmental change and social transformations are tightly intertwined. Current research trends on how to meet global challenges focus on societal dynamics as both the root of environmental problems and the potential solution to them [IHDP, 2007]. Environmental problems should not be defined as discrete problems and are increasingly being understood as symptoms of a particular economic and social growth path.

References

Assadourian, Erik. 2010. 'The Rise and Fall of Consumer Cultures'. In *'State of the World 2010,* World Watch Institute New York: W. W. Norton & Company, 2010, pp. 3–20.

Brandt Commission. 1980. North–South: A Program for Survival.

_____. 1983. Common Crisis: North–South Cooperation for World Recovery.

Costanza, R. Gar Alperovitz and Herman Daly. 2012. *Building a Sustainable and Desirable Economy-in-Society-in-Nature.* New York: United Nations Division for Sustainable Development.

Environmental Audit Committee. 2014. Third Report – Growing a circular economy: Ending the throwaway society, July 2014, London, UK.

ICSU. 2010. Earth System Science for Global Sustainability: The Grand Challenges, International Council for Science, Paris.

IHDP. 2007. Strategic Plan 2007–2015, International Human Dimension s of Global Environmental Change Programme, 2007.

Jackson, Tim. 2009. *Prosperity Without Growth: Economics for a Finite Planet.* London: Earthscan.

Lars-Göran Engfeldt. 2009, Towards a World Summit on Sustainable Development 2012, "Uniting for Sustainability": Overview of state of the implementation of the sustainable development commitments already taken in 1992 and 2002, European Economic and Social Committee and Stakeholder Forum, Brussels, 1 October 2009.

Levin, Simon A. and William C. Clark, ed. 2010. Towards a Science of Sustainability, Report from Toward a Science of Sustainability Conference, Airlie Centre, Warrenton, Virginia, November 29–December 2, 2009. CID Working Paper No. 196, Centre for International Development at Harvard University, May 2010, USA.

Linner, Bjorn-Ola, and Henrik Selin. 2003. How it all Began: Global Efforts on Sustainable Development from Stockholm to Rio. Paper presented at the 6th Nordic Conference on Environment and Social Sciences, Finland, June 12–14.

Maddison, Angus. 2001. *The World Economy: A Millennial Perspective,* OECD, Paris.

Sanwal, Mukul. 2012. 'Rio +20, Climate Change and Development: The Evolution of Sustainable Development (1972–2012)'. *Climate and Development* 4 (2): 157–166.

Seyfang, Gill, and Andrew Jordan. 2002. *The Johannesburg Summit and Sustainable Development: How Effective Are Environmental Mega-Conferences?* Yearbook of Environment and Development 2002/2003. London: Earthscan.

Sachs, Wolfgang ed. 2010. *The Development Dictionary.* London: Zed Books.

UNEP. 2011. *Towards a Green Economy: Pathways to Sustainable Development and Poverty Eradication. A Synthesis for Policy Makers,* UNEP, 2011.

WBGU. 2011. World in Transition: A Social Contract for Sustainability, *German Advisory Council on Global Change.* Berlin, March 2011.

WCED, 1987, *Our Common Future.* 1987, World Commission on Environment and Development, Oxford Paperbacks.

Politics within the United Nations

13

13.1 Setting the agenda

The economic model of industrialization–urbanization led to the environment as an input to be used and exploited for human well-being, defined as increasing production, and it was only in the 1970s with the fear that modern science may not be able to resolve the concern with substitution and that the pattern of economic growth was damaging the environment that scarcity was first raised as a global concern [Meadows et al., 1972]. The term sustainable development was first used in the World Conservation Strategy with a focus on environmental damage [IUCN, UNEP, WWF, 1980]. During most of the late twentieth century, sustainable development evolved as a set of observations about nature, and the relations of humans with it, but it was clear to many that the key to understanding this lay in the relationships reviewing consumption and production patterns, that is, how human society was evolving in its use of natural resources as a consequence of the industrial revolution and urbanization. As the sustainability debate became more mainstream in the 1980s, much of it was influenced by economics and the move to translate environmental choices into market preferences. A necessary addition was the need for measurement, and as the emphasis shifted to practical ways in which sustainability could be incorporated into existing policies and structures, policy professionals and business began to take an interest in the dialogue.

The growing environmental concerns soon became part of the mainstream debates on development and economics, without resolving the two main ambiguities in the definition relating to socio-economic needs and environmental stability. The notion of 'sustainable growth' was criticized as 'an oxymoron in a world where ecosystems are finite' [Daly, 1993]. At the same time, natural and manufactured capital were seen as interchangeable with technology filling human produced gaps, and the success in dealing with the depletion of the ozone layer modifying production and consumption patterns tended to support this view. While the World Conservation Strategy, 1980, concentrated entirely on environmental damage without discussing socio-economic concerns, their 1991 report [IUCN et al., 1991], although still concentrating on environmental issues considered social issues proposing increasing participation in decisions, improving the quality of human life and modifications to the world economy.

This process of bringing together environmental and socio-economic questions was taken up in the Brundtland Report, in 1987, which made a number of observations out of which one was picked up by the industrialized countries indicative of their intellectual capacity to see that it would also be acceptable to emerging countries, as it allowed for different interpretations without being specific in requiring any national actions in industrialized countries, and became the definition of sustainable development for meeting 'the needs of the present without compromising the ability of future generations to meet their needs' [WCED, 1987]. The report – *Our Common Future* – also stressed that human needs should be seen in a broader context than merely exploiting natural resources: 'ecology and economy are becoming ever more interwoven – locally, regionally, nationally and globally', and industrialized as well as rural subsistence societies depend for their well-being on the natural environment. It pointed to the planetary connections, with environmental problems having an impact at not just the local but increasingly at the global level, making it a multilateral issue. It linked the pattern of growth to environmental degradation and to the 'downward spiral of poverty', calling for 'changing the quality of growth, meeting essential needs, merging environment and economics in decision making' with an emphasis on human development but rejected the idea that there were environmental limits. The Brundtland Report shifted the debate from resource scarcity to meeting the needs of the poor, protecting the environment and more rapid economic growth, making the notion acceptable to emerging countries. The inherent ambiguity enabled a global consensus on three pillars of sustainable development – environmental, economic and social – at the Rio Conference in 1992.

With the shift in emphasis towards implementation and operational aspects, academic research began to look at synergies and trade-offs between the three goals. An important early initiative was taken by Non-Governmental Organizations. Product certification – through which industry would endorse the more sustainable use of resources – provided accreditation for businesses that meet defined standards of compliance. For example, the World Wide Fund for Nature (UK) established the '1995 Group' of companies with the objective of making the timber industry more sustainable. The management systems introduced defined targets and devised a system of informal self-regulation, under the control of managers appointed for the purpose. The benefits of achieving more sustainable production of wood, via the Forest Stewardship Council, included the right to use the logo of the FSC on appropriate products. The World Business Council for Sustainable Development (WBCSD) proposed the concept of eco-efficiency [Schmidheiny, 1992], and the Wuppertal Institute emphasized resource use efficiency Factor Four [Weizsacker et al., 1997]; the focus remained on production patterns. In essence, instead of viewing activities in a new framework, existing practices and policies were re-branded, and the policy thrust remained on actions in emerging countries. The reality is that because of the leverage exercised by the World Bank on all countries, except China, the emerging countries lacked the power to disagree with the agenda put forward by industrialized countries and continued to focus on securing additional finance for any national implementation while largely ignoring the implications on their natural resource use at the global level because of low rates of industrialization and lack of knowledge of the importance of requirements of transboundary resources.

Sustainable development was framed in institutional terms by industrialized countries to support multilateral decision-making for global natural resource management at the Rio Conference of 1992. The United Nations Secretary General described the real purpose of the United Nations Conference on Environment and Development (UNCED) 'as mobilizing and sensitizing world public opinion to environmental issues, which would itself be a contribution' (*UN Archives*). Brundtland, at that time the Prime Minister of Norway, voiced concern with the Secretary-General of the United Nations about how the sustainable development agenda would need to be integrated into the existing structure because real power lay in the United Nations specialized agencies. The concern of the United Kingdom was also on the machinery for follow-up, targets and monitoring arrangement. The United States made an informal proposal for restructuring, in which the authority for intergovernmental policy management was to be transferred from Governing Councils of the Specialized Agencies to the Economic and Social Council (ECOSOC), it found no support in 1992 and such a step has now been taken in 2012.

13.2 Evolution of the issues

At the end of World War II, the United States established the international order in which international cooperation was based around agreed global goals and priorities, as well as a political, legal and institutional framework for meeting them. Acknowledgement by the emerging countries of a concern for the global environment placed the issue on the international political agenda. Negotiation of multilateral treaties on an issue-by-issue basis served to maximize participation, giving the priorities of the developed countries greater legitimacy by protecting the principle of national sovereignty. The framework, at the insistence of emerging countries, included provision of financial and technical assistance to emphasize that the environmental goal needed to be balanced by development goals of countries, but not to support emerging countries in meeting their development goals. This delicate balance meant that the concept was vague enough to be open to different interpretations but the way specific issues were framed by the industrialized countries set the agenda.

At the first conference to discuss the global commons, in 1972, a tentative beginning was made towards developing a global constituency around the environment, with some questioning of the dominant system and structures without becoming overly ideological, or a threat to the existing economic model. The agenda also challenged the concept of absolute state sovereignty. For almost two decades, these issues were not prominent on the global agenda, and in 1992, climate change revived the old 'systems' concerns that were first articulated at the time of the 1972 Stockholm UN Conference on the Human Environment. At that time, scientists linked environment-related issues to and, initiated the debate on, limits to growth, the sustainability of dominant patterns of production and consumption and drew attention to global distributional and equity issues. In 2012, the second Rio Summit, now being held in a multipolar world, moved away from treaties to goals, and the new understanding also focused on the individual's personal behaviour and responsibilities, on the environmental footprint and its cumulative implications at the global level; re-visiting the issues that were first raised in 1972 and have remained unresolved.

Despite continuing the North–South debate on economic issues, a working relationship was established on global environmental issues between the emerging countries, who by now had a voting majority in the United Nations, and the smaller group of industrialized countries, which provided the finance. The institutional framework established at Stockholm was based on a balance between different objectives of the two groups of countries, with the United Nations acting as a facilitator. The United Nations was given the role of a catalyst for developing global rules around multilateral concerns related to the environment, monitoring implementation in the early period of global governance, and sponsoring interdisciplinary research on the changing state of the global environment and likely impacts. However, the focus was on the symptoms rather than the causes of the environmental problems, because redistribution, which any discussion of patterns of resource use implied in the context of scarcity, was kept out of the United Nations. The architecture of global environmental governance set up at Stockholm in 1972 continues till today, with varying degrees of success, with emerging countries, at least the majority, remaining reluctant partners.

At Stockholm, China more clearly than the others saw their future in industrialization and were afraid of the implications on their nascent industry of any attempt to impose global environmental standards and expressed this concern in terms of national sovereignty This perspective was also reflected in their decision not to join the G77 but be linked in institutional terms – G77 and China. For the other members of the G77, having recently emerged from a century of colonial domination, the global issue was securing additional finance. They equated environmental and developmental concerns, defined in terms of their present situation as agricultural and poor countries which they expected would continue. The position that the South adopted – that 'poverty is the worst form of pollution' in the words of Indian Prime Minister Indira Gandhi – gained prominence at Stockholm. In contesting the framing of the global environmental concern, the intellectual leadership of the South defined the developing country position at this conference, as well as until 1992, in terms of continuing poverty rather than future industrialization:

'The developing countries would clearly wish to avoid, as far as feasible, the [environmental] mistakes and distortions that have characterized the patterns of development of the industrialized societies. However, the major environmental problems of the emerging countries are essentially of a different kind. They are predominantly problems that reflect the poverty and very lack of development in their societies ... These are problems, no less than those of industrial pollution, that clamour for attention in the context of the concern with human environment. They are problems which affect the greater mass of mankind ... In [industrialized] countries, it is appropriate to view development as a cause of environmental problems ... In [the Southern] context, development becomes essentially a cure for their major environmental problems' [Founex Report, 1971]. In 1990, the Report of the South Commission also defined the term in a decidedly political context by talking not merely about economic poverty but about the poverty of influence [The South Commission, 1990].

The idea of independent funding for the United Nations was also first formally raised as long ago as at the 1972 Stockholm Conference on the Human Environment, but did not find favour with industrialized countries. It was then agreed by governments that the matter should be explored and was subsequently elaborated in a number of specific studies and proposals, but it has not been possible to translate these ideas into the functioning of international organizations; for example, the Brandt Commission in 1983. These suggestions included international taxation of economic activities that are made possible by and depend on globalized processes and of the use of global public goods, for example, communications and cyberspace. At the same time, at the insistence of the industrialized countries, the World Trade Organization (WTO) was institutionally located outside the United Nations system, on the lines of the International Monetary Fund (IMF) and the World Bank; governed by the 'one dollar one vote' arrangement rather than the 'one country one vote' system of the United Nations. Similarly, the ongoing global processes of trade and financial integration and growing interdependence of humankind in the use of natural resources were considered as one in terms of keeping prices down and at the same time, drawing attention away from the consumption patterns in developed countries. The newly established WTO – which the General Agreement on Trade and Tariffs (GATT) evolved into on the basis of the institutional design prepared at the OECD and brought to the negotiating table by developed countries in the closing stages of the Uruguay Round – was not mandated to deal with 'trade and development', while protection of intellectual property rights was included [Boutros Boutros-Ghali and Branislav Gosevic, 2011].

Attempts were also made by the industrialized countries early on to deal with as many of these issues as possible outside the United Nations in institutions in which they exercised greater control; and shift decisions that had to be taken to still more favourable forums. Therefore, moves were made within the IMF and the World Bank for the establishment of the Third Window, of the Joint Fund/World Bank Development Committee, and of the IMF Interim Committee on the International Monetary System, in the 1970s, which were at least partly in response to some of the immediate concerns of the Group of 77 raised in the United Nations. These moves were also inspired by the wish to divert issues from the United Nations and to diminish its importance, as a response to the G77 trying to keep various ongoing processes linked to the United Nations at least in procedural terms.

The G77 were not successful in issue linkage, largely because the constituents were at different stages of development and therefore with different interests, unlike the G7 countries. Efforts at restructuring the UN system in its economic and social sectors and revising the International Development Strategy continued wherever an opportunity arose, but the institutional structure of the United Nations was not modified in order to accommodate the political power of the votes with the emerging countries. The Bretton Woods institutions and WTO were not formally covered by the exercises within the United Nations of an expanded concept of development, including general patterns of economic growth and development and the quality of life in all societies, developed and developing. The linkages with outcomes from the financial and trade bodies were kept limited to procedural matters – presentations by these bodies in the United Nations ECOSOC – rather than leading to any substantive change in their priorities as a result of those discussions.

From the 1970s, the pattern of negotiations emerged where the G77 initially presented a united position based on principles, and as negotiations progressed into the specifics of the issue related to implementation divisions emerged. A steadily decreasing number of the emerging country diplomats continued to see the United Nations as the means for global economic reform by changing terms of trade and raising prices of commodity exports to buy industrial technology. Issue-by-issue negotiations exposed them to economic and political pressure – debt and aid. In this arrangement, the lack of capacity was largely ignored and compliance with the treaties, including environmental ones, remained selective. Issues of concern to emerging countries, like ban on export of toxic wastes, did not succeed in getting a global consensus despite the vigorous effort of some emerging countries.

As the emerging countries, with the organization of the cartel of oil producers, Organization of the Petroleum Exporting Countries (OPEC), sought to take advantage of their potential for disrupting certain international economic flows that were vital for the finely tuned economies of the industrialized countries, they became vulnerable to systematic efforts aimed at weakening their solidarity and unity of action, with the industrialized countries offering measures and making gestures sufficient to reach out to and engage the interest of the moderates within the Group of 77, without, at the same time, yielding to the more far-reaching demands of a structural character. This interesting compromise within the G77, of unity at the beginning with divergences appearing later to dilute that common position as the negotiations progress, continues.

As it became clear to the industrialized countries that the 'new' environmental issues related to rights to natural resources outside national boundaries – biodiversity and atmosphere – which required greater cooperation from emerging countries, the developmental issues that they had raised in 1972 were sought to be reintroduced into a new framework in terms of what was described as 'sustainable development'. In 1982, the Canadian government called for a special commission to 'look at long term environmental strategies for achieving sustainable development by the year 2000 and beyond'. This led to the World Commission on Environment and Development being set up by the UN General Assembly under the chairmanship of Gro Brundtland in 1986 called for 'a new era of economic growth, one that must be based on policies that sustain and expand the environmental resource base ... essential to relieve the great poverty that is deepening in much of the developing world' [Our Common Future, 1987]. The political motivation of the exercise was clear, as sustainable development was more neutral than environment and development, and more readily acceptable to emerging countries.

At the same time, trade rather than protection of infant industry from competition became the priority for emerging countries, increasingly worried about the imposition of 'non-tariff' barriers on the basis of environmental standards. At the end of the Seventh Session of the General Assembly, held in 1975, called to discuss the development strategy, the United States reiterated its position emphatically that it 'cannot and does not accept any implication that the world is now embarked on the establishment of something called the "new international economic order"' [UN, 1976]. The response of the emerging countries was to use multilateral agreements to set limits to the push from industrialized countries for

184 | The World's Search for Sustainable Development

bilateral treaties that would secure them more favourable terms. This was one reason why Singapore and Malaysia, which had developed by the 1990s, played important coordination roles at the Rio Conference, in 1992, and why trade and environment started getting linked.

At the Rio Conference, in 1992, the major emerging countries – China, India and Brazil – remained reluctant to enter into agreements that would put constraints on their development. In biodiversity, the initial hope of emerging countries to secure their genetic resources from patenting by multinational companies without sharing the benefits also met economic obstacles in the industrialized countries unwillingness to share the profits of new biotechnology companies with the countries of origin of the genetic resources on which they were based. In climate change, emerging countries could limit their own commitments to 'communicating information' only when they agreed to diluted emission reduction commitments of the industrialized countries. Annual reporting processes had to be funded, with guidelines that remained vague and allowed room to provide general information, and the process remained consultative – essentially allowing emerging countries to report on their own terms. However, they had to accept climate change and its adverse effects as a 'common concern' rather than treat the atmosphere as an economic resource to be shared equitably, leading to continuing tension between countries at different levels of development. Negotiations on a Forest Convention were still-born when emerging countries refused to consider tropical forests as a global concern, or resource to be shared, and successfully argued that all forests should be considered as a global resource, if at all. Essentially, the United Nations was used to present an appearance of environmental concern to secure economic interests, including access to natural resources outside national boundaries.

For example, in the case of the climate convention, different patterns of natural resource use in terms of energy efficiency levels, urban design and settlement patterns, use of personal transport and consumption patterns meant that similar targets for industrialized countries led to countries avoiding ratification (United States), walking out of the Kyoto Protocol (Canada, Australia), and avoiding a second commitment period (European Union, Japan). Differentiated responsibilities related to the levels of development that have shaped the framework have been the stumbling block in evolution of multilateral agreements and have also emerged within the expanded European Union. Targets, indicators and national reports have not led to compliance. Financial transfers, the original motivation for emerging countries to join international environmental agreements, are also declining. The unresolved issue of using the authority of the United Nations for economic rather than environmental reasons remains true even today.

In addition to the way the issues were framed, it has now become clear that only when countries adjust their national interests against global objectives will a different mode of global politics emerge. Decision-making among actors with different capabilities, views and often opposing interests has led to an adversarial relationship requiring deal-making and *quid pro quo* modes of negotiation around global concerns as a reflection of what the least forthcoming major partner is willing to agree to, the lowest common denominator. This development only underlined the basic objective of the exercise to secure recognition of a global concern rather than strong national action to deal with it.

13.3 Multilateral negotiations

Increasingly, in addition to environment and trade, the work of the United Nations was moved towards specific areas with separate agendas but related outcomes. These included dealing with economic concerns, domestic situations and problems within emerging countries, in particular humanitarian and emergency assistance, natural disasters, human rights, and the improving of domestic governance. This was later broadened to include 'threats' seen to emanate from emerging countries, including terrorism, drugs, infectious diseases, and, most recently conflicts, or fragility, arising from climate change. With the result that once negotiations began under an agreed framework, all emerging countries could expect to achieve were establishing claims for 'special treatment' or exceptional grounds for assistance on a case-by-case basis. Problems were also defined and treated as national failures in emerging countries, shifting policy attention away from industrialized countries and placing the onus for action on emerging countries. The universalism, or harmonization of policies, which was an essential part of the framework supported leaving solutions to the market. Emerging countries soon realized that resistance to external conditionality could lead to accusations of undermining 'investor confidence', giving scope to multilateral financial institutions to further open markets through the leverage of aid and debt relief. The use of selected words and terminology – 'development round' in the WTO – enabled policy bundles to be set up for trade-offs at a high level.

This pattern of negotiations soon became representative of the emerging mode of international decision-making. If one compares the seemingly issue-by-issue negotiations, for example, United Nations conferences on the Environment, Population, Food, Law of the Sea, and others, several interesting similarities are apparent. This collective decision-making mode was increasingly inter-sectoral, and no longer simply confined to the sector-by-sector approach and to the socio-economic local issues of the past but increasingly also included global implications of natural resource use. Since it was concerned with relationships among several sectors, this mode of decision making put an incremental strategy at a disadvantage, as it necessitated the construction of more holistic perspectives and the formulation of broader policy bundles on the basis of which to calculate trade-offs. Moreover, this new decision-making mode tended to take place at an increasingly high political level, one at which general parameters for relations across sectors were defined and then left to technically competent bodies and individuals within each sector to operationalize. This type of international decision making increasingly became institutionalized, in the sense that the same high-level representatives, from both industrialized and emerging countries, often negotiated different agreements in different forum. A further element of institutionalization was that the representatives increasingly drew upon a growing network of common bureaus and secretariat bodies. The functionally specific and technocratic system of international socio-economic decision making constructed after World War II has been increasingly superseded by a more integrated and directly political mode. Consequently, substantive issue linkage was increasingly expressed in institutional terms as common goals and monitoring arrangements, with some flexibility in terms of timing of the measures required to be taken by emerging countries. The parallel negotiations on climate change and sustainable development goals are examples of the way the issues were framed around related concerns to give maximum advantage to the industrialized countries [Gosovic et al., 1976].

This trend in agenda-setting solely by the industrialized countries has evoked two divergent assessments, which stress the importance of the conceptual framework and the disunity of the emerging countries, respectively, as the key issue. This dominance has been described as an exercise of power – 'Marshalling the power of their nations, they have been able to project and impose their preferred vision of the world order and marginalize the United Nations and the multilateralism that this organization embodies ... With no compelling reason to change or even discuss the nature of their preferred version of the world order ... Key developed countries had the final say in what was promoted and prioritized on the international agenda. They worked hard to filter out and neutralize what was deemed undesirable, achieving an almost worldwide censorship of ideas and control of prevailing thinking and perception. International rules, regimes and institutions and ongoing programmes were shaped and used in a manner consistent with the interests and political outlook of the industrialised countries' [Boutros Boutros Ghali and Branislav Gosovic, 2011].

186 | The World's Search for Sustainable Development

Acceptance of the framework by emerging countries has also been described as a lack of strategic thinking on their part – ' … They came together in a political movement against imperialism's legacy and its continuance. To read the texts produced by the political project of the Third World can be gravely misleading. Most of the documents and speeches are triumphal, and few of them reveal the fissures and contradictions within the Third World. … By the 1970s the new nations were no longer new. Their failures were legion. Popular demands for land, bread, and peace had been ignored … borrowings from commercial banks could only come if the states agreed to "structural adjustment" packages from the International Monetary fund and the World Bank … in 1989 a few NAM states created the Group of Fifteen, and they wanted a more urgent response to the debt crisis, although there was no mention of debt forgiveness. The main themes were to increase world trade, open up Northern markets to southern goods, and increase growth rates only … This was not a genuine agenda for the South' [Vijay Prashad, 2008].

The underlying factor in agenda – setting was the science–policy interface which served to define the problems and solutions in particular ways. It shaped the thinking of the diplomats and policy-makers in emerging countries, so that they did not question the framework itself and focussed negotiations on how it applied to them; they did not realize that setting the agenda is half the outcome.

13.4 Governance arrangements

Understanding of the interdependence of environmental challenges and economic and social systems in a globalized world reflects geopolitical shifts, highlighting the limitations of existing knowledge and inadaquacy of governance arrangements to deal with them. Global environmental governance involves more than just signing a treaty, creating new rights and meeting individual obligations. It also involves establishing and maintaining new rules, organizations, and decision-making procedures – 'regimes' – around the issue areas. A consensus on the goals and the means of implementation was expected to be the basis for continuing cooperation, securing mutual gains over time. Increased transparency through mechanisms for national reporting and assessment was expected to reduce the possibility of cheating, or free-riding, on the part of states. The hope was that states will accept common international norms of environmental protection and enact national legislation to support collective action. Actually, the political struggles over 'principles' and decision-making procedures reflected the existing balance of power, and interests of industrialized countries for universalism and markets, ignoring the need for differentiation based on different levels of development.

Global environmental politics looks different from the perspective of many emerging countries. The framework of negotiations was carefully crafted to reflect interests of industrialized countries. Experts developed reports prescribing 'appropriate' behaviour for states by framing issues couched in terms concerning humanity but in effect transforming the understanding and practices of territorial sovereignty, with states giving up certain powers, autonomy and even rights to natural resources. The mechanism of the G77 while providing collective power also concealed an inherent weakness in its being open to those who favoured the status quo against those who wished to change basic economic relations. Since the scientific, and supposedly neutral, reports indicated the issues under consideration were technical in nature, the interests of all countries were considered to be the same, despite different levels of development, and emerging countries were reduced to 'cutting the best deal'.

Globalization, and the extent to which global environmental governance and global economic governance have become intertwined, was unanticipated by the architects of the governance order – at Rio in 1992, the industrialized countries were very particular to ensure that there is no reference to multinational corporations in Agenda 21. This changed with the re-emergence of China, and at the

World Summit on Sustainable Development (WSSD), in 2002, a new framework was introduced which considered the role of the private sector in terms of a partnership. By that time environmental and social issues, the way they had been framed, were on the agendas of the Bretton Woods Institutions, in step with the dilution of the principle of common but differentiated responsibilities in the environmental negotiations within the United Nations.

The outcome has been that agreement on priorities, targets and obligations are defined under a common legal framework as part of a political agreement, but would be different for countries in implementation and the basis of that differentiation would be capability. The issue of the global environment was not reframed, and did not shift the elements from the earlier transfer of financial resources and technology as a form to aid rather than as compensation, but diluted the polluter pays principle. The re-emergence of China and India also allowed industrialized countries – most often the United states – to argue for universalism, and elimination of the differentiation between countries that was the basis for the transfers and later for sharing the costs of the transition, ignoring their historical responsibility for having caused the global environmental problem.

For example, the principle of differentiation led to the collapse of the 1997 Kyoto Protocol of the Climate Convention. The United States and its allies in the 'Umbrella Group' – Australia, Japan, and Canada – argued that as countries such as China and India were going to increase their emissions and share of global greenhouse gas emissions, they were not entitled to any major concessions. The industrialized countries had with skilful diplomacy first framed the issue in terms of shifting the focus from their historical emissions, which had caused the climate problem, to reductions in current emissions. Though the protocol required emission reduction commitments only from industrialized countries, and that too what they very prepared to commit and not what they should have done according to science, the refusal of the United States to ratify it later led to its collapse, increasing the pressure on emerging countries later.

The Rio+20 Summit on environmental sustainability in late June 2012 did not produce any breakthrough agreements or commitments, reflecting the changed balance of power. But it provided an international platform to shed light on issues to secure global sustainable development, making global sustainable development goals a universal priority on the international agenda. It also shifted the focus to the 'green economy' with an agenda for action at the national and domestic level, rather than at the global level. Lack of a clearly defined path to a 'green economy' allowed emerging countries critical national policy space to formulate their own paths for urbanization, industrialization and energy, while also discussing industrialized countries' willingness to undertake responsibilities for committing to a sustainable global future, but still without a focus on the consumption patterns of industrialized countries.

The Sustainable Development Goals for the first time encompass specifics on all three aspects of sustainable development – economic, social and environmental – and seek to perpetuate momentum in international development work beyond the poverty-eradicating mission of the Millennium Development Goals, which will lapse in 2015. Part of the green economy involves potentially placing economic value on environmental services provided by nature, an approach that some argue 'financializes nature'. Attention is also shifting from sole reliance on the carbon market, which seemed for a while to drive change now seems far divorced from its sustainability roots, commoditized and unable to drive long-term change. The World Bank alone continues with its push for a price on carbon.

What Rio+20 achieved was bringing attention to the fact that the path to a green economy lies at the national and local levels. Global goals will enable, rather than direct these actions. In a multipolar world, the focus has shifted away from the vision of an international legal framework aiming to solve global environmental problems through global governance and toward global goals for the promotion of domestic and local action. At the institutional level, the separation between environment and development established at Rio in 1992 has given place to global sustainable development goals, and a corresponding coordinating role to the United Nations Economic and Social Council (ECOSOC), in place of sole reliance on multilateral environmental agreements. The weakening of the old framework is illustrated by developments around a new fund. As in 1972 and 1992, one important outcome expected from the Rio+20 Conference in 2012 was an international fund that would supplement the Global Environment Facility established in 2012 to promote a worldwide green economy. Emerging countries were reluctant to accept it as they would have had to contribute, and industrialized countries recognized that emerging countries had more power and influence but were no longer one single and uniform group reducing the leverage from a new fund. As a result, a strong agreement was not possible. Instead, achievements were limited to a document with vague language and few concrete steps, with the divergences focused around climate change and consumption and production patterns as global goals, but without linking them and with the means of implementation now expressed as partnerships.

A High-Level Political Forum (HLPF) has been established to provide political leadership to implement sustainable development at the global level. It has a unique hybrid structure, with universal membership. It will meet every 4 years at the level of Heads of State and Government under the auspices of the United Nations General Assembly and every year under the auspices of the United Nations ECOSOC. The ECOSOC meetings will also conduct regular, voluntary and State-led reviews on the follow-up and implementation of sustainable development commitments and objectives, including those related to the means of implementation. In terms of current United Nations processes, there are two examples of monitoring and accountability mechanisms: the Universal Periodic Review process of the Human Rights Council and the Annual Ministerial Review process of ECOSOC, which serve as possible models. The hybrid nature of the HLPF (General Assembly-ECOSOC) lends itself to a hybrid formulation of review and monitoring processes – the universality and legitimacy of the General Assembly and the convening power and experience of ECOSOC are naturally advantageous. The theme of the June 2014 meeting of the HLPF was 'urbanization' reflecting the emergence of a new framework around social development rather than natural resources.

In June 2013, the United Nations General Assembly also passed a resolution on global economic governance that may move to resolve some of the fractured and disconnected practices between intergovernmental bodies (GA/67/L.73). This resolution was proposed by Chile and co-sponsored by more than 60 countries from all geographic regions. Chile's goal was to position the General Assembly and the ECOSOC as a common communication centre for the various multilateral bodies on economic, social, and environmental issues. The resolution addresses in a new way: (a) the role of the United Nations in 'inclusive, transparent and effective' multilateral economic governance; (b) the relationship of bilateral and regional trading regimes to the international trading system; (c) the role of emerging countries in economic norm setting; (d) engagement of the United Nations with 'international groupings that make policy recommendations or take policy decisions with global implications, including the Group of 20' and (e) the role of regional and sub-regional economic bodies 'dealing with global matters of concern to the international community'. It also calls for elevating academia to the same level as civil society and the private sector as participants in United Nations dialogues on global challenges recognizing – for the first time – a connection between the United Nations and the Financial Stability Board (FSB) and the Bank for International Settlements (BIS) in Basel.

Early establishment and diffusion of global environmental norms was driven by issue-specific intergovernmental meetings, other norms were generated through intergovernmental consultative processes and later intergovernmental regimes adopted market mechanisms for meeting obligations to reduce the costs of measures in the industrialized countries. Now environment and development have been brought together within the United Nations leading to a hybrid system of global governance. The result has been the shifting nature of global governance architectures over time and the possibility of several types of governance orders coexisting, sometimes uneasily. It remains to be seen whether an integrated approach to global governance will evolve within the United Nations.

Emerging countries have begun a serious attempt to set the global agenda. They succeeded in promoting a resolution, titled 'Towards the establishment of a multilateral legal framework for sovereign debt restructuring processes' at the United Nations General Assembly which recognized that a state's efforts to restructure debt should not be impeded by hedge funds that seek to profit from distressed debt. The General Assembly, by a vote of 124 in favour, 11 against (including United States, Germany and the United Kingdom) and 41 abstentions (including most of the EU), also decided to set up a multilateral legal framework for sovereign debt restructuring by the end of 2014, giving recourse to an international court or system (A/68/L.57/Rev.2). Another resolution, also initiated by Argentina with 74 co-sponsors, in the United Nations Human Rights Council condemned the activities of vulture funds 'for the direct negative effect that the debt repayment to those funds, under predatory conditions, has on the capacity of Governments to fulfil their human rights obligations, particularly economic, social and cultural rights and the right to development', and requested its Advisory Committee, composed of 18 experts, to prepare a research-based report on the activities of vulture funds and the impact on human rights (A/HRC/27/L. 26, 2014). The Council noted that 'the international financial system does not have a sound legal framework for the orderly and predictable restructuring of sovereign debt, which further increases the economic and social cost of non-compliance'. It expressed its concern about the voluntary nature of international debt-relief schemes that has created opportunities for vulture funds to acquire defaulted sovereign debt at vastly reduced prices and then seek repayment of the full value of the debt through litigation, seizure of assets or political pressure. Condemning the activities of vulture funds, the Council reaffirmed, in this context, that 'the activities of vulture funds highlight some of the problems in the global financial system and are indicative of the unjust nature of the current system, which directly affects the enjoyment of human rights in debtor States.' The Czech Republic, Germany, Japan, United Kingdom and the United States voted against the resolution, while Austria, Estonia, France, Ireland, Italy, Montenegro, Republic of Korea, Romania and the former Yugoslav Republic of Macedonia abstained. The deliberations mark a democratization of the United Nations in two aspects; first, diluting the resistance of industrialized countries of keeping discussions of finance outside the United Nations and, second, considering socio-economic rather than only environmental–humanitarian issues and trends. The shift is on-going, and will not be easy.

This is because sustainable development has been defined within the United Nations, reflecting its 'political' origins, shaping rights to natural resources outside national boundaries and new markets but having only a marginal impact on the basic causes of the problem itself, which is based on urban consumption patterns in an increasingly urbanized society worldwide. Over the 40-year period, industrialized countries were able to maintain the framework where the social concerns expressed by the emerging countries were accommodated as means of implementation in an incremental manner leading to successive negotiations, which then served to advance the claims of the industrialized to additional natural resources at the global level.

The political, rather than the environmental, underpinnings have shaped the way sustainability has been framed since 1972. Over the 40-year period, the current framework has also not lessened the North–South divide in international cooperation nor the global environmental consequences of natural resource use. The problems lie with the rules, institutions and policies for international cooperation under which sustainability has evolved since the Stockholm Conference in 1972 and the Rio Summit in 1992, as compared with the more successful national approach based on shifts in growth pathways adopted in the re-emergence of China and India, for example, the stress on rail transport, dense urban clusters and declining subsidies for energy. These geopolitical shifts are replacing the continuing erosion of public trust in expert institutions specifically servicing intergovernmental negotiations with more broad-based studies from the United Nations and management consultancies. The integrity of this research is necessary if we are to manage global change more effectively, and this is happening with emerging country experts playing a greater role in the deliberations and framings. The implications of the changing global balance of power for the United Nations is the emergence of new type of institutions where international cooperation would be based on designing networks to support innovation and respond more effectively to the scale and speed required to meet the challenge of the growth of the global middle class. A globally shared vision for the strategic shift will be necessary, where patterns of natural resource use will in principle be common for all countries.

13.5 Evolving institutional arrangements

At the 1972 United Nations Conference on the Human Environment held in Stockholm, industrialized and emerging nations came together in recognition of the need to protect and use the global commons leading to recognition of 'common concerns' and the creation of global institutions within the United Nations system. In 1980, the International Union for the Conservation of Natural Resources (IUCN) published the World Conservation Strategy, which asserted that conservation of nature cannot be achieved without development to alleviate the poverty and misery of hundreds of millions of people, and stressed the interdependence of conservation and development, pointing out that unless the fertility and productivity of the planet are safeguarded at the local level the human future is at risk. In 1982, 10 years after the Stockholm Conference, the World Conservation Strategy initiative culminated with the adoption of the World Charter for Nature. The Charter asserted that mankind is a part of nature and life depends on the uninterrupted functioning of all natural systems, global and local (General Assembly resolution 37/7, annex).

In 1983, the World Commission on Environment and Development was created; by 1984, it was constituted as an independent body by the General Assembly, and asked to formulate a 'global agenda for change'. In 1987, in its report, 'Our Common Future', the Commission advanced the understanding of global interdependence and the relationship between economics and the environment previously introduced by the World Conservation Strategy. It reaffirmed that the environment does not exist as a sphere separate from human actions and needs, and therefore it should not be considered in isolation from human concerns. The environment is where we all live; development is what we all do for our well-being, and the two are inseparable (A/42/427, pp. 13–14).

The Brundtland Commission also paid special attention to social development, noting that it was necessary for sustaining both economic development and environmental protection. The Commission observed that a world in which poverty is endemic will always be prone to ecological and catastrophes, and that 'the distribution of power and influence within society lies at the heart of most environment and development challenges'. It also emphasized that sustainable development is not a goal applicable only to emerging countries and must be a goal of developed countries as well. It observed that, although the exact nature of a sustainable society is difficult to know in advance, the basic conditions for that society (e.g., absence of large scale poverty and environmental degradation and intergenerational responsibility) can be stated [WCED, 1987]. These views went on to shape the United Nations resolution establishing the Rio Conference in 1992.

In June 1992, the UNCED was held in Rio de Janeiro and adopted an agenda for environment and development in the twenty-first century, comprising the Rio Declaration on Environment and Development, which recognizes each country's right to pursue social and economic progress and assigned to States the responsibility of adopting a model of sustainable development; Agenda 21, a programme of action for sustainable development and the Statement of Principles concerning forests. At the same time, separate multilateral agreements were also reached in the Convention on Biological Diversity and the Framework Convention on Climate Change. Since the Rio Conference, sustainable development has become part of the international lexicon. The 'Three Pillars' approach of 'Social,' 'Environment,' and 'Economic' dimensions of sustainability emerged as a well-recognized and established model for evaluating sustainability, without defining the linkages.

The Rio Declaration, in 1992, reflected an increasing concern with the management of global environmental issues. This concern was based on three assumptions. First, enhanced scientific assessment was expected to lead to increased efforts to protect the environment through binding agreements. Second, that international environmental problems – climate change and biodiversity loss – needed new mechanisms and countries had a shared interest in ensuring that future economic development was not prejudicial to the environment. Third, at the same time, the environment, including what was defined as the global common inside and outside national boundaries, was also seen as a strategic resource, extending the principle of national sovereignty through the concept of 'common concern of mankind' giving all countries a right over these resources. This raised distribution questions which remain unresolved.

Agenda 21 and the Rio Declaration were not simply agreements about sustainability ideas; they were also agreements to achieve sustainability. The most widely used set of principles in the world are the sustainable development principles from the Rio Declaration of 1992, which stress intergenerational and intragenerational equity and justice and a holistic approach to environmental problems. Professor Edith Brown Weiss had earlier explained intergenerational equity as having three elements, including an intragenerational aspect. First, each generation should conserve the options of future generations by conserving 'the diversity of the natural and cultural resource base'. Second, each generation is entitled to a quality of planet enjoyed by prior generations, and also has an obligation to pass to the next generation a quality of planet that is no worse than it received. Third, all people in the current generation should have the same minimal level of access to this legacy. Because poverty and environmental degradation are inseparably linked, equity within the current generation is necessary for equity between generations, this aspect has not been placed on the agenda of the United Nations. For the first time also, the lifestyle of the current civilization was addressed in principle 8 of the Rio Declaration, in which the urgency of a deep change in consumption and production patterns was expressly and broadly acknowledged by State leaders, but Agenda 21 reaffirmed that sustainable development was delimited by the integration of the economic, social and environmental pillars, and the Rio Conference did not shift the focus to socio-economic trends as the root cause of the environmental problem [Weiss, 1989].

One of the principal features of *Agenda 21* was the call for partnerships between business and environmental groups. The business community helped conceptualize the phases through which corporate involvement in the environment had passed: the prevention of pollution in the 1970s, measures to encourage self-regulation in the 1980s and a concern to incorporate sustainability into business practices in the 1990s. The 1990s and the period post-Rio was seen as a turning point in the relation between corporate business and the environment, in which environmental concerns

192 | The World's Search for Sustainable Development

(at least in the case of the largest global players) became internalized and a part of corporate governance. The 'Caring for the Earth definition' focused on the capacity of ecosystems: 'improving the quality of life while living within the carrying capacity of supporting ecosystems'. Once the new framework of legally established rights of access to transboundary resources had been established, the market had become more important than governments in dealing with the global environment.

The United Nations Commission on Sustainable Development (CSD) was established in 1992 for effective follow-up of UNCED, enhance international cooperation, and examine progress in implementing Agenda 21 at the local, national, regional and international levels, and its subsequent multi-year programme ensured it would adopt a sectoral role rather than focus on cross-cutting issues that really affect sustainability. The 2002 WSSD Johannesburg Plan of Implementation (JPOI) shifted attention to partnerships, as voluntary multi-stakeholder initiatives, that would contribute to the implementation of inter-governmental commitments in Agenda 21, the Programme for the Further Implementation of Agenda 21 and the JPOI. Post-Rio+20, in 2012, discussions on how to define, design, and implement sustainable development goals (SDGs) have taken centre stage in the United Nations. The global goals for the first time include measures for setting the agenda for the whole United Nations system and international cooperation in relation to sharing experiences at the regional level, reviewing commitments, monitoring goals and ensuring coherence in efforts that include transformation of the rural economy and shift of population to urban areas, signified by the increasing number of studies on urbanization, and in the agenda of the first meeting of the new high-level forum, held in 2014. There is as yet no common understanding on an overriding meta-goal to share responsibility for the Planet and prosperity of the People.

References

Daly, Herman. 1993. 'Sustainable Growth: An Impossibility Theorem'. In *Valuing the Earth: Economics, Ecology, Ethics*, edited by Daly H., Townsend K. MIT Press, Cambridge, MA.

Daly, Herman. and Cobb J. 1989. *For the Common Good: Redirecting the Economy towards Community, the Environment and a Sustainable Future*. London: Green Print. pp. 267–73.

Founex Report on Development and Environment, 1971, Stakeholder Forum.

Ghali, Boutros Boutros and Branislav Gosevic. 2011. Global Leadership and Global Systemic Issues: South, North and the United Nations in a 21st Century World, *Mainstream*, XLIX No. 18, 23 April 2011.

Gosovic, Branislav and John Gerard Ruggie. 1976. On the Creation of a New International Economic Order: Issue Linkage and the Seventh Special Session of the UN General Assembly. *International Organization*. Vol. 30, Issue 02, March 1976, pp. 309–45.

Guha R. 1989. *The Unquiet Woods: Ecological Change and Peasant Resistance in the Himalaya*. Oxford University Press, Oxford.

Hecht S, Cockburn A. 1990. *The Fate of the Forest: Developers, Destroyers and Defenders of the Amazon*. Penguin, London.

Huber J. 2000. 'Towards Industrial Ecology: Sustainable Development as a Concept of Ecological Modernisation'. *Journal of Environmental Policy and Planning* 10: 2–11.

IUCN, UNEP, WWF. 1980. *World Conservation Strategy: Living Resource Conservation for Sustainable Development*. Gland, Switzerland: IUCN.

Meadows D, Meadows D, Randers J, and Behrens W. 1972. *The Limits to Growth: a Report for the Club of Rome's Project on the Predicament of Mankind*. Earth Island: London.

Meadows D, Meadows D, and Randers J. 1992. *Beyond the Limits: Global Collapse or a Sustainable Future*. Earthscan, London.

NRC. 2011. *Sustainability and the US EPA, Committee on incorporating sustainability in the US Environmental Protection Agency*. National Research Council, National Academies Press, Washington.

Pearce D. 1991. *Blueprint 2: Greening the World Economy*. Earthscan: London.

Pearce D., Markandya A., and Barbier E. 1989. *Blueprint for a Green Economy*. Earthscan: London.

Prasad, Vijay. 2008. *The Darker Nations: A Peoples History of the Third World*. The New Press, New York.

Rowell A. 1996. *Green Backlash: Global Subversion of the Environmental Movement*. Routledge: London.

Schmidheiny S. 1992. *Changing Course: A Global Business Perspective on Development and the Environment*. MIT, Cambridge, MA.

The South Commission. 1990. *The Challenge to the South: Report of the South Commission*. Oxford University Press, New York.

UN. 1976. United Nations General Assembly Resolution 31/178, dated 21 December 1976.

WCED. 1987. *United Nations World Commission on Environment and Development. Our Common Future*. Oxford University Press, Oxford.

Weiss E.B. 1989. *In Fairness to Future Generations: International Law, Common Patrimony, and Intergenerational Equity*. Tokyo: Hotei Publishing.

Weizsacker E, Lovins A, and Lovins L. 1997. *Factor Four: Doubling Wealth Halving Resource Use*. Earthscan: London.

Limitations of the Building Blocks of Sustainability 14

The thrust of the Rio+20 Conference on a green or low carbon economy in the context of eradication of poverty focuses global attention on total planetary biophysical limits. Moving from prices to quantities and the economics of human development as the basis for international cooperation will require focus on consumption patterns. For the first time global goals are being considered not just for emerging countries but for all countries. These shifts bring out the limitations of the conceptual framework of sustainable development based on three pillars – economic, environmental and social – even when they are not seen as silos. The current framework focuses on production patterns in emerging countries while efforts to incorporate consumption patterns of all countries enhances the understanding of the concerns, and also serves to emphasise the need for a new framework that will respond to the aspirations of the rural poor to shift to urban areas and the needs and impacts of the growing urban middle class.

14.1 Economic sustainability: modifying natural resource use

With all economies being increasingly driven by the urban services sector, and not just by industrialization, global environmental change is being driven by the lifestyles of the wealthy citizens worldwide. The International Energy Agency points out that in industrialized countries, on the consumer side of the economy, technological and lifestyle changes combined with higher incomes have significantly altered energy use patterns since the Convention on Climate Change was negotiated in 1992, with over two-thirds of carbon dioxide emissions now coming from the services, households and travel sectors, they account for more than half the increase in global emissions since 2005, and it is expected that emissions from transportation (largely for leisure) will exceed half of global emissions in 2050. There is also a high correlation between per capita GDP and municipal solid waste [UNEP, 2011]. In industrialized countries, energy use in manufacturing has remained unchanged in the period 1990–2004, while buildings consume 40 per cent of the electricity generated. Energy consumption has increased by 50 per cent in the services sector, by 35 per cent in households, and by 25 per cent in transportation, as a result final energy use – and emissions of carbon dioxide – have each increased by 14 per cent [IEA, 2007]. Driven by these consumption patterns, energy consumption is growing most quickly in the transport, household and service sectors, driven by rising passenger travel and freight transport, appliance energy use by households and a rapid expansion in the service economy [IEA, 2003].

In emerging countries, energy use per capita is just one-fifth of industrialized country levels, currently transportation accounts for only one-fifth of total energy use, and this situation is going to change. For example, in the period 1990–2005, passenger travel tripled in China, while freight haulage more than doubled, and per capita energy use has increased nearly 50 per cent. In India, just 10 per cent of emissions are from the transport and residential sectors, and the main driver of energy demand up to the year 2050 will be the movement of nearly 1 billion people into towns. As two-thirds of final energy consumption is in cities, urbanization must be the focus of global policy development. As emerging countries build their infrastructure, modified patterns of land use, new technologies and behavioural changes will play a key role in the transition to sustainable development, rather than develop global rules on costly alternatives to fossil fuels for generation of electricity that are more suited for industrialized countries.

Challenging conventional assumptions that focus only on production processes and regulation throws up new commercial solutions for making the transition to a low carbon economy. For example, McKinsey research shows that the growth of worldwide energy demand can be cut in half or more over the next 15 years, without reducing the benefits that energy's end-users enjoy – and while supporting economic growth – by focussing on demand-side management [McKinsey, 2007]. A recent analysis of transportation emissions in the United States also shows that transportation represented 31 per cent of carbon dioxide emissions in 2008, vehicle miles travelled are expected to increase by 40 per cent by 2050, and existing federal programmes do not take this metric into account. The report argues that the rate of technological progress is uncertain and the stress should be on public transportation and land-use strategies that provide alternatives to driving. The report concludes that technology alone will not solve the energy and emissions problem, and there is a need to moderate driving habits, with implications for infrastructure development [WRI, 2011].

Consequently, the strategic policy issue for decoupling energy use from economic growth will not only be developing efficiency standards and fuel substitutes – 'impact decoupling' as industrialized countries are doing – but also a modal shift in transport patterns and modifying the nature of the urbanization process itself, in particular, new land-use and consumption patterns that minimize personal transportation and maximize natural resource use, or, 'resource decoupling' as many emerging countries are doing.

14.2 Environmental sustainability: enhancing ecosystem services

One way to avoid ineffective and contentious discussions around arrangements for integration of environmental issues in current economic policies in an equitable and cost-effective manner is to focus on economic and welfare gains from ecosystem services that will provide the framework for modification of patterns of natural resource use and have so far been ignored as they are outside the market.

The Millennium Ecosystem Assessment, a comprehensive assessment of ecosystem services, concluded that two-thirds of the environmental services studied are being degraded faster than they can recover. Ecosystems provide society with a wide range of services – from reliable flows of clean water to productive soil and carbon stability and sequestration. Societies rely on these services for their well-being. Since many of these ecosystem services either have no financial value at all or are undervalued, they are often not taken into account in policymaking, investment decisions of companies and in the daily life of citizens, all of whom focus on short-term financial returns. The result is that many ecosystem structures and functions are being lost.

The Millennium Ecosystem Assessment also pointed out that 'most resource management decisions are most strongly influenced by ecosystem services entering markets ... the most important public policy decisions affecting ecosystems are often made by agencies and policy arenas other than those charged with protecting ecosystems'. For example, it noted that 'forest management is influenced more strongly by actions outside the forest sector, such as trade policies and institutions, macroeconomic policies, and policies in other sectors such as agriculture, infrastructure, energy and mining, than those within it' [MEA, 2005].

The way the issue is framed around ecosystem services will determine strategic goals related to economic growth, impact on environmental policy arenas and alter policy objectives for eradication of poverty and growth of the middle class. There should be recognition of the limited capacity to absorb waste with payments for allocation of the available space (carbon dioxide, chemicals); establishing community rights of forest dwellers and valuation of ecosystem services will provide resources to the poor removing dependence on exploitation of natural resources (forests); the economic and social gains from new products need to be identified and shared with forest dwellers who have conserved these resources (biodiversity); and, the role of forests in augmentation of water supply and agricultural productivity providing alternatives for energy-intensive engineering and cultivation practices needs to be considered (watershed management). For example, in such a re-framing, dealing with poverty will go beyond sustainable farming to conserve soil and water to reducing consumption of natural resources in urban areas, and for dealing with climate change emissions trading would not be an 'international flexibility mechanism' supporting cost-effectiveness of policies but rather a 'national allocation mechanism' to implement carbon budgets supporting sustainable development.

Similarly, the annual losses of biodiversity and ecosystems are typically estimated as equivalent to a few percentage points of GDP. If, however, we re-express these in terms of ecosystem services, and social well-being, then the argument for reducing such losses gains considerable strength. It is estimated that we are losing forest ecosystem services, including carbon sinks, with a value equivalent to around $28 billion each year, which could serve to eradicate poverty [The European Communities, 2008]. There are ethical choices involved not only between present and future generations but also between people in different parts of the world.

Conventional economic indicators, such as GDP, provide a distorted lens for economic performance particularly since such measures fail to reflect different levels of development and the extent to which production and consumption activities may be drawing down natural capital by either depleting natural resources or degrading the ability of ecosystems to deliver economic benefits, in terms of provisioning, regulating or cultural services; economic activity is often based on the depreciation of natural capital. National accounting systems need to be more inclusive and measure the significant human welfare benefits that global and national ecosystems provide [Vuuren, 2009]. Modern society's focus on market-delivered components of well-being and its reliance on market prices to indicate value have together led to many environmental services not being given any significance at all despite being essential for human well-being. Making nature's flows economically more visible, mainstreaming such valuations into policymaking and into business practices at different scales and recognition that economic value is only one of the relevant values for society can become a powerful feedback mechanism for a society that has distanced itself from the biosphere on which its survival depends. Eco-system services have quantifiable economic value, and this value can be used to enable investment in restoration and maintenance, as well as equitably sharing the global commons for eradication of poverty.

The United Nations Millennium Ecosystem Assessment has provided a clear indication that we are living beyond our means and require an economic system that accounts for the health of the natural environment. This new reality also demands a new approach to the way nations value the global commons and their national ecological assets – not as stocks to be liquidated for economic growth, but as natural resources to be equitably shared and as an important source of ongoing wealth in their own right. The World Bank has formed a global partnership, building on the United Nations project 'The Economics of Ecosystems and Biodiversity (TEEB)' to enable emerging countries to quantify the value of their natural resources through green 'national accounting systems' and reverse the 'invisibility' of nature's contribution to the economy. The United Nations statistics division also maintains a satellite system called the System of Integrated Environmental and Economic Accounting (SEEA). It evaluates changes in stocks of natural capital in monetary terms and incorporates this in national accounts to measure the contribution of the environment to the economy and the impact of the economy on the environment; the emphasis is shifting to water and food security and indicators of sustainable development. A report by the Netherlands Environmental Assessment Agency, 'Growing within Limits' 2012, recommends that broad win-win solutions can be achieved by implementing policies aimed at zero carbon energy options, energy efficiency, ecosystem conservation, higher agricultural yields and lifestyle changes.

The focus on the economic, social and environmental shared benefits of less resource intensive and environmentally damaging economic systems needs to be articulated effectively at a global level to include the global commons. Even though 'new' economic thinking is gaining in popularity, the concepts and benefits are not well recognized, or adapted to, equitably sharing global resources. More work is required to start or further build on the existing dialogue to achieve collective global prosperity by reforming the existing economic system that has human and environmental well-being at its core [Vuuren van and Faber, 2009], and the United Nations should take the lead in generating this new knowledge. National carbon budgets can be adopted as an interim indicator for measuring sustainability – sustainable use of atmospheric, ocean and terrestrial natural resources, and assessing national strategies for the transformation to sustainable development, till such time as more research leads to a new composite indicator of human well-being.

14.3 Social sustainability: local development and conservation

The livelihoods of the rural poor and the conservation and sustainable use of natural resources are so intimately intertwined that they are best addressed through an integrated approach, irrespective whether the primary motivation is development or environmental conservation. It is estimated that environmental wealth accounts for 26 per cent of the total wealth of low-income countries, versus 13 per cent of wealth in middle-income countries and only 2 per cent of wealth in developed countries [Hamilton et al., 2005]. For example, it is now recognized that fighting climate change, including adaptation, conservation of biological diversity and fighting poverty have to be addressed together [CCCD, 2009].

The World Conservation Congress, organized by the International Union for Conservation of Nature (IUCN) in 2008, discussed non-regulatory longer term approaches to restoring, protecting and sustainably using natural resources that can lead to new livelihood and economic opportunities and renewed environmental vitality. A transition is also taking place from a donor-driven NGO-Corporate Social Responsibility-Government dominated framework to one where governments, capital markets and technology companies see the poor as consumers, and as part of core economic activities. New business models and investment opportunities can stimulate new production practices that lead to sustainable management of the environment. Market creation for biodiversity is an example of lessons learned about overcoming obstacles.

The review of the Millennium Development Goals by the United Nations underlines the reality that after over 50 years of international cooperation, analysis and action by governments on 'sustainable development' the world still has nearly 4 billion poor, who subsist on less than $2 a day and do not

198 | The World's Search for Sustainable Development

have access to adequate energy, food, education, health and employment that underpin human well-being, and inequality is steadily increasing. The International Food Policy Research Institute also points out that while early impacts of climate change can be reduced by adaptation, options diminish and associated costs increase with increasing impacts. Socio-economic development is, therefore, essential for improved resilience by reducing over dependence on ecosystems, strengthening local coping strategies through the built environment and technology and moving populations to cities. Fundamental shifts in traditional outputs – from crops to livestock management, switching crop types or livestock species – will require investment and innovating crop varieties, for example, drought-resistant varieties and urbanization [Munang et al., 2011]. Joint research and development, as well as sharing of technologies, is needed for agriculture and health as much as it is needed for the generation of electricity and personal transportation.

Increasing investment in natural assets that are used by the poor enhances livelihoods temporarily in many low-income areas. For example, India's National Rural Employment Guarantee Act 2006, a social protection and livelihood security scheme for the rural poor invests in the preservation and restoration of natural capital in the form of a public works programmes guaranteeing at least 100 days of paid work per year to every household who wants to volunteer an adult member. The scheme has grown fourfold since its inception and investment in 2010 amounted to over US $8 billion, creating 3 billion workdays and benefiting 59 million households, and about 84 per cent of this investment has been made in water conservation, irrigation and land development. While there are challenges with implementation, the programme is proving to be effective, replicable and scalable [ILO, 2010].

New conceptual frameworks and strategies tailored to social value creation, where the objective is for the maximum number to benefit from the effort have begun to emerge. The 'Bottom of the Pyramid' provides new growth opportunities for innovation and entrepreneurship, with new products, services and payment models to make finance and technology affordable and accessible to the poor, while enhancing local natural resources. For example, well-managed trade in wildlife products, as against a ban, not only promotes species conservation but also provides cash and food for the world's poorest people – these groups, and their business, should be seen as a solution, not a problem [Roe, 2008]. An independent evaluation of the International Finance Corporation also concludes that economic growth, poverty reduction and environmentally and socially sustainable development can have mutually reinforcing development and financial benefits [World Bank Group, 2008].

Consequently, a new approach to innovation, development of infrastructure, financial inclusion and political decentralization to the local level will be needed to create self-sustaining pathways out of the vicious circle of poverty and will also be seen as the preferred strategy for conservation of natural resources. Current trends locate around 90 per cent of economic growth in emerging countries in urban areas, with resulting conflicts over sharing of services provided by the ecosystem – land, energy and water resources. Recognition of a more decentralized urbanization process that also augments ecosystem services will support new growth pathways that will enhance the natural resource base of economic growth, by reducing reliance of the poor on biomass energy and as a result augmenting forest 'sinks' and national carbon budgets. This shift will transform global rules for addressing climate change, conservation of biological diversity and eradication of poverty, which emerged independently in the first Rio Summit in 1992.

References

CCCD. 2009. Report of the Commission on Climate Change and Development, Ministry of Foreign Affairs, Sweden, May 2009.

European Commission. 2009. GDP and beyond: Measuring progress in a changing world; see also, Beyond GDP indicators: Beyond GDP fact sheets.

IEA. 2007. *Global Energy Trends 2007*. International Energy Agency, 2007.

Global Footprint Network. 2010. The Ecological Wealth of Nations: Earth's biocapacity as a new framework for international cooperation.

Hamilton, K., G. Rutta, A. Markandaya, S. Pedroso, P. Silva, M. Ordoubadi, G-M Lange, L. Tajibaeva, L. Gronnevet and M. Dyoulgerov. 2005. Where is the Wealth of Nations? Measuring Capital for the 21 Century, Washington, DC: World Bank.

IEA. 2003. *Understanding CO2 emission trends in IEA countries*, International Energy Agency, 2003, Paris.

IEA. 2007. *Energy in the New Millennium: Trends in IEA Countries*. International Energy Agency, 2007, Paris.

ILO. 2010. NREGA – A Review of Decent Work and Green Jobs. International Labour Organization, Geneva.

McKinsey. 2007. Curbing the Growth of Global Energy Demand. McKinsey Quarterly, July 2007.

MEA. 2005. *Ecosystems and Human Well-being: Synthesis*. Millennium Ecosystem Assessment. Island Press, Washington, DC.

Munang, Richard, Ibrahim Thiaw and Muke Rivington. 2011. Ecosystem Management: Tomorrows Approach to Enhancing Food Security Under a Changing Climate. *Sustainability*. 3(7): 937–54.

New Economics Forum. 2006. Growth isn't Working: The unbalanced distribution of benefits and costs from economic growth;

Roe, Dilys. 2008. Trading Nature. TRAFFIC.

Sanwal, Mukul. 2012. 'Rio +20, Climate Change and Development: The Evolution of Sustainable Development (1972–2012)'. *Climate and Development* 4 (2): 157–166.

Sanwal, Mukul. 2013. 'The Rise and Fall of Global Climate Policy: Stockholm to Rio 1992, to Rio + 20 and Beyond'. *Chinese Journal of Environmental and Urban Studies* 1 (1).

The European Communities. 2008. The Economics of Ecosystems and Biodiversity: An Interim Report

UNEP. 2011. *Towards a Green Economy: Pathways to Sustainable Development and Poverty Eradication: A Synthesis for Policy Makers*, United Nations Environment Programme, Nairobi.

Vuuren D.P. van and Faber A. Netherlands Environmental Assessment Agency. 2009. *Growing within Limits*.

World Bank. 2010. Global Partnership to "Green" National Accounts; United Nations Statistical Division, Integrated Environmental and Economic Accounting (SEEA).

World Bank Group. 2008. Independent Evaluation of IFC's Development Results 2008, World Bank Group, Washington, DC, USA.

WRI. 2011. The Role of Driving in Reducing GHG Emissions and Oil Consumption: Recommendations for Federal Transport Policy. World Resources Institute, July 2011, Washington, DC, USA.

Use of Natural Resources

15

Human well-being depends on the consumption of goods and services and production depends on the transformation of natural resources, and both impact on the environment in very different ways. There is now a call for a new 'economics of sustainable development', or 'new type of investment', where, for example, transport is more than just road building and should be environmentally sustainable; adoption of long-term strategies needs to give importance to social capital or trust [Sachs, 2014]. There are calls for 'a new social contract that rethinks global environmental change research in the 'new intellectual climate' to encompass a deeper analysis of societies affecting and affected by global environmental change [Carey et al., 2014]. There are also many calls for the proper integration of the social sciences into the climate change research agenda as a crucial step to fill the science-policy gap [Editorial, 2014]. The fundamental transitions in consumption and production systems will require major changes in institutions, technologies, practices and thinking because these systems rely on infrastructure and investment decisions with long term implications.[1]

15.1 Urbanization

No country has substantially reduced poverty without urbanization and greatly increasing the use of energy; most economic activity would be impossible without energy. Over the past two centuries, fossil fuels have made possible mechanical power, lighting and heating substituting animal and human muscle power. In urban areas, changes in consumption patterns, mobility and changes in the diet all lead to changed patterns of natural resource use in increasing levels that are causing ecosystem scarcity at the global level; slow growth increases local environmental impacts.

The distinguishing feature of economic development is the population shift from rural to urban areas, and rising levels of GDP per capita correlate with levels of urbanization, as they generate four-fifth of GDP. In 2007, over one-quarter of the human population lived in cities, consuming three-quarters of all natural resources and was responsible for three-fourth of the world's energy-related carbon dioxide, with transport, industry and building sectors being the largest contributors; this population level will rise to half by 2030 as urbanization continues. Spatial organization, density and lifestyle choices determine trends in natural resource use. Currently, average per capita carbon dioxide emissions embodied in the infrastructure of industrialized counties is five times larger than for developing countries.

---

[1] Parts of this chapter were first published in Sanwal (2012, 2013).

Cities have major potential to modify longer term trends in natural resource use through transformation in spatial and urban planning and management that reduces energy and water demand, and food wastage. Although statistics are not maintained on trends in consumption patterns, it is estimated that already between 60 and 80 per cent of world energy use is in cities. This proportion will increase as population shifts from rural to urban areas and the patterns of energy use shift from biomass, which is degradable and carbon neutral, to electricity, with a more intensive consumption of energy and other natural resources. Urban areas contain most of the production and consumption activities, and almost all growth, both demographic and economic, is occurring in and around urban areas. Though the challenges are immense, the urban transformation in developing countries will need to be driven locally, enabled nationally and supported internationally.

While urbanization in industrialized countries covered only 400 million shifting from rural areas, as much as 4 billion could move to urban areas in developing countries by 2050, as the global population stabilizes around 9 billion from the current level of less than 7 billion. Urban property development has been a driver of growth in industrialized countries since the 1950s, leading to an increase of 40 per cent in extraction of construction and industrial minerals. These trends are also emerging in developing countries. Global construction is a $4.2 trillion industry, worth 10 per cent of global GDP, employing 100 million persons, accounting at the global level for 50 per cent of natural resource use, 45 per cent of energy (with only 5 per cent used during construction), 40 per cent of water and 70 per cent of timber products. This urbanization trend has largely been market-driven through land and real estate speculation rather than governed (UNEP, 2010).

Mega, secondary and tertiary cities have become the hub of the global economy in the form of concentrated clusters of industrial and service sector activities. Improved infrastructure leads to concentrated commercial and population centres providing economic opportunities, in turn enabling resource efficiencies. The clusters are dispersed around the world, but are networked into an international division of labour, facilitated by globalization – trade and information technology. Cities have always been political, cultural and economic centres; they have now become networked into the global economy as centres for natural resource use because of their consumption and production patterns.

As cities are spearheading the major global trend in driving the unsustainable use of natural resources, in particular ecosystem scarcity and planetary limits, the future growth of cities in emerging countries also provides opportunities for modifying this longer term trend. Urban infrastructure and consumption patterns of urban dwellers needs to be viewed from the perspective of patterns of natural resource use to identify trends that need to be modified with respect to demand for electricity, transportation and diet accessed from the local areas to develop high density and compact form, integrated living, working neighbourhoods and zero waste systems.

Cities also cluster knowledge, financial, institutional and social resources, and have the potential to become centres for innovation to support the transformation, and the focus on consumption patterns is likely to be a more effective model for 'de-coupling' to the one being practised around production patterns. As households and businesses shift expenditures from the natural resource use and capital-intensive sectors, there will be a multiplier effect towards more labour-intensive decentralized service sectors, where new jobs will be created with a distributive impact, in turn leading to redesign of tax and subsidy regimes with a greater role for local governments. Local governments can change longer term trends in natural resource use through land-use planning impacting on urban form and growth, transportation planning for mass transit transport, building regulations for low-energy use buildings, changes to education curricula and campaigns to influence individual behaviour and values.

Infrastructure related to urbanization is primarily in the construction sector related to buildings. The buildings sector is the largest energy-consuming sector, accounting for over one-third of final energy consumption globally and an equally important source of carbon dioxide emissions [IEA, 2013]. The transformation of the buildings sector will have positive benefits for other sectors, most notably the power sector, as over half of all electricity consumed today is used in buildings, and will translate into avoided electrical capacity additions, as well as reduced distribution and transmission network expansion, with potentially huge savings for utilities. Within buildings, two-thirds of the energy consumption is for room temperature control and heating of water, and here improved insulation is important. A high-performance building envelope in a cold climate requires just 20 to 30 per cent of the energy required to heat the current average building in industrialized countries. In hot climates, the energy savings potential from reduced energy needs for cooling are estimated at between 10 and 40 per cent. With better use of natural lighting and adoption of highly efficient lamp technologies, buildings energy consumption for lighting could be reduced by 40 per cent in 2050 compared to current levels. Since two-thirds of the emissions of carbon dioxide in the use of the buildings are from electricity and heat, reducing the demand could be a substitute for decarbonization of the fuel supply from power plants. This has the added advantage that steps can be taken for a transformation even in the absence of technological breakthroughs.

Another trend is the increased use of small appliances through new kinds of appliances and more and larger appliances. In many countries, appliances and other electrical equipment represent the fastest-growing end-use for energy in buildings. Consumption of electricity in households can be reduced by increasing the efficiency of refrigerators, improved computers and home media appliances, the elimination of the stand-by losses of all appliances and shift to LED-based lighting. Without behavioural change, however, the savings in costs resulting from improved efficiency can lead to increased operations and consumption.

Consumption patterns are also leading to escalating electricity demand from devices in network standby mode where strong market drivers for energy efficiency are absent and policy action will be needed for societal change. In 2013, around one-fifth of the total population relied on more than 14 billion network-enabled devices in homes and offices, and being in 'network standby' mode they are 'always on' and are projected to expand exponentially. As more people use a wider range of devices for increasingly diverse purposes, the total number is expected to skyrocket to 50 billion network-enabled devices by 2020, possibly rising to 100 billion by 2030 and 500 billion over the following decades. By 2025, the corresponding energy demand is expected to rise to 1,140 terawatt hours per year (TWh/yr) – more than the current annual electricity consumption of Canada and Germany combined. The vast majority of this energy is consumed when devices are 'ready and waiting', but not performing any particular function, and up to 80 per cent of their electricity consumption is used just to maintain a network connection. While the quantity of electricity used by each device is small, the anticipated massive deployment and widespread use makes the cumulative consumption considerable. Two-thirds of the energy used by these devices can be saved with existing technologies and solutions, and the global energy efficiency potential that could be achieved by reducing standby electricity consumption is estimated at almost 600 TWh annually by 2025 – more than the current electricity consumption of Canada, Denmark, Finland and Norway combined.

If no action is taken to improve energy efficiency in the buildings sector, energy demand is expected to rise by 50 per cent by 2050. This increase is driven by rapid growth in the number of households, residential and services floor area, higher ownership rates for existing electricity-consuming devices and increasing demand for new products. However, this growth could be limited to just over 10 per cent without changing comfort levels or requiring households to reduce their purchases of appliances and other electronic equipment. An estimated 40 exajoules (EJ), equivalent to current energy use in Russia and India combined could be saved in the buildings sector in 2050 through the wide deployment of best available technologies. Examples include high-performance windows, optimal levels of insulation, reflective surfaces, sealants, heat pumps, solar thermal heating, co-generation, energy-efficient appliances and equipment, efficient cook stoves and LED lighting. Growth in electricity demand could be halved compared to a near doubling under a business-as-usual scenario. A combination of efficiency standards, greater use of heat pumps, solar thermal and co-generation with waste heat and renewables could reduce growth in electricity demand by 2 000 terawatt-hours (TWh) in 2050. This is equivalent to half the final electricity consumption of the United States in 2010, or the final electricity consumption of South America, Africa and the Middle East combined in 2010 [IEA, 2014].

Urban infrastructure over the next 20 years at the global level is estimated to require US $41 trillion investments, including US $22.6 trillion on water and sanitation, US $9 trillion on energy, US $7.8 trillion on road and rail services and US $1.6 trillion on air/sea ports. The scale is such that a societal transformation can modify longer term trends in natural resource use. This is one reason why local authorities were prominent in the discussions in the run up to the Rio+20 World Conference.

15.2 Transport

Transport sector emissions of greenhouse gases have more than doubled since 1970 and have increased at a faster rate than any other energy end-use sector, even though only 10 per cent of the global population accounts for 80 per cent of the vehicle-kilometres, with much of the world's population hardly travelling at all; the gasoline consumption of New York equals that of the entire continent of Africa. Transport in total currently accounts for about 23 per cent of global energy-related GHG emissions of which 75 per cent are derived from land transport. Driven by motorization, urbanization, economic and population growth land transport GHG emissions are set to double by 2050 if current trends persist. Emissions from freight were 40 per cent of all land transport emissions in 2010, and are likely to double by 2050, while passenger transport is projected to increase by three-fourth of current levels. A combination of technological and behavioural measures could decrease final energy demand in 2050 for urban passenger transport by at least 55 per cent below the baseline and some of these mitigation measures could be tapped at very low or even negative costs from a societal perspective, along with generating substantial sustainable development benefits [IPCC, 2014].

Since two-third of all travel made is within urban environments, and is expected to triple by 2050, public transport infrastructure has to be considered at an early stage in urban planning. As cities grow, and the incomes of the middle class rise, car ownership increases, pushing public transport to a low priority. The purchase price of motor cars has been raised less than average consumer prices, and even though fuel costs impact on the cost of transportation, the evidence is that even at high prices there is growing demand for personal transportation. Developing an integrated public transport system to meet the needs of a large population is difficult in existing cities and is subject to delays in acquiring costly land. Integrating the city by linking together underground railway systems, metropolitan railway systems and bus lanes can be carried out only in capital cities, and where new cities are planned. The alternative of dedicated lanes for bus rapid transit systems also has to be planned in advance to be efficient because space has to be reserved for the dedicated lanes. Express bus systems are particularly suited for small- and medium-sized towns in emerging countries that will grow and where open spaces exist for planning infrastructure development, which can include cycling and walking.

With economic development, and rising incomes, transport becomes the most energy-consuming sector, accounting for almost one-third of final energy consumption; in terms of trends the fastest growing sector, and could increase to half of final energy consumption. Sales of vehicles follow trends in economic development. Personal transport also provides a good example of the 'rebound effect', where the benefits of energy efficiency have been negated by increasing demand. For modifying these trends, technological improvement alone will not be sufficient, and citizens will have to change their daily habits. In industrialized countries, there is a debate whether the shift will result from voluntary actions or regulations would be needed. The policy change will happen only when there is a readiness on the part of each citizen to accept change and the new level of responsibility for safeguarding ecosystem services. Personal transport – cars – accounts for more than three-quarters of all transport for the European Union, and a higher percentage in the United States.

The evolution of transport modes, driven by consumption patterns in industrialized countries, shows an interesting pattern of resource use. Since 1990 long-distance transport has grown the most, including shipping, because of increasing demand for commodities and shifts in industrial capacity overseas, and air transport, because of lifestyles, leisure travel and holiday trips. International aviation doubled in the period 1990–2010. The fastest growing mode of transport with economic development is aviation. For distances less than 500 km aviation is not the preferred mode, aviation has only a tiny share (1 per cent), and cars make up the majority of trips (72 per cent), because of the time taken up by check-in procedures and travel to airports. At the same time, rail transport has decreased, by as much as a quarter in the European Union for passenger travels.

A new development is the introduction of high-speed rail travel, which already accounts for a quarter of rail passenger travel in the European Union. For example, in the most popular air route in Europe in terms of passengers carried, between Barcelona and Madrid demand decreased by a quarter with the introduction of the high-speed rail link, and there are very few flights now between Brussels to Paris because of a high-speed rail link. Rail is also more competitive for long-distance freight, if problems concerning interoperability are dealt with, as in the case of China. Considerable increase in efficiency can be achieved using rail transport for long-distance passenger and goods transport, compared with transport by road or air.

Infrastructure related to transport has a longer lifespan than capital goods in buildings, with respect to use of energy services. Land-use planning for transport systems has to be done in advance or innovative and difficult means used to reframe use. For example, redevelopment of the inner cities can feature mixed residential and commercial buildings, car-free pedestrian zones, cycle paths, and dedicated buses. Mixed usage can also be extended to regional planning, with teleconferencing and home working reducing the need to travel. The driver here, too, is not technology but social change, and modifying certain activities does not mean sacrifice of the quality of life for inhabitants.

New forms of infrastructure and business models can support the shift from households owning cars. These models can combine goods and services in one package for all the four areas of production, consumption, housing and mobility, as against the current practice of producing consumer goods for sale. The goods remain the property of the provider (car, electricity, heating-cooling system) and are only rented or used communally and paid for on the basis of actual use of the service. For example, the infrastructure for car sharing will need to ensure easy accessibility to information, low costs and flexibility in use to be integrated seamlessly in daily schedules for work, or recreation visits. Currently, information technology-led solutions are being planned for the first-order operations, like route planning to include charging stations and integration with public transport, in Singapore. Switzerland has a countrywide car sharing system linked with public transport, and books cars at the destination along with the rail ticket.

France, Japan, the UK and Germany have experienced a decline in transport GHG emissions in recent years, with stabilized or even decreased road GHG emissions despite growth in both the economy and road-freight over the same period, which can be attributed to saturation in the travel demand. Absolute reductions are required in GHG emissions from land transport in the industrialized economies so that relative reductions in the emerging countries would allow for a limited growth in absolute emissions in these countries. This will enable these countries to meet growing travel demand in support of poverty alleviation, economic growth and social development, but doing so more efficiently.

Three approaches have been adopted in a complimentary manner for optimum results and are known as the Avoid–Shift–Improve (ASI) approach. These include avoided journeys, modal shift resulting from behavioural change, and use of improved vehicle and engine technologies, low-carbon fuels, improved infrastructure and other changes to the built environment. Although the overall economic impact of low-carbon transport is found to be highly positive, there are substantive costs linked to the transformation of the current, mostly car-dependent transport infrastructure and systems. Part of these transformational costs can be passed on to the users of transport, for example, in the case of improved fuel economy. In other cases, beneficiaries of low-carbon transport will be able to contribute through, for example, capture of increased land values resulting from public transport. The IPCC Fifth Assessment Report also concluded that the mitigation potential of transport is greater than in previous assessments.

The transition is compounded because of major difference in mobility levels between the United States, all industrialized countries and developing countries, with yearly per-person per capita travel in 2010 on the order of 24,000 km, 16,000 km and 4,000 km, respectively; the United States has 2.8 times the transport emissions per capita than Japan. For light-duty vehicle kilometres of travel per capita, the differences are even more significant at 12,000 km, 7,000 km and 1,000 km, respectively. There is very low availability of cars, and a low level of car-based travel, in developing countries. Motorized travel will have to significantly decline in industrialized countries to compensate for the increase in developing and emerging countries. Fuel efficiency, in particular in industrialized countries and choices on infrastructure and technology made in the emerging economies will be important. The aim will need to be for countries around the world achieving an average urban mobility level close to 8,000 km per person in 2050 [Allen, 2014].

There is increasing evidence of behavioural change, documented for the European Union and United States. Owning high capacity and more powerful cars is no longer considered by many as the preferred option and is becoming less popular with the younger generation. The United States has introduced measures to reduce single occupancy travel to work, including by introducing special lanes. In the Netherlands, three-quarters of the drivers curtailed peak time driving with introduction of road user charges, and it is estimated that it could amount to reducing travel by as much as a fifth. An ageing population is also leading to saturation levels in industrialized countries. Instead of one type of vehicle meant to do everything, smaller vehicles with no tailpipe emissions are being considered specifically for urban travel, with larger, extended-range vehicle used for longer routes. Car sharing is spreading from the United States to India, where the consumer pays to use vehicles only as needed. These shifts could transform the automotive industry and even alter our very concept of what an automobile is, as a means of self-expression, in the re-emerging countries and developing countries [Gao et al., 2014].

Public transport offers an immediate route to a better future, by doubling the market share of public transport worldwide by 2025, cities will be able to boost growth, help fight climate change and create pleasant urban environments. Cities will need to have a clear vision and strategy on how their mobility systems should look in the future, for at least three reasons. Part of the reason is that management of urban mobility is fragmented. This is partly because the initiative needs to be taken at a very different level towards shared mobility in terms of complementing conventional public transport, more cars and bikes are being shared in cities and new business-to-consumer models emerging. Part of the reason is also that transport infrastructures were historically designed to serve regional needs and have now to be adapted to local contexts [Little, 2014].

15.3 Electricity

While it is now agreed that individuals' access to electricity should be seen in incremental levels of basic human needs, productive uses and modern society needs, 'basic human needs' is the level that is commonly used for forecasts related to emerging countries, as it is linked to growth in GHG emissions from universal energy access. Global emissions will increase by as much as one-third to half of current levels by 2050, and peaking of carbon dioxide emissions will depend on shifts in patterns of resource use in industrialized countries and the availability of innovative energy technologies in emerging countries, not by underestimating demand. Between 1972 and 2012 electricity generation has gone up three-and-half times and the industrialized country share has come down from nearly three-fourth to slightly less than half and China's generation has increased seven times to less than a quarter – with similar population numbers – and the share of Asia and Africa has doubled while the share of Latin America has declined [IEA, 2014].

The Millennium Development Goals, agreed in 2000, did not include electricity as a basic need, ignored its essential role in establishing infrastructure necessary for the growth of the middle class, and the unique role of electricity with respect to planetary limits has only now come onto the global agenda. Residential electricity consumption in Sub-Saharan Africa is equivalent to the consumption in New York City, and the per capita generation of electricity in India is one-fifteenth that of the United States. Estimates suggest that currently, worldwide 3 billion people lack access to assured electricity, and they are also below the poverty line[2]. As part of the re-appraisal of current approaches, a new poverty index recently developed by the United Nations stresses lack of services such as electricity as a key factor in determining poverty.

Placing energy poverty, and related carbon space, as a central element in the framework of sustainable development/low-carbon green economy also requires political decisions for enhancing ecosystem services to overcome the limits imposed by the 'sink' constraints of the planet. Reconciling competing resource needs with respect to maintaining lifestyles and eradication of poverty is at the centre of the deliberations on modification of longer term trends in patterns of resource use for the transition to global sustainability. A policy objective of enhancing end-use energy efficiency and spread of renewable energy is more likely to obtain public support than an exclusive focus on reducing carbon dioxide, particularly the use of coal to generate cheap electricity, and curtailing use of energy by the middle class that will move into cities in developing countries.

Access to affordable and adequate electricity is a human right and coal is the most abundant source of electricity. In the United States, coal has provided over 50 per cent of electricity for the last century and according to the United States Energy Information Administration's latest projection in its Annual Energy Outlook 2014, coal will still supply 11 per cent more in the generation of electricity in 2040 than it did in 2012. The United States National Academy of Engineering identified societal electrification as the 'The Greatest Engineering Achievement' of the twentieth century. At the global level from 1990 to 2010, coal-based generation nearly doubled from 4,400 to 8,700 terawatt hours (TWh) to account for over 40 per cent of all electricity supply. Since 1990, in China, power generation from coal increased 700 per cent and GDP per capita rose 630 per cent. Each of the United Nations' Millennium Development Goals depends upon adequate energy, as it is essential

---

[2] One-third of the world still lives on less than $2 per day and lacks access to affordable and adequate electricity. For example, more than 300 million in India – equal to the population of the US – are without access to electricity. Currently biomass energy meets one-fourth of the energy needs of developing countries and they are also being advised by some analysts not to move to electricity–Bundles of energy: *The case for renewable biomass energy*, International Institute for Environment and Development (IIED), July 2011, Canada.

for enhancing the quality of life, for example, water supply, sanitation, and child mortality. Cities are built with electricity, steel, cement and associated materials, and the production required for these materials depends on adequate coal power and metallurgical coal for steel being available. Clean coal technologies are spreading where pulverized coal combustion systems, utilizing supercritical technology, operate at increasingly higher temperatures and pressures and therefore achieve higher efficiencies than conventional plants, emit up to 40 per cent less carbon dioxide.

15.4 Energy transformation

Energy – electricity and transportation – is a basic requirement for human well-being, as it is essential for the socio-economic activities of all societies, in the form of light, heat, mechanical power or electricity. At the same time, energy use is responsible emissions of carbon dioxide. The use of energy use is currently imbalanced, with around half of global primary energy demand in industrialized countries, which have only one-seventh of the global population, while generating around three-quarters of global GDP. World energy demand is projected to be nearly 40 per cent higher in 2035 with virtually all the growth taking place in developing countries, and with China and India accounting for half that growth, two-third of which will be in electricity generation. Global energy efficiency is expected to be half of what it was in 1995 and one-third lower than in 2013. Renewable energy is likely to account for less than 10 percent of total energy consumption in 2035. At that time total global carbon dioxide emissions are expected to increase by 25 per cent, with three-quarter of the emissions produced in developing countries, although per-capita emissions will be less than half levels in industrialized countries [BP, 2015].

In industrialized countries, energy demand continues to increase, because while electricity demand has stabilized, demand for personal transport continues to rise. At the same time, half of the human population has yet to enjoy the benefits of industrialization, urbanization and growth in incomes, as some 2.8 billion people still depend on traditional biomass as their primary energy source for cooking, and 1.4 billion people do not have access to electricity and transportation. Energy demand in developing countries for modern energy services – electricity and transportation – will continue to grow till at least 2050. Most of urban transport energy use and one-third of all urban direct energy use is attributable to economic activity, transport costs, geographic factors and urban form [Creutzig, 2015].

Coal will remain important as coal deposits are geographically widespread and the cheapest energy carrier. Coal is therefore preferred by many national states for reasons of strategic supply security, and frequently enjoys subsidies. Germany and the United States currently generate approximately 48 per cent of their electric power from coal. In India, the share is 68 per cent, and in China as high as 81 per cent. In the period 1990–2013, there has been little change in emissions intensity of electrification, and fossil energy carriers still accounted, in 2011, for two-thirds of primary fuel in the global electricity mix. Change is taking place, and legislation in China has taken close to 100 GW of inefficient plants offline since 2006, decommissioning of old plants continues, and the United States is proposing a 30 per cent cut in emissions from coal-fired power plants. Compared with coal-powered plants, nuclear energy causes very low levels of GHG emission.

Oil is the most important energy carrier for the transport sector, with limited potential for substitution. Between them, supertankers and coal freighters make up more than half of the total sea freight volume. The United States has already outstripped Russia as the world's largest gas producer and is expected to become the world's largest gas exporter by the end of the decade, fundamentally changing pricing and trade patterns in global energy markets. The United States is also expected to again become the world's largest oil producer. It looks as though the world will again see plentiful energy at low prices. Since shale resources are found around the world, many countries, including China, are developing this natural resource, and will change the geopolitics of energy. The 'Golden Age' of natural gas that is now firmly established in North America will expand to China over the next 5 years with the projected near-doubling of Chinese gas demand through 2019, and half of its new gas demand will be met by domestic resources, most of them unconventional. Both developments will lead to more efficient natural gas markets.

Globally, 442 nuclear reactors with a capacity of around 375 GWe were in operation in 2011, of these, 46 per cent of these are located in Europe (including Eastern Europe and Russia), 30 per cent in North America, and 21 per cent in the Far East (Japan and China), and 72 reactors were under construction in 2013. Together, the United States, France and Japan produced around 57 per cent of electricity generated by nuclear power in 2010. Globally, nuclear reactors provide 8 per cent of installed power generating capacity and contribute around 13 per cent to power generation, as the output capacity can be utilized approximately 80 per cent of the time. Nuclear energy is therefore often used for base load supply in power grids. China is expected to overtake the United States as the biggest nuclear producer with its share of the world total rising to 30 per cent in 2035.

Renewable energy sources are growing but are characterized by requirement for large areas of land to cover the major share of the energy supply. Wind and solar powers are also subject to considerable fluctuations in terms of energy availability. Hydropower is renewable energy that is particularly relevant in terms of system integration, as they can also be used to balance fluctuating feed-in.

The technical potential of solar power alone exceeds the current overall consumption by more than one order of magnitude. There has been a marked shift in activity towards emerging economies in 2010, as it was the first year that overall investment in solar came close to catching up that in wind. Asia as a whole deployed more than half of global solar PV additions in 2013. The price of PV modules per megawatt (MW) has fallen by 60 per cent since the summer of 2008, according to Bloomberg New Energy Finance estimates, putting solar power for the first time on a competitive footing with the retail price of electricity in a number of sunny countries. Wind turbine prices have fallen 18 per cent per MW in the last 2 years, reflecting, as with solar, fierce competition in the supply chain. Further improvements in the cost of energy for solar, wind and other technologies have begun to mark a shift from using fossil fuel for generation of electricity.

In 2013, commercial solar power reached grid parity in Italy, Germany and Spain and will do so soon in Mexico and France. Increasingly, solar PV can compete without subsidies: power from a new 70 MW solar farm under construction in Chile, for example, is anticipated to sell on the national spot market, competing directly with fossil fuel-based electricity. Onshore wind electricity is the cheapest source of new electricity in a wide and growing range of markets. More than 100 countries now use wind power. Offshore wind is also expected to grow rapidly as costs fall, with the United Kingdom leading the market with 4.2 GW of installed capacity as of mid-2014. These and other developments have made renewables increasingly attractive in many more markets. In 2013, for the first time, new renewable capacity installations were higher in emerging countries. China's deployment of solar PV and wind in 2013 was estimated at 27.4 GW: nearly four times more than the next largest, Japan. Worldwide, renewable power capacity has grown 85 per cent over the past 10 years, reaching 1,700 GW in 2013 and renewables today constitute 30 per cent of all installed power capacity. Global perceptions on renewable energy have shifted with the need for a level playing field in the entire energy sector and the importance of long-term and differentiated policy frameworks to sustain and increase investment levels; 144 countries have renewable energy targets and at least 138 countries have renewable energy policies, out of which 95 are in developing countries [IRENA, 2014]. Energy from renewable sources met 15 per cent of gross energy consumption in the European Union 2013, according to the European Union's statistical office, Eurostat, up from 8.3 per cent in 2004. In the China–United States climate deal, in November 2014, China has committed to increase the non-fossil fuel share of all energy to around 20 per cent by 2030, putting up additional 800–1,000 GW of nuclear, wind, solar and other zero emission generation capacity; that is more than all the coal-fired power plants that exist in China today and close to total current electricity generation capacity in the United States.

According to Bloomberg New Energy Finance, China's investments in renewable energy in 2014 increased by 32 per cent, to US $89.5 billion, and in the United States and Japan, totalling US $51.8 billion and US $41.3 billion respectively. In Europe, which collectively accounted for the second largest investment, US $66 billion, investments only grew by 1 per cent in 2014. China is currently the world's largest market for solar power and among the biggest for wind, owing to support from the Government, which aims to diversify the national energy supply. Globally, funding for wind and solar power, biofuels and other low-carbon energy technologies grew by 16 per cent to US $310 billion. Nearly half of the investments went into solar energy, at US $149.6 billion, while wind energy attracted US $99.5 billion, driven by offshore projects. Investment in distributed power grew by 34 per cent, to US $73.5 billion, reflecting a move away from large, centralized power stations.

Resource productivity improvements are shifting to be greater than economic growth driven less by economics than by technological innovation, resource efficient and low material intensity manufacturing and living, and appropriate attitudes and consumption patterns. Improving the efficiency of consumption and applying demand-side management is vital to limiting the need for capacity expansion and reducing investment costs across the electricity chain. Some European countries have adopted zero-energy goals for new residential construction around the 2020 time frame. The United States recently approved its most stringent energy-saving building code, which includes mandatory day lighting and automated lighting controls. With global electricity demand associated with network-enabled devices growing at an alarming rate, and network-enabled devices use up to 80 per cent of their electricity in 'standby mode' just to maintain a network connection, a range of existing technologies and solutions can be implemented to prompt devices to power down or reduce energy requirements without compromising the services that network connectivity enables. China's bold measures to support clean transport as a means of improving urban air quality has led to some 150 million electric two wheelers on the road and greater deployment of electric buses. Car-sharing programmes being launched in cities around the world are indicative of behavioural changes that could have far-reaching consequences for urban mobility solutions. It is estimated that half of emission reductions by 2035 can be delivered by end-use energy efficiency largely based on consumption patterns [IEA, 2014].

The last time the energy supply was changed was in the industrial revolution. Germany aims to power the country almost entirely by renewable energy by 2050; currently renewable energy is meeting 27 per cent of the demand, double the electricity powered by renewables in the United States. China aims to generate 20 per cent of its electricity from renewable sources by 2030. With respect to reducing demand, experience shows that there are no technical and economic obstacles in the first 25 per cent but 50 per cent and beyond can only be achieved by combining this penetration with energy efficiency measures and finally by modifying consumption patterns; and this is what China is aiming to achieve.

References

Allen, Heather, Manfred Breithaupt, Lew Fulton, Kain Glensor, Sanjing Han, Cornie Huizenga, Oliver Lah, Katie Millard, Michael Replogle, Shritu Shresta. Land transport's contribution to a 2°C target-bridging the gap: pathways for transport in the post-2020 process, Report jointly developed by the Bridging the Gap Initiative (BtG) and the Partnership on Sustainable, Low Carbon Transport (SLoCaT), September 2014.

BP. 2015. BP Energy Outlook 2035, British Petroleum, February 2015.

Carey, Mark, Lincoln C. James and Hannah A. Fuller. 2014. 'A new social contract for the IPCC'. *Nature Climate Change*. 4: 1038–39.

Creutzig Felix, Baiocchi Giovanni, Bierkandt Robert, Pichler Peter-Paul Seto, Karen. 2015. 'A Global Typology of Urban Engergy Use and Potentials for an Urbanization Mitigation Wedge'. *Proceedings of the National Academy of Sciences*. doi: 10.1073/pnas.1315545112.

Editorial. 2014. 'Science that Matters'. *Nature Climate Change*. 4: 841.

Gao, Paul, Russell Hensley, and Andreas Zielke. 2014. *A Road Map to the Future for the Auto Industry: As the Sector Transforms Itself, will the Automobile Keep its Soul?* McKinsey and Company, October 2014.

IEA. 2013. *Transition to Sustainable Buildings: Strategies and Opportunities* to 2050 International Energy Agency, Paris, 2013.

IEA. 2014a. *More Data Less Energy: Making Network Standby more Efficient in Billions of Connected Devices.* International Energy Agency, Paris, 2014.

IEA. 2014b. *Energy Technology Perspectives*, International Energy Agency, Paris, 2014.

IRENA. 2014. *Rethinking Energy: Towards a New Power System.* International Renewable Energy Agency, Abu Dhabi.

Little, Arthur D. 2014. The Future of Urban Mobility 2.0: Imperatives to Shape Extended Mobility Ecosystems of Tomorrow, Arthur D. Little, Boston, January 2014.

Sachs, Jeffery. 'Sustainable Development Economics'. Project Syndicate 2014.

Sanwal, Mukul. 2012. 'Rio +20, Climate Change and Development: The Evolution of Sustainable Development (1972–2012)'. *Climate and Development* 4 (2): 157–166.

Sanwal, Mukul. 2013. 'The Rise and Fall of Global Climate Policy: Stockholm to Rio 1992, to Rio + 20 and Beyond'. *Chinese Journal of Environmental and Urban Studies* 1 (1).

UNEP (2010), *Assessing the Environmental Impacts of Consumption and Production: Priority Products and Materials*, United Nations Environment Programme, 2010, Nairobi.

Distribution of Natural Resources

16

Lifestyles of the urban middle class impose disproportionate burdens on the global ecosystem requiring a policy focus not only on globalized material flows and related scarcity but also on the social, economic and environmental systems that structure society's use and distribution of natural resources. The fundamental drivers and tends are increasingly internationalized through globalization of supply chains so that impacts occur in other parts of the world, and interdependencies and lock-ins require systemic transitions.

16.1 Mega-trends and the decreasing stock of natural resources

Human well-being has always been, and will be in the future, dependent on the availability of natural resources such as energy, materials, water and land. Economic development in a globalized world is associated with a rapid increase in the use of natural resources. In 1998, the richest one-fifth of the world's population was responsible for more than four-fifth of consumption expenditure while the poorest one-fifth had to settle for less than one-fiftieth of such expenditure. The 500 million richest people, who constitute only 7 per cent of the world population, are responsible for half of all greenhouse gas (GHG) emissions. In contrast, the poorest 3.1 billion people are responsible for only 5–10 per cent of the total. However, the research and policy focus so far has been on impacts caused by direct interventions into natural systems such as resource extraction, land cover change and fishing in rural areas where the poor live. The effects of consumption in urban areas, such as electricity use in buildings and ecological footprint of food and transport, have been treated as unintended side effects and largely ignored. The degree to which natural resource use affects ecosystem services and causes adverse impacts on the environment depends not only on the amount of resources used, but also on the types of resources used and on the ways in which they are used [UNEP, 2011].

Humans have converted about a quarter of the Earth's potential net primary production, half through direct cropping and the rest through land-use-induced productivity changes, or industrialization and urbanization. The combined impact on natural ecosystems is biggest in North America and Europe. Reflecting this trend, historical large-scale forest loss has stabilized in temperate regions and is decreasing in the tropics, and the net area lost to deforestation annually has halved compared with the forest loss 20 years ago [FAO, 2010]. For much of the twentieth century, biomass has dominated among the four material types: in 1900, biomass accounted for almost three-quarters of total material use, and its share has now declined to only one-third. This decrease in biomass extraction, while the world population needing food quadrupled, is mainly due to a substitution of biomass use for combustion by fossil fuels and the shift towards mineral resources.

The global stock of natural resources is decreasing, largely because of urban consumption. Humans already use almost a quarter of the biomass produced globally each year on all land, and nearly half of the renewable, accessible water resources. Around half of the world's oceans are severely affected by human activities, and about three-quarters of the world's marine fish stocks for which information is available are fully exploited or overexploited. Collectively, various anthropogenic global material and energy fluxes by now exceed any natural flows. As a consequence, water resources, soils, forests and oceans have been overexploited or are being destroyed, biodiversity is undergoing a drastic reduction, and important biochemical flow patterns have been radically changed by humankind; for example, the carbon and nitrogen cycles. The loss of natural ecosystems damage a wide range of ecosystem services, including cycling carbon and water, and providing food and fibres, leading to food and water scarcity.

16.2 Myth of the environmental impact of the rural population

Global population has grown from just under 1 billion in 1800 to 7 billion in 2012 and is likely to stabilize at 9 billion around 2050. Population is considered a major driver of the overall increase in natural resource use, because it has been common to compute per capita resource use as an overall measure of material standard of living. This ignores the nature and consumption patterns of resource use, which varies by a factor 10 or more between rural areas where most of the population resides today and urban areas where most of it will be in the next 50 years [Marina Fischer-Kowalski and Helmut Haberl, 2007].

Average global rates of natural resource use stagnated in the period from 1900 to 1950 and have grown rapidly from the end of World War II up to the early 1970s, when urbanization had been completed in industrialized countries. The period after the early 1990s marks a new phase in patterns of natural resource use in which a number of developing countries have adopted growth strategies for industrialization that make it possible for the rural population to move to urban areas into a rapidly expanding middle class, and begin to achieve convergence with high consumption levels achieved between 1970–1990 in industrialized countries. Globalization has facilitated much of the recent reduction in material and energy intensity of output in industrialized countries by relocating material- and energy-intensive manufacturing to developing countries.

Over the last 100 years, industrialized countries accounting for only one-seventh of the global population have had levels of energy use above the levels in developing countries. It was only in 2010 that developing countries accounted for over half of global energy use, because of the strong growth in China, and are likely to account for only between two-thirds to three-quarters of total global energy use in 2100; per capita energy use will continue to be much higher in industrialized countries than in countries that are now industrializing. Some two billion people in developing countries continue to rely on non-commercial biomass as the principal source of energy, and levels of energy use at the level of pre-industrial societies, requiring more quantity of energy use and qualitative change in the structure of the energy system in light of global ecological limits.

The global transition in the use of natural resources is still incomplete. Infrastructure, essential for urbanization and economic development, accounts for most of the materials used as well as emissions of carbon dioxide. The energy-intensive industries alone (iron and steel industry, metals, chemicals industry, cement, glass) were responsible for more than four-fifth of the concentration of GHGs in the atmosphere [IPCC, 2007]. With increase in wealth delayed impacts from consumption are becoming more important than immediate ones and global impacts on the environment are becoming more important than local ones, affecting global ecosystem services.

More research is needed to study the links between societal needs, the natural and economic processes involved in meeting these needs, and the associated environmental and social consequences. For example, population numbers in rural areas, who are mostly poor, do not cause degradation of the natural environment, as they live in balance with nature; consumption patterns of the urban dwellers, largely in the middle class, are de-linked from nature through trade and responsible for excessive natural resource use. For example, three commodities, soy, beef and palm oil for urban consumption, have been responsible for close to 80 per cent of tropical deforestation worldwide; they also account for 12–15 per cent of global GHG emissions [Global Environment Facility, 2014].

The global impact of increasing natural resource use in emerging countries is now the subject of new research focusing on social capital and resource productivity, from very different perspectives. For example, population growth and natural capital depreciation are considered to constitute the main driving forces of declining wealth per capita in the majority of countries. Population increased in 127 of 140 countries, while natural capital declined in 127 of 140 countries. Although both factors, with each negatively affecting growth in wealth, changes in population were responsible for greater declines. Produced capital, the capital type for which by far the most exhaustive (and reliable) data exists, represents only about 18 per cent of the total wealth of nations. The remaining capital types, which together constitute 82 per cent of wealth (54 per cent in human capital and 28 per cent in natural capital), are currently treated as, at best, satellite accounts in the System of National Accounts. Investments in human capital, in particular education, it is argued, would generate higher returns for 'inclusive wealth' growth, as compared to investments in other capital asset groups in countries with high rates of population growth [UNU-IHDP and UNEP, 2014]. As against this perspective for emerging countries, for industrialized countries it is argued that "the current way our economy consumes resources is not sustainable", the European Union has ambitious targets for improving resource productivity by 30 per cent and countries like the United Kingdom are moving towards a 'circular' approach of re-using resources, maximising their value over time as it makes environmental and economic sense [Environmental Audit Committee, July 2014]. The transformation of poor rural societies into the urban middle class is still not at the centre of the global agenda, and the social scientists are nudging the United Nations in that direction with their contribution to the formulation of the global sustainable development goals, calling for the meta goal of 'a prosperous, high quality of life that is equitably shared and sustainable' [ICSU, ISSC, 2015].

16.3 Land-use change and statistics

Three trends in the environmental impact of land-use change, where also local populations have not been the drivers, have largely been ignored.

First, the land-use systems (agriculture and forestry, including deforestation), which are currently responsible for almost a quarter of global GHG emissions have to provide enough food for a world population that continues to grow wealthier, but around half of the emissions are generated subsequent to agricultural production, for example, through storage and preparation for urban areas [EEA, 2012]. Even more important, though corn is the biggest crop economically and takes up nearly one-third of United States cropland, in 2013, nearly three-quarters of the corn crop is used either to feed animals or to fuel cars – just 10 per cent was used for direct human consumption.

Second, in large parts of the world, food systems were shaped to a considerable extent by the so-called green revolution of the 1960s and 1970s, which pushed agricultural yields as much through intensive use of irrigation water and environmentally harmful chemical fertilizers and pesticides, and the introduction of new seed varieties, as a result agricultural irrigation accounts for some 70 per cent of all water withdrawals, largely to provide food for urban areas.

Third, the shift in diets from cereals to meat as wealth increases is likely to cause demand for agricultural production to rise steeply and to meet this demand, food, feed and fibres could grow by 70 per cent by 2050, which will be offset if the current pattern of food wastage, as one-third of the food produced is wasted, is modified along with avoiding dietary changes. Agricultural productivity will also have to increase from the current rates, and global agricultural area is likely to expand only by about 10 per cent to meet the new urban demand. Biotechnology, genetic engineering, food irradiation, hydroponics and anaerobic digestion can improve the resistance of food crops to pests and extreme weather and increase productivity.

Carbon dioxide emissions (and, to a certain extent, GHG emissions) are the only well-documented environmental impact indicator available at the global level, as existing land-use statistics are not easily applied to an analysis of patterns of natural resource use. While measuring consumption of energy resources is fairly established, seeking a consistent methodology for documenting the extent of use of other natural resources is still under development. With land, the statistical situation is much better, at least as far as cropland is concerned. The main focus of accounting for land resources is put on land cover (such as cropland, grassland or forest) and its change over time. However, the coupling of economic activity and land use is reflected not only in land cover change, but also in the intensity of use. An increase in yields or multi-cropping on existing arable land, or an increase in livestock grazing on grassland, does not necessarily lead to change in land cover types, but nevertheless represents an increased use of natural resources. For assessing the use of water and land in relation to economic activities, the data situation is even less well developed. This paucity of data is related to the fact that water use is often considered a free common good not reflected in economic statistics. System boundaries also raise problems, as the same water can be used many times over. As a rule of thumb, total extraction is about double total used material [UNEP, 2014]. The statistical system now being developed in the United Nations does not take into account these elements related to consumption patterns even though the United Nations acknowledges that there will be water and food scarcity in 2050 only if demand, or consumption, patterns do not change.

16.4 Globalization and sustainable natural resource management

It has become harder for consumers to continue enjoying de facto gains in living standards resulting from ever-falling import prices, reduced availability of low cost capital enabled by developing countries and mounting environmental risks. During most of the nineteenth and twentieth centuries, commodity prices declined by more than 50 per cent and have already doubled in this century, altering the relative importance of resources compared to other inputs into production and changing the basis of relative competitive advantage of industrialized countries; the 'terms of trade' led to annual material extraction that grew by a factor of eight through the twentieth century. The policy focus, particularly in industrialized countries with high levels of natural resource use, has shifted to resource productivity, to achieve economic output from fewer resources and reducing waste by reducing per-capita consumption; material use is linked to energy use and carbon dioxide emissions. However, the legacy of past policy decisions and technological, behavioural, organizational and institutional biases against innovation in resource productivity present significant barriers to decoupling. This includes lock-in by resource-intensive consumption patterns, production systems, infrastructure and institutions.

Global scientific assessments are now stressing that industrialized countries would need to absolutely decouple their growth from their greenhouse gas emissions, at a rate that would give more room to developing countries to raise living standards until they too can achieve absolute decoupling [UNEP, 2014]. This implies, for these countries, that each unit of production is produced using between 25 per cent and 10 per cent of its current resource inputs by 2050 [World Business Council for Sustainable Development WBCSD, 2010]. Steps are being taken in this direction. Sweden introduced an energy efficiency programme in 2005 for its energy-intensive industries. A recent analysis showed average payback periods of less than 1.5 years [Stenqvist and Nilsson, 2013]. High-efficiency motors could potentially save 28–50 per cent of motor energy use, with a typical payback period of 1–3 years [CADDET, 1995]. Sub-surface drip irrigation systems that deliver water directly to crop roots can reduce water use by 30–70 per cent and raise crop yields by 20–90 per cent, depending on the crop [Postel et al., 2001].

These initiatives, while important, do not amount to the new framework that some had envisioned when issues related to the environment came onto the global agenda. Maurice Strong had voiced this concern and hope over 40 years ago – 'Will the growing awareness of the concepts of "one earth" and "one environment" in fact lead – as it should – to the nobler concept of "one humanity", and to a more equitable sharing of environmental costs and a greater international interest in, and responsibility for, the accelerated development of the less industrialized world? Or will it become a narrow concern of the industrialized world, leading to many awkward confrontations with the developing countries rather than to a new era of international cooperation?' [UN. 1972]. The global mega-trend of the spread of urbanization to the developing countries is now, 40 years later, shaping a new framework for understanding global concerns, this time taking also into account the interests of the emerging countries and new form of international cooperation.).

References

CADDET. 1995. *Saving Energy with Electric Motor and Drive*. Sittard: CADDET Energy Efficiency
Environmental Audit Committee. 2014. Growing a Circular Economy: Ending the Throwaway Society, Third Report of Session 2014–2015, July 2014.
EEA. 2012. *Consumption and the Environment: 2012 Update*, European Environment Agency, Copenhagen.
FAO. 2010. *Global Forest Resources Assessment* 2010, Food and Agriculture Organization, Rome.
Fischer-Kowalski, Marina and Helmut Haberl, editors. 2007. Socioecological Transitions and Global Change: Trajectories of Social Metabolism and Land Use, Institute of Social Ecology, Klagenfurt University, Vienna, Austria, Edward Elgar Publishing, Vienna.
Global Environment Facility, Supply Chains, Supply Change: The Future of Sustainable Commodities, December 2014.
ICSU, ISSC (2015): Review of the Sustainable Development Goals: The Science Perspective. Paris: International Council for Science (ICSU).
IPCC. 2007. *Climate Change 2007: Synthesis Report. Summary for Policymakers*, Intergovernmental Panel on Climate Change, Geneva.
Postel S., Polak P., Gonzales F., Keller J. 2001. Drip Irrigation for Small Farmers: A New Initiative to Alleviate Hunger and Poverty *Water International*. Vol. 26, no 1, p. 8.
Report on Development and Environment by Secretary-General for UN Conference on the Human Environment to the General Assembly, Maurice Strong, UN General Assembly Document A/CONF.48/10, 22 December 1971.
Report on Development and Environment by Secretary-General for UN Conference on the Human Environment to the General Assembly, Maurice Strong, UN General Assembly Document A/CONF.48/10, UN, 1972
Stenqvist, C and L. J. Nilsson. 2013. Energy Efficiency in Energy-Intensive Industries – An Evaluation of the Swedish Voluntary Agreement PFE. *Energy Efficiency* 5(2): 225–41.
UNEP. 2011. *Decoupling Natural Resource Use and Environmental Impacts from Economic Growth*, A Report of the Working Group on Decoupling to the International Resource Panel. Fischer-Kowalski, M., Swilling, M., von

Weizsäcker, E.U., Ren, Y., Moriguchi, Y., Crane, W., Krausmann, F., Eisenmenger, N., Giljum, S., Hennicke, P., Romero Lankao, P., Siriban Manalang, A., Sewerin, S.

UNEP. 2014. *Decoupling 2: Technologies, Opportunities and Policy Options*. A Report of the Working Group on Decoupling to the International Resource Panel. von Weizsäcker, E.U., de Larderel, J., Hargroves, K., Hudson, C., Smith, M., Rodrigues, M, United Nations Environment Programme; Nairobi.

UNU-IHDP and UNEP. 2014. *Inclusive Wealth Report 2014 Measuring Progress Toward Sustainability*. Cambridge University Press, Cambridge.

World Business Council for Sustainable Development WBCSD (2010) Vision 2050. WBCSD, Conches-Geneva.

CONSUMPTION IN A MORE EQUAL WORLD: SHAPING SOCIETAL FUNCTIONS

'... International cooperation and the resulting governance mechanisms are not working well. First, the current global governance system is not properly equipped to manage the growing economic integration and interdependence among countries, both of which are compounded by the current globalization process. Globalization tends to accentuate interdependencies among countries. Second, global governance structures and rules are characterized by severe asymmetries in terms of access, scope and outcomes. While developing countries must abide by and/ or shoulder the effects of global governance rules and regulations, they have limited influence in shaping them. Meanwhile, the unbalanced nature of globalization implies that important areas of common interest are currently not covered, or sparsely covered, by global governance mechanisms, while other areas are considered to be over determined or overregulated by a myriad of arrangements with different rules and provisions, causing fragmentation, increased costs and reduced effectiveness. These deficiencies have contributed to the generation of asymmetric outcomes among countries and have had important implications for inequality at the national level as well. Finally, current approaches to global governance and global rules have led to a greater shrinking of policy space for national Governments, particularly in the developing countries, than necessary for the efficient management of interdependence; this also impedes the reduction of inequalities within countries'.

Committee for Development Policy, 2014, Policy Note, Global governance and global rules for development in the post-2015 era, Department of Economic and Social Affairs, United Nations, June 2014. The Committee for Development Policy (CDP) is an expert body of the Economic and Social Council composed of 24 members serving in their personal capacity.

'Today an average European consumes 40–60 tons of material each year. A sustainable level of material use per individual has however been calculated at 7–10 tons per year which means that the average individual lifestyle material use needs to be reduced by about 80%. ... A main challenge to achieve these changes is that future individual consumers will not compromise on quality, convenience, price or status when it comes to purchasing decisions. ... New transformative approaches towards sustainable consumption and production are thus needed ... identifying solutions that can reduce the volume rather than the value of what we consume'.

'Changing Production and Consumption Patterns through Transformative Action', the 4th Global Green Growth Forum held in Copenhagen on 20–21 October 2014, The 3GF, a partnership of seven governments (Denmark, the Republic of Korea, Mexico, China, Kenya, Qatar and Ethiopia) and several businesses and international organizations.

'The longer we wait to take action towards sustainable production and consumption, the more it will cost to solve the problem and the greater the technological challenges will be'.

Synthesis Report of the Secretary-General on the Post-2015 Agenda, The Road to Dignity by 2030: Ending Poverty, Transforming All Lives and Protecting the Planet, 4 December 2014, United Nations New York.

Geoeconomics of Human Well-being

17

Global consumption drives exhaustion of natural resources and environmental systems, and this is primarily the impact of the expanding urban middle class. The drivers represent increased needs for mobility rather than increased population, diet based on livestock farming which has the highest global anthropogenic impact on land use and community and social norms in the way electricity is used in buildings[1].

17.1 Urban Design

Urban planning shapes travel distances between people and places they need to go to work, school, shopping and recreation. A focus on increased population densities and on accessibility; mixed use areas rather than only establishing more roads to enable speedier movement of goods and services reduces natural resource use. The current 'zoned' cities make inefficient use of infrastructure and do not support a modal shift to public transport, which needs greater efficiency and acceptability as well as a reduced need to travel. 'Streets' serve many purposes other than as transport arteries, as they also encourage non-motorized mobility.

With respect to personal transport, it is now being accepted that technical solutions alone will not lead to a reduction in emissions of greenhouse gases (GHGs) in the transport sector, and demand-side management, including modal shifts will be an essential part of the strategy, and can also be cost effective. Accessibility does not depend so much on affordability of the transport network as on the quality and efficiency of reaching places. This perspective will serve to change public attitudes to personal mobility and the automobile. The reframing extends to considerations of shifting the focus of policy away from redefining needs – not just reaching destinations but also accessing opportunities, making a distinction between transportation, or motorization, and trips and travel distances, or mobility. The key issue in shaping transport patterns is urban design.

Transport volume growth responds to economic development in the sectors using transport. Economic growth leads to a demand for more transport; growth means more goods to be produced and traded, and wealth leads to more services consumed. For example, in the European Union, transport GHG emissions have risen 27 per cent between 1990 and 2007, total transport energy consumption increased by over one-third, and in 2009, transport contributed one-quarter to GHG

---

[1] Parts of this chapter were first published in Sanwal (2014).

emissions from all sectors in the European Union. Road transport represents the largest energy consumer, accounting for three-quarters of total demand.

Government policies play an important role in shaping transport use. In the United States, heavy investment was made in high capacity highways, from the 1950s, and subsidised home mortgages, leading to low density urban design and increased dependence on personal transport. In Europe, funds were spent on urban rail systems and social housing near public transport stops. Consequently, the role of public transport in cities varies widely, from 45 per cent trips in East Europe and Asia to 25 per cent in Europe and 5 per cent in North and Latin America. In the 2000s, Japan brought in reduced ownership charges by as much as 25–50 per cent for fuel efficient cars while increasing those for large engine vehicles, and 40 per cent of all trips are now made by public transport. However, except in China, the share of trips by public transport is declining with increase in wealth and low public investment. This is leading to increased congestion as increase in road width and length has not kept up with increase in traffic, which results from increased needs for mobility rather than increased population. GHG emissions per passenger are one-twelfth for public transport as compared with personal transportation.

17.2 Diet

We now know that changed eating habits in line with increasing prosperity, rather than population growth, results in substantial natural resource use and emissions of GHGs, which is much more than the technical emissions reduction potential of agriculture through improved land management. The lifecycle emissions of meat, dairy products, and eggs – in particular beef – are up to 10 times higher than those of an equal weight of plant-derived foodstuffs in the United States; these values are half as much, or less, for cattle production in emerging countries, as they are range animals. Overall, around three-quarter of the world's cultivated land is used for livestock farming (as pasture, or for feed production) and provides only 15 per cent of global calorie supply, while contributing 18 per cent of global GHG emissions. The current ecological footprint of North American and European eating habits is around twice as large as Africa's or Asia's because of the important part which animal products play in their diets. This ratio is changing, as the per capita consumption of meat in the developing countries has more than tripled over the past 50 years, except in India, where more than half of the population is vegetarian. It has been estimated that in 2050, global GHG emissions from agriculture have the potential to be below 1995 figures, if eating habits were to change towards a diet with a lower proportion of animal products. The shift to a healthier diet according to nationally approved guidelines, but not fully vegetarian, with less animal products would have a significant impact on natural resource use and ecosystem services [FAO, 2013].

According to Food and Agriculture Organization, one-third of the food produced in the world is wasted, with impacts on resource use and food security. Food wastage is the third top emitter after China and the United States, representing 30 per cent of the world's agricultural area. Wastage of meat generates a substantial impact on the environment in terms of land utilization and carbon footprint, as two-third is wasted in developed countries, because of inadequate planning and exaggerated concerns over 'best-before' dates. The direct economic cost of all the wastage is estimated to be about $750 billion in terms of producer prices and the food supply chain has impacts on climate, water, land and biodiversity. Reduction in food wastage has the potential to reduce pressure on land and decrease the need to raise food production by half to meet the increased demand in 2050.

Food wastage occurring at the consumption stage, high for industrialized countries, impacts on all the phases that the product has gone through. The carbon footprint of wastage in the United States is nearly two times that of Japan and three times that of France. The consumption of water in the food wasted amounts to over three times the total human consumption of the United States, as cattle's relatively low conversion efficiency leads to a large water footprint. Most of the water footprint comes from the animal feed. In general, animal products have a larger water footprint per tonne of product than crops. From a freshwater resource perspective, it is more efficient to obtain calories, protein and fat through crop products than animal products. The food wastage of milk and meat involves three-quarters of the agricultural land area. China with low demand for beef and India, largely vegetarian, have a low food carbon footprint compared to other major economies.

Products from animals account for about one-third of the total carbon footprint, even though their contribution to food wastage volumes is only 15 per cent. Pulses, such as peas and beans, are also efficient sources of protein, as compared with animal protein, because pulses need fewer inputs per kilograms of protein produced. In addition, the ability of grain legumes to fix nitrogen from air means that only a very small amount of nitrogen fertilizer is applied in the cultivation, which lowers the emission factors of these products. Livestock represents 14 per cent of GHG emissions, of which beef production is nearly half, mainly from feed production and processing, enteric fermentation and use of fossil fuel over the supply chain. A 30 per cent reduction of GHG emissions would be possible, for example, if producers in a given system, region and climate adopted the technologies and practice currently used by the 10 per cent of producers with the lowest emission intensity; the potential can be achieved as a result of improving practices rather than changing production patterns [FAO, 2013].

In India, meat accounts for about 4 per cent of food wastage but accounts for 20 per cent of the wastage costs. In contrast, fruit and vegetable losses run to 70 per cent, but account for about 40 per cent of economic costs. India is the world's largest producer of milk and the second largest producer of fruits and vegetables after China. High wastage rates are often responsible for doubling of fruits and vegetables prices, and making the cost of milk 50 per cent higher. It is not only perishable food that is wasted but also staple grains such as wheat and rice. It is estimated that each year around 21 mt of wheat, equivalent to the entire production of Australia, rots or is eaten by insects. Around 35 to 40 per cent of the food is not consumed and the problems lie in inadequate supply chains, storage and management; limiting wastage can bring about food security in 2050 even with rising wealth and urban demand.

Changes in consumption patterns are important for food security, related land use patterns and production trends in agriculture. However, the focus so far has been on modifying production patterns, through greater productivity, to increase supply and for food security to meet the rising demand with growth in incomes. Trends in the use of food grains show the greater impact of changing food habits and the shift to increasing consumption of meat products in driving land use change and agriculture production. Meat production also leads to substantially higher levels GHG emissions than plant-based agricultural food grains, and current consumption patterns of this demand have shown a continuing growth trend.

17.3 Behaviour

Governments will need to take the lead to make sustainable living the 'default option', and this will require innovative technology, infrastructure, regulation, pricing, marketing and new social norms used in combination in policy packages. Public discussion is needed on different pathways to happiness than offered at present, along with a wider vision of well-being that considers community aspects and sustainable resource use, because individual choices are influenced by the social context [Mont et al., 2013].

Infrastructure shapes sustainable behaviour, and public acceptability can be increased by building appropriate social norms for the acceptance of regulatory measures, while providing practical alternatives.

The policy focus should be on high impact consumption areas like flying, meat and car driving to shift to lower impact activities like vegetarian diets, public transport and local leisure and cultural activities and personal development. To support and enable new ways of living, a new metrics of societal prosperity needs to be developed; referring to people as citizens rather than consumers and appealing to the national and societal, in addition to individual interest, as legitimate reasons for action. The policy focus, however, remains on the supply side of the production–consumption continuum, for example, greening products and eco-labelling, while leaving the demand side to the preferences of individuals.

Existing policies promoting 'green' consumerism aim to promote sustainability through the existing consumer culture, even though it is becoming clear that these approaches do not lead to reduced natural resource use and aggregate reductions of environmental and social impacts associated with consumption. The focus on efficiency, mainly of production, reflects government's reluctance to directly target consumption and outsource these concerns to the private sector to show that something is being done.

Well-being and high quality of life do not depend on high resource consumption. Sustainable consumption needs to be reframed so it is viewed as a progressive path to societal development. Policy initiatives will need a broad spectrum ranging from technological and efficiency improvements, promoting pro-social and pro-environmental values, and modifying longer term trends to de-link material consumption from societal status, identity and notions of well-being. Policies influence public perceptions of what is normal and desirable, both by providing resources and incentives to act in a particular way and by providing information and messages that encourage particular interpretations of society and politics, for example, shift from conventional light bulbs and other energy using products. It will be important to deal with both the practical barriers to green living (e.g., why is flying often cheaper than taking the train?) and the emotional and psychological barriers (e.g., camping holidays in your own country are not generally seen as attractive or fun). Public opinion and values linked to consumption are responsive to government policy [ECT/SCP, 2011].

The total number of products per household is constantly on the rise and people nowadays tend to own more than one product in a certain product category (computers, mobile phones, TVs). What used to be a product for satisfying needs of a family rapidly became a product for satisfying individual needs and wants. Alternative perspectives are now emerging across countries that place less focus on the ownership of products per se by using information technology to provide access to products and services in different forms and shapes. There are a number of examples of these developments – car sharing and communal washing rooms, toy libraries and DIY tools and garden equipment sharing schemes, renting of equipment and sport goods. The shift from services to a knowledge-based economy is leading to innovation that reduces natural resource use to provide the same level of service.

References

ECT/SCP. 2011. The role of values and public perceptions in policymaking for sustainable consumption, Working Paper 2/2013, European Topic Centre on Sustainable Production and Consumption, Copenhagen.

FAO, 2013. *Tackling Climate Change Through Livestock – A Global Assessment of Emissions and Mitigation Opportunities*. Food and Agriculture Organization, Rome.

Mont, Oksana, Eva Heiskanen, Kate Power and Helka Kuusi. 2013. *Improving Nordic Policymaking by Dispelling Myths on Sustainable Consumption*. Nordic Council of Ministers.

Sanwal, Mukul. 2014. 'Global Sustainable Development Goals are about the Use and Distribution, Not Scarcity of Natural Resources: Will the Middle Class in the USA, China and India Save the Climate as Its Incomes Grow?' *Climate and Development*. 4(4).

Social Science – Policy – Society Interface

18

18.1 Interrelated systems and the environmental perspective

Since the Stockholm Conference on Human Development, held in 1972, sustainable development has been seen as a practical tool for achieving incremental improvements in environmental protection. It also had a visionary impact with its stress on human needs and social justice, dependence of human well-being on the environment, characterization of limits, strong economy and support for future generations. The conventional viewpoint is now facing the challenge of a growing global economy meeting ecological limits in the sink constraints of the atmosphere. It is being stressed that there is a need for a transformation of the economic system itself, for which the industrialized countries must take a primary responsibility because in recent years the affluence factor has exceeded the population factor in driving natural resource use[1].

The structure of economies forces them to grow, and sustainable development demands a new economics, informed by a broader vision of human nature and human well-being. A world in which 9 billion people all achieve the level of affluence and the consumption patterns in developed countries would need an economy 40 times bigger than today's (200 times bigger than in 1950) by the end of the century [Jackson, 2009, p. 14]. Consequently, the existence of ecological limits poses the moral question – if this cannot be achieved through technological efficiency, how much of the world's resources does any one nation or individual have a right for their well-being?

Twenty years after the Rio Summit on Environment and Development, held in 1992, the world is still facing two challenges: meeting the demands for better lives by tripling the size of the global middle class by 2050 and keeping this growth within planetary limits. The global policy response to these interlinked challenges does not require slowing growth, by modifying longer term trends to enable the right kind of growth policies have had a clearer impact in improving resource efficiency than in reducing environmental impacts or enhancing ecosystem resilience. The global policy response for dealing with the 'sink' constraints of the planet requires a strategic shift from merely considering environmental damage and resource productivity to enhancing and equitably sharing ecosystem services. Emerging countries must now take the leadership in evolving a new paradigm, because in the coming years, they will be making increasing demands on carbon space, to absorb emissions of

---

[1] Parts of this chapter were first published in Sanwal (2012, 2013).

carbon dioxide, as they consume vast quantities of steel, cement, aluminium, chemicals and fertilizers needed for infrastructure, urbanization and food security essential for the eradication of poverty in an environmentally sustainable manner. While each country has its own vision of what is fair in defining the criteria for sharing the global commons, an analysis of patterns, trends and drivers of national resource use since 1972 suggests that transforming societies towards living in balance with the natural environment will also lead to more equity.

The United Nations has acknowledged the importance of efforts to 'live in harmony with nature'. At present, alternatives are being examined to devise a more sustainable model for production, consumption and the economy as a whole so as to promote harmony with nature. In February 2008, at the request of the Government of France, Joseph Stiglitz, Amartya Sen, and Jean-Paul Fitoussi established the Commission on the Measurement of Economic Performance and Social Progress. The motivation was that GDP, as an expression of purely economic growth, no longer meets societies' concerns with welfare and sustainability. This is especially the case as the metrics do not take into account sustainability, as current consumption puts in jeopardy, for instance, future living standards. The most obvious cases involve depletion of resources and the degradation of the environment. The Commission acknowledged that no single number can summarize anything as complex and variegated as 'society'. But, inevitably, certain numbers – in particular GDP – have taken centre stage. The Commission agreed that such a number may be misleading if it were applied to all purposes, and especially as a broader measure of societal performance [UN, 2010].

The 'population question' is also taking on a new dimension, with increasingly aging populations in industrialized countries and China. Global population has more than doubled since the 1960s, it is unlikely that it will double again during the current century, and it is expected to peak at approximately nine billion by around 2050 [UN Population Division, 2009]. Like other industrialized countries, but in this case not because of urbanization but because of its 'single-child' policy, in China a demographic transformation with a massive shift in age structure is taking place; In 2040 36 percent of Japan's population will be aged over 65 years. China's population is projected to start declining around 2030 and the working age population, which currently provides one of the biggest drivers of economic growth, will decline rapidly both in absolute terms and as a proportion of the total population. By 2050, China's population will have fallen to its size in 2000 and by the end of the century, it is likely to be half of the 2000 level. Aging, rather than stabilization of the global population towards the middle of the century, will enable sustainable development.

Increasing levels of energy use is also a characteristic of economic development, and the relationship cannot be determined for any country based on the experience of other countries. For example, different development pathways, and the 'path dependency' they create, have led to highly energy intensive (e.g., the United States) to highly energy efficient (e.g., Japan) end use at comparable levels of income. Path dependency in energy systems arises from both contextual factors, such as availability of the natural resource, and political, social, economic and institutional factors that lead to urban design, type of infrastructure and different consumption patterns.

These trends show that energy transitions have been policy-enabled rather than policy-driven. The perspective that regulation, externality pricing and other supporting policies will drive low carbon technology diffusion is different to the way technological transformation has taken place in energy systems. Scenarios modelling the future also assume globally integrated markets and stronger growth in Asia, consequently suggesting action in that region. Fossil fuels are likely to have for some time cost and performance advantages over low carbon technologies, and the magnitude of decarbonization required in the future does not take into account the timescale in the spread of such technologies. However, the ranking of different 'mitigation wedges' is quite strong across the scenarios explored, with energy efficiency and conservation the single most important option, contributing over half to cumulative emission reductions over the twenty-first century; a conclusion now supported by the International Energy Agency.

Energy end-use technologies, at the centre of consumer demand and markets, are already driven by innovation and change, and this explains why the largest efficiency improvement potentials do not lie in energy supply but in energy end-use sectors [Grubler and Riahi, 2010]. Consequently, the costs of change will be much less on the demand side than modifying energy supply technologies and related systems. This also suggests that public expenditure supporting research and development should include smaller-scale end-use technologies within technology portfolios. Support for such technologies in the past has proven both cost-effective and successful, generating high social returns on investment [Fri, 2003]. The form of urbanization that requires less input and generates less waste will be one of the deciding factors for the end-use demands that a future energy system must meet.

18.2 Policy implications of current patterns of natural resource use

We need transformative change because we now have to deal with resource scarcity not so much in terms of 'sources' but rather in terms of 'sinks' – the limited capacity of the planet to absorb waste carbon dioxide, as the global commons are a strategic resource for all countries. Sustainable development/climate governance can no longer be considered only in terms of environmental damage, and has now become a part of the political, economic and security debate because of the competition for scarce resources, in the form of the global commons. Consequently, the central concern in international cooperation is equitably sharing of ecosystem services provided by the planet outside national boundaries making it a social process rather than a physical problem.

There are five policy implications of current patterns of natural resource use. First, global resource use in the period 1900–2005 increased 8-fold while per capita use doubled, because 20 per cent of the global population used 86 per cent of the resources (in 1998) and the bottom 20 per cent used less than 2 per cent of the resources [UNEP, 2011]. In the context of global limits, the case for the wealthy to reduce resource use is obvious.

Second, it has been computed that two-third of the global environmental impact has been caused by carbon dioxide, cities account for three-quarter of these emissions, and the construction sector accounts for more than a third of global material resource consumption. The strongest increase in resource use in the last century has been in construction material and minerals and ores (34 and 27 times, respectively), while oil increased 12 times and biomass only 3.6 times; during this period, resource prices declined some 30 per cent. The rate of resource use accelerated sharply in the period 1950–1970 driven by the establishment of urban infrastructure in the industrialized countries. While this urbanization involved a population shift of half billion, in emerging countries, this could amount to over 5 billion by 2050 with the attendant growth in emissions – in India, over 500 million are expected to shift to urban areas by 2025. The global community has to recognize the increase in resource use, and carbon dioxide emissions, resulting from industrialization to provide employment and the scale of the infrastructure for urbanization, including everything from energy, housing, roads, trains, airports and ports to education and health care needed by the new middle class.

Third, carbon dioxide emissions are driven ultimately by consumption. Over two-thirds of global emissions of carbon dioxide occurred in the period after 1970, caused by urban lifestyles, rather than from industrialization [TISS, 2010]. In industrialized countries, while industrial emissions have remained steady since 1990, over two-thirds of carbon dioxide emissions are now coming from the services, households and travel sectors, they account for more than half the increase in global emissions since 2005, and it is expected that emissions from transportation (largely for leisure) will exceed half of global emissions in 2050 [IEA, 2007]. However, global attention continues to be focused on the increasing emissions from generation of electricity, largely from coal, in China and India, where three-quarters of the electricity generated goes for industrial production and any reduction in emissions will have a direct impact on economic growth[2], unlike in developed countries (the United States also gets most of its electricity from coal) where consumption by household's accounts for two-thirds of the electricity generated, and reductions will impact only on (wasteful) lifestyles.

Fourth, as there are limits to the total ecological burden the planet can sustain, without industrialized countries sharply reducing their resource use immediately other countries cannot get their fair share of the global commons for eradication of poverty. As the Nobel Prize winner Joseph Stiglitz pointed out in his address to the International Economics Association, held in Istanbul in June 2008, the transition to a low carbon economy will require a new economic model – changed patterns of consumption and innovation, as 'only through changes in patterns of demand will adverse effects of climate change on emerging countries be mitigated'[3].

Fifth, the implication for international cooperation is that in industrialized countries, frameworks will be needed to change particular kinds of resource consumption, not middle-class lifestyles or human well-being, and in emerging countries, the type of infrastructure, or urban design, to be established will largely determine emission levels in 2050. The policy focus has to be on urban design to eliminate excessive emissions from buildings as well as modal shifts in transport and modify consumption patterns to reduce wastage of food and conserve water. Such national actions, or bottom-up, efforts conceptualize sustainability in terms of strategies that will modify patterns of resource use rather than in terms of multilaterally negotiated burden sharing of the costs of measures in developed countries, through a carbon tax or a price on carbon.

18.3 Longer term trends in natural resource use

It has now become clear that alternative patterns and processes in the human use of nature in industrialized and emerging countries result in trade-offs for socio-economic systems that are very different to those focusing only on environmental systems, and international cooperation based on multilateral agreements around long-term economy-wide issues, like climate change needs changes in consumption and production, like the successful tackling of the ozone problem [Levin and Clark, 2010].

Trends in industrialized countries highlight the limitations of only considering production patterns, for example, the carbon dioxide emissions from the fuel mix of electricity generation, ignoring the growing consumption patterns. The paradox here is that while global energy intensity – final energy use per unit of GDP, largely driven by technology – fell by 26 per cent in the period 1990–2005, energy use per capita – largely driven by increase in consumption and wealth – increased more

---

[2] According to the National Energy Administration of China, six high energy consuming industries contributed 42.7 per cent to the growth of electricity consumption in the first 5 months of 2011 – electric power, steel, building materials, non-ferrous metals, chemicals and petrochemicals. Manufacturing constitutes 45 per cent of the GDP of China and uses 74 per cent of its energy, while manufacturing is 16 per cent of the GDP of India and uses 45 per cent of its energy demand.

[3] Stiglitz also stressed that in the case of global carbon management, the key problem is how to allocate emission rights, currently valued at about $2 trillion annually, that is, 5 per cent of global GDP, and the 'only serious defensible principle is equal emission rights per capita, adjusted for past emissions … as a process of slowly easing in emission rights would increase inequities associated with past emissions'. Even if this entails large redistribution, it is not clear why this should be treated differently than other property rights.

than 6 per cent in developed countries and less than 1 per cent in emerging countries. Consequently, even though carbon dioxide emissions from manufacturing have not increased, overall emissions increased 15 per cent in developed countries, in this period [IEA, 2009]. Recent research establishes that growth and sustainable development/climate protection are rival objectives only in high-income countries, which are called upon to share their resources to enable a global sustainability transition. The political difficulties of this are obvious, and the crucial, still unresolved questions are how far from the global welfare and climate optimum is it necessary to deviate in order to win acceptance of sustainability policy/low carbon green economy in developed countries [SEI, 2011].

A more holistic view has also led to the recognition that hypothetical global scenarios on which international cooperation is based bear no relationship to trends in resource use and the real options confronting policy makers [Perrings et al., 2011]. Existing models focus on specific policy areas and sectors such as energy and transport, and they cannot capture fully the impact of resource use on ecosystems, enterprises, the economy and society as a whole, or the interdependence of policy measures and longer term trends [EC, 2011]. For example, different energy economies and greenhouse gas emission profiles lead to different economic and environmental impacts for countries in pursuing a harmonized policy approach [NRTEE, 2011].

Scenarios are not able to capture the 'decoupling' taking place in emerging countries driven by social rather than environmental considerations. Recent reviews of China's actions to reduce energy and carbon intensity challenge the many analyses projecting continued exponential growth for China as energy demand is likely to plateau around 2030 and 2040 because of the saturation effects (appliances, residential and commercial floor area, roadways, railways, fertilizer use, etc.), deceleration of urbanization, low population growth, and change in the export mix to high value-added products, and carbon dioxide emissions are expected to stabilize around 2030 owing to continuous energy efficiency improvement as well as decarbonization in the power sector with the spread of renewable energy [Zhou et al., 2011]. In China, and in other emerging countries, with societal notions of well-being, consumption patterns and technological shifts very different to those in developed countries per capita carbon dioxide levels are not likely to increase significantly despite rising per capita GDP [Eichengreen et al., 2011]. Emerging countries are likely to settle into the status of well-being of Germany, and this could well be the global norm in terms of 'happiness' in 2050.

China's production patterns have significant potential for end-use efficiency. For example, electric motors used in industry in China account for around 60 per cent of the country's total electricity consumption, their operational efficiency is 10–30 per cent below international best practice and have a potential to save 28–50 per cent of motor energy use depending on the industry. China currently consumes 60 per cent of global steel reinforcement bar production, and use of higher strength steel achieves an average 25 per cent reduction in the weight of steel. Agriculture is responsible for 70 per cent of freshwater withdrawals, and efficiency savings can be as high as 50–80 per cent, sub-surface drip irrigation systems that deliver water directly to crop roots can reduce water use by 30–70 per cent and raise crop yields by 20–90 per cent, depending on the crop [UNEP, 2014].

References

EC. 2011. Communication from the Commission to the European Parliament. The Council, The European Economic and Social Committee of the Regions: A Resource-Efficient Europe – Flagship Initiative Under the Europe 2020 Strategy. COM(2011) 21, 26 January 2011, Brussels.

Eichengreen, Barry, Donghyun Park, Kwanho Shin. 2011. When Fast Growing Economies Slow Down: International Evidence and Implications, NBER Working Paper No. 16919, March 2011.

IEA. 2007. *Energy in the New Millennium: Trends in IEA Countries*. International Energy Agency. 2007, Paris.

IEA. 2009. *Worldwide Trends in Energy Use and Efficiency: Key Insights from IEA Indicator Analysis.* International Energy Agency, Paris.

Levin, S. A. and W.C. Clark. 2010. Toward a Science of Sustainability, Centre for International Development Working Paper No. 196, May 2010, Harvard University, USA.

NRTEE. 2011. Parallel Paths: Canada-U.S. Climate Policy Choices – Climate Prosperity, Report 03, National Round Table on the Environment and the Economy, Jan 2011.

Perrings, Charles, Anantha Duraiappah, Anne Larigauderie and Harold Mooney. 2011. 'The Biodiversity and Ecosystem Services Science-Policy Interface'. *Science.* 17 February 2011.

Sanwal, Mukul. 2012. 'Rio +20, Climate Change and Development: The Evolution of Sustainable Development (1972–2012)'. *Climate and Development* 4 (2): 157–166.

Sanwal, Mukul. 2013. 'The Rise and Fall of Global Climate Policy: Stockholm to Rio 1992, to Rio + 20 and Beyond'. *Chinese Journal of Environmental and Urban Studies* 1 (1).

SEI. 2011. Comparing Climate Strategies: Economic Optimization versus Equitable Burden-Sharing. Frank Ackerman, Ramón Bueno, Sivan Kartha, and Eric Kemp-Benedict, Stockholm Environment Institute, Working Paper US-1104, Feb 2011.

TISS. 2010. Conference on Global Carbon Budgets and Equity in Climate Change. 28–29 June 2010, Tata Institute of Social Sciences, Mumbai, India.

UN. 2010. Report of the Secretary General, Harmony with Nature. A/65/314 dated 19 August 2010.

UNEP. 2011. *Decoupling Natural Resource Use and Environmental Impacts from Economic Growth*, A Report of the Working Group on Decoupling to the International Resource Panel. Fischer-Kowalski, M., Swilling, M., von Weizsäcker, E.U., Ren, Y., Moriguchi, Y., Crane, W., Krausmann, F., Eisenmenger, N., Giljum, S., Hennicke, P., Romero Lankao, P., Siriban Manalang, A. Copyright © United Nations Environment Programme, 2011, Nairobi.

UNEP. 2014. *Decoupling 2: Technologies, Opportunities and Policy Options.* A Report of the Working Group on Decoupling to the International Resource Panel, von Weizsäcker, E.U., de Larderel, J, Hargroves, K., Hudson, C., Smith, M., Rodrigues, M.

Zhou, Nan, David Fridley, Michael McNeil, Nina Zheng, Jing Ke, and Mark Levine. 2011. China's Energy and Carbon Emissions Outlook to 2050, LBNL-4472E, China Energy Group, Lawrence Berkeley National Laboratory.

Reframing the 'Common Concern' From a Physical to a Social Problem

19

19.1 Measuring sustainability and human well-being

The context in which sustainability has been discussed at the multilateral level has changed since the issue first came onto the global agenda in 1972. Globalization, urbanization, increasing consumption patterns and continuing poverty despite the sustained economic growth of industrialized countries and some emerging countries have broadened perspectives. However, the response at the multilateral level to the transformative impact of the re-emergence of China has largely been of a scarcity mentality, seen as a zero-sum game, rather than develop a shared vision where everyone can become better off. The challenge everywhere is not limited to increase resource productivity – using fuel, water and raw materials more productively, as some have argued [The Economist, 2008], but also conserving and sharing resources by modifying patterns of global natural resource use[1].

Limits to growth concerns not just ecosystem scarcity but also the impact on individual welfare, through reduced freedom, or options. These are not unbearable restrictions and costs, for example, in the context of climate change. Since these are societal issues, ultimately it is society that has to change, and, therefore, different indicators are needed to complement the GDP indicator in order to generate a more balanced understanding of sustainable development. The 1970s study on 'The Limits to Growth' [Meadows et al., 1972], produced by the Club of Rome, had also discussed how to measure human welfare and changes to the natural environment. There is a broad agreement that the indicator GDP, or GDP per capita, is suitable for reflecting economic activity, but not social progress, national welfare and sustainable development. These discussions have been based in part on the parallel debates on quality of life and social indicators as inputs to state-related planning and international cooperation.

The choice of indicators and assumptions made to complement GDP and determine future 'qualitative' growth, is a political issue, and will be based on a clear understanding of what sustainability means. GDP, or GDP per capita, measures only market activities and monetary value. It does not provide information on income distribution, welfare or well-being. In making these choices, it is now being realized that exclusive focus on environmental damage should shift to enhancing standards of living, and its implications for use of natural resources. This would lead to considering the socio-economic as well as environmental trends in different countries, and the interaction within and between them.

---

[1] Parts of this chapter were first published in Sanwal (2012, 2013).

Two methodologies have generally been adopted in measuring sustainability. One approach determines or assumes certain critical thresholds and aims to keep the stock above that level. The second approach computes a value to each stock and converts it to a monetary equivalent. It, therefore, also assumes substitutability between the different stocks, implying that a decrease in one can be offset by increase in another. Recent work is stressing the social dimension and shifting the focus from measuring ecosystem services to measuring human well-being within ecological limits. Living standards are related to income and consumption. However, average levels do not tell us what is happening at the bottom, or at the top, and indicators to reflect their distribution provide a better picture. Median levels provide a better measure than average levels of the status of the 'typical' household or individual.

The assessment and valuation of environmental damage, or loss of ecosystem services, also remains controversial. The 'consumption of natural capital' is sought to be measured and valued using methods that are indirect and depend on 'what if' scenarios to develop a 'Green GDP', computing environmental damage or estimating prices for environmental functions, and not at all accurate. Environment has a global dimension, where the contribution of each country to the loss of ecosystem services, at least with respect to the global commons, has to be measured, and remains controversial. There is also no common understanding of the future well-being of all – it could be the average global GDP or the convergence of the well-being of all, where the global policy implications will be very different. Assessing a future state requires projections to be made of trends – environmental and technological and how they interact with socio-economic trends and policies, recognizing the inherent uncertainties. Since it is difficult to define thresholds for all ecosystem services, the usual practice is to identify risk assuming the continuation of current trends. For example, representative nature reserves are considered a suitable indicator as well as the optimum measures for the conservation of biodiversity and ecosystem services. Another example is a carbon footprint, if one is adopting consumption-based approach, or a carbon budget, if a national-level approach is adopted because it is only for greenhouse gases that global data is available and responds to both production and consumption patterns in each country. Measuring sustainability is different to statistical observations.

Alternative concepts for measuring welfare and sustainability have also been developed. The Genuine Progress Indicator (GPI) uses the GDP as a basis and modifies it by giving a money value to environmental degradation and even voluntary work. Other approaches do not use the GDP at all, but develop a composite index to add various monetary and non-monetary factors together to give one index of indicators for the areas of health, education, and material living standard – the United Nations Development Programme's Human Development Index (HDI), and the Index of Economic Well-being (IEWB). There are also approaches that measure current level of welfare and the sustainability aspect of economic activities, focusing on ecological sustainability, or other dimensions of sustainability. A recent approach is the 'Gross National Happiness' index in Bhutan. This extends the indicators to other values, such as 'spiritual well-being', 'good government' and 'biodiversity' are included. Some approaches consider only the ecological dimension, for example, the European Union's Sustainable Development Indicators. In response to concerns about measurement, markets are also emerging for ecosystem services related to carbon, water, and forests and in addition, commercial transactions are being made to invest in restoration and maintenance of particular ecological systems and the services that they provide. These alternative indicators of growth essentially support decoupling economic growth from environmental degradation, but say little about the social issues of use and distribution of natural resources.

GDP as a unit of measure has also not kept pace with the changing nature of economic activity. It was designed to measure the physical production of goods in the market economy, and is not suited to accounting for private- and public-sector services where there is no output that can be counted in terms of number of units produced. It cannot assess improvements in the quality and diversity of goods and services or degradation of the environment associated with consumption. Transformative change in technology is also not easy to measure using GDP because the real benefit accrues at the consumption rather than production level. GDP was not meant to be a measure of national economic performance or well-being because of trade-offs required in defining the ultimate goal [Dobbs et al., 2015].

19.2 Re-defining ecological limits and global interdependence

Forty years after the Stockholm Conference on the Human Environment, in 1972, a new framework for global interdependence has yet to get a consensus. The recognition of planetary limits is supporting the view that benefits accruing from the world's limited supply of global commons must be distributed more equitably. As important as the size and duration of the supply of resources is who should have access to them and who should consume what. The difficulty lies in agreeing on an agenda for a more equitable allocation of the global commons, if indeed they are limited.

Earlier predictions of the limits to growth have been proved wrong; this time it may be different because the impact of urbanization in the emerging countries rather than the impact of the limited population of industrialized countries is involved, even though they are not adopting the old patterns and trends in natural resource use. Thomas Robert Malthus, in the late eighteenth century, in his *Essay on Population* argued that growth in population will always be more than growth in the available resources, making it impossible to provide food and shelter to people. He did not foresee the implication of the impact of cheap fossil fuels which enabled new technology to increase use of natural resources through trade and that rising incomes lead to declines in the rate of growth of the population. In the 1970s, with the completion of urbanization in industrialized countries, the Club of Rome asked two ecologists, Donella and Dennis Meadows and their colleagues, to look at the increasing growth in resource use since the industrial revolution to see whether the trend in rates of economic growth would continue in emerging countries. Their conclusion was that because of the production and consumption patterns of urbanized societies, and three-fourth of the population in developed countries had by then shifted to cities, resource scarcities would push prices up and slow down the possibilities for future growth, and the natural resource base of economic growth would collapse. It was in the context of urbanization, and not just in terms of population numbers, that they expected significant scarcities before the end of the century, because they assumed that existing trends would continue into the future in emerging countries. This has not happened.

Since sustainability is about the distribution and use, rather than scarcity, of natural resources, it is inherently political. Economists in industrialized countries point out that there are easy solutions, and spending as little as I per cent of GDP now can avoid losses of up to 20 per cent of GDP later, with the measures being taken by emerging countries as they grow. Economists in emerging countries see environmental degradation as a result of over-consumption, and growing inequalities, shifting the focus from cheating, or free riding, to sharing global resources. A very different response has now come from scientists at the multilateral level in the IPCC, for example, with reference to climate change, that what really matters is the total greenhouse gas budget we allow ourselves, because global atmospheric concentrations are already at 435 ppm [IPCC, 2013]. If we want a 75 per cent chance of staying below the 2°C level, the global economy can only afford to emit a total of 1 thousand billion tonnes of carbon dioxide between the year 2000 and the year 2050. Crucially, they show that by 2008, we had already used up a third of this budget. Staying within the budget is going to be even more demanding than 450 ppm stabilization scenarios of the IPCC suggest, and the ecological limits could be reached before the poor are able to raise their levels of income to comparable levels with those who have over-utilized these ecosystem services to their advantage; the solutions are equally a matter of ethics and justice and economic efficiency.

Adequate carbon pricing at the global level is considered essential by those who believe that market forces will drive the transformation. This measure is considered only for carbon, and not for other global concerns like biological diversity. It is argued that greenhouse gases have not been valued and in fossil fuel using sectors consumption is highly subsidized, making adoption of innovation difficult, because the price distortions favour fossil fuel use. According to this view, the objective of international cooperation should be to establish a global carbon price, even as the inequities of this arrangement are recognized. The approach adopted, by implication and not an express statement, by the re-emerging countries is that mitigation and adaptation are an integral part of urbanization, and the shift in population from rural areas to become consumers can be achieved without leading to 'dangerous' climate change. The United Nations is now recognizing that the distinguishing feature of economic development is urbanization. With cheap commodities and mass production material wealth has been equated with a 'good life', and market principles affect all other institutions. However, relying on short-term costs and benefits ignores the longer term social implications. Therefore, modifying longer term patterns of natural resource use, especially energy, will need a broad spectrum of support to gain social acceptance. In this transformation, international cooperation will be an important, even a deciding, element because of the interdependence created by the overuse of the global commons by some and the need for all to keep within the global carbon budget; the China–US climate agreement, November 2014, seeks to achieve this goal.

19.3 Redistribution in the use of natural resources

Consumption lies at the heart of current global environmental change. Individuals shape resource use by their consumption patterns, societies define the boundaries and character of their environments, while affecting and reacting to their environment with only a limited and biased understanding of it. The current arrangements do not steer societies towards preventing, mitigating, and adapting to global and local environmental change and, in particular, earth system transformation, within the normative context of sustainable development. There is a gap in assessing what societies need for their physical well-being, and what they understand as their needs based on their beliefs and values of what constitutes well-being.

While carbon dioxide is the immediate trigger, or symptom, the strategic shifts have to go deeper. Urbanization itself has to follow a different path to the one followed by industrialized countries of planning settlements, mobility patterns and design of buildings to enable energy conservation and not just energy efficiency. Modifying lifestyles in the industrialized countries will also require a structural change. People have to be convinced of both the merit and the necessity of the changes before they will change their consumption patterns. The relative roles of societal change and of markets in the transformation continue to be a matter of debate.

The transformation will be enabled by a societal change and will not just be a technological change or instituting new business models. Increased awareness of high energy usage and waste is already leading to new attitudes and values. For example, the G20 has considered removal of consumption subsidies on fossil fuels, which could be as much as $500 billion annually. The real problem is that the changes have to take place within a tight time frame. It will not be easy because the current system follows an economic model established over 200 years ago, and at present we do not have another working model.

A societal transformation will catalyze reform in three areas. First, globalization, with increasing dependencies in trade and information technology is already creating a global identity modifying notions of state sovereignty and greater importance will need to be given to the role of cities, individuals and the behavioural changes they should make more appropriate for a service and knowledge-based economy. Second, internationally agreed political, human and socio-economic rights already stress the equality of all, and this should evolve to patterns of natural resource use being common to all. Third, the new type of international cooperation will have to be supported by science that relies more on the social than the natural sciences to overcome the difficulties inherent in achieving consensus in a multipolar world.

The transformative impact of the rise of China provides a new model. For example, climate change is viewed in China as more than just an environmental issue, to becoming an economic and innovation challenge to move to a higher and more technologically stage of economic growth, while increasing human well-being. China already has the world's largest capacities to manufacture solar modules and high speed rail network. It is also experimenting with new models of public transport, establishing that dealing with the scarcity of ecosystem services, economic growth and competitiveness are mutually supportive. The key message is that an exclusive concern on one dimension, like climate change, will not lead to sustainable development.

The global community will have to develop a vision of the world in 2050, in which there is a broad agreement of the objectives of the transformation to bring about convergence in standards of living. Since normative decisions have to be taken this will be a cooperative effort between countries, as well as between science, politics and society. It will be important to explore different pathways that are both practical and affordable in terms of the societal and technological innovations with respect to urbanization, energy use and diet, or lifestyles. Since societal and technological innovations interact with respect to changed behaviour and need, the diffusion and development of alternative science must focus more on the societal objectives to determine the goals themselves through dialogue with society, only then would the solutions be credible and relevant.

A key goal has to be changing certain consumption patterns, rather than middle-class lifestyles, which are in turn shaped by urban design, energy efficiency in buildings and appliances, diets and personal transportation. These shifts, can augment ecosystem services (establishment of low-carbon societies, modifying the energy system) and also natural capital (land and water use) because of diets based on livestock and food wastage. For example, a new website, Uber uses technology to increase the supply of cars in the taxi market and has also improves their utility and efficiency. By monitoring ridership, Uber can smartly allocate cars in places of high demand, and by connecting with users' phones, it has automated the paying process, and no parking requirement frees up parking lots for housing. Ride sharing is a fast and cost effective alternative way of connecting to public transport in emerging countries. Such a transformation moving away from owning a resource to sharing it is based on new welfare concepts and will impact on both national institutions and international mechanisms. While technologies help, they are not the key because the transformation will have to review the relationship between humankind and nature requiring a normative reorientation.

Interactions between social institutions and technological changes lead to social transformations, with changes in individual behaviour preceding diffusion of innovations. The two are mutually dependent leading to multiple changes, some of which are not interrelated. Unlike the past transformation, the current one has a defined objective, of moving to a sustainable economy and society by modifying identified longer term trends. Therefore, it is important not only to understand these trends but also to identify global goals that will lead to a better life for all. There is scope for optimism as the emerging knowledge-economy, unlike all earlier transformations, is not dependent on increasing use of energy and other natural resources.

References

Dobbs, Richard, James Manyika, Jaana Remes, and Jonathan Woetzel, 2015, Is GDP the best measure of growth? No matter how we measure economic growth, it needs to be pursued in a smart way. McKinsey Global Institute, January 2015.

Meadows D, Meadows D, and Randers J. 1992. *Beyond the Limits: Global Collapse or a Sustainable Future.* Earthscan: London.

Meadows D, Meadows D, Randers J, and Behrens W. 1972. *The Limits to Growth: A Report for the Club of Rome's Project on the Predicament of Mankind.* Earth Island: London.

Sanwal, Mukul. 2012. 'Rio +20, Climate Change and Development: The Evolution of Sustainable Development (1972–2012)'. *Climate and Development* 4 (2): 157–166.

Sanwal, Mukul. 2013. 'The Rise and Fall of Global Climate Policy: Stockholm to Rio 1992, to Rio + 20 and Beyond'. *Chinese Journal of Environmental and Urban Studies* 1 (1).

The Economist. 2008. A Bigger World: A Special Report on Globalisation, September 20 2008.

Developing a Shared Global Vision

20

20.1 New role of the social sciences

Assessments of Rio+20, held in 2012, largely focus on institutional issues, for example, conference diplomacy, institutional redesign and multilateralism and this restricts the analysis to what was agreed by states. For example, researchers who have been reviewing the evolution of international law consider the agreement on developing global sustainable development goals as important, but within their treaty-based framework global goals are not considered a significant achievement with implications for the longer term future. Rio+20 should really be seen as a milestone in the evolution of sustainable development, since sustainability is about the use and distribution not scarcity of natural resources, it is highly political, and new thinking already emerging from within the United Nations, government think tanks and private sector consultancies reflects the emergence of a new kind of broad-based social, rather than natural, science 'epistemic community', their input gives hope for a successful transformation as the global middle class triples by 2050[1].

In 1972, states agreed that the global commons were a 'common concern' and needed consideration distinct from national economic development, which was causing environmental degradation. In 1992, the need for international cooperation was cemented through multilateral environmental agreements, for example, on climate change and biological diversity. Now, in 2012, states have agreed that global environmental concerns and national economic development should be encompassed within a common set of global goals for all countries, described in terms of sustainable development. The explanation of these shifts is provided by the 'World Social Science Report, 2013', produced by the United Nations Education, Social and Cultural Organization (UNESCO), prepared jointly with the International Council for Social Science Research (ICSSR) and the Organization for Economic Co-operation and Development (OECD) – a wide cross-section of opinion – which concludes that 'the social sciences must help to fundamentally reframe climate and global environmental change from a physical into a social problem'.

Global sustainable development goals reflect this reframing. The scale of global change requires policy choices and trade-offs in the face of conflicting priorities, particularly with respect to three related but distinct global drivers – urbanization, energy, and the middle class – as they depend on natural resource use with a global impact. A set of global goals is important because relations between

---

[1] Parts of this chapter were first published in Sanwal (2012, 2013, 2014).

countries are now being shaped by geoeconomics rather than geopolitics, and the emerging issue is to what extent the United States, China and India, all populous countries and top tier economies, see their national interest in giving a new meaning to words like 'responsibility', 'development' and 'growth' by shifting the focus from the 20-year-old formula of burden-sharing for environmental degradation to modifying longer term trends in resource use, and developing a global vision for 'sharing responsibility and prosperity'.

With the global middle class expected to triple by 2050, we are faced with three inter-related global limits – carbon budget, consumption by the rich and comparable standards of living for the poor. How these limits are approached will not depend on burden-sharing but on what is regarded as essential for human well-being.

Geopolitical shifts are contributing to the rethinking of the science–policy interface in understanding underlying processes and the context in which the activities impacting on the environment take place. Risk-based regulatory approaches are not able to deal with aspects of sustainability because it is cross-cutting in nature, involves a high degree of uncertainty and requires data that is just not available. Risk assessment works best for chemical and physical agents that have already been emitted, partly because the nature and degree of impact is better understood and can be monitored. Instead of asking the question 'what action can be taken given the risk', the approach should be to 'maximize social, economic and environmental benefits with as little harm as possible'.

Four related but distinct perspectives are emerging, with the lead being taken by the United Nations, intergovernmental and government think-tanks, business and consultancies:

First, attention is shifting to global drivers such as urbanization, technologies, trade patterns and consumption along with demographics. Many of these changes are interdependent and likely to unfold over decades and we are very far from understanding them completely. Identification of trends in natural resource use has relied on quantitative forecasting even though the systems addressed and their linkages are not fully understood. What is now suggested is an approach based on historical patterns of natural resource use to identify the longer term trends that need to be modified [FAO, 2013a, 2013b; ISSC/UNESCO, 2013].

Second, the transformation of energy systems, which will be a central component of a transition to sustainability, has taken centuries for full coverage, and even more important, all past energy transitions have been driven by the development of end products or services that were made possible by the new forms of energy but not by the old ones. So far end-use services and technologies have not been adequately considered in the sustainable development, climate and energy scenario analysis, in public investments in research and development and in policy development; they are now regarded as the most promising emission reduction and conservation of natural resources option [IEA, 2013; WEC, 2013].

Third, while there is no consensus on whether the way the institutions of the global economy operate can be modified to deliver more sustainable outcomes or that a societal transformation will be needed, it is now being stressed that absolute decoupling in resource use will require significant changes in government policies, corporate behaviour, and consumption patterns by the public, which are very different to technological innovation in industrial units [IIED, 2013; Nordic Council of Ministers, 2013; OECD, 2013; UN, 2013; WSJ, 2013].

Fourth, urbanization is seen as the driver for increasing levels of natural resource use by humans; rural populations are largely in balance with nature. Urban design shapes the three areas which account for nearly three-quarters of carbon dioxide emissions and natural resource use and which have high levels of wastage and potential for reductions, without affecting middle-class lifestyles. These areas are energy efficiency – electricity use in buildings and personal transport, as well as diet. Instead of framing the question as one of scarcity of natural resources, the key issue is now considered as use and distribution; that is, 'access' to energy, transport and food for the global middle class, and it is being defined differently than was done by those who urbanized earlier [McKinsey, 2013; UN-HABITAT, 2013; Urban Land Institute and Ernst & Young, 2013].

The global goal of ensuring human well-being provides a new perspective to the international debate as the United Nations struggles to find a consensus and suggests a broader focus centred on patterns of resource use that can in principle be adopted by all countries, and where measures have to be taken at the national level around common goals rather than negotiated obligations under multilateral environmental agreements.

20.2 New policy framework

At Stockholm, in 1972, and in Agenda 21, in 1992, environment was not considered only in terms of industrial pollution and conservation of rural natural resources, but a broad view was adopted to include social considerations, like water and health, with an emphasis on 'rights'. This makes the developmental and environmental agendas quite similar only if the focus remains agrarian. Energy – electricity and transport – infrastructure and related urban consumption, which requires trade-offs with global environmental concerns, were left out of both the global development and environmental agenda, and also not included in the Climate Change Treaty in 1992 and in the Millennium development Goals in 2000, because of the global implications and are now the subject of considerable debate, as they are a part of the Sustainable Development Goals.

The new global goals will have to go back to the Brundtland view of 'needs' and debate the related limits to arrive at a consensus. The forces unleashed by the industrial revolution, in the form of its economic model and urbanization, leads to population moving to cities and shifts the drivers of natural resource use from production to consumption, resulting in a new relationship between society and nature. As in the case of the Montreal Protocol, the focus on production and consumption alone enables sustainability to become a part of business strategy and goes a long way towards solving the problem at its roots.

An assessment of patterns, trends and drivers of the activities that led to the utilization of the global carbon budget over the previous 200 years shows that the most important trend to be modified worldwide is urban design and the resulting consumption shaped by urban lifestyles. How China and India shape their urban future will be critical, and the global impact of such transformation could well take as long as 50 years. For example, lower consumption immediately can stabilize the rate of impact on all parameters of environmental degradation by 2030, while high density cities and a modal shift to rail transport will modify longer term trends in levels of use of energy, food and transportation later by 2050. A genuine commitment is needed to global goals that make the pie bigger rather than enable some to seize a larger slice.

Global environmental conferences in the period 1972–2012 were not able to build a political commitment for change because they were focused on 'burden sharing'; did not define the issues in social terms where the obstacles lie, or the allocation of scarce natural resources amongst competing uses; did not recognize new science that questioned how the relationship between society and nature had been organized with industrialization, urbanization and the middle class; and kept re-distribution out of the agenda of the United Nations, even though poverty eradication has been central to its work since 1960 – the First Development Decade. The conceptual framework for the sustainable development goals is now capturing the key social and economic factors of value to individuals everywhere.

The shift in global power, national interests and ideas of those who need to ensure well-being of nearly 6 billion, will support a new multilateralism, or global vision, for 'sharing responsibility and prosperity', as it is the only kind of economic development that is truly sustainable. Acting collectively in the face of long-term and uncertain threats will now be an essential element in solving global problems in an equitable fashion in a manner that is in the long-term interests of all, and that is why global sustainable development goals are so important.

20.3 New understanding of global interdependence

We need new forms of international cooperation for transformative change in order to directly address the modification of patterns of consumption and production necessary for equitable sustainable development. This shift will also blur the distinction between addressing climate change, conservation of biological diversity and eradication of poverty that emerged in the first Rio Summit in 1992. The building blocks of global sustainability will need to ensure a transformation in the way we use natural resources, in five areas.

First, the growing importance of the service sector and consumer demand in economic growth worldwide requires political agreement on a shift beyond modifying production patterns seeking greater efficiency in resource use, to modifying consumption patterns for ensuring conservation of resources, largely in industrialized countries.

Second, recognition of the value of ecological and energy services, and their contribution to eradication of poverty – infrastructure, job creation, food security and pharmaceuticals – will support new growth pathways, largely in emerging countries.

Third, new market-based employment opportunities and infrastructure development, as part of the global shift to a low carbon green economy, need to be provided for the poor to shift activities away from relying on, and causing harm to, natural resources to augmentation of local ecosystems, as a part of human well-being, in all countries. This will need the evolution of global sustainable development, not environmental, standards so that global rules support, rather than hinder, international cooperation through open trade, including sharing of innovative technologies, as well as supporting and enabling urbanization.

Fourth, the focus of international cooperation would then shift from burden sharing through funds, mechanisms and programmes to support implementation in emerging countries through public – private networks for "innovation" supporting, for example, joint development and sharing of energy technologies, agricultural seed varieties and medical benefits of biodiversity as well as exchanging experiences on new forms of urbanization – driven by wider societal interests that reach larger proportions of the global population.

Lastly, national accounting systems need to measure the significant human welfare benefits, or services, national and global ecosystems provide and develop an economic yardstick that is more effective than GDP for assessing human well-being, while GDP remains as a measure of economic activity. In the interim, national carbon budgets are a good indicator for developing and assessing national strategies, the sustainable use of natural resources and the transition to global sustainability.

At the United Nations Conference on Environment and Development, in 1992, the objective was integration of environment in development at the sector level, with a focus on regulation over the production of goods and technology. The World Summit on Sustainable Development, in 2002, laid emphasis on policy-level approaches for the 'cross-sectoral aspects of sectoral issues', including consumption and production patterns, and modified the role and function of the Commission on Sustainable Development for the issues to be framed differently than they were in the preceding decade, in three key areas, which are now gaining importance.

First, the focus shifted from regulating on-going activities to identifying and monitoring 'win-win' strategies, seen largely in terms of sustainability. Second, the top-down approach based on national commitments agreed at the multilateral level was supplemented with a focus on regional level actions and public-private partnerships. Third, a re-balancing of the relationship between formal and informal institutions was initiated for sharing experiences of best practices emerging from the local level. However, since different groups of countries continued to stress the economic, environmental and social dimension of sustainable development selectively, efforts to reconcile divergent visions have not been successful. Since sustainable development provides the integrating theme for deepening coherence of the global agenda, these discussions have now shifted to the United Nations, and the Economic and Social Council.

The United Nations performs three types of functions – normative, operational and review – to support implementation in 'poor', or developing countries. In the context of growth prospects of these countries driven by investment from other emerging countries, the United Nations must now modify its role and functions and become a 'knowledge organization' by rearranging the mandate and structure of existing organizations to support the transition to global sustainability in all countries. While the review function should be strengthened to take on a global character, the operational programmes should gradually be limited to the Least Developed Countries, and the normative role should give way to expert groups analysing and developing options on the OECD model, rather than harmonized policy approaches, for all countries. Learning from the evolution of the climate regime, the new paradigm that is emerging must evolve new types of collaboration around innovation, with emerging countries as partners rather than passive aid recipients [Clean Energy Group, 2011].

Obtaining agreement among countries on the public policies needed to establish a global technology sharing regime to accelerate invention and diffusion of innovative technologies is going to be critical in the future, just as aid was important for development in the past. Currently, protecting private intellectual property rights by enforcing exclusive use and deployment by its owner is the main approach.[2] Internationally, spurring green technological development will require a wider mix of public sector strategies, which guarantee a commercial incentive substantial enough to enable private parties through the use of subsidies and public purchases of technology at reasonable cost in their research undertakings, while constraining monopolistic practices which restrict diffusion and further development. Public policy tools could include global funding for research, to be placed in the public domain for widespread dissemination under the same modality utilized in the green revolution in food agriculture in the 1960s and 1970s. With technology funds, it should be possible to establish international innovation networks within different areas of technology. The overall strategy could also include global awards for the formulation of technical solutions to well-defined problems, and public purchase at appropriate prices of private technology for deployment in the public domain. Where exclusive private-sector rights of use to vital technology are a hindrance to the development of other needed technology or to widespread use, the technology regime must have a mechanism (such as exists in certain areas of public health) for granting a 'compulsory license' that places such technology in the public domain [United Nations, 2011]. International public technology policymaking will also promote greater coherence between the disparate entities of the multilateral system whose common objective is to support the transition to global sustainable development.

---

[2] There has been a rapid increase in international patenting of climate mitigation and plant genes, unlike in the 1960s and 1970s when 'miracle seeds' were placed in the public domain to assist in the global objective of raising food production to meet the requirements of a growing population. How to embody the 'common but differentiated responsibilities' principle in the application of trade disciplines promoting sustainable development remains an unresolved issue. Jurisprudence in the many industrialized countries, including the United States of America, is an abundant source of precedents and grounds for the application of compulsory licensing.

The new global rule-based system would be based around three programmes peer reviewing national actions to ensure that the vision, as well as agreed global goals, is followed through:

- Shifts in consumption patterns, including progress in reaching national carbon budgets,
- Joint research, development and sharing of innovative renewable energy, agricultural and health technologies, including progress in bringing energy services, adequate food and good health to the poor who do not have adequate access to them at present, and
- Progress in development of a metric, more effective than GDP, to measure human well-being; a development that will also serve to evolve long-term sustainable development goals, indicators of progress in making the transition to global sustainability and blur the distinction between industrialized and emerging countries.

A common vision will have to drive the transformation. It is still not clear whether global governance structures will support national implementation, or a knowledge-based institution will enable countries to design appropriate strategies. The G20 will play a major role in determining the agenda, reflecting a common political willingness to act. International cooperation will be an indispensable part of the arrangements for identifying trends that have to be modified and reports analysed to set standards that can then be reviewed, with the focus on urbanization.

An integrated strategy for dealing with global environmental and development issues will require the establishment of a global system that puts equity, or ethics and justice, at the centre. Intergovernmental cooperation will involve appreciation of the interactions between the environmental and the socio-economic trends. The objective will be to ensure that half of humanity that has so far not benefited from industrialization, urbanization and increase in incomes can reach levels of well-being currently enjoyed by industrialized societies. This will only be possible when the availability of ecosystem services in the global commons is ensured. It will also have to be accepted that patterns of resource use are in principle common for all. New concepts and strategies will have to be developed for the use and distribution of resources, only then will the new structures have legitimacy.

The shift involves new concepts of sovereignty and national interest, where power will be used to ensure equity and the availability of the global commons for all. In political terms the shift will be as significant as the establishment of constitutional states in place of feudalism. Just as markets enabled a new form of society to be formed following the industrial revolution, new social norms will guide consumers and the market towards sustainability. The concepts of the welfare state will extend to develop new social standards of cooperative, rather than individual, behaviour, and an amended Universal Declaration of Human Rights which includes responsibilities to each other and to the global ecosystem on which life itself depends. Building up trust will be important because policy will need to be made based on scientific analyses and reports, rather than react to events after they have occurred. The new type of multilateralism will also serve to bring countries together.

Redefining global interdependence away from burden sharing to collective benefits will now need to be done in a multi polar world, overcoming formidable barriers. This will require leadership around a common vision, building on small gains in specific areas. As outcomes will be based on equity, the multilateral negotiation process should also be speeded up. Similarly, decision making for identifying priorities will be quicker and more effective, rather than be distracted by considerations of competitive advantage, for example, because, for the first time, the 'global interest' and 'global public goods' coincide with national interests, as ecosystem scarcity and its use is itself a common resource.

A multilateral framework will remain important because the transformation must include all countries. At the same time, the role of the United Nations would need to change from being a mere service provider for facilitating cooperation and implementation to monitoring and reviewing the 'stock' of ecosystem services, and the impact of national action rather than national action itself. The broadening of the energy debate to include issues of its role in economic development and of consumption patterns is an example of moving from purely technological considerations to include social concerns. The current narrow definition of distinction between environment and development has also to be reviewed, as poor countries move out of the post-colonial stage to taking advantage of globalization and increasing levels of income and wealth, needing ecosystem services to be able to move the rural poor into the urban middle class. The new pathways will need positive incentives, like technology cooperation, and will be driven by information provided by the United Nations based on patterns, trends and drivers of natural resource use, rather than rely only on prices fixed by the market. Distributional issues will have to become more important and could even lead to a review of the United Nations Charter for ensuring the availability of ecosystem services for all, instead of appropriating them for the use of some countries.

The starting point has to be a global consensus on the objective or goal. The opportunities presented by recent technological and social innovation, are driving the emergence of more participatory network governance approaches, based on more informal institutions and instruments. Cities and other sub-national levels of government are increasingly engaged in cross-border networking and governance. Consumers and shareholders can also influence production practices across the world through their purchasing choices and investment decisions. Exactly how the change will take place and the sequence of strategies and actions that will be needed should be the subject of research. The focus must remain on fostering global cooperative behaviour and well-being of all; at the multilateral level, technology will be a key element in the transformation.

20.4 New forms for sharing technology

The multilateral agreement on Trade-related Aspects of Intellectual Property Rights (TRIPS) emerged in the World Trade Organization (WTO, 1994). Since then it has involved numerous bilateral and regional trade and investment regimes. At the international level, under the agreement member States of the World Trade Organisation undertake to recognize and enforce nationally created private intellectual property rights. At the national level, the regime categorises intellectual property as private property with respect to use and deployment and establishes a State-enforced monopoly of use as the main approach to motivate private investment. Others have to pay to use, adapt and undertake innovations related to the technology.

The dependence on the private sector for transfers of technology was mitigated in the TRIPS Agreement with flexibilities and safeguards. For example, domestic objectives were to determine national interpretation of the criteria for patentability – novelty, inventive step and industrial applicability. For stated social objectives, States can issue compulsory licences for local production and undertake 'parallel imports', after paying adequate compensation. In practice, these flexibilities have been difficult to use because of a possible adverse impact on foreign direct investment and on multinational corporations providing investment to those countries. At the same time, there has been limited impact on industries, which largely involve product assembly, other than the pharmaceutical industry, because of the nature of the innovation. The arrangement has led to dependence on private transfers making the international intellectual property regime a potentially decisive determinant of technological upgrading in emerging countries. This situation is very different to the publicly led rapid diffusion where 'miracle seeds' were placed in the public domain in response to the global concern of raising food production.

A balance must be struck between a sufficient commercial incentive to private parties to undertake research while constraining monopolistic practices which restrict both diffusion and further development. It has been suggested that subsidies and public purchases of technology at reasonable cost can be used for this transfer. A number of steps have been suggested to treat identified technologies as 'global goods' by the international community. The technology could be placed in the public domain, with expert committees determining which technologies meet the criteria. The technologies could be purchased at a reasonable rate of compensation and compulsory licensing could be resorted to. Many national laws recognize the power to convert private property to public use on grounds of eminent domain.

The international community can determine the technologies whose use needs to be discontinued, with the alternative technology listed in a pool with funds. Countries can draw upon this pool to purchase technology and conduct research. In these transactions, the private sector would continue to play the major role, including adapting and developing inventions for application, with only monopolistic tendencies being checked. Prizes can also be awarded for solutions to defined problems. In all these cases, users would pay royalty at agreed rates when the application is commercialized and there is a reasonable return on the investment.

The discussion on Intellectual Property Rights in the negotiations for the post-2015 global agenda signals its relevance for efforts to achieve sustainable development. In the workshops conducted by the President of the United Nations General Assembly convergence was achieved on an information and knowledge sharing platform, a United Nations Technology Coordination platform for synergies among United Nations entities and 'possibly' assessment of technology needs. However, beyond the procedural steps, a stalemate has developed about how to further characterize the role of Intellectual Property Rights in relation to green technologies. The Rio+20 document adopted in 2012 mandates the setting up of a Technology Facilitation Mechanism. These discussions are based around three distinct but related areas, stressing technology cooperation rather than transfer and improving coordination within the United Nations system rather than with the private sector:

- "enhance North-South, South-South and triangular regional and international cooperation on and access to science, technology and innovation, and enhance knowledge sharing on mutually agreed terms, including through improved coordination among existing mechanisms, particularly at UN level, and through a global technology facilitation mechanism when agreed" (target 19.6).
- "promote development, transfer, dissemination and diffusion of environmentally sound technologies to developing countries on favourable terms, including on concessional and preferential terms, as mutually agreed" (target 17.7), and
- fully operationalize the Technology Bank and STI (Science, Technology and Innovation) capacity building mechanism for LDCs by 2017, and enhance the use of enabling technologies in particular ICT". The discussion is shifting to Science, Technology and Innovation, with no consensus on a facilitation mechanism beyond a mapping and on-line platform, multi-stakeholder partnerships and capacity building. (target 17.8).

At the same time, since UNCED in 1992, there has also been is a rise of technological capabilities in China and other emerging economies, and clean energy technologies such as gas turbines, advanced batteries, solar photovoltaics, and coal gasification emerged have spread to China. Of the top 10 wind power companies in the world, four are Chinese (Sinovel, Goldwind, Dongfang Electric and United Power) and one is Indian (Suzlon). Among the top 10 solar energy producers worldwide, seven are from China (LDK Solar, Suntech, JA Solar, Trina Solar, Yingli Green Energy, Hanwha Solar One, and Jinko Solar). However, despite the increase in manufacturing capabilities in emerging economies, industrialized countries continue to dominate innovation in clean energy technologies.

Six OECD countries (Japan, United States, Germany, the Republic of Korea, the United Kingdom and France) account for nearly 80 per cent of patents filed in clean energy technologies. While there were only 25,419 applications under the Patent Co-operation Treaty (PCT) overseen by WIPO in 1992, they reached a total of 182,120 PCT applications in 2011. In a globalized knowledge-based economy, Intellectual Property Rights – and patents in particular – have become strategic assets for companies seeking to secure market shares and dominate competitors. Contradictory trends and the absence of a global consensus can be seen in this vital area for the transition to sustainability.

Whereas the first generation of innovation investments had focused on labour productivity through the application of knowledge embedded in information systems, the second generation will need to focus on resource productivity. International cooperation around technology can be a defining factor in the transition in emerging countries. Emerging countries may also enjoy a strategic advantage because they do not face the same market and institutional rigidities that stem from a dependence on technological and physical infrastructures that are rapidly becoming obsolete as more ecological thresholds are breached.

20.5 New global rules

International distribution issues are the most important inadequacy of the global rules created in the 1950s. Increased power and level of participation of the emerging countries is likely to focus on this issue, even though there is multi rather than bi-polarity. So far there has been a dichotomy between the national interests of the big powers and preferences of the others striving for the least common denominator in the multilateral negotiations. Such an arrangement is not suitable for providing solutions for the problems of high level of global interdependence, limits as well as wide range of risks the planetary system and a global society that will soon be experienced with 9 billion people. New global rules will be needed. Cooperative and collective learning will stimulate action at the national level and help to define a global identity, to support the transformation. As in the case of the welfare state, disadvantaged groups are to be supported to enable them to increase their incomes through self-help, with state action supporting the market and action by civil society. Demographics will also enable the transformation, as the most difficult period is likely to be the next 30 years, with increasing incomes in the emerging countries balanced by declining numbers in the industrialized counties with higher incomes. For example, after initially increasing, by mid-century, China's population is expected to fall to its size in 2000 and by the end of the century it may have halved from the 2000 level, and the population of Germany, Japan and Russia will be a quarter less than now in 2050.

Four distinct but related trends are emerging:

- Shift towards regional cooperation and integration, for example, in Asia;
- Shift in global agenda setting and decision making: shifting from bodies of leading countries such as the G7 to the more broad-based G20;
- Shift from reliance on international law from codifying new rights and responsibilities addressing 'common concerns' to a focus on common vision and goals and the attendant 'softer' form of coordination, in the form of codes, frameworks and guidelines;
- Shift to sharing governance and decision making with cities, with related concerns about the legitimacy, credibility and accountability of new approaches. In parallel with the diffusion of technology, diffusion of regulatory practices and standards is gaining ground leading to convergence without relying on multilateral treaties and negotiations.

It is still not clear how these shifts will interact with current and future global rules in the United Nations. It is likely that ad hoc coalitions of relevant countries come together to raise issues, concerns and address specific challenges.

Trade and environment, in terms of resources, will continue to dominate international relations because of the positive effects. International policies and regulation will continue to be seen in terms of impacts on comparative advantage and competitive edge in global markets. For example, the ratio of global exports to global GDP rose from 5.5 to 19.4 per cent in the period 1950–2005. Therefore, new forms of cooperation will not replace the multilateral approach of international decision-making. Emerging countries will, however, continue to seek reform of existing global governance structures as well as new rules around resource use in the context of the needs of a larger number of countries with increasing levels of income which have to be accommodated within planetary limits. Asia, where future growth is going to be concentrated with two-third of global wealth by 2050, will likely develop its own rules that are not shaped by the North–South divide.

There will be a shift away from reliance on international environmental law consequent on the changed objectives, and lack of progress in international negotiations in areas such as trade and environment. The trade agreements now being pushed by the industrialized countries (the trans-pacific and the trans-atlantic partnerships) include planned efforts to tackle illegal wildlife trade, protect forests and oceans, and enforce multilateral environmental commitments as well as an investment chapter that it could give companies grounds to challenge domestic laws geared towards protecting the environment. This will lead to greater reliance on regional integration. The financial crisis in industrialized countries will also lead them to rely more on non-state actors to help with policy formulation and implementation, giving them space in global decision making. Parallel with this development is the inadequate appreciation of the shift and lack of coherent response on the part of emerging countries, because they are undergoing fundamental socio-economic change in a much shorter time than industrialized countries did, and have yet to appreciate the importance of focusing on ideas – strategic visions – and to formulate global policies and approaches that stress on the long term, and which are valid over decades.

Even as emerging countries have taken the leadership, and are in a position to shape the outcomes, there is as yet no consensus whether political decisions on equitably sharing the global commons, (the new paradigm) are a precondition for agreement on a global rule-based system, or, incremental steps to develop a rule-based system (the old paradigm) will lead to equitable outcomes. There is, however, an emerging global consensus that the key drivers for equitable sustainable development should now be defined in terms of enhancing services provided by the global ecosystem for human well-being, rather than in terms of merely controlling global environmental degradation.

The global vision for the future will be defined in terms of achieving universal human well-being within the planetary limits by 2050. To achieve this goal, new global rules should focus on reviewing progress in terms of equitably sharing the global commons and innovative technologies, to support and enable adequate energy, food, employment, shelter and water for all. It is still not clear how many of these elements, and in what detail, will be included in the sustainable development goals. Patterns of natural resource use that are in principle common for all will lead to a more prosperous and safer world. A common understanding is needed of resultant shifts in global economic models, working with a range of actors at different levels, exchanging experiences for understanding and modifying longer term trends in consumption and production patterns. The objective has to be enabling human well-being through a societal transformation, supported by a new paradigm, partnerships, priorities and programmes for generating strategic knowledge. As in 1972, the United Nations will best support this societal shift by generating and sharing new knowledge, this time based on the social sciences and not the natural sciences, to meet the speed and scale of the transformation.

References

Clean Energy Group. 2011. Moving Climate Innovation into the 21st Century: Emerging Lessons from Other Sectors and Options for a new Climate Innovation Initiative, May 2011, Washington, DC, USA.

FAO. 2013a. *Food Wastage Footprint: Impacts on Natural Resources*. Food and Agriculture Organization, Rome.

FAO. 2013b. *Tackling Climate Change through Livestock*. Food and Agriculture Organization, Rome.

IEA. 2013. *Redrawing the Energy-Climate Map: World Energy Outlook Special Report*, International Energy Agency, Paris.

IIED. 2013. 'Post-2015' International Development Goals: Who Wants What and Why', IIED Issue paper, June 2013.

ISSC/UNESCO. 2013. *World Social Science Report 2013: Changing Global Environments*. OECD Publishing and UNESCO Publishing, Paris.

McKinsey Global Institute. 2013. *Urban World: The Shifting Global Business Landscape*, October, 2013.

Nordic Council of Ministers. 2013. *Improving Nordic Policymaking by Dispelling Myths on Sustainable Consumption*, Terma Nord 2013:553.

OECD. 2013. *Looking to 2060: Long Term Global Growth Prospects*, OECD, Paris.

Sanwal, Mukul. 2012. 'Rio +20, Climate Change and Development: The Evolution of Sustainable Development (1972–2012)'. *Climate and Development* 4 (2): 157–166.

Sanwal, Mukul. 2013. 'The Rise and Fall of Global Climate Policy: Stockholm to Rio 1992, to Rio + 20 and Beyond'. *Chinese Journal of Environmental and Urban Studies* 1 (1).

Sanwal, Mukul. 2014. 'Global Sustainable Development Goals Are about the Use and Distribution, Not Scarcity of Natural Resources: Will the Middle Class in the USA, China and India Save the Climate as Its Incomes Grow'. *Climate and Development* 4 (4)

UN HABITAT. 2013. *Global Report on Human Settlements 2013 – Planning and Design for Sustainable Urban Mobility*, United Nations Human Settlements Programme, Nairobi.

UN. 2013. United Nations. *World Economic and Social Survey* 2013: Sustainable Development Challenges.

United Nations. 2011. *See also, World Economic and Social Survey: The Great Green Technological Transformation*, Department of Economic and Social Affairs, United Nations, New York 2011.

Urban Land Institute and Ernst & Young. 2013. *Infrastructure 2013: Global Priorities, Global Insights*. Washington, DC: Urban Land Institute.

WEC. 2013. *World Energy Trilemma 2013: Time to get real – the case for sustainable energy investment*, World Energy Council, 2013.

WSJ. 2013. Beijing to Limit Car Ownership to 6 Million, *Wall Street Journal*, September 23.

GEOPOLITICS TO GEOECONOMICS: RURAL–URBAN DIVIDE, RATHER THAN BETWEEN COUNTRIES

"… Living well within ecological limits will require fundamental transitions in the systems of production and consumption that are the root cause of environmental and climate pressures. Such transitions will, by their character, entail profound changes in dominant institutions, practices, technologies, policies, lifestyles and thinking … The overall challenge for the next decades will be to recalibrate mobility, agriculture, energy, urban development, and other core systems of provision in such way that global natural systems maintain their resilience, as the basis for a decent life … the most fundamental shift in modern society in the 21st century will be to reinvent what it means to have a high level of societal well-being, while accepting and embracing the limits of the planet".

The European Environment: State and Outlook 2015 – Assessment of Global Megatrends, European Environment Agency, March 2015.

"… the broader debate to define and implement post-2015 Sustainable Development Goals (SDGs) … addressing fragility in the new framework will be crucial if strides in reducing poverty are to be made … fragility as an issue of universal character that can affect all countries, not only those traditionally considered "fragile" or conflict-affected … violence, access to justice, accountable and inclusive institutions, economic inclusion and stability, and capacities to prevent and adapt to social, economic and environmental shocks and disasters … making headway on the targets will require building a new portfolio of tools and interventions, and an understanding of the role the international community should and can play in assisting this process.

States of Fragility 2015: Meeting Post-2015 Ambitions, OECD, March 2015

'… The 18th Party Congress of the Peoples Republic of China, in 2012, incorporated in the Party Constitution the statement that promoting ecological progress is a long term task of vital importance to the people's well-being and China's future … key principles entail conserving resources, protecting the environment and promoting its natural restoration … the objective is to work hard to build a beautiful county, and achieve lasting and sustainable development of the Chinese nation.

An ecological civilization is considered a governing idea and national strategy for the whole society. The effort is to shift from industrialization led economic development and urbanization to a services and high technology led development and urbanization, which will also stress the services provided by ecological systems along with resource conservation and efficiency to ensure that waste and pollution from production and living are within ecological limits.'

China Human Development Report: 2013 – Sustainable and Livable Cities: Towards Ecological Civilization, UNDP, June 2013, China; Beautiful China: Eco-Cities Indicators Guidebook, Blue path City Consulting, Tong Xin Press, 2013, China.

Urban Areas: Sustainable Development and Human Well-being

21

21.1 Consumption more important than production

How should global governance be organized to support the societal transformation? In a multipolar world, bilateral understandings and regional arrangements have already begun to supplement global multilateral agreements. The overriding issue is not whether the current economic development model can be, and should be, sustained. It is also not just a question of energy, because half of humanity has yet to benefit from industrialization, urbanization and increase in incomes, and they amount to some 5 billion people. As the world continues to urbanize, sustainable development challenges will be increasingly concentrated in cities, particularly in the lower-middle-income countries where the pace of urbanization is fastest' [UN, 2014]. The unresolved issue is the use and distribution of natural resources. How the integration of these concerns into institutions and review arrangements will supplant or supplement current arrangements with those more suited to the post-industrial, or services and knowledge based, economy and society is now the subject of debate within the United Nations. The economic and power shift to Asia will also shift geopolitics to geoeconomics around the rural–urban divide, rather than between countries and the North–South divide. The overriding issue is how to manage the transformation over the next 20 years, as by then urbanization will be the dominant trend in all countries[1].

Global sustainable development goals are currently the subject of extensive debate and divergent interpretations, as the scale of global change requires policy choices and trade-offs in the face of conflicting priorities. How global limits are approached will depend on what is regarded as essential for human well-being; as the United Nations has stressed, climate and global environmental change must be fundamentally reframed from a physical into a social problem [ISSC/UNESCO, 2013]. What form global governance structures will take to establish cause-effect relations and transition pathways, it is being suggested, should be based on a meta-science panel [Steven Bernstein et al., 2014] or around a meta-goal for 'a prosperous, high quality of life that is equitably shared and sustainable' [ICSU, ISSC, 2015]. In a multipolar world, emerging countries favour policy space for nationally determined action.

---

[1] Parts of this chapter were first published in Sanwal (2012, 2014).

First, the fundamental issue in the design of the new global framework is whether in 2050, emerging countries will remain agrarian societies or between three-fourth and two-third of their populations would have shifted to urban areas; this shift had taken place in North America, Europe and Japan by 1970, and is expected to take place in China by 2030 and in India around 2050. Expert opinion is divided between those who hold that the Millennium Development Goals' (MDGs) emphasis on social protection of rural populations, a 'rights'-based approach, should continue with the new goals limited to eradication of extreme poverty [Kashambuzi, 2013], and those who stress the global historical model of industrialized societies establishing the built environment, with whole industries and cities as the notion of development 'needs' for prosperity [McKinsey Global Institute, 2013]. Urbanization is the product of a major long term, worldwide, socio-economic process – centuries old evolution in man's way of life from the rural agricultural life pattern to the urban–industrial way of life [U.S., 1971]; no country has moved to even middle-income status while remaining agrarian, and this is a trend that will get stronger.

Second, despite the Rio+20 outcome documents recognizing the critical role that energy plays in the development process, there is still no consensus on energy as the primary sustainable development goal. Energy, in particular electricity, along with urbanization, encompasses and enables the other MDGs in terms of both 'basic needs' and 'productive uses' for employment and well-being. Currently, the poorest three-quarters of the global population uses 10 per cent of global energy, and 'scientific' models using traditional baseline or incremental growth approach assume that emerging countries will remain predominantly rural, only 'extreme' poverty will be eradicated by 2030 and there will be a maximum demand of 750 kWh per year per capita for new connections [IEA, 2013]; the global average in 2010 was just under 3,000 kWh per capita per year; the average for the United States is 13,400 kWh, Germany consumes about 7,200 kWh and Greece about 5,200 kWh per person per year. Historical patterns show that countries with large population have in the past experienced fast growth in energy access, and rapid economic growth, in a period of 30 years – United States, China, Thailand, Vietnam and South Africa. The trade-offs related to energy and climate need to be discussed in terms of the transformations the global goals will require because access to adequate and affordable energy is the basis for economic and social development [World Energy Council, 2013], and energy efficiency is now considered a critical tool to relieve pressure on energy supply and global emissions [World Energy Outlook, 2014].

Third, the global vision will have to go much beyond eradication of extreme poverty, as urbanization itself accounts for half of the decline in poverty and removing economic inequality is an essential condition for good governance. Currently, the richest 1 per cent of the world's population, largely in developed countries, owns 40 per cent of global assets, while the bottom half, largely in emerging countries, holds just 1 per cent and since 1998–2008 their income increased by 60 per cent while the bottom 5 per cent had no change; the top 8 per cent also take home 50 per cent of the global income. One-seventh of the human population in industrialized countries accounted for half of global energy use in 2000. The primary cause of this disparity is the continued dependence of emerging country populations on uncertain incomes from agricultural cropping patterns. The new global goals require an approach to social mobility for achieving middle-class status; one that goes beyond a limited focus on 'rights' to stress education, urban housing and transport, and steady income which only industry and cities can provide, even as high unemployment, widening inequality and climate change have remained key challenges for countries [UN, 2013].

With the global middle class expected to triple by 2050, it is not just a question of shifting the energy system to zero or near-zero carbon levels through improvements in efficiency and technology but also considering limiting the end-user demand for high levels of natural resource use beyond electricity and transportation. Sustainability on the supply side can only be achieved by limiting energy for consumption. This essential element, or precondition, of the transformation has largely been ignored in policymaking, scenarios and technological research and development. Similarly, in the transport sector, along with gas and electricity, modal shifts to rail need to be considered. Biotechnology may soon replace energy as the primary global concern with respect to sustainable development; it has the potential to provide the means to address some of the pressing issues of global concern by contributing to ensuring a safe environment through bio-conservation and remediation methodologies, research for health, as well as for food production and security. This is particularly important in framing mitigating and adapting to the effects of climate change as an integral part of urbanization, and thus on sustained food production, while also focusing on employment, as well as addressing re-emerging diseases and newly emerging pandemics [UNESCO, 2011].

Energy models that are focused on the supply side consider demand-side management indirectly, if at all. Urban areas, where most of the global population will soon be residing, are centres for consumption of energy, goods and services, and raise demands for buildings and mobility. This infrastructure has a longer lifespan than power generation and patterns of natural resource use must take into account longer term trends that are not sustainable that can have a significant, even decisive, impact because of the huge potential to make a transformation without compromising well-being, as only some trends need to be modified.

For this transformation to become acceptable, it is argued, consumers will have to learn to regard low-carbon actions and goods as desirable [Urry, 2013]. In this context, the China-United States deal of November 14, 2014, is significant: United States President, Barack Obama, described China's commitment on peaking of its carbon dioxide emissions by 2030, as 'important because if China, as it develops, adopts the same per capita carbon emissions as advanced economies like the United States or Australia, this planet doesn't stand a chance, because they've got a lot more people [China Daily, 2014]. By 2030, no country – whether the US, China, or any other large country – will be a hegemonic power, restoring Asia's weight in the global economy, ushering in a new era of 'democratization' at the international and domestic level. In addition, two megatrends will shape our world out to 2030: demographic patterns, especially rapid aging about which we can do little and growing resource demands which, in the cases of food and water, might otherwise lead to scarcities [NIC, 2012]. These developments can be enabled and supported by geoeconomic[2] shifts.

21.2 Shaping the transformation

Social scientists are now arguing that the requirement is to reverse the apparently inexorable growth of high-carbon systems and related social practices. This reversal has to be both social and economic and requires 'reversing' most systems set in motion during the twentieth century, finding the equivalent of a reverse gear while going forwards very fast. Low-carbon systems will reduce the short-term levels of measured income and consumption, which will make it difficult to persuade people to embrace low-carbon social practices.

At the global level, integrated scenarios are now dominating the debate as the means to resolve the most important trade-off between economic, social and environmental considerations, but remain inadequate to the requirement. They base their models on the Intergovernmental Panel on Climate Change

---

[2] Geoeconomics is the overwehlming dependence of all countries on the global economy, at the same time countries are focussing on the challenges as well as on the benefits and multilateral regimes are becoming regional rather than global.
'Geo-economics: Seven Challenges to Globalization', Global Agenda Councils, World Economic Forum, January 2015

(IPCC) scenarios and focus on a single issue with carbon dioxide peaking by 2020; renewable energy providing around half of primary energy by 2050; view technological progress as the most important lever; consider shifts only from current levels in emerging countries rather than seek comparable levels with developed countries in 2050; and have little agreement amongst themselves on specific policy suggestions [GEA, 2012; SEI, 2012; PBL, 2013; OECD, 2013]. For example, the Organization for Economic Co-operation and Development (OECD) considers climate change, biodiversity, water and health as the highest priority challenges ignoring energy and inequality. The Stockholm Environment Institute (SEI) specifically considers the energy transformation that would be needed for poor countries to double GDP and reach at least $10,000 per capita incomes by 2050, and even this may be on the lower side, when compared with the GDP of $30,000 of Spain, a mid-level country of the European Union. The International Energy Agency considers only the eradication of 'extreme' poverty, as they do not see energy demand exceeding 750 kWh per year per capita in 2030, which is just one-quarter of the global average in 2010 and is not likely to be acceptable as a global goal. There are also problems with the structure of these models as future scenarios leave out alternative pathways of technological change in energy end-use, shifting the focus to decarbonization of electricity generation.

Reliance on risk analysis and quantitative forecasting deals with the symptoms rather than the causes of the problem, and even though most analyses recognize the key role of consumption, they do not make it a central feature of the recommendations. For example, 'wasteful energy use in buildings, transport and industry as the single most important strategy' has been identified for achieving energy sustainability [GEA, 2012]; dietary changes and 'eradicating inequality in access to food' are considered as the main challenge for achieving food security and biodiversity conservation as well as addressing 'energy-intensive lifestyles' [PBL, 2013]; and the recognition that 'global environmental problems arise primarily from over consumption amongst the richest segments of the population worldwide' [SEI, 2012]. The 'Limits to Growth' Report in 1970 had also stressed an upper limit on per capita consumption [Meadows, 2004]. Reviewing these models, the United Nations concludes in its report to the High-level Policy Forum, that has replaced the Commission on Sustainable Development, that 'at some point in time we will be forced to make more drastic behavioural changes' [UN DESA, 2013].

Human well-being is now based on the availability of the carbon budget, and the global policy issue is to determine the implications of consumption patterns in urban areas reaching planetary limits in order to identify the longer term trends that need to be modified. An analysis of patterns of natural resource use shows that urbanization patterns should be modified, as they drive energy, land use, and even technology, while still enabling comparable levels of human well-being. It is now recognized that considering ecological limits in isolation without linking it to consumption patterns of resource use and the drivers of change will not modify longer term trends [UNEP GEO 5, 2012].

The degree to which resource use causes adverse impacts depends not only on the amount of resources used but also on the types of resources used and the ways in which they are used. According to the Millennium Ecosystem Assessment, two-thirds of the ecosystems have been degraded [MEA, 2005]; of the nine planetary boundaries, three (climate change, biological diversity and the nitrogen cycle) have already been crossed and the others (ozone, land-use change, freshwater use, ocean acidification, aerosol loading and chemical pollution) are under threat [Rockstrom, 2009]; and natural resource consumption is expected to rise to 150 per cent of the earth's bio-capacity by 2030, if present trends continue [Jackson, 2009]. However, which trends need to be modified remains contested as international trade and investment, because of globalization, expands supply chains and aligns global consumption and production patterns. For example, with respect to deforestation in Brazil, two-third of the area is now under cattle ranching and one-third under soybean and around one-third of the emissions are exported, linking global patterns of resource use leading to demand-driven deforestation [Karstensen, 2013]. Similarly, climate change considers sink constraints as global goods to absorb waste of human activity leading to linkages between consumption and production patterns at the international level, while its description in terms of 'industrial emissions' focuses solely on national production patterns and the symptoms, rather than the causes of the problem.

The debate centres on the extent to which people are able to substitute one good or service for another, and whether depletion of natural capital can be overcome by the accumulation of knowledge, manufactured capital and human capital. There are ecological limits to the availability of degradable natural resources, for example, sink constraints, and as ecosystem services are underpriced in markets the distortions affect research and the character of technological change, providing insufficient market pressure to develop alternatives. In this situation, well-functioning markets need policy support if they are to stimulate substitution with technological and societal innovation providing alternatives, and a number of diverse approaches are being implemented and analysed worldwide [Burns, 2012]. We now know that the social and bio-physical sub-systems are intertwined such that the system's conditions and responses to external forcing are based on the synergy between the two sub-systems. Consequently, the full global system has to be studied rather than its individual components, as none of the challenges can be fully considered without addressing the other challenges [Bierman, 2012].

The debate continues to be typified by those who stress that population is the source of unsustainable trends. It is argued that in 1900, at the global level, 0.5 billion tons of carbon was emitted when the population was 1.6 billion, and in 2000, 7.3 billion tons were emitted when the population had increased to 6.1 billion. Alternatively, resource use can be stressed, because while the population increased 4 times, emissions increased 15 times; global population increased 7 times since the industrial revolution while global energy use has grown 25 times and water withdrawal 15-fold, much more rapidly than population growth and more in accordance with urbanization and increasing number of urban dwellers in industrialized countries. For example, transport emissions have doubled in industrialized countries since 1990. Moreover, half the world's population now lives in countries with replacement level fertility or below, leading to stabilization of the population and a shift in the age structure around 2050, challenging the assumptions based on projecting past trends in population growth into the long-term future.

Population becomes important in the context of large-scale migration from rural to urban areas, as the nature of industrialized societies – urbanization – is the major driving force for increasing demands for material and energy. Cities concentrate and integrate investment and employment opportunities, supporting rapid economic growth and access to goods, services and public facilities, with economies now being driven by the urban services sector and not just by industrialization. In ancient civilizations, less than 5 per cent of the total population lived in cities in China, India and the Middle East, while the proportion of people living in urban areas has increased from one-third in 1950 (out of a total population of 2.5 billion) to half in 2005 and is expected to reach three-quarters in 2050 when the population will be 9 billion – an increase from 1 billion to 6 billion people in cities. The sole focus on population numbers in rural areas has kept the attention on their poverty and production patterns and diverted attention away consumption patterns, trends and drivers of natural resource use in cities where the population has shifted or is in the process of doing so. Already cities produce three-quarters of global greenhouse gas (GHG) emissions, which are directly related to household consumption – shelter, mobility and food [UN Habitat, 2013].

Average global rates of natural resource use stagnated in the period from 1900 to 1950 and then grew rapidly till the 1970s because of infrastructure development – urbanization – following World War II; in the United States, in the decade 1960–1970, carbon dioxide emissions rose 4.5 per cent annually and once saturation level was reached, the energy intensity of the economy (energy consumption per unit of GDP) fell by more than half. Global carbon dioxide emissions again increased from the 1990s when China, and other emerging countries, began developing their infrastructure, and global inequality began to decline for the first time since the industrial revolution. Infrastructure accounts for most of the resource use and emissions till date, it is essential for human well-being and urban infrastructure development will continue till 2060, when saturation levels are likely to be reached. Urbanization has been in the past, and should be for the future, the first concern of any analysis on environmental resources as it is an inexorable trend and a precondition for sustainable employment and elimination of global social and economic inequality.

Urbanization involves two transitions – the establishment of infrastructure, or consumption of material resources, as a necessary part of the process of economic development, and later higher incomes support changes in consumption patterns that are largely non-material goods and services based on specific lifestyles. Both are direct inputs to human well-being, and each is responsible for roughly a doubling of the rate at which resources are used. However, most of the first is essential and some of the second is discretionary, or optional, and can vary by a factor of three for countries at similar levels of income and well-being.

Land-use systems are computed to cause a quarter of total global emissions, but half the emissions are generated subsequent to agricultural production in storage, preparation and transport. The highest impact is from livestock farming, which uses nearly three-quarters of the agricultural land, while providing only 15 per cent of the global calorie supply and contributing 18 per cent of global emissions. The lifecycle emissions of meat, dairy products and eggs which the city dwellers demand are up to 10 times higher than those of an equal weight of plant-derived foodstuffs on which the rural population continues to depend. If urban eating habits change, global GHG emissions from agriculture can come down to below 1990 levels, even though the demand for food is expected to go up by three times during the next 20 years, as one-third of food is currently wasted [FAO, 2013].

The current focus on the use of fossil fuels for the generation of electricity ignores the fact that transport emissions will soon equal the energy share of electricity, and overall levels depend on urban design, type of infrastructure and consumption patterns; energy efficiency has the highest potential for the reduction of emissions, not changing the fuel mix [IEA, 2013]. In industrialized countries, two-thirds of the electricity generated is used in buildings as saturation levels have been reached in infrastructure development, while in emerging countries, three-fourth of the electricity is still used in manufacturing, as infrastructure development is continuing, and with population shifting from rural to urban areas, employment and consumption is still taking place. Transport volume growth, which has doubled since 1990 and contributes one-quarter to total EU GHG and one-third of total US emissions, is also linked to urbanization and continues to increase in industrialized countries. It is estimated that emissions from transport will exceed half of total global emissions in 2050, out of which passenger transport is likely to be more than half. Spatial organization, density and lifestyle choices determine natural resource use – electricity demand, transport use and urban goods and services.

Recent analysis is focusing on urban consumption patterns as the driver of global change, and the intellectually challenging question is why it is generally assumed that all countries aspire to adopt the consumption patterns of the United States. The United States with 5 per cent of the world population uses nearly one-quarter of the world's energy. As an early developer, it benefitted from cheap commodities; in the United States, between 1950 and 1970, the real price of oil again declined steadily – and a barrel of oil cost less in 1970 than 50 years ago, when the oil price hiked four times in 1973 petrol use per capita dropped by more than one-third [Ross, 2013], and from 1990 the price of oil dropped by a third. An extensive land mass and low population led to an urban design and technology ignoring resource use implications – fossil fuel combustion wastes equal to two-thirds of the heat content in electricity generation and vehicle engines. The future is going to be different to the past because for the re-emerging countries and new developers, the global context is very different.

Even more important, a sustainable development framework provides for a dialogue and sharing experiences on modifying longer term trends, instead of pitting old against new emitters. For example, there is more potential for non-transport energy efficiency in the United States than anywhere else in the world, with a potential saving of around $1.2 trillion; the reduction in energy use would also result in the abatement of 1.1 gigatons of GHG emissions annually – the equivalent of taking the entire United States fleet of passenger vehicles and light trucks off the roads [McKinsey, 2009]. Through a combination of policies and improved technologies, it is possible to cut GHG emissions from the transportation sector in the United States cost-effectively by up to 65 per cent below 2010 levels by 2050 by improving vehicle efficiency, shifting to less carbon-intensive fuels, changing travel behaviour, and operating more efficiently [PCGCC, 2012]. Getting food from the farm to the United States family fork eats up 10 per cent of the total U.S. energy budget, uses 50 per cent of the land and swallows 80 per cent of all freshwater consumed in the United States, yet 40 per cent of food in the United States today goes uneaten, and has now been taken up as a challenge by the United States Department of Agriculture [NRDC, 2013]. Per capita energy consumption in the transport sector is more than three times higher in the United States than in Japan and Germany; in Japan, 40 per cent of all urban motorized trips are by public transport; in the United States, it is 4 per cent; Austria's urban areas are over four times denser than Australia's, and generate only 60 per cent of the amount of carbon dioxide per person than Australia's urban areas do; GHG emissions per passenger of bus, rail and trams is about one-twelfth that of the car [UN Habitat, 2013]. The legal definition of 'responsibility' in the climate treaty, with implications for others seeking compensation, has prevented any discussion in that forum on natural resource use and economic issues have been kept out of the United Nations.

A new dimension to the 20-year-old debate is emerging as China plans to shift 250 million from rural areas to dense urban clusters on the lines of New York City, where emissions are one-third of the average in the United States. China has built 10,000 km of high speed rail equal to the length of interstate highways in the United States, modifying earlier global trends in resource use. This explains why China, with four times the population, uses just three-fourth more energy than the United States, while the per capita energy consumption is less than half the level in the United States. The major reason is that the carbon dioxide emissions per capita from transportation in the United States are 12 times higher than in China, constituting one-third and one-tenth of total emissions, respectively, and China has begun to limit vehicle ownership in major cities [WSJ, 2013]. Similarly, while global livestock production was responsible for 14.5 per cent of GHG emissions, the carbon intensity is highest for beef contributing half of those emissions, which the Indians do not eat at all and is not a key part of the diet in China [FAO, 2013]. With infrastructure reaching saturation levels, in 2012, China's emissions rose 3 per cent, well below the 10 per cent growth in the previous decade. China has set a policy of a maximum level of energy consumption by 2015, has invested nearly $70 billion in renewable energy, which is 50 per cent more than the United States and is shifting to natural gas, opening the possibility of declining global emissions [PBL, 2013]. China, India and other emerging countries aspire to reach per capita levels of income of a European country, like Germany, and their resource use will remain one-third to half that of the United States; a trend that has yet to be recognized by the economic and environmental models.

21.3 Middle class as the driver of global change

The implication for the global rule-based system is that the consumption patterns of the rich in cities, not just countries, affects the availability of resources for others. The shift to the longer term objectives of a more equal society across the world will go beyond political boundaries and revisit current notions of state responsibility and accountability for the environment.

As in the case of the Montreal Protocol – the most successful global cooperation on the environment – the focus on production and consumption alone enables sustainability to become a part of business strategy and goes a long way towards solving the problem at its roots [Patchell, 2013]. Business has begun to recognize the link between environmental impacts, increasing wealth and society-based drivers. Immediately, technological fixes and the market are shifting from a 'take, make and dispose' economy to a 'circular' economy that would have a low material throughput and re-use waste and is being stressed in a number of developed countries as a model for the future. The recent report of the IPCC – that the recent rate of increase in global temperature may not be as much as what was thought earlier [IPCC, 2013] – gives hope that modifying longer term trends in resource use will be successful in addressing limitations in availability of the carbon budget.

For industrialized countries particular forms of resource consumption, not middle-class life styles, will need to be modified. Food and drink have the highest ecological footprint, followed by energy used in household equipment and housing, and transport. However, the stress in industrialized countries is on improvements in technology to redesign products and services and secure more output for any given input – 'decoupling', rather than on conservation of resources. While the concept of a 'Green Economy' with its co-benefits is an attempt to reframe the debate, it still focuses on production factors [OECD, 2013]. This is important, as the most promising emissions reduction options, in end-use services and technologies are not being adequately considered. It is only the Nordic countries that are seriously exploring behaviour change to modify consumption patterns and markets [Nordic Council of Ministers, 2013].

For emerging countries, the overriding question is how to move away from the historical patterns of resource use and design new structures for well-being. The type of new infrastructure will determine sustainability as they will be building the equivalent of a city of one million people every day from now till 2050. Sustainable growth will depend upon high-density communities responding to land becoming a scarce resource, higher cost of commodities and using fewer resources by designing living and working places close to one another, allowing people to walk rather than use cars and providing public transportation. Other measures include mandatory energy efficiency in building, reducing waste and encouraging water reuse and conserving rain water. Conservation frees resources for the use of those who will shift in the subsequent years from rural poverty into the middle class.

Despite the available social science research on drivers of resource use, the dominant ideas everywhere continue to focus on the supply side of the production–consumption continuum, leaving the demand side to the preference of individuals and limited set of tools providing information. It also continues to be debated whether technology induces societal and economic change or societal change drives adoption of new technology. While energy transitions have been driven by end products or services that were made possible by new forms of energy but not by the old ones. More research is needed on the role of technology in increasing the sustainability of consumption through increased efficiency, elimination of waste with recycling and reuse and exploitation of alternative resources, and providing renewable energy. Ultimately, behaviour change will be critical in the choices made on urban layout and apartment size, transport mode, changing away from excessive meat consumption and energy conservation. These drivers are increasingly being recognized in the way sustainability is increasingly being seen in terms of measuring a society's wealth and not just economic activity [UNU-IHDP and UNEP, 2012]. It is now being recognized that barriers will not be overcome solely by technology, but in combination with changes in usage and governance.

The 'new' goals will need to recognize four enabling conditions – innovation and technological change as the main driver of economic growth, energy as a basic requirement of human well-being, urban consumption patterns shaping trends of natural resource use and reducing the rural–urban divide as essentials for good governance. The essential characteristics of a sustainable society will need to recognize that utilization of the remaining global 'carbon budget' is interlinked with urbanization – providing a comparable level of infrastructure, energy services (electricity and transport) and food, and these together constitute the most important global goals, as other goals for social development are subsets of these environmental and economic goals.

The transformation will include a discussion on limits to the consumption of the rich, so that the inequality gap can be bridged within ecological limits. We know that economic growth by itself does not satisfy societies concerns with welfare and sustainability. A high consumption level does not guarantee happiness: above a minimum level there is no correlation between per capita GDP and life satisfaction [Jackson, 2009]. Human development increases hugely as per capita electricity increases to 3,000 units, but levels off at the level of European consumption, which is half that of the United States [Martinez, 2008]; and quality of life also does not improve significantly beyond $30,000, the GDP of Spain, and the average for the European Union. Therefore, societal change will be the critical driver for the transition to sustainability, with a change in value systems reflected in the way we measure progress, for example, a shift away from owning consumer goods to sharing them with others – the growing use of 'zip' cars in the United States is an example.

A sustainable society and economy within global ecological limits will be shaped more by governments than by markets, because the 'new' economy will also need to create jobs that do not require much material consumption, as full employment is important for stabilizing debt-based financial systems and maintaining high-quality public services, which are dependent of constant growth. However, the current governance institutions, including the United Nations, are not able to adequately respond to the scale, speed and scope of change in the absence of a common vision of the future based on the elimination of disparity in resource use. Reliance on law, or treaties, ignores these societal trends and focuses on areas of cooperative agreements essentially monitoring the symptoms, and research on regime effectiveness leaves out the causes of the problems where there has been no agreement. Targets become wish lists difficult to prioritize, ignoring interrelationships, trade-offs and synergies. Economic models focus more on efficiency rather than equity; for example, indicating 'pathways' that require a 'peaking' in energy demand unrelated to inequality in levels of infrastructure and well-being. Even setting a price on carbon under the emissions trading regime has not modified long-term consumer behaviour or led to technological shifts in Europe.

At the same time, carbon management provides an integrating theme; it links the national and international levels reflecting interdependence that extends to patterns of resource use; it is the only area where data for global trends are available and an indicator that the existing framework has outlived its relevance. An assessment of patterns, trends and drivers of the activities that led to the utilization of the global carbon budget over the previous 100 years shows that the most important trend to be modified worldwide is consumption shaped by urban lifestyles. As it is closely linked to current economic models, real change will only occur in the long term and could well take as long as 30–50 years. As we have also not been able to incorporate the concerns in the existing socio-economic system to a degree that they may start bending the trends in the right direction, and because of this delay, the problem will be 'managed' rather than 'solved'. For example, lower consumption immediately can stabilize the rate of impact on all parameters of environmental degradation by 2030, while high density cities and a modal shift to rail transport will modify longer term trends in levels of use of energy, food and transportation later by 2050.

Population decline, itself an outcome of urbanization, could well mean that limits to growth will not be reached, and the shifts will most likely be based on a combination of diverse factors. For example, new global rules on technology transfer linking commercial objectives with societal needs; rising commodity prices leading to irreversible impacts on the well-being of the rich; and policy directed investment with respect to urbanization, public transport and shaping usage to support a societal and technological transformation that could extend over a period of 50 years.

A new approach to global rules will be a pre-condition of early and sustainable transformation. For example, the World Health Organizations' constitution states that the highest attainable standard of health is a fundamental human right of every human being. This raises the question: should a drug be described as 'blockbuster' by a billion dollar label or a billion patients' label? If drugs are developed only for those who can afford them, but not for those who need them, is it unethical? In 2012, USFDA approved 39 drugs. Of the 12 for cancer, 11 cost $1,00,000 a year, and in 2013, a breakthrough Hepatitis C pill won approval with a $1,000-a-day price tag. Drug innovation is expensive and the long-drawn-out approval process needs to be compensated through market mechanisms to allow pharma companies to recoup such investments. But the question is how much should the return on investment be?

The geopolitical shifts are leading to three related but distinct developments with respect to global agenda setting, review of global rules and taking advantage of national benefits in global rules. First, the WHO has already taken up coordination of research as an essential function. It established a Commission on Intellectual Property Rights, Innovation and Public health in 2003, and Expert Groups to consider the recommendations in 2006 and 2010, and the second group's report was released in 2012. The Report on 'Research and Development to meet Health Needs in Developing Countries' suggests mandatory government funding for research and draws attention to health needs of emerging countries as well as international coordination of priorities and implementation through a binding agreement, on the lines of global environmental agreements and their funds. In the Expert Working Group, the United States desired to obtain a wide range of non-governmental perspectives on the funding and coordination of global health research, even though, in the United States, the government finances most health-related drug research and public purchases and insurance covers most of the medicines. Improved medicines are a public good as they stop epidemics and limit the economic and human toll of illness.

Second, the United States is also considering reforming the innovation system with a shift from the patent regime that gives a temporary monopoly to innovators to a government supported prize-based system, where innovators will be rewarded for new knowledge but there will be no monopoly on its use. Instead of hoarding the knowledge to avoid competition, markets can ensure that the drug will be made available at the lowest possible price. Open source research will encourage sharing.

Third, the provision of compulsory licensing in the Trade-Related Aspects of Intellectual Property Rights, as part of the Uruguay Round of trade negotiations establishing the World Trade Organization, has a provision for compulsory license to domestic firms if the patent holder did not provide medicines at an affordable price, and India invoked this provision for the first time in 2012 enabling the liver and kidney cancer drug, Nexaver, to be available at 3 per cent the price Bayer was charging. Sensing the threat to future profits, the United States put pressure on India and placed it on the 'priority watch list'.

Generic producers in India have brought down the prices of lifesaving drugs used to treat diseases such as HIV, TB and cancer by as much as 90 per cent. In the 1990s, HIV/AIDS drugs cost $12,000 per patient a year which saved patients in the United States but not in Africa. In 2001, an Indian pharma company produced a three-in-one HIV/AIDS treatment for $1 a day. Today, most antiretroviral medicines purchased by the United States global AIDS programme come from India and more than

80 per cent of HIV drugs that Medecins Sans Frontieres, UNICEF and Clinton Foundation use are generics from India. India is a vital producer of affordable medicines and the world's largest producer of generic drugs. The Indian pharma industry accounts for 20 per cent of the world's pharma industry in value terms and constitutes a significant 80 per cent in volume terms. Indian generics account for a 30 per cent share of the United States market. Data from the 2013 Generic Drug Savings in the U.S. report shows that generic pharmaceuticals saved the American health system and patients $217 billion in 2012 and a staggering $1.3 trillion in the most recent decade.

It is sustainable for pharma companies to innovate without the need for exorbitant pricing, taking advantage of globalization for ensuring a global right to health care. Helped by a significantly lower cost base and a large talent pool of scientists and engineers, India's research engine is now driving a new model of innovation that focuses on quality and affordability through outsourcing, risk-sharing, and co-development partnerships. This can also extend to quality health care, for example heart and eye operations, where economies of scale make medical care accessible and affordable to the masses, irrespective of national boundaries.s

The future global goals will have to consider where the current consensus lies with respect to global rules that balance national interests with global legitimacy for human well-being. Since a genuine commitment to global goals that transcend national interests will be a politically difficult issue, it may be best to identify enabling conditions and characteristics of sustainability, defined in terms of changes in rules for sharing technological innovation, modifying urban patterns of consumption and production, and recognize the rural–urban divide to make the pie bigger rather than goals that enable some to seize a larger slice. The shift in global economic power, and national interests of those who need to ensure well-being of nearly 6 billion, will support a new multilateralism, or vision, for 'sharing responsibility and prosperity', as it is the only kind of environmental, economic and social development that is truly sustainable. Acting collectively in the face of long-term and uncertain threats will now be an essential element in solving global problems in an equitable fashion and in a manner that is in the long-term interests of all.

References

Burns, Thomas, R. 2012. 'The Sustainability Revolution: A Societal Paradigm Shift'. *Sustainability* 4: 1118–34.
China Daily, 'Obama Hails Climate Deal', November 18, 2014.
FAO. 2013. *Food Wastage Footprint: Impacts on Natural Resources.* Food and Agriculture Organization, Rome, 2013.
FAO. 2013. *Tackling Climate Change through Livestock.* Food and Agriculture Organization, Rome, September 2013.
GEA. 2012: *Global Energy Assessment – Toward a Sustainable Future.* International Institute for Applied Systems Analysis, Laxenburg, Austria. Cambridge University Press, Cambridge, New York.
ICSU, ISSC (2015): Review of the Sustainable Development Goals: The Science Perspective. Paris: International Council for Science (ICSU).
IEA. 2012. *World Energy Outlook* 2012. International Energy Agency, Paris.
IEA. 2013. *World Energy Report*, International Energy Agency, Paris.
ISSC/UNESCO (2013). *World Social Science Report 2013: Changing Global Environments.* OECD Publishing and UNESCO Publishing, Paris.
Jackson, T. 2009. *Prosperity without Growth.* Earthscan, London, UK.
Karstensen, Jonas, Glen P. Peters and Robbie M Andrew. 2013. 'Attribution of CO2 Emissions from Brazilian Deforestation to Consumers between 1990 and 2010'. *Environmental Research Letters.* 8: 024005.
Kashambuzi, Eric. 2013. Accelerating Growth to End Poverty without Damaging the Environment, Guest Article #3, Post-2015 Policy and Practice, International Institute for Sustainable Development. Posted on 16 October, 2013. http://post2015.iisd.org/guest-articles/accelerating-growth-to-end-poverty-without-damaging-the-environment/

Martínez, D.M., Ebenhack, B.W. 'Understanding the Role of Energy Consumption in Human Development through the Use of Saturation Phenomena'. *Energy Policy* 2008, 36: 1430–35.

Mckinsey. 2009. *Green Unlocking Energy Efficiency in the US Economy*, McKinsey Global Energy and Materials, Mckinsey and Company, July 2009.

McKinsey Global Institute. 2013. *Urban World: The Shifting Global Business Landscape.* October, 2013, Washington, DC.

Meadows, D., Randers, J. 2004. *Limits to Growth – The 30-Year Update.* Vermont: Chelsea Publishing Company.

MEA. 2005. *Millennium Ecosystem Assessment, 2005. Ecosystems and Human Well-being: Synthesis.* Island Press, Washington, DC.

NIC, 2012, *Global Trends 2030: Alternative Worlds.* National Intelligence Council, December 2012, NIC 2012-001

Nordic Council of Ministers. 2013. Improving Nordic Policymaking by Dispelling Myths on Sustainable Consumption. TemaNord: 553.

NRDC. 2012. *Wasted: How America is Loosing upto 40 per cent of Its Food from Farm to Fork to Landfill.* Issue paper August 2012, IP:12-06-B, Natural Resources Defense Council.

OECD. 2012. *Environment Outlook for 2050,* Organization for Economic Cooperation and Development, Paris.

OECD. 2013. *Putting Green Growth at the Heart of Development.* Organization for Economic Cooperation and Development. June 2013, Paris.

PBL. 2012. *Making Ends Meet – Pathways to Reconcile Global Food, Energy, Climate and Biodiversity Goals.* PBL Netherlands Environmental Assessment Agency, The Hague.

PBL. 2013. *Trends in Global Carbon Dioxide Emissions: 2013 Report,* Netherlands Environmental Assessment Agency, The Hague, 2013.

PCGCC. 2012. *Reducing Greenhouse Emissions from US Transportation,* Report prepared for the Pew Center on Global Climate Change, Washington.

RITE. 2012. Akimoto, K., Sano, F., Hayashi, A., Homma, T., Oda, J., Wada, K., Nagashima, M., Tokushige, K., and Tomoda, T. 2012. *Consistent Assessments of Pathways Toward Sustainable Development and Climate Stabilization.* ALPS Scenarios Project, RITE, Japan.

Rockström, J., Steffen, W., Noone, K., Persson, A., Chapin, F.S., Lambin, E.F., Lenton, T.M., Scheffer, M., Folke, C., Schellnhuber, H.J., Björn Nykvist, Cynthia A. de Wit, Terry Hughes, Sander van der Leeuw, Henning Rodhe, Sverker Sörlin, Peter K. Snyder, Robert Costanza, Uno Svedin, Malin Falkenmark, Louise Karlberg, Robert W. Corell, Victoria J. Fabry, James Hansen, Brian Walker, Liverman, D., Richardson, K., Crutzen, P., and Foley, J.A. 2009. 'A Safe Operating Space for Humanity'. *Nature* 461: 472–75, 24 September 2009.

Ross, Michael L. 2013. How the 1973 oil embargo saved the planet. *Foreign Affairs,* 15 October 2013.

Sanwal, Mukul. 2012. 'Rio +20, Climate Change and Development: The Evolution of Sustainable Development (1972–2012)'. *Climate and Development* 4 (2): 157–166.

Sanwal, Mukul. 2014. 'Global Sustainable Development Goals Are about the Use and Distribution, Not Scarcity of Natural Resources: Will the Middle Class in the USA, China and India Save the Climate as Its Incomes Grow'. *Climate and Development* 4 (4).

SEI. 2012. Nilsson, M., Heaps, C., Persson, A., Carson, M., Pachauri, S., Kok, M., Olsson, M., Rehman, I., Schaeffer, R., Wood, D., van Vuuren, D., Riahi, K., Americano, B., Mulugetta, Y. 2012. *Energy for a Shared Development Agenda: Global Scenarios and Governance Implications.* Stockholm Environment Institute, Sweden.

Steven Bernstein, Joyeeta Gupta, Steinar Andresen, Peter M. Haas, Norichika Kanie, Marcel Kok, Marc A. Levy, and Casey Stevens. 2014. Coherent Governance, the UN and the SDGs. POST2015/UNU-IAS Policy Brief #4. Tokyo: United Nations University Institute for the Advanced Study of Sustainability.

UN. 2013. United Nations, *World Economic and Social Survey 2013: Sustainable Development Challenges.*

United Nations, *Department of Economic and Social Affairs.* 2014. 'World Urbanization Prospects: The 2014 Revision – Highlights', ST/EA/SER.A/352

UNEP-GEO 5. 2012. *GEO 5: Global Environmental Outlook: Environment for the Future we want,* United Nations Environment Programme, Nairobi.

UNDESA. 2013. *Sustainable Development Scenarios for Rio + 20: A Component of the SD21 Project.* United Nations Department of Economic and Social Affairs, Division for Sustainable Development, February 2013.

UN Habitat. 2013. *Gobal Report on Human Settlements 2013 – Planning and Design for Sustainable Urban Mobility*, United Nations Human Settlements Programme (UN-Habitat), Nairobi.

UNESCO. 1985. *World Modeling, Report* (August 1985), by Heinrich Siegmann, Wissenschaftszentrum Berlin. International Institute for Comparative Social Research, Berlin. BEP/GPI/2.

UNESCO. 2011. *From Green Economies to Green Societies: UNESCO's commitment to sustainable development,* United Nations Education, Scientific and Cultural Organization, Paris.

UNESCO. 2013. UN Secretary-General's Scientific Advisory Board to strengthen connection between science and policy, Press release, 18 October 2013, UNESCOPRESS.

UNU-IHDP and UNEP. 2012. *Inclusive Wealth Report 2012: Measuring Progress towards Sustainability.* Cambridge University Press, Cambridge.

Urry, John. 2013. Are increasing greenhouse gas emissions inevitable? In ISSC/UNESCO (2013). *World Social Science Report 2013: Changing Global Environments.* Paris: OECD Publishing, UNESCO Publishing.

U.S. 1971. *National report on the human environment. Prepared for: United Nations Conference on Human Environment*, Dept of State, June 1972, Stockholm, Sweden.

WSJ. 2013. *Beijing to Limit Car Ownership to 6 Million.* Wall Street Journal, September 23, 2013.

WEF. 2012. *Global Risk Report.* World Economic Forum.

World Energy Council. 2013. *World Energy Trilemma – Time to get real – the agenda for change.* Project Partner Oliver Wyman, October 2013.

Rural Areas: Climate Change, Fragile States and Human Security

22

A new rural–urban divide is emerging at the global level because of the adverse impacts of climate variability, and also climate change. The global debate on climate change has evolved through four phases – status of the atmospheric resource, patterns of anthropogenic use of natural resources with global implications, adverse impacts of climate change on both natural resources and economic activity and now as a contributing factor to increased human security risks globally, particularly in rural areas which remain vulnerable to the adverse impacts of climate change. For example, even though Africa's economic growth has been more than 5 per cent on average since 2002 rural–urban inequality has been increasing. This imbalance is most pronounced in social groups living in inhospitable agro-climatic zones, small food crop farmers, workers in the informal sector, the unemployed youth; all of whom together constitute the majority of the population in Africa. These are the symptoms of deeper structural problems that are exasperated by climate variability, but not apparent in the risk-management framework that continues to be adopted which now re-frames adaptation in terms of fragile states[1].

The industrialized countries that have shaped the evolution of climate change within the United Nations now support a discussion in the United Nations Security Council and the General Assembly on the impact of climate change on maintenance of human security as that would reinforce their thrust on a new principle of shared rather than differentiated responsibilities. Human Security is defined as 'security' because it undermines livelihoods, compromises culture and identity, induces migration that people would rather have avoided, and challenges the ability of states to provide the conditions necessary for human security. This shift reflects the recognition that all countries must not only adopt national policies for emissions reductions but also respond to the impact of climate change on national development expressed in terms of human security and vulnerability in rural areas. This re-framing has been put on the agenda of the Security Council.

The United Nations Development Programme in 1994 articulated the concept of 'human security', shifting the focus on securing individual people, creating the space to incorporate non-traditional threats into the security agenda and moving away from opportunities and adaptive capacity – a focus on the symptoms rather than the root causes. For example, countries dependent on agriculture with weak institutions are particularly vulnerable to socio-economic impacts of climate change and at the

---

[1] Parts of this chapter were first published in Sanwal (2012, 2013, 2014).

same time 1.6 billion have no access to modern energy. The United Nations is also now stressing that the world could suffer a 40 percent shortfall in water by 2030 unless countries dramatically change their use of the resource. The report from Working Group II of the Fifth Assessment Report, in 2014, contains a chapter on Human Security which reports high agreement and robust evidence that human security will be progressively threatened as the climate changes, but as far as the impact on armed conflict is concerned, it states that 'collectively the research does not conclude that there is a strong positive relationship between warming and armed conflict'.

The new sustainable development goals being negotiated within the United Nations are also considering climate change in terms of risk management and vulnerabilities in rural areas rather than human well-being within ecological limits. The scientific, academic and policy debate is shifting in the way the issue has been framed in terms of scarcity rather than use of scarce resources at the global level to considering individual rather than country-level impacts. Consequently, redistribution, which has yet to be accepted within the United Nations, is also framed in terms of vulnerable citizens and human rights at the local level in rural areas. The OECD has now developed a new understanding of fragility beyond fragile states. It assesses fragility as an issue of universal character that can affect all countries, not only those traditionally considered "fragile" or conflict-affected. To do so, it takes three indicators related to targets of SDG 16 and two from the wider SDG framework: violence, access to justice, accountable and inclusive institutions, economic inclusion and stability, and capacities to prevent and adapt to social, economic and environmental shocks and disasters. It applies them to all countries worldwide, and identifies the 50 most vulnerable ones in all five dimensions. The group of countries most challenged on all five fronts differs little from the traditional list of fragile states and economies with several middle-income countries with disproportionately high levels of crime-related violence, sub-national conflict or poor access to justice included. These countries cover half the world's population living in absolute poverty, that is 1 billion people, and supports a new role for the international community by focusing development aid to these countries for institution building. The report points out that remittances constituted the largest aggregate financial flow to fragile states and need to be facilitated and channeled better (OECD, 2015). The future global objective is being defined, in the words of the Secretary-General of the United Nations, as a life of dignity for all and to develop national and local solutions to seemingly intractable problems, with a focus on those who have yet to move to urban areas, rather than view the global societal transformation to urbanization and industrialization as an opportunity for middle-class levels of well-being for all, in the context of sustainable development.

The report on Human Security of the UN Secretary-General to the United Nations General Assembly (A/68/685 dated 23 December 2013) highlights the centrality of human security to the activities of the United Nations system and underlines its importance as a universal framework to respond to a wide range of challenges and opportunities for achieving inclusive social and economic development, environmental sustainability and peace and security in the twenty-first century. It is initially being projected as a response to addressing multiple insecurities in remote and isolated areas, representing special problems of States rather than relations between States, but will gradually impact on and shape a new framework for multilateral relations. The concept includes the need for people-centred, comprehensive, context-specific and prevention-oriented solutions. The argument is being made that the human security approach has tremendous potential in the determination to reduce the likelihood of conflicts, overcome the obstacles to sustainable development, and promote a life of dignity for all. A comprehensive approach is being sought for interlinkages among the three pillars of the United Nations – now defined as attainment of peace and security, development and human rights, and improved coherence among goals and responsibilities.

In removing obstacles to sustainable development and tackling poverty, in addition to climate change, two other interlinked trends, at the local and not global level, have been identified – transboundary water flows and water scarcity in rural areas as more and water is drawn into cities. As population shifts to cities, the demand for water to produce food, energy and goods increases and by 2050 the world's demand for water is expected to grow by 55 per cent. About 50 per cent of all available water is transboundary – water located in the rivers, lakes or groundwater systems of two or more countries – and cooperation over this water is often troublesome. Around two-thirds of the world's transboundary rivers lack agreements between the countries that share them. In the context of climate change, this situation, linked to political conflicts in many of the sharing regions, has meant that transboundary waters are being presented as a reason for violent conflict and even war.

However, the water wars that were feared a decade ago have not materialized, because consumption patterns and the loss and waste of food represent a much greater proportion of water use in production supply chains. Some 20 years ago, the UN International Conference on Water and the Environment had agreed that water should be recognized as an economic good, but water is not just another commodity, it is both a public and a private good. Governments are struggling with these issues and rather than focus on urbanization and industrialization as the guiding principle of the post-2015 agenda an international consensus is being sought in the United Nations around human security, with local or rural concerns, rather than rural-urban flows and global trends as the guiding principle.

22.1 Political dimension

The policy question in considering climate change as a 'threat multiplier' is the nature of the threat – environmental or developmental – and whether the risks are addressed better by promoting cooperation or by preventing conflict? The related questions are whether mediating disputes between States can best be done in the Security Council because it has delegated responsibilities for 'maintenance of peace and security' giving the permanent five members immense power to react urgently and set the agenda, or whether this composition reflecting the victors of World War II will not build a global consensus? And, whether other regimes can set appropriate norms and standards for enforcement short of sanctions and use of force? A global consensus has yet to emerge on these issues, as the perspectives of the different countries have political rather than scientific or legal dimensions.

Human security has a broader meaning than conflict for an essential resource such as water and includes livelihoods and well-being, including access to modern energy, as well as having a potential for cooperation between nations. For example, there are a range of assessments of the scope and scale of the problem of use, distribution and scarcity of water in Asia. A consensus is emerging that a broader understanding of demand-side management is needed rather than focus only on scarcity, which seeks to 'securitize' water. This view questions approaches that look at resource scarcity solely in environmental terms, that is, variability or shortage, and leads to the conclusion that managing changing water relations in Asia will become difficult.

Reframing the issue in terms of sustainable development, that is, distribution and use, provides solutions that will be based on the transformations needed in domestic growth pathways as the urban middle class in Asia triples in size by 2050; even as the population is also expected to achieve replacement levels around 2015. Both water availability and carbon space, as essential and interlinked natural resources, call for reviewing urban design as new cities are planned so that they use fewer natural resources than existing cities and reshape consumption patterns, modifying longer term trends in natural resource use. California, for example, faced with water scarcity, as limits to growth become apparent, has decided to cut down usage by one–fifth – which will primarily affect the excessive watering of the lawns! and Albuquerque, in New Mexico, also in the United States, with farmers turning to technology and ingenuity, has cut its water consumption by a quarter in 20 years even as its population has grown by a third.

Academic debate on the issue of environmental security is divided, with some concluding – on the basis of either case studies or quantitative analyses of historical and present-day climate–conflict relations – that anthropogenic warming is likely to exacerbate conflict dynamics, with others finding only circumstantial evidence of linkages between the two, and still others refuting the climate–water conflict thesis altogether. The range of recent analyses – assessments, methodologies, definitions and strategic reviews – focus on the environmental aspects and the rising demand ignoring new patterns of resource use; but are much less alarming than the models that have so far been adopted to project and assess scarcity.

The focus of the strategic security dimension of water scarcity in Asia is based on the international definition of water stress, which is 1,000 cubic metres of usable water per person per year, and the increasing demand in China where the average northern Chinese has less than a fifth of that amount. China has 20 per cent of the world's population but only 7 per cent of its fresh water. This view focuses on the projects for damming or diverting rivers and argues that such diversions have the potential to deprive other countries of their assured supply – increasing available water by capturing more of what flows through rivers or by moving water from one river to another.

A recent strategic analysis argues that three interconnected crises – a resource crisis, an environmental crisis, and a climate crisis – are threatening Asia's economic, social, and ecological future. This analysis is based on the impacts of climate change and argues that the Tibetan Plateau, which contains the world's third-largest store of ice, is warming at almost twice the average global rate, owing to the rare convergence of high altitudes and low latitudes – with potentially serious consequences for Asia's freshwater supply [Brahma Chellaney, 2013]. This conclusion is not supported by recent scientific assessments, which have not detected any abnormal changes in the Himalayas compared with glaciers in other regions [IPCC, 2014].

The problem of water scarcity is also framed in terms of water security. According to the Asian Development Bank's 'Asia Water Development Outlook 2013', 37 of 49 countries assessed were suffering from low levels of water security, including those which lacked measures to tackle the problem. Twelve countries are shown to have established infrastructure and management systems for water security, while no country in the region was found to have reached the highest model level of water security. More than 60 per cent of households in Asia and the Pacific still live without a safe, piped water supply and improved sanitation. The conclusion, however, adopts a sustainable development perspective, stating that more than 75 per cent of Asia–Pacific countries will face an imminent water crisis only they do not take steps to improve resource management. An analysis of water basins with treaties has also found that higher water variability leads to greater cooperation, where allocation and institutional mechanisms serve to bring countries together [World Bank Policy Research Working Paper 6916, 2014].

Moving from describing what is happening to analysing the causes, the Asian Development Bank has also pointed out that the majority of Asia's water development problems are attributable to 'poor water governance and not to water scarcity'. The report acknowledges that conservation of resources is also a societal goal – with potential to improve quality of life around the world. According to the Asian Development Bank, the important thing is a dramatic reduction in waste, and it has urged countries to invest in 'reduce, re-use, recycle systems' to better make use of dwindling water resources and better sanitation and other infrastructure, mobilize additional resources to clean up rivers and modernize irrigation systems. Governments must also step up campaigns to educate people on water scarcity. This view argues that it would be better to focus on demand, reducing consumption of water in order to make better use of limited supplies. Water is too cheap in most cities, industry recycles too little water and agriculture wastes too much. Asia has the highest water scarcity and also one of the lowest levels of water efficiency and productivity in the world.

The problem is now being framed in terms of sustainable development, with an equal focus on demand and supply. According to the report, Global Trends 2030, released by the Office of National Director of Intelligence, United States, demand for food, water, and energy will grow by approximately 35, 40 and 50 per cent, respectively, owing to an increase in the global population and the consumption patterns of an expanding urban middle class. Climate change will worsen the outlook for the availability of these critical resources. This report also points out that scarcities in availability of resources can be avoided, but only if steps are taken by a number of industries and economies in a coordinated manner to improve productivity and efficiency. According to this report, 'we are not necessarily headed into a world of scarcities', but policymakers and their private sector partners will need to be proactive to avoid such a future. It has also stressed that most scientists are not confident of being able to predict climatic events. Rapid changes in precipitation patterns – such as monsoons in India and the rest of Asia – could sharply disrupt that region's ability to feed its population. At the same time, key technologies likely to be at the forefront of maintaining energy, food and water resources in the next 15–20 years are available and will include genetically modified crops, precision agriculture, water irrigation techniques, and solar energy.

In the case of the Himalayas, though the amount of ice on the plateau of Tibet and its surrounding mountains, Himalayas, Karakoram and Pamirs, is a lot smaller than that at the Poles, it is still huge. The area's 46,000 glaciers cover 100,000 square kilometres (40,000 square miles) – about 6 per cent of the area of the Greenland ice cap. Another 1.7 m square kilometre is permafrost, which can be up to 130 m deep. That is equivalent to 7 per cent of the Arctic's permafrost. The area is known by some as Asia's water tower, because it is the source of 10 of the continent's biggest rivers. About 1.5 billion people, in 12 countries, live in the basins of those rivers.

An unresolved scientific issue is whether the glaciers are retreating, as is happening in parts of the Arctic, and their pace of withdrawal. The Intergovernmental Panel on Climate Change's report in 2007 incorrectly suggested that the Himalayas' glaciers could disappear as early as 2035, with an official statement acknowledging the error. A 2012 study published in *Nature* by Thomas Jacob of the University of Colorado, in Boulder, showed that glaciers in the Himalayas and Karakoram had lost little ice between 2003 and 2010, and that those on the Tibetan plateau itself were growing [Thomas, 2012]. According to the recent Intergovernmental Panel on Climate Changes report in 2013, glaciers in Europe and North America are more affected by climate change than glaciers in Asia.

22.2 Scientific dimension

Climate change will impact on human security in Asia with respect to reduced water availability primarily because of increasing demand, with Asia expected to account for two-third of global wealth in 2050. Water supports food production, industry and urban living, and these different uses can no longer be seen in isolation from each other. Unless these competing needs are balanced, the resulting water stress will undermine the quality of life for billions of people in the region. Technological solutions include desalination, drip irrigation, and new crop varieties alone will not be a solution in the absence of societal changes. Reduced access to water is not expected to affect urban migration and geopolitical tensions.

The driest continent in the world is not Africa but Asia, as availability of freshwater is not even half the global annual average of 6,380 cubic metres per inhabitant. When the estimated reserves of rivers, lakes, and aquifers are added up, Asia has less than one-tenth of the waters of South America, Australia and New Zealand, not even one-fourth of North America, almost one-third of Europe, and moderately less than Africa per inhabitant. Yet the world's fastest-growing demand for water for food and industrial production and for municipal supply is in Asia, which now serves as the locomotive of the world economy.

Asia more than doubled its total irrigated cropland between 1960 and 2000. Once a continent of serious food shortages and recurrent famines, Asia has emerged as a net food exporter. Three sub-regions of Asia – South Asia, China, and Southeast Asia – by themselves account for about 50 per cent of the world's total irrigated land. Today, the fastest-growing Asian economies are all at or near water-stressed conditions, including China, India, South Korea, Vietnam, and Indonesia. Looking three or four decades ahead, it is clear that the water situation will only exacerbate, carrying major implications for rapid economic growth and inter-riparian relations.

That concern has helped give rise to grand schemes – from China's Great Western Route to divert river waters from the Tibetan Plateau to its parched North and South Korea's politically divisive four-river project, to India's proposal to link up its important rivers to conserve the monsoon run-off and Jordan's plan to bring water from the Red Sea through a 178-km-long canal to the Dead Sea, which is also to serve as a source for desalinated drinking water – a significant share of which is in transboundary watercourses. As rural populations move to urban areas consumption rises, and Asia is consuming an increasing share of global resources, including water, food, oil and energy.

Only 4 of the 57 transnational river basins in Asia have a treaty covering water sharing or other institutionalized cooperation. These are the Mekong, Ganges, Indus and Jordan River basins. Dam building for energy has only intensified intrastate and interstate water tensions, with implications for regional security and stability. Security analysts consider the absence of a cooperative arrangement in most Asian transnational basins a potential source of conflict making transboundary water competition a major security risk, increasing the likelihood of geopolitical tensions. They suggest that institutionalized cooperation on transboundary basin resources is needed for strategic stability, continued economic growth, and environmental sustainability. Actually, the future prosperity of Asia requires political and technological partnerships for greater water efficiency, conservation strategies, and clean-water technologies.

In seeking clarity through specificity, the Himalayan Rivers provide an interesting case study of the lack of authoritative statements on the adverse effects of climate change. With respect to water scarcity in Asia the contribution of Himalayan and snow melt varies greatly for the rivers flowing on the Northern and Southern aspects. For example, the Yellow, Mekong and Salween rivers get less than 10 per cent of their flows from the glaciers, while the Indus and the Ganges get up to 70 per cent prior to and during the monsoon. For South Asia, the monsoon, including the resulting snow fall in the upper reaches, is the determining factor in water flows. Conclusions on water flow are usually made on the basis of a few studies and researchers from India and China are only now, in 2014, beginning to work together with respect to the Himalayas and for joint monitoring of transboundary water flows. There are as yet no authoritative scientific assessments, as they depend on whether natural science or a social science perspective has been adopted.

For example, with respect to water scarcity in South Asia even the scientific and the intelligence community of the United States differ widely in their conclusions on how climate change impacts interact with political, economic and social dynamics.

The National Research Council has adopted a sustainable development framework [National Research Council, 2012]. It recognizes that the Hindu Kush Himalayan region is the location of several of Asia's great river systems, which provide water for drinking, irrigation and other uses for about 1.5 billion people. The study draws upon scientific evidence to show that 'glaciers in the eastern and central regions of the Himalayas appear to be retreating at rates comparable to glaciers in other parts of the world, while in the western Himalayas glaciers are more stable and may even be increasing in size', and that the consequences for the region's water supply are unclear. Their assessment, based on the natural sciences, is that shifts in the location, intensity, and variability of rain and snow due to climate change will likely have a greater impact on regional water supplies. They also conclude, on the basis of social science research, that 'social changes such as changing patterns of water use and water management decisions, are likely to have at least as much of an impact on water demand as environmental factors do on water supply'.

A recent assessment for the Central Intelligence Agency adopts a climate-centric approach [Intelligence Community Assessment, 2012] and concludes that 'it is prudent to expect that over the course of a decade some climate events – including single events, conjunctions of events occurring simultaneously or in sequence in particular locations, and events affecting globally integrated systems that provide for human well-being – will produce consequences that exceed the capacity of the affected societies or global system to manage and that have global security implications serious enough to compel international response'. Its framework is that in Asia as a whole with 60 per cent of the world's people, there is only 36 per cent of the world's renewable freshwater, and between now and 2040 'fresh water availability will not keep up with demand'. It assumes that effective management of water resources will not take place with agriculture continuing to use approximately 70 per cent of the fresh water supply 'posing a risk to global food markets and hobbling economic growth'. It sees the Brahmaputra basin as an area of potential conflict because of uncoordinated land use and development plans.

The strategic community has ignored current scientific consensus on how to meet the challenge of global change, which focuses on societal dynamics as both the root of environmental problems and the potential solution to them. The academic and policy discourse with respect to water security has been framed too narrowly around the intersection with rural poverty and state fragility in Sub-Saharan Africa and the long-term problems in certain small island states, without understanding the complexity of interlinked processes like glacial melt, precipitation and modifying consumption patterns. Even within the United Nations the multilateral discourse on climate change, sustainable development, conflict and security has so far been highly climate-centric and fails to contextualize climate impacts in relation to other broader processes of economic and social change and the urban transformation.

22.3 Legal dimension

Within the United Nations Security Council, the discussion on human and environmental security has so far also been around the symptoms and not the causes of the global challenge of climate change, and an example of how issues come onto the global agenda.

On 17 April 2007, the United Kingdom initiated a debate in the Security Council on the relationship between energy, security and climate, and both the Non-Aligned Movement and the Group of 77 + China argued that the matter should be discussed within the General Assembly. On 3 June 2009, on the initiative of the small-island developing states of the Pacific Ocean, the General Assembly held a debate and requested the Secretary-General to submit a report on the possible security implications of climate change.

On 11 September 2009, the Secretary-General identified climate change as a 'threat multiplier' that exacerbates a number of existing threats, such as persistent rural poverty, weak institutions for resource management and mistrust between communities. The report identified five ways in which climate change might affect security:

- climate change could threaten food security and human health and increase exposure to extreme events;
- it could undermine the stability of states by slowing or reversing development;

- it could increase the likelihood of domestic conflict due to rural migration and depleting resources, with possible international ramifications;
- disappearance of territory might raise issues of sovereignty, rights and security; and
- international conflict might be a result of climate change's impact on shared or demarcated international resources.

The current concern is only with environmental dimension even though the Security Council had stressed the importance of 'contextual information'. Germany, with the strong support of Portugal, initiated an open debate on 20 July 2011, on the 'security implications' of rising sea level and its impact on coastal and small island states, from the loss of coastal territory to the disappearance of certain islands completely, and threats to food security, while ignoring the impact on national development which was included in the Report of the Secretary General. The most significant Council outcome to date on the issue, in the form of a presidential statement was a compromise and expressed concern over the adverse effects that climate change may have on existing threats to both peace and security.

A 23 November 2012 debate on 'New Challenges to International Peace and Security' also touched on the theme of climate change and security, ignoring possibilities of cooperation to promote peace. A narrow climate-centric focus around scenarios continued to be taken when the Security Council heard climate experts from the United Kingdom and Germany on the 'security dimensions of climate change' on 19 February 2013, initiated by Pakistan and the United Kingdom, ignoring the impact of climate change on sustainable development. The Annual Security Council Retreat with the Secretary-General held on 22–23 April, 2013, discussed the security implications of climate change, going beyond peace-keeping operations and field missions to exploring questions of how the Council can encourage states or other actors to work to mitigate the deleterious effects of climate change on security, again ignoring prevention and the impacts on development. The Annual Retreat in April 2014 explored the challenges and opportunities of managing crisis in failed or fragile nascent states.

The response of those who have been reluctant to discuss the issue in the Security Council has largely been defensive, and procedural, in nature. China and Russia objected to the deliberations in February 2013 being held in a formal session and 130 emerging countries shared this view. Others, like Brazil, have stressed the developmental elements in the Report of the Secretary-General and argued that there is no direct link established between climate change and peace and security and that social and economic development provides adequate tools to tackle climate change's impact.

Immediately after this Summit, in the Security Council open debate, initiated by the UK presidency on the theme 'Conflict prevention and natural resources' on June 19, 2013, India cautioned against the 'concerted push to bring several normative issues into the Council's agenda under the pretext of their affecting international peace and security' and pointed out that the system would only run correctly and effectively if the division in roles and responsibilities between the Council, the General Assembly, the Economic and Social Council and other specialized bodies was respected. The G8 foreign Ministers in their statement of 11 April, 2013, continued with this trend and stressed the potential consequences of climate change and associated environmental and resource stresses as a contributing factor to only increased security risks globally, ignoring approaches that would promote peace through enhanced international cooperation. Just prior to this debate, the G8 summit held between 17 and 18 June 2013 recognized for the first time 'climate change as a contributory factor in increased economic and security risks globally', and that a better response is needed to this challenge considering 'international climate policy and sustainable development as mutually reinforcing'. The G7 Foreign Ministers' Meeting

Communique, Lubeck, 15 April, 2015, stressed " integrating climate change – fragility considerations across foreign policy portfolios" linking climate change adaptation, development and humanitarian aid and peace building. Climate change is now a part of the security, or conflict, discussion, and re-emerging countries must shape the discussion towards sustainable development and peace, rather than restrict their response to blocking a discussion.

22.4 Policy dimension

The outcome of the deliberations in the Security Council should be to call upon the Secretary-General to prepare a new report taking account of the post-Rio+20 deliberations on the post-2015 global development agenda by integrating climate change, sustainable development and human security. That is, based on the most recent scientific assessment in the Reports of the Intergovernmental Panel on Climate Change, cover the relationship between climate change and resource use and access to modern energy, infrastructure and urbanization that could impact on standards of living as well as sparking or aggravating existing tensions from natural resource use that could lead to conflict. In the context of global ecological limits, the global concern should focus on prevention and requires sharing responsibility as well as prosperity in promoting collaboration between concerned States and the international community for the transformation to urbanization.

The legitimate concern of the non-permanent members of the Security Council is that sovereignty no longer exclusively protects States from foreign interference, and environmental or human security should not adopt the principle of 'sovereignty as responsibility' where collective action for crimes against humanity is extended to protect rural vulnerable populations from loss of habitat, starvation and mass migration. The emerging trend in the negotiations around the post-2015 global agenda is to stress the principle of 'sustainable development' with respect to the global impacts of natural resource use. Environmental, technological and societal transformations are interlinked and cannot be considered in isolation, and it would be within the mandate of the Security Council to support peace and security by looking at the longer term urban future of the planet, and sharing responsibility as well as prosperity for human well-being.

In the case of climate change, the choice for the collective response should be characterized as a choice between rules for societal and technological urban transformation and intervention in the face of rural environmental risks, access to resources and State fragility. The international community should define 'responsibility to protect' in terms of equal rights of all populations to sustainable development with new platforms for cooperative responses to deal with longer term global change, of which climate change is only a part.

22.5 Development dimension

As in the case of the global environment in the 1970s, which was described broadly as the 'human environment', human security is being broadly defined by the United Nations as 'the right of people to live in freedom and dignity, free from poverty and despair', and as providing a new way of thinking about the range of twenty-first century challenges and how to respond to them, with a people-centred approach, rather than the earlier state-centric approach, which is now considered as vital to ensuring sustainable development for all. For example, a human rights perspective on environmental protection is being suggested, including the ways that environmental harm prevents individuals and communities from living lives of dignity, equality, and freedom; procedural requirements for environmental policy-making; minimum substantive standards that environmental policies must meet; with human rights institutions (and even trade agreements) providing remedies for environmental harm.

Environmental risk from the re-emerging countries is now being stressed. For example, the United States Department of Defence in its 2014 Quadrennial Defence Review identifies the nature of climate change as a 'threat multiplier', including its impact on political instability: 'Climate change poses another significant challenge for the United States and the world at large. As greenhouse gas emissions increase, sea levels are rising, average global temperatures are increasing, and severe weather patterns are accelerating. These changes, coupled with other global dynamics, including growing, urbanizing, more affluent populations, and substantial economic growth in India, China, Brazil, and other nations, will devastate homes, land, and infrastructure. Climate change may exacerbate water scarcity and lead to sharp increases in food costs. The pressures caused by climate change will influence resource competition while placing additional burdens on economies, societies, and governance institutions around the world. These effects are threat multipliers that will aggravate stressors abroad such as poverty, environmental degradation, political instability, and social tensions – conditions that can enable terrorist activity and other forms of violence' The 'Wales Summit Declaration' of NATO, in September 2014, noted that 'key environmental and resource constraints, including health risks, climate change, water scarcity, and increasing energy needs will further shape the future security environment in areas of concern'. The United States Department of Defence has since expanded its concern to 'the probability that climate change will increase the likelihood of conflict in strategically significant parts of the world' [Department of Defence, 2014; Maplecroft Global Risk Analytics, 2014].

The approach of the industrialized countries continues to focus on scarcity, rather than use and distribution, of water as well as other natural resources. For example, water problems are closely tied to the structure of the global economy. The interest in the water footprint is rooted in the recognition that human impacts on freshwater systems can ultimately be linked to human consumption, and that issues like water shortages and pollution can be better understood and addressed by considering production, supply and demand chains as a whole. Many countries have significantly externalized their water footprint, importing water-intensive goods from elsewhere. This puts pressure on the water resources in the exporting regions, where too often mechanisms for wise water governance and conservation are lacking. Therefore, not only governments but also consumers, businesses and civil society communities need to play a role in achieving a better management of global water resources in the rural areas of countries with the adverse impacts of climate change.

An approach considering use and distribution will have three elements. First, examining the relationship between income distribution and economic, social and environmental dynamics to address the multiple dimensions of continuing rural poverty – including underemployment; poor health; lack of access to education; inequality, including gender inequality – in a more coherent and systemic manner. Second, a focus on early prevention and risk mitigation strategies rooted in human security to strengthen state–society relations and empower rural communities as active agents of change. This approach is being regarded to be particularly useful in the context of human-centred threats with a global character, such as climate change or large-scale pandemics. Third, by underscoring the importance of inclusive, targeted and comprehensive solutions to widespread and cross-cutting challenges, social science is considered as providing a useful methodology for the analysis and development of policies and programmes in formulating the sustainable development goals for the extreme poor in rural areas while linking it to urban consumption. However, the way the issue has been framed implementation is focused at the national and local level, or rural areas, just as the earlier environmental concern was focused on developing countries whereas new social science research focusing on consumption patterns and trans-boundary impacts.

For example, according to the United Nations Food and Agriculture Organization,

- The production of 1 kg of beef requires 15,000 L of water, and the water footprint of a 150 g soy burger produced in the Netherlands is about 160 L. A beef burger from the same country consumes about 1,000 L.
- The water footprint of Chinese consumption is about 1,070 cubic meters per year per capita. About 10 per cent of the Chinese water footprint falls outside China embodied in the goods exported.
- Japan with a footprint of 1,380 cubic meters per year per capita has about 77 per cent of its total water footprint outside the borders of the country.
- The water footprint of United States citizens is 2,840 cubic meters per year per capita. About 20 per cent of this water footprint is external. The largest external water footprint of United States consumption lies in the Yangtze River basin, China.
- Water scarcity affects over 2.7 billion people for at least 1 month each year.

Water use in China is half that in the United States. China, India and other emerging countries aspire to reach per capita levels of income of, for example, Germany, and their natural resource use will remain two-third to half that of the United States; a trend that has yet to be recognized by the economic and environmental models. The implication for transboundary sharing of water resources, and the global rule-based system, is that the consumption patterns of the urban dwellers, not the entire population affects the availability of resources for others. The shift to the longer term objectives of a more equal society across the world will have to go beyond political boundaries and revisit current notions of state responsibility and accountability for the use of natural resources at the global level.

For countries in Asia, the overriding question is how to move away from the historical patterns of natural resource use and design new structures and support productivity norms for urban well-being. The type of new infrastructure will determine sustainability as they will be building the equivalent of a city of 1 million people every day from now till 2050. Sustainable growth will depend upon high density communities responding to land and water becoming a scarce resource, higher cost of commodities and using fewer natural resources by designing living and working places close to one another, allowing people to walk rather than use cars and providing public transportation. Other measures include mandatory energy efficiency in building, reducing waste and encouraging water reuse and conserving rain water; in 2015 California has cut water use by one-fifth of 2013 usage, essentially reducing the watering of lawns.

New technology will also help to reduce resource stress. For example, in Beijing, the supply of water available per person is 100 cubic metres, far lower than the international average of 1,000 cubic metres. China faces an annual shortfall of some 600 million cubic metres of water. To address its water shortage, China plans to double its desalination capacity to 2.6 million cubic metres of water by 2015. China is already one of the fastest growing markets in desalination, and ranks ninth in the world in terms of seawater desalination capacity. The Chinese government is looking into a project that will deliver 1 million cubic metres of desalinated water to Beijing every day by 2016. Improvements in technology have greatly reduced cost; desalination is now a viable solution to China's water shortage.

Water is increasingly being seen as a source of cooperation, even in situations of political tension. There are a number of benefits from cooperation in transboundary regions: economic, environmental and social. There are also a wider range of less tangible benefits, like trust building. This suggests that the transboundary aspects of water can generate a wide range of benefits, and resource stress is best dealt by not limiting efforts within national borders but considering them in a regional and global context.

After over 40 years of debate in multilateral forums with limited impact, the scientific understanding, now based on research by social rather than natural scientists, suggests that global environmental change, climate change and sustainable development are fundamentally about recognizing, understanding and acting on interconnections between national urban societies and global natural resource use – earlier expressed as interactions between the economy, society and the natural environment. Under the Charter of the United Nations, the Security Council has primary responsibility for the maintenance of international peace and security. Initiating a discussion on identifying the longer term social transformations associated with the responses to urban pathways to sustainability is now an essential element in the global rebalancing and rise of the global urban middle class in a peaceful manner responding to geoeconomics – in a globalized world with respect to rural communities and not countries. This re-framing is best done in the Security Council, with special invitees from the G20 who are urbanizing, rather than in the Economic and Social Council which is a coordinating body, and then taken to the United Nations General Assembly for a broader discussion.

References

Chellaney, Brahma. 2013. *Water, Peace, and War: Confronting the Global Water Crisis*. Rowman and Littlefield Publishers, Lanham.

Jacob, Thomas, John Wahr, W. Tad Pfeffer, and Sean Swenson. 2012. Recent Contributions of Glaciers and Ice Caps to Sea Level Rise. *Nature* 482: 514–18.

Department of Defence. 2014. Climate Change Adaptation Roadmap, 2014.

Intelligence Community Assessment. 2012. Global Water Scarcity. CIA 2012-08, 2 February 2012, United States.

Maplecroft Global Risk Analytics. 2014. 'Climate Change and Environmental Risk Atlas 2015'. October 2014.

National Research Council. 2012. 'Himalayan Glaciers: Climate Change, Water Resources and Water Scarcity'.

OECD. 2015. *States of Fragility - 2015: Meeting Post-2015 Ambitions*, March 2015, OECD Paris.

Sanwal, Mukul. 2012. 'Rio +20, Climate Change and Development: The Evolution of Sustainable Development (1972–2012)'. *Climate and Development* 4 (2): 157–166.

Sanwal, Mukul. 2013. 'The Rise and Fall of Global Climate Policy: Stockholm to Rio 1992, to Rio + 20 and Beyond'. *Chinese Journal of Environmental and Urban Studies* 1 (1).

Sanwal, Mukul. 2014. 'Global Sustainable Development Goals Are about the Use and Distribution, Not Scarcity of Natural Resources: Will the Middle Class in the USA, China and India Save the Climate as Its Incomes Grow'. *Climate and Development* 4 (4).

World Bank Policy Research Working Paper 6916. 2014. Climate Change, Conflict, and Cooperation: Global Analysis of the Resilience of International River Treaties to Increased Water Variability, Shlomi Dinar, David Katz, Lucia De Stefano, Brian Blankespoor, Washington.

Global Sustainable Development Goals

23

23.1 Societal well-being in the twenty-first century

For the first time global goals that will impose some obligations on all countries are being considered, because the re-emergence of China and India is leading to a spread of prosperity and power very different to the post-colonial world. The current model for sustainable development is three separate but connected pillars of environment, society and economy, with the implication that each sector is, at least in part, independent of the others. This framework reflected the natural resource use patterns of an industrializing economy that shaped urbanization and growth in the twentieth century. In the twenty-first century, re-emerging countries are increasingly adopting a new growth model and urban design stressing the social dimension and the knowledge economy, which is the first transformation since the beginning of civilization not based on increasing use of natural resources. Services already contribute a large part of GDP in emerging countries. Even in low-income countries, young workers leaving the farm for the cities are increasingly absorbed into urban services jobs instead of only in manufacturing. International trade in services has tended to expand more rapidly than trade in goods. Service industries could serve as a growth escalator, the role traditionally assumed by manufacturing, with much less natural resource use in their consumption patterns and different notions of well-being[1].

Defenders of the status quo, largely in industrialized countries, see the root cause of the problems with achieving sustainable development in the lack of capabilities – scientific knowledge, information and appropriate mechanisms – rather than in the overlap and interaction between the three pillars. The growing involvement of the social sciences, in part because of the issues raised by the re-emerging countries, is now emphasizing that the scope of the impact of human activities on the life support system, consequential on the shift in the population from rural to urban areas, is such that the biophysical and socio-economic forces are interdependent and interconnected across sectors and countries with the trends shaped by levels of development, or urbanization.

The nature of the change with urbanization, industrialization and middle-class levels of well-being, or economic development, involves a fundamental linkage in patterns of natural resource use across international borders. Sustainable development requires modification of certain consumption patterns and 'lifestyles' of urban dwellers, which drive ecological change at the global as well as local

---

[1] Parts of this chapter were first published in Sanwal (2012, 2014a, 2014b).

level. Historical experience is the relevant factor to identify patterns, trends and drivers of natural resource use that need to be modified. The past, however, will not be a sufficient guide to the future, which requires reshaping collective and individual human behaviour. This perspective suggests a focus on distribution or significant decrease in material consumption in wealthy communities and nations to provide space for the emerging global middle class [Young et al., 2014].

Various concepts exist to describe global environmental constraints: 'carrying capacity', 'guardrails', 'tipping points', 'footprints', 'safe operating space', 'planetary boundaries', 'protection of the world's life support system' or 'sustainable consumption and production'. They differ in the emphasis they put on scarcity, patterns of use or distribution of natural resources. The choices are essentially political in nature as they will shape goals and targets and emphasize with very different characteristics. These can focus at the local-level ecosystem services, for example, the nexus between food, water and energy, or at global ecological limits, for example, access to adequate carbon budgets and the related provision of telecommunications, transportation, power and water, or at natural resource use for public buildings such as schools and hospitals, infrastructure touches every aspect of the way we live, and all of these elements play a critical role in reducing the gap between the rich and the poor. The different perspectives shape governance of the implementation of the Sustainable Development Goals at the national, local or international levels, and will largely dictate the success or failure of the global sustainable development agenda. These perspectives respond to different dimensions of sustainable development and represent the continuing dialogue between industrialized and emerging countries for a global consensus [UNEP, 2012].

Over the last 60 years, industrialization, urbanization and energy use has led to half the global population achieving middle-class levels of well-being – described as economic development – accompanied by widespread negative environmental and social impacts. A new definition of sustainable consumption and production is needed, as the earlier perspective ignored use and distribution of resources. The current formulation has stressed – 'the use of services and related products, which respond to basic needs and bring a better quality of life while minimizing the use of natural resources and toxic materials as well as the emissions of waste and pollutants over the life cycle of the service or product so as not to jeopardize the needs of further generations' [Oslo Symposium, 1994]. As the remaining global population moves into the middle class, these problems are going to get worse because supply chains are global and consumption patterns in one country can have negative impacts on the biophysical and social environment in neighbouring or even distant ones. Addressing a specific sustainability issue can easily become ineffective when it drives that particular activity to other parts of the world or other parts of a product life cycle. The volume of internationally traded materials has increased over 5 times since 1970, the rise of income inequality is now higher than in the 1970s, and we are reaching ecological limits to absorb waste carbon dioxide because of the consumption patterns of those who are already in the middle class. Patterns of natural resource use are global and need multilateral cooperation to shape their distribution and overcome adverse impacts.

Three important trends have become apparent over the last 10 years. First, attempts to reduce environmental degradation through gains in eco-efficiency, as sustainable production has been defined in industrialized countries, have been reversed by the overall increase in consumption. Second, the focus on environmental problems during production is not enough and problems that arose during the use of products, or consumption, needed to be addressed, as the impacts are different. Third, advances in technology modifying the life cycle of a product – from conception through consumption and to the end of its life – have not led to better integration across all three pillars of sustainable development. It is now being recognized that the fundamental objective has to be to decouple economic growth as we currently understand it from environmental degradation. A joint report by the McKinsey Global Institute and McKinsey's Sustainability & Resource Productivity Practice, March 2015, shows that the resource challenge can be met through a combination of expanding their supply and a step change in the way they are extracted, converted, and used. Resource productivity improvements that use existing technology would satisfy nearly 30 percent of demand in 2030. Fifteen areas, from more energy-efficient buildings to improved irrigation, could deliver 75 percent of the potential for higher resource productivity. However, the assessment of the value chain from an environmental as well as social perspective is still not questioning the lifestyles of urban dwellers but stressing identifying impacts on local communities, with a focus on the poorest, who are considered to be the most affected by these changes.

By the beginning of the twentieth century, the percentage of the world's urban population had increased to 10 per cent, and during the first decade of the twenty-first century it reached the 50 per cent mark, thus making urban centres for the first time the dominant habitat of humankind. The process of urbanization is considered a mega-trend. But this is not simply a demographic phenomenon. Rather, it is a force which, if effectively steered and deployed, could potentially help the world to overcome some of its major challenges arising from natural resource use. With the world urban population estimated to increase from 3.5 billion today to 6.2 billion in 2050, urbanization constitutes both a challenge and an opportunity for sustainable development.

The United Nations considers 'sustainable urbanization' as an integration tool, as urbanization presents both challenges and opportunities for sustaining development gains in the future; they, however, continue to focus at the local level ignoring drivers, trends and patterns of natural resource use. Urban areas are faced with problems of unsustainable geographical expansion patterns (especially urban sprawl); ineffective urban planning, governance and financing systems; inefficient resource use (especially energy use); poverty, inequalities and slums, as well as inadequate delivery of basic services (including water, sanitation and waste management). Extreme deprivation remains a major concern with 1 billion people living in slums. Cities also continue to be the major contributor to the total greenhouse gas emissions and excessive consumption of natural resources. Despite these challenges, as centres for business and innovation, urban areas are also a source of growth, development and jobs. Urban densities offer opportunities for economies of scale and scope in development efforts, in particular in addressing environmental, poverty, health and education issues. In fact, the positive correlation between urbanization and development has long been recognized and, throughout history, urbanization has been, and continues to be, a source rather than simply an outcome of development.

Today, urban centres account for 70 per cent of the world's gross domestic product (GDP), that is, 55 per cent in low-income countries, 73 per cent in middle-income countries, and 85 per cent in high-income economies. Thus, Governments can use urbanization as a powerful tool for transforming production capacities, income levels, living standards and natural resource use, especially in emerging countries as they are undergoing the transformation. However, this requires a shift in the mindset of the decision makers, away from viewing urbanization as a local problem, towards viewing urbanization as a tool for sustainable development. While in the past, it was sometimes thought that focusing on urban areas could jeopardize the progress made in rural areas by attracting the rural population to urban centres, it is now recognized that urbanization is inevitable.

There is no common understanding of the challenges and opportunities for achieving sustainable development through urbanization. In 2014, the Economic and Social Council focused on urbanization as a part of its overall theme of 'Addressing on-going and emerging challenges for meeting the Millennium Development Goals in 2015 and for sustaining development gains in the future'. Its discussion was general and did not establish a common understanding of the role of urbanization in sustainable development and natural resource use and also did not define the fundamental attributes of the 'sustainable city' that Member States and United Nations system organizations could collectively promote, from the perspectives of their different responsibilities and mandates. It also did not draw policy recommendations that could advance the achievement of the Millennium Development Goals through sustainable urbanization.

Sustainable development has a transformational potential, as it questions current patterns, trends and drivers of natural resource use as well as notions of the absolute sovereignty of states and of individualism, reviving in some ways the old post-colonial development dialogue with its stress on collective benefits. With four-fifths of the world's population, key natural resources and ecosystems and growing economies, the emerging countries are in a position to support a shared understanding of global problems caused by the forces unleashed by the shift of rural populations to urban areas and the industrial revolution with a new global vision for sharing responsibility and prosperity in post-agricultural-industrial societies. This transformation is in line with the core objectives of the Charter of the United Nations 'to save succeeding generations from the scourge of war', 'to promote social progress and better standards of life in larger freedom', 'to employ international machinery for the promotion of the economic and social advancement of all peoples', and 'to be a centre for harmonizing the actions of nations in the attainment of these common ends'.

The concept of sustainable development represents a shift in understanding of humanity's place on the planet from the view that emerged in industrialized countries with the shift of population from agriculture to urban areas, of conquering nature for human well-being. Now, there is a broad agreement that society needs to change, though there are major debates as to the nature of the outcome, the changes necessary and the tools and actors for these changes. In most cases, people bring to the debate already existing political and philosophical outlooks, and use similar words to mean a wide divergence of perspectives on the goals and methods of moving towards sustainable development.

The emerging view, largely in states with large number of rural poor, is that the process of global change is driven by three distinct yet interrelated factors – urbanization, energy/natural resources linkages and scientific and technological advances; interdependence in a globalizing international economy is shaped by patterns of natural resource use; and the direction and nature of human society and civilization is towards greater equality. In this view, the international community in the United Nations is the forum for collective review and management of the process of global change to enable well-being of all.

23.2 Integrated global agenda

Sustainable development goals are now considering people and planet, rather than countries. There is also an ongoing debate within the United Nations whether a sustainable development and a security lens will be needed for dealing with climate change, characterized as the most important challenge of our times. Responding to emerging challenges, scientific consensus and geopolitical shifts, the G8, in their communiqué of 18 June, 2013, have recognized climate change and sustainable development as 'mutually reinforcing', while also describing climate change as a security threat. Emerging countries have yet to formulate a comprehensive response to the new global agenda developing in the four parallel negotiations – in the Climate Convention, General Assembly, Security Council and the G20 – that will take place in the coming years. A strategic view is important because the perspectives of the different countries have political rather than scientific or legal dimensions.

Current strategic thinking in the industrialized countries focuses on the strength of the economy rather than the size of the military as determinants of the influence countries exert in world affairs, as well as the role of global rules in maintaining that influence. The design of new global sustainable development goals provides an opportunity for re-emerging countries with a bold vision to build a coalition and ensure that the new order also serves their interests of supporting the urban transformation and movement of their population into the middle class. The world is at a defining moment much like at the end of World War II when the United States established the multilateral system, putting economic concerns under the Bretton Woods Institutions with 'one dollar one vote' and keeping political concerns in the Security Council where the victors had a veto, while humanitarian concerns went to the United Nations with its 'one country one vote'. The leverage that went with that arrangement is now unravelling – China's aid to Africa exceeds the amount provided by the World Bank, the BRICS have established a New Development Bank for infrastructure development and China has established the Asian Infrastructure Investment Bank. It has also become clear that in a multipolar world, the new global challenges can no longer be dealt with in a fragmented system. A new global vision is needed.

The developed countries in the G7 see the collective response for sustainable development in terms of new rules for intervention to meet environmental risks associated with human security rather than for societal and technological urban transformations. A redefinition of national security is being pushed by raising the question whether traditional roles of national states and international agreements will prove adequate for dealing with the adverse effects of climate change as a 'threat multiplier' or 'catalyst' of conflict in fragile states, vulnerable areas and populations who remain rural. The deliberations in the Security Council mirror those in the other forums and have ignored the complex interactions between human activities, ecological limits and international cooperation.

The policy issue for emerging countries, with China and India in the lead, is whether to continue with the comfortable but fraying principle of environmental law, 'common but differentiated responsibilities and respective capabilities' agreed in 1992, even as the deliberation shifts to other forums, or rephrase their quest for a recognition of diversity that acknowledges the significance of the different concerns coming together around human well-being, rather than human security, and take a more forward looking approach towards the urban transformation. For example, new research, like the World Economic Forum's '*Global Risk Report, 2013*, concludes that severe income disparity is a greater disruptive risk by likelihood and impact than climate change. By shifting the global agenda from the universalism that environmental risk implies as the overriding concern to seeking human well-being within ecological limits, these countries can shape the new global goals to focus on the gaps in the Millennium Development Goals, for example, energy, because eradicating poverty has been central to the agenda of the United Nations since it was established in 1948 with little to show by way of results.

The design of a fair climate agreement is already drawing on the wider scientific and policy debate around new global goals, because keeping global emissions within agreed limits has very different implications for fast growing economies and economies where growth has stabilized. Emissions, standards of living and global ecological limits are inter-linked and cannot be considered in isolation.

First, in the face of continuing reluctance of the industrialized countries to modify longer term trends in consumption and production patterns, which they had committed to under the Climate Convention, and geopolitical shifts in the power of emerging countries, a rigid global environmental perspective giving sole consideration to risk management is giving place to a more flexible national sustainable development perspective of economic growth within ecological limits. Temporarily over-shooting of the global temperature limits using the carbon budget or paths over time rather than an end point is gaining prominence amongst scientists and is likely to be reflected in any new agreement.

Second, fairness is no longer sought to be defined as differentiated commitments for burden sharing but rather in terms of methodologies for reviewing national actions. There is, however, no agreement on whether this would be based on common accounting rules and a consultative process to periodically enhance commitments or reviewing modification of patterns and trends of natural resource use based on levels of development, for example, between 1970 and 2050; environment first came on the global agenda in 1972 at the Stockholm Conference and global growth is expected to continue till at least 2060 before population and growth stabilize. The fear in emerging countries is

Global Sustainable Development Goals | **279**

that international approval should not be accorded to a lack of ambition on the part of industrialized countries to the detriment of the others as energy use reaches the planet's ecological limits before comparable levels in standards of living are achieved and the demographic transition occurs.

China and India are still building their infrastructure and according to BPs forecasts in its *Energy Outlook 2030,* energy use per capita is predicted to increase at a similar rate to that in developed countries in the period 1970–2011, and despite energy intensity of GDP in 2030 being less than half of the level in 1970, incomes and population are expected to drive a 40 per cent increase in global primary energy use. This implies that the international review of national actions should consider national circumstances, or stages of development. The Green Book, produced annually by China Meteorological Administration, in its release on November 6, 2014, articulates this approach – 'by looking into the trend of China's industrialization, urbanization, population growth, energy development and consumption, and employing a historic and systematic approach, it projects that emission peak of China may occur between 2025 and 2035'.

Third, the specificity of the global goals and the monitoring arrangements will depend on the extent to which redistribution, which has so far been kept out of the United Nations, becomes a part of the global agenda. Given the complexity and uncertainty surrounding the environmental, social and economic processes upon which pathways to sustainable development depend, the guiding principle for the new partnership will update the principle of 'common but differentiated responsibilities and respective capabilities' to focus on a functional sharing of responsibility and prosperity. International cooperation will then be seen in terms of sharing technological development and exchanging experiences on societal transformations that will lead to emissions reduction, and not the other way round. The China–US Climate Agreement, November 2014, is an example of the blurring of the post-colonial North–South divide as consensus emerges around a common set of global goals for all countries. Recognizing each other's concerns as a part of the architecture, the agreement moves away from the 40-year-old universalism that international environmental law established, with the resulting divide between countries at different levels of development. The implication is that countries do not have to choose between opposing perspectives, and groups, and this understanding may well spill over into other areas, like the sustainable development goals.

23.3 Redefining national security

A redefinition of national security has been gaining political momentum worldwide away from state-centred and military-focused definitions raising the question whether traditional roles of national states and international agreements prove adequate for human security. There is as yet no universally agreed definition of environmental security as it involves complex interactions between human activities, ecological limits and international cooperation making it difficult to determine causal relationships other than environmental degradation as a 'threat multiplier', with human security defined in terms of a range of elements such as freedom from threats, disruption of daily lives and resource scarcity.

In the context of growing disagreement on sharing responsibility for climate change, the emerging powers are blamed for these threats in the thinking of analysts in the old powers, by extending what originated as the strategic concern of impact on military operations to international relations. Analysts in Asia, despite considering climate change as a sustainable development concern, have not developed a coherent response by extending this perspective to see these threats in terms of equitably sharing global ecological resources so that development, in all its dimensions, is not constrained. The academic and policy discourse within the United Nations on climate change, sustainable development, conflict and security has so far been highly climate-centric and fails to contextualize climate impacts in relation

280 | The World's Search for Sustainable Development

to other broader processes of urban economic and social change. The strategic community has also ignored current scientific consensus on how to meet the challenge of global change, which focuses on societal dynamics as both the root of environmental problems and the potential solution to them.

The CNA Corporation's Military Advisory Board report, titled 'National Security and the Accelerating Risks of Climate Change', 2014, points out that choices regarding how the finite resources of water, food and energy will be produced, distributed and used will have increasing security implications, given their inextricable links. It identifies climate change as a 'catalyst for instability and conflict,' and concludes that improvements in resilience will be critical in removing long-term risk and that the potential security consequences of climate change should serve as catalysts for cooperation and change, rather than as catalysts for instability and conflict. Climate change is now increasingly being seen as creating new opportunities for multilateral cooperation.

This brings new light on the question of the link between poverty and conflict. The report of the Intergovernmental Panel on Climate Change, in 2014, has warned for the first time that climate change, combined with poverty and economic shocks, could lead to war and drive people to leave their homes. However, in the on-going negotiations on Sustainable Development Goals, many emerging countries are against the inclusion of a goal on 'peaceful and inclusive societies, rule of law and capable institutions', arguing that notions of fragile states shifts the focus away from sustainable development and includes security issues that are under the purview of the Security Council. The global community should really be looking at the global dimensions of patterns and trends of natural resource use as a means of channelling aid to the Least Developed Countries, who are also the most vulnerable. The least developed countries (LDCs) are a group of countries that have been classified by the UN as "least developed" in terms of their low gross national income (GNI), their weak human assets and their high degree of economic vulnerability; since 1971 only four countries have graduated from this list - Botswana, Cape Verde, Maldives and Samoa.

23.4 Reviewing governance reform

The United Nations High Level Panel of Eminent Persons on the post-2015 global agenda argued that sustainable development governance is best seen as a stand-alone goal that would help accomplish 'a fundamental shift – to recognize peace and good governance as core elements of well-being, not optional extras', broadening the scope of development to include peace. The argument is that longer term transformations required in the twenty-first century will include the capacity of institutions to engage in long-term planning for sustainable development as well as planetary stewardship, to deal with interconnected social, physical and regional problems of global ecological limits [UNEP, 2013]. These are challenges shared by countries at all stages of development as the poor rural population shifts to cities and adopts middle-class consumption, that is, at every point of the economic growth spectrum. Discussions on this issue have so far been limited to 'means of implementation', stressed by emerging countries, or 'rule of law', stressed by industrialized countries. The deliberations are likely to move towards fragility at the national level and equitable governance and reform of the multilateral political and economic system, including bringing issues of redistribution onto the agenda of the United Nations.

The political challenge is to create a new global framework – in the form of a common global vision, goals and rules. The voting rights and shares in many international institutions reflect the world as it was after the Second World War and not the world as it is today. This imbalance has to be addressed so that global institutions can speak with greater legitimacy. At the same time, today's emerging economies will need to take greater responsibility for global public goods more generally.

The ethical foundation of sustainable development is equity, or convergence of living standards: that all of the world should enjoy similar benefits of human knowledge, technology and well-being. It is also true that emerging countries will not be able to sustain economic growth simply on the basis of the same technologies, business models and lifestyles as the industrialized countries and will need sharing of technological innovation as a first step to developing the capacity for strategic analysis. For example, the world needs a new low-carbon energy system that uses fewer natural resources, and it is the responsibility of all countries to jointly enable that transformation.

Emerging countries, as their rural population shifts to urban areas, cannot deal with the crisis in the earth system themselves because rising urban demand for resources is less a consequence of population growth and more a product of rising incomes and associated global consumption in all cities worldwide and requires that citizens of all nations make the transition to sustainable lifestyles. So far research has been focused on reducing extreme poverty in emerging countries rather than supporting and enabling their shift into the middle class in cities, and that focus has been on local resource use rather than global asymmetry in power for control of the key natural assets. Right now, in emerging countries, poor groups – forest dwellers, smallholders, pastoral livestock keepers, fisherfolk – are being squeezed out and left without land or livelihood, while later as the shift to urban areas gets underway in these countries they will be affected by the scarcity of global ecological resources, like the carbon budget. Life on Earth is dependent on a basic life-support system, while the food–water–energy nexus has local impacts energy use in urban areas plays a key role in urbanization and is affected by global ecological limits.

Cities currently occupy only 2 per cent of the earth's land, yet account for 60 to 80 per cent of energy consumption and 60–75 per cent of carbon emissions, and as the shift continues, some estimates suggest that by 2030 $40 trillion will need to be invested in urban infrastructure worldwide. As incomes and consumption grow, there will be a bigger resource gap between what is available from domestic resources and what is consumed. This means that market forces now stretch into most parts of the world, conferring global market values on land, water, energy, forests and minerals. For example, between 2005 and 2010, Chinese food imports grew by 24 per cent a year, China now imports 60 per cent of global soy bean production and more than 40 per cent of the United States maize crop is currently being used for production of bio-ethanol. Traded goods and services already constitute 60 per cent of world production, indicating the very high level of interconnectedness between national economies, and the role of trade in balancing locations of urban demand with sources of rural supply. By 2030, over 80 per cent of the world's 4.8 billion middle class is projected to be living in cities in Asia, Africa and Latin America, adding a very different dimension to patterns, trends and drivers of natural resource flows and to trade [IIED, 2013].

Economic growth over the last 20 years, which has taken place largely in cities, has doubled real global GDP. The number of corporations with sales turnover exceeding U.S. $25 billion (inflation-adjusted 2010 dollars) increased from fewer than 20 in 1970 to 320 in 2010. The combined receipts of top 20 public and private corporations by annual revenue add up to about United States $5.8 trillion, or 10 per cent of global GDP. Of these, 10 of the top 20 are in the oil and gas business, with combined turnover of United States $3.4 trillion, followed by motor vehicles ($662 billion) and commodities ($483 billion) – reflecting patterns of natural resource use. Aid continues to remain a significant component, at 40–60 per cent of government budget expenditure, only in the Least Developed Countries[2]. Investment flows and private finance already dwarf overseas development assistance, and is part of the geopolitical shift taking place with multilateral financial institutions losing their leverage in influencing multilateral negotiations and global governance.

---

[2] The first group of LDCs was listed by the UN in its resolution 2768 (XXVI) of 18 November 1971 and since then only four countries have graduated out of this category; currently there are 48 countries designated as LDC's.

There has been a similar shift in spending in the industrialized countries from public and into private-sector financed research, so that most of the cutting edge science and its results are now under private ownership, protected globally and rewarded by the intellectual property and patents system. One perspective is that too much protection is assured, offering super-profits to investors. Others argue that insufficient investment is now coming forward to ensure a pipeline of new discoveries, especially in fields such as pharmaceuticals – based on biological diversity – making the world ever more vulnerable to major diseases and the risk of antibiotic resistance. For global well-being, the strategic issue with respect to technology is really to ask whose knowledge and priorities count in deciding where resources will be invested, and who controls research resources. For example, China, India and Brazil have invested further in public-sector agricultural research, seeing the value for their own economies in getting higher productivity and incomes from this sector, and with characteristics of global public good.

Another sign of change is that traditional indicators such as GDP that form the backbone of national income accounts do not place any value on the depletion of natural resources or social capital. Alternative accounting methods, such as those used in the internationally agreed System of Environmental-Economic Accounts, are emerging but national accounts based on GDP still remain dominant. Countries are also experimenting with indices that capture broader social progress include the Human Development Index of UNDP, the Gross National Happiness Index in Bhutan, the Sufficiency Economy in Thailand, and the Harmonious Society and Circular Economy in China. Asia has taken the lead in investing in collecting new data and developing alternative metrics of well-being, because there is where urbanization has advanced considerably.

In response to these shifts, new global rules will be needed to ensure that both urban centres and urban governance play a central role in building a fairer more sustainable world. Part of these rules will involve the new accountability of multinational companies, the main drivers of the world economy today, as the majority will now be located in cities in Asia. The technological challenge is also clear: consciously steer the direction of technological change rapidly and on a global scale for developing an effective global partnership through joint research, by shifting industrial-age technologies to new information-age technologies, in energy, food production, transport, finance, health, education, and other sectors.

Research initiatives such as Future Earth, a 10-year programme coordinated by the International Council for Science, are refining our understanding and targets to provide sustainable solutions for human well-being. There are many gaps and uncertainties in our knowledge of global environmental risks and how to enable societies to become resource-efficient, sustainable and wealthy within global ecological limits. A first step is for policymakers to embrace a unified environmental and social framework in the design and implementation of the Sustainable Development Goals, so that today's advances in development are not lost as the planet ceases to function for the benefit of the global population which has so far been deprived of the fruits of urbanization, industrialization and middle-class levels of well-being.

Alongside shifts in political power have been shifts in ideas, currently for national level reform but increasingly looking at global change. China, India and Brazil provide an alternative development model to the Washington 'Consensus' for the other emerging countries, in which governments, infrastructure and information and biotechnology play a more central role. Many innovations now stem from outside the developed countries, such as agricultural research in China and Brazil, mobile banking in Kenya, the experiences of BRAC, one of the largest enterprises in Bangladesh and now working in 12 African nations, and the design of social protection programmes in Brazil and India. South–South connections are expanding greatly on the business, political and investment front. Investment flows are growing in a similar manner, and three-quarters of all foreign exchange reserves acquired in the period 2000–11 were accumulated by the emerging countries. These very real shifts are leading to a more equal world where the way the issues were framed 40 years ago is being questioned – Is the strategic issue in the global crisis natural resource scarcity and planetary boundaries, or should the debate be around distribution and use and who manages and controls resources? How does a shift from a local or community-based perspective change to analysing global historical patterns of change the analyses and prospects? How can emerging countries use the rapid urbanization ahead to build sustainable cities and secure the transformation to sustainability? [IIED, 2013].

Emerging countries, particularly in Asia, will have to think about global ecological limits in new ways. In an interdependent and multipolar world, global strategies are more likely to be based on negotiated political agreements in the United Nations High Level Policy Forum that has replaced the Commission on Sustainable Development, rather than legally binding commitments in the Climate treaty. As China reshapes its urban future, with its planned urbanization over the next 5 years involving 250 million farmers, and its willingness to lead by example in reforming global financial institutions with the establishment of new banks, rather than the United States defending the current arrangements, will determine the outcome and the new global rules. It may well be a complete break with the past, equitable and democratic. By agreeing to cap its carbon dioxide emissions, China is showing the strategic planning this role requires; unlike the United States in the 1970s, this approach is not based on ensuring cheap flow of commodities but on renewable energy technology.

There is as yet no overarching common vision of the future. The main problem with the process for agreeing on global sustainable development goals has been identified by social scientists as the absence of a common understanding on how broader social change will take place. The 'ultimate end' of the SDGs in combination is not clear, nor is how the proposed goals and targets would contribute to achieving that ultimate end; how achieving specific goals would lead to broader social change and in terms of how this change actually takes place. There is no clear means-ends continuum or 'theory of change' underpinning the framework. It has been suggested that this meta-goal of what would the world look like once all the goals are fully achieved, should be 'a prosperous, high quality of life that is equitably shared and sustainable' [ICSU, ISSC, 2015].

At the global level, the issue that must be debated is how a continually growing economic system will fit within a finite ecological system, and identify areas for innovation as well as longer term trends in production and consumption patterns that need to be modified to raise standards of living. Given the complexity and uncertainty surrounding the environmental and economic processes upon which pathways to future well-being depend, the guiding principle for the new partnership should be 'sharing responsibility and prosperity' to enable a societal transformation. The focus will then be on political agreements in the United Nations General Assembly rather than on legal commitments in an environmental treaty or enforcement through the World Trade Organization and the Security Council. All the organs of the United Nations should now consider the transformation to sustainability by modifying consumption and production patterns, as the central item in their agenda. This will really amount to going back to the beginning, as scientists in the United States, studying the global impact on natural resources of the urbanization process of the United States, had come to this very same conclusion in 1972.

References

ICSU, ISSC (2015): Review of the Sustainable Development Goals: The Science Perspective. International Council for Science, Paris.

IIED. 2013. 'Future World? Addressing the Contradictions of Planet, People, Power and Profits'. IIED Discussion Paper, International Institute for Environment and Development, May 2013, London.

IRENA. 2014. *RE Map 2030: A Renewable Energy Roadmap*, International Renewable Energy Agency, Abu Dhabi.

OECD. 2013. *Looking to 2060: Long Term Global Growth Prospects*. OECD, Paris.

Oslo Symposium. 1994, *Oslo Roundtable on Sustainable Production and Consumption, Norwegian Ministry of the Environment. Oslo, Norway.*

Sanwal, Mukul. 2012. 'Rio +20, Climate Change and Development: The Evolution of Sustainable Development (1972–2012)'. *Climate and Development* 4 (2): 157–166.

Sanwal, Mukul. 2014a. 'Global Sustainable Development Goals Are about the Use and Distribution, Not Scarcity of Natural Resources: Will the Middle Class in the USA, China and India Save the Climate as Its Incomes Grow'. *Climate and Development* 4 (4).

Sanwal Mukul. 2014b. Post-2015 Global Agenda: Are the Political Decisions on Climate Change Shifting to a New Forum in the United Nations as It Comes Together with Sustainable Development and Security? *Climate and Development* 6 (2).

UNEP. 2012. *Global Outlook on SCP Policies: taking action together*, co-financed by the European Commission, United Nations Environment Programme.

UNDESA. 2013. A New Global Partnership: Eradicate Poverty and Transform Economies Through Sustainable Development, the Report of the High-Level Panel of Eminent Persons on the Post-2015 Development Agenda. United Nations Department of Economic and Social Affairs. United Nations.

UN HABITAT. 2013. *Global Report on Human Settlements 2013 – Planning and Design for Sustainable Urban Mobility*, United Nations Human Settlements Programme (UN-Habitat).

Young, Oran R., Arild Underdal, Norichika Kanie, Steinar Andresen, Steven Bernstein, Frank Biermann, Joyeeta Gupta, Peter M. Haas, Masahiko Iguchi, Marcel Kok, Marc Levy, Måns Nilsson, László Pintér and Casey Stevens. 2014. Earth System Challenges and a Multi-Layered Approach for the Sustainable Development Goals. POST 2015/UNU-IAS Policy Brief #1. Tokyo: United Nations University Institute for the Advanced Study of Sustainability.

Transformative Impact of the Re-Emergence of China

24

The transformative change over the last 40 years has been the re-emergence of China as the world's largest economy, leading to a reconsideration of the way we understand the world, global governance, the process of natural resource use and human well-being. In this period, China's economy has increased over 18 times, more than 680 million have been lifted out of poverty and the increase in its annual average per capita GDP from around $300 to $7000 has reshaped the world economy and geopolitics leading to the emergence of a multipolar world order. In 2015, China's outward foreign direct investment is likely to exceed its inward flows, powerfully symbolizing the degree to which China has matured as a global economic power. China has catalysed new financial institutions in Asia, where two-third of future global growth is going to take place, directly challenging the Bretton Woods institutions established by the United States after World War II. At the meeting of Asian and African nations in Jakarta to mark the 60th anniversary of a conference that made a developing-world stand against colonialism and led to the non-aligned movement, in April 2015, China called for "a new type of international relations" that leaves the "obsolete ideas" of Bretton Woods institutions in the past. The multilateral system has not been challenged but there is the call for new rules that are not based on universalism and recognize diversity and levels of development as essential elements of the architecture[1].

As the China–US Climate Agreement, signed in November 2014, demonstrates the initial emphasis is on a reframing of global environmental change, climate change and sustainable development because of the magnitude of energy, material and financial resources that will be needed for global well-being to converge around 2050. China's long-term goal is the realization of the 'two centenary goals' – doubling the 2010 GDP and per capita income of urban and rural residents and achieving the renewal of the nation by the 100th anniversary of the Communists gaining power in 2049, even as its carbon dioxide emissions peak by 2030. On March 5, 2015, Premier Li Keqiang announced the "Made in China 2025" strategy as a 10-year guideline to lay the foundation for the next two decades, to boost "innovation in China," as an essential step for the country to achieve medium-high-level economic growth. Premier Li said China will implement the "Made in China 2025" strategy alongside an "Internet Plus" plan, based on innovation, smart technology, the mobile Internet,cloud computing, big data and the Internet of Things. Following this, informatization and industrialization will be unified and priority will be given to restructuring of the traditional manufacturing industry, and support enterprises' mergers and

---

[1] Parts of this chapter were first published in Sanwal (2012, 2013).

reorganization, as well as market competition. Industrialization and informatization will be deeply integrated to make breakthroughs in some key fields for green development. More efforts will also be made to boost the integrated growth of productive services and the manufacturing sector; the 'Beijing Consensus' is replacing the 'Washington Consensus'.

As the largest energy consumer in the world, how China meets the demands of its growing middle class will shape the global energy transformation, determine whether the world meets the challenge of climate change and makes sustainable development a reality: China has already become a global leader in renewable energy [IRENA, 2014a]. Even as its energy consumption increases 60 per cent, it is expected to achieve a 20–30 per cent share of modern renewable energy in its energy mix by 2030. This would be both technically and economically feasible and require an investment of US \$145 billion, and result in savings of between US \$50 billion and US \$228 billion, if benefits from improved health and lower carbon dioxide emissions are factored in. China accounts for two-thirds of global solar panel production, 90 per cent of installed biogas systems, 40 per cent of newly installed wind capacity in 2013, will be fully deploying hydroelectricity, expanding its grid and transmission capacity, undertaking electricity market reform and already provides 2.6 million jobs in its renewable energy sector [IRENA, 2014b].

Five developments are shaping China's urban future.

First, China's urban population is increasing by more than 20 million inhabitants each year. Though farm output remains high, rural living standards have stagnated compared with the cities, and few in the countryside see their future there. The most recent figures show a threefold gap between urban and rural incomes; annual per-capita household electricity consumption in rural China is around 200 kWh, 8 times less than in large coastal cities and about 5 per cent of the United States average [Zhao 2011]. China has now unveiled a new blueprint for economic reform with agricultural policy as a central focus and leading to increased incomes and food self-sufficiency despite the urbanization [UN Habitat, 2013].

Second, China has also begun implementing some innovative measures in the cities focusing on the sector where carbon dioxide emissions are increasing most rapidly globally. For example, a 5-year Clean Air Action Plan (2013–2017) for Beijing rules that out of the 600,000 new vehicles to be allowed in the city in the next 4 years, 170,000 should be battery electric, plug-in hybrid or fuel cell vehicles, and in 2014, a quota of 20,000 new car registrations will be given to such vehicles [McKinsey Global Institute, 2013].

Third, China is moving into the post-industrial services and knowledge-based economy and society, which is much less natural resource intensive in securing middle-class levels of well-being. Biotech, pharmaceutical, consumer electronics, medical tech, drones, graphene, and tele-communications equipment are just some of the sectors where aggressive Chinese midsize companies lead the way in their field [KPMG International, 2014].

Fourth, by 2035, China is projected to consume 70 per cent more energy than the United States, while on a per capita basis, its energy consumption will be half of levels in the United States [IEA, 2012]; China's population in 2050 is expected to be at the same level as today. According to the International Energy Agency, 38 per cent of the cumulative emission reductions required by 2050 could come from efficiency improvement, making energy efficiency essentially a fuel [IEA, 2014].

Fifth, China recognizes that for society to urbanize, maintain human well-being and successfully pursue together the larger quest for global sustainability deep social transformation is needed. Ecological civilization is part of China's search for a revived Confucianism is enabling individual self-transformation with social values that are not based on monetary, and Western, values [Osnos, 2014].

This approach to focus on infrastructure has impacts on world commodity prices and flows different in scale to the arrangements that led to urbanization and well-being in the industrialized countries. Over the past century, there have only been three periods of widespread commodity price increases – in the early 1950s, in the early 1970s and since 2002. The increases in the twentieth century were short-lived, each of 2–3 years duration, the recent one in the twenty-first century, continued till 2012, because in China, the most important user sector is not manufacturing but construction and infrastructure and prices reflect demand instead of the earlier trend of relying on international agreements and arrangements which kept prices from rising. For example, China buys nearly 40 per cent of Chile's copper, and its demand helped push copper prices from $1 to $4 a pound. In 2010, Chinese lending to Latin America roughly equalled that of the World Bank, the Inter-American Development Bank and the United States Ex-IM Bank combined. The increase in global commodity prices has also had major implications for Africa's resource-rich economies; China's trade with Africa in 2012 at $198 billion was double that of the United States, four-fifth of which constituted crude oil, raw materials and resources. Chinese companies are interested not only in raw materials but also in vast public works to transport the raw materials, including rail links across Brazil and a proposed $50 billion, 171-mile canal across Nicaragua. One result has been the creation of regional production chains to serve regional markets; for example, buying commodities and investing in solar panels in the region, sharing prosperity.

China considers 'ecological civilization' a governing idea and national strategy for the whole society. The effort is to shift from industrialization led economic development and urbanization to a services and high technology led development and urbanization, which will also stress the services provided by ecological systems along with resource conservation and efficiency to ensure that waste and pollution from production and living are within ecological limits [China Human Development Report, 2013]. The 18th Party Congress, in 2012, incorporated in the Party Constitution the statement that 'promoting ecological progress is a long term task of vital importance to the people's well-being and China's future ... key principles entail conserving resources, protecting the environment and promoting its natural restoration ... the objective is to work hard to build a beautiful county, and achieve lasting and sustainable development of the Chinese nation'.

A century ago, the economist Thorstein Veblen coined the term 'conspicuous consumption' to characterize the materialism of newly well-to-do Americans. In 1976, Daniel Bell, in 'The Cultural Contradictions of Capitalism' argued that capitalism undermines itself because it nurtures a population of ever more self-gratifying consumers. The term 'conspicuous accomplishment' has been suggested for China's young nouveaux riches, which typically work hard and want to establish their social status not only through what they wear but also through what they do. The compressed time frame and memories of previous austere lifestyles are leading to behaviours and expectations different to those in the industrialized societies, in terms of urban spaces, social status, lifestyles and identities [LiAnne, 2014].

24.1 Urbanization as the global mega trend

There are three related yet distinct global trends – urbanization, energy, and the middle class – which depend on natural resource use with a global impact, and the degree to which resource use causes adverse environmental impacts depends more on the types of resources used and the ways in which they are used than on the amount of resources used. A comparison with the United States shows the transformative changes that have taken place and are going to take place in China's 'urbanization plan 2014–2020', which aims to integrate 'ecological civilization into the entire urbanization process'. For example, the average U.S. citizen consumes more than four times the electricity of the average Chinese; in the United States, floor space per inhabitant is roughly twice and energy use per square meter of floor area in the residential sector is three times that in China. Car ownership is 10 times higher in the United States than in China; though the difference is declining China has much lower emissions per car and stronger vehicle emission standards [Climate Action Tracker, 2014].

Refrigeration

Lifestyles of the middle class influence the choice and consumption levels of energy and materials, and vary significantly across countries. For example, cooling is responsible for 15 per cent of global emissions worldwide. The United States currently has 10 cubic feet of cold storage per capita, and China currently has one-third of this space. The difference lies in what is known in the logistics business as the 'cold chain' – the seamless network of temperature-controlled space through which perishable food is supposed to travel on its way from farm to refrigerator. In the United States, at least 70 per cent of all the food eaten each year passes through a cold chain, and refrigeration in the United States has tended to merely change when the waste occurs, impacting on the use of energy. Americans throw away 40 per cent of their food, and nearly half of that waste occurs at the consumer level, meaning in retail locations and at home. Over the longer time frame, the cold chain encourages consumers to buy more than they are going to eat. Americans have become so used to associating refrigeration with freshness that soy-milk manufacturers have actually paid extra to have their product displayed in a refrigerated case, despite the fact that it is perfectly shelf-stable. In Europe and North America, there is nearly 15 times the level of wastage of food compared with Asia and Africa.

In China, less than a quarter of the country's meat supply is slaughtered, transported, stored or sold under refrigeration. The equivalent number for fruit and vegetables is just 5 per cent. In its Development Plan for Cold-Chain Logistics of Agricultural Products, China set itself the 5-year goal of reducing the loss rate for vegetables, meat and aquatic products to less than 15 per cent, 8 per cent and 10 per cent, respectively, by 2015, by modifying social habits and through energy efficiency. If the nation achieves those targets, the effort could save a large part of the more than $32 billion in food that is now wasted. Nearly half of everything that is grown in China rots before it even reaches the retail market. For all the food waste that refrigeration might forestall, the uncomfortable fact is that a fully developed cold chain (field precooling stations, slaughterhouses, distribution centres, trucks, grocery stores and domestic refrigerators) requires a lot of energy. In the 12 years between 1995 and 2007, China's domestic refrigeration ownership increased from 7 to 95 per cent of urban families. China had 250 million cubic feet of refrigerated capacity in 2007 and is expected to be 20 times this figure in 2017. Driven by urbanization demand for refrigeration services have increased by more than 30 per cent year-on-year in China's major coastal cities. Efforts are underway to reduce consumption of this electricity by 25 per cent by designing an energy-efficient, automated control system.

The evidence so far is that the Chinese will not follow the lifestyle of the United States, where the size of the average domestic refrigerator has increased by almost 20 per cent since 1975. This development leads to the 'full-cupboard effect', as supermarkets are usually a long drive from a home and to conserve gas one has a tendency to stockpile food in not just one but in multiple refrigerators with additional wastage, something that is not evident in Chinese homes. There is also evidence that not all Chinese are ready to embrace the refrigeration revolution, as they continue to prefer the regional variety and specificity of Chinese fruits and vegetables rather than the homogeneous American produce aisle, which is often limited to three tomato varieties and five types of apple for sale, all hardy (and flavourless) enough to endure lengthy journeys and storage under refrigeration, and individual unpacked food is always more expensive than packed food, which is not the case in China [Twilley, 2014].

Residential electricity

Residential electricity consumption in China is also likely to remain well below levels in industrialized countries. Demand has not grown despite growth in the housing sector, with only 13 per cent of total use, and the consumption breakdown has remained relatively static for a decade. Some 300 million moved to cities in 1990–2010 and a further 300 million are expected to move from rural to urban areas in 2010–2030, and in 2011, the decision was taken to construct 36 million low cost dwelling units by 2015. Future urbanization is also not going to be led by heavy industry but by 'emerging strategic industries' – energy conservation and environment protection, new information technology, bio-industry, high-end equipment manufacturing, renewables and alternative energy, new materials and new energy vehicles – which will make cities more 'eco-efficient'.

Infrastructure

There are three significant differences in infrastructure development in China compared with the United States. Without large-scale infrastructure investment, especially in transport, the productivity gains that enabled America's emergence as an industrial power would not have been possible. Similarly, China's massive infrastructure investment is contributing to boosting the country's productive capacity and constitutes a critical contribution to the country's economic modernization, while adopting a very different approach. First, the total value of infrastructure investment in China amounts to only about 240 per cent of GDP, less than half of Japan's 551 per cent – and with a much younger population. China's capital stock remains below $10,000 per capita; that figure is above $90,000 in the United States and more than $200,000 in Japan (at 2011 prices). Second, institutional innovation has enabled the reconstruction of hundreds of Chinese cities, connected by airports, highways, high-speed rail, and advanced telecommunication systems. Supported by these structures and linkages, one-third of Chinese cities have already attained per capita GDP of more than $10,000. Third, roughly 1 per cent of China's population – about 10–12 million people – are migrating to cities each year, and levelling the infrastructure gap enlarges the range of options from which people and companies can choose when deciding where to live or establish factories and offices making for a more resilient economy in the long run.

Building codes

China has a rapidly growing building stock, including rapid urban development and demolition of older buildings, and new building energy codes are highly effective at reducing energy consumption. China's building energy efficiency standards require new buildings to be up to 65 per cent more efficient than buildings from the early 1980s. China also has enforcement mechanisms that include incentives and penalties for non-compliance; the energy efficiency policy is driven at the federal level and carried out by provinces and municipalities. Several building labelling efforts are led by China's Ministry of Housing and Urban-Rural Development (MOHURD), which has developed an official Chinese Green Building Design Label also known as 'Three Star' to certify and rate buildings. Labelling in China is mandatory for many commercial buildings including large office buildings and those undergoing publicly funded retrofits. China also has mandatory appliance and equipment standards and a labelling program that covers a significant number of products.

Transportation

China has a clear vision and strategy on how the mobility systems should look in the future. China's railway system is the world's third largest network, with 6 per cent of the world's track length carrying about 25 per cent of the world's traffic. It is expected that China will lay about 16,000 km of high-speed rail by 2020 adding to the 10,000 km at present. China is also investing heavily in metro and light rail systems, particularly in some of its larger cities, and is expected to have 3,000 km of urban rail networks by the end of 2015. Such policies to promote public transit and freight shipment through rail are helping improve the energy conservation and efficiency of its transportation system.

In China, 72 per cent of travel is completed by public transit; in United States, it is 10 per cent, in the EU, 17 per cent and in Japan, 37 per cent. The ratio of rail versus road or investment in rail transit in China is 0.94 compared with United States 0.004. The United States stands out negatively in this metric with an average Vehicle Miles Travelled (VMT) per person that is more than twice that of most countries and is 30 per cent greater than the next highest country, Australia. China has a VMT of 510, compared with Japan 3,000, Germany 4,600 and United States 9,300; India has an exceptionally low VMT per capita reflecting its low state of urbanization and high state of poverty. While supply-side improvements are being undertaken by cities, including expansion and improvements of public transport and integrated ticketing and fares policies, congestion charging and cycling pathways, the more effective number plate auctioning is being implemented in Beijing and Shanghai (and Singapore).

Energy intensity

China has a goal to reduce energy intensity, the European Union has an energy-savings goal, and the United States has no national energy-saving targets. China also scores well on its energy intensity in residential and commercial buildings, appliance and equipment standards, and appliance and equipment labelling and is followed by Germany. The United States, once considered an innovative and competitive world leader, has moved slowly, while China, Japan and European countries have surged ahead in energy efficiency [Young et al., 2014].

Diet

The impact of urbanization will not be disruptive as China's food production and consumption are expected to stabilize after 2030. Unlike other East Asian and developed countries food self-sufficiency will still be above 97 per cent for rice and wheat, balance of supply-demand for pork, the most important animal product, fishery products, poultry and eggs; only feed grain may need to be imported. China has scope to increase grain production capacity [The World Bank, 2014].

Per-capita emissions and energy use

In 2000, China's emissions were 40 per cent below the United States, China surpassed the United States in 2008 and its emissions in 2014 are 60 per cent higher than the United States, with per capita emissions half those of the United States. It is expected to reach saturation levels in development of infrastructure by 2030 and carbon dioxide emissions because of its energy policy, urban design, role of high-speed rail, urban metro's and 'lifestyles' very different to that in the developed countries. China's per capita carbon dioxide emissions are remarkable in their relatively 'flat' path of development indicating that per capita emissions may not increase significantly despite rising per capita GDP. These policies, actions and behaviour provide the confidence to China to announce that it will cap its carbon dioxide emissions in 2030 while its per capita well-being of 2010 levels doubles by 2030 and again doubles by 2050.

Forty years after the 'common concern' for the transition to global sustainability came on the global agenda a new paradigm is emerging as China plans to shift 250 million from rural areas to dense urban clusters on the lines of New York City, where emissions are one-third of the average in the United States. China already has 10,000 km of high speed rail equal to the length of interstate highways in the United States, modifying a critical global trend in natural resource use. This explains why China, with four times the population, uses just three-fourth more energy than the United States, as the per capita energy consumption and carbon dioxide emissions are less than half the level in the United States. The major reason is that the carbon dioxide emissions per capita from transportation in the United States are 12 times higher than in China, constituting one-third and one-tenth of total emissions, respectively, and China has begun to limit vehicle ownership in major cities [WSJ, 2013]; China's industry is also on average more energy efficient – cement is produced with less emissions per tonne of cement in China compared to the United States.

Energy technology development

China is already the world's largest energy consumer, but its energy use is rising only two-third as fast as real GDP. In 2005–2011, there was a 33 per cent gain in energy efficiency and the target for 2011–2015 is another 15 per cent gain, which is achievable. The policy focus is clear that future growth will be of non-traditional fuels, which are currently growing 20 per cent faster and expected to be 4 times faster than growth of traditional energy. The world's biggest nuclear power programme is underway with 17 reactors operating, 29 under construction and 51 one gigawatt plants planned. China is becoming the world leader in solar and wind, with wind far bigger than solar in size, surpassing the United States. Massive new R&D programmes are underway in manufacturing and transmission. The Energy Development Strategy Action Plan (2014–2020), announced in November 2014, has the aim to keep annual coal consumption below 4.2 billion tonnes by 2020. In 2013, China consumed 3.61 billion tonnes of coal, and coal made up 66 per cent of the primary energy mix, and in the new proposed energy mix, the share of natural gas will be raised to above 10 per cent as China has the largest shale gas reserves in the world. China accounts for the highest percentage of patent filings in biofuels, solar thermal and solar PV for the period 2006–2011, and in solar thermal accounting for more than half of applications [WIPO, 2014]. China has the world's largest installed capacity of wind farms. It is the world's leading manufacturer of solar PV modules, and it produces more hydroelectricity than any other country. The significant role that energy efficiency policies and renewable energy use play, along with continuing improvements, will decrease the growth of energy demand leading China on a lower carbon development pathway.

The National Development and Reform Commission of China describe sustainable development as the development of a socio-economic system that can realize low carbon emissions [UNDP, 2014]. In the on-going climate negotiations, China has stressed that solutions will lie in reforming socio-economic systems 'where we invest, consume, and conduct trade in certain patterns and style' [TWN, 2014]. China is successfully reducing the per capita rate of depletion of nature as its population reaches middle-class levels of well-being and it transitions to a service-based economy; its emissions increased only 3 per cent in 2012 after an annual growth rate of 10 per cent over the last decade [PBL, 2013]. More than 70 Chinese smaller cities and counties have dropped GDP as a performance metric for government officials, in an effort to shift the focus to environmental protection and unequal income distribution. The move, which follows a central directive in 2013, is among the first concrete signs of China switching its blind pursuit of economic growth at all costs towards measures that encourage better quality of life. Evaluation will instead be based on raising living standards for poor residents, reducing the number of people living in poverty and shifting the focus to quality of life.

24.2 Stress on modifying consumption patterns: case studies

The re-emergence of China, as well as India, is shaped by adopting a very different trajectory of consumption of natural resources that is not based on industrialization but a services and knowledge economy using resources with greater efficiency and concern for others. The urbanization of India will take further steps towards a knowledge-based economy making the possibility of sustainable development and societal values a reality. China is adopting, and shaping, global best practices in the sustainability transformation and the future demand, as the global middle class triples, and is leading to new social science research asking new questions; China has one of the world's all-time lowest consumption as a share of GDP – about one-third and by comparison the United States secures more than two-third of its GDP from consumption. As the political process engages social science research more closely reports of United Nations bodies and business analysts are producing policy-relevant conclusions that are taking account of this transformation.

We now know that the middle-class label is as much about aspirations as it is about economics – the psychological frame – how people feel about their security and prospects – and the sociological – how they relate to their parents, friends, neighbors and colleagues – are just as important as purely economic criteria of jobs and incomes. The policy focus is, therefore, shifting from the sole focus on energy and incomes to urbanization and middle-class lifestyles, and disentangling the analysis from politics in industrialized countries will be difficult, as the following case studies demonstrate.

CASE STUDY: Energy efficiency

'Young, Rachel, Sara Hayes, Meegan Kelly, Shruti Vaidyanathan, Sameer Kwatra, Rachel Cluett, Garrett Herndon. 2014. The 2014 International Energy Efficiency Scorecard, Report Number E1402, American Council for an Energy-Efficient Economy, Washington, DC.*

The three primary sectors responsible for energy consumption in an industrialized country are buildings, industry, and transportation, and efficiency of electricity generation cuts across these sectors. Countries that use energy more efficiently use fewer resources to achieve similar goals, reducing costs, conserving natural resources, and securing a competitive edge over other countries by making their economies more efficient.

In a recent analysis based on the energy consumed per square foot of floor space in residential buildings, fuel economy standards for vehicles, and energy-efficiency standards for appliances, ratio of energy consumed by a country to its GDP, overall China was the highest-scoring country in terms of performance, while other countries are failing to adopt best practices. The analysis shows that some countries are significantly outperforming others, but the more important finding is that there are substantial opportunities for improvement in all major economies.

China received the maximum possible points for buildings performance metrics due to its low energy use in both residential and commercial buildings. In the research, total energy consumption in buildings was divided by the floor space of the building stock. To normalize these results, differences in seasonal temperatures were factored in by taking average of the total population-weighted heating and cooling degree days for each country, in terms of efficiency of buildings, size of buildings and how heavily buildings are heated and cooled. As a result, the lowest energy intensity does not necessarily equate to the most energy-efficient buildings nor does energy intensity indicate the level of comfort experienced in buildings.

India and China are among the lowest energy per capita but highest energy consumption per unit GDP, and by contrast Spain is ranked the same in both – that is the consumption pattern that China, and India, are aiming to achieve.

CASE STUDY: Food Wastage

FAO. 2013. Food Wastage Footprint: Impacts on Natural Resources, Food and Agriculture Organization, Rome, 2013.

Food wastage ranks as the third top emitter of greenhouse gases (GHG) after United States and China; the FAO estimates that each year, approximately one-third of all food produced for human consumption in the world is lost or wasted. This food wastage represents a missed opportunity to improve global food security, but also to mitigate environmental impacts and resources use from food chains. Today, although there is a wide recognition of the major environmental implications of food production, no study has yet analysed the impacts of global food wastage from an environmental perspective. This FAO study provides a global account of the environmental footprint of food wastage (i.e. both food loss and food waste) along the food supply chain, focusing on impacts on climate, water, land and biodiversity. A model has been developed to answer two key questions: what is the magnitude of food wastage impacts on the environment and what are the main sources of these impacts, in terms of regions, commodities, and phases of the food supply chain involved – with a view to identify 'environmental hotspots' related to food wastage.

The scope of this study is global: the world has been divided in seven regions, and a wide range of agricultural products – representing eight major food commodity groups – has been considered. Impact of food wastage has been assessed along the complete supply chain, from the field to the end-of-life of food. The global volume of food wastage is estimated to be 1.6 Gt of 'primary product equivalents', while the total wastage for the edible part of food is 1.3 Gt. This amount can be weighed against total agricultural production (for food and non-food uses), which is about 6 Gt. Without accounting for GHG emissions from land-use change, the carbon footprint of food produced and not eaten is estimated to 3.3 Gt of CO2 equivalent: as such, food wastage ranks as the third top emitter after United States and China.

Globally, the blue water footprint (i.e. the consumption of surface and groundwater resources) of food wastage is about 250 km3, which is equivalent to the annual water discharge of the Volga River, or three times the volume of Lake Geneva. Also, produced but uneaten food occupies almost 1.4 billion hectares of land; this represents close to 30 per cent of the world's agricultural land area. While it is difficult to estimate impacts on biodiversity at a global level, food wastage unduly compounds the negative externalities that mono-cropping and agriculture expansion into wild areas create on biodiversity loss, including mammals, birds, fish and amphibians.

The loss of land, water and biodiversity, as well as the negative impacts of climate change, represent huge costs to society that are yet to be quantified. The direct economic cost of food wastage of agricultural products (excluding fish and seafood), based on producer prices only, is about U.S. $750 billion, equivalent to the GDP of Switzerland. With such figures, it seems clear that a reduction of food wastage at global, regional, and national scales would have a substantial positive effect on natural and societal resources. Food wastage reduction would not only avoid pressure on scarce natural resources but also decrease the need to raise food production by 60 per cent in order to meet the 2050 population demand.

This study highlights global environmental hotspots related to food wastage at regional and sub-sectoral levels, for consideration by decision-makers wishing to engage into waste reduction. Wastage of cereals in Asia emerges as a significant problem for the environment, with major impacts on carbon, blue water and arable land. Rice represents a significant share of these impacts, given the high greenhouse gas (GHG) intensity of rice production methods (e.g. paddies are major emitters of methane), combined with high quantities of rice wastage. Wastage of meat, even though wastage volumes in all regions are comparatively low, generates a substantial impact on the environment in terms of land occupation and carbon footprint, especially in high income regions (that waste about 67 per cent of meat produced), and Latin America. Fruit wastage emerges as a blue water hotspot in Asia, Latin America, and Europe because of food wastage volumes. Vegetables wastage in industrialized Asia, Europe, and South and South East Asia constitutes a high carbon footprint, mainly due to large wastage volumes. By highlighting the magnitude of the environmental footprint of food wastage, the results of this study – by regions, commodities or phases of the food supply chain – allow prioritizing actions and defining opportunities for various actors' contributions to resolving this global challenge.

294 | The World's Search for Sustainable Development

CASE STUDY: Livestock

Gerber, P.J., Steinfeld, H., Henderson, B., Mottet, A., Opio, C., Dijkman, J., Falcucci, A. and Tempio, G. 2013, Tackling Climate Change through Livestock – A Global Assessment of Emissions and Mitigation Opportunities, Food and Agriculture Organization of the United Nations (FAO), Rome.

The global livestock sector contributes a significant share to anthropogenic GHG emissions, and it can also deliver a significant share of the necessary mitigation effort. The need to reduce the sector's emissions and its environmental footprint has indeed become ever more pressing in view of its continuing expansion to ensure food security and feed a growing, richer and more urbanized world population.

With emissions estimated at 7.1 Gt CO_2-eq per annum, representing 14.5 per cent of human-induced GHG emissions, the livestock sector plays an important role in climate change. About 44 per cent of the sector's emissions are in the form of methane. Emissions from the production, processing and transport of feed account for about 45 per cent of sector emissions. Cattle are the main contributor to the sector's emissions with about 4.6 Gt CO_2-eq, representing 65 per cent of sector emissions. Beef cattle (producing meat and non-edible outputs) and dairy cattle (producing both meat and milk, in addition to non-edible outputs) generate similar amounts of GHG emissions. Pigs, poultry, buffaloes and small ruminants have much lower emission levels, with each representing between 7 and 10 per cent of sector emissions. Beef and cattle milk production account for the majority of emissions, respectively, contributing 41 and 20 per cent of the sector's emissions, while pig meat and poultry meat and eggs contribute, respectively, 9 and 8 per cent to the sector's emissions. Feed production and processing, and enteric fermentation from ruminants are the two main sources of emissions, representing 45 and 39 per cent of sector emissions, respectively. Manure storage and processing represent 10 per cent. The remainder is attributable to the processing and transportation of animal products. Included in feed production, the expansion of pasture and feed crops into forests accounts for about 9 per cent of the sector's emissions. The consumption of fossil fuel along the sector supply chains accounts for about 20 per cent of emissions from this sector.

Emission profiles show that cattle alone account for two-thirds of the sector's emissions. When all ruminants are considered together, this share increases to 80 per cent. At the global level, specialized beef meat production is most emission intensive (67.8 kg CO_2-eq), followed by small ruminant meat (23.8 kg CO_2-eq) and dairy meat (18.4 kg CO_2-eq). Mitigation policies focusing on subsectors where emission intensities are comparatively low but absolute levels of emissions are high would also be highly effective. In these situations, small additional reductions in emission intensity can still yield sizeable mitigation outcomes. This is, for example, the case for milk production in Organization for Economic Co-operation and Development (OECD) countries and pork production in East Asia.

Technologies and practices that help reduce emissions exist but are not widely used. Their adoption and use by the bulk of the world's producers can result in significant reductions in emissions. Emission intensities (emissions per unit of animal product) vary greatly between production units, even within similar production systems. Different farming practices and supply chain management explain this variability. Within the gap between the production units with the lowest emission intensities and those with the highest emission intensities, lies an important potential for mitigation. A 30 per cent reduction of GHG emissions would be possible, for example, if producers in a given system, region and climate adopted the technologies and practice currently used by the 10 per cent of producers with the lowest emission intensity.

Possible interventions to reduce emissions are thus, to a large extent, based on technologies and practices that improve production efficiency at animal and herd levels. They include the use of better quality feed and feed balancing to lower enteric and manure emissions. Improved breeding and animal health help to shrink the herd overhead (i.e. unproductive part of the herd) and related emissions. Manure management practices that ensure the recovery and recycling of nutrients and energy contained in manure and improvements in energy use efficiency along supply chains can further contribute to mitigation. Sourcing low emission intensity inputs (feed and energy in particular) is a further option. Most mitigation interventions can provide both environmental and economic benefits.

Practices and technologies that reduce emissions can often simultaneously increase productivity, thereby contributing to food security and economic development. The potential can be achieved as a result of improving practices rather than changing production systems (i.e. shifting from grazing to mixed or from backyard to industrial).

While many of the mitigation practices are likely to be profitable in the mid-term, public policies should ensure that farmers can face initial investment and possible risks. This is particularly important in least affluent countries. Public and private sector policies also have a crucial role to play in supporting research and development to improve the applicability and affordability of existing technologies and practices and to provide new solutions for mitigation. Significant additional research is also needed to assess the costs and benefits of mitigation options in practice.

The most affluent areas of the globe usually combine low emission intensity per unit of product with high emission intensity per area of land. Here, relatively marginal emission intensity gains can result in a significant mitigation effect, given the sheer volume of emissions. Climate change is a global issue and livestock supply chains are increasingly internationally connected.

CASE STUDY: Mobility

UN HABITAT. 2013. Planning and design for sustainable urban mobility: global report on human settlements 2013. United Nations Human Settlements Programme, Nairobi.

Globally, carbon dioxide emissions from the transport sector have increased by 85 per cent from 3.593 billion tonnes in 1973 to 6.665 billion tonnes in 2007. With respect to the targets of the Kyoto Protocol, the emissions have increased by over 47 per cent during the 1990–2007 periods. There is considerable variation in the amounts of carbon dioxide produced by different countries and regions. A similar variation applies to the emissions from the transport sector. Transport emissions per capita in North America are more than four times the global average, and more than double that in other OECD countries. The carbon dioxide emissions from transportation are much lower in emerging countries, and the emissions in most of Asia and Africa are about a third or a quarter of the global average. Even more striking: while the overall carbon dioxide emissions per capita in the United States are some 2.5 times higher than in China, the carbon dioxide emissions per capita from transportation in the United States are 12 times as high as in China.

The report argues that the development of sustainable urban transport systems requires a conceptual leap. The purpose of 'transportation' and 'mobility' is to gain access to destinations, activities, services and goods. Thus, access is the ultimate objective of all transportation (save a small portion of recreational mobility). The construction of more roads for low-income cities and countries is paramount to create the conditions to design effective transport solutions. However, urban planning and design for these cities and others in the medium- and high-income brackets is crucial to reduce distances and increase accessibility to enhancing sustainable urban transport solutions. If city residents can achieve access without having to travel at all (for instance through telecommuting), through more efficient travel (online shopping or car-sharing), or by travelling shorter distances, this will contribute to reducing some of the challenges currently posed by urban transport. Thus, urban planning and design should focus on how to bring people and places together, by creating cities that focus on accessibility, rather than simply increasing the length of urban transport infrastructure or increasing the movement of people or goods.

The issue of urban form and functionality of the city should be a major focus of urban policy. Not only should urban planning focus on increased population densities; cities should also encourage the development of mixed use areas. This implies a shift away from strict zoning regulations that have led to a physical separation of activities and functions, and thus an increased need for travel. Cities should encourage mixed land use, both in terms of functions (i.e. residential, commercial, manufacturing, service functions and recreational) and in terms of social composition (i.e. with neighbourhoods containing a mixture of different income and social groups).

Such developments also have the potential to make better use of existing transport infrastructure. Most of today's cities have been built as 'zoned' areas, which tends to make rather inefficient use of their infrastructure; as 'everyone' is travelling in the same direction at the same time. In such cities, each morning is characterized by (often severe) traffic jams on roads and congestion on public transport services leading from residential areas to places of work. At the same time, however, the roads, buses and trains going in the opposite direction are empty. In the afternoon the situation is the opposite. Thus, the infrastructure in such cities is operating at half capacity only, despite congestion. In contrast, in cities characterized by 'mixed land-use' (such as Stockholm, Sweden), traffic flows are multidirectional – thus making more efficient use of the infrastructure – as residential areas and places of work are more evenly distributed across the urban landscape.

Furthermore, the report argues with strong empirical information that increased sustainability of urban passenger transport systems can be achieved through modal shifts – by increasing the modal share of public transport and non-motorized transport modes (walking and bicycling), and by reducing private motorized transport. Again, an enhanced focus on urban planning and design is required, to ensure that cities are built to encourage environmentally sustainable transportation modes. While encouraging a shift to non-motorized transport modes, however, the report acknowledges that such modes are best suited for local travel and that motorized transport (in particular public transport) has an important role while travelling longer distances. However, in many (if not most) countries, there is a considerable stigma against public transport. The private car is often seen as the most desirable travel option.

There is thus a need to enhance the acceptability of public transport systems. More needs to be done to increase reliability and efficiency of public transport services and to make these services more secure and safe. The report also notes that most trips involve a combination of several modes of transport. Thus, modal integration is stressed as a major component of any urban mobility strategy. For example, the construction of a high-capacity public transport system needs to be integrated with other forms of public transport, as well as with other modes. Such integration with various 'feeder services' is crucial to ensure that metros, light rail and bus rapid transit (BRT) systems can fully utilize their potential as a 'high-capacity' public transport modes. It is therefore essential that planners take into account how users (or goods) travel the 'last (or first) mile' of any trip. By way of an example, it is not much use to live 'within walking distance' of a metro (or BRT) station, if this implies crossing a busy eight lane highway without a pedestrian crossing, or if one is unable to walk to the station (due to disability, or lack of personal security). Likewise, it is unlikely that urban residents will make use of metros (and BRTs), if the nearest station is located beyond walking distance, and there is no public transport 'feeder' services providing access to these stations or no secure parking options for private vehicles near the stations.

It is essential that travel is recognized as a 'derived demand' – i.e. derived from the need for people to socially and economically 'interact'. The end or objective of most travel is to meet a friend, earn income, attend school or purchase a good, not movement per se. Cars, trains, buses and bikes are simply the means to achieve these ends. Making this distinction shifts the focus to 'people' and 'places' and away from 'movement'. This realization envisages cities, neighbour hoods, regions and mobility systems as tools that promote desired societal outcomes – such as live ability and affordable access – with transport playing a supportive role. Operationally, this can take the form of compact, mixed-use communities that dramatically shorten trip distances and improve pedestrian and bicycling infra-structure. Compact cities are less reliant on private cars and minimize distances travelled, thereby conserving energy, and land and environmental resources. They are also more resilient, enabling them to better adapt to the vagaries and uncertainties of climate change and other global unknowns.

CASE STUDY: Cities

'Climate Change Implications for Cities: Key findings from the Intergovernmental Panel on Climate Change Fifth Assessment Report', May 2014, University of Cambridge, Institute of Sustainability Leadership and ICLEI – Local Governments for Sustainability.

Large amounts of primary resources are used in the initial construction of cities, which contributes to lifecycle emissions. Energy use in human settlements mainly concerns urban areas. Cities account for about 71 per cent of energy related CO_2 emissions, but only 37–49 per cent of global GHG emissions (other sources of GHG emissions are predominantly associated with rural areas). The long lifetime of the built environment limits the speed at which emissions in some sectors (such as buildings and transport) can be reduced.

Substantial new construction in dynamically growing regions presents a great opportunity from a mitigation perspective as emissions can be virtually eliminated for new builds. Approaches in industrialized countries are also generally cost-effective but barriers remain to their widespread implementation. Retrofitting existing buildings can lead to potential reductions in heating energy requirements of 50–75 per cent in single family housing and 50–90 per cent in multifamily housing at costs of about US $100 to 400 per square metre. Emissions from transportation can be reduced by avoiding journeys where possible, a modal shift to low-carbon transport systems, lowering energy intensity by enhancing vehicle and engine performance, and reducing carbon intensity of fuels by substituting oil-based products by natural gas, bio-methane or bio fuels, or with electricity or hydrogen produced from low GHG sources. Options for mitigating emissions in urban areas include

- Increasing the efficiency of buildings, appliances and distribution networks will reduce energy demand. Changes in the awareness and behaviour of residents can also reduce demand. Projections suggest demand may be reduced by up to 20 per cent in the short term and 50 per cent by 2050.
- The greatest potential for mitigating GHG emissions lies in rapidly developing cities in industrializing countries. City-based sectors with potential for mitigation include buildings, energy, transport, and industry. Steps that build resilience and enable sustainable development in urban areas can accelerate successful climate change adaptation globally. Adaptation options exist in areas such as water, food, energy and transport

CASE STUDY: Behavioural Changes

McKinsey Insights
America the frugal: US Consumer Sentiment Survey
December 2014

McKinsey's latest Consumer Economic Sentiment survey in the United States finds that some 6 years after the recession of 2008, because inflation-adjusted median household income has dropped over the past few years, consumers are reluctant to increase spending and are instead remaining thrifty, affecting the American economy which is heavily dependent on consumer spending.

The significant economic pressure that families earning less than $75,000 a year feel has caused many of them to make spending adjustments in order to make ends meet. Roughly 40 per cent of these households say they are making changes, including cutting back and delaying purchases, as compared with 22 per cent of those in households earning at least $150,000 a year.

While the number of consumers cutting back on spending has stabilized, Americans are still pinching pennies in 2014. Decreasing purchases of high-end brands and doing more one-stop shopping to reduce the number of trips are just as popular as they were last year, with 40 per cent of consumers saying they have cut their spending over the past 12 months. An even bigger proportion of Americans (55 per cent) say they continue to look for ways to save money, including paying more attention to prices, using coupons more often, shopping around to get the best deals, and buying more items in bulk.

With food as the second-largest household expense after housing, many Americans say they are cutting back on the most costly eating options: dining at restaurants and ordering takeout. Forty-seven per cent say they have eaten out less often over the past 12 months, on par with those who said this in 2013. Money-saving, in-home dining options, such as eating leftovers, cooking from scratch, and packing lunches from home, remain popular, as consumers discover they like these thrifty dining habits more than they expected.

Throughout the recession consumers saved money on grocery and household products by trading down to less expensive brands, often private-label or store brands. Nearly three-quarters say they do not intend to go back to purchasing more expensive brands. For one-third of Americans, this is because they no longer prefer the more expensive brand, having realized that the cheaper product offers better value for the money than expected and is of higher-than-expected quality. Another 39 per cent of Americans say they would like to buy the more expensive brand, but that doing so is not worth it.

Multiple years of austerity have left consumers with altered views about spending. Almost 40 per cent say they will probably never go back to their pre-recession approach to buying. Twenty-nine per cent say they now have new attitudes and values about spending, a figure that is up from 17 per cent in 2010. An additional 24 per cent claim that their opposition to increased spending is the result of a change in their economic situation.

American consumers continue to cut back on spending by delaying purchases, trading down to lower-priced brands, and eating more meals at home. Cautious spending behaviour is the new normal and is unlikely to change in the near future.

24.3 Weakening natural science framework

Until 1500, Asia accounted for two-thirds of the global GDP, and now a decisive geopolitical geoeconomic shift is taking place in favour of Asia. China's economic transformation resulting from urbanization and industrialization is happening at 100 times the scale and 10 times the speed achieved earlier in the United Kingdom, the first country to urbanize. However, globally around 1.3 billion people still live in extreme income poverty and the human development needs of many more are still not met; more than 1.5 billion people live in countries affected by violent conflict. Over 1 billion of these persons should move to cities over the next 30 years, as the global middle class triples. Patterns of natural resource use in the past have led to a situation where the challenges of meeting the consumption needs of the new middle class for infrastructure, goods and services are universal and interrelated and need to be addressed together by all countries, and it will require all to cut down on consumption for equitable use and distribution of natural resources.

It is in this context that the terms sustainability and sustainable development have become common currency in the international science and policy community. The most frequently cited definition of sustainable development is that of the Brundtland Commission, which in 1987 wrote, among other phrases that 'sustainable development is development that meets the needs of the present without compromising the ability of future generations to meet their own needs'. For many scholars and practitioners, there are three pillars of sustainability: environmental (or ecological), social and economic with others seeing sustainable development as based in a respect for nature, human rights and economic justice. The World Summit on Sustainable Development in 2002 rephrased these concerns from considering development as a technical issue to address the three overarching objectives of sustainable development: poverty eradication, changing unsustainable consumption and production patterns and protecting and managing the natural resource base of economic and social development. Sustainable development is fundamentally about recognizing, understanding and acting on interconnections between the economy, society and the natural environment. However, outside the re-emerging countries, there has been little impact of these shifts on actual policy, while at the multilateral level in a multipolar world nothing can now be done without the full engagement and the final agreement of China.

The earlier neglect of the social dimension of sustainable development has led to social scientists now asserting that the true achievement of sustainable development is human well-being within ecological limits. Social sustainability has not been given sufficient importance even though environmental and social processes interact as part of a single complex system. For example, despite two-third of the services provided by nature – including fertile land, clean water and air – in decline and climate change and biodiversity loss close to the limits beyond which there are irreversible effects on human society and the natural environment, development indicators have shown only some improvement, and about a billion people remain poor and hungry and many more experience chronic threats to their livelihoods, health, and well-being, and inequality is increasing. The global environment has been considered by natural scientists as part of a discrete problem. For example, UNEPs recently published Global Environmental Outlook-5 [UNEP 2012] assesses the state of the environment in different regions, for different sectors and for the world as a whole, and concludes that we are not moving towards sustainability, with only 3 of 90 indicators showing significant improvement. We now know that development is not a technical problem founded on physical problems and the problems raised by global environmental change cannot fully be grasped without understanding the human drivers of change. Nor can the importance of such problems be judged without understanding what they mean for people and in what contexts they unfold.

The most discussed global environmental change is climate change, and even this concern is now stressing human well-being and adopting a sustainable development perspective as the focus shifts to responses; the China–United States Climate Agreement of November 2014 is an example. These challenges are connected to increasing consumption and production, socio-economic globalization, population growth and increasing inequality, requiring innovative policy that challenges existing worldviews, ethics and equity and power dynamics. Efforts have so far stressed incremental change in a situation where transformative change is needed, largely because there is as yet no agreement on the meaning of this transformation and the pathways towards sustainability.

24.4 Emerging social science framework

The fundamental issue in the design of the new global framework, with the integration of climate change and sustainable development goals, is whether in 2050 emerging countries will remain agrarian societies or around three-fourth of their populations would have shifted to urban areas and into the middle class; this shift had taken place in North America, Europe and Japan by 1970. Urbanization and per capita GDP tend to move together as countries develop. Since cities produce three-quarters of global GHG emissions, which are directly related to household consumption – shelter, mobility and food – resource use and carbon emissions are going to increase in these countries, providing both a threat and an opportunity as new cities will be established. With the global middle class expected to triple by 2050 [OECD, 2013] sustainability is being seen in terms of distribution and use, rather than scarcity, of natural resources.

In the current 'anthropocene' era it is the way, not the extent, of natural resource use that has caused the global crisis. Ecological limits, including the global carbon budget, considered in terms of physical quantities are really symptoms of the impact of patterns of natural resource use. How these limits are approached should depend on identifying the drivers and modifying longer term trends in consumption patterns in both industrialized and emerging countries, to reduce per capita levels of resource use and enable well-being of all. The 'World Social Science Report; 2013', also concludes that 'the social sciences must help to fundamentally reframe climate and global environmental change from a physical into a social problem' [ICSSC/UNESCO, 2013], suggesting the need for a new paradigm.

Social scientists are now reframing global sustainability. While the state has traditionally been seen as the guarantor of public and collective goods, there is now a growing role for the private sector, civil society, citizens and consumers. This shift from government to governance is important for social science's understanding of who governs and how governance happens. As the role of government is redefined, there are new practical questions about how the vitality and capacity of various groups in society can be aligned to achieve sustainability goals, while ensuring openness and equity in the distribution of environmental goods and bads. Top-down governance processes can set overarching policy directions and address large-scale drivers of environmental change, but they often fail because they are ignorant of realities on the ground and are not sensitive to national capabilities, perceptions and interests. Bottom-up, participatory approaches, by contrast, are intended to lead to legitimate and effective decisions, but can get stuck because they do not have the power, legitimacy or scope needed to achieve global change. This dichotomy has become particularly acute in the context of climate change and sustainability, where problems and solutions must often span different scales of governance. It remains a challenge to find the right combination of top-down and bottom-up governance, and the right public, private and public – private arrangements to go with them (Future Earth: Research for global sustainability, April 2013).

24.5 Governance focus on use and distribution, not scarcity, of natural resources

With the re-emergence of China and India the world is now at a defining moment, much like at the end of World War II when the United States shaped the international order to serve its interests. China, South Korea, Taiwan, Malaysia and Singapore put early emphasis on industrialization and urbanization to move rural populations into the middle class and Asia has now created a global situation similar to the one in the 1970s, as three-fourth of their population moves into towns. This model, as the Brundtland Commissions stated in 1987, is based on 'economic needs' and not 'political and social rights' and will now be expressed in terms of achieving middle-class levels of well-being. The post-2015 global sustainable development goals are comparable with the Universal Declaration of Human Rights; this time focusing on socio-economic issues, just as environmental concerns are being reframed from considering physical conditions and limits to a focus on urban areas, social issues and human well-being.

For example, New York plans to reduce its GHG emissions 80 per cent by 2050. Nearly three-quarters of the city's emissions come from powering, heating and cooling its 1 million buildings, and they are a primary focus of this initiative. New York is equipping 24 public schools with solar roofs, the first of 300 solar projects the city plans to pursue between now and 2025. New York city currently spends $800 million a year on energy costs, but by retrofitting its own buildings, it expects, by 2025, to save $180 million a year.

Forty years after the global environment came on the agenda of the United Nations geopolitical and geoeconomic shifts with the re-emergence of China, and India, are reshaping the discourse around patterns, trends and drivers of natural resource use as well as the nature and scope of the shift from rural agriculture to urban industry and services and middle-class levels of well-being, and away from the sole focus on the natural resources and extreme poverty. The one clear lesson for action on sustainable development, and what can be done for human well-being, is that the future will be very different to the past, as the focus shifts from access to natural resources to their use and distribution. The reliance will continue to be on the multilateral system, and as distribution has so far been kept out of the agenda of the United Nations, new institutions and rules, this time catalysed by China, will lead to more legitimacy, equity and coherence in the agenda as well as enabling implementation, and go a long way is ensuring that the future of the planet is not at risk. These institutions will largely focus on Asia, as that is where future growth is going to take place, rather than challenging existing global institutions, while supporting new rules that will go on to shape new global rules. Much will depend on how China shapes its 'ecological civilization', urbanization and knowledge economy to cap carbon dioxide emissions in 2030 and reduce natural resource use while doubling per capita GPD by 2050, when its demographic transition will lead to stabilization.

References

Climate Action Tracker. 2014. China and the US: How does their climate action compare? Policy Brief, 21.

China Human Development Report. 2013. Sustainable and Liveable Cities: Towards Ecological Civilization, UNDP, June 2013, China; Beautiful China: Eco-Cities Indicators Guidebook, Bluepath City Consulting, China: TongXin Press.

FAO. 2013a. *Food Wastage Footprint: Impacts on Natural Resources*, Food and Agriculture Organization, Rome.

FAO. 2013b. *Tackling Climate Change through Livestock*, Food and Agriculture Organization, September 2013, Rome.

GEA. 2012: *Global Energy Assessment – Toward a Sustainable Future*, International Institute for Applied Systems Analysis, Laxenburg, Austria, Cambridge University Press, Cambridge, UK and New York, NY.

IEA. 2012. *World Energy Outlook*. International Energy Agency, Paris.

IEA. 2013. *Energy Technology Perspectives*. International Energy Agency, Paris.

IEA. 2014. *Redrawing the Energy-Climate Map: World Energy Outlook Special Report*, International Energy Agency, Paris.

Institute of Sustainability Leadership and ICLEI. 2014. Climate Change Implications for Cities: Key findings from the Intergovernmental Panel on Climate Change Fifth Assessment Report, May 2014, University of Cambridge, Institute of Sustainability Leadership and ICLEI – Local Governments for Sustainability.

IRENA. 2014a. *RE Map 2030: A Renewable Energy Roadmap*, International Renewable Energy Agency, Abu Dhabi.

IRENA. 2014b. 'Renewable Energy Prospects: China', RE map 2030 series, International Renewable Energy Agency, prepared in association with the China National Renewable Energy Centre, Abu Dhabi.

KPMG International. 2014. Future State 2030: The global megatrends shaping governments. KPMG 2014.

LiAnne, Yu. 2014. Consumption in China: How China's New Consumer Ideology Is Shaping the Nation (China Today Series) Polity Press, UK.

McKinsey Global Institute. 2013. Urban World: The Shifting Global Business Landscape., Richard Dobbs, Jaana Remes, Sven Smit, James Manyika, Jonathan Woetzel, and Yaw Agyenim-Boateng. McKinsey Global Institute.

McKinsey Insights. 2014. America the Frugal: US Consumer Sentiment Survey, December 2014.

Sanwal, Mukul. 2012. 'Rio +20, Climate Change and Development: The Evolution of Sustainable Development (1972–2012)'. Climate and Development 4 (2): 157–166.

Sanwal, Mukul. 2013. 'The Rise and Fall of Global Climate Policy: Stockholm to Rio 1992, to Rio + 20 and Beyond'. Chinese Journal of Environmental and Urban Studies 1 (1).

Nordic Council of Ministers. 2013. Improving Nordic Policymaking by Dispelling Myths on Sustainable Consumption, Terma Nord 2013:553.

NRDC. 2012. Wasted: How America is loosing upto 40 per cent of its food from farm to fork to landfill. Issue paper August 2012, IP:12-06-B, Natural Resources Defense Council.

OECD. 2013. Looking to 2060: Long Term Global Growth Prospects. OECD, Paris.

Osnos, Evan. 2014. The Age of Ambition: Chasing Fortune, Truth and Faith in the New China. Farrar, Straus & Giroux.

PBL. 2013. Trends in Global CO_2 Emissions: 2013 Report, PBL Netherlands Environmental Assessment Agency, The Hague.

PCGCC. 2012. Reducing Greenhouse Emissions from US Transportation, Report prepared for the Pew Center on Global Climate Change, Washington.

SEI. 2012. Nilsson, M., Heaps, C., Persson, A., Carson, M., Pachauri, S., Kok, M., Olsson, M., Rehman, I., Schaeffer, R., Wood, D., van Vuuren, D., Riahi, K., Americano, B., Mulugetta, Y.2012. Energy for a Shared Development Agenda: Global Scenarios and Governance Implications. Stockholm Environment Institute.

The World Bank. 2014. 'China Economic Update – June 2014: Special Topic – Changing Food Consumption Patterns in China: Implications for Domestic Supply and International Trade'. World Bank Office, Beijing.

Twilley, Nicolla. 2014. What do Chinese Dumplings have to do with Global Warming. Wall Street Journal.

TWN. 2014. TWN Bonn News Update No.7, 2014.

UNDESA. 2013. Sustainable Development Scenarios for Rio + 20: A component of the SD21 Project, United Nations Department of Economic and Social Affairs, Division for Sustainable Development, February 2013.

UNDP. 2014. 'Low Carbon Development in China and India', United Nations Development Programme.

UN HABITAT. 2013. Planning and design for sustainable urban mobility: global report on human settlements 2013. United Nations Human Settlements Programme, Nairobi.

UNEP. 2012. Urban Land Institute and Ernst & Young. Infrastructure 2013: Global Priorities, Global Insights. Washington, DC: Urban Land Institute, 2013.

WEC. 2013. World Energy Trilemma – Time to Get Real – The Agenda for Change, World Energy Council, Project Partner Oliver Wyman, October, 2013.

WIPO. 2014. Global Challenges Report – Renewable Energy Technology: Evolution and Policy Implications— Evidence from Patent Literature, World Intellectual Property Organization, Geneva.

WSJ. 2013. 'Beijing to Limit Car Ownership to 6 Million'. Wall Street Journal.

Young, Rachel, Sara Hayes, Meegan Kelly, Shruti Vaidyanathan, Sameer Kwatra, Rachel Cluett, Garrett Herndon. 2014. The 2014 International Energy Efficiency Scorecard, Report Number E1402, American Council for an Energy-Efficient Economy, Washington, DC.

Zhao, C., Niu, S., and Zhang, X. 2011. 'Effects of household energy consumption on environment and its influence factors in rural and urban areas'. Energy Procedia 14: 805–11

THE ASIAN CENTURY

The Asian Century: In 2025, two-thirds of the world's population will live in Asia. The population of the European Union will account for less than 7 per cent of the world's population with the highest proportion of people over 65 years old in the world (more than 30 percent of the population). The center of gravity of world production will move towards Asia, reaching more than 30 percent of the world GDP, and would surpass that of the EU, estimated at slightly more than 20 percent. In 2030, the middle class (with an income between 4000 and 17,000 dollars a year) could account for 1 billion people, of which 90 percent will be living in developing countries. If recent trends continue, in 2025, the United States and Europe will have lost their scientific and technological supremacy for the benefit of Asia, and India and China could account for 20 percent of the world's R&D.

'The World in 2025: Rising Asia and Socio-Ecological Transition', European Commission, Directorate General for Research, Socio-Economic Sciences and Humanities, European Communities, 2009.

'By nearly doubling its share of global GDP (at market exchange rates) from 27 percent in 2010 to 51 percent by 2050, Asia would regain the dominant global economic position it held some 250 year ago, before the Industrial Revolution. Some have called this possibility the "Asian Century". ... The key policy implication for all Asian countries is that their future competitiveness and well-being will depend heavily on improving the efficiency of natural resource use and winning the global race to a low carbon future ... a greater focus on personal satisfaction and harmony with nature, rather than more wealth, will be important for the affluent countries. This requires a dialogue within Asia to understand what can be done to improve well-being and what that implies for the region's growth model'

Asia 2050: Realizing the Asian Century, Asian Development Bank, 2011, Manila.

The global economic power shift from the established advanced economies in North America, Western Europe and Japan will continue over the next 35 years. China is already the world's biggest economy in PPP terms and India has the potential to overtake the US as the world's second largest economy in 2050 in PPP terms. In 2014, the third biggest economy in PPP terms (India) is around 50 per cent largest than the fourth biggest economy (Japan). In 2050, the third biggest economy in PPP terms (U.S.) is projected to be approximately 240 per cent larger than the fourth biggest economy (Indonesia). However, income per capita will still be significantly higher in the industrialized economies than the emerging economies in the 2050s.

'The World in 2050', Price Waterhouse Coopers, February 2015.

Moving from Ideas to Reality will Depend on How Asia Structures its Urban Future

25

In 2015, the world stands roughly halfway between the initiation of a global sustainable development policy in the early 1970s and a global vision of middle class well-being within the limits of the planet by 2050. The consumption systems for meeting basic social needs such as food, energy, housing and mobility rely on costly and long-lasting infrastructure, and their production depends on the transformation of natural resources. The transformation of both consumption and production systems, that are at the root of the environmental crisis, has begun with the new model of well-being emerging in China and India. Sustainable development goals are intertwined with the core systems that societies depend on for their welfare and the related transitions in institutions, technologies and lifestyles is moving sustainable development from ideas to reality.[1]

The search for natural resources is a driving force of human well-being. For example, after 1500, as frontiers became global, the rise of the United Kingdom as an industrial nation was enabled by new patterns of resource exploitation – founded largely on the buying and selling of enslaved Africans – that helped move Western Europe economically ahead of natural resource rich, but inward looking, civilizations in China and India [Barbier, 2011]. One-third of the 12 million slaves imported into the United States arrived between 1793 and 1808 and produced 85 per cent of the cotton requirement of the textile mills in Lancshire and when that supply dried up with the Civil War the East India Company expanded its territory into cotton growing areas and within 5 years met the entire requirement from India. As the European market could not sustain the factories cheap milled textiles were introduced into the Indian market; earlier the center of the cotton industry, peasants were made into share croppers producing raw cotton for export to British mills. This industrial revolution was the beginning of the great divergence between the West and the rest. [Beckert, 2014]. After 1950, following World War II, the unprecedented prosperity of the United States was enabled by the multilateral system it established – securing access to commodities at low prices from developing countries emerging from colonialism – as well as the global financial rules that maintained that arrangement; the real price of oil declined in the period 1950–1970 and averaged less than $1.5 a barrel at current prices. The Asia Infrastructure Investment Bank, established by China, in 2014, is

---

[1] Parts of this chapter were first published in Sanwal (2014).

now challenging that arrangement.[2] The international system – as constructed following the Second World War – will be almost unrecognizable by 2025 owing to the rise of emerging powers, a globalizing economy, an historic transfer of relative wealth and economic power back from West to East, and the growing influence of cities. The players are changing, but so too are the scope and breadth of transnational issues important for continued global prosperity. Aging populations in the industrialized world; growing energy, food, and water constraints; and worries about climate change will limit and modify what will still be a historically unprecedented age of prosperity [NIC, 2008].

Concern for the global environment emerged in the 1970s as a response to patterns, trends and drivers of natural resource use. Following the shift of three-fourth of their population to the urban middle class, the United States in 1972 developed a conceptual framework to manage the global environment in terms of shared values, rights and obligations. This framework took shape in 1992 and focused on rights to what was defined as 'common concerns' – declaring biological diversity and access to genetic material as a global public-good to support the new growth sector of biotechnology. The Millennium Development Goals in 2000, whose framework also largely emerged in industrialized countries, defined progress in terms of social, humanitarian and political human development outcomes – did not include energy despite its essential role in industrialization and correlation with GDP growth because of the implications for sharing the global carbon budget. Attempts to partition the atmosphere, at Copenhagen in 2009, was thwarted by China, reflecting its growing power. Following the global conference in 2012, the post-2015 Sustainable Development Goals, with the global urban middle class set to triple in size by 2050, are being negotiated with inputs from both industrialized and emerging countries in terms of sharing responsibility for both the planet and prosperity of all inhabitants.

According to a recent analysis, by 2030, no country – whether the United States, China, or any other large country – will be a hegemonic power, restoring Asia's weight in the global economy, ushering in a new era of 'democratization' at the international and domestic level, and in addition two megatrends will shape the world out to 2030: demographic patterns, especially rapid aging; and growing resource demands which, in the cases of food and water, might lead to scarcities [NIC, 2012]. The beginning of this shift has led the United Nations to call for a new 'people-centred and planet-sensitive agenda', which includes for the first time a 'transformation of our economies' and for 'our global intellectual property regimes to contribute to the goals of sustainable development'. The earlier formulations, in 1992, of a 'grand bargain' have now been replaced with a 'Global Compact' [United Nations, 2014]. In place of global rules based on the universalism, the new framework is suggesting global goals that recognize different levels of development, making diversity a part of the architecture. The nature and scope of this shift continues to be contested.

The new conceptual framework stresses the use and distribution of natural resources, including equitably sharing the global commons. Half of the cumulative emissions of carbon dioxide from human activity in the period 1750–2010 have occurred in the period after 1970; urban areas are responsible for three-quarter of these emissions and energy use. In an interdependent world, urban dietary patterns have changed with meat production accounting for 15 per cent of world's greenhouse gas (GHG) emissions, and one-third of world food production is wasted. The value of world trade in natural resources is a quarter of world merchandise trade and world transport energy use doubled in the last 40 years and is expected to double again by 2050. Buildings and the transport sector are each responsible for about one-third of final energy consumption. Modification of longer term trends at

---

[2] The Asian Development Bank first flagged, in 2009, that Asia would need $8 trillion in infrastructure spending; the World Bank's total investment in 2014 was $11 billion, and the Asia Infrastructure Investment Bank has an authorized capital of $100 billion.

the national level will be enabled, rather than directed, by new global goals. They will also provide policy coherence in a multipolar world to support the transformation, this time China, with four times the population of the United States, will show the way.

Questions are being raised within the United Nations on the 'institutional' approach to sustainable development that was adopted in 1972, which is based on new rights to the global commons and periodic review of national economic and environmental action. The emerging paradigm stresses the social dimension of sustainable development, moves away from law as an integrating theme and redefines global goods in terms of collective benefits, for example, sharing technological advances in identified sectors, placing SDRs at the centre of the global monetary system and trade rules that shift their focus to consumption sectors and support structural change [Committee for Development Policy, 2014].

A re-framing is underway because the transformative impact of the re-emergence of China has led to new analysis and evidence on the asymmetry in the use of natural resources, including in the world's two largest economies. For example, the average citizen in the United States consumes four times more electricity than the average Chinese citizen [Ecofys, 2014]. At the same time, while median American wages are flat since 2007, after having risen by 7.7 per cent in real terms in 1995–2000 and have fallen in Britain and much of the euro zone despite a 45 percent increase in economic output, China aims to double 2010 GDP *and* per capita levels of rural and urban residents by 2050 as well as cap emissions of carbon dioxide by 2030, providing a new model for other countries; the 'Beijing Consensus' is replacing the 'Washington Consensus'.

The re-framing will not be a complete break from the past as it will integrate the United Nations Universal Declaration of Human Rights, 1948, the Declaration on the Right to Development, 1986, and the Rio Declaration, 1992, into the Sustainable Development Goals, 2015, to respond to the increasing interdependencies of the twenty-first century. The focus will, however, shift from institutions – multilateral environmental treaties, harmonization and global markets–that require universalism to global goals – managing diversity, recognizing different national pathways for sharing prosperity that will make sustainable development a reality. As India and other developing countries urbanize, they are likely to follow the Chinese model and compensate for their larger populations. Consequently, even greater intergovernmental cooperation will be required in the future for sharing, rather than appropriating, natural resources; now in a South–South rather than North–South context, and these terms are losing their relevance.

The shift currently making Asia – once again – the world's economic centre of gravity is 1,000 times larger than was witnessed during the Industrial Revolution. The visible aspect of this socio-economic–political revolution is the shift of the population from the rural to urban areas and into the middle class, along with stagnation of the middle class in many industrialized countries and rising income inequality. As two-third of global growth is going to take place in Asia, a rural–urban divide will replace the current divide between industrialized and emerging countries. The establishment of Asia-centred financial institutions by China to support this urbanization is reshaping global governance as cities become nodes for 'universal' economic, social and political activity with 'diversity' continuing in rural areas according to national circumstances. Speaking at the Boao Forum for Asia, on 28 March 2015, (the forum is conceived as the Asian version of the World Economic Forum, at Davos, and its theme was "Asia's New Future: Toward a Community of Common Destiny") President Xi Jinping sketched out China's vision for a new Asian order, and presented China as a partner willing to "jointly build a regional order that is more favourable to Asia and to the world" and he was careful not to place China at the centre of this emerging order. China also released an action plan for "one belt, one road linking Asia and Europe," which will include roads, rail, ports, oil and gas pipelines, fibre optic networks as well as funding for information technology, biotechnology and new energy. Customs and other regulations that might impede trade and investment are also to be smoothed out, making the Asian Century a cooperative venture for sharing prosperity.

According to McKinsey and Company, a feature of this transformation will be the growing power of cities and the extreme concentration of wealth in a limited number of megacities. The world's top 600 cities (measured by absolute GDP) are expected to drive nearly two-thirds of global economic growth by 2025; in 60 megacities – more than double the current number – GDP will exceed $250 billion, accounting for a full one-quarter of global GDP. Out of the 25 largest growth-contributing cities, 21 are likely to be in today's emerging countries with a significant number of them in China. This represents a great leap from the current situation, in which only 4 of the 25 wealthiest cities are in the developing world [Dobbs et al., 2012].

Urbanization is a global mega-trend associated with human well-being and correlated with higher consumption of natural resources, energy and carbon dioxide emissions. Urban areas in 2050 will hold three-fourth of the global population, and most of its built assets and economic activities. Therefore, the next two decades present a window of opportunity for sustainable development moving from ideas to reality as a large portion of the world's urban infrastructure will be established and inhabited by the middle class, largely in Asia; 1 billion in India by 2030 [Brar et al., 2014]. With the urban population projected to increase from 3.4 billion in 2005 to 6.3 billion in 2050 (estimates vary, but the trend is clear), urban design that builds resilience can also accelerate successful climate change mitigation and adaptation globally.

Urbanization, industrialization and middle-class levels of living in North America, Europe and Japan in the twentieth century led to a 20-fold increase in the demand for commodities, which is likely to go up a further 3–5 times in the twenty-first century with the re-emergence of China and India. The extent of use of natural resources, and resulting waste carbon dioxide, will proportionately be less than in the previous phase of urbanization as it is now also shaped by services overtaking goods which will enable new urbanization patterns, values, worldview and global rules. Global flows of data, finance, talent, and trade are poised to triple in the decade ahead and technology is no longer being seen primarily a tool for cutting costs and boosting productivity. For example, the shift in viewing climate changes not as a global but as a country, city level and personal problem is reflected in the China–United States deal on climate change announced in November 2014 and the 2014 UN Climate Summit in New York launched the Compact of Mayors, a coalition of mayors and city leaders voluntarily committing to cut emissions, track progress and prepare for the impacts of climate change, through consistent, public reporting of efforts.

An area of special focus is urban design, especially in terms of density, land-use mix, connectivity and accessibility; all of which are tightly related. While individual measures of urban form have relatively small effects on vehicle miles travelled, they become more effective when combined. There is consistent evidence that co-locating higher residential densities with higher employment densities, coupled with significant public transit improvements, higher land-use mixes and other supportive demand management measures can lead to greater emissions savings. Highly accessible communities are typically characterized by low daily commuting distances and travel times, enabled by multiple modes of transportation. Industrialized country urban residents produce 2 to 10 times more carbon dioxide emissions than those in the emerging countries. Residents in Sydney, Calgary, Stuttgart and several in the United States urban areas produce more than 15 tons of carbon dioxide per capita per year. Compare this with the global average output of 4.8 metric tons of carbon dioxide per capita and 6.5 metric tons in New York, which is about half the United States average. Residents of urban areas in emerging countries typically produce even lower emissions per capita levels than the global average. For example, Mexico City, Buenos Aires and Delhi produce, 4.3, 3.8, and 1.5 tons carbon dioxide per capita, respectively (Hoornweg et al., 2011). Re-emerging countries are experimenting with new urban design, and important research is being done to understand and quantify how changes to the existing urban infrastructure, lifestyles and governance institutions interact and can drive reduced emissions and natural resource use while enhancing human well-being [CEPS, 2014]. For example, India's Aravind Eye Care System, which, by applying principles of industrial engineering to its work flow, has become the world's largest eye-care provider. Aravind can carry out two-thirds the number of operations conducted by the United Kingdom's entire National Health Service at one-sixth the cost – and with a lower infection rate. Changes in business models, awareness and behaviour of residents can further reduce demand for natural resources without affecting the quality of services they provide.

The growing stress on distribution is leading to a questioning of conventional economic theories of the past century on the working of capitalism that focus on the role of markets and prices for the efficient allocation of society's resources. Assumptions of what a good life consists of/and the reliance on money, energy, global rules and asymmetry of power to achieve it are being challenged. The consumerist myths of market economies and linkages between happiness, quality of life and greater consumption are being explored; notions of a 'global citizen' that require equal access to energy and imply limits are being discussed. Changes in urban dwellers' behaviour – for example, their choice of transport, the walk-ways in urban spaces and the use of household and community gardens for food and aesthetics – will be of increasing importance, as individual lifestyles and attitudes become more austere and frugal. Historically, the 'middle class' construct is a product of the forces of industrialization and urbanization.

Interpreting global environment change, climate change and sustainable development as a human challenge, in terms of social development, focuses attention on a global meta-goal as well as patterns, trends and drivers of natural resource use to determine how best to achieve it , rather than on the management of the global commons, scarcity of ecosystem services and planetary limits. Scientific opinion in the 1970s also considered global environmental change as the result of national unsustainable models of consumption and production; implying individual and collective choices, values, beliefs and assumptions about what it is to be progressive, modern and developed. The political implications led to the emergence of a natural science perspective of an environmental crisis, for example, climate change framed by atmospheric science for global attention which new technologies, it was suggested, can solve. The current focus on the causes instead of the symptoms lays stress on the development pathways that have been adopted and have led to massive inequalities in incomes, access to resources and power between countries. Climate change is increasingly being seen as the negative effect of a particular world view – of well-being as consumption and the accumulation of material possessions based on low-cost commodities as well as production processes and services with a high degree of waste.

It is not only the social science perspective that is re-framing global environment change, climate change and sustainable development. Within the natural sciences also the problem of planetary limits is being re-framed. There is an emerging view questioning the science of climate change based exclusively around climate models because observation-based estimates in a global energy budget shows lower average forcing, as over 90 per cent of the heat is absorbed by the oceans [Nicholas Lewis and Judith Curry, 2014]. The recent reduction in surface warming indicates that the climate is responding to higher concentrations of carbon dioxide in ways that had not been properly understood before. The climate system involves non-linear coupling of the atmosphere and ocean making it hard to predict how the intensity of tropical cyclones will change as the climate warms, the rates of sea-level rise, or the prevalence and severity of future droughts and floods over the next 50 years. The IPCC now concludes that a 2°C rise in temperature could result in worldwide economic losses of only 0.2–2 per cent of GDP a year – but the poor are more vulnerable. By then the global population will be in cities requiring a very different approach to the longer term changes. The inherent uncertainties suggest that till 2050, the policy issue is climate variability.

The increasing number of models and their sophistication has also not served to reduce uncertainty, for example, the simulation of clouds and soot in climate models for temperature changes and orbital forcing for sea level rise. As a result of climate variability, regional sea level change is likely to differ significantly from the global average. Since efforts at mitigation will have an impact only in the twenty-first century, climate policy, it is being suggested, should be thought as 'climate insurance' taken out against the most severe and irreversible potential consequences of climate change [United States Global Change Research Programme, 2014]. It is also suggested that climate sensitivity may have been overestimated in the past and that the science is too uncertain to justify a single estimate of future impacts, making adaptation the optimum policy response [The Economist, 2013], including through urbanization patterns, as the IPCC now suggests. Recent research supported by the United Nations University Institute for Environment and Human Security concludes that adaptation to the adverse effects of climate change should not be considered in terms of resilience as an ecological concept and the research and policy emphasis shift to social systems considering adaptive livelihood systems in the context of wider transformational changes [Tanner, 2015].

The leadership emerging countries are now showing is reflected at the national level in modifying urban design and personal consumption, as against the earlier view of industrialized countries of sharing the burden to minimize costs, for the rich countries. The new measures could save the planet while eradicating poverty as the new urbanization, and the vastly bigger new markets it creates, provides an opportunity for the global community to begin modifying consumption patterns. The continuing resistance of industrialized countries to share authority in global governance institutions is also not leading to a confrontation with the re-emerging countries as the institutions established at the end of World War II are losing their relevance. These institutions helped secure the well-being of one-fifth of the global population through the 'Washington Consensus', while the others benefitted from the globalization that the international system of rules brought even though their growth is not based on the imbalances that were created. A new generation of multilateral institutions and rules will now respond to the multipolar world shaping the transformation based on the equitable distribution and use, and not just ensuring asymmetric flows, of natural resources. Examples are the BRICS Development Bank and the Asia Infrastructure Investment bank, both promoted by China, to enable urbanization, which the existing multilateral institutions still do not support.

However, there is as yet no agreed 'global vision' and broad consensus on the kind of society all countries should be striving for, pathways for achieving that objective and more meaningful ways of thinking about living standards than GDP as a measure of prosperity. We know that the global population will plateau and it is greying; China's working age population has peaked and Germany's population in 2060 could shrink by one-fifth, and a smaller workforce means lower consumption and savings; the United States and European Union will be using 25% less energy per capita than today. We also know that, for example, in the United States, most cars spend more than 95 per cent of their time in garages or parking lots and, the heat-rate efficiency of the average coal-fired power plant has not significantly improved in more than 50 years – an extreme version of conditions in many industries over the past century. The industrial revolution focused on labour and capital, and ignored land, or natural resource use. A sustainable society will require a transformation involving changes in productivity solutions, efficient use of capital, economic strategy, policy action parameters, social structures and lifestyles. Cities will be where success and failure of resource productivity and distribution will be determined, and global sustainability depends largely on how China and India define their urban future, and shape the Asian Century.

Much will also depend on how the interplay between universality and diversity evolves within the United Nations in line with geopolitical shifts. The architecture of post-2015 global governance is recognizing the diversity of national circumstances and policy approaches as an intrinsic feature, not as an exception to general rules. The outcome of these shifts is also that recent science within the United Nations and its Specialised Agencies and Programmes, now led by officials from emerging countries, is supporting a stronger focus on the restrictions universal agreements impose on the policy space in emerging countries and are seeking supportive rules, standards and norms to enable the shift of rural populations into cities and into the middle class, while keeping within planetary limits.

For example, the United Nations IPCC in its Fifth Assessment Report, 2014, has for the first time highlighted ethics and justice; the United Nations Education, Scientific and Cultural Organization, in its World Social Science Report–2013 has characterized climate change as a social and not a physical problem; and the United Nations Economic and Social Council's expert group–Committee for Development Policy in its Policy Note: Global Governance and Global Rules for Development in the Post-2015 Era has called for reforming severe asymmetries in the effects of global governance structures and rules to achieve sustainable development. The stress on social concerns is in addition to the shift from analysing natural resource use solely in universal terms to consideration of diversity and distribution in sector domains by the United Nations Industrial Development Organization–UNIDO (access to energy), United Nations Human Settlements Programme–HABITAT (urbanization), and the United Nations Food and Agriculture Organization–FAO (impact of food wastage and livestock). The International Social Science Council - ICSU has suggested the need for a global meta-goal: "a prosperous, high quality of life that is equitably shared and sustainable".

The new research also brings out the emergence of a very different conceptual framework to the one that framed natural resource use in the mid-twentieth century. First, differences within the group of developed and emerging countries have now become as significant as those between industrialized and emerging countries in the 1970s. Second, the emerging trends are significant to the extent of re-defining 'happiness', 'well-being' and 'global public goods'. Third, very different consumption patterns of the re-emerging countries are driving the global economy with trends in natural resource use very much less inefficient and wasteful than in the past. The stress now is on innovation and sharing, whereas the earlier focus of international cooperation was on depressing commodity prices and ensuring supply. In a more equal world, the emerging middle class recognizes that it has to live within planetary limits for the new global order to have legitimacy within the country and in the other emerging countries as the urban - rural becomes more salient than a continuing the focus on the North-South divide.

The way forward will be a stronger focus on the new infrastructure that is being established in Asia, as well as national and regional action, which distinguishes between natural resources, ecosystem services and planetary limits with respect to urbanization, the middle class and energy, respectively. Since two-third of future global economic growth is going to take place in Asia, countries in that continent will need to support this shift by recognizing diversity in the architecture of universal rules equally applicable to all countries to support local measures. As against the earlier focus on harmonized global rules, norms and standards that ignored historical context in patterns of natural resource use and relied on markets to deliver social outcomes the focus will now be on infrastructure and urban design, knowledge economy, consumption patterns and human behaviour. The challenge for China, India and other countries in Asia in managing this transformation will be to shape a global vision for the design of cities, sharing technology, responsibility and prosperity through new institutions in Asia, and then transferring that vision and experience to the United Nations.

The scale and speed of the transformation will depend on the re-emerging countries taking the intellectual and conceptual lead for a more democratic United Nations, where distribution has so far been kept out of the agenda. The challenge will be to avoid replacing either the existing global institutions or the consumption patterns, or lifestyles, which were established more than 50 years ago. They will be able to do so by focusing on modifying certain consumption patterns as they shape their own transformation and develop new institutions and rules in Asia, and then take them to the global level. The post-2015 global agenda will signal the end of the North–South divide, and the China–United States climate deal in November 2014 is the first step in that direction. In a more equal and urbanized world, with a globalized services and knowledge-based market economy and not just the earlier industrial economy dependent on cheap natural resources, capital and labour supporting well-being of a few, sustainability has a real chance of moving from ideas to reality.

References

Barbier, Edward B. 2011. *Scarcity and Frontiers: How Economies Have Developed through Natural Resource Exploitation.* Cambridge University Press, Cambridge.

Beckert, Sven, 2014, *Empire of Cotton: A Global History*, Knof.

Brar, Jaidit, Shishir Gupta, Anu Madgavkar, Barnik C. Maitra, Sunali Rohra, and Mithun Sun dar. 2014. India's Economic Geography in 2025: States Clusters and Cities–Identifying the High Potential Markets of Tomorrow, October 2014, McKinsey Global Institute.

CEPS. 2014. Orchestrating Infrastructure for Sustainable Smart Cities. Centre for European Policy Studies, White Paper, 10 November 2014.

Committee for Development Policy. 2014. Policy Note, Global governance and global rules for development in the post-2015 era, Department of Economic and Social Affairs, United Nations, June 2014. New pillars for global governance would include rules on agriculture, capital flows and international taxation, and labour mobility.

Dobbs, Richard, Jaana Remes, James Manyika, Charles Roxburgh, Sven Smit, and Fabian Schaer. 2012. *Urban World: Cities and the Rise of the Consuming Class.* McKinsey Global Institute.

Ecofys. 2014. China and the U.S: How does their climate action compare? Climate Action Tracker, Policy Brief, 21 October 2014.

Hoornweg, Daniel, L. Sugar, C. Lorena, and T. Gomez. 2011. Cities and Greenhouse Emissions: Moving Forward, *Environment and Urbanization*, 23(1) January 10 2011.

NIC. 2008. *Global Trends 2025: A transformed world*, National Intelligence Council's 2025 Project, USA.

NIC. 2012. *Global Trends 2030: Alternative Worlds a publication of the National Intelligence Council*, USA December 2012, NIC 2012-001.

Nicholas Lewis and Judith Curry. 2014. The implications for climate sensitivity of AR5 forcing and heat uptake estimates. *Climate Dynamics*, September 2014.

Synthesis Report of the Secretary-General On the Post-2015 Agenda, The Road to Dignity by 2030: Ending Poverty, Transforming All Lives and Protecting the Planet, 4 December 2014, United Nations New York.

Tanner, Thomas, David Lewis, David Wrathall, Robin Bronen, Nick Cradock-Henry, Saleemul Huq, Chris Lawless, Raphael Nawrotzki, Vivek Prasad, Md. Ashiqur Rahman, Ryan Alaniz, Katherine King, Karen McNamara, Md. Nadiruzzaman, Sarah Henly-Shepard, and Frank Thomalla. 2015. 'Livelihood Resilience in the Face of Climate Change'. *Nature Climate Change* 5: 23–26.

The Economist, Climate Science: Sensitive Information, July 20, 2013.

United States Global Change Research Programme, The Cost of Delaying Action to Stem Climate Change, July 2014.

Index

Agenda 21   97, 98, 166, 191
Asian Development bank   265, 303
Asia Infrastructure Investment Bank   305
Barack Obama   14, 92, 161
Basel Convention   46, 47
Belmont Challenge   64, 65
Belmont Forum   63
Behaviour   3, 25, 64
Brandt Commission   172, 182
Bretton Woods   15, 50, 155
Brundtland Commission   7, 31, 96
Carbon budget   8, 21, 60
China   154, 225, 267
Cocoyoc Declaration   172
Commission on the Measurement of Economic
   Performance and Social Progress   224
Commission on Sustainable Development   106,
   158, 192
Common but Differentiated Responsibilities   50,
   94, 156
Consumption Patterns   3, 7, 213
Convention on Biological Diversity   44, 101, 191
Copenhagen Conference   58, 158
Diet   13, 290
Economic and Social Council   5, 75, 155
Electrification   206
Energy   3, 16, 29
European Union   22, 125, 184
Food and Agriculture Organization   45, 311
Finance   56, 132

Forests   6, 53, 196
Founex Meeting   76, 79
Future Earth   18, 68
GATT   80, 182
Governance   8, 84, 186
High Level Policy Forum   15, 106, 252
International Energy Agency   6, 118, 141
International Monetary Fund   6, 15, 186
Intellectual Property Rights   15, 45, 137
Inter Academy Council   59
ICSU   63, 64
IPCC   38, 57, 59
IPBES   40, 41
ISSC, International Social Science Council   39,
   66, 84
IUCN   72, 190, 197
Japan   19, 28, 155
Johannesburg WSSD   99, 187
Kyoto Protocol   96, 118, 128
Middle Class   121, 147
Millennium Development Goals   69, 137, 206
Millennium Ecosystem Assessment   19, 102, 195
Montreal Protocol   48, 50, 94
Narendra Modi   163, 164
New International Economic order   77, 172
OECD   22, 48, 102
Rio Conference   5, 44, 180
Rio + 20 Conference   21, 35, 194
Rio Declaration on Environment and
   Development   16, 19, 191

SAB Scientific Advisory Board on Science and Technology 39
South Commission 83, 182
Stiglitz, Joseph 118, 224, 226
Stockholm Conference 41, 74, 89
Strong, Maurice 11, 73, 215
Sustainable Development Goals 249, 274
System of Integrated Environmental and Economic Accounting (SEEA) 197
Technology transfer 46, 96, 138
The Economics of Ecosystems and Biodiversity (TEEB) 197
Tolba, M 50, 97
Trade-Related Aspects of Intellectual Property Rights (TRIPS) 241, 258
Transport 203, 219
Truman, Harry 15
United Nations charter 241
UNCED 53, 180, 242

UN HABITAT 35, 237
UNESCO 35, 63, 157
United Nations Conference on Trade and Development (UNCTAD) 75, 171
United Nations Conference on the Human Environment 42, 82, 190
United Nations Environment Programme 44, 132, 171
United Nations General Assembly 75, 151, 188
United States 171, 181, 203
Urbanization, urban design 26, 200, 219
Water 18, 24, 78
World Bank 6, 27, 125
World Conservation Congress 197
WMO 64
World Summit on Sustainable Development 5, 101, 174
World Trade Organization 5, 155, 182
Xi Jinping 84, 307

For EU product safety concerns, contact us at Calle de José Abascal, 56–1°,
28003 Madrid, Spain or eugpsr@cambridge.org.

www.ingramcontent.com/pod-product-compliance
Ingram Content Group UK Ltd.
Pitfield, Milton Keynes, MK11 3LW, UK
UKHW030659060825
461487UK00010B/885